Architects
of the
Underworld

Architects
of the
Underworld

Unriddling Atlantis, Anomalies of Mars,
and the Mystery of the Sphinx

Bruce Rux

Frog, Ltd.
Berkeley, California

Published by Frog, Ltd.
Frog, Ltd. Books are distributed by
North Atlantic Books
P.O. Box 12327
Berkeley, California 94712

Cover design by Paula Morrison
Cover illustration by Spain
Book design by Catherine E. Campaigne

Library of Congress Cataloguing-in-Publication Data

Rux, Bruce, 1958–
    Architects of the underworld : unriddling Atlantis, anomalies of
Mars, and the mystery of the Sphinx / Bruce Rux.
        p.   cm.
    Includes bibliographical references and index.
    ISBN 1–883319–46–3
    1. Life on other planets.   2. Unidentified flying objects—Sightings
and encounters.   3. Conspiracies—United States.
    I. Title.
QB54.R89   1996
001.9'4—dc20   96–814
                                                                  CIP

To all the researchers whose names are mentioned herein, for having had the courage to explore the outer limits; and especially to the memory of my father, Victor Sheldon Rux, a dedicated teacher and seeker after the truth, who I am sure would have been pleased.

Acknowledgments

First and foremost, thanks to my family: my mother, Georgia Garkie, my brother, George, and my sister, Dr. Victoria Seitz-Norton. A special debt of gratitude goes also to my "families away from home," the Ken and Paul Strauss families, Bud and Heloise Peak, and especially Joel and Zoe Climenhaga, who took such good care of me throughout grad school (and ever after).

Thanks, on the professional level, to Zecharia Sitchin and David Jacobs for their time, advice, and courtesy, and to Linda Moulton Howe for providing some helpful comments and suggestions while the manuscript was in its earliest draft. Thanks also to Abbas Nadim and Visions Travel, my Cairo roomie Lloyd Pye, Harvey Hagman and Kathy La Combe, Fritz Meyer, and all my other friends from the "Invisible College." Thanks to the Culture God, RAW. And certainly, thanks to everyone at North Atlantic Books for all their patience and help in getting the book out: Richard Grossinger, Lindy Hough, Kathy Glass, Marianne Dresser, Anastasia McGhee, and Anniken Høyer-Nielsen.

On the more personal level, thanks to all those who have provided so much moral support to me over the years: Sandra Broad and Sean Emery (who made Detroit bearable), the Fabulous Five (who know who they are), James Bernard and Todd Suiter (for help on figuring the irregularities of the Martian orbit), Tim and Elizabeth Hogan, Julie Rumney, Lou Fails, Mike Franzen, Lori Clark, Jeri Daetwiler, Denise Groves, Tom and Amy Harm, Karl and Mary Gross, and Elizabeth Ivory (for carrying me through the bad times and listening to all my theories as I was in the process of formulating them), Wade Wood (the only other person I know who was asking archaeoastronomical questions about ancient Egypt at the same early date I was), Steve Wright (who came to the same UFO conclusions I did when we were only pre-adolescents, that—lo and behold—appear to have been correct, after all) and all the other Village Inn Irregulars of the past quarter century.

Special regards to Paul Dini and Arleen Sorkin, who have flattered my work as sincerely as possible, along with something only they and a fellow chap will be able to answer: *Riddle Me This!* On what dark D.C. night during the days of our lives converged the animals of the month of Mars, a venomous viper, a rabid dog, and a stolen Egyptian gem? (Regards, Ra's)

Lastly, to whom it may concern:

Who meet on the angle must meet on the square
To acknowledge the Architect only is fair
All labors ascend to a Grand Master Plan
The most Divine handiwork of which is Man.

Contents

Introduction: Anomalies

Investigation of any mystery begins with the recognition of anomalies—the existence of something where it shouldn't be, or the absence of something where it should. This study began as an investigation into anomalies of the planet Mars—specifically, with the unusual findings of NASA's *Viking* probes in 1976, their subsequent loss of *Observer* in 1993, and the loss of the Soviets' *Phobos 1* and *Phobos 2* probes four years earlier, in 1989. Chief among *Viking's* findings was an item seemingly sculpted in stone, larger than the Golden Gate Bridge: a controversial sphinx face photographed in the Cydonia region of the Red Planet, the presence of which was downplayed from the start by the Space Agency even as its own members were admittedly amazed by its existence.

The Face shouldn't have been so surprising. Former *Mariner* probes had photographed what very much appeared to be pyramidal structures in the planet's Elysium region, in 1972. For that matter, the man who televised the Elysium pyramids for a mass audience the same year, Carl Sagan, had told the American Astronautical Society six years prior—following his examination of data from the same planet, beamed back from *Mariner 4*—that it was entirely possible Earth had been visited in antiquity even up to ten thousand times by a technologically advanced race, and that not only might they have left behind artifacts from those visits, but they may even have automated bases still functioning in our solar system for continuity in successive expeditions.

Memory is short, however, and common interest in space matters being of negligible concern to the public anyway, these interesting observations and anomalies were quickly consigned to oblivion. Had anyone remembered them, interest would surely have been rekindled by the fate of the next Mars probes, the Soviets' and the European Space Agency's *Phobos 1* and *Phobos 2.* America's presence in these missions was not absent either, though virtually no news about their loss was to be found in the mainline U.S. media. This was especially curious, since not only was American technology in the probes, but many United States defense experts had even complained that a laser and ion beam emitter included in the probes' equipment were nothing more than a transparent Soviet ploy to experiment with their own counter-Star Wars weaponry, a complaint which the White House itself overrode.

These were all anomalous occurrences, in themselves. Why would the United States contribute technology to its supposedly most rabid cold war foes, let alone condone the Soviet use in space of equipment so advanced and dangerous that their own defense experts would register objection? And why would the White House overrule those defense experts in the matter? Ostensibly, the reason for the latter was a gesture of trust in improved U.S./U.S.S.R. relations, and the former because the equipment was needed to obtain samples from the Martian moonlet, Phobos. This made for another curious anomaly: why was Phobos of more concern to all the various space agencies than Mars itself? Especially since Mars appeared to show evidence, in at least two regions, of former habitation? Moreover, since this evidence potentially links its inhabitants with our own, by virtue of the type of intelligent construction discovered there? Why would a mere moon—and a very small one at that, only about twelve by sixteen miles across—elicit such interest?

Far more curious, still: what happened to the Phobos probes? Both were suddenly and inexplicably lost, the first seemingly due to failure of the radio link, and the second due apparently to impact. *Impact?* Another anomaly. Loss of the radio link was virtually ruled out in the case of *Phobos 2,* and the odds against its having been struck randomly by a meteor were astronomical. What, then, could have caused such an impact? The dead probe provided its own answer, in its very last seconds of life, apparently having photographed its killer even as it expired in the best suspense-filled tradition of a pulp thriller: the Soviets revealed that an unidentified symmetrical ellipse, between twelve and sixteen miles in length, was the last object seen by *Phobos 2.* This same ellipse—or something nearly identical to it—had also been photographed days before. The Soviets have since refused to speculate on what the object or objects might have been, and still have not shared the last images captured by the ill-fated device. But simple definition itself provides part of the answer: at least one unidentified object was photographed between Mars and Phobos, on more than one occasion, and both times the object or objects were flying. In simplest terms, *Phobos 2* photographed at least a single unidentified flying object—a UFO.

By itself, this might perhaps mean nothing at all, or at least be written off as only a temporary anomaly, which could be expected to be more clearly understood in terms of some natural phenomenon at a future date. But such objects, even of the same dimensions, are not isolated to Mars. They have also been witnessed over the Moon—and not only in recent years, but as far back as 450 years ago. NASA compiled at least two catalogues of these curious "Lunar Transient Phenomena" (LTP), witnessed by reliable professional astronomers, between 1958 and 1967.

And failed space probes were not limited to Soviet experience, or new to the United States when it lost the *Observer* under the most highly suspicious of circumstances. The Soviets lost not only all their earliest Mars probes, but many to the Moon, as well—as did the United States, in the latter case. And just as anomalous geometric surface structures were found in the historical record of Mars observation, they were also found in the history of lunar observations. In fact, respectable scientists of both Russia and the United States have been on record, for at least the past three decades, as having expressed the opinion that the moons of both Earth and Mars could well be somebody's space stations—and while the Soviets may have been the first to deliver Star Wars technology to Phobos, the Pentagon was seriously proposing the detonation of nuclear devices there in the late 1960s. More recently, the Pentagon launched a probe to the Moon called *Clementine,* under the auspices of the BMDO (Ballistic Missile Defense Organization—the new designation for the Star Wars program), for the express purpose of lunar mapping. *Clementine* was also subsequently lost, with a full tenth of its returned photos publicly withheld. Why? Of what use is a supposedly dead chunk of rock to the military? Either beside our own planet, or Mars? And why would any pictures be kept from public view, at all?

Such questions are both obvious and pressing, especially in light of the fact that the vast majority of the ever-dwindling national budget is given over to the same military that is withholding evidence—and the largest portion of that budget, for going on two decades now, has been spent on space weaponry. Answers are not too commonly sought, however, for the simple reason that these very questions have been forcefully and pervasively relegated to the fringe. That mere fact, alone, should make obvious that there is something deliberately being hidden and make finding the answers all the more interesting.

But we live in a world ruled by economy, which has a severe dampening effect on inquiry into subjects which have clearly been labeled "off limits," whether overtly or covertly. And it is not only the government and its protective shroud of "national security" that threaten interlopers, but also the halls of science, theology, and academia. Vested interests go beyond the economic, to the spiritual or psychological. Pyramids on Mars would prove that man was technologically advanced in antiquity, as opposed to the hunting-gathering primitive we have assumed our ancestors to be. It is simply beyond the realm of possibility that two races evolved identical building concepts on two separate worlds, entirely independently of each other. If those pyramids—and that disturbing Face—actually exist on the next planet from the sun, it could well mean that what we understand of religion would have to be intelligently reexamined in a new light, which is upsetting even to many more stalwart psyches.

A massively growing body of evidence that the Old and New Worlds sprang from a common source has been continually suppressed, or more often simply ridiculed or ignored, by academics for 150 years. To attempt to prove to those same academics that not only did mankind have a single original civilization on this planet, but that in fact that same civilization came from another, is all but impossible. This has been ably demonstrated by the work of John Anthony West, Robert Schoch, and an increasing number of geologists, who have proven even to skeptical Egyptologists that the Giza Sphinx has been eroded not by wind, but by water—which cannot have occurred more recently than the last 10,000 years, contradicting the accepted date given for its construction at 4,500 years ago. To acknowledge this discrepancy, while simultaneously refusing to revise previous erroneous assumptions, is the height of absurdity. Nevertheless, it is exactly the current state of things in Egyptology.

And even those who are reexamining Egypt's past, due to such discoveries, suffer from a blind spot themselves. A small number are coming to realize that if the pyramids and Sphinx are far older than previously believed, and such structures may also exist on at least one other planet in our solar system, then attempting to make a connection between the two is only logical. Far fewer in number are those who are taking that examination a single step further, in wondering if there just might be a connection between Earth and Mars not only in antiquity, but in the present day as well. John Anthony West and Richard Hoagland, to varying degrees, are examining the possibility (or probability) of ancient contact, but even they refuse to consider that the present UFO phenomenon could have anything to do with it. However, the evidence—if thoroughly examined with an open mind—leads to exactly that conclusion. The only reason this has not been discovered previously is that those investigating into the question have limited themselves only to study of one or the other of the two areas: the evidence of past contact, or of present. The two do not contradict each other at all, but rather provide each other's proof. The purpose of this book is to demonstrate this very point.

The style of presentation in this study is intended to allow the reader to share in the process of discovery as it naturally unfolds, simultaneously providing as much related information as possible along the way to enrich the experience. The information is put forward in such a way as to establish patterns of evidence which will emerge of their own accord, then be collated and summarized concisely. The methodology employed is that used by any academician, or any detective. The record is fully examined, going always to original sources and testimony (where possible), and allowing the witnesses their unadulterated voice. From there, the evidence is compared and contrasted, to discover common elements. These are then combined with the archaeological and historical record, to establish precedent. When all combined, they come to a single, overpowering, but simple conclusion: not only do the origins of man inextricably connect to the planet Mars, but that relationship is ongoing; and not only are we not alone in the universe, but we never have been.

The best place to begin examining the evidence for this conclusion is in its most overlooked area: the modern UFO phenomenon. Specifically, with that much abused and ridiculed—but equally undeniable—reality, the flying saucer. Part 1, *ARQ*, provides in great detail the history of flying saucers in the modern era. The word signifies many things, not the least of which is an exotic ship. It also is the word for the vessel of God's covenant, both in salvation from the Flood and in subsequent military campaigns of the children of Israel. Lastly, it is a word connected to the enigmatic Sphinx itself, and also to the completion of a long, great, roundabout journey—all of which this study will show to be vitally connected.

UFOlogists who believe they already know this material will discover much that is new in going over it again. A "mystery" is almost always nothing more than an inadequately studied set of facts, with the answers overlooked the whole while they are hiding in plain sight. The initial investigation usually contains everything necessary to discover the seemingly elusive answers, which are present in the original facts and testimonies but simply have not been comprehended. Jim Marrs and Oliver Stone amply demonstrated this point in the book *Crossfire: The Plot that Killed Kennedy* and the movie *JFK*. More than enough evidence exists to prove that the CIA and the Mafia were primarily responsible for John F. Kennedy's assassination in Dealey Plaza, with complicity on the parts of Vice President Lyndon Baines Johnson and FBI head J. Edgar Hoover, but the facts still continue to be ignored by people who can't conceive of their own government running in equally corrupt fashion to a banana republic. It isn't that the facts and the truth aren't there—they always have been. It is just that they remain overlooked due to bias and preconception. The UFO mystery is no different.

Architects of the Underworld's trail of investigation begins with Kenneth Arnold's infamous sighting of UFOs in Washington State, and the recovery of at least one flying saucer in New Mexico, in 1947. While the story of this famous crash recovery has become better known in recent years, its two most salient points have continued to be overlooked. Those points are *(a)* the inscriptions reported on the wreckage by every witness, without exception, and *(b)* the nature of the occupants from the downed craft. The latter will prove to be of paramount importance, since their continued mislabeling as "aliens" by everyone studying them has proven to be perhaps the greatest stumbling block to proper comprehension of the entire phenomenon. The inscriptions are an equally telling clue—especially in light of the artifacts witnessed on Mars—being described by virtually everyone who saw them as "Egyptian hieroglyphics."

Chapter 2 continues with the history of "official" government investigations into the UFO phenomenon, showing an identifiable pattern of deception and manipulation from the outset. It will be shown that as recovered material from flying saucer crashes was investigated behind the scenes by the U.S. military for purposes of weapons exploitation, palliative research groups were erected before the public to speciously examine the problem and offer conventional explanations. The Central Intelligence Agency, the Air Force, and the National Security Agency were all formed to deal—in varying degrees—with the real questions and problems raised by the UFO reality. These government offices, and their counterparts around the world, encountered increasing difficulty in keeping the subject quiet due to more frequent and public appearances of UFOs. In addition, certain unsettling truths about UFOs began to emerge, the most notable being their occasional permanent bodily abduction of pilots. Recurrent reports of occupants from these craft—frequently similar in description to the ones at Roswell, New Mexico—began to surface in the 1950s, coincidentally with idiotic stories from self-styled "contactees" almost certainly sponsored by the CIA. The result of these occurrences together created an unrealistic circus aura around the entire subject, deflecting both amateur civilian investigators and their government counterparts from any reality involved. This area continues to be explored in Chapter 3, adding the interrelated UFO activities of cattle mutilation and military-industrial sabotage, as well as active disinformational campaigns undertaken by the government to keep civilian investigators confused.

Chapters 4 and 5 study UFO abductions in depth. The first of the two chapters looks into the more common variety performed by the much-publicized Roswellesque "Grays," and begins to explore the nature of their being and activities. Human reproduction seems to be their central focus of intent, for purposes not entirely known, and is conducted through either laboratory manipulations in a sterile environment or direct sex with altogether human occupants. The human UFO occupants often reported (but little publicized) contrast markedly with the Grays, beginning to show a critical clue as to just what the Grays really are. This becomes more evident in Chapter 5, when the Grays and other "humanoid" (but obviously not "human") UFO occupants are examined in more detail. Consistent clues emerge from analysis of these beings, showing them to be of metallic look and feel, bulletproof and blade-proof, with physically cold bodies, hobbling walks, antennae, camera-like eyes, and computer-like (or "telepathic") voices, leading to the unmistakable conclusion that they are not living beings at all, but robot servants of the human intelligence behind UFOs.

Part 2, *UR*, takes the clues presented in Part 1 and follows them to where they lead: the origins of mankind and his civilization, and the ancient history of not only planet Earth, but the entire solar system. The name is that of the traditional birthplace of the biblical Abraham, which has long been considered also to be the birthplace of civilization—even though archaeological evidence continually pushes civilization's beginnings back to much earlier epochs. These earlier epochs are the subject of man's mythologies, which are examined in this section as nothing less than forgotten history, written in advanced riddles which are encoded in elaborate etymologies and numerical ciphers. The mythologies studied in this section will prove to be the final solution to the enigma of UFOs.

Chapter 6 picks up where the last section ended, studying the folkloric and anthropological history of robotlike mythological beings from a great variety of cultures around the world. Their activities are shown to be identical to those of the UFO occupants of today. Chief among these activities is biological maintenance, not only of human beings, but of Earth itself. In addition to this function, the beings serve as intermediaries, initiators, and occult teachers, monitoring entire tribes of people in what is essentially a social-control function. In this capacity, they can be found in such supposedly diverse histories as those of China, North America, Europe, Great Britain, and most especially ancient Egypt. In Egypt, they were specifically designated as "animated figures," and can be proven to have performed exactly the same activities as are witnessed by today's UFO occupants—including aerial flight, the leaving of physical marks on their targets, and the erasure of people's memories. This, combined with numerous testimonies from today's UFO abductees of Egyptian symbols and revelations witnessed aboard the craft they are taken aboard, lead into Chapter 7.

In this chapter, the connection of Mars to the modern UFO phenomenon is demonstrated. The history of possible Martian contact with Earth is studied back to the beginning of the century, when such eminent names as astronomer William Pickering, and inventors Nikola Tesla and Guglielmo Marconi, stated the belief that intelligent signals were being transmitted from that planet. The Siberian aerial atomic explosion of 1908 is recounted, directly connected to a UFO speculated by prominent Russians to have been a crashing Martian spaceship. Jacques and Janine Vallée's findings connecting the planet Mars with UFO sightings are explored in depth, and a substantial history of observed Martian and lunar anomalies is related. These include geometric features discovered on both of these planetary bodies by notable scientists and astronomers, going into depth on the findings of science writer Richard Hoagland, Erol Torun of the Defense Mapping Agency, Russian Laureate State Prize winner S. Ivanov, and the Boeing Institute's William Blair. The author presents his theory that the sphinx on Mars and a similar companion structure are actually the faces of Ra and Thoth from Egyptian mythology. The mathematical correlations discovered by Scottish astronomer Duncan Lunan and coauthor M. W. Saunders between the Great Pyramid, the Pyramid of the Sun at Teotihuacán, and the planet Mars are disclosed. Some bizarre details recorded by the Apollo astronauts regarding the Moon are considered in light of interplanetary atomic war fought in antiquity, which are bolstered by similar archaeological findings from Earth and Mars.

In light of Egyptian artifacts on Mars and the connection of hieroglyphics to the modern UFO phenomenon, ancient history is reexamined in Chapter 8. The fallacies of modern Egyptology are exposed and demolished, with the Great Pyramid and the Sphinx shown to be far older than today's historians are willing to accept in spite of the evidence. Theories for the construction of these two edifices are considered, delving into etymology and mythology to find alternative answers in lieu of historians' failure to provide any credible ones of their own. The potential use of sound wave technology to levitate megalithic blocks is discussed—this technology's use being implied by the ancients, and modern technologies showing that it is entirely possible to accomplish. The biblical Ark of the Covenant is considered as an item of precisely such technology, and the God of the Bible as a master architect and technological wizard. This leads to comparison and discussion of the works of two central figures in ancient astronaut theory, Robert Temple and Zecharia Sitchin, and the study of "culture gods" who arrived from the skies (and/or seas) in ancient civilizations around the world. The myth texts of the Middle East are paid special attention in light of Sitchin's theories, showing them to be a cosmological history of the solar system's origins, and of the creation of man by a superior race of humans from another planet. Ancient sites are shown by Sitchin and ex-NASA scientist Maurice Chatelain to be "footprints" for astronautical travel.

Chapter 9 tells the story of wars between the gods in many cultures, the interbreeding of fallen angels and men, and the apocalyptic destruction of Earth. The mythology of the ancient Celts is shown to be the same as that of the ancient Egyptians, and the Egyptian origins of the Judaeo-Christian religion begin to be discussed. The etymology of the word "Watchers" is shown to be a universal constant in referring to this superior race of men in Earth's ancient history, as is the title "Sons of the Sun." Numerical and linguistic connections between the Middle East, Ireland, and Mexico are illustrated. "The Wild Hunt" is considered as a time of war or ethnic purge conducted by the gods, and witchcraft and demonology are cited as examples of degenerating awareness of this race's existence into superstition. Universal myths are explored, showing the history of wars first between the god races, then between those "gods" and the present human race of their creation, ending with the ultimate withdrawal of the vanquished gods back to their original "other world," leaving chosen kings and established institutions in their stead as an ongoing liaison. The Great God of the Underworld is introduced as a metaphor for this race, leading into the final chapter, on the subject of that Underworld.

The Celtic Fairy Folk are shown to have strong connections to the Bible's angels, and the Celtic god Manannan Mac Lir is shown to be the same as the Egyptian Thoth and the biblical Yahweh. This Great God's role as occult initiator of children and other chosen humans is demonstrated, as is the tremendous similarity his methods bear to UFO activities. The Underworld is shown to have universal constants, being located to the west and beneath Earth or under the sea, and referred to as a sunken "Red Land." Its colors are consistently found to be red, white, and black—the colors of Plato's Atlantis, and of ancient Egypt. Further evidence for the face of Ra on Mars is presented, and for connections between Mars and Egypt. Occult tradition is shown to similarly provide numerous proofs of a connection between Earth and Mars. A multitude of overwhelming coincidences is brought to light, demonstrating that all of Western civilization and tradition, Judaeo-Christian religion in particular, stem from Egypt. In conclusion, several final items of evidence are offered of a worldwide race of technologically superior travelers in antiquity.

Finally, Part 3, *ARQ UR,* renders a straightforward conclusion based on all the foregoing evidence. The term refers to a "great completion," and is a name for the "Mystery of Mysteries," the Sphinx—which, after all, is the final key to the puzzle of UFOs, ancient civilization, and the origins and destiny of man, being the connecting point between Earth and Mars.

ARQ

The Modern Phenomenon:
Saucers in the Skies

1

Recoveries

AT APPROXIMATELY 3 PM on June 24, 1947, while flying over Mt. Rainier in Washington, Lieutenant Kenneth Arnold witnessed what he referred to as an echelon formation of objects looking like "saucers skipping across water," inadvertently coining a new phrase via the press: "flying saucers." There were nine of them, forty-five to fifty feet in length, looking like shiny pie tins, estimated by Arnold to be traveling at seventeen hundred miles per hour. Despite the appellation, and the multitude of subsequent and prior sightings of saucer-shaped objects, Arnold specifically described these aerial unknowns as crescent-shaped, with a third-of-a-curve fore-edge sweeping back into streamlined wings and two curved cutouts meeting together as a cusp in the rear. Arnold pursued the objects as long as he could, but their advanced speed did not allow him to get much closer. "It is the personal opinion of the interviewer," wrote one FBI investigator, whose report belies the Bureau's later claim that it never had any interest in the phenomenon, "that [Arnold] actually saw what he states he saw in the attached report . . . [He] would have much more to lose than gain and would have to be very strongly convinced that he actually saw something before he would report such an incident and open himself up for the ridicule that would accompany such a report."

In fact, even at the time, unknown flying objects were not all that new. Many reports from as early as 1943, on all sides of the world conflict, were given of fiery spheres in the air following fighter and bomber formations. After the war, it was discovered from obscure intelligence reports and press clippings that each combatant thought these spheres were experimental secret weapons of an opposing power, generally believed to be some kind of remote-controlled aerial bombs, even though none ever detonated or caused an injury. They paced flight formations to the side of their wingtips at up to 360 miles per hour, flew in front of planes, and sometimes merely formed groups of about fifteen in the distance, seeming to hover and watch. Some supposedly entered through the fuselage, maneuvering slowly about inside the planes. Small and flickering, in a variety of colors (usually red or white), these fiery spheres were nicknamed "foo fighters" after the French word for fire *(feu)*.

Ten years earlier, Scandinavia, Britain, and the United States investigated "ghost aircraft," sometimes called "ghost rockets," that were being frequently reported by reliable observers performing low-level maneuvers in complete silence and running powerful searchlights over the ground. The two terms came from the objects' behavior at different times, appearing sometimes to be more like aircraft, and other times like rockets. They were unmarked, of no identifiable origin, and superior in flight performance to any known aircraft of the time. By January of 1934, more than forty reports a day were being registered in Sweden and Norway. Despite massive and serious research, no satisfactory explanation was ever found, even when the objects briefly reappeared in 1946. Like the later foo fighters, they were attributed to foreign powers, even though no known powers were capable of such feats of engineering. If these apparitions were piloted, their flying alone was remarkable. Journalist John Keel estimated that approximately 35 percent of the mystery objects sighted in Scandinavia flew dangerously low over uncertain land conditions during severe weather.

The year before the first foo fighters were reported, one of the most striking UFO incidents on record occurred over Los Angeles. At 2:25 AM on February 25, 1942, the city was blacked out as air-raid sirens summoned twelve thousand wardens to their posts. One thousand four hundred and thirty rounds of 12.8-pound anti-aircraft shells were fired intermittently at the aerial invaders until 4:15 AM, severely damaging several homes in misfires and causing three fatal heart attacks. No Japanese aircraft were spotted during that entire time, and no craft of any kind were downed or even seen to be damaged. Thousands of witnesses, including a *Herald Express* staff writer, saw a large stationary object in the sky sustain direct hits with no effect. It casually cruised for twenty minutes along the California coastline at about sixty miles per hour, then disappeared.

The next day, General George Marshall issued a memorandum for the president giving all known details, concluding that in the absence of hostile action they were probably commercial aircraft being employed by enemy agents to spread confusion and betray antiaircraft locations. He estimated there had been "as many as fifteen airplanes . . . flying at various speeds from . . . 'very slow' to as much as 200 mph and at elevations from 9,000 to 18,000 feet," and began his concluding paragraph with "Investigation continuing." Marshall failed to mention how twelve thousand air wardens and 1,430 rounds of 12.8-pound antiaircraft shells, often scoring direct hits, did not succeed in even dislodging a piece of fuselage or an aileron for examination, let alone bring down a single one of those "commercial airplanes flying 'very slow,'" in fact, almost stationary. He also failed to mention eyewitness testimony from at least one source, Douglas Aircraft Company employee Paul Collins, who said, "Taking into account our distance from Long Beach, the extensive pattern of firing from widely separated antiaircraft batteries and the movement of the unidentified red objects among *and around* the bursting shells in wide orbits, we estimated their top speed conservatively to be five miles per second." Considering he gave a correct estimate of the altitude, his reckoning of the speed cannot be considered spurious.

Other trained observer reports of equally startling aerial phenomena continued throughout the war. Sergeant Stephen J. Brickner of the First Marines' First Paratroop Brigade witnessed an extremely unusual display over Tulagi in the Solomon Islands on August 12, 1942. Approximately 150 objects, in tight lines of ten to twelve each, appeared seemingly out of nowhere. They triggered the air-raid sirens without the customary preceding "Condition Red." Brickner said they moved "a little faster than Jap planes," and made "a mighty roar [that] didn't sound at all like the high-pitched 'sewing machine' drone of the Jap formations . . . A few other things puzzled me: I couldn't seem to make out any wings or tails. They seemed to wobble slightly, and every time they wobbled they would shimmer brightly from the sun. Their color was like highly polished silver. No bombs were dropped, of course. All in all, it was the most awe-inspiring and yet frightening spectacle of my life." Given countless later reports of the same appearance and wobbling motion associated with such objects, Brickner's sighting is not likely to have been imaginary, especially at a time when no other reports existed from which to borrow.

As evidence of how seriously the Air Force took flying saucer reports, it offered a reward of three thousand dollars to anyone who could provide any "proof that flying saucers were real." Hundreds of UFO sightings from Glen Falls, New York, to Yakima, Washington, were reported coincidentally, preceding and following Kenneth Arnold's now-infamous pursuit, and if for no other reason than to reassure the public and reduce the potential panic factor, the Air Force had already more or less embarked on a debunking campaign. And needless to say, they must have been as anxious, if not more so, as anyone else to discover the reality behind the elusive phenomenon that was playing cat-and-mouse with them, as it continues to today.

They didn't have to wait very long. Sometime on the night of July 2, 1947, during a severe lightning storm, something crashed down out of the sky near Roswell, New Mexico. The Army wasted no time trying to convince the world that it was a weather balloon as soon as they found out about it, but not before one of their own, First Lieutenant Walter Haut, the Roswell Base Public Information Officer, had broadcast to the world on July 8 a press release carried by more than thirty afternoon newspapers: "The many rumors regarding the flying discs became a reality yesterday when the intelligence office of the 509th Bomb Group of the Eighth Air Force, Roswell Army Air Field, was fortunate enough to gain possession of a disc through the cooperation of one of the local ranchers and the Sheriff's office of Chaves County. The flying object landed on a ranch near Roswell sometime last week. Not having phone facilities, the rancher stored the disc until such time as he was able to contact the Sheriff's office, who in turn notified Major Jesse A. Marcel of the 509th Bomb Group Intelligence Office. Action was immediately taken and the disc was picked up at the rancher's home. It was inspected at the Roswell Army Air Field and subsequently loaned by Major Marcel to higher headquarters."

A radio transmission of the story was ordered to be stopped during broadcast: "ATTENTION ALBUQUERQUE: CEASE TRANSMISSION. REPEAT. CEASE TRANSMISSION. NATIONAL SECURITY ITEM. DO NOT TRANSMIT. STAND BY . . ." Well-known T.V. broadcaster and ex-Royal Canadian Air Force pilot Hughie Green personally attested, to researcher Timothy Good, that he heard the interrupted broadcast in his car while driving across New Mexico on his way to Philadelphia. By the time he got to his destination, "the story had been killed."

Who would have given a "Cease Transmission" order that could stop radio broadcasters from giving out one of the biggest stories ever to break? Who would have authority to say that it was "an item of national security"? While the issuer of the cease transmission order has not been identified, an FBI document of the same date—July 8, 1947, even giving a time of 6:17 PM—was acquired by UFO researcher Brad Sparks via the Freedom of Information Act, which seems to indicate the Bureau as the likeliest source: "Disc and balloon being transported to Wright Field by special plane for examination. Information provided this office because of national interest in case and fact that National Broadcasting Company, Associated Press, and others attempting to break story of location of disc today." Physicist and well-known UFO researcher Stanton Friedman even succeeded in finding the actual agent who wrote the memo. When asked for details, the agent's only response was to write, "Happy in my retirement. No guys in black suits on my doorstep. I cannot talk to you." As Friedman drily put it, this was "an interesting response indeed."

That details of the incident were withheld from the public can be found in an FBI memorandum dated July 10, 1947, two days following the interrupted Albuquerque story, which is signed by both J. Edgar Hoover and Clyde Tolson. It concerns a conversation between "special agent Reynolds" with Colonel L. R. Forney of MIB (Military Intelligence) as to whether or not "the Bureau . . . should accede to General Schulgen's request" to study "flying disks, [since they] are not the result of any Army or Navy experiments." The author of the memo recommended against the Bureau getting involved, "it being noted that a great bulk of these alleged discs reported found have been pranks." It is signed by David M. Ladd, assistant director. Clyde Tolson wrote his response at the foot of the memo, five days later: "I think we should do this." Beneath his signature is Hoover's: "I would do it, but before agreeing to it we must insist upon full access to discs recovered. For instance in the La. case the Army grabbed it and would not let us have it for cursory information." And given that as late as 1976, the FBI director's (C. M. Kelley) public response to all queries concerning UFOs was that "the investigation of Unidentified Flying Objects is not and never has been a matter that is within the investigative jurisdiction of the FBI," it is even more interesting. Two years after this denial, in a February 10, 1978, letter, Kelley did an about-face and admitted, "Investigation of UFO sightings does not fall within the investigative jurisdiction of the FBI; however the FBI for a limited period of time did assist the Department of the Air Force in investigating alleged UFO sightings."

Researchers Lawrence Fawcett and Barry J. Greenwood are quick to note that the signed Hoover-Tolson document is not proof of military-recovered flying disks, since the "La." case probably refers to an obviously hoaxed saucer recovered in Shreveport on July 7, 1947, according to declassified Project Blue Book files. But the dating here is something to take into account. On July 6, 1947, farmer Mac Brazel reports the crashed object near Roswell, and conveniently on the very next day in Shreveport, Louisiana, an obviously manufactured fake with a label reading "Made in U.S.A." is recovered; on July 8, 1947, the official Air Force press release from Roswell confirms that the object recovered there was in fact a flying saucer, and a radio news bulletin to that effect is interrupted by someone with authority to a national security claim, while an FBI memo of the same date confirms that a "disc *and* balloon" are being transported by special plane and that news services "*attempted* to break the story of the location." On July 15, 1947, one week after these occurrences and five days after a special meeting with a military agent, J. Edgar Hoover and Clyde Tolson both sign a memo attesting to "recovered disks" the military would not let them examine, despite the *military's* request that the Bureau get involved in such investigation.

That balloons were deliberately hoaxed by the Air Force, not only in subsequent cases but specifically at Roswell, has since been testified to by those involved in the hoaxes. Kevin D. Randle located a sergeant who "faked solutions to keep the local civilians calm and to keep the sightings from reaching the wire service, the press, or network news broadcasts." More to the point, when questioned whether he had been involved in a possible hoax in El Paso, he answered specifically, "I never went to El Paso to do it, I went into Roswell, New Mexico ... The orders for all these units were from the Pentagon. They weren't really orders and some of us believed that we were telling the truth. If you tell someone a lie and they repeat it then they are not lying. They are passing false information, but they believe it too ... as I said, they weren't really orders, but they were about the same thing. Well, yes, they were orders. We knew that someone at higher headquarters knew what the UFOs were and that they were trying to hide the answers. After all, it is all one Air Force. I only did it once, but it did become common. In the meantime, this [UFOs] all became balloons which was ridiculous. And we were sworn to secrecy and all scared stiff."

At the time of writing their groundbreaking book *Clear Intent,* Fawcett and Greenwood did not have access to either the testimony unearthed by Kevin D. Randle or the July 8 FBI memo acquired by Brad Sparks, as is evidenced by their comment, "The first document of any consequence [in FBI UFO records] was filed July 10, 1947," which refers to the Hoover-Tolson memorandum. The authors explicitly state that the FBI did not release all documents in their possession to them: "Many documents have been withheld to protect the personal privacy of eyewitnesses who had reported sightings, a legitimate exemption which we did not challenge. Another reason given for withholding information was the . . . 'national security' exemption, though this was not used extensively by the FBI."

Whether by disingenuous design or simple bureaucratic compartmentalization, Clarence Kelley may or may not have known about such documents being missing, or even existing in the first place. Released documents must first be searched for on request, then given out after receiving clearance, both of which take time. Approximately seventeen hundred pages came out of the FBI over a two-year period from 1978 to 1980. It is possible that further documentation may continue to surface. In any event, the FBI and all other government agencies later proven to have massive involvement in UFO investigations initially and vociferously denied any such involvement, indicating at the very least an extremely secret policy, if not cover-up.

Given later testimony by Blue Book scientists and FBI memos signed by Hoover, it is also likely that each investigative agency's right hand did not know what its left was doing. Hoover asked in a March 1950 note, "Just what are the facts re 'flying saucers'? A short memo as to whether or not it is true or just what Air Force, etc. think of them." He got the same response the public always has, which was that they were temperature inversions, swamp gas, and the like, though a memo from Guy Hottel dated March 22 did give the more detailed (but impossible to verify) report that "An investigator for the Air Forces [*sic*] stated that three so-called 'flying saucers' had been recovered in New Mexico. They were described as being circular in shape with raised centers, approximately 50 feet in diameter. Each one was occupied by three bodies of human shape but only three feet tall, dressed in metallic cloth of a very fine texture. Each body was bandaged in a manner similar to the blackout suits used by speed flyers and test pilots."

Hottel said that his informant reported military radar being the suspected cause of the saucer crashes, an idea which was soon to be circulated by ex-Marine Major Donald E. Keyhoe in his writings. Internationally renowned astrophysicist, computer scientist, and UFO investigator Jacques Vallée considers radar destabilization unlikely, and it is very difficult not to agree with him; but given our ignorance of the saucers' propulsion system—and some indicators, to be encountered later, that sound waves may figure in the crafts' levitation—the possibility does remain open. No one knows whether the information in the Hottel memo is spurious or not. The special agent who was Hottel's informant was named in the document but is blacked out. Former Director of Central Intelligence (DCI) Admiral Stansfield Turner advised researcher Timothy Good in 1986 that "anything written in intelligence channels that gives any credence whatsoever to UFOs, when released to the public, may be highly distorted," which seems sensible.

The earlier request by the military for FBI involvement was intended to prod the Bureau into investigating the more obvious hoaxes, thereby leaving the Army free to look into more serious cases, a fact attested to by Hoover's reference to Louisiana, special agent Reynolds' recommendation against Bureau involvement, numerous subsequent complaints by Bureau agents that they were being wasted on idiotic investigations of exactly this sort and that the military was excluding them from the really important cases (preserved in a great many memos), and the eventual withdrawal of the FBI for all the foregoing reasons. Given this evidence, it is entirely possible that Hoover and the Bureau were being deliberately used as a smokescreen to assure the public that all UFOs and flying saucer crashes were hoaxes, while the real things were being examined in private. Jacques Vallée repeatedly charged, during and after his involvement with Project Blue Book, that his and J. Allen Hynek's work was being used for precisely this purpose, and Blue Book head Captain Edward J. Ruppelt voiced similar suspicions. Both men's well-reasoned arguments and evidence will soon be examined.

The full facts regarding the Roswell case, insofar as they can be known, are best presented in Kevin D. Randle and Donald R. Schmitt's *UFO Crash at Roswell*. A condensation of its relevant facts to this study follows. It must be noted that the authors dispute some of their own precise dates and findings in a follow-up book, clouded by suspiciously convenient new witnesses, but the substantive testimonies remain the same. Reliability is difficult enough to gauge in cases this old, especially when most of the information conveyed is secondhand and there are disinformationalists with motives for wanting to keep the facts concealed, but sufficient firsthand testimony is still available from which to verify the basic story.

After the rainstorm the night before, rancher Mac Brazel inspected his fields on July 3, 1947, so that he could move his stock to the best pasture for grazing. He found a debris field so thick that his sheep refused to cross it for water. Remembering a loud crashing sound heard during the storm, he collected some pieces of the wreckage to show his friends Floyd and Loretta Proctor, who suggested due to the strange nature of the material that it might be the remains of a saucer. "A little sliver" of it proved impossible to burn or cut. Loretta told Brazel about the standing reward for proof, and he returned to the crash site to transport the largest circular piece of debris to his livestock shed three miles north.

Brazel waited until Sunday morning, July 6, to drive the seventy-five miles to the sheriff's office in Roswell, where George A. Wilcox inspected the wreckage he brought along. "Contrary to published reports," as Randle and Schmitt note, Sheriff Wilcox was quite excited and recommended the find be brought to the attention of the military. That Brazel could have manufactured the evidence for the reward money is impossible on the face of it, since no one ever identified the material involved, and Brazel neither made any great haste to report it nor took it straight to the military. He waited, and then reported it to the sheriff for him to decide how it should be handled. Wilcox told KGFL announcer Frank Joyce that he might want to get Brazel's story, but Joyce was too busy to pay serious attention. If Brazel had been seeking publicity, he certainly didn't press the point.

Phyllis McGuire, Sheriff Wilcox's daughter, testifies that the military arrived almost as soon as her father hung up the phone. Commander of the 509th Bomb Group, Colonel William Blanchard, and Air Intelligence officer Major Jesse A. Marcel interviewed Brazel, inspected the material, and went with Brazel to his ranch. Blanchard's first wife, Ethyl, states that her husband called his next higher-up in the chain of command and said they might have found something belonging to the Soviets, but never mentioned anything about any type of balloon. He bagged the material Brazel gave him, on the orders of General Clements McMullen via Colonel Thomas DuBose, and had it flown to Fort Worth Army Air Field. In that time, Wilcox's two deputies, who had scouted the area in advance of those arriving, reported that they hadn't been able to find the crash site without Brazel's help, but had discovered a burned area where the sand had blackened and turned to glass; it appeared something circular had touched down. Major Marcel ran a Geiger counter over Brazel's shed, but found no radiation.

Brazel took Marcel and Blanchard to the actual site the next morning, July 7. The entire previous day had been taken up with phone calls and preliminaries. Marcel estimated that the debris field was two or three hundred feet wide and three-quarters of a mile long, beginning with a huge gouge at the northernmost end that extended four to five hundred feet to the southernmost end, looking according to Brazel as if something "had touched down and skipped along."

Marcel and Blanchard knew they had seen something out of the ordinary. There were paper-thin sheets of metal that couldn't be bent or dented, I-beams with what appeared to be hieroglyphic writing that could be slightly flexed, and foil that rolled into a ball and unfolded itself back flat again without a crease (a property now known as "molecular memory"). More than thirty years later, Marcel unqualifiedly asserted that what he saw was "nothing from the Earth." Walter Haut later testified that Marcel told him, "It was something he had never seen and didn't believe it was of this planet. I trusted him on his knowledge. He felt very sincerely about it. He felt that it was something that was not made or mined or built or manufactured here on this earth." Descriptions of the debris have been confirmed by Brazel, Loretta Proctor, Tommy Tyree, Walt Whitmore, Sr., Jesse Marcel, Jr., Mrs. Viaud Marcel, Robert Shirkey, Robert Smith, O. W. Henderson, and Lewis S. Rickett.

Marcel and a CIC agent (counterintelligence) spent the entire day until dusk loading up Marcel's '42 Buick and the CIC Jeep car-ryall with all the debris they could, and returned to Roswell. For reasons never specified, General Nathan F. Twining suddenly changed his plans that day and flew to Alamogordo Army Air Field, a short drive from Roswell. Twining was chief of Air Materiel Command, the parent organization at Wright Field (now Wright-Patterson) in Ohio, where all the Roswell crash remains eventually ended up.

Senator Barry Goldwater, himself a brigadier general in the Air Force reserve with a top-secret clearance from the war, had heard rumors over the years and attempted sometime around 1964 to gain access to the flying saucer material stored at Wright-Patterson in an effort to understand the phenomenon. Explaining his denied access in a letter to a constituent in 1975, Goldwater specified, "It is still classified above Top Secret." Later, in 1981, he wrote, "I have long ago given up acquiring access [*sic*] to the so-called blue room at Wright-Patterson, as I have had one long string of denials from chief after chief, so I have given up . . . it is just impossible to get anything on it." As recently as 1988, in the *New Yorker's* April 25 issue, he commented that his friend General Curtis LeMay gave him "holy hell" over broaching the subject, and warned him never to do it again. Goldwater's letters and remarks would seem to confirm Canadian government scientist Wilbert Smith's top-secret memorandum of November 21, 1950, brought to light by Stanton Friedman: "I made discreet enquiries through the Canadian Embassy staff in Washington who were able to obtain for me the following information: a. The matter is the most highly classified subject in the United States Government, rating higher even than the H-bomb. b. Flying saucers exist. c. Their modus operandi is unknown but concentrated effort is being made by a small group headed by Doctor Vannevar Bush. d. The entire matter is considered by the United States authorities to be of tremendous significance."

Early on the morning of the eighth, Marcel arrived home and woke up his wife to show her the debris before it might become classified material. He took it then to the base, where he and the CIC man briefed Blanchard, who in turn called Provost Marshal Major Edwin Heasley, ordering him to post guards at the site and deny access to anyone without clearance. He also alerted Eighth Air Force Headquarters in Fort Worth, which relayed his communication about the find to the Pentagon, which in turn arranged a special flight out from Andrews Air Force Base. The regular morning staff meeting was moved up to decide how best to handle the situation.

Walter Haut later said that Blanchard had "a very sincere interest in the relationship between the base and the community. If anything unusual happened or anything he felt the community should know about, he would call me and say, get this thing out. He did that with many, many things." Blanchard told Haut, "Jess

Marcel [*sic*] has brought something in that looks like a flying disc or saucer or parts of it. Put out a press release on this that it was discovered on a ranch outside of Roswell, near Corona. Basically, that's all I'm going to tell you. Jesse's going to take it and is flying it down to Fort Worth." Like everyone else, Haut was impressed that the remains were nothing earthly, and prepared and released the famous statement.

At this juncture in history, policy was decided at a higher level than the local and democratic. The base in charge had analyzed the materials present, come to the unshakeable professional and personal opinion that it was of extraterrestrial origin, and decided there was no reason not to inform the public of that fact. But, as the author of that remarkably open and honest press statement so trenchantly observed, "Once it got to Fort Worth it became a weather balloon." Why the secrecy? If the public had been notified, the government and the military could have cemented a bond of trust with the public they were sworn to serve and protect. Instead, almost a full half-century of suspicion, distrust, allegations of varying accuracy, and an atmosphere of fear and ridicule were institutionalized. The representative republic began an erosive and pervasive change, from open to secret government. Arguably, this was just one more step in a process that had begun as early as the world wars, but that is the subject for another study.

The Central Intelligence Agency was formed weeks after the Roswell crash, and the National Security Agency, the largest and most secret intelligence agency in the world, was formed on November 4, 1952 (with no announcement, any word that might leak out concealed behind election results), only a little over three months after UFO violation of White House airspace. The timing and secrecy of the NSA's formation are telling, it being inconceivable that they would not have in their domain a matter more highly classified than the H-bomb. UFO documents show the NSA on their distribution list as early as June 26, 1953, only seven months after its creation as a separate agency, and Project Blue Book head Captain Edward J. Ruppelt said in his memoirs that orders came from "The Puzzle Palace"—the NSA's then-unknown nickname—on UFO material. Until the Foreign Intelligence Surveillance Act (FISA) of 1978, no official body watched over the NSA's often illegal spying, and even today FISA is essentially token legislation, not affecting the Agency at all. From the beginning, they monitored "watch-lists" of all sorts, ". . . which contain information on foreign governments, organizations, or individuals who are attempting to influence, coordinate, or control U.S. organizations, or individuals who may foment civil disturbance or otherwise undermine the national security of the U.S." Obviously, these conditions would apply to the UFO intelligence, and anyone it might contact.

It has been suggested that such incredible secrecy was imposed to avoid creating a panic, such as was engendered by Orson Welles' 1938 *The War of the Worlds* Mercury Theatre radio broadcast. There can be no doubt that this was one reason, since Edward Ruppelt testified in *The Report on Unidentified Flying Objects* that the UFO files were full of references to exactly that. It has also been suggested that what the government and/or military discovered about flying saucers was so terrifying, or potentially terrifying, that they themselves were afraid, and have spent all the intervening years attempting to militarily prepare for a confrontation, perhaps partly explaining the rationale behind a project like Reagan's "Star Wars." General Douglas MacArthur is on record as having told the *New York Times* in October of 1955, "The nations of the world will have to unite, for the next war will be an interplanetary war. The nations of the earth must someday make a common front against attack by people from other planets." Such a statement could have been hyperbole, especially coming from so theatrical a general, but MacArthur's name has been linked to the IPU, or Interplanetary Phenomenon Unit, also formed only months after the Roswell crash. The IPU unquestionably existed and is not mere rumor, since there is a March 12, 1987, letter from the Directorate of Counterintelligence to researcher Timothy Good concerning "information on the Interplanetary Phenomenon Unit of the Scientific and Technical Branch . . . Please be advised that the aforementioned Army unit was disestablished during the late 1950s and never reactivated." Ronald Reagan made a famous speech while president concerning possible "enemies from outer space," and even Jimmy Carter, who promised full disclosure of UFO materials to the public in his campaign, having seen and reported one himself in previous years, mysteriously changed his mind once he was in office, presumably in regard to what he learned concerning the subject.

This possibility is not incredible, but it is unlikely for the time in question. On July 8, 1947, no hostility had been demonstrated by any UFOs on record, and documents of the time profess confusion and interest, but no fear. In fact, no acts of overt hostility have been recorded since, though there have been injuries and even occasional fatalities directly or indirectly attributable to UFO activity, extremely few of which appear to have been deliberate, and many of those can be classed under "self-defense"—i.e., firing after having been fired upon. Captain Thomas Mantell, for instance, crashed and was decapitated in his P-51 Mustang in 1948 after having been ordered to pursue "a bright, disc-shaped object" by military ground control, automatically exposing as a lie the military's later claim that he and his squadron were chasing the planet Venus and/or weather balloons. His last words were that it was "metallic and tremendous in size," and that he would continue to climb in his intercept attempt. His last two wingmen turned back at twenty-two thousand feet, their oxygen not working properly, and Mantell—who did not have the recently ordered new oxygen masks installed in his craft—presumably passed out from anoxia and crashed. But that incident was due, to all appearances, to pilot error and occurred exactly six months *after* the Roswell recovery.

A more credible explanation, backed by documents signed by General Twining—the man who made a sudden flight to the Roswell area and whose jurisdiction included the base which then housed the recovered wreckage—is that the military both wanted to understand fully what was in their possession before issuing statements, and wanted to exploit in private whatever technological edge it might give them. In a memorandum dated September 23, 1947, Twining gave the specific recommendation that "It is possible within the present U.S. knowledge—provided extensive detailed development is undertaken—to construct a piloted aircraft which has the general description of the object . . . which would be capable of an approximate range of 7,000 miles at subsonic speeds. Any developments in this country along the lines indicated would be extremely expensive, time-consuming and at the considerable expense of current projects and therefore, if directed, should be set up independently of existing projects." The "object" to which he refers has only two specifications not found on any known aircraft at the time. One was "normally no associated sound" and the other, "circular or elliptical in shape, flat on bottom and domed on top." We have nothing approximating such a craft today, except perhaps the Stealth bomber. Or, if we do, it is interesting it has not made an appearance, the purpose of such weaponry being primarily to intimidate potential opponents. It is interesting, too, that what Twining describes would be nearly impossible to assess from mere visual sightings alone, but would almost of necessity indicate having had direct material examination.

The memo in which all this is stated is an AMC (Air Materiel Command) "Opinion Concerning 'Flying Discs,'" from Twining to Brigadier General George Schulgen. Acknowledging that "some of the incidents may be caused by natural phenomena, such as meteors," his assessment was that "The phenomenon reported is something real and not fictitious. There are objects probably approximating the shape of a disc, of such appreciable size as to appear to be as large as man-made aircraft. The reported operating characteristics such as extreme rates of climb, maneuverability (particularly in roll), and action which must be considered *evasive* when sighted by friendly aircraft and radar, lend belief to the possibility that some of the objects are controlled either manually, automatically or remotely."

Twining states, "Due consideration must be given . . . the lack of physical evidence in the shape of crash recovered exhibits which would undeniably prove the existence of these objects," but given the overwhelming Roswell evidence, this must be considered disingenuous. His memo says that "this [AMC] opinion is based on interrogation report data furnished by AS/AS 2 and preliminary studies by personnel of T-2 and aircraft Laboratory, Engineering Division T-3. This opinion was arrived at in a conference between personnel from the Air Institute of Technology, Intelligence T-2, Office, Chief of Engineering Division, and the Aircraft Power Plant and Propeller Laboratories of Engineering Division T-3." He concludes, "Awaiting a specific directive AMC will continue the investigation within its current resources in order to more closely define the nature of the phenomenon. Detailed Essential Elements of Information will be forwarded immediately for transmittal thru channels."

Again, the long list of technical experts, and the conclusions reached, sound more like the product of direct examination of material than an assessment based on radar and visual sightings alone. The specific references to a "lack of physical evidence in the *shape* of crash recovered exhibits," and *"probably approximating the shape of a disc,"* are interesting in their wording. At Roswell, wreckage almost certainly of a flying saucer was recovered, but no one would be able to reconstruct the craft as it had originally appeared—i.e., its exact "shape"; they would, however, have sufficient material to put through a battery of laboratory tests, which the long list of experts seems to indicate.

Once again we see indications that any given investigative branch on the subject was operating in smaller fragmentary groups, keeping the body politic unaware of its working. If there was recovered wreckage, why would Twining tell the Air Force there wasn't? But if there wasn't, why his abrupt trip to the Roswell area and all the documented and ongoing hugger-muggery associated with it?

Supposing the military initially was unsure of what it had, and so began with secret flights and transports to examine their find, then any subsequent secrecy would be entirely unnecessary if they did in fact discover the wreckage to be only that of a mundane object. But this would also mean that not only didn't Mac Brazel or Sheriff Wilcox know a weather balloon when he saw one, but neither did a major, a colonel, a CIC man, at least two MPs, and General Nathan F. Twining himself. If the Roswell wreckage had turned out to be identifiable, it would have been included in the declassified Project Blue Book—which it isn't. Ed Reese, at the National Archives in Washington, informed Donald Schmitt, "We have all of the other explained reports, many of them involving weather balloons, but not Roswell," and Pentagon personnel told Schmitt as late as 1990 to "leave it alone." He and Kevin Randle cite at least eleven specific instances where witnesses refused to talk, either because of sworn secrecy oaths or some form of coercion. And no weather balloon could leave as much wreckage as the Roswell crash did. It is not possible that any recognizable object crashed out of the sky on that fateful New Mexico night in 1947.

Which leaves us again with the question: why would the Air Force be keeping secrets from the Air Force, or the FBI keep secrets from J. Edgar Hoover? For one thing, to keep the fewest possible people from knowing, thus ensuring the minimum number of security leaks. Several former military and private sector scientists have told stories about being involved in what they were sure was UFO research, as a matter of course in their given jobs. These reports are most likely not apocryphal, since they corroborate each other, gain nothing for those relating them, and make sense in and of themselves. Additionally, there is some external confirmation from CIA authors.

A typical story goes like this: a lab is given material for analysis by a private company or the military, either as standard contract work or on an independently contracted basis. They are given few or no particulars concerning its origin, and nothing suspicious is betrayed. The results prove unusual, and the analyst's request for further information is either denied for lack of security clearance or the material is admitted to be of "unknown origin," specifically from an aerial vehicle or not specified at all. Depending on the persistence of the analyst, they are either told to ask no further questions, or are given a bare minimum of information and asked or sworn not to discuss it. Since such incidents do not occur frequently in any given individual's life, they are not thought about much unless the subject of UFOs should come up—which, generally speaking, it doesn't.

The word for this method of maintaining secrecy is "compartmentalization," and is especially common in hierarchies and bureaucracies. Multiple examples of it abound in the Roswell case alone. "As you will be aware," *CIA* author Brian Freemantle told Timothy Good, "intelligence agencies are strictly compartmented . . . I was told at one stage, however, that the Agency contracted out some of their [UFO] research through Stanford University, in Palo Alto, California." Freemantle also stated that, while the CIA was the agency most involved in initial "concentration of inquiries" on UFOs, since the early 1950s (which would correspond with the NSA's formation) UFO research has been "under the umbrella of Air Force intelligence and the National Security Agency—through its electronic expertise—rather than the CIA itself." Former director of Central Intelligence Admiral Stansfield Turner and former NSA employee Todd Zechel, however, both claim that the NSA merely collects and processes information which is then turned over to the Agency's Office of Scientific Intelligence and the director of Central Intelligence for comprehensive analysis. In other words, while the NSA may be the eyes and ears of UFO investigation (Turner does not admit the Agency's involvement in that particular subject, but Zechel does), the CIA remains the brain studying it.

When information is compartmentalized, any given witness interviewed knows only one or two items of information, not the whole. Mac Brazel and Sheriff Wilcox knew about the wreckage at Roswell, for instance, but wouldn't know what happened to it after they reported it to the military. One witness could attest to the fact that he loaded crates of unknown contents on a secret flight on a given date, but not as to why or what the contents were. Another could state that the military asked professional questions of him at a given time which seemed suspicious, but have no idea why. Only someone following a concrete trail of evidence, and with some idea of what he was looking for in the first place, could begin to figure out the story behind the events.

Each witness, when their information is compartmentalized, becomes a single puzzle piece to whatever story is being concealed. And the more puzzle pieces there arc, the smaller they can be made, ensuring increased difficulty on the part of any investigator attempting to put the whole story together. Adding to the confusion are the factors of time and distance. Memories fade, over the years. People move, and become more difficult to track down. They die, and anyone they may have related their part of the puzzle to over the years may or may not recall it correctly. The trail grows cold much faster and much easier when compartmentalized.

The executive branch of government assisted in compartmentalizing Roswell, and the subject of UFOs in general. At the time of the Roswell recovery, there was neither a Central Intelligence Agency nor an Air Force. The Air Force was merely a division of the Army, the United States Army Air Force, which is why it used to be referred to not as the "USAF," but the "USAAF." Five months after Roswell, on December 17, 1947, the United States Air Force became a separate bureaucracy from the Army. And much sooner, on September 18, 1947, two months after the New Mexico incident, the CIA was formed by the National Security Act. From its inception, it was an investigative branch with unidentified flying objects as part of its curriculum, but of course nowhere is this mentioned in its charter. In fact, the CIA has always been extensively involved in the subject, incessantly fighting to preserve the illusion that it is not. On August 1, 1952, the acting chief of CIA's Weapons and Equipment Division wrote in a memo, "It is strongly urged ... that no indication of CIA interest or concern reach the public" on the matter of UFOs. Then, as already mentioned, the NSA was formed in 1952, entirely by executive order and with no charter at all, answerable solely to the president and not properly overseen by anyone, following the highly publicized Washington, D.C., flap of that year, and documented to be involved in UFO investigation within its first seven months. Disputed documentation exists for President Truman's alleged formation of an extremely elite investigative unit solely devoted to the examination of the UFO question, called MJ-12 and occasionally referred to under the name "Majic" (with a "j," and not to be confused with the WWII designation) "Majority" or "Majestic."

Dr. Pierre Guérin of the French Institute of Astrophysics and senior director of CNRS (National Center for Scientific Research) concurs that MJ-12, or at least some group fitting its specifications, exists, adding the weight of his opinion to the belief that secrecy has always been maintained due to private weapons research: "To the extent that the presence of a hyper-sophisticated non-human technological activity within our Terrestrial Space could not possibly be regarded with indifference by those who have the task of governing the world, these latter will attempt to exploit, each party for themselves, any data that is in their possession, while at the same time publicly denying that they have such data [and] publicly suffocating all ufological research in a haze of 'psychological' interpretations! *That is not to say that the 'Invaders' may not be engaged in a pretty bit of suffocation of the subject themselves.*" This latter point has been noticed by many investigators over the years, and will be discussed later.

"Certainly, if there wasn't an MJ-12, we'd have to invent one," Stanton Friedman concurs. So does author Paris Flammonde, who states that, in light of the murders of President John F. Kennedy and his brother Robert, the attempted murders of George Wallace and Gerald Ford (to which possibly could be added Ronald Reagan), and the collapse of the Nixon White House, "It . . . requires little imagination to conceive that the creation of a modest, private air force by a non-government cabal, or the sequestering of some amazing advance in flying technology, or even the arrival of one, or many, extraplanetary vehicles, could be achieved with virtually no effort. The public would respond with an aroused curiosity about lights in the sky. It would be told that it was seeing conventional craft, ball lightning, and Venus."

For our purposes, the existence of a top-secret UFO investigative body—whether called MJ-12 or not—is established independently of the controversial documents attesting to such a group's existence, those documents standing as evidence of concealment whether genuine or forged. The difficulty of authenticating the documents is proof of a cover-up, either way. If genuine, then the information associated with the documents is true, proving the government's involvement in private research and deliberate deception from the start in only one more of a great many sources; if forged, then they could only have been forged by someone with excellent inside knowledge on too wide a variety of related subjects to have been manufactured for any other reason than disinformation. Excellent testimony by such eminent persons as General Arthur Exon and Dr. Robert I. Sarbacher is on record stating that such a group exists, the names associated with it stand to reason as being not unlikely, and some are even confirmed by separate testimony. The forest is clearly visible despite the trees.

The names given for the membership of MJ-12 in the documents, as of September 24, 1947, are the following: General Hoyt S. Vandenburg, CIA Director Admiral Roscoe H. Hillenkoeter, Dr. Vannevar Bush, Secretary of Defense James V. Forrestal (replaced in August of 1950, after his apparent suicide in May 1949, by General Walter Bedell Smith), General Nathan F. Twining, Dr. Detlev Bronk, Dr. Jerome Hunsaker, Sidney W. Souers, Gordon Gray, Dr. Donald H. Menzel, General Robert M. Montague, and Dr. Lloyd V. Berkner. These names, as Kevin Randle notes, will repeatedly be found wherever obfuscation occurs in UFO research. The appearance of the MJ-12 documents themselves is discussed in Chapter 3 of this book. For the moment, it can be said that they are almost certainly illegitimate, but are important for the simple fact that someone obviously took a great deal of time and trouble forging them, indicating a desire of interested parties to obscure behind half-truths any actual secret government UFO investigative group.

Brigadier General Arthur Exon, a lieutenant colonel at Wright Field when the Roswell material was brought in, confirmed many years later that the wreckage did in fact exist, that it was experimented with in a "special project" there by the lab chiefs, and that "there was a top intelligence echelon represented and the President's office was represented and the Secretary of Defense's office was represented and these people stayed on in key positions even though they might have moved out." And, demonstrating compartmentalization even at the highest levels, Exon himself "never heard what the results were" of the secret lab tests, even though he did know "the overall consensus was that the pieces were from space. They knew they had something new in their hands. The metal and material was unknown to anyone I talked to." Even when he was made base commander in 1964, "We were never informed about any reports [by special teams]. They all went to Washington."

Exon also confirmed the immediate cover-up. "Blanchard could have cared less about a weather balloon. I know that at the time the sightings happened, it went to General Ramey . . . and he along with the people out at Roswell decided to change the story while they got their act together and got the information into the Pentagon and into [*sic*] the President." Exon was quite positive that no elected official, excluding the president, was ever privy to the top echelon's existence or findings. One reason he gave for the secrecy was that the "oversight committee" had among its duties "to design studies to exploit it [the technology]." Here we have additional confirmation that secrecy was maintained to privately experiment on and exploit superior extraterrestrial technology.

Dr. Hermann Oberth, one of the great pioneers in astronautics, who unequivocally stated his belief publicly that UFOs are extraterrestrial spacecraft, also believed private exploitation was occurring. He said in 1974, "We cannot take the credit for our record advancement in certain scientific fields alone; we have had help." Asked by whom, he answered, "The people from other worlds." And Dr. Wernher von Braun, commenting from Germany on the unexpected deflection of U.S. rocket *Juno 2* in 1959, said, "We find ourselves faced by powers which are far stronger than we had hitherto assumed, and whose base is at present unknown to us. More I cannot say at present. We are now engaged in entering into closer contact with those powers, and in six or nine months' time it may be possible to speak with more precision on the matter." Von Braun's comment, especially, has been taken by some to mean that secret arrangements of one sort or another exist between world superpowers and alien beings, but he may have meant by "closer contact" the handling of further crash recoveries. Roswell was probably not an isolated incident. Good cases can be made for more than one recovery over the years, both in America and abroad, but since the documentation for those cases is less certain than that of Roswell, it would not do to spend time on them here. And, as will be discussed later, such mysterious "deflections" are still occurring, most recently in two Soviet and one United States probes to Mars.

While elected officials may not have been included in the top echelon's knowledge, there is some indication that at least one congressional member may have been part of the reason the Albuquerque transmission was interrupted. New Mexico's Senator Dennis Chavez called KGFL staff member Jud Roberts on July 9, from Washington, D.C., "suggesting" that the station not air a recorded interview with Mac Brazel—acquired when they quickly realized their missed opportunity with Frank Joyce on the seventh—on threat of losing their license. Earlier the same day, Roberts and his reporting team had been among the many civilians turned away from the crash site by the cordon of military police. As a result of Haut's press release the day before, every news organization's phone in Roswell was ringing off the hook, "calls from London and Paris and Rome and Hong Kong," as *Roswell Morning Dispatch* editor Art McQuiddy recalled, and someone very high up did not want any more news getting out than already had.

The official weather balloon story was obligingly posed and issued from General Roger M. Ramey's office, by Ramey, Jesse Marcel, and Thomas DuBose, at 6 PM on the eighth. Seventeen minutes later, as documented by the FBI memo, the "disc and balloon" were winging their way to Wright Field. DuBose later confirmed that earlier debris had gone on to Washington via Fort Worth and General Clements McMullen on the night of the sixth, which would have been the sample Brazel gave Sheriff Wilcox: "Nobody, and I must stress this, no one was to discuss this with their wives, me with Ramey, with anyone. The matter as far as we're concerned was closed." More evidence of compartmentalization from the very start, and at the highest levels.

Conveniently, Sherman Campbell and his daughter found a downed weather balloon in Circleville, Ohio, on July 6, which was immediately identified. Despite the quick identification, a picture of the two with the object appeared in the paper, and the public associated both cases in their mind, giving the Roswell cover-up story greater credence. Though the military did not involve themselves in the investigation, which was over before they could be called, they were plainly aware of it and hoped to exploit it. Given the extreme convenience of the report, and confirmation from Thomas DuBose that wreckage from the Roswell crash was sent out on the same night the Ohio story was reported, there is added reason to believe the Army staged the Circleville weather balloon themselves. The *Roswell Daily Record* of July 9 reported that Brazel, Marcel, and Blanchard had been unable to configure the wreckage into a "kite" to explain it, and a kite is precisely what the downed Ohio weather balloon was reported to look like. The "Louisiana" case referred to in the Hoover memo was also much too neatly timed on July 7 to avoid suspicion as a deliberate military fraud for the FBI's, and so the public's, benefit. Two weather balloons downed in two days is highly unlikely; three, in three days, unlikelier still. But the public, and even other governmental investigative branches, were being conditioned to accept "weather balloon" as a probable explanation not only for suspected downed craft, but also unidentified objects in the sky. In the papers, explanations began mentioning hallucinations and illusions as well.

Colonel Blanchard abruptly went on leave, and Mac Brazel was taken into military custody on the ninth. KGFL interviewer Frank Joyce could see in a second interview with the rancher on that day that he "was under a great deal of stress." The interview concluded with the military escorting him away, but before he left, Brazel turned back to Joyce and said, "Frank, you know how they talk of little green men? . . . They weren't green."

That bodies of a flight crew were recovered at Roswell has been much disputed, but turns out to be easily proven not only by numerous eyewitnesses, but also countless corroborative accounts. These will be examined in coming chapters, proving the existence of the occupants, and the veracity of the witnesses, by leaving no question as to the occupants' exact nature. Once the crashed saucer was discovered, everyone who had become part of the investigation was convinced there had to be a flight crew somewhere. This was an erroneous assumption on their part, since the possibility existed that the saucer was an entirely automated craft of some sort, as at least a few later ones seem to have been. But, for the time, it wasn't a bad guess. It appears to have been correct.

A Washington CIC agent named Thomas told Frank Kaufman at the Roswell base, on July 8, "We don't know if there are bodies, but we're looking for them." Mac Brazel had accompanied two CIC men in an aerial reconnaissance on the same day, looking for a second crash site. At least three other flights over the desolate area were made the same day. They finally found what they were looking for about two and a half miles southeast of the main crash site.

Archaeologist Grady "Barney" Barnett and other university archaeologists were already there, before a cordon could be thrown up. Some researchers have discredited Barnett's account, because the date and site they incorrectly investigated were July 3 and the Plains of San Agustin near Magdalena, neither of which could have been the case because Barnett stayed home and wrote in his journal that day. Barnett told friends in secrecy that he had found the bodies on the third, but—like Mac Brazel, who later altered the date he claimed to have found "the balloon" to June 14, for members of the press—he had almost certainly been intimidated by the military beforehand.

"It amounted to humiliation and detention when there wasn't any good reason," Brazel's neighbor and friend Marian Strickland recounted for the documentary, *UFOs: A Need to Know*. "He [Brazel] had come in, in good faith. And they didn't accept it that way, or didn't appear to. He said they threw him in jail. He said if he ever found anything like that again, he would never show it to them. He would never bring it in, he had done so as what he thought was a good citizen, and he had been humiliated and mistreated. And he was very disturbed." Brazel asked friends to accept his new story after being intimidated. "It'll go hard on me," he would say. Paul Brazel, one of Mac's sons, insists that Mac never got any sort of payoff money from the military, but his neighbors noticed that soon after his week's detention, Mac suddenly had enough money to buy a new pickup truck, a meat locker in Las Cruces, and a new house in Tularosa.

Accepting, then, that Barnett may have changed the date and/or location of his discovery when relaying the story of his find to friend L. W. "Vern" Maltais, that story as related to Randle and Schmitt was, "They [sic] were three or four of them, all wearing one-piece gray suits with no sign of buttons, snaps or zippers. They were small creatures, four to five feet tall, with large, pear-shaped heads, small bodies, and skinny arms and legs." He had seen "pretty good sized" wreckage that had "burst open," but didn't much notice it because of the bodies. Very soon after he discovered them, a small group of people also claiming to be archaeologists working the same site said they had seen the bodies and wreckage. Before Barnett could discuss it any further with them, the military arrived and told them it was their "patriotic duty" to remain silent about their find because it was part of a "classified project," and escorted the lot of them away.

Randle and Schmitt succeeded in finding two witnesses to seemingly confirm Barnett's account. Cafe owner Iris Foster came forward as the result of an *Unsolved Mysteries* broadcast. She knew an amateur archaeologist and pottery hunter called Cactus Jack, who had told her in the early 1970s that "he had been there when the spaceship had come down." He described four bodies as small, in silver uniforms and covered in blood that was "like tar, thick and black." And on February 15, 1990, the late archaeologist Dr. W. Curry Holden of Texas Tech University, whose anonymity was maintained by request until his death in April of 1993, stated that he and a team had been north of the Capitan Mountains in central New Mexico seeking evidence of pre-American and -Spanish occupation of the area, and discovered what he took to be "a crashed airplane without wings." They drove closer and saw three bodies matching the previously given descriptions, even mentioning that one arm was bent at an odd angle, which was noted by the nurse at the air hospital who claimed later to have examined them. They had silvery suits, which sounds like the one-piece gray suit described by others. The faces were not close enough to be visible, that of the closest one being turned away from the witness. A military Jeep arrived before too long, carrying armed officers who ordered them away and escorted them from the site. They were ordered not to discuss what they had seen for reasons of national security. Their names were taken, and they were clearly threatened with the loss of their government grants if they talked. Those threats were sufficient to cause the witness to continue his anonymity until his death. As the researchers relating the account say, "He was sure that if he told stories of crashed saucers and a dead flight crew it could come back to haunt him," adding, "it establishes just how powerful the government's threats have been. Those threats have silenced people for more than forty years." In fact, it is now almost fifty.

Admittedly, it is not possible to be certain whether any or all of these individuals are telling the truth, and a great deal of debate has been undertaken by respected UFOlogists concerning the places and dates given by various witnesses in regards to their reliability. The "Cactus Jack" story is the least possible to corroborate, the man being either dead or his present whereabouts unknown, perhaps even being entirely fictitious, the story related secondhand. The testimony of the archaeologists is, in any event, secondary to the greater mass of evidence provided by military witnesses and mortician Glenn Dennis, soon to be encountered. Subsequent descriptions to the same effect by abductees of UFO occupants make for the good possibility that some of the claimed witnesses at the crash site did see the bodies, and so the alleged Roswell witnesses' testimony is included for the reader to make his own decision concerning each.

The site was cleared and cordoned by the military, and a truck of ice arrived, into which the bodies were put and covered with a tarpaulin. Both Sergeant Melvin E. Brown and Captain Darwin E. Rasmussen told of having seen them at the location. Rasmussen's cousin, Elaine Vegh, testifies that he told her father "that he had no doubt flying saucers were real because he'd helped to retrieve the bodies from one that crashed." Brown, who replaced another soldier on watch at dusk, disobeyed orders and looked beneath the tarp. He described the bodies as smaller than human and yellowish orange, possibly hued strangely by the lighting, with leathery and beaded skin. Brown was dismissed after the bodies arrived at the Roswell Army Air Field base hospital, but stood guard over them again outside the hangar where they were placed later that night.

Roswell mortician Glenn Dennis arrived soon after. The military had been calling all day asking him questions about preservation. He was eventually told that there had been three fatalities in a crash, two mangled but one "in fairly good shape," and they wanted to know if all of them could be put into a single hermetically sealed casket. Later in the afternoon, he was summoned to convey a pilot to the hospital with only a broken nose and the most superficial of head injuries, all of which could easily have been faked for the same reason the weather balloon had been. At the rear of the hospital, where the man was escorted by an MP up the ramp, Dennis noticed "there was some wreckage" in the back of three old-fashioned boxy ambulances, which he did not find at all unusual under the circumstances, since a little crash wreckage sometimes got thrown into ambulances during recoveries. "Looked like some particles or pieces from a crashed airplane," he said. "In the second, there looked to be some almost identical pieces. In the third ambulance, I don't believe there was any debris, but there was an MP by the door." When he got a better look at it, he found some of it unusual. "What I saw reminded me of the front part of a canoe . . . about three feet long and lying up against the side . . . tipped [so that] the open side was against the floor. There were some inscriptions on [a] border around part of it . . . three inches maybe . . . going along the contour of the wreckage. . . .[which] reminded me of Egyptian inscriptions."

He stepped into the lounge for a Coke, and a new nurse waylaid him, "very excited," saying, "How did you get in here? You're going to get into trouble. Get out of here as fast as you can." Having said her piece, she immediately disappeared through a side door. Dennis did not leave, and was confronted by a prematurely graying middle-aged officer who asked him, "Who are you? What are you doing here?" He responded that he had brought a pilot in on an emergency call. Had he left it at that, he might have been left alone, but he added, "Looks like you've had a crash. I see some debris in the ambulance there." The officer summoned two MPs and ordered them to get Dennis out, which they did, first threatening him. "There was a big, tall, six foot-three or -four redheaded captain," Dennis later related. "And he came up to me and [tapping me] like that, he said, 'Mister, don't go in Roswell, and don't say there's been a crash or anything, cause nothing's happened out here.' I said, 'Look, Mister, I'm a civilian. And you can't do a damned thing to me, and you know that.' And that's when he said, 'Mister, somebody'll be diggin' your bones outta the sand.'"

The next day, Dennis phoned the nurse who had warned him away, asking "if it would be all right if I could drive out because I would like to know more about the incident." It took him two or three hours, at about 11:30, to get a return call. "I understand you've been trying to call me," she said. "I don't want you coming to the hospital. I would rather see you at the officers' club." Over Cokes and lunch—which the nurse never touched—she said, "I want to tell you what this is all about, but you have to give me a sacred oath that you won't ever mention this or my name and get me into trouble. I can't believe what I've just seen. This is the most horrible thing I've ever seen in my life."

"I don't think she said alien bodies," Dennis specified, recounting the story almost fifty years later for witnesses. "I think she said foreign bodies. Then she described to me what happened when she got involved in it." Performing her normal duties at the hospital, she entered an examination room for supplies and encountered two doctors she'd never seen, who said, "You stay here. We've got to have you." Three bodies were in the room, two badly mangled and the other mostly in one piece. The nurse explained to Dennis that they had been examining the bodies of small beings that weren't human. They "didn't know what they were or where they came from." She gave no medical specifics of the examination, saying only that the shock and the overpowering smell finally drove her out of the room, and that the bodies were sealed in mortuary bags to be taken to the morgue before being sent on to Wright Field. "She said it was so gruesome and so horrible," recounted Dennis. "She was in a state of shock . . . she looked like she was going into total shock. She never touched her food."

It must have been an unusual autopsy, to say the least. The nurse saw no indication of gender. The doctors didn't tell her, nor did she ask. Her only response to Dennis when asked about their sex was, "I didn't pay any attention and was so sick." She wasn't even sure whether the bodies were dressed or not, meaning she must not have seen them medically opened up—if she had, they would unquestionably have been naked. Her nausea and horror overpowered her professional ability, which must be taken into account when considering her report, as must the fact that it is being rendered secondhand by Glenn Dennis. If she did see anything internal, she never said. She did give some particulars of their exteriors. She said that their arms were consistently different from human arms, in that they were longer from wrist to elbow than from elbow to shoulder, and that she wasn't sure, but she thought they only had four fingers—she only saw one hand turned over, and it looked like the thumb was "missing"—with hollowed-out suction cups on their tips. Whatever they had for a bone structure (the only indication she gave of having seen anything inside the bodies, possibly as the result of crash damage) was no thicker than a human finger, brittle, and more "like real thick cartilage." The heads, oversized with sunken eyes, were "very pliable. It was like a newborn baby . . . You could push the sides and it would be movable." They bore a markedly concave nose with two small orifices, and two small orifices were all that were noticed on either side of the heads to function as ears. The mouth was ". . .very thin. [It] didn't have a full lip . . . hardly any lip at all. In place of teeth, it looked like a piece of rawhide. The doctors said it was even harder than the bone structure." This last comment implies that she may not have seen the bones herself, or felt them, since she clearly specified in this instance that she was repeating what she was told, not what she had personally experienced. Pressed for more details, she had nothing more she was able to tell Dennis, but did provide a sketch for him before excusing herself— saying she felt sick—to go to her barracks and lie down.

Dennis never saw her again, and her whereabouts from that time to the present remain entirely unknown. He called the base the following day to see if she had recovered and was feeling better. "They told me she wasn't working," Dennis said, "she wasn't available that day. The next day I made two or three calls, and it was also that she was unavailable. On the third day I called again. They said she'd been transferred out. They didn't know where, but she was no longer at the air base. About ten days to two weeks later, I got a letter from her . . . just a note . . . [that said] 'I can't write right now, but here's an APO number you can send mail to.' I wrote a letter back . . . probably two weeks [later] . . . [it] was returned to me, and the envelope said 'Return to sender,' and it had big red print that said, 'Deceased.'" The only answer he was ever given, to repeated queries, was that she had died on a plane crash with five other nurses while on maneuvers, despite the fact that the *New York Times Index,* the National Transportation and Safety Board, and the Army's own records have never shown evidence of any such crash. Dennis' father was warned by Sheriff Wilcox that "Glenn is in some kind of trouble at the base. I don't know what it is, but I've had a black sergeant inform me to tell you to tell your son to keep his mouth shut, because he didn't see anything out at the base." The sergeant referred to had been with the redheaded captain who told Dennis they'd be "digging his bones out of the sand" if he talked, gratuitously adding that Dennis "would make good dog food." Wilcox had been threatened as well, despite his having cooperated with the military from the beginning. Wilcox's granddaughter testified in 1991 that her grandmother, George Wilcox's wife, Inez, had told her that military police had come to the jailhouse in 1947 "and told George and [Inez] that if [they] ever told anything about the incident, talked about it in any way, not only would [they] be killed, but they would get the rest of the family."

Captain Pappy Henderson, one of Blanchard's most trusted officers, also saw the bodies. He told friend and confidante, military physician Dr. John Kromschroeder, about them while the two were fishing in 1978. Henderson was "clearly nervous" discussing it, and only brought the subject up because Kromschroeder would respect the classification of the material. He hadn't even told his wife, Sappho, in all the intervening years. Kromschroeder relayed that Henderson said they were "kinda little guys" he hadn't gotten a good look at, having wanted to get away from them as quickly as possible. To the best of his knowledge, they had been put in deep freeze, and in a later 1986 conversation he still thought they were at Wright-Patterson. Kromschroeder believed him without proof at the time, but in 1979 Henderson showed him a sliver of metal he claimed was from the craft. Kromschroeder, familiar with metallurgy, had never seen its like. After reading an article on the Roswell crash in 1982, Henderson told his daughter, Mary

Katherine Groode, that the bodies recovered "were little men, gray, with slanted eyes and tiny mouths," giving no other particulars.

General Exon also confirmed that the bodies ended up at Wright-Patterson, though he had not seen them himself: "They did say there were bodies . . . they were all found, apparently, outside the craft itself but were in fairly good condition. In other words, they weren't broken up a lot. One of them went to a mortuary outfit . . . I think at that time it was in Denver. But the strongest information was that they were brought into Wright-Pat."

Former executive assistant to the deputy director and special assistant to the executive director of the CIA, Victor Marchetti, author of the first tell-all book on the Agency, *The CIA and the Cult of Intelligence,* said in 1979 that the subject had always come under the heading "very sensitive activities." Though never having seen any conclusive evidence of UFOs himself, he did admit to having heard "high level" rumors of "little gray men" kept at Wright-Patterson's Foreign Technology Division.

The most comprehensive report of the bodies is a composite by Randle and Schmitt in *UFO Crash at Roswell,* combining pathologist Dr. Jesse Johnson's claimed eyewitness autopsy report with other supposed eyewitness testimony given to researcher Len Stringfield: "The bodies measured between three and a half and four and a half feet and weighed about forty pounds. There were two large, almond-shaped eyes without pupils that were under a heavy brow ridge. The eyes were elongated and appeared slightly slanted, giving the face an Oriental look. They were set deep and wide apart and without an eyelid, just a slight fold. The head was large by human standards, which meant it was not in proportion to the body. Instead of ears, there were small openings on the side of the head. The nose was indistinct, almost invisible, with only a slight protuberance. The mouth was small and described as a slit without lips. According to the doctor, the mouth didn't function as a means of communication or as a way of eating. In fact, the mouth appeared to be a wrinkle-like fold and was only about two inches deep. The head seemed to be hairless . . . The bodies themselves were hairless. The torso was small and thin. The arms were long and thin, reaching down to the knees. The length from the shoulder to the elbow was shorter than the length from the elbow to the wrist [the "broken" appearance noted by the nurse and the archaeologist]. The hands had four digits and no opposable thumb and seemed to have sucker pads at the end. Two fingers appeared longer than the others. This is consistent with the descriptions given by the nurse at Roswell. The legs were short and thin. The feet were covered, though one source did say that the feet didn't have toes . . . The skin, as everyone who ever saw the bodies pointed out, was not green. The skin was a pinkish gray . . . [and] was tough and leathery. Under magnification, it had a mesh-like structure . . . Most of the firsthand sources who reported seeing the bodies had no opportunity to see any internal structures. One of Stringfield's sources did. He said there were no teeth and no apparent reproductive organs . . . There was a colorless liquid prevalent in the body but without red blood cells. There was no evidence of a digestive system or upper gastrointestinal tract and no lower intestinal or alimentary canal or rectal area."

Dr. Robert I. Sarbacher, who according to Timothy Good was at least one of Wilbert Smith's informants for his top-secret Canadian government memorandum in 1950, was asked about his knowledge on the subject by researcher William Steinman in 1983. Sarbacher had been consultant to the Research and Development Board during the Eisenhower administration, and was president and chairman of the board of the Washington Institute of Technology. He wrote to Steinman that he "had no association with any of the people involved in the recovery and have no knowledge regarding the dates of the recoveries," indicating certainty of one such recovery and the strong possibility of others. He verified, concerning the top-secret group rumored to be investigating such material, that "John von Neuman [*sic*] was definitely involved. Dr. Vannevar Bush was definitely involved, and I think Dr. Robert Oppenheimer also . . . This is all I know for sure." Von Neumann and Oppenheimer are not on the MJ-12 documents, and are likelier names to be associated with that theoretical group than many of the ones that are found listed there.

"My association with the Research and Development Board . . . was rather limited," Sarbacher reported, "so that although I had been invited to participate in several discussions associated with the reported recoveries, I could not personally attend the meetings . . . About the only thing I remember at this time is that certain materials reported to have come from flying saucer crashes were extremely light and very tough. I am sure our laboratories analyzed them very carefully." Again, he makes references to more than one recovery, verifying at least that the former reference was not an accident.

Sarbacher's report of the occupants is the most interesting of all, and may ultimately stand as the best evidence of their existence: "There were reports that instruments or people operating these machines were also of very light weight, sufficient to withstand the tremendous deceleration and acceleration associated with their machinery. I remember in talking with some of the people at the office that I got the impression these 'aliens' were constructed like certain insects we have observed on earth, wherein because of the low mass the inertial forces involved in operation of these instruments would be quite low."

The "insectoid" appearance was noted in the autopsy report that prompted Republican New Mexico Representative Steven Schiff to open a congressional investigation into the Roswell crash. In a late 1993 *Denver Post* article, the supposed autopsy report was said to describe one of the bodies slightly differently than the lengthy description in Randle and Schmitt's book. The exception was said to be black, with an exoskeletally hard body, and a face like an insect. Interestingly enough, the discrepancy is marginal, and does more to confirm the bodies' existence than to deny them, as will be seen in numerous cases to be encountered in the coming chapters.

If no other testimony existed about the reality of a flying saucer crash near Roswell, New Mexico, on the night of July 2, 1947, the occupant reports, compiled by Randle, Schmitt, and Stringfield, and the Sarbacher letter would prove it. Not only does each prove the other's validity, but they all manage to prove the nature and truth behind the vast majority of all saucer occupant reports to follow. They are the smoking gun evidence of the reality of flying saucers, in that they provide the single underlying detail that matches in all reports.

But before this is demonstrated, the best UFO cases after Roswell should be examined, to better tie together the answers to the entire mystery in due course. Chief among these cases is the compartmentalization and duplicity of the official government investigations themselves. What began at Roswell and continues into the present day is, itself, extremely revealing.

2

Investigations

B
Y THE END of July 1947," wrote Edward J. Ruppelt in his book, *The Report on Unidentified Flying Objects,* "the UFO security lid was down tight. The few members of the press who did inquire about what the Air Force was doing got the same treatment that you would get today [1956] if you inquired about the number of thermonuclear weapons stock-piled in the U.S.'s atomic arsenal. No one outside of a few high-ranking officers in the Pentagon knew what the people in the barbed wire enclosed Quonset huts that housed the Air Technical Intelligence Center [ATIC] were thinking or doing." Ruppelt does not mention Roswell, but what else explains the particular timing of this sudden security?

On September 23, 1947, ATIC sent a letter in response to the commanding general's verbal request for an assessment of unidentified flying objects. "The reported phenomena were real," was its conclusion. "The question, 'Do UFO's exist?' was never mentioned," says Ruppelt. "The only problem that confronted the people at ATIC was, 'Were the UFO's of Russian or interplanetary origin?' Either case called for a serious, secrecy-shrouded project. Only top people at ATIC were assigned to Project Sign." The controversial MJ-12 documents give September 24, 1947—one day after this letter—as the date for the formation of that group.

ATIC officers sent the report, referred to as the "Estimate of the Situation," up the chain of command. Its conclusion, based on the best available information from military sources, was that flying saucers were extraterrestrial spacecraft, meaning controlled devices that travel both inside the earth's atmosphere and outside of it. General Hoyt S. Vandenburg in the Pentagon summarily pronounced that the conclusions were not supported by the evidence, and ordered the document declassified and burned. Such an order is a standing contradiction: a declassified document can be read by anyone; it does not need to be destroyed. Only a document of the highest security would need to be burned.

"The general said it would cause a stampede," Ruppelt told Major Donald Keyhoe. "How could we convince the public the aliens weren't hostile when we didn't know it ourselves?" Captain Edward Ruppelt, who had already been sent out to investigate early reports and soon was to head Project Blue Book, saw the supposedly destroyed "Estimate" four or five years later. Some copies were not burned, either because the officers ordered to do so found the evidence convincing enough to save for further research, or simply because they wanted the report as a curiosity. Ruppelt never specified details of the report, but portions of it are found in the declassified Project Blue Book.

The "Estimate of the Situation" was the concluding report of Project Sign—sometimes referred to by the press as "Project Saucer"—the Air Force's first official UFO investigation. Another military-headed investigation paralleled it, Project Twinkle, which will be discussed in the next chapter. Twinkle was not a general study on the phenomenon, but a specific attempt to answer the question of what aerial unknowns were traversing the airspace of atomic energy sites. Twinkle never reached any conclusions, finally disbanding for lack of evidence to study. Project Sign, though it preceded Project Twinkle, could be said to have been an extension of it, since the logical conclusion was that the unknowns over the installations were the same unknowns being spotted elsewhere.

Subsequent investigations fared no better. They weren't meant to. They were designed to satisfy the public that the objects reported were all either misidentifications, hoaxes, or the product of sick minds. Project Sign might have been different from the others in one regard, being the first. It could have been an attempt by the Air Force and the Pentagon to see what their own best investigators' conclusions would be concerning the phenomenon *without* the hard physical evidence already in their possession. In other words, it might have been a test to see if concealment of the routine facts was even necessary to maintain secrecy. As Hoyt Vandenburg's treatment of Sign's conclusions proves, it was.

The beginning paragraph of the "Estimate," as it came to be known, underscored not the determination of the reality or nonreality of unidentified flying objects, but rather the fact that so long as no physical evidence was given to investigators to examine, they would be "proved non-existent" in the face of any alternative explanation provided: "No definite and conclusive evidence is yet available that would prove or disprove the existence of these unidentified objects as real aircraft of unknown and unconventional configuration. It is unlikely that positive proof of their existence will be obtained without the examination of the remains of crashed objects. Proof of non-existence is equally impossible to obtain unless a reasonable and convincing explanation is determined for each incident."

The report continues, "Evaluation of reports of unidentified objects is a necessary activity of military intelligence agencies. Such sightings are inevitable, and under wartime conditions rapid and convincing solutions of such occurrences are necessary to maintain morale of military and civilian personnel. In this respect, it is considered that the establishment of procedures and training of personnel is in itself worth the effort expended on this project." For this, one could read: *It is impossible to keep people from seeing the unknown aircraft we have been seeing ourselves and that we have determined are most likely to be interplanetary. However, so long as investigators never acquire such hard physical evidence as we have sequestered, our trained program of debunking will suffice to explain them away.*

In 1949, Project Sign became Project Grudge, with the name changed because the Air Force believed the original had been compromised. Grudge specifically treated all UFOs as misidentifications to be explained. Any report that *could* be a weather balloon was determined to *definitely* be a weather balloon, whether the facts really fit the given answer or not. The official policy of debunking was formally institutionalized.

"This attitude can be readily seen in the 'Montana Movie' case," Kevin Randle writes in *The UFO Casebook.* "Air Force analysis of the films didn't take very long. It was reported that two jet fighters might have been in the area at the time of the sighting. Air Force officers picked this up in the initial report, circled it, and wrote next to the remark, 'This is probably it.' They simply did not care that witnesses said they saw the jets just after the objects disappeared and that they viewed the UFOs at relatively close range. A later Air Force study revealed that for the objects to be mistaken for jets, they would have to be over twelve miles away. But the jet theory remained the official Air Force explanation."

This particular case concerns a home movie made by the manager of the Great Falls, Montana, baseball team, Nick Mariana. He and his secretary, Virginia Raunig, were inspecting the field and saw two bright discs in the sky. Mariana obtained close to twenty seconds of footage, showing the objects flash brightly over a building and behind a water tower. Virginia immediately called the papers. For the next couple of months, Mariana showed the film to civic groups. One of his audience members wrote to Wright Field, after suggesting it to Mariana, on his behalf. The Air Force labeled the objects as misidentified airplanes and returned the film, but public interest in the case resulting from publication of the results caused them to request a second examination in 1952. The second verdict has already been mentioned above.

Mariana insisted that more than thirty frames of his film had been excised before its return. The frames were from the beginning, showing clearly the elliptical shape of the objects, and their transition from nearly stationary to mobile, which were crucial to the film's credibility. The Air Force admitted to removing a single frame for damaged sprockets, but not to any more than that. This was not the first or last time the Air Force misplaced evidence. In numerous instances, such items as metal samples were never returned at all.

The Robertson Panel, a CIA-convened group of scientists brought together in 1953 to publicly debunk UFOs, dropped the word "probable" from the aircraft explanation, but Dr. Robert Baker from Douglas Aircraft ran his own exhaustive test in 1955 concluding that no known natural phenomena were responsible. His tests included movies of his own, filming known airplanes in differing circumstances, the results of which he was not satisfied with.

The Condon Committee, the next decade's version of the Robertson Panel, reviewed the film again in 1966, once more concluding "aircraft," even as they admitted that the explanation was impossible. They hoped no one would notice that no airplane could have been filmed on August 5; the date in their file incorrectly showed August 15, a date when planes could have been in the area. In fairness, they were at least honest enough to admit the discrepancy in dates, but they still attempted a little sleight of hand with them. They also admitted that the objects filmed were clearly elliptical, unlike any airplane either then or now. Still, the answer was "aircraft." Such an answer is the equivalent of saying, "It doesn't look like a bird, act like a bird or sing like a bird. Therefore, it's a bird." The declassified Project Blue Book carries this case as one of its admitted unidentifieds, and officially answers the claim of debunkers that no undeniable photographic evidence of unidentified flying objects exists.

Late in 1951, Project Grudge became Project Blue Book, renamed by its new head, Captain Edward J. Ruppelt, because "the word 'Grudge' was no longer applicable. For those people who like to try to read a hidden meaning into a name, I'll say that the code name Blue Book was derived from the title given to college tests. Both the tests and the project had an abundance of equally confusing questions." Ruppelt was also the first person to use the term "UFOs" in place of "flying saucers," in an attempt to remove the derogatory and somewhat silly connotations that had become attached to the latter. It was a noble attempt, but history has shown it to be a wasted effort. As Jacques Vallée noted eleven years later, that term also soon wore out its welcome. "I still would like us to call it the 'Arnold Phenomenon,' or any such term that would break with the sensational and somewhat pejorative term 'flying saucer,' or the overly used and abused acronym 'UFO,'" he wrote in his journal, though interestingly enough—even despite his frequent later insistence that the physical nature of the objects goes beyond our full understanding—Vallée almost never referred to them during his association with Blue Book as anything other than "flying saucers." By any other name, UFOs would probably be as emotive and repelling to the public at large.

Whether Ruppelt was expected to continue a policy of debunking or to follow his own inclinations toward finding a serious answer, he chose the latter. For his own part, he was convinced they were physically real objects, and he intended to get the best possible data on them. He had little over a year to do so, before the hastily convened Robertson Panel debunked the entire phenomenon for the sake of the public and caused drastic federal policy changes concerning its investigation. Two of its more severe results were AFR (Air Force Regulation) 200-2 and JANAP (Joint Army/Navy/Air Force Publication) 146, which simultaneously criminalized the release by any military personnel of UFO-related information but made the reporting of all sightings to immediate superiors mandatory. Shortly after the Robertson Panel disbanded, Ruppelt was replaced.

Blue Book continued until 1969, when it was declassified. By that time, it had become only a glorified Grudge, identifying all sightings with whatever explanation could be manufactured, credible or not. The cases it examined were controlled. No one knows exactly who was doing the controlling or how, but everyone associated with Blue Book was convinced of it. But at least in its first year, Ruppelt did what he could to run an honest and thorough investigation. Like his contemporary, USMC Major Donald Keyhoe, he found himself outspokenly at odds with his superiors and the official military stance. He had ample opportunity to make waves, since 1952 was one of the biggest flap years in UFO history—hence the January 1953 Robertson Panel. The most significant occurrence of the year was the violation of White House airspace, nicknamed "The Washington Nationals" after the airport that made the initial sightings.

At 11:40 PM on July 19, 1952, seven blips were detected near Andrews Air Force Base by Washington National Airport fifteen miles to the north. Controller Ed Nugent assumed they were military aircraft. Abruptly, the blips accelerated from 100 or 130 miles per hour to a speed that took them off the screen in seconds. Senior controller Harry Barnes and secondary radar men Howard Cocklin and Joe Zacko were called into observation and confirmed the sighting. They alerted Andrews Air Force Base. The blips were moving at approximately 7,000 miles per hour at their fastest, stopping suddenly and then cruising about. And they were doing all this over the White House.

The military's response to the threat was inexplicable. Barnes was told that there was "not enough information" for a scramble. When he persisted, he was told that the situation was "in hand" and "being taken care of." Plainly, it was not. Between 1 and 3 AM two civilian planes in the vicinity reported blue-white whizzing lights and orange streaks, and one of Andrews' ground personnel saw a "huge, fiery-orange sphere." It took until almost dawn for a single jet interceptor to arrive, and when it did, it came all the way from Delaware, not Andrews. By that time, of course, there was nothing to intercept.

That a military air base would show no concern and take no action for six hours, while its country's executive building is flown over by seven unidentified aircraft, is inexcusable. Nevertheless, it is precisely what happened. The military's own observers confirmed the sighting made and reported by multiple witnesses of the professional civilian air sector. The Air Force's behavior is even more incomprehensible in light of the standard operating procedure to attempt "intercept and destroy" with all unidentifieds. Why the sudden exception? And for the nation's theoretically most secure airspace, no less?

Ruppelt flew to Washington at once, where of course the event was front-page news. The military gave him no cooperation. This would be odd enough in and of itself, since he was a captain, after all, but he was also much more than that: he was the man in charge of the national military investigation of exactly such incidents as this. But not only did they not assign him a staff car to interview witnesses, they actually told him to use the bus and pay for it out of his own pocket. Worse still, he was quickly informed that he was spending too much time away from Wright-Patterson (he had been gone less than a week), and would be listed as AWOL if he didn't immediately return. Aside from which, how could he conduct his investigation, and of so obviously important a matter, from his desk in Ohio?

Anyone needing proof of an official military cover-up and public deflection policy on the matter of unidentified flying objects need look no further than this single case. By any standard it makes no sense, except for one: that the military had two investigative groups—one for public appearance that was deliberately intended to deceive, and the other behind the scenes, of the highest security nature possible. Ruppelt was left with no choice but to give "no comment" as his terse response to the waiting press concerning the White House flyover. He was given no information himself from which to draw conclusions. And if he was the official investigator for the Air Force, then only orders from someone higher up could block his authority to conduct that investigation. The only explanation is that someone higher up did not want him finding any answers. In other words, Project Blue Book, like its predecessors, was a lie from the very beginning.

The treatment of the 1952 Washington, D.C., case is the best evidence for the existence of Blue Book as a purely cosmetic investigative group, scarcely more than a glorified public relations outfit. The creation soon after the White House flyovers of the most secret and least publicly accountable organization in the world, the National Security Agency, is evidence that the secret investigators still did not have the answers themselves, and were as intensely concerned in private over the Washington occurrences as they were publicly unconcerned. And the formation of the Robertson Panel immediately thereafter is proof that the private investigative group wanted the public as highly deflected from the subject of UFOs as was humanly possible.

The July 19 flyover must have been alarming enough to the military and governmental powers that be, behind closed doors. The only thing that could have rattled them more severely would be a sequel. One week later, at about 9:30 PM on July 26, they got exactly that: the uninvited guests made a return visit.

The local press were immediately on it. They rang Ruppelt in no time, punctuating the fact that the Air Force did not call him at all. They asked him what the Air Force was doing about it, and he angrily replied, "I have no idea what the Air Force is doing; in all probability it is doing nothing."

Ruppelt, however, did do something. The Air Force may not have taken his job seriously, but he did. He called one of his technical Blue Book consultants at the scene, Major Dewey Fournet, and asked him to assemble as many reliable men as possible. Fournet and civilian Air Force press agent Albert M. Chop arrived at the airport radar screens—not the military's—to witness the unknowns and monitor the ground-to-air contact of the jets sent by the military to intercept the intruders. Those planes, two F-94s, did not arrive until 11:25, two hours later, which is again an extreme delay, especially given that Andrews Air Force Base, being adjacent to the nation's capital, should have interceptors scrambled after unknowns in a matter of minutes. The press had also arrived, convinced that proof of flying saucers was finally at hand. The airport evicted everyone as the jets came on the scene, on the pretext (the Air Force's very word, according to author Jenny Randles) that interceptor communications had to remain confidential, but Albert Chop was present to subsequently report that one of the F-94s was suddenly rushed by the UFOs en masse, surrounding it in no time, causing badly shaken pilot Lieutenant William Patterson to radio Andrews Base for orders on whether or not he should fire upon them. "Stunned silence," according to Chop, was their reply. The UFOs broke the tension themselves, withdrawing a few moments later.

The historic cat-and-mouse game played out over the White House that night has been replayed many times since over military bases, evidenced by multiple eyewitness testimonies as well as actual documentation. For the next several hours until dawn on July 27, radar tracked "very probably solid metallic objects" being closed in on by F-94s. Every time the jets neared their targets, the objects disappeared—one second there, the next not—both visually and on radar. And every time the jets then started back to base, the objects suddenly reappeared as if they had never been gone. This behavior clearly denotes intelligent design. Natural phenomena do not camouflage themselves when threatened.

Later occurrences of exactly this sort will be examined in the next chapter, such as the Malmstrom Air Force Base incidents of 1975. There is a clear pattern established by these actions. American Indian tribes would call it "counting coup." It is a display of prowess precluding war. They play it as a game with sticks. Winning is accomplished by touching one's stick harmlessly between an opponent's shoulder blades: *gotcha*. A variation of this same game was until recently (and is perhaps still) going on between Russian and American ships at checkpoints, aircraft carriers of each side being sighted by the other's submarines, each sighting silently conveying a message: "I could have had a torpedo through your hull and gotten away before you even knew I was here."

The intelligence behind the UFOs was delivering a clear message to the military in July of 1952: *We traverse any airspace of our choosing. You have no say in the matter. The only reason you see us now is because we allow it, and we allow it only to communicate this message. It is useless to oppose or combat us. Leave us be.* An addition could be deduced from the highly visible encore performance: *And do not deceive yourselves into believing you can keep us concealed to preserve the myth of your power.*

The intuitive observer may note another clear message conveyed by these actions, and it is a most reassuring one. It has been more than forty years since the White House flap. With as much obvious technical superiority as the unknowns possess, they could have invaded or harmed our world in 1947 had that been their intention. So what are they waiting for? Christmas? And of what year? Unless, as seems plainly apparent, they intend us no harm at all.

Forty-eight hours after this second White House incident, Major General John Samford, the director of Air Force Intelligence, held the biggest press conference since WWII. Ruppelt, Fournet, Albert Chop, and another Blue Book specialist named Holcombe sat in the background, failing to protest the official Air Force verdict that their interceptors had spent close to eight hours chasing temperature inversions, and any lights seen in the sky during that time had been coincidental meteors. Ruppelt does not comment on this in his memoirs other than to state independently in his conclusion that, "When a ground radar picks up a UFO target and a ground observer sees a light where the radar target is located, then a jet interceptor is scrambled to intercept the UFO and the pilot also sees the light and gets a radar lock on only to have the UFO almost impudently outdistance him, there is no simple answer. We have no aircraft on this earth that can at will so handily outdistance our latest jets." He might have added that Nature also lacks such a capability.

Such an irresponsible oversight must rank with T.V. newscaster Dan Rather's completely reversed report on the direction Kennedy's head snapped when shot. Considering that Ruppelt left Blue Book very shortly afterward to write a serious work attesting to the reality of UFOs, and that he met not only with a complete lack of cooperation from the Air Force in his efforts but also was demonstrably threatened by them as well, we can only conclude that he and his retinue were present at the Samford conference under duress. Could Ruppelt have been part of the conspiracy of silence? By definition, he was—at least during the Samford conference. The controversial MJ-12 documents state that the head of Project Blue Book—who would have been Ruppelt—was an adjunct member of that theoretical group, serving as their liaison. While this is not impossible, it is unlikely. Ruppelt's actions belie the theory.

For instance, while only five pages in Ruppelt's book are devoted to the Washington Nationals, and his only reference to the Samford conference is that "It did take pressure off Project Blue Book— reports dropped from fifty a day to ten a day inside of a week," he devotes most of that space to disproving the Air Force's verdict. "We found out that the UFO's frequently visited Washington. On May 23 fifty targets had been tracked from 8:00 PM till midnight. They were back on the Wednesday night between the two famous Saturday night sightings [the Washington Nationals], and again the night of the press conference; then during August they were seen eight more times. On several occasions military and civilian pilots saw lights exactly where the radar showed the UFO's to be . . . Then there was another interesting fact: hardly a night passed in June, July, and August in 1952 that there wasn't a temperature inversion in Washington, yet the slow-moving 'solid' radar targets appeared on only a few nights." He adds that professional radar men like those at Washington National Airport certainly know the difference between weather conditions and solid aircraft.

Ruppelt even throws in, "Had the press been aware of some of the other UFO activity in the United States during this period, the Washington sightings might not have been the center of interest.... In fact, less than six hours after the ladies and gentlemen of the press said 'Thank you' to General Samford for his press conference, and before the UFO's could read the newspapers and find out that they were natural phenomena, one of them came down across the Canadian border into Michigan. The incident that occurred that night was one of those that even the most ardent skeptic would have difficulty explaining. I've heard a lot of them try and I've heard them all fail."

In short, Ruppelt called a press conference of his own to counter Samford's, which was his book *The Report on Unidentified Flying Objects.* However, Samford's press conference was front-page news, widely repeated over the years in books on the UFO subject; Ruppelt's book garnered some high-powered blurbs from major newspapers at the time of its publication, but who read it? It's falling apart from age and disuse on a few library shelves and used paperback cutout bins. Its only reprint, immediately before Ruppelt's death in 1960, added three new chapters completely reversing his previous stance on the subject, making him oddly his own debunker. "Most of the press, with some relief," writes Jenny Randles in *The UFO Conspiracy,* "accepted the [Samford] solution. After all, they presumed, the U.S. Air Force would surely not pretend there was nothing to worry about if the nation's capital really had been invaded by unknown phenomena."

Ruppelt wasn't the only disgruntled ex-Blue Booker. Fournet quit and joined a civilian UFO group, and Albert Chop also left, becoming an advisor on the 1955 Hollywood documentary, *U.F.O.,* about the early years of official investigation. Ruppelt said straight out that he considered it entirely possible he had been used by the Air Force as a "front man," and complained (before his abrupt and inexplicable recantation) that "there appear to be no confirmed saucer fans in the hierarchy of the professional societies. I continue to follow the subject of UFO's primarily because of my being requested for comment on the interplanetary flight aspects. My personal feelings have not changed [since leaving Blue Book] although I continue to keep an objective outlook."

The United States was not the only country to have sightings over its capital. England's Parliament and the Kremlin had similar occurrences, about which not enough is available for further comment here. China had what might have been one of the largest mass UFO sightings in modern times, when several hundred military personnel of Lintiao Air Base in Gansu Province saw a flight of UFOs on October 23, 1978, matching the description given two days earlier of a large aircraft seen by vanished pilot Frederick Valentich over the Bass Strait in Australia. Neither Valentich nor his plane were ever found, and his last words were, "Ah, Melbourne, that strange aircraft is hovering over me again . . . it is hovering and it's not an aircraft."

In 1954, Rome had some of the most remarkable UFO appearances on record. On October 30 of that year, Italian diplomat Dr. Alberto Perego and perhaps a hundred people watched two white dots at about two thousand meters, which seemed to those present to be aircraft of some type but not that anyone recognized. On November 6, dozens of the objects reappeared in formations. "At first I calculated that there were about fifty of them," Perego said, "but later I realized that there were at least one hundred. Sometimes they were isolated, sometimes in pairs, or in threes or fours or sevens or twelves. Frequently they were in diamond or 'lozenge' formations of four, or in 'V' formations of seven." If he was having hallucinations, then they were geometrically artistic hallucinations, and thousands of other people were hallucinating the same thing. The display started at about 11 AM. At noon, two formations of twenty unidentifieds each, coming from opposite directions, converged in the form of a St. Andrew's cross directly over Vatican City. The display grew and moved to new locations for the next hour before dispersing. The objects ejected massive amounts of the filament material called "angel hair" preceding their exit, none of which has apparently stayed intact for more than a few hours before dissolving and the content of which this author has never found published. No news of the display appeared in the next day's papers, but the objects reappeared and repeated the previous day's performance, as they did again on November 12.

The only press given to the events of November 6 was an *Il Messagero* report that squadrons of unidentified aerial objects had been detected that day *in England,* stating that "At the British War Office, they are concerned." In between the first and last of the Rome sightings, Dr. Perego contacted the chief of the cabinet of the Ministry of Defense, the principal secretary of Foreign Affairs, and the commander of the Italian Air Force, drawing a blank on the incidents from everyone except the last, who told him there was nothing to report because their radar didn't cover the altitudes of the unknowns in question. Perego did, however, manage to get visual confirmations of at least one of the incidents from the Vatican Observatory. The Air Force response is most interesting, for exactly the same reason it is interesting in the U.S. The Italian Air Force saying that its radar doesn't cover certain altitudes over Rome or the Vatican is the equivalent of a Washington homicide captain refusing to investigate a murder because it happened on the Senate steps.

But then, their actions are consistent with those of the USAF, and France's GEPAN. GEPAN, the *Groupe d'Etudes Phenomenes Aerospatiaux Non-Identifies,* was formed in 1977 as a committee of seven headed by Dr. Claude Poher, CNES (*Central Nationale d'Etudes Spatiales,* the French equivalent of NASA) director of the Sounding Rockets Division. CNES was the essential founding organization of GEPAN, cooperating with the Gendarmerie Nationale, who take UFO sightings quite seriously. In the beginning, GEPAN was more open to public comment, but soon it became another Blue Book, serving as public relations to front for more thorough— and private—investigations behind the scene. The French Gendarmerie is allied to the Air Force, unlike our own police forces, and a tighter lid can be maintained on secrecy. French UFOlogist Fernand Lagarde called them "the Masters of Silence." By 1984, their purpose was not even being kept a secret. Public relations officer Monsieur Metzle admitted, at a *France-Inter* press conference that year, "In 1977 it was necessary to tranquilize public opinion concerning the UFO phenomenon. And it was in that spirit that GEPAN was created."

UFOs have been witnessed all over the world, sometimes by massive numbers of people. If the Fátima miracles of 1917 were, as Jacques Vallée believes, UFO incidents, then seventy thousand people, from a great many nations, witnessed a single incident, and it was front-page news around the world. Closer to our era, on September 18, 1954, several thousand people saw a "green fireball" that passed right over a crowded football stadium in Santa Fe, lighting up the sky all the way into Colorado and jamming every switchboard in both states with reports. Neither of these examples could be attributed to natural phenomena or weather balloons, and few such incidents received any major news coverage except to dismiss them as exactly that. While such large-scale incidents cannot have failed to gain the attention of the authorities, news of any such official attention was very rarely publicized. And every country responded to them in the same way: with palliative research groups for public relations, showing evidence of more detailed investigations behind the scenes. In the case of Russia, one Soviet general was so staggered by the sheer weight of incoming reports that he openly advertised to the entire nation that he wanted all help possible in figuring out the UFOs, from any and every citizen, only to have his program appropriated three weeks later by the KGB, who continued it entirely in secret.

And then began the occupant reports. The most classic of these that was without an abduction—a separate phenomenon that will be discussed at length in coming chapters—was the 1964 Socorro sighting in New Mexico. Police patrolman Lonnie Zamora detoured from chasing a speeder at about 6 PM on April 24, to investigate a flaming roar that he took for an exploded dynamite shack. He found two small humanoids digging up plant and soil samples beside an egg-shaped craft in a gully, the description of which matched previous and later occupant reports. They were child sized, wearing white outfits. He couldn't make out anything in the way of features. Before he had much chance to look at them further, they saw him and quickly got back in their craft, which then took off with a roaring burst of flame. Understandably shaken by the incident, Zamora immediately reported it and was one of the few UFO witnesses in history not ridiculed by friends, peers, the press, or the public. The object left physical landing traces, and was considered by Blue Book scientific adviser J. Allen Hynek to be the single best case arguing for UFOs as physical "nuts and bolts spacecraft." The dimensions of the landing traces and the insignia observed on the craft showed up later in other investigations.

In its early years, Blue Book did not want to consider occupants. Solving the saucer problem invited enough paranoia and ridicule without mixing whatever occupants they might have into the equation. That occupants had already been recovered at Roswell, and perhaps other crash sites, was of course not available information to them, and tracking down precisely to whom that information was available is demonstrably difficult even today.

"Why is Blue Book rejecting all the landing reports?" Blue Book scientist Jacques Vallée complained in January of 1964, when such incidents had been reported for at least ten to fourteen years. "Why ignore Aimé Michel's well-documented accounts of humanoids simply because they seem fantastic? That is not a scientific criterion." Aimé Michel was one of the earliest UFO researchers in France, who discovered a later verified series of UFO landing patterns (called "orthoteny"), and Paleolithic cave drawings in his country with a remarkable resemblance to modern saucer configurations and their reported occupants.

"I don't know what makes me want to automatically look down on these creature cases," J. Allen Hynek admitted. "Maybe this involves an atavistic fear of the unknown, or of rivalry with another species."

Adding to the problem was the introduction of numerous "contactees," beginning with George Adamski, who claimed special liaisons with "space brothers." Adamski presented himself as a friend of "the Venusians," and showed home movies of what looked very much like a plastic model with light bulbs beneath it, as an alleged flying saucer. (Adamski's footage has never been satisfactorily demonstrated to be false, bearing witness to just how difficult it is to fully investigate even the seemingly most fallacious of cases.) Other claimants followed, virtually all, like Adamski, seeming to be colorful, middle-aged, uneducated kooks. Howard Menger claimed he ate "space potatoes" on the moon. Another man claimed an ongoing relationship with a Venusian woman named "Aura Rhanes," who was "tops in shapeliness and beauty." Their stories invariably sounded like the fantasies of sad, lonely, somewhat pathetic men, which indeed they may have been.

Considering the effect the contactees' reports had on serious UFOlogical study in the public eye, however, it cannot be ruled out that they were put up to their stories by parties interested in creating exactly the aura of ridicule and idiocy that resulted. The Air Force had deliberate hoaxsters and a vested interest, as Roswell and the conclusions of Project Sign prove—not to mention the outright later confession of some of the hoaxsters themselves. An excellent example of just such activity is the Glassboro, New Jersey, case of 1964. A suspected landing site at that location left a crater with sand fused into glass, and burned and broken trees, but no radioactivity. The military stated that firecrackers had caused the damage. When that answer failed to be accepted, "broke college students" suddenly stepped forward and announced they had hoaxed the landing to try and sell their story for money. The press made a big deal of the confession, but none of it stood up to examination. For one thing, the students claimed to have spread radium dioxide over the site, and no radiation showed up—aside from which, it is much too dangerous and expensive a chemical for poor college students to get their hands on. Furthermore, the burns went beyond what could have been caused by anything except perhaps a flamethrower, and the branches above and the roots of the trees beneath the crater had been crushed by a weight far greater than any team of hoaxsters could make even with heavy machinery. But, like the Roswell weather balloon, the "college students" story stuck in the public's mind. Though not conclusively proven to be an Air Force hoax, that explanation for the Glassboro "confession" is the easiest to accept.

Various effective civilian UFO organizations have been rendered impotent, and sometimes inactive, after ex-CIA members have joined their board of directors, the best example being the ousting of Major Donald Keyhoe from NICAP (National Investigations Committee on Aerial Phenomena). APRO (Aerial Phenomena Research Organization) head Jim Lorenzen was put under CIA surveillance in 1953, after the recommendations of the Robertson Panel. APRO's Paul Bennewitz, whose case will be considered at length in the next chapter, was skillfully fed disinformation by a false friend in the service of several intelligence agencies, until he was nearly driven out of his mind with paranoia.

In light of these and other hoaxes and probable disinformation ploys to be examined, the suggestion that some of the colorful "contactees" of the 1950s and '60s were government plants cannot be rejected out of hand. Vallée considers, in *Messengers of Deception,* that "the *contactees* . . . could have been set up in their roles . . . George Adamski gave credit to four U.S. government scientists for launching his career as an ambassador for the Space Brothers. They were from the Point Loma Naval Electronics Laboratory near San Diego, and from a 'similar setup' in Pasadena. They allegedly asked him if he would 'cooperate in the collective attempt to get photographs of the strange craft moving through space.' Adamski's major supporter abroad was a former intelligence officer with the British Army, and a Cambridge engineering graduate, who now lives in Mexico. And according to a man who hosted Adamski during his tour of Australia, he was traveling with a passport bearing special privileges." Indeed, when Howard Menger later recanted his outlandish space stories, he did so "muttering about a CIA experiment."

Author-journalist Howard Blum related his research into official UFO investigations in *Out There:* "After months of weary-eyed reading . . . I found myself recalling with some amusement a line in the secret CIA monograph that had been my starting point. *The Investigation of UFOs* huffily complained that in the twenty years following Kenneth Arnold's first sightings 'it became fashionable to accuse the Air Force of censorship or of withholding UFO information from the public.' And now I could understand why. For it was all preserved in the official files; they were a monument to the birth of a long and abrasive era of national skepticism. One day I would read military task force reports proclaiming there was no need for concern, no unanswered questions about UFOs. On the next, the Freedom of Information Act would unlock padlocked cabinets stuffed with secret trails, swarming with leads and false leads, classified documents pregnant with lingering problems. In those memos written for a restricted membership, there was always something—a fact, an ambiguity, an opinion—that was deliberately held back from the public. A succession of generals, CIA administrators, FBI officials, and presidential advisers had believed that their investigations should move forward behind the scenes. To tell all, their attitudes and actions suggested, would be a sin, a betrayal of institutional covenants. A fundamental law of spook behavior, as inviolable as an axiom of physics itself, guided the bureaucrats: For every story shared, there was one buried; for every truth announced, there was one suppressed. And so, perhaps inevitably given the cast of official characters involved, given their fears and concerns, from the first a cover-up had begun."

Professor J. Allen Hynek, director of Ohio State University's Department of Astronomy, was perhaps the only original scientific expert on Blue Book. Ruppelt was not fully satisfied with him, considering at least one of his important reports to be "weasel-worded." Hynek was often charged, even by his friends, with lacking the courage of his convictions. If he privately maintained a belief that evidence he had examined was indicative of some sort of interplanetary craft, he would publicly waffle and say he just wasn't sure some natural phenomenon wasn't the culprit as soon as the cameras and mikes were on him. Harsher critics overtly accuse him of aiding and abetting the Air Force cover-up, and there is sufficient available evidence for such an interpretation. For instance, he was a scientific adviser on the Robertson Panel, and approved of the debunking policy. Hynek's greatest gaffe was attributing the March 1966, Ann Arbor, Michigan, series of UFO reports to "swamp gas," which even the Air Force didn't believe but was more than happy to accept. If he had said "elephant farts," he couldn't have met with more derision—and the Air Force would have been equally happy. "Swamp gas" remains, to this day, the phrase used by many disbelieving the sincerity of a government report, especially on the subject of UFOs.

Hynek's protégé, Jacques Vallée, who maintains that his friend Hynek was a sincere and conscientious scientist to the end, nevertheless also unearthed evidence that he was, at the very least, weak willed. "Hynek has been charmed and neutralized by the Air Force," he wrote in his journals. "The Air Force kept Hynek around only as long as he was silent. I . . . put pressure on him, urging him to change his stance [in 1963]. A string of important cases forced the issue. When he started talking, arguing for a new study, the Air Force simply pushed him aside. First they defused the issue by getting their most vocal opponents to testify before bogus Congressional Hearings; then they selected Ed Condon, a physicist who was about to retire, and he signed his name to a report which was a travesty of science, yet reassured the establishment. They used that report to bring about the liquidation of Hynek's position, but they were careful not to fire him." Vallée concludes that Hynek enjoyed the prestige of his position sufficiently to make him fearful of losing it. "Hynek remains very prudent. He is clearly afraid of antagonizing the Air Force and losing his contract, hence access to the files, if he makes any waves. I have no such reservations, so I speak up against the Blue Book approach."

Vallée met Hynek in 1962 at Northwestern University, where he got his degree in computer science five years later. Born in France and trained in astrophysics, Vallée got involved in Blue Book more or less as Hynek's secretary the year after meeting him. Later, he became the principal investigator on Department of Defense computer networking projects. The biography in one of his books states that Vallée's initial interest in UFOs was sparked "when he witnessed the destruction of tracking tapes of unknown objects at a major observatory." In his own journals of the time, which make for excellent reading and should be required for any student on the UFO subject, Vallée relates a different story: "My interest in 'flying saucers' goes back to the Fall of 1954 when there was a deluge of sightings in France, and indeed throughout Europe, from England to Italy . . . As a kid I remember hearing one of the earliest French witnesses, a railroad worker named Marius Dewilde, telling his story to radio broadcaster Jean Nohain in a live interview on the evening news: 'I had gone out to piss . . . ' he bluntly told the whole nation. He had seen two little robots next to a dark machine resting on the nearby railroad tracks. The air police found traces of a large mass. A strange ray issued from the object and paralyzed Dewilde. I believed his story at the time. I still do . . . It was during the following year, a Sunday in May 1955, that I observed a flying saucer in Pontoise . . . What I observed was a gray metallic disk with a clear bubble on top. It was about the apparent size of the moon and it hovered silently in the sky above the church of Saint-Maclou. I have no recollection of seeing it go away. My mother says it flew off, leaving a few puffs of white substance behind." The same object had been independently witnessed by Vallée's college friend, quite some distance away, not long after.

Vallée noticed that something was fundamentally flawed with Blue Book, nearly from the start. In 1965, he wrote in his journal that a man he knew in the Italian Secret Service had made an extremely important report, the handling of which demonstrated the problem: "Luciano has sent me information about a near-landing that took place on 20 August 1963 at 9:32 PM and which he investigated with a secret service team under a special clearance from the Italian government. The witness was the trusted chauffeur of the Italian President, driving his official car. The site was the hunting preserve of the President, not far from Rome. A disk-shaped object resembling an upside-down saucer with a turret on top hovered at low altitude above the car. The case created quite a stir among the Intelligence services, understandably. The report was communicated to the U.S. authorities in Washington, who never followed up with the Italians but gave assurances they had passed it on to Hynek for evaluation. Yet Hynek has never seen the report, never heard of it! *I have used this case to point out to him again that he didn't see all the reports, that there must be another study somewhere, using Blue Book as a mere front.*"

Two months before, Vallée encountered similar suspicions among his colleagues. "Aimé [Michel] does not trust any of these shadowy people (Intelligence, any branch), whose very business is lying and cheating in the first place . . . Someone is using us to 'snow' somebody else, he thinks. But the sudden renewal of interest in the topic, the fact that they even talk about it, is very curious indeed."

Vallée's youthful integrity in attempting to conduct an honest scientific approach toward studying UFOs is more evident than Hynek's, and it is left to the observer to determine the reason for that or the extent of it. It appears very much as if Hynek was willing to deliberately play the part of the Air Force public relations man by being a front for the scientific community, in order to be allowed to conduct his own investigation in private. In other words, that he sacrificed the truth for the public in order to be allowed the opportunity to find it out for himself. "Dissatisfied as he may have been [with his Robertson Panel association] . . . Hynek apparently offered his cooperation with the CIA in the debunking program, as the report shows," notes author Timothy Good. He adds later, "I do not know if Dr. Hynek was actually employed as a CIA consultant subsequent to the Robertson Panel but it seems evident that he was in the best position to perform such a function, with worldwide contacts at official and unofficial levels. Many fellow researchers in a number of countries agree with me that while Hynek was always interested in gathering information, he seemed reluctant to give out much in return."

Like most other researchers, Good is reluctant to besmirch the name of a man long supposed to be a guiding light in the field, and gives Hynek a nod of thanks for "his contribution in putting over this controversial subject to the skeptical scientific fraternity." Good does, however, bring to light other valid criticisms of the man. For instance, he quotes APRO consultant Dr. Robert Creegan's comment, "Professor Hynek was never asked to be a member of either the Robertson Panel in 1953 or the Condon Committee, 1966-1969. Yet he was able to sit in on at least some of the meetings of both. He made no evident criticism of the evasiveness of the conclusions in either case. As a matter of fact the astronomer has been able to attend many or most UFO conferences in the U.S. and abroad, and has gone to the locales of major flaps. Obviously funds were adequate." Good also brings up Hynek's failed 1974 attempt to acquire a list of APRO's field investigators' home addresses and telephone numbers from the board of directors. "Hynek's motives may well have been innocent, and perhaps we should give him the benefit of the doubt . . . Yet certain questions remain unanswered."

Whatever his failings, Hynek was at least sufficiently impressed with Vallée to get him involved in Blue Book. Hynek appeared to agree with Vallée's approach, even when not openly seeming to embody it himself. "Comets seemed utterly fantastic in the Middle Ages," Vallée pitched to Captain Hector Quintanilla and Sergeant Moody, then heads of Blue Book, in January of 1964. "Artists have left us engravings that show comets as the hand of God holding a bloody sword in the sky. Yet competent scientists took the trouble to study them. If they had rejected them just because the reports sounded weird, where would astronomy be today? A scientist is supposed to be able to go beyond the report to the phenomenon itself." His views were not shared. "Hynek is impressed by this argument but I can see I am not getting through to Quintanilla, who has made it clear he wasn't concerned with science, or to Moody, who keeps looking at his watch." Vallée reminded them that stated opinions do not necessarily reflect the thoughts of those expressing them, something that would soon enough become evident in Hynek in a way other than Vallée meant. "You underestimate the level of interest which exists among scientists in private, even if they deny it in public," he said, to which Hynek added, "Carl Sagan himself is more interested than he would admit to his colleagues. At a recent astronomy meeting he walked up to me and told me privately that he had learned of my association with the Air Force." Sagan's strangely schizophrenic stance will be noted again later by author/lecturer and science writer Richard C. Hoagland.

After a year of not exactly promising work with Blue Book, Vallée had more pointed observations of his military colleagues. "[Moody's] universe is a world where neatly-ordered catalogues of Rational Events furnish well-behaved Models of Authorized Phenomena. Hynek jokes that the Air Force must have sent him to an elementary psychology class, from which he seems to remember only that the world is made for 'normal' people like him, and that anyone who reports an unusual phenomenon is simply 'nuts.'" At another time, Vallée added that "Moody deserves a Nobel Prize for his bold UFO 'explanations.' Thus he is the discoverer of a new species of *birds with four blinking lights.* It was also Moody who once decided that a certain observation was without merit because 'the reported object did not match any known aerial maneuvering pattern'!"

Quintanilla's attitude, from the start, was even less encouraging: "The Mission of the Air Force is to *identify, intercept and destroy* any unauthorized object that violates U.S. air space ... It's none of our business if a Martian shakes hands with a baker in Brittany. Our responsibility is limited to reports from U.S. citizens. What we are looking for? Enemy prototypes, spy craft, anything unusual that we can understand in terms of technology." This sounds like the regurgitation of a memorized order, and is especially interesting for its final sentiment in light of all the previous indications of private technological exploitation. It is also interesting in that it belies General Twining's comment that UFOs display evasive maneuvers when pursued by "friendly aircraft," itself a curious phrase since "pursuit" would hardly seem to be indicative of "friendliness."

Vallée gives an example of how Blue Book was sabotaged at the source: "In December 1964 a huge craft is said to have landed in Harrisonburg, Virginia, after flying over a car whose engine stalled. Some local college teachers measured strong radioactivity at the site. A few days passed, and a report was duly sent to the Air Force. More days went by. Quintanilla eventually sent two sergeants to investigate the case. They came back to Dayton and stuffed the report in the 'psychological' category ('the witnesses were nuts'). This neatly explained everything except for the radioactivity readings. One of the college professors, one Dr. Gehman, got angry and mailed his own observations to NICAP [the civilian UFO organization headed by former Major Donald E. Keyhoe]. He also reported on the unusual investigative technique used by the two sergeants, who had arrived on the scene no less than three weeks after the events. They carried a Geiger counter, but all they did with it was to sweep it over the field, which was now covered with a thick blanket of snow. Yet they seemed to be detecting something. Every time the needle of the counter hit the top, they would reset the calibration, saying reassuringly: 'That's all right, it does that all the time! There's no radiation here!'"

It should be noted that even though a great many sites where UFOs have reportedly landed do show a rise in radioactivity, the lack of it could not be expected to prove that nothing had been there. For instance, in one case Captain Ruppelt sent a machete alleged to have been involved in a UFO close encounter to the Wright-Patterson lab. "The question we asked was, 'Is there anything unusual about this machete? Is it magnetized? Is it radioactive? Has it been heated?' No knife was ever tested so thoroughly for so many things ... They found nothing, just a plain, unmagnetized, unradioactive, unheated, common, everyday knife." One cannot assume that a lack of radiation by itself is proof that no

UFO activity has been present at a given site. This presupposes that radiation must be present in an unidentified aerial object, which may or may not be the case but has yet to be established beyond a doubt. Criticisms of abductee cases based on the fact that the witnesses report regular-looking scalpels or hypodermics in place of something more exotic or "futuristic" equally presuppose that anyone capable of space flight must have developed the bloodless medical scanning beds in the sickbay on *Star Trek*. Since no one can evaluate evidence they don't have, coming to these conclusions in advance could only be the work of a prophet with a crystal ball, not a scientist. Perhaps, when all is said and done, advanced space flight can be accomplished without radiation leaks, and no matter how superior the technology, blood removal will still require needles.

Vallée stated, "To study UFOs is like studying meteorites, or an epidemic disease: the research has to cross national and cultural boundaries." It was to just such a comment that Quintanilla responded with his chauvinistic remark about bakers in Brittany. But true to his word, Vallée at least attempted to get the French military to help him break through the U.S. military resistance to studying the problem, and perhaps work on joint research. He met with a Colonel Cluerin, who listened to him, neutral but not unfriendly. Cluerin said he would see what he could do. A short time after, Cluerin rendered the French Air Force verdict: "We in the French Air Force, we are sick and tired of hearing all those unjustified attacks against the USAF experts who are impeccable scientists. Their investigations are top-notch . . . There is another point which is even more important. Why should we embark on doing a job no one is asking us to do? The Pentagon is perfectly right to downplay the whole thing. *Society is working just fine the way it is, why should we encourage all this saucer business?* It might stir up social repercussions we couldn't control. So the longer we wait the better it is for everybody. Let the scientists do something about it if they want to." Which would be a hell of a trick, considering that the military had all the evidence locked up, and no scientist can study what he can't see.

The emphasis in Cluerin's statement is given by Vallée in his relation of it. This clearly shows that Vallée had given thought to the reasons for the cover-up—or, perhaps, more accurately put, "lockdown"—of information, and that at the time of the writing, which was June of 1967, had picked up from the military that one of the important reasons was *fear.* Donald Keyhoe claimed that Captain Ruppelt once told him, "We're ordered to hide sightings when possible, but if a strong report does get out we have to publish a fast explanation—make up something to kill the report in a hurry, and also ridicule the witness, especially if we can't figure a plausible answer. We even have to discredit our own pilots."

Ruppelt expands on the fear factor in his comments concerning the Robertson Panel in his memoirs: "Another question the panel had was about Orson Welles' famous *War of the Worlds* broadcast of October 1938, which caused thousands of people to panic. Had we studied this to see if there were any similarities between it and the current UFO reporting? We had. Our psychologist had looked into the matter and gave us an opinion—to make a complete study and get a positive answer would require an effort that would dwarf the entire UFO project. But he did have a few comments. There were many documented cases in which a series of innocent circumstances triggered by the broadcast had caused people to completely lose all sense of good judgment—to panic. There were some similar reports in our UFO files." He concludes with, "But we had many reports in which people reported UFOs and obviously hadn't panicked," but no one seemed interested in that perspective, or to weigh in the fact that in 1938 the fictional broadcast that was mistaken for a real one "reported" that the unidentifieds were on a military attack, where no actual sightings on record show any demonstrable hostility.

Another, perhaps more credible, concern voiced by the Robertson Panel and even earlier by General Twining was the potential influence on the masses various organizations might manipulate if the UFOs became openly witnessed. Because of this, the Psychological Strategy Board (PSB) had been consulted from the beginning, and the Robertson Panel agreed with the Office of Strategic Intelligence (OSI) that even if no direct threat came from the unidentifieds, there were potential related dangers in "(a.) Misidentification of actual enemy artifacts by defense personnel. (b.) Overloading of emergency reporting channels with 'false' information . . . (c.) Subjectivity of public to mass hysteria and greater vulnerability to possible enemy psychological warfare."

Vallée dealt heavily with this issue in *Messengers of Deception,* showing how various mystical sects and cults already wield influence on large numbers of people, even in the absence of mass open sightings. French expatriate Claude Vorilhon is one example.

Just beginning to acquire an audience for his contactee-style reports of alien fraternization in 1979, when Vallée wrote his book, Vorilhon has since grown in popularity to the point that Geraldo Rivera has had him on his T.V. shows. Renaming himself "Rael," Vorilhon has attracted a substantial number of followers for his Raelian Society. Rael is only one among many. There are a number of groups around the world awaiting the arrival of friendly Space Brothers, such as the Aetherians. Arguably, media religion shows such as *The 700 Club* wield far greater power without bringing saucers into the equation, but still the point about potential cult manipulation in relation to UFOs is a valid one. The question of course comes to mind whether or not mind control to combat mind control isn't a worse form of mind control, but that is beyond the scope of this book.

There is some reasonable fear in suspecting the possible long-range goals of such groups, but the Robertson Panel used that fear to create the draconian AFR 200-2 and JANAP-146, and to cause civilian UFO organizations to be monitored and put under surveillance for subversive activities as if they were foreign spy cells in the midst of the body politic. The panel recommended "That the national security agencies immediately take steps to strip the UFOs of the special status they have been given and the aura of mystery they have unfortunately acquired" by institution of a debunking policy, which Hynek obligingly suggested could be helped along by proselytizing amateur astronomers to "spread the gospel." This program was partly an attempt to "educate" the public by showing how all seemingly mysterious reports ultimately have a mundane explanation—which was, specifically in the matter of UFOs, blatantly untrue. Giving the devil his due, it is to be admitted that both the Robertson Panel's and the later Condon Committee's conclusions, as utterly contrived and illegitimate as their bogus investigations had been, were at least essentially honest in proclaiming that UFOs were to all appearances nonhostile and that the public should be made to know that. They were fundamentally dishonest in everything else, but not that.

There is some indication that part of the debunking program went well beyond the proposed use of documentaries and Walt Disney cartoons (actually one of the panel's suggestions) to more organized, massive, and subtle propagandizing. The seeds for this can be found in the panel's specific recommendation: "The 'debunking' aim would result in reduction in public interest in 'flying saucers' which today evokes a strong psychological reaction. This education could be accomplished by mass media such [as] television, motion pictures, and popular articles." British UFOlogist Jenny Randles was told almost thirty years after the panel's 1953 recommendations by a high-ranking individual in the House of Lords that Hollywood films such as *Close Encounters of the Third Kind* were part of a deliberately funded government program to begin educating the populace to the reality of UFOs. The available evidence is plentiful that exactly such a program was in effect almost from the very beginning of UFO research. Jimmy Carter, who included a promise of full disclosure of UFO material in his campaign, spent twenty million dollars on "research" of the topic that almost certainly went into the dissemination program, as is evidenced by the number of excellent movies on the subject that came out during his term as president.

The specific recommendation of Disney is interesting in light of the recent revelation by Marc Eliot, in *Walt Disney: Hollywood's Dark Prince,* that Disney may well have been recruited as an FBI informant by Special Agent E. E. Conroy as early as November 10, 1940, after a vigorous four-year attempt by J. Edgar Hoover to enlist Disney in Bureau ranks. He was recommended to Hoover for SAC (Special Agent in Charge) status in memo #S-186, dated December 16, 1954, reading, "Because of Mr. Disney's position as the foremost producer of cartoon films in the motion picture industry and his prominence and wide acquaintanceship in film production matters, it is believed that he can be of valuable assistance to this office and therefore it is my recommendation that he be approved as an SAC contact." Under "Services Contact Can Perform," half of the total information is blacked out, as is more than 60 percent of his entire file, under the listed exemption "b-7d." Ninety percent of the total blacked-out material was on the b-7d. A b-7d exemption includes withholding of material when it "could reasonably be expected to disclose the identity of a confidential source, including . . . any private institution which furnished information on a confidential basis . . . or by an agency conducting a lawful national security investigation." And "national security" and "private institution" would, of course, include the National Security Agency. Disney helped compose the Motion Picture Alliance for the Preservation of American Ideals' "Statement of Principles," which "pledged to fight" against "domination by Communists, radicals, and crackpots." Numerous later FBI documents, such as Document #80-294-24, dated October 11, 1960, refer to Disney as "a valued contact of this office," and J. Edgar Hoover wrote a personal letter of condolence to Disney's widow, Lillian, on December 15, 1966, specifically ending with the note: "Mr. Disney was on the Special Correspondents' List on a first-name basis."

A thorough examination of the U.S. government's educational/disinformational program on UFOs is not necessary to prove its existence, since a few brief examples are sufficient to make the point. RKO's 1951 movie *The Thing from Another World* was drastically changed from its fictional source material by executive decision, and the changes all but duplicate the known facts of Roswell. Though the location of the story is moved to the Arctic Circle, the discovery of a crashed saucer is identically presented: it leaves a shiny skid to a circular patch in the ice, where the Roswell saucer did the same to the sand in the desert; the saucer is destroyed, but the occupant is recovered; the occupant is a bald humanoid with a heavy brow ridge, clear fluid for blood, no internal organs, unusual hands, and a skintight outfit, and a great many more features in common with actual UFO occupants—numerous examples of which will be cited in Chapters 4 and 5—such as being bulletproof. The 1953 Paramount production of *The War of the Worlds* differs substantially from its source material as well: H. G. Wells' Martian death-machines were tripodal tanks, where the movie makes the three legs invisible to make the machines appear to be flying, and their look is identical to the crescent-shaped UFOs reported by Kenneth Arnold, which cannot be accidental. Where the appearance of Arnold's flying saucers was publicly known at the time, that of the movie's Martians was not—Wells' Martians were tentacular blobs, where those in the movie are bipedal humanoids with three-lobed eyes (the significance of which will be discovered later) and fingers with suction-cup tips, just like those the nurse described at Roswell. The same year, 20th Century Fox's *Invaders from Mars* showed identical creatures from the Red Planet abducting people by night into a limbo environment aboard a flying saucer, where they are subjected to implants and hypnotic mind control, thirteen years before publication of the Betty and Barney Hill case (discussed in Chapter 4) revealed even half of these elements as standard components of actual UFO abduction. Other UFO films were deliberately made to be as bad as possible, in order to make the subject hopelessly ludicrous to the average viewer. The best example is Ed Wood's infamous *Plan 9 from Outer Space*. Wood was a patriotic ex-Marine with FBI secret clearance, and a great many other makers of bad UFO movies also had (and have) strong connections to the intelligence community. The ratio of educational to disinformational or deflectional Hollywood pieces appears to have varied according to the political power in office at any given time, with the laughable or overly scary movies and television shows coming out during Republican administrations, and the more educational or realistic ones during Democratic tenures, as a general rule.

Vallée finally found the evidence he sought, proving that Blue Book was a mere front. One day while straightening out Hynek's files, he found a document he referred to as the Pentacle letter. He does not accuse Hynek of deliberate concealment, or even hint of it, but it must be noted that this important letter had been both overlooked and "misplaced." He relates the story in his journal entry of June 13, 1967: "The worst section of [Hynek's] files concerned the history of the Air Force projects themselves, from Sign and Grudge to Blue Book. Hynek had misplaced many of these documents. And it is in that section that I found a letter which is especially remarkable because of the new light it throws on the key period of the Robertson Panel and of *Report #14.* It is stamped in red ink 'SECRET—Security Information.' It is dated 9 January 1953. It is signed by a man I will call Pentacle. It is addressed to Miles E. Coll at Wright-Patterson Air Force Base for transmittal to Captain Ruppelt. It begins with a statement that the document contains a recommendation to ATIC regarding future methods of handling the UFO problem, based on experience in handling *several thousands of reports.* This opening paragraph clearly establishes the fact that *prior to the top-level 1953 Robertson Panel meeting somebody had actually analyzed thousands of UFO cases on behalf of the United States government.*"

After emphasizing the point, he ponders the full implications of its meaning. "Let us go back to 1953: the Intelligence agencies have determined that unknown objects are flying over the United States. If these are controlled machines they are far beyond anything we have. Public opinion demands some action. What could be simpler than assembling a panel of scientists? Perhaps not the best informed, but the most prestigious. They are shown a sample of the reports, pre-selected by the Air Force. They find no reason, of course, to revise the current edifice of science on the basis of what little they are shown. And once the panel has been disbanded and public opinion quieted, what a wonderful opportunity for the military to resume its research in secret, with its own scientists, its own laboratories ... if such a research project exists it certainly does not need the Blue Book data. It could operate independently, at a much higher level."

When he brought this letter to Hynek's attention, Hynek seemed genuinely shaken. But, as usual, he did next to nothing about it. It took him over nine months to confront Pentacle with the evidence. When he did, he did it very badly. He met with Pentacle alone, where Pentacle had four colleagues. He made the confrontation on Pentacle's ground, the Battelle Corporation. And he handed the evidence straight to Pentacle, who predictably did not return it. "When he started reading from his notes," Vallée says, "Pentacle snatched the paper out of his hand and said it was an old story, it was all over and forgotten. Pentacle got rid of him as fast as possible, but did not return his notes. Always fearful of confrontations, Hynek left Battelle with his tail between his legs. Such a violent reaction may in fact indicate that something important is going on. Why should Pentacle worry so much about a simple letter written fifteen years ago?"

At the time of the bungled meeting, the Condon Committee was in progress. Like the Robertson Panel before it, it was a palliative. The University of Colorado received the actual committee, which was headed by Dr. Edward Condon in 1966. The committee's *Scientific Study of Unidentified Flying Objects* was published in 1969, with predictably negative conclusions. Whether or not the CIA was as directly responsible in this case as it had been with the Robertson Panel, it was at least unquestionably concerned with keeping its tremendous interest in UFOs from the public. Condon and members of his committee visited the CIA's National Photographic Center (NPIC) in February of 1967, to which a CIA memo of the time referred: "Any work performed with NPIC to assist Dr. Condon in his investigation will not be identified as work accomplished by the CIA. Dr. Condon was advised by Mr. Lundahl to make no reference to CIA in regard to this work effort. Dr. Condon stated that if he felt it necessary to obtain an official CIA comment he would make a separate distinct entry into CIA not related to contacts with NPIC."

Vallée knew that Condon was going to be no help. "The Condon Report is going to be a public relations fortress built up by the military, the press people, the scientific establishment, accompanied by a fanfare of editorials in major newspapers and the scientific press. How do you expect to counter all that?"

"The cold, hard fact is that Condon has no interest in UFO's whatsoever," Hynek commented in 1967. "Never did. From the beginning he thought it was all a big joke. Recently he entertained himself by attending a meeting of so-called 'scientific ufologists' in New York. That episode reinforced his impression that all believers were crackpots, jokers or fast-buck artists. He talks about nothing else for hours, repeating how ridiculous these folks are."

How interesting, then, that Condon asked Dr. James Harder his advice on how to handle a report's conclusions that might confirm UFOs as extraterrestrial spacecraft. According to Harder, "I said that I thought there would be other issues than the scientific ones, notably international repercussions and national security. He smiled the smile of a man who sees his own opinions reflected in the opinions of others and said that he had given the matter much thought, and had decided that if the answer was to be a positive finding of ETH (Extraterrestrial Hypothesis), he would not make the finding public, but would take the report, in his briefcase, to the President's Science Advisor, and have the decision made in Washington."

The public was not really deceived either. A year before the committee's report was published, John Fuller exposed evidence of its contrivance in *Look* magazine. Vallée commented, "[Fuller] reveals the evidence of a deliberate bias . . . It is worse than a bias, it is a smoking gun. An official University of Colorado memo by Bob Low, dated August 9, 1966, discussed the research proposal they were getting ready to submit to the Air Force in the following terms: '*The trick would be* to describe the project so that, to the public, it would appear a totally objective study but, to the scientific community, it would present the image of a group of nonbelievers trying their best to be objective but having an almost zero expectation of finding a saucer.'"

As was to happen numerous times after, the Condon Committee made a badly bungled attempt at connecting modern UFO phenomena with ancient historical sources. "The Condon Report assembled an argument for a similarity between [one] record and the passages in the Book of the Prophet Ezekiel," says UFOlogist Paris Flammonde. "The comparisons are forced and often false, and the citations drawn from a dozen points, not sequential in the

Bible, despite the writer saying that they are. In fact, the resemblances claimed are strained, arbitrary, or unrecognizable. The proposition has absolutely no value and is, in reality, far less useful for the Report's purposes than an accurate and honest analysis would have been."

Erich Von Daniken, the author of *Chariots of the Gods* in 1970 and numerous later books advancing the same evidence rejected by the Condon Committee, would later be similarly charged by critics, mostly by way of attempting to get the public to throw out the baby with the bath water. Von Daniken was a poor scholar, and the worst spokesman for the subject of ancient extraterrestrial contact. Making matters worse, he was caught inventing facts in his later books, causing his new phrase "ancient astronauts" to be discredited in the same pejorative tone as "flying saucers" or "UFOs."

In fact, ancient astronaut theory has been credibly argued by scholars and scientists, from France's Aimé Michel and England's Earl of Clancarty, to Russia's Dr. Felix Zigel and Alexander Kazantsev. Probably the foremost scholar publishing in the field today is Zecharia Sitchin. Some of these men's findings—Sitchin's, especially—will be discussed throughout Part II of this book, but for the moment it is interesting to note that not only was the Condon Committee discrediting ancient astronaut theory along with that of modern UFOs, but they were actually studying it in the first place, in anticipation of research to come.

Official reaction to the Condon Committee's predetermined negative findings was sharply critical. Congressman J. Edward Roush expressed openly to the House of Representatives his "grave doubts as to the scientific profundity and objectivity of the project ... We are $500,000 poorer and not richer in information about UFOs ... I am not satisfied and the American public will not be satisfied." They weren't. Lockheed's cofounder, eighty-year-old aviation pioneer and later founder of his own aircraft company, John Northrup, predicted that "The 21st Century will die laughing at the Condon Report," and his seems to represent the consensus opinion.

Many years later, proof that Blue Book and its predecessors had been a front surfaced in an October 20, 1969, Air Force memo from Brigadier General C. H. Bolender, plainly stating that "...reports of unidentified flying objects which could affect the national security are made in accordance with JANAP 146 or Air Force Manual 55-11, and are not part of the Blue Book system."

Except for the Rommel Report, which will be encountered in the next chapter, the Condon Committee and Project Blue Book ended all official government study into the UFO question in 1969. The resounding verdict: No extraterrestrial phenomenon. All is attributable to misidentification, hoax, and hallucination. Whatever few genuine unidentifieds remain will eventually be proven to fit into one or another of these categories. Science confirms it, Government ratifies it, and That Ends It.

Unimpressed with having been pronounced nonexistent, the spacecraft continued to fly. Unless it was weather balloons sabotaging military bases, or swamp gas mutilating cattle. Or, for that matter, temperature inversions abducting human beings.

3

Installations, Mutilations, and Disinformations

I N LATE NOVEMBER 1948, a great many reports were made in Albuquerque, New Mexico, of "green fireballs" in the sky. The Air Force initially ignored them, but they increased both in number and quality and developed an alarming pattern.

On December 5, two separate airplanes had close encounters with the green fireballs. One was an Air Force C-47 piloted by a Captain Goede. He and his crew had seen one fireball near Las Vegas, New Mexico, then twenty-two minutes later, at 9:27 PM, saw another ten miles east of Albuquerque. Unlike any meteor they had ever witnessed, it had the ability to maneuver. They radioed a report to Kirtland Air Force Base, which gave it to their intelligence people. A few minutes later, at 9:35 PM, Pioneer Airlines Flight 63 also radioed Kirtland from Las Vegas, reporting that a ball of fire which turned from green to red flew straight at them, forcing the airplane to take a hard bank to the left to avoid collision. The object then altered course.

"No matter what these green fireballs were," wrote Edward J. Ruppelt in his memoirs, "the military was getting a little edgy. They might be common meteorites, psychologically enlarged flares, or true UFO's, but whatever they were they were playing around in one of the most sensitive security areas in the United States. Within 100 miles of Albuquerque were two installations that were the backbone of the atomic bomb program: Los Alamos and Sandia Base. Scattered throughout the countryside were other installations vital to the defense of the U.S.: radar stations, fighter-interceptor bases, and the other mysterious areas that had been blocked off by high chain-link fences."

The next morning, Dr. Lincoln La Paz, an expert on meteorites,

67

was called in on what was about to become "Project Twinkle." Interviewing dozens of people in northern New Mexico, La Paz and an intelligence team determined that eight separate fireballs had been witnessed, one especially spectacular in size and brightness. They also found no trace of meteorite fragments at any of the locations La Paz was certain they would be, had the objects sighted in fact been meteors. Finding fragments based on triangulated trajectories was La Paz's specialty, and to have found nothing from such a great number of excellent reports was virtually impossible. But just to be sure, the team scoured the area repeatedly. When they still found nothing, La Paz "seriously doubted" the fireballs were meteorites.

The green fireballs returned several nights later, then to appear almost nightly. Again, they left no fragments. And this time, their trajectories were even better plotted by skilled observers.

Kirtland Intelligence decided to fly around and see if they could spot one of the green fireballs themselves. At 6:33 PM on December 8, they succeeded. "The object was similar in appearance to a burning green flare," Ruppelt reports, "the kind that is commonly used in the Air Force. However, the light was much more intense and the object appeared considerably larger than a normal flare. The trajectory of the object, when first sighted, was almost flat and parallel to the earth. The phenomenon lasted about 2 seconds. At the end of this time the object seemed to begin to burn out and the trajectory then dropped off rapidly. The phenomenon was of such intensity [estimated at 5200 angstroms] as to be visible from the very moment it ignited."

Wright-Patterson tried to find similar reports elsewhere in the country. There weren't any. There were UFO reports, yes, but no green fireballs. These were unique to the particular region of New Mexico—the region where the defense installations and weapons development plants were.

Through December of 1948 and January of 1949, the green fireballs persisted, witnessed at one time or another by everyone involved in the investigation. In mid-February, a conference was held to discuss the green fireballs, which included atmospheric expert Dr. Joseph Kaplan and Dr. Edward Teller (the later inventor of the H-bomb), in addition to everyone who had so far been involved. The group was split as to whether or not the fireballs could be meteors. La Paz was certain they were not. Though they exhibited some of the characteristics of meteors, their trajectory was consistently too flat, their color too green, their intensity too bright, and no fragments could be found despite excellent scientific information and a great multitude of sightings. By December 13, 1948, the investigative team was satisfied that the green fireballs had to be under intelligent control. By that date, as authors Tad A. Sherburn and Harvey M. Haeberle remarked in their article "Los Alamos Overflights," in the January-February 1996 edition of *UFO,* "these green fireballs were on [at least two] occasions [witnessed to be] trailed by red lights that maintained a constant relationship with the main body as it traversed the sky. So now the meteorite theory had to be abandoned by any objective person." As if to emphasize the point, on December 20, 1948, a silent green fireball descended at a forty-five-degree angle from ten miles above Earth to 2.3 miles, and continued at level flight from 3.75 to 7.5 miles per second.

An FBI memo of the time attests to the fact (emphasis original) that *"This matter is considered Top Secret by Intelligence Officers of both the Army and the Air Forces."* These included the FBI (because of possible sabotage implications), Fourth Army, Armed Special Weapons Project, University of New Mexico, the Atomic Energy Commission, the University of California, the Air Force Office of Special Investigations (AFOSI), Scientific Advisory Board, and Geophysical Research Division Air Materiel Command. These parties were all present at the two major conferences discussing the phenomenon, on February 17 and October 14, 1949. Two hundred and nine reports were evaluated, all falling into three listed categories: Green Fireballs, Disk or Variation, and Probable Meteor. At least one photo was obtained by Dr. La Paz, of a small white object that was definitely ruled out as either a planet or a meteor.

The Air Force's Cambridge Research Laboratory was also stumped, establishing Project Twinkle in late summer of 1949 to try to photograph the green fireballs. Three photographic stations were set up near White Sands to accomplish this. They failed. Wherever they set up, the green fireballs weren't. When they relocated to where the fireballs were, the fireballs moved to where the cameras weren't. It was proposed that the best strategy (as in duck hunting) would be to simply choose a single location and wait for the green fireballs to come to them, but by then it was too late. The Korean War began, and morale and budgetary problems caused a cessation of Project Twinkle.

UFOs were far from finished with the military, however. Several repeats of the Mantell case can be found in official files, reporting little more than the fact that pilots were found crashed and dead—or sometimes not found at all—after UFO pursuits. One, the Kinross case of November 23, 1953, over Lake Superior, has still never been explained satisfactorily. Two years later, Donald Keyhoe broke the story in his bestseller, *The Flying Saucer Conspiracy,* and in 1958 he acquired a leaked Air Force document quoting a radar observer of the incident as saying, "It seems incredible, but the blip just swallowed our F-89." No trace of either the plane or its crew, pilot Lieutenant Felix Moncla, Jr., and radar observer Lieutenant R. R. Wilson, was ever found. Blue Book representative Master Sergeant O. D. Hill told civilian UFO investigators Tom Comella and Edgar Smith in 1959 that other such incidents had occurred, and that officials were worried about a possible interplanetary Pearl Harbor. Confronted with this testimony, Captain George T. Gregory, at Blue Book headquarters, got a shocked look on his face and left the room for a short while before returning to say, "Well, we just cannot talk about those cases."

Then there were the intrusions at military installations, and the "Faded Giants." Faded Giant is a code phrase used to indicate that a nuclear device has been tampered with. How many times this has occurred is a matter for speculation, since the Air Force has not exactly been forthcoming with documents on the subject. It is only through legal battles utilizing the Freedom of Information Act that most of what little documentary evidence exists has come to light.

Raymond Fowler describes two incidents of this type in *Casebook of a UFO Investigator.* In the early spring of 1966, Malmstrom Air Force Base in Montana developed simultaneous malfunction in all ten of its Minuteman nuclear missile guidance and control systems, shortly after ground personnel had witnessed UFOs in the area. The inference of sabotage was all but impossible to avoid. The guidance system is the most highly secured area of the missile, and whatever had been done to them at Malmstrom, all ten of the missiles were rendered incapable of launch. The week of March 20, 1967, the UFOs were back and confirmed on radar, and ten new missiles were sabotaged. Interceptors were dispatched, but the result of their pursuit is not on record.

Malmstrom was revisited in 1975, along with many other bases. SAC (Strategic Air Command) instituted a series of northern tier base Security Option Three Alerts from fall of that year into the coming winter, as Air Force nuclear weapons storage depots were flown over by UFOs. NORAD's (North American Defense Command) commander in chief sent a confidential memo to all units: "Suspicious Unknown Air Activity."

It read: "Since 28 Oct 75 numerous reports of suspicious objects have been received at the NORAD COC [Combat Operations Center]. Reliable military personnel at Loring AFB, Maine, Wurtsmith AFB, Michigan, Malmstrom AFB, Minot AFB, and Canadian Forces Station, Falconbridge, Ontario, Canada, have visually sighted suspicious objects.

"Objects at Loring and Wurtsmith were characterized to be helicopters. Missile site personnel, security alert teams and Air Defense personnel at Malmstrom Montana reported object which sounded like a jet aircraft. FAA advised 'There were no jet aircraft in the vicinity.' Malmstrom search and height finder radars carried the object between 9,000 ft and 15,600 ft at a speed of seven knots . . .

"F-106s scrambled from Malmstrom could not make contact due to darkness and low altitude. Site personnel reported the objects as low as 200 ft and said that as the interceptors approached the lights went out. After the interceptors had passed the lights came on again. One hour after the F-106s returned to base, missile site personnel reported the object increased to a high speed, raised in altitude and could not be discerned from the stars . . .

"I have expressed my concern to SAFOI [Air Force Information Office] that we come up soonest with a proposed answer to queries from the press to prevent overreaction by the public to reports by the media that may be blown out of proportion. To date efforts by Air Guard helicopters, SAC and NORAD F-106s have failed to produce positive ID."

Linda Moulton Howe, documentary producer and three-time regional Emmy Award winner, was in Boston working on a medical script in late October of 1975. She had no interest in either UFOs or animal mutilations at the time. Now she is an authority on the latter subject and an avid researcher on the former. Her introduction to the subjects came when her brother, a helicopter pilot at Malmstrom, called her up and told her what had just happened at the base.

She relates the entire story on camera in *UFOs: A Need To Know:* "One night, that fall of October of '75, I had a phone call . . . and it was my brother, and he was extremely excited, and the first words out of his mouth were, 'Linda, a UFO has set down on the base,' and I rarely heard my brother speak with such energy . . . That particular night he had been at a wing party, when beepers started going off all over. It was an emergency. And the emergency, as it turned out, was that an electronic signal had quit and it had gone off over a missile silo known as Kilo Seven, at Malmstrom, and a Sabotage Alert Team was reporting that a football field-sized—that'd be 300 feet in diameter—orange, glowing disc, was hovering, or stationary, whatever word you want to use, very low to the top of the missile silo. And that it was casting light that was brighter than daylight. . . . My brother said that the Sabotage Alert Team actually had an argument with the command unit, saying, 'You want us to go closer than where we are'—which was a quarter of a mile away—'then *you* come out here.' And that kind of insubordination got people's attention, too, that something serious was out there, at that missile silo. Jets were scrambled. When the jets got above whatever this orange glowing thing was [*snaps fingers*], it blinked out. The Sabotage Alert Team said, 'We know it must still be there, it's just disappeared.' As long as the jets were there, couldn't see it. The jets were called back [*snaps fingers*], back on it came. It began to rise, and was picked up by radar until it dopplered off at 200,000 feet. Well, the next day, my brother said that they sent a team out there to investigate that missile. And that they found that the targeting information in the computer head, about where the warhead would go in the world, had been changed. And the next day, they took out that whole missile and put in a new one."

The story is confirmed by the official documentation and the history preceding the event. And for Ms. Howe's brother to defy JANAP-146 and AFR 200-2 and call his sister up to tell her all of this must have "got people's attention, too." It was officially documented that Wurtsmith Air Force Base saw a UFO and "lights," more than once, "near the Weapons Storage Area," around November 1, 1975, and that on July 30, 1976, several military personnel of Fort Ritchie, Maryland, saw "an object . . . about the size of a 2½ ton truck . . . over the ammo storage area at 100-200 yards altitude." Several well-documented intrusions at Loring Air Force Base in Maine occurred in the same time period. The UFOs in question, as in many other cases, were believed to be helicopters because of their size and maneuvering patterns (but were capable of sudden acceleration away from pursuers at one thousand knots), and were seen hovering about the weapons storage areas. One object witnessed, as at Malmstrom, was "reddish orange" and incredibly bright, becoming invisible when it turned out its lights.

Other tantalizing bits of confirmation concerning operations capabilities of the intruders emerged in official reports. Chief Warrant Officer Bernard Poulin aerially patrolled the region in that time period, accompanied by Air Security Police, Canadian Royal Mounted Police, and Maine Police. "We would launch," he reported to researcher Barry Greenwood in 1981, ". . . with the idea that it was a rotary-type craft we were searching for. We were vectored in by ground personnel to different spots on the base where the ground personnel were seeing or hearing it. All this time we were being tracked by base radar, and radar was not painting the object that was being reported. Ground personnel would call and say the object is at this location, but radar would not pick it up . . . They maintained all along up there, you know, those are pretty sensitive places and they have to know what the hell is going on." In other words, not only could the UFOs in question sometimes render themselves invisible to sight, but they could also at times render themselves invisible to radar.

Retired USAF Lieutenant Colonel Wendelle C. Stevens reports that as early as 1948, Arctic survey mapping B-29s under his command not only photographed numerous UFOs with specially mounted cameras, but were taken over by remote control upon occasion, in the most unusual ways, by unknown sources. "We had reports . . . that engines quit running in place and then started up again, by themselves. We had radio interference on the communications lines where they experienced complete communications blackout, [and] for no reason at all, the communication would come back again. We had surges on all the lines, including the closed lines . . . We had electrical interference on all frequencies at times, we also had selective interference on different frequencies. We never knew what was causing this, because it always cured itself in flight—which true failures don't do. And it indicated the potential for somebody else to selectively interfere with frequencies and functions aboard an operational vehicle in flight. And these are supposed to be our best military equipment, they're supposed to be foolproof, and somebody was fooling with the systems . . . I'm sure this got a lot of attention in Washington." Stevens never saw any of the photographic evidence, which was immediately downloaded, undeveloped, into a steel box which was picked up twice a month by a government courier who hand-cuffed it to his wrist. "All I ever ended up with were the stories—but they were some very exciting stories."

Captain Lawrence Coyne gave a report confirming exactly such a cockpit-control incident when his Air Force helicopter out of Columbus, Ohio, headed for Cleveland, was suddenly flooded by green light from a sixty-foot-long, cigar-shaped UFO, at 10:30 PM on October 28, 1973. "I could hardly believe it," he said seven minutes later, when his radio resumed working. "The altimeter was reading 3,500 feet, climbing to 3,800. I had made no attempt to pull up. All the controls were still set for a 20-degree dive. Yet we had climbed from 1,700 to 3,500 with no power in a couple of seconds, with no G-forces or other noticeable strains. There was no noise or turbulence, either." The UFO left as abruptly as it had appeared, with Coyne and his crew none the worse for wear. Green light from a UFO commandeering piloted aircraft, interestingly enough, appeared in the 1955 Hollywood sci-fi epic *This Island Earth,* another among many of the curious coincidences to be found in the entertainment industry as a result of the Robertson Panel recommendation that the entertainment media be used to minimalize any serious attention which might otherwise be paid to UFOs.

The assistant professor of Radio-Film-TV at the University of Wisconsin, Dr. Robert Jacobs, was a first lieutenant at Vanden-burg Air Force Base on September 15, 1964, in charge of a crew of 120 men who installed and monitored a camera tracking missile launches. On that day, an Atlas F missile malfunctioned and crashed. "A couple of days later," he reported in 1982, "I was ordered to go and see my superior, Major Florenz J. Mansmann, Chief Science Officer of the unit. With him there in his office were a couple of men in plain clothes. He introduced them to me only by their first names and said they had come from Washington, D.C." Mansmann ran a film of the test, saying "Watch this bit closely." Jacobs had missed the excitement at the time, too busy congratulating himself and his fellow crew members on the success of their camera. Now, "Suddenly we saw a UFO swim into the picture. It was very distinct and clear, a round object. It flew right up to our missile and emitted a vivid flash of light. Then it altered course and hovered briefly over our missile . . . and then there came a second vivid flash of light. Then the UFO flew around the missile twice and set off two more flashes from different angles, and then it vanished. A few seconds later, our missile was malfunctioning and tumbling out of control into the Pacific Ocean, hundreds of miles short of its scheduled target." Confronted then by "three very intense faces," Jacobs was asked by the Major, "Lieutenant, just what the hell was that?" After several repeat viewings and microscopic analysis, Jacobs said that in his opinion it was a UFO. Mansmann smiled and said, "You are to say nothing about this footage. As far as you and I are concerned, it never happened! Right . . . ?" Reminded of "the seriousness of a security breach," the film was handed over to the plainclothesmen, who Jacobs took to be CIA, and he waited seventeen years before ever discussing it.

Engine failures and remote controlling have been frequently reported around UFOs. The "selective interference" might account for the sabotage at military weapons sites and missile silos, unless occupants of some sort are actually disembarking from the craft and performing the sabotage manually. In any event, the sabotage is performed one way or another, and UFOs are present at the time.

One report by Italian science writer Alberto Fenoglio, condensed and translated by Robert Pinotti in the mid-1960s, says that UFOs hovered over the Russian Tactical Missile Command at Sverdlosk for twenty-four hours in 1959, eventually chased by Soviet fighters firing machine guns at them, which they easily evaded. Then, in 1961, a huge disk-shaped object surrounded by smaller aerial objects was reported to have had two salvoes of missiles fired at it by "a nervous battery commander" near Moscow. They both exploded about two kilometers premature of their target. "The third salvo was never fired," reported Fenoglio, "for at this point the smaller 'saucers' went into action and stalled the electrical apparatus of the whole missile base. When the smaller discoidal UFOs had withdrawn and joined the larger craft, the electrical apparatus was again found to be in working order." Fenoglio claimed his sources included a well-known Russian diplomat. Such reports have since been verified by Russian Air Force officers on the October 6, 1994, edition of ABC's *Prime Time,* including photos of the UFOs. One colonel claimed that the base instrumentation went out of control for no detectable reason, either at the time or in subsequent investigation, and that missile silos were sabotaged as they have been in the U.S.

UFO researcher Stanton Friedman unearthed a Cuban report by an Air Force Security Service specialist with the 6947th Security Squadron, which monitored all Cuban military communications. In March of 1967, two MIG interceptors were scrambled after a bogey in Cuban airspace: "The wing leader reported the object was a bright metallic sphere with no visible markings or appendages. After a futile attempt to contact the object for identification, Cuban Air Defense headquarters ordered the wing leader to arm his weapons and destroy the object. The wing leader reported his missiles armed and his radar locked-on. Seconds later the wing man began screaming to the ground controller that the wing leader's aircraft had exploded. After regaining his composure he further reported that there was no smoke or flame; the aircraft had disintegrated . . . A spot report was sent to National Security Agency headquarters, which is standard procedure in any case involving aircraft loss by an enemy country . . . Within hours we received orders to ship all tapes and pertinent intelligence to the Agency and were told to list the incident in the squadron files as aircraft loss due to equipment malfunction."

This report is interesting for a number of reasons. It shows that the intruders are quite capable of defending themselves, which adds verification to the Soviet incidents, and once more shows no hostile action other than justifiable self-defense. Most interesting is the NSA's handling of the incident. They confiscated the evidence and specifically ordered a cover-up story released to conceal the truth. Also, while it is clearly stated that the report was filed with the NSA because it dealt with the destruction of enemy aircraft, NSA did not request the evidence be sent to a different agency—and the evidence unquestionably concerns an unidentified flying object.

A less violent and more widely witnessed encounter occurred over Iran in 1976, according to another document acquired through the Freedom of Information Act belonging to the DIA (Defense Intelligence Agency). The distribution list on the document included the White House, secretary of state, NSA, and CIA, originating from the defense attaché at the U.S. Embassy in Teheran. An F-4 had been dispatched from Shahrokhi Air Force Base at 1:30 in the morning on September 19, to intercept an object approximately the size of a Boeing 707. It was visible from seventy miles away, though its shape could not clearly be discerned due to the object's intense brilliance. Nearing the object, the F-4's instrument and communications panel went dead, coming back on after the pilot had turned back to base. A second interceptor was launched ten minutes later. Another object emerged from the first and flew at the second plane with remarkable speed. The pilot armed his AIM-9 missile, but at that moment his instrument panel also went dead. When he turned back to base, his instruments returned to normal as had the first pilot's. The second object returned to the main body, and several smaller objects emerged from it, one landing in a dry riverbed. Some of the objects, like those reported by NORAD the year before, were characterized as helicopters by the display they put on radar. No trace of the landed object was ever found, but multiple witnesses both on the ground and in the air, including a civil airliner, swore to having seen it.

"An outstanding report," the DIA's own evaluators said of it. "This case is a classic which meets all the criteria necessary for a valid study of the UFO phenomenon: a) The object was seen by multiple witnesses from different locations ... b) The credibility of many of the witnesses was high ... c) Visual sightings were confirmed by radar. d) Similar electromagnetic effects (EME) were reported by three separate aircraft. e) There were physiological effects on some crew members (i.e. loss of night vision due to the brightness of the object). f) An inordinate amount of maneuverability was displayed by the UFOs." The DIA was slow in releasing the report and its evaluation, and the agency has others it has not released. If they would release a report this solid, Timothy Good notes, "One wonders just how many other positive evaluations remain classified in the DIA files at the Pentagon."

Congress was never directly informed of the U.S. military base incidents. The 1975–76 intrusions only came to their attention when *Parade* uncovered them in a story by Michael Satchell, "UFO's vs. USAF, Amazing (but True) Encounters," published on December 10, 1978. Congressman Samuel S. Stratton (D-NY), chairman of the Armed Services Investigations Subcommittee, wrote to the Air Force ten days later, "... The article proceeds to quote from Air Force documents to the effect that the intruding aircraft had 'a clear intent in the weapons storage area' at Loring Air Force Base ... This Subcommittee is concerned by the alleged ability of unknown aircraft to penetrate air space and hover over SAC bases, their weapons storage areas, and launch control facilities, and the inability of Air Force personnel to intercept and identify such aircraft. Accordingly, it is requested that all Air Force reports relating to each of the incidents described in this article be furnished to the Subcommittee. It is further requested that all reports of any similar incidents, either before or since the October-November 1975 events, be furnished to the Subcommittee."

Various internal Air Force groups noted in a January 8, 1979, memo that the Air Force had been "unable to find any official information regarding the incidents described," literally concluding with "some of these incidents may not have happened at all." For its official response to Stratton, on February 9, the Air Force gave the runaround answer that the reports had been "of transitory interest" and that "permanent files are not maintained." Since the *Parade* article had been written entirely from official documents acquired through the Freedom of Information Act, plainly the response was a complete lie. Stratton, however, military-friendly, blithely accepted the answer and did not apply any pressure or make waves. The matter simply dropped.

It is important to note that however much cover-up exists of UFO evidence or activity, there is little or no pressure from government bodies for anyone to reveal it. Individual interest or attempts made to discover hidden truths from such governmental figures as Barry Goldwater, Gerald Ford, or Jimmy Carter do not seem to be shared by enough of their peers or constituents—at least not for any sustained period of time—to force open any doors or reveal much of any great consequence. The investigation of UFOs continues as it began, a matter of individual research and effort, sporadically assisted by the Freedom of Information Act, and fueled almost solely by the interest of those few citizens who can maintain their drive in the absence of everyone else's. Representative Steven Schiff's official inquiry into the Roswell events of 1947 ran into official stonewalling and runarounds from the Air Force, from the start. The military's initial response, on page one of the September 18, 1994, Sunday National *New York Times,* was simply to manufacture a new balloon story to replace the old one. Ultimately, the six hundred-page report ending the congressional inquiry in 1995 upheld the new story, claiming that the Roswell wreckage was nothing more than the remains of a classified project called Mogul, which utilized specially equipped balloons to sense Soviet atomic experiments. The most vital bit of information about that particular crash got overlooked in the midst of accusations and counteraccusations: in July of 1947, Roswell Air Force Base's 509th Bomb Group was the only such unit to be in possession of an atom bomb.

But the military base intrusions were not even the most alarming of UFO incidents in the 1960s and '70s. Running concurrently with them—and seeming to increase in proportion to the base intrusion activity—was another phenomenon, also closely associated with strange lights in the sky: cattle mutilations.

The oldest known record in the United States of cattle mutilation and UFOs is from 1897—one of the biggest flap years in history—left to us by a farmer named Alexander Hamilton (a former congressman, but not the statesman) of Le Roy, Kansas: "Last Monday night, about 10:30, we were awakened by a noise among the cattle. I arose, thinking that perhaps my bulldog was performing some of his pranks, but upon going to the door saw to my utter astonishment an airship slowly descending upon my cow lot, about forty rods from the house . . . It consisted of a great cigar-shaped portion, possibly three hundred feet long, with a carriage underneath. The carriage was made of glass or some other transparent substance alternating with a narrow strip of some material. It was brilliantly lighted within and everything was plainly visible—it was occupied by six of the strangest beings I ever saw. They were jabbering together, but we could not understand a word they said . . . When about three hundred feet above us it seemed to pause and hover directly over a two-year-old heifer, which was bawling and jumping, apparently fast in the fence. Going to her, we found a cable about a half inch in thickness made of some red material, fastened in a slip knot around her neck, one end passing up to the vessel, and the heifer tangled in the wire fence. We tried to get it off but could not, so we cut the wire loose and stood in amazement to see the ship, heifer and all, rise slowly, disappearing in the northwest."

Hamilton was "so frightened I could not sleep" after the incident. He rode all the next day looking for any trace of the heifer, but it was a neighbor three or four miles away who "found the hide, legs and head in his field that day. He . . . had brought the hide to town for identification, but was greatly mystified in not being able to find any tracks in the soft ground." Hamilton identified the carcass by his brand. But after the incident, "every time I would drop to sleep I would see the cursed thing with its big lights and hideous people. I don't know whether they are devils or angels, or what; but we all saw them, and my whole family saw the ship, and I don't want any more to do with them."

In recent years, a family relative claimed Hamilton's story

had been made up as a Liar's Club joke, based on the then-current mystery airship appearances (to be examined in Chapter 6), but since this can no more be verified than the original account, and that account does seem to bear some similarities to the present phenomenon, it is included for the reader to consider for himself.

In the modern era, the first recorded animal mutilation associated with UFOs was on the morning of September 9, 1967, when the corpse of a mare named Lady—misidentified by the press as "Snippy"—was found on Harry King's ranch in Colorado's San Luis Valley. Lying on her side, her body was completely intact, except for the fact that she had been stripped to the bone from the neck up. The cut was so clean that no one who saw it believed it could have been done with a knife—including pathologist Dr. John Altshuler, multiple award-winner for contributions to the study of blood coagulation and holder of seven patents for medical inventions. Altshuler was so frightened by Lady's remains in 1967 that he didn't speak of them fully until Linda Moulton Howe interviewed him for her 1989 book, *An Alien Harvest*.

Altshuler had been satisfying his curiosity concerning reports of strange lights in the San Luis Valley night sky. He broke the law by staying in Alamosa's Great Sand Dunes National Monument after ten o'clock, about ten days after Lady's mutilation. To his surprise, "About 2:00–3:00 AM, I saw three very bright, white lights moving together slowly below the Sangre De Cristo mountain tops . . . They were definitely not the illusion of stars moving . . . At one point, I thought they were coming toward me because the lights got bigger. Then suddenly, they shot upward and disappeared. At the time, I was both elated and disbelieving in a way. I knew the lights were not my imagination, that the stories about UFOs were true."

Park police found him there in the morning, and he begged them not to give out his name for the sake of his career and reputation. When they found out he was a medical hematologist, they took him to the King ranch to examine Lady's remains. Alamosa Sheriff Ben Phillips had never even gone out to view the remains, so accustomed to predators being the cause of animal deaths that he didn't much care. Upon hearing the state of Lady's corpse, he simply wrote the incident off as having been caused by lightning.

Altshuler noticed the incredibly clean stripping from the neck up, and also a "cut from the neck down to the base of the chest in a vertical, clean incision . . . Then inside the horse's chest, I remember the lack of organs. Whoever did the cutting took the horse's heart, lungs, and thyroid. The mediasternum was completely empty—and dry. How do you get the heart out without blood? It was an incredible dissection of organs without any evidence of blood." The lack of blood was "most amazing" to him. "I have done hundreds of autopsies. You can't cut into a body without getting some blood. But there was no blood on the skin or on the ground. No blood anywhere. That impressed me the most."

The wounds were not the result of any standard cutting instrument. "At the edge of the cut, there was a darkened color as if the flesh had been opened and cauterized with a surgical cauterizing blade. The outer edges of the cut skin were firm, almost as if they had been cauterized with a modern day laser. But there was no surgical laser technology like that in 1967. Today when we use cauterizing to control bleeding, the flesh still has a soft pliable feeling. But the edges of that horse cut were stiff, leathery and a bit hardened. I cut tissue samples from the hard, darker edge. Later, I viewed the tissue under a microscope. At the cell level, there was discoloration and destruction consistent with changes caused by burning."

At the time, Altshuler was "unbelievably frightened. I couldn't eat. I couldn't sleep. I was so afraid I would be discovered, discredited, fired, no longer would have credibility in the medical community . . . Today I have enough confidence in my reputation and ability that I am no longer afraid to say that I saw three UFOs that night above the sand dune valley in September 1967, and examined the horse that was surgically worked on with some kind of burning instrument."

Lady's owner, Nellie Lewis, King's sister, was sure UFOs had something to do with the horse's death. "We see something—I won't say what it is—every night," she told a reporter of the *Pueblo Chieftain* for its October 7 article on the incident, entitled "Dead Horse Riddle Sparks UFO Buffs." Lewis had seen lights in the sky for about two weeks before Lady's mutilation, and they had not gone away since. A week before the article ran, the National Atmospheric Research Center near Palestine, Texas, confirmed sighting a UFO that matched the description given by a Colorado witness in the same time period.

"High levels of radiation also were reported in the area of the animal's body," the report tantalizingly revealed, without giving any further details as to who had done the testing or why. In 1974, a sheriff named Richards in Cochran County, Kimball, Minnesota, investigated two mutilations a quarter of a mile apart, one a heifer, the other a steer, both in the middle of thirty-foot circles in the center of fields, commonly called "crop circles" for their appearance overnight in the crops. As with Lady, no meat had been touched or taken and no blood was anywhere on the animals or on the ground. Richards thought it was certainly mysterious, and "went back to town and got a Geiger counter. I checked the circles and it showed that there was radiation present. I called Reese Air Force Base and they sent a team to check this out." When the Air Force said that yes, there was radiation, but it was low (for a body with no official interest in UFOs, the Air Force certainly seems to get around to the sites and the witnesses), Richards said, "What I want to know is how it got there in the first place? I have had reports of UFOs in this area, but have not seen any myself. The people that have been reporting this all tell the same story. It [the UFO] is about as wide as a two-lane highway, round and looks the color of the sun when it is going down and has got a blue glow around it. When these people see this thing, in two or three days we hear about some cows that have been mutilated. I don't know what is doing this, but it sure has got everyone around here uptight."

The huge, reddish UFO described ("the color of the sun when it is going down") sounds not unlike the object seen over Malmstrom's missile silo in 1975, and also matches the description of "the Red Sun that rises straight up into the sky after devouring some of the tribe's cattle" in Zulu legend, as well as the Cherokee *Atsil-dihye gi,* or "Fire-carrier," a nocturnal aerial light. When Alexander Hamilton described the huge aerial object abducting his heifer in 1897, he remarked that "Every part of the vessel that was not transparent was of a dark reddish color." A consistency seems to be emerging from these reports, both in our time and from legends before our time. And this is hardly the description of a temperature inversion or a weather balloon.

Lady was mutilated the year after Malmstrom AFB was first documented to suffer UFO intrusions and sabotage. The next documented year of air base sabotage, much more widespread, coincided exactly with a massive wave of cattle mutilations across the United States. The mutilations had not ceased in the intervening years, nor have they since, but like UFO flaps—and seeming to correspond directly with them—they come and go in waves of greater and lesser regularity.

"Around the base," said Linda Moulton Howe in a 1990 interview, "ranchers were finding mutilated animals. And my brother had a firsthand conversation with a flight surgeon at Malmstrom Air Force Base, in 1975, when a rancher brought, in the back of a pickup truck, a cow in which the lips alone had been beveled so perfectly, so surgically, that the flight surgeon talked to my brother about it, and said that the tissue of this particular cow had been drained so thoroughly of blood that it was not even red, but the palest of pink-white, and that he, as a flight surgeon, had no idea what had happened to that cow."

Frederick W. Smith, in *Cattle Mutilation,* underscores the connection between military installations and animal incidents with the most remarkable of that year's mutilations—at NORAD: "The steep hillside up to the electronically controlled high entrance gate to the huge tunnel into this worldwide intelligence nerve center is covered with rock and brush. Surprisingly, a few cattle are also grazed here, no doubt to lower any possible fire hazard. So right there, overlooking thousands of military buildings, the protective covering of hundreds of planes and helicopters and 20,000 soldiers, and immediately in front of the electronic brain and senses that survey the entire North American continent so that even a needle couldn't get in undetected, plus monitoring of all of space from here to the Moon ... someone thought this would be a neat place to have a cattle mutilation." It was June 6, 1975. The mutilated cow had been due to calve in six months, and was found right outside the unmarked and unmapped entrance to this most secure of installations. Certainly it was no accident. It could not be construed in any fashion other than a clear message to the military: *Ignore this.*

Colorado was extremely hard hit with animal mutilations in 1975–76, especially in Elbert County, close to most of Colorado's military bases. At the time, it was one of the most militarily active states in America. Rocky Flats, manufacturer of H-bomb triggers and warehouse of half of the country's fifteen tons of plutonium, was located there. So was Lowry Air Force Base bombing range; the U.S. Air Force Academy; Buckley Air National Guard and Naval Air Station; the Rocky Mountain Arsenal, manufacturer and storehouse of nerve gas; Ent Air Force Base; Fort Carson Army Base; Peterson Field; and, of course, the target of this message delivery, the Canadian Air Defense Command and NORAD's Combat Operations Center, carved deep into Cheyenne Mountain, probably the most secure military fortress in the world.

A clear pattern emerges, looking over the decades: the foo fighters followed military planes in the latter half of WWII; the Los Angeles UFOs of 1942 did all but sit completely still, taking a mammoth barrage of antiaircraft fire without suffering a scratch; the green fireballs of 1948 were seen only in New Mexico, which was the most concentrated nuclear and military industrial state at the time; in 1952, UFOs prominently buzzed White House airspace on more than one occasion, ensuring extremely high visibility and publicity, while effortlessly eluding and baffling Air Force pursuers that were obviously reluctant to engage them in the first place. In various years, they have continued the same behavior over military bases in Cuba, Iran, China, Russia, Britain, France, South America, and elsewhere. In 1967 and 1975, U.S. missile silos were sabotaged by UFOs, concurrent with cattle mutilations, in some instances literally on the military's doorstep. Considering that only an estimated one in ten UFO sightings or cattle mutilations are reported, according to most authorities, and given the extreme reluctance of any parties involved to release their documents concerning UFOs, it seems a safe bet to say that, whoever the guiding intelligence is behind the phenomenon, it has something of a grudge-match going on with Earth's military forces.

Some researchers, not without a degree of prompting from inside sources, have inferred hostility from the cattle mutilations and abductions associated with UFOs, the latter of which will be discussed in Chapters 4 and 5. It is too premature for such a judgment. If anything can be deduced from these strange actions, it is less hostility than simply a proclamation of *superiority*—again, "counting coup." Though disinformation campaigns have been actively attempting to convince researchers of human mutilations associated with UFOs, none have been reported or corroborated by any reliable source. Despite some legitimate horror stories associated with UFO abductions, no one has been physically injured by them. We have seen instances of pilots presumably passing out during pursuit of UFOs and crashing, and in some cases being destroyed by the UFOs; but in these latter cases, it is clearly after the UFO has been armed against, if not actually fired upon. Planes have also disintegrated by flying directly into UFOs, but that can hardly be held against the UFO any more than a car's driver can be faulted for hitting a man who leaps before him out of nowhere. There have been permanent disappearances associated with UFOs, as in the case of pilot Frederick Valentich in Chapter 2, but we have no evidence of harm having come to these individuals even in the form of damaged vehicles. There have been harmful contacts with UFOs, even fatalities, but the question of intent is unclear in these rare instances.

The military has been intimated by various researchers to be performing the cattle mutilations, possibly to analyze salt samples in the animals' body tissues for the absorption of suspected petroleum or valuable minerals in their grazing land. Author George C. Andrews, in *Extra-Terrestrials Among Us,* cites a researcher named David DeWitt as publicizing this very science under the name of "biogeochemistry," which DeWitt stated was beginning to develop in 1973. This is possible, since the UFOs seen over mutilation sites are frequently reported as unmarked helicopters, and in at least one instance recounted to researcher Lawrence Fawcett in 1982, unmarked black helicopters strongly appear to have been part of a military nuclear recovery unit. In mid-February of 1995, Kimberly Drake of Denver's "News 4" did a piece on the unmarked helicopters in a series called "Colorado Mysteries," in which Major Shawn Flora of the Colorado Army National Guard admitted that the Army has them at both Fort Collins and Buckley Air Bases, and the News got pictures of them up close. They are not black, but dark green, their markings painted over in black. "It's standard," said Flora. "It reduces some of the infrared signature; also it's for camouflage." Flora claimed the helicopters are flying secret maneuvers, performing training missions, and helping law enforcement fight the war on drugs.

Training missions flown at night in camouflaged and unmarked helicopters make no sense at all. From whom or what are they being camouflaged? Secret Iraqi spies? That they are helping law enforcement is not credible, since Las Animas County, Colorado, Sheriff Lou A. Girodo—who has witnessed the helicopters himself around cattle mutilation sites after the event—has never been told by the military about such helicopters, even though they have now been seen on the nightly news. If they are helping the law, wouldn't he be the first to know? Or at least be informed, when he asked about them?

Colorado's Senator Jim Roberts also has reported seeing the dark helicopters, according to the *Longmont Daily Times-Call* of

August 2, 1994, in the article entitled "Copters and Roberts." Like Girodo, he has been denied any information about their existence, even after specific requests to the military. Why would the military deny a senator affirmation of their helicopters, which he has seen with his own eyes?

United Airlines ramp serviceman Greg Hix reported seeing "an unidentified black helicopter ... hovering over the baggage cart parade from Stapleton to Denver International Airport," in the *Rocky Mountain News* article "Mystery Chopper Turns Out," on February 28, 1995, the day Denver's new airport opened. "Black. No serial numbers. It was there," he affirmed.

A retired university professor and his wife, known to the author, saw three extremely low-flying helicopters that were "very dark greenish-black ... with no markings at all," flying west directly over deserted U.S. Highways 62 and 180 in Texas on the midafternoon of May 2, 1995, "plenty close enough to see ... [all three] had a big boxy shape, hefty." The highway was "[unusually] frequently marked as hazardous," which they thought may have had some bearing on the helicopters' presence, and a "quasi-road block," presumably seeking the recent Oklahoma City bombing suspects, had stopped the couple about thirty minutes before. Norm Franz and Ed Prout, of Fort Collins First American Monetary Consultants, stated during the "News 4" report that they believe the helicopters are in training for civilian crowd control in a coming economic collapse.

One of the extremely few serious UFO injuries on record involved up to twenty-three unmarked black helicopters, identified specifically as Boeing CH-47 Chinooks, seen surrounding a diamond-shaped flying object that appeared to be having trouble keeping aloft on December 29, 1980, in southern Texas. The helicopters and UFO were witnessed by Betty Cash, Vickie Landrum, and Vickie's seven-year-old son, Colby, all of whom suffered varying degrees of irradiation, causing burns and cancer. The UFO is generally believed to have been an Air Force project gone wrong, and lawsuits have been filed over the incident.

But we have also seen that some of these suspected helicopters perform in ways no such aircraft could. And even supposing that the biogeochemistry tests exist to determine oil content on grazing land from tissue samples, couldn't the government afford its own cattle to experiment upon, thereby keeping the public ignorant of the occurrences and avoiding alarm? Especially

NORAD, which has its own animals at the Cheyenne Mountain Zoo? Not to mention, how does a helicopter slip into a farmer's field without making a sound? A great many mutilations have occurred where neither owners nor animals were disturbed in the night by any sort of commotion, yet in the morning the grisly remains bear mute testimony to the mutilators' presence. And why would the military savage some citizen's cattle, then drop it on one of their own bases? Let alone NORAD?

One extremely dark motive for possible military involvement in cattle mutilations—supposing their ability to accomplish some of these acts, since obviously others go beyond their capability—comes from AIDS researchers Drs. Robert Strecker and Allan Cantwell, as reported by author Jim Keith. Strecker discovered expert testimony that the AIDS virus consists of genes found in two animal retroviruses: visna, and bovine leukemia. On an inspired hunch, he and Cantwell asked a medical library computer for information on "bovine visna," and "out came articles describing a virus identical to the AIDS virus . . . [with] the same morphology (shape), the same magnesium dependency, it has the same ability to kill cells, it has the same T-cell tropism (it attacks T-cells), it has the exact same characteristics in cattle that AIDS does in humans . . . and subsequently, 5–7 years later, the cows [die] of a wasting disease—and immune deficiency." No matter how alarming, this idea cannot be rejected completely—biological weapons development has long been a matter not of science fiction, but science fact. In any event, the information can be independently investigated, and it is mentioned here in the hope that it will be.

All of which merely begs the question: just what use do UFOs, or the military, have for the parts of the cattle they are taking? The mutilations vary to some degree, and animals other than cattle are mutilated, as well. Dogs, geese, rabbits, pigs, and other animals have suffered, but the vast majority are cattle. Typically taken are one eye, one ear, the tongue from deep down in the throat, the reproductive organs and the cored rectum, and half of the face from the mouth area up. Sometimes evidence of simple or serrated cutting tools is found, but in every instance the cut is considered by examining pathologists to be the cleanest they have ever seen. More often, the cut areas appear to have been burned with something like a laser beam, though there are differences—for instance, the heat generated in the process is actually sufficient to cook the hemoglobin.

Occasionally there are peculiarities—once a scalpel was left on a mutilated carcass, and another time a hollowed-out teat was filled with ten gallons of sand. In at least one instance in New Mexico, chlorpromazine—a medical tranquilizer—was found in a mutilated cow, which, as state police officer Gabe Valdez noted, "is made here, and it isn't from outer space. Whoever is doing it is highly sophisticated, and they have a lot of resources. They're well-organized." One cow was found in Colorado in 1978 with straight lines marked on its back in a strange, puttylike substance, and police officer Ted Oliphant discovered a cow in 1993 with an unusual substance on it which Linda Moulton Howe had analyzed. It turned out to be an unknown manufactured product with high levels of aluminum, titanium, silicon, and oxygen that was non-water soluble. The remains are usually found right in the middle of the animal's own field or pen, or sometimes in a removed location, with no sign of blood or footprints anywhere around them. In the majority of cases, scavengers and predators will not touch the remains, and maggots will not touch the damaged areas. In some instances, the animals have definitely been dropped from a height: legs are found broken, or the carcasses are in the middle of a body of water or literally in the treetops.

We are left with insufficient evidence to answer the question of why the mutilations are occurring, but with a surfeit of proof that the phenomenon is going on and is at least sometimes UFO-related. One speculation—in light of scientific findings in the past ten years and the fact that much of UFO abduction activity seems to be oriented toward human reproduction—concerns the amazing similarity between human and cattle chromosomes. Humans have twenty-three chromosomal pairings and cattle thirty, but "big chunks of cattle chromosomes [are] identical to large regions of human chromosomes," according to Texas A&M geneticist Dr. James Womack in a February 27, 1984, *Texarkana Gazette* article carried by UPI. He called these "perfect match" chromosomes. The implications for medical research are enormous. It is certainly not impossible that someone with such a technological aerial superiority over our terrestrial science might have discovered uses for bovine tissue along these biological lines that we are only beginning to suspect. In 1986, Dr. Mario Feola at Texas Tech University reported that the match is so close between human and cow hemoglobin that the latter can be used for human transfusions in medical emergencies, so long as it has first been purified and is not used in any given patient more than once. In fact, Jacques Vallée reports in *Revelations* that a firm called Biopure processes cow hemoglobin for exactly that purpose.

One thing seems clear: the purpose of the mutilations is to acquire specific tissue samples; the occurrence of the activity around military bases may be considered a fringe benefit for the extraterrestrials, or merely a convenience, though there seems little question that in the case of NORAD a clear message was being sent. Perhaps the UFO intelligence is merely killing two "cows" with one stone. The acquisition of biological samples is part of their program, disarming or harassing our military is another. If the purpose of the mutilations were simply to terrorize the military, then the mutilated animals would be dropped at NORAD more often, instead of being left in isolated fields, sometimes not to be reported at all. Jacques Vallée believes that these bizarre acts are intended to terrorize the civilian population, since the mutilators do not pick animals in the wild but rather those on private farms. But if such is the case, it seems more likely that the goal is to foment dissatisfaction with the government, which, after all, either willfully does nothing about it or else is shown to be powerless. If the extraterrestrials wanted to scare people, they would mutilate people, not animals.

It is, however, admittedly difficult to dismiss a sense of menace regarding mutilated cats—which, as house pets, are more personal. Cat mutilations are reported in the first volume of Linda Moulton Howe's *Glimpses of Other Realities,* and her documentary, *Strange Harvests 1993.* These have occurred in waves in Canada, California, and Texas, since the 1970s. The cats' remains are sometimes left on their owners' lawns, and other times are found blocks away. John Altshuler confirms that at least one of these was performed with high heat, like the cattle mutilations. The cats are uniquely butchered, invariably being cut neatly in half, and only one of those halves is ever found. Occasionally, other cats that are skinned or disemboweled are also discovered in the same time period. In tandem with cat mutilation waves come a great many missing cat reports, the bodies of which are never found at all. As with the cattle, no blood is about the carcasses, no disturbance or sign of resistance is evident, no outcry is ever heard, and surgical precision is noted in the cuts. Investigator Janet Hampson, in Tustin, California, reports that "paws and other body parts are often left on the ground in strikingly similar arrangements" at different mutilation scenes, indicating a single intelligence behind each act.

Reliable figures are not available to assess the actual extent of damage done in this ongoing concern. There are thousands of animal mutilation cases in police files across the country, none of them solved. One confession from a cult member is on record, but unfortunately it turned out to be false; Satanist groups have been investigated, but no evidence at all has been found. No one has been arrested, let alone convicted, of any of these crimes, despite government indignation and demand for results. "The mutilations are one of the greatest outrages in the history of the western cattle industry," Colorado Governor Richard Lamm said in 1975, with a gift for understatement. Senator Floyd Haskell (D-CO) asked the FBI to help investigate, but as reported in the Colorado Springs *Gazette Telegraph* of September 24, 1975, Director Clarence Kelley declined, "since there is no evidence of interstate movements in connection with the reported mutilations." This was a neat bit of sophistry, considering that the problem has been encountered not only in nearly every state of the Union, but in several other *countries,* as well. Mutilations fitting the same M.O. have occurred in Canada, Mexico, Panama, Puerto Rico, Brazil, the Canary Islands, Australia, and parts of Europe. It is not unreasonable to assume that, like UFO activity itself, they have probably also occurred in countries with less accessible news reporting.

The FBI's official waffling became even more noticeable in 1979, when the Justice Department convened an open conference in Albuquerque, New Mexico, to discuss the problem. That state's Senator Schmidt confronted the Bureau on its inactivity, to which its representative claimed it only had jurisdiction over cases occurring on Indian reservations. The senator brought up the obvious fact that this simply was not true, but the representative stuck to his guns and the senator backed down. Captain Keith Wolverton, an expert on the phenomenon who had come all the way from Montana to present evidence, was forbidden by his superior officers to do so. "The amateur researchers" in the audience, George C. Andrews notes, "came away from the conference with the impression that it had been convened for a different purpose than the one that had been announced: that it was not really to encourage communication between official and unofficial investigators, but rather to find out how much the unofficial investigators really knew about what was going on." In short, the conference seemed to be a "damage-control" test, like Project Sign in the 1940s.

"The conference was designed to embarrass the sincere and legitimate mutilation investigators," said one participant, "by sprinkling the meeting with bizarre, dubiously relevant presentations and information. This would make it easier for the media and the public to reject the whole matter by throwing out the baby with the bath water." Just like the Robertson Panel, the Condon Committee, and Project Blue Book, he might have added. One deputy sheriff resigned in disgust over the refusal of the conference to look at his masses of evidence, which included pictures taken over 130 consecutive days of the same dead horse which did not decompose. *Denver Post* publisher/editor Palmer Hoyt pronounced, "The FBI and/or the CIA (and/or some other agency or agencies) were and still are protecting the mutilators."

Whoever was doing the protecting also decided that the sham Albuquerque conference was insufficient to the task. The official verdict was that no federal investigation would be undertaken of the mutilation phenomenon, but recently retired FBI agent Ken Rommel was given $50,000 to conduct a year-long investigation in a single district of New Mexico, which—interestingly enough— was one of the few places in the country that year that *didn't* have a single mutilation. More than twenty other states were hard hit, including other regions in New Mexico than the one Rommel "studied."

One rested and relaxed year and 297 pages later, Rommel predictably reported that all animal mutilations were the result of predators following natural deaths, despite the simple fact that absolutely none of the evidence warranted such a conclusion. He actually stated that police officers had perpetrated deliberate hoaxes and filed falsified and erroneous reports. His final recommendation was that no further federal funds be wasted on researching the matter . . . and they weren't. Almost twenty years later, no one in the world is any closer to solving the problem, or answering its mysteries. At least, no one who didn't already know at the time. And whichever agency or agencies they belong to, they haven't broken their silence.

At least one of those agencies wasn't satisfied with the sham investigations, the destabilized civilian UFO organizations infiltrated by former CIA personnel, the Air Force balloon hoaxes, and the probable contactee scams, and moved into a highly active disinformation campaign. "Disinformation," writes Howard Blum, "as the Soviet term *desinformatsiya* was anglicized by admiring Western intelligence agencies, is the propagation of false, incomplete or misleading information to targeted individuals. But for a disinformation campaign to be truly successful, it must accomplish two related goals. One, the target must act on these new 'facts.' And two, the target must be irrevocably diverted from the more fruitful path he had previously been following."

William L. Moore, NICAP member since 1965 or 1966 and director of APRO by 1981, is the coauthor of two books with Charles Berlitz and Stanton Friedman: *The Philadelphia Experiment* and *The Roswell Incident.* Moore was approached in September of 1980 by Master Sergeant Richard C. Doty, an agent of the Air Force Office of Special Investigations (AFOSI), and asked to "cooperate" with them on an undercover assignment. Doty introduced himself as "the Falcon," one of a faction within the government intelligence community supposedly at odds with their peers on the issue of official UFO cover-up. Moore had first been called by a man who said he was a colonel, claiming, "You're the only person we've ever heard who seems to be on the right track," in response to a radio talk show promotion of *The Roswell Incident.* Until another caller in another state said exactly the same words to him in response to a promotion about a week later, he didn't think much about it. But the caller suggested a coffee shop meeting, and "the Falcon" showed up.

The undercover assignment Moore was asked to "cooperate" with was to assist "counterintelligence officers from a variety of agencies" in their ongoing disinformation campaign against a man named Paul Bennewitz, which had begun as early as two years before. Their interest was "systematically to confuse, discourage and discredit Bennewitz." Their man in question was a physicist/inventor who was president of a small Albuquerque electronic company called Thunder Scientific Corporation, working on his own UFO investigation, which he called Project Beta. Beta was the nightly film and radar tracking of UFOs that appeared with predictable regularity after sunset. The UFOs sent strange signals that Bennewitz recorded even though he could make no sense of them and performed reconnaissance over Kirtland Air Force Base, Manzano Nuclear Weapons Facility, and the Coyote Canyon test area. Bennewitz had the signal tapes and more than twenty-six hundred feet of film of the objects locked in a cabinet, the result of two years of work.

He was also intensely paranoid, a fact which Doty's team planned to exploit to maximum advantage. Bennewitz's mental disintegration began when he called New Mexico psychologist Dr. Leo Sprinkle on May 6, 1980, to hypnotize a purported female abductee whose case he was investigating for APRO. While several elements in the witness' story were common enough, even Sprinkle found some of her testimony suspicious. She made an unlikely reference to Roswell and hinted at secret underground bases where gray aliens and Earth scientists conducted experiments, something not reported in other abduction cases. She also said she was sure the aliens were hostile to the human race and kept human body parts in containers, that they put a metal plate in her head, controlled her mind and beamed thoughts of suicide to her, followed her home in their mothership after the abduction, and more statements not common to other reports. But abduction research was still in its infancy among all but secret government circles, and there was an insufficient data base at the time from which to determine case legitimacy. Bennewitz, however, bought it all. In the space of a few months, he became convinced that aliens were taking over and controlling the populace with sinister technology. By the time APRO head William Moore met Bennewitz, Bennewitz had for the most part already convinced himself of an elaborate and virtually groundless scenario based entirely on spoon-fed disinformation from Doty and his associates.

"Their work had been remarkably successful," Howard Blum succinctly summarizes in *Out There.* "It was government agents, pretending to be friendly coconspirators or using other more convoluted covers, who had first passed on to a gullible Bennewitz 'official' documents and stories detailing the secret treaty between the U.S. government and evil aliens, the existence of underground alien bases, the exchanges of technology, the wave of brain implants, and even the tale about the spaceship that had crashed into Archuleta Peak. These 'facts' became the linchpin of [Bennewitz's] grand theory; and, fulfilling all the government's hopes, Project Beta—the filming of airship maneuvers in the vicinity of nuclear bases and the monitoring of the unusual signals emanating from these craft—had now been relegated to a secondary concern."

But having sold Bennewitz on these false stories was insufficient to the AFOSI plot. Moore's assignment was to keep Doty and his friends briefed on how effectively their lies and deceptions were continuing to be bought by Bennewitz. In intelligence parlance, this is called a "Little Aunt" role: gaining the trust and friendship of a given target for the purpose of keeping tabs on him. Moore did exactly that, for four long years, by the end of which Bennewitz was a nervous wreck with extra locks on his doors, guns and knives hidden throughout the house, chain-smoking twenty-eight cigarettes in forty-five minutes (while eating), surrendering his business to his son, fretting over phone taps and office break-ins that may or may not actually have occurred, and finally ending up hospitalized for sheer nervous exhaustion. Far from being merely a passive observer in this process, Moore knowingly passed on once-legitimate documents to him from Doty, skillfully altered to give the impression that an alien invasion was imminent.

In public statements, years after the fact, Moore claimed that Bennewitz was monitoring nothing more than government helicopters on secret maneuvers which the military simply did not want photographed, and since Bennewitz refused to comply with their open request to him to cease his Project Beta, they were then somehow justified in using Moore to destabilize and discredit the man. The story came to light at the July 1989 MUFON (Mutual UFO Network) conference, in Las Vegas, Nevada, when Moore openly admitted the entire affair in response to an audience member's question. Moore's revelations were met with angry yells from the crowd. Jacques Vallée, who was present, reported one man loudly calling out to Moore, "What about the Constitution? What gives you the right to drive someone crazy?" One woman simply got up and left in disgust.

"If the Air Force," summarizes Vallée on the matter, "or any other government organization, has in fact encouraged its agents to act in such ways, then the result is a scandal on the scale of the disinformation and mind-control operations of the Sixties and the Seventies that culminated in the FBI's Cointelpro and the CIA's MK-Ultra, a very dark chapter in American history. With these programs, citizens of the U.S. and other countries, notably Canada, were systematically exposed to disinformation, to anonymous letters that used every possible racist and sexual insinuation to discredit them, or to dangerous drugs that turned them into vegetables and sometimes led to their death. MK-Ultra has been documented in the courts and in several books. But the scandal of the manipulation of the belief in UFOs has not been documented at all."

Putting aside the criminality of such behavior, the obvious question remains: why would AFOSI go to such extreme lengths to conceal helicopter activity that could be witnessed by anyone? Answer: it wouldn't. Not only was Bennewitz recording all of this material, but he was passing it on in a concerted letter-writing campaign to UFO researchers, congressmen, military commanders, members of the scientific establishment and even the president of the United States. It didn't matter that Bennewitz's paranoid ravings made him "his own worst enemy," as Moore put it. He was gathering evidence. And he was talking. And no matter how crazy he sounded, someone might eventually listen to him and look at the evidence he had. If that evidence was of nothing more than Air Force helicopters, even if they were on secret maneuvers, it would be unimportant. The Air Force would simply come right out to whatever authority asked them about it, put them on their "need-to-know" list, and explain it all, showing required documentation or proof.

But the documentation does not point to military helicopters on maneuvers, and it did not emerge from a need-to-know official investigation at the time, but from a Freedom of Information Act request filed late in 1982 with Kirtland AFOSI/Washington OSI, by *Clear Intent* coauthor Barry J. Greenwood. The seven-page file he received, stamped "For Official Use Only," and titled "Kirtland AFB, NM, 8 Aug–3 Sept 80, Alleged Sightings of Unidentified Aerial Lights in Restricted Test Range," stated that three base personnel "first thought [an] object was a helicopter, however, after observing the strange aerial maneuvers (stop and go), they felt a helicopter couldn't perform such skills. The light landed in the Coyote Canyon area. Sometime later, [the] three witnessed the light take off and leave proceeding straight up at a high speed and disappear."

More interesting revelations come two paragraphs later. A security guard at Sandia, whose name was withheld by request, reported seeing a bright light near the ground in Coyote Canyon, which was called in the report "a large restricted test range used by the Air Force Weapons Laboratory, Sandia Laboratories, Defense Nuclear Agency and the Department of Energy." He approached and "also observed an object he first thought was a helicopter. But after driving closer, he observed a round disk shaped object. He attempted to radio for a backup patrol but his radio would not work. As he approached the object on foot armed with a shotgun, the object took off in a vertical direction at a high rate of speed. The guard was a former helicopter mechanic in the U.S. Army and stated the object he observed was not a helicopter." This occurrence came exactly one week after the other Coyote Canyon event. Some time later, identical phenomena were witnessed by three more base personnel other than the security guard or the previous three witnesses, and at least one civilian policeman who filed a report. Another security guard at a later date witnessed the same, "but did not report it until just recently for fear of harassment." The succeeding paragraph contains the intriguing comment that "The two alarmed structures located within the area contain HQ CR 44 material," which somehow sounds important, especially given the sort of area and complex they are in.

The report is written by Major Ernest E. Edwards, commander 1608 Security Police Squadron. It is signed by Special Agent Richard C. Doty. The report confirms in two "Multipurpose Internal OSI Forms" dated October 28 and November 26, 1980, that Doty personally contacted Bennewitz. Doty went with former Blue Book officer Jerry Miller to look over Bennewitz's material on October 26, in response to correspondence by Bennewitz to the base commander two days prior, relating "he had knowledge and evidence of threats against Manzano Weapons Storage Area . . . from Aerial phenomena over Manzano." All indications show Bennewitz being taken quite seriously, and he was asked to attend a second meeting at the base on November 10 with several important military and scientific personnel, including Brigadier General William Brooksher, to discuss his material in greater depth. It was even recommended that Bennewitz apply for a USAF research grant to continue his work. The November 26 OSI form claims Bennewitz "allegedly had a number of conversations with Senator Schmidt during the last few months," and Schmidt did contact General Brooksher to discuss base security nine days after Bennewitz's research grant was turned down by Doty on the 17th of November. Another senator, Peter Domenici, met with Doty in July of 1981, interested in knowing if a formal investigation of Bennewitz had ever been conducted, to which the response was that none had ever been undertaken by AFOSI, but if the senator wanted further information he could contact AFOSI headquarters at Bolling Air Force Base. This last is most interesting, since the October 28 Multipurpose Internal OSI Form has listed: "Request a DCII check be made on Dr. Bennewitz," and "This is responsive to HQ CR 44."

On the surface, it would appear that the AFOSI team could not have set up the abduction testimony that began Bennewitz's downward spiral, given that the purported abductee's hypnotic session came five months before the official Air Force documentation of UFOs over Kirtland. But both forms confirm that "Dr. Bennewitz has been conducting independent research into Aerial Phenomena for the last 15 months," and the November 26 form expresses that Bennewitz might have been in touch with Senator Schmidt several months prior to the initial meeting between Bennewitz and Doty. In other words, Project Beta—and probably Bennewitz's letter-writing campaign—had begun ten months before Dr. Sprinkle was called in by Bennewitz to hypnotize the purported abductee with the suspicious testimony. Since Doty told William Moore that "counterintelligence officers from *a variety of agencies*" were involved in destabilizing Bennewitz, that could well mean that some intelligence office higher than AFOSI had begun work on the man before Doty and his team got involved.

There can be no question that people falsely claiming to be abductees are used to sow disinformation or discredit abduction researchers. Pulitzer Prize-winning Harvard psychiatrist Dr. John Mack, probably the front-runner in this kind of research at present, was infiltrated by a phony named Donna Bassett. In 1994, *Time* magazine ran an article on the woman, plainly designed to discredit Mack and providing no rebuttal from the man under attack. "What's interesting here is why *Time* magazine would . . . discredit [my] work on the basis of somebody whose chief claim is that they lied to me consistently," Mack commented to *UFO* magazine in September of 1994. "The writer never indicated that he would build the story on a person who was not an abductee, by her own claim, and who would lie her way into our confidence. *Time,* in a little squib, a few weeks later said they'd received a lot of letters supporting [my] work and admitted something must be going on here that they hadn't acknowledged in their article. By that time the damage was done."

Soon after, at a four-day CSICOP (Committee for the Scientific Investigation of Claims of the Paranormal) conference in Seattle, Bassett turned up as a "surprise speaker" to confront Mack in public. "I faked it," she said. "Women have been doing it for centuries." She said she found "no methodology whatsoever in Mack's therapy," and belittled the abductees in his research by calling them "intelligent, imaginative, but poorly educated" and "very needy," which is to politely say that, like the 1950s "contactees," they were kooks. To his credit, Mack refused to rise to the bait, declining to publicly discuss anything about her owing to doctor-patient privilege, other than commenting that his other patients did not believe her story and felt she was "deeply troubled," and had told him she attempted to turn them against him. He did, however, state openly that Bassett's husband was a friend of notorious UFO debunker Philip J. Klass, both men having worked together during Klass' days at *Aviation Week and Space Technology* magazine. Conveniently close at hand, Klass barged into the room minutes later, raging that Mack was making "false innuendos," and Mack coolly responded, "Yelling at me doesn't get anywhere, Phil. You just knew each other, and that's a possible channel for her coming here."

There are also indications that novelist Whitley Strieber may have been someone's "Little Aunt" against abduction researcher Budd Hopkins, and that Hopkins may still have other wolves in his fold—his current research concerns a purported abductee with the highly questionable claim that her abduction from a New York high-rise was witnessed by two members of an unspecified government agency. Strieber's case is extremely interesting, less for the possibility that he may actually be an abductee than the probability he is not. His claims of abduction have earned him well-timed millions of dollars on a growing number of books that pulled him out of bad financial problems at the time of their initial appearance. Where he was widely accepted by the UFOlogical community at first, Strieber is now virtually a pariah among them. He befriended Budd Hopkins early in 1986 under the guise of being an abductee, but his case was atypical from the start. Hopkins considered him completely unlike more than two hundred abductees he had worked with, Strieber being abnormally afraid and even suicidal. Hopkins "absolutely" refused to deal with him until he had first been to a psychiatrist. This, together with Strieber's later behavior and statements, gives the impression that Strieber is either legitimately deranged or, more likely, putting on an act, though Hopkins continues to believe—even after their falling-out—that Strieber's abduction claim is not false. About a year after their meeting, Strieber went behind Hopkins' back to his publisher, trying to delay the appearance of *Intruders* on the market until Strieber's own *Communion* had its run. The act severed relations between the two men as soon as it was discovered, and Strieber's pretenses of noble intentions are utterly unbelievable. It is not incredible to suppose that Strieber is an informed fraud, a cat set among the pigeons by interested parties to keep a close tab on abductees, not to mention researchers. He claims to receive a tremendous amount of mail annually from abductees, which would certainly make him a valuable asset to anyone who wanted to compile a list.

In the matter of Paul Bennewitz, the worst that might be said of him is that he tried to get a government grant—or, given the close proximity of Senator Schmidt's call to Brooksher after it was denied, that he tried to shake the Air Force down—but he didn't even do that until after freely reporting what he had discovered. For that matter, the grant had been the Air Force's suggestion in the first place, not Bennewitz's. However one wants to look at it, one fact remains: for his patriotic concern, the very man to whom Paul Bennewitz made his report—Richard Doty—conspired to destroy him, essentially succeeding in that aim with the help of civilian UFO organization head William Moore.

It was that same William Moore who, years later in 1987, trumpeted to the world that he had proof of the U.S. government UFO cover-up: the MJ-12 documents. The documents are almost certainly a forgery, given the highly suspicious nature of their appearance, the people to whom they appeared—most notably William Moore—and the inability of the FBI to find duplicates of them anywhere, which no doubt adds fuel to the fire of conspiracy buffs. However, like any good disinformation, they are almost equally certain to contain at least some truth. The difficulty in proving them false testifies to inside knowledge on the part of the forgers.

In brief, the documents appeared just after noon on December 11, 1984, in the home of Hollywood producer Jaime Shandera, a friend of Moore's with experience in documentaries for Time-Life Broadcast and RKO General, who had once considered doing a film version of *The Roswell Incident.* Someone had personally deposited the envelope, shortly after Shandera got off the phone with Moore to arrange a lunch date. His first thought was that someone was returning his wallet, which he had noticed missing two weeks before. Finding instead the envelope, he opened it (there were several envelopes inside of envelopes) to reveal a roll of undeveloped black-and-white Triex 35-millimeter film. Suspecting it was important, Shandera rushed to meet Moore at the restaurant with the film, and they took it to Moore's house to develop it. On it were the MJ-12 documents.

The timing and circumstances of the film's appearance are suspicious, to say the least. The missing wallet may have significance, or it may not; Moore's call may have been to assure Shandera was home, or it may not. But certainly whoever was behind dropping off the film wanted to make it all seem mysterious, or else they wouldn't have put it inside so many envelopes. In any event, they had the film developed in a hurry, at Moore's house, almost as if he was already expecting it. Given that Moore is a self-admitted AFOSI asset, and that long-suspected CIA asset Philip J. Klass is the other primary party to have fanned the flames of the MJ-12 controversy, the entire affair is suspicious beyond belief.

Their effect has certainly been detrimental to serious UFO research, which is the purpose of disinformation. The wilder claims of Paul Bennewitz—the ones that had been developed with calculated precision by Doty and his AFOSI associates—became closely intermingled with the MJ-12 documents, which have essentially been utilized as if they corroborated those claims. The result has been a steadily growing UFOlogical mishmash over the past ten years, with amateur researchers pro and con taking up sides over the authenticity of the documents and the purported wild claims that have become associated with them, which can all be traced back to Richard Doty.

Doty approached Linda Moulton Howe in 1983, approximately concurrent with his campaign against Paul Bennewitz, trying to hook her into making a documentary "exposing the cover-up" with proof of extraterrestrial biological entities, nicknamed "EBEs" (pron: EE-bee), recovered from crashed saucers and in shadowy collusion with various government personages. She told Jacques Vallée that she felt she "had been the victim of a neat 'bait-and-switch' trick engineered by the Air Force to make sure that the same filmmaker who had created an excellent documentary on cattle mutilations *(A Strange Harvest)* did not focus the sharp eye of her camera on the UFO phenomenon for a national television audience." Unfortunately, where she was smart enough not to buy it from Doty, other formerly excellent researchers wasted valuable time and their reputations publicizing more or less the same story from other "inside sources," namely ex-ONI (Office of Naval Intelligence) man William Cooper and CIA-connected John Lear, son of the inventor of the Lear jet and holder of seventeen world speed records. The worst victim is Timothy Good, author of the extraordinary *Above Top Secret*. He devoted his entire next book, *Alien Liaison,* to uncorroborated accounts selling precisely these disinformation stories, all of which can be directly traced back to AFOSI's campaign against Paul Bennewitz.

Having its origination in at least two prior sources—Robert Emenegger's 1974 book, *UFOs: Past, Present and Future,* describing a purported landing of aliens in an uncertain year at Holloman Air Force Base, and Stan Deyo's 1978 book, *The Cosmic Conspiracy,* about subterranean saucer bases in Australia—the revamped and expanded MJ-12 conspiracy story, which is the "EBE" or "Area 51" story, has slight variations according to who tells it, but goes something like this: The Roswell wreckage (or any other crash of a flying saucer) contained X number of dead aliens and one live one, called EBE, who was cared for and questioned for X period of time, until he got sick and died because no one on Earth knew how to take care of him and his own race didn't respond to distress calls. EBE's race is evasive in answering questions, and notorious for not telling the truth. Since the original EBE's death, members of the U.S. government secretly established private liaison with EBE's race, whose leader is named "Krlll" or "Crlll" (with no vowels and three "l's," but apparently pronounced "Krill"), who arranged a deal to abduct private citizens for medical experiments and mutilate cattle for never clearly specified reasons. In return, Krlll/EBE's race provides technological advances to the global powers, which are experimented with in a huge secret underground base in New Mexico or Arizona or Nevada called "Area 51." (The Air Force does have a maximum-security, top-secret test range called Area 51 in Nevada, but there is no evidence of an underground alien base either there or anywhere else.) However, notorious liars that they are, the aliens have reneged and are doing God-knows-what horrible things to our citizenry, and we are powerless to stop them. Implied along with this story is a "Thank God people like Reagan support Star Wars, our only hope," which is probably the subliminal intent of the story in the first place. The EBEs are said to have atrophied digestive tracts, needing cattle (and maybe human) parts to supplement their diet, and atrophied genitalia, requiring them to use our race to help them reproduce. They were the engineers of the human race in antiquity, and recycle souls in different "containers." They are not animal, mineral, or vegetable, and more or less consume chlorophyll like plants, but—as a matter of fact—they just love strawberry ice cream.

This story has so many flaws, it is difficult to know where to begin picking it apart. Just on the surface of it, the script sounds like a radio show being read by Ronald Reagan and John Wayne before an American flag, with H. P. Lovecraft feverishly churning out new pages of dialogue as they go along. William Cooper's EBE-related conspiracy book, *Behold a Pale Horse,* has a whole series of letters supposedly written by a loyal underground of brave rebel military men fighting the sinister conspiracy to sell out the human race, all of whom have a rather comical tendency to overuse adolescently melodramatic phrases such as, "The report is all true! Devastatingly true!" The EBEs are not supposed to be classifiable into any animal category we know. Meaning what? That they have scales *and* feathers? Or that one day they're a mammal and the next a protozoan? And if their food is synthesized chlorophyll, what use do they have for either cattle or human edibles, let alone strawberry ice cream? The aliens are reputed to be telepathic, and yet their names are written without vowels; if they are telepathic, did they spell their names in their listeners' minds, or did the names just *sound* like they had no vowels in them? And just what would a name with no vowels sound like? Hiding an underground base is completely impossible, given the state of the art in satellite surveillance, aside from which, as Jacques Vallée asks, "Who takes out the garbage?" Any sizeable base will have sizeable supplies. And, most obviously, what need would any race with such technological superiority over our own have for making agreements with our political leaders in the first place? It seems pretty plain that they can take whatever they want with impunity, entirely without our consent.

There is a companion scenario forerunner to the EBE/Area 51 story, a pseudodocumentary aired in Britain in June of 1977, called *Alternative 3.* Like its near-contemporaries, it has no evidence at all to back its conclusions, only purportedly real transcripts of supersecret conversations provided by shadowy intelligence people who hide themselves behind names like "Trojan," "the German," and "the Instigator." According to this one, the leaders of the world are working together in secret, having discovered at the time of the first landing that aliens were on the Moon and conspiring with them ever since. They abduct useless members of society to Mars and the Moon for slave labor, where they are preparing a base for the habitation of the rich and powerful when life on Earth ends, which will be any day now. The world leaders and certain intelligence personnel meet occasionally beneath the Arctic icecap in a modified Permit nuclear submarine, marking people for death who know too much about them. These unfortunate souls are fried with a microwave beam that makes them appear to have spontaneously combusted, or are hypnotized into committing suicide.

What is most interesting about these stories—none of which have a single shred of supporting evidence—is not that anyone believes them, but that everyone who can be shown to have originated them is connected to Intelligence work. Not only "Falcon" and "Condor," but John Lear who flew missions for the CIA by his own admission, another proponent of the story named Bill English who was an information analyst for the Air Force, William Moore the AFOSI asset, and William Cooper, who claims in his book to be hiding from former ONI buddies and ratting on them, but who admits he has worked only for ONI-owned businesses since leaving the military. (Where does he hide from them during office hours? The broom closet?)

What makes such stories especially insidious is that they stem from small grains of truth. *Alternative 3* ostensibly began as a legitimate investigation into the "Brain Drain" from the United Kingdom to the United States, a steady emigration of Britain's best minds that was going on at the time. Unfortunately, the "Intelligence Insiders" very quickly either duped innocent investigators or else made use of media assets in the first place to disseminate false information. Ten scientists listed as having disappeared and committed suicide (at least three of whom were given complete biographies in the later book version of the show) were all "invented," according to investigator Jim Keith in his *Casebook on Alternative 3: UFOs, Secret Societies and World Control;* yet exactly the kind of mysterious accidents, murders, and suicides suggested in the script did actually occur to at least thirty different scientists named by Keith beginning five years *after* the show's airing—in America's Strategic Defense Initiative (SDI) program. Keith called it "an example of strange prescience" on the scriptwriters' part. *Alternative 3*'s before-the-fact hints that the MK-ULTRA program—which was just coming to light in America—was responsible for such suicides may well have diminished legitimate later investigations of illegal mind-control experiments, by attaching trumped-up stories and unprovable conspiracy theories in a ballyhooed British television documentary. The *Sunday Telegraph* astutely made that exact observation, speculating that it may have been an intentional "fiendish double bluff inspired by the very agencies identified in the program." And since little has been written about the telecast outside of the book version of the show, released after the fact, some particulars concerning even this much information are suspect.

After more than ten thousand irate complaints following the show, *Anglia TV* formally declared the next day that it had been a spoof, denying that they had been irresponsible and adding, "We are delighted by the response." The head of a renowned T.V.-programming activist group said she "had hundreds of calls. The film was brilliantly done to deceive." That the various intelligence agencies had at the very least been monitoring *Alternative 3* is confirmed by the June 20, 1977, *Daily Mirror* article (the same day the broadcast occurred) headlined "WHAT ON EARTH IS GOING ON?" In its advertisement of the show based on an advance copy of the script, it said, "The programme will be screened in several other countries—but not America. Networks there want to assess its effect on British viewers."

Similar false catastrophe programs were later undertaken in America, advertising in advance—as had the 1938 radio dramatization of *The War of the Worlds*—that the events shown were entirely fictional. One show in the early 1980s presented documentary/live-action enactment of nuclear terrorists threatening to detonate an atomic warhead near a major city if their demands for unilateral disarmament were not met, concluding with an extremely realistic explosion and its aftermath of horror and misery. The 1994 network T.V. broadcast *Without Warning*—also fictionalized and advertised as such in advance—dramatized a number of meteor strikes on Earth announced by actual T.V. news figures. *Alternative 3* featured professional actors, billed at the show's end, but it still managed to deceive its audience by airing on the usually nonfiction show called *Science Report*. The excuse given for this neat bit of sophistry was that the show had originally been intended to air on April Fools' Day, and was delayed for unspecified reasons. Both broadcasts triggered a tremendous number of calls from concerned and frightened viewers. These programs seem almost certain to have been experiments to gauge the effect of television on a mass audience.

If one of the reasons the Air Force wanted to keep flying saucers out of the public eye was to avoid potential panic, as has so often been said by such reputable officers as Edward Ruppelt, it is of the utmost interest that it is Air Force Intelligence and CIA/ONI members who seem to spread all the panic stories. One might note that Richard Doty and his associate Captain Robert Collins, long since exposed as the mystery sources "Falcon" and "Condor," are both still quite alive and well, despite their refusals to reveal any source of the deadly knowledge they are publicizing for fear of the reprisals that will be made against them. One might also note that William Cooper says, in all seriousness, in the preface of his book, that he actually saw Kennedy's driver shoot him on November 22, 1963, on T.V.—which is a neat trick, since all stations blacked out across the country before the shots were fired. The Kennedy assassination was not actually seen by the public until Geraldo Rivera televised the Zapruder film more than a decade later. Not only are these people blatantly manufacturing untrue material, but they actually seem to *want* to get caught at it. And why not? Once they are, they show up whoever believed them, discrediting whatever good work those individuals might already have done.

Also, what private UFO organization is going to start calling these disinformation experts on their nonstories? "Most UFO organizations," says Jacques Vallée, "are led by people who are independent and sincere. In the cynical and blunt terminology of Intelligence, I have heard them referred to as 'useful idiots.' . . . Such sincere individuals are surrounded with people who have links to the world of espionage or to military intelligence. I found that some of the links were open and obvious: for instance, the Board of Directors of NICAP lists among its members the former head of the CIA; and it is no secret that CUFOS (J. Allen Hynek's Center for UFO Studies) has several 'former' agents among its associates. Sometimes the link is less obvious but is known to members of the organization, who admit it when confronted with the fact . . . In yet other groups, the link to such an organization can only be suspected. But the conclusion is inescapable: all the UFO groups are closely watched by several agencies."

Such scrutiny was a recommendation of the Robertson Panel all the way back in 1953. Their concern then was the potential mind control such organizations might wield; in fact, the only people who seem to be exercising mind control in these groups are the intelligence plants, which shouldn't be surprising considering the phenomenal amount of time and money they invested in such studies as MK-ULTRA. Perhaps the intelligence agencies are not as concerned with whether or not someone might influence a great many people, as they are concerned with the fact that whoever might wield such influence could be someone other than the intelligence agencies themselves. In at least one instance, a member of the French Air Force admitted to Vallée that a "UFO abduction" (the Franck Fontaine case) had been a deliberate intelligence experiment, later aborted, having nothing to do with UFOs but purposely made to look as if it did.

More circumstantial evidence leading to this conclusion can be found in the media handling of the EBE story. Seligman Productions in Hollywood purchased interviews with "Falcon" and "Condor," which had been turned down by the major networks. The result was an extremely shoddy two-hour broadcast on October 14, 1988, called *UFO Coverup?: Live,* hosted by Bill Bixby and syndicated by WGN—and derogatorily dubbed "The Strawberry Ice Cream Show" by journalist John Keel. The production values were so ridiculously bad that suspicion is unavoidable as to their having been deliberate. The choice of Bixby is especially interesting in that his most famous role was the bumbling idiot in T.V.'s *My Favorite Martian,* the early 1960s sitcom which made "spacemen" laughable. And the same production team, again hosted by Bixby, later did an "Is Elvis Alive?" show. In both instances, tabloid-style reporting abounded. Witnesses refusing to give their names and/or with electronically altered voices and blacked-out faces gave testimony with no evidence, alleging that their sources were legitimate but offering none of them up for scrutiny. Cheap music was played in the background for a soundtrack, and the script was often woodenly read off a teleprompter. And in both cases, live call-ins tabulated a vote at the beginning and end of the shows to the questions "Do you think the government is covering up UFOs/that Elvis is still alive?" For both shows, Bixby subtly prompted the audience as "evidence" was presented along the way, until by the end of the productions he literally emphasized to them, "*Now* how many of you believe. . . ?" to which both the live and call-in audience registered a marked increase from negative or noncommittal to the "believing" category. If the shows had been designed not as legitimate forums of information, but instead as demonstrations of media persuasion on a mass audience by the skillful deployment of propaganda, they could not have been more effective.

Most importantly, the subject of UFOs was linked by association in the public mind with irrational beliefs concerning dead superstars. As if this weren't enough, the same thing was done in a Kennedy assassination show which came out about the same time as Oliver Stone's movie *JFK,* again with the end result of showing mass audience persuasion during two hours' worth of propagandizing. And again, by association, it linked the subject publicly to fringe or irrational beliefs.

The most recent of the EBE-related media programs has been *Alien Autopsy: Fact or Fiction?* which Fox aired twice in one week, on August 28, 1995, and then again on Labor Day. Hosted by *Star Trek: The Next Generation's* Jonathan Frakes, the aired footage was supposedly that of the 1947 Roswell "autopsy." Secondhand eyewitness testimony from a purported Roswell witness stated, at alternate times, that her father had witnessed either one or three living aliens outside of the crashed ship before the arrival of the military, who cruelly hit one in the head to force it to relinquish a black box it clutched to its chest. The inconsistency in the number of aliens is difficult enough, but it is impossible to believe that even the most violent backwoods redneck would cold-cock an alien life form with a rifle butt, let alone a well-disciplined military man who would have to be under orders not to harm any life form encountered even if he felt threatened. Aside from which, if there had been aliens discovered outside the ship, they would have been doing nothing but hanging around for close to a week after the crash, which is not credible in any scenario. The film itself looked pristine, which would be impossible if it had been shot in 1947—the silver nitrate in the film stock would have badly deteriorated in the ensuing fifty years. And where any of the footage looked grainy, it was superimposed graininess such as is routinely employed by Hollywood. Worse, the authentic 1947 phone in the background was terribly beat up, making painfully obvious that it was a fifty-year-old authentic 1947 phone. In short, film that should have been deteriorated was perfect, and a background item that should have been perfect was deteriorated. The autopsy itself, despite obviously staged and carefully edited shots of amazed Hollywood special effects men watching the film, was far less convincing than better stagings seen in such movies as 1979's *Alien,* just to name one example among many. All of this is obvious even without considering contradictory evidence in the next two chapters, which provides much better explanation as to the nature of both the Roswell and other UFO occupants. As frauds go, it wasn't even a remotely convincing one— merely the latest incarnation of the old EBE-disinformation hoaxes.

"The expectation of extraterrestrials," writes Jacques Vallée, "is a sociological effect which in itself can be, and is exploited for down-to-earth, sophisticated psychological warfare. While little money has been spent researching UFOs, considerable effort has been made to study, document and exploit the belief in extraterrestrials. Someone has been using (and is still using) the sociological impact of the phenomenon for his own purpose, muddying up the waters and making the life of the objective researcher very difficult."

But however much various world intelligence agencies might have used the UFO phenomenon for their own mind control or group-persuasion test experiments, they certainly aren't sabotaging their own bases, or mutilating their own cattle to create unrest among the populace. And just because one Franck Fontaine abduction is an intelligence fraud doesn't mean that other people aren't being taken aboard flying saucers, or other controlled aerial craft not from the local neighborhood.

At the 1992 MUFON Conference in Albuquerque, New Mexico, Vallée gave an address, implying the disinformationists along with legitimate UFO researchers, when he said, "The American public is being taught to expect an imminent landing by extraterrestrials and to recognize them as short, gray aliens with big dark eyes. The fact that real UFO witnesses actually describe a wide variety of other shapes has been censored, to such an extent that some research groups do not even accept these shapes into their data base."

It is precisely the study of those various "shapes" that holds the most crucial clue to answering the mystery of UFOs: both the commonly known, media-advertised, Roswell-described Grays and the multitude of seemingly more absurd—and almost never discussed—others to which Vallée refers. Far from contradicting each other, these vastly different kinds of reports actually provide mutual corroboration, by defining just what the unperceived nature of the UFO occupants must actually be. To prove this, we must study the reports describing those occupants, given by the witnesses who have most closely encountered them: UFO abductees.

4

Abductions

T HE FIRST RECORDED incident of what is called a UFO abduction in the modern age happened to twenty-three-year-old Antonio Villas Boas in Brazil, on the night of October 15, 1957. Reluctant to tell his story, Boas was convinced by Dr. Olavo T. Fontes, Professor of Medicine at the National School of Medicine of Brazil and also an APRO representative, to publicly relate what happened, which he did on February 22 of the following year to Fontes, journalist Joao Martins, and a Brazilian military intelligence agent. Boas had been found to be suffering from radiation poisoning, and Fontes was curious. Among the symptoms were "pains throughout the whole body, nausea, headaches, loss of appetite, ceaseless burning sensations in the eyes, cutaneous lesions at the slightest of light bruising . . . which went on appearing for months, looking like small reddish nodules, harder than the skin around them and protuberant, painful when touched, each with a small central orifice yielding a yellowish thin waterish discharge." The skin surrounding the wounds presented "a hyperchromatic violet-tinged area." The military intelligence man interrogated Boas, and he was subjected to a battery of physical and psychological tests. The most conservative of UFOlogists accept his abduction as an actual occurrence.

The first incident of Boas' experience happened ten days before, on the night of October 5. It was a little after eleven at night, following a party at his house, and Boas saw a bright white light up in the sky when he opened his window to relieve the heat. His brother did not come to look, but sometime later in the night, after both had slept awhile, Boas rose and looked again to find that not only was the light still there, but it actually moved toward him when he looked at it. Frightened, he slammed the shutters, waking his brother, who watched with some astonishment as the bright light played through the shutters awhile before leaving.

Boas' family owned a farm with several fields and plantations, and to beat the heat, he tended to sleep by day and farm by night. The night of the 14th, Boas was out tilling with his tractor between about 9:30 and 10 PM, again with his brother. They both witnessed an extremely bright light a little over three hundred feet above their heads. Boas set out in its direction, curious if he could see the source, but his brother stayed behind. As he got close, it suddenly darted away at tremendous speed to the opposite end of the field. He approached it again, and again it darted away, back to where it had started from. This maneuver was repeated "no less than twenty times." At last discouraged, Boas returned to his brother.

"The light kept still for a few minutes longer in the distance. Now and again it seemed to throw forth rays in all directions, the same as the setting sun, sparkling. Then it suddenly disappeared, as if it had been turned off. I am not quite sure if this is what actually happened, for I cannot remember if I kept looking in the same direction all the time. Maybe for a few seconds I glanced elsewhere so it may have lifted up and disappeared before I had the time to look back again." In light of the descriptions so often recounted years later in relation to military base intrusions and cattle mutilation sites, Boas' description of the light being "the same as the setting sun," moving with sudden speed, and being able to instantaneously disappear is certainly consistent.

The next night Boas worked the fields alone, and when he was at the same spot he and his brother had witnessed the light the night before, he saw a reddish light in the sky which zoomed toward him at remarkable speed, "so quickly that it was on top of me before I could make up my mind what to do about it." It stopped suddenly, about 160 feet over his head. The light was so bright, he couldn't see his tractor's headlights through it at 1 AM. It looked like "a large elongated egg" with several technical features about it. Three legs extended from beneath it, and as it settled to land, Boas ran to his tractor in terror. The tractor and its lights died when he reached it, and as he got out the other side to run back to the house, his arm was grabbed by "a small figure (it only reached to my shoulder) in strange clothes," which he violently shoved away. Three more of the figures surrounded him and lifted him off the ground by the arms.

"All . . . of them [the abductors]," reported Boas, "wore a very tight-fitting siren-suit, made of soft, thick, unevenly striped gray material. This garment reached right up to their necks where it was joined to a kind of helmet made of a gray material (I don't know what it was) that looked stiffer and was strengthened back and front by thin metal plates, one of which was three-cornered, at nose level. Their helmets hid everything except their eyes, which were protected by two round glasses, like the lenses in ordinary glasses. Through them, the men looked at me, and their eyes seemed to be much smaller than ours, though I believe that may have been the effect of the lenses. All of them had light-colored eyes that looked blue to me, but this I cannot vouch for. Above their eyes, those helmets looked so tall that they corresponded to what the double of the size of a normal head should be. Probably there was something else hidden under those helmets, placed on top of their heads, but nothing could be seen from the outside. Right on top, from the middle of their heads, there sprouted three round silvery metal tubes (I can't tell whether they were made of metal or of rubber) which were a little narrower than a common garden hose. The tubes, which were placed one in the middle and one on each side of their heads, were smooth and bent backward and downward, toward the back. There they fitted into their clothes; how I cannot say, but one went down the center, where the backbone is, and the other two, one on each side, fitted under the shoulders at about four inches from the armpits—nearly at the sides, where the back begins. I didn't notice anything at all, no hump or lump to show where the tubes were attached, nor any box or contrivance hidden under their clothes.

"Their sleeves were narrow and tight-fitting to the wrists where they were followed by thick five-fingered gloves of the same color, that must have somewhat hindered their movements. As to this, I noticed that the men weren't able to double their fingers altogether, so as to touch the palms of their hands with the tips of their fingers. The difficulty did not prevent them from catching me and holding me firmly, nor from [later] deftly manipulating the rubber tubes for extracting my blood. Those overalls must have been a kind of uniform, for all the members of the crew wore a red badge the size of a pineapple slice on their chests, and sometimes it reflected a shiny light. Not a light of its own, but reflections such as those given by the rear lights of a car, when another car lights it up from behind. From this center badge there came a strip of silvery material (or it might have been flattened metal) which joined onto a broad tight-fitting claspless belt, the color of which I can't remember. No pocket could be seen anywhere, and I don't remember seeing any buttons either. The trousers were also tight-fitting over the buttocks, thighs, and legs, as there was not a wrinkle nor a crease to be seen. There was no visible hem between the trousers and shoes, which were actually a continuation of the former, being part of the selfsame garment. The soles of their shoes were different from ours: They were thick, about two or three inches thick, and a little turned up (or arched up) in front, so that the tips looked like those described in the fairy tales of old, though the general appearance was that of common tennis-shoes. From what I saw later, they must have fitted loosely, for they were larger than the feet they covered. In spite of this the men's gait was free and easy, and their movements were swift indeed. Perhaps the closed siren-suit they wore did interfere slightly with their movements because they kept walking very stiffly. They were all about my height [1.64 meters tall, in shoes], perhaps a little shorter because of those helmets, except for one of them, the one who had caught hold of me out there—this one did not even reach my chin. All seemed strong, but not so strong that had I fought with them one at a time I should have been afraid of losing. I believe that in a free-for-all fight I could face any single one of them on an equal base."

Boas took the shortest one to be a female he encountered later aboard the object, not because he saw her face, or even a configuration other than those just described, but simply because of the height. His description is one of the most thorough on record. The "unevenly striped" uniforms sound not unlike the sort of parti-colored clothing design one might expect on an elf, or perhaps a mediaeval jester—even with bent "hoses" sticking out of the head like tasseled bells on jesters' caps—"like in the fairy tales of old," which may be of some significance in later analysis.

Resisting as best he could, Boas was pulled up a flexible metallic rolling ladder into a hatchway, which closed behind them so neatly that no seam was visible to the naked eye. He found himself in a small square room, bare of furnishings, but brightly and evenly lit—"the same as broad daylight"—by recessed square lights in the smooth metallic walls. An opening mysteriously appeared, presumably from a door as seamlessly and tightly fitted as the outer hatch, to a room Boas was then led into. "The only furniture visible was an oddly shaped table that stood at one side of the room surrounded by several backless swivel chairs (something like barstools). They were all made of the same white metal. The table as well as the stools were one-legged, narrowing toward the floor where they were either fixed (such as the table) to it or linked to a movable ring held fast by three hinges jutting out on each side and riveted to the floor (such as the stools, so that those sitting on them could turn in every direction)."

Boas' abductors held him in place for a while, communicating in sounds with "no resemblance whatever to human speech ... I can think of no attempt to describe those sounds, so different were they from anything I have ever heard before ... Those sounds still make me shiver when I think of them! It isn't even possible for me to reproduce them ... my vocal organs are not made for it." The sounds were compared to animal grunts, "some ... longer, others shorter, sometimes containing several different sounds at the same time, at other times ending in a tremor."

The figures—there were five of them—then forcibly undressed him, despite his resistance and loud vocal opposition. "They obviously couldn't understand me, but they stopped and stared at me as if trying to make me understand that they were being polite. Besides, though they had to employ force, they never at any time hurt me badly, and they did not even tear my clothes, with the exception of my shirt perhaps (which I believe had already been torn before; this I cannot be sure of)." Stripped naked, they rubbed him all over with a thick, clear, odorless liquid, and prompted him into another small square room with red inscriptions over the door Boas could make no sense of, "like scribbles of a kind entirely unknown to us." Again, the door closed so flush to the walls that it could not be discerned by the naked eye. Soon two of the figures joined him, carrying apparatuses with which they took some blood from his chin, leaving small scars that were later noticed by the doctors at the hospital but that caused him no pain and only minimal discomfort.

He was left alone for perhaps an hour, making himself comfortable on the only piece of furniture there, which was a large, featureless foam rubber-like gray bed or couch in the middle of the room, with no legs. From holes in the wall at about the height of his head came tufts of gray smoke that quickly dissolved, with a smell "like painted cloth burning," which finally made him throw up. Then he turned to discover the door had opened again and "received a terrible shock ... *a woman* was coming in, walking toward me."

Like him, she was entirely naked. "She came in slowly, unhurriedly, perhaps a little amused at the amazement she saw written on my face. I stared, open-mouthed . . . she was beautiful, though of a different type of beauty compared with that of the women I have known. Her hair was blonde, nearly white (like hair dyed in peroxide)—it was smooth, not very thick, with a part in the center and she had big blue eyes, rather longer than round, for they slanted outward, like those pencil-drawn girls made to look like Arabian princesses, that look as if they were slit . . . except that they were natural; there was no makeup. Her nose was straight, not pointed, nor turned-up, nor too big. The contour of her face was different, though, because she had very high, prominent cheekbones that made her face look very wide, wider than that of an Indio native. Underneath her cheekbones her face narrowed to a peak, so that all of a sudden it ended in a pointed chin, which gave the lower part of her face a very pointed look. Her lips were very thin, nearly invisible in fact. Her ears, which I only saw later, were small and did not seem different from ordinary ears. Her high cheekbones gave one the impression that there was a broken bone somewhere underneath, but as I discovered later, they were soft and fleshy to the touch, so they did not seem to be made of bone. Her body was much more beautiful than any I have ever seen before. It was slim, and her breasts stood up high and well-separated. Her waistline was thin, her belly flat, her hips well-developed, and her thighs were large. Her feet were small, her hands long and narrow. Her fingers and nails were normal. She was much shorter than I am, her head only reaching my shoulder . . . Her skin was white (as that of our fair women here) and she was full of freckles on her arms. I didn't notice any perfume . . . except for a natural female odor . . . Another thing I noticed was the hair in her armpits was bright red, nearly the color of blood." A later recounting of Boas' story included the mention that her pubic hair was also bright red, which may have been omitted from the original publication of Boas' encounter due to the sexual mores of the time. Details of his encounter which followed were not published either, but apparently he did discuss them—albeit with some embarrassment—when relating his story to Dr. Fontes and Mr. Martins.

"The woman came toward me in silence," Boas related, "looking at me all the while as if she wanted something from me." She pressed herself to him, "clearly giving me to understand what her

purpose was, [and] I began to get excited . . . I ended up by forgetting everything and held the woman close to me, corresponding to her favors with greater ones of my own." They had two
sexual encounters and performed a variety of acts together for
about an hour, after which the woman pulled away to leave. "[A]ll
they wanted [was] a good stallion to improve their own stock," or
so was Boas' impression, though he wasn't complaining. He had
enjoyed the encounter, even if the woman refused to kiss (he had,
after all, just thrown up), preferring to bite his chin, and even
though he found her "animal growls" off-putting. She never spoke.
When their time was up, one of the other figures entered and
called out to the woman. "But before leaving, she pointed to her
belly, and smilingly (as well as she could smile) pointed to the
sky—southward, I should say. Then she went away. I interpreted
the signs as meaning to say that she intended to return and take
me with her to wherever it was that she lived." He was a little concerned, even afraid about the last, for he took the meaning quite
seriously and wasn't sure if he was anxious to leave his familiar
surroundings or his family.

The figure who had fetched the woman returned Boas' clothes
to him, which were intact and missing nothing except his lighter,
which he thought might have been lost outside in the scuffle. He
was led back to the room with the stools and table, where the crew
sat and communicated with each other in their strange way, ignoring him. Boas was "by now feeling altogether calm for I knew no
harm would come to me." He took stock of his surroundings, trying to remember all he could, and noticed that the walls were
smooth, metal and hard, and that there were no windows anywhere. He attempted to conceal a box-shaped, clocklike object as
proof of his visit, but one of the crew seized it instantly and shoved
him back. "Obviously . . . only when I behaved properly did they
respect me," he observed.

They led him through the ship, pointing out various interesting features which Boas described at length with a remarkable
amount of detail. He referred to it always as a "machine." There
was no doubt whatsoever in his mind that he was aboard a metal
aerial craft. The tour finally over, one of the figures gestured him
down the ladder, then pointed to itself, to the ground, "and then
in a southerly direction in the sky," the same direction the woman
had pointed. Boas was signaled to step back, and the ladder
retracted, the ship rose, the tripod landing struts retracted—once

again, so smoothly that once in place no sign of the opening through which they had emerged was visible—and stopped a little over a hundred feet above his head, "[growing] increasingly brighter. The buzz formed by the dislocation of air grew louder, and the revolving saucer began to rotate at a terrific speed, while the light turned to many different shades of color, finally settling on a bright red. As this happened the machine abruptly changed direction by turning unexpectedly and producing a yet larger noise, a kind of 'shock' ... When this was over, the strange airship darted off suddenly like a bullet southward, holding itself slightly askew, at such a heady speed that it disappeared from sight in a few seconds." This description of the craft's departure is almost identical in every particular with that of a famous suspected UFO at a U.S. air base in Rendlesham Forest, England, in 1980.

It was about 5:30 in the morning when Boas returned to his tractor, by his reckoning four and a quarter hours from the time he had been picked up. He discovered the tractor had been sabotaged, presumably during the scuffle, meaning that his abductors were smart enough to know he would try escaping and that they had knowledge of how a tractor works: the battery wires had been detached. For about three months after his encounter, Boas suffered various mild medical ailments such as those described above, and excessive sleepiness, a trait commonly found in subsequent abduction cases.

The British subscription-only magazine *Flying Saucer Review* printed the story for the first time in English in March 1965. It was first published for a wide audience in 1967 (the year after the much more famous Betty and Barney Hill case was written about in detail by John G. Fuller) by APRO head Jim Lorenzen in *Flying Saucer Occupants,* which Lorenzen coauthored with his wife, Coral. A geneticist who read the book wrote the Lorenzens offering a scientific observation that is simple and obvious, but has since been completely ignored by UFO abduction researchers in favor of more exotic theories: "It is an utter impossibility for living organisms of separate evolutions to sexually unite their genes ... unless they were of common genetic background." Human beings share more than 98 percent of their genetic background with chimpanzees, but cannot mate with them. "The overall genetic distance between us and chimps," writes Jared Diamond in *The Third Chimpanzee,* "is even smaller than the distance between such closely related bird species as red-eyed and white-eyed vireos." This is a critical point to keep in mind, in light of the claims of the majority of contemporary UFOlogists that abductions are being carried out in order to create hybrids between us and alien beings. If we cannot mate with chimpanzees, less than 2 percent chromosomally removed from us, how could supposed life forms so vastly different in appearance from human beings be creating hybrids between our species and theirs? Even if superior technology enabled them to tinker with the two dissimilar genetic materials, any offspring could only be a surrogate of one or the other race, not a hybrid. And if, as this EBE-related theory goes, the supposed alien race needs our stock to revitalize its own, then doesn't it seem more reasonable to assume that any intelligence with technology superior enough to hybridize completely dissimilar genetic structures could much more easily just repair whatever deficiency existed in the first place?

But in the Boas case, especially, we have only a suggestion of aliens, not a confirmation of them. Boas assumed all of his abductors were of the same race, the female simply being out of her spacesuit when he had his unquestionably sexual encounter with her. There were discrepancies in his relation of their appearance, but only on the basis of his assumptions—for instance, he believed the hoses coming out of their oversized helmets must have been hooked to a breathing apparatus, even though he could not see any bulge where such an apparatus should be beneath their suits. Since he never for a certainty saw the woman with a helmet on, and never saw any of the others with their helmets off, it is possible they were entirely dissimilar types of beings.

Since to all appearances—and apparently functions—the female who approached Boas was a human being, the most logical conclusion that can be reached, just on the basis of the facts related (assuming, of course, that they are true), is that "the Boas affair was in actuality a breeding experiment," as Jim Lorenzen put it, adding that such a conclusion would be "not emotionally acceptable to most." As added weight to the theory, he relates another UFO sighting which may or may not have been connected to what happened to Boas, but was contemporaneous and, to say the least, suggestive. Exactly three hundred miles in a straight line from Boas' home, at about 8 PM on the night of October 10, 1957—five days after Boas' first encounter, and five days before his abduction—coffee export agent Miguel Navarette Fernandez and his friend Guido were suddenly confronted by a hovering light they first thought was "the body of a helicopter." It maneuvered about them and pursued them, causing Guido to run the truck off the road, where it immediately stalled, the lights going out. Guido shouted, "My God, that ball is going to hit the truck!" But it came to a halt about 120 feet from them, hovering perhaps eighteen feet off the ground. The craft was at least 420 feet wide and 120 feet high (making it egg-shaped, since Guido by then referred to it as "that ball"). A hatch door opened in the bottom of the craft, forming more or less a short bridge, "like the door of a Convair plane," according to Fernandez, and again matching one of Boas' descriptions. Seven short and slim figures, all appearing to be human with long hair, stood in the bright hatchway and looked the two men over for about three minutes. They wore outfits with glowing red badges on their chests (once more matching the testimony of Boas) that made it difficult to discern their features. Then they withdrew, the hatch closed, and the ship rose to approximately 1,500 feet, ejecting a smaller discoidal object in the direction from which the ship had come, at which point the truck's lights and engine started up again and Guido drove away as fast as possible.

"Did the female part of the experiment pick her companion?" Lorenzen asks, pondering the possible relevance. "Was she looking for an acceptable mate on October 10 and were Fernandez and his companion rejected? Did the group then scout the Boas farm and did the woman choose Boas? Were there other similar incidents in which humans were observed and considered for a part in the experiment?"

There are other important points to note in these reports. One is the initial impression of the craft as a helicopter, which we have seen is quite common. Another is the ejection of smaller discoidal objects from the main, apparently for the purpose of stalling electrical systems and/or devices. Most important is an element overlooked in every analysis of Boas' story, which ties it to such sightings as those made at Malmstrom in 1975 and over Washington in 1952: the significance of the cat-and-mouse behavior of the object in relation to its observers.

For supposed aliens, the operators of unknown flying objects demonstrate remarkably human behavior. They know how to dismantle a tractor battery, which indicates knowledge of its function. They understand the nature and purpose of ICBMs, and how to incapacitate them. They know how to lure interceptors, and perform a consistent "peekaboo" game with them. Rather plainly a demonstration of superiority when engaging military craft, the almost identical behavior of the object with Boas, when taken into account with its benign and enjoyable end result, takes on a new aspect: *playfulness.* The night before his abduction, Boas was led a merry chase by the unidentified strange light in the sky, "no fewer than twenty times." Since the very beautiful woman aboard clearly had designs on him, what would be the purpose of such deliberate and repetitive elusiveness on her part the night before? The woman seemed "amused," smiled at him when "caught" the next night, and (seemingly, at least) having gotten her desired pregnancy from him, left him essentially with a wink and a smile, indicating she would be back for him. Especially if she had, in fact, been scouting Fernandez and possibly others before settling on Boas, the entire pattern of behavior suggests very strongly a ritual of courtship.

There are several instances of UFOs containing identifiably human crews, or crews dressed extremely similar to those just described. On April 24, 1950, Italian Abbiate Buazone witnessed a dark object hovering between a pole and a tree close to his house, at about 10 PM. Attracted to it by sparks that he first attributed to an electrical storm, he saw four figures "dressed in tight fitting clothes and wearing [helmets] . . . about five feet nine inches tall . . . in gray diving suits with an oval transparent glass in front of their faces, which were concealed behind gray masks. From the fore portion of the masks a flexible pipe emerged at the level of the mouth. They wore earphones . . . [and] talked among themselves in guttural sounds." Except for the height, they sound very much like Boas' abductors. His had three hoses leading out of the top of what he called their "helmets," bending back and down to attach into their backs, and these had a single hose at the mouth area. It is naturally an item of some curiosity why faces already covered by helmets and faceplates should also be wearing "gray masks." The occupants appeared to be welding or soldering something, and knocked Buazone back several yards with a flash from a "camera-like device" around one of their necks. Before reembarking and taking off, Buazone noticed the occupants' craft had "a series of oxygen type containers and many dials." There were other witnesses to the event who testified privately to the police, when Buazone went to a doctor to get his bruises seen to, and evidence was found: four circular imprints and patches of scorched grass, and some of the metal from the "soldering operation," which turned out to be "anti-friction material very resistant to heat," according to the Ministry of Defense.

Among those cases involving what appear to be entirely human occupants, at least one involves a craft similar to that observed by Boas. On October 23, 1954, at about three in the morning, another Italian farmer near Tripoli witnessed a craft land near him, "shaped like an egg laid horizontally." It was much smaller than the vessel Boas encountered, and had an undercarriage of six seemingly ordinary rubber wheels which left imprints two feet long. The crew of six, dressed in yellowish coveralls and "gas masks," appeared quite human, one's features becoming visible as he removed his mask to blow in some sort of tube, which is evidence that he could breathe our atmosphere. The other crew members wore earphones and sat at a variety of instrument panels with visible wiring. The farmer got close enough to touch the object, which threw him back with an electrical shock. The crew made gestures to warn him to stay away. After about twenty minutes, the craft rose silently and departed with tremendous speed, as did that witnessed by Boas.

Other human occupants were witnessed by sixty-year-old chicken farmer Joe Simonton, near his home in Eagle River, Wisconsin, at about 11 AM on April 18, 1961. He heard a sound like "knobby tires on a wet pavement," and found a twelve-foot-high and thirty-foot-long saucer-shaped object, "brighter than chrome," hovering close to the ground. Smooth-shaven and five feet tall, the occupants "resembled Italians," in tight two-piece black outfits with turtleneck tops and "knit helmets." One man aboard was "frying food on a flameless grill of some sort," and another saw Simonton and gestured at him with a metal jug, which he took to mean they needed water. He took it in the house and filled it, and when he showed interest in their food, one of the crew gave him three cookies about three inches in diameter and perforated with holes. No evidence remained of the encounter, which lasted about five minutes, but the sheriff taking his report had known Simonton for fourteen years and was convinced he was telling the truth. The Air Force took the report seriously enough to run a laboratory analysis on the "cookies," finding them to be "ordinary pancake[s] of terrestrial origin," which, as a matter of fact, "tasted like cardboard" according to Simonton. Both J. Allen Hynek and the Air Force's spokesperson on the matter, Major Robert Friend, were as convinced as the sheriff that Simonton "felt that his contact had been a real experience." Given the lack of any evidence, this is the occupant report most in the apocryphal realm, but it is worth including for the seriousness with which it was treated and its possible potential as evidence in later cases.

Jacques Vallée investigated a 1966 case from Temple, Oklahoma, where an aircraft electronics instructor at Sheppard Air Force Base sighted what he first thought was a stalled car at five in the morning on Highway 70. It turned out to be "an aluminum airliner with no wings or tail and with no seams along the fuselage," about the size of a cargo plane. Kneeling beside it holding a flashlight was "a man ... dressed in military fatigues, which I thought was a master sergeant ... this insignia was on his right arm, and he had a kind of cap with a bill turned up, weighed approximately 180 pounds and about 5'9". ... he was just a plain old G.I. mechanic ... or a crew chief or whatever he might happen to be on that crew." The man got in the craft, which rose vertically and took off silently at approximately 720 miles per hour, illuminating several barns across the valley. The event was witnessed independently by another motorist farther down the road. The instructor was interrogated by officers at the base.

But these cases—unlike that of Boas—were without abductions. The case of Betty and Barney Hill, probably the most famous on record, was not. Their story first appeared in serialized form in *Look* magazine, beginning in the October 4, 1966, issue. Journalist John G. Fuller—who first wrote about UFOs when his attention was called to recent New Hampshire sightings that resulted in the book *Incident at Exeter*—wrote a full-length book on the Hills the same year, *The Interrupted Journey.* The 1975 T.V. movie, *The UFO Incident,* based on this book has been blamed by skeptics and debunkers as the cause of hysterical contagion in later abduction cases. While in some instances this possibility must be considered, as must the occasional fraud, hoax, or deliberate disinformation story, it does not account for other evidence pointing to the reality of later abductions, such as matching testimony (down to details) not published or commonly known coming from witnesses who do not know each other, inexplicable medical ailments that come and go for no apparent reason, recovered implants, identical markings on witnesses, and the like.

On the night of September 19, 1961, Betty and Barney Hill were on their way home to Portsmouth, New Hampshire, from a trip to Canada. They left at 10:05 PM, expecting to arrive no later than three in the morning. They didn't get home until five. Neither could account for the two hours of missing time, since they hadn't stopped for more than a few minutes—just enough time to take a few looks at a strange airplane. Soon after, they both had troubling nightmares, and Barney discovered a ring of venereal warts that had not been there before. There were other anomalies in their lives, all traceable back to the night they drove home from Canada, and finally Barney went to see psychiatrist Dr. Benjamin Simon on December 14, 1963. At first suspecting some tension resulting from their mixed marriage—she was white, he was black, and racial tolerances were very poor at the time—Simon soon came to believe some other buried trauma was bothering them. He used hypnotic regression to find out what had happened to the two on the mysterious night in question. Through June of 1964, when their treatment was terminated, their remarkable story unfolded in a number of hypnotic sessions, first conducted separately and with posthypnotic suggestions to keep the two from contaminating each other's testimony, then later conducted together for comparison.

Barney's sessions were first, and were more traumatic and less revealing than Betty's. Both had been very badly frightened, even terrified, but Betty overcame her fear more easily and seemed to have better recall. Except for minor details, their stories corroborated each other in the main. Barney fainted or fell unconscious early on in the experience and was the more frightened of the two, which would account for his lesser memory of the incident. He was highly resistant to lowering the mental blocks protecting him from what had happened that night.

Traveling along isolated U.S. Highway 3, Betty and Barney had both more than once noticed a hovering bright light, at first indistinguishable from the stars in the clear night sky. They stopped a few times to get a better look, also periodically looking at it through a pair of binoculars as they drove. Barney first decided it was an off-course satellite, but its behavior and the length of time it was visible precluded that possibility. At about 11 PM, near Cannon Mountain, the object performed a series of maneuvers, suddenly approaching them fast enough to cause Barney to hit the brakes and pull off into a rest area. They used the opportunity to get a closer look through the binoculars, and determined it was some sort of airplane fuselage without wings. It had rotating lights of red, amber, green, and blue, and even though it wasn't very close to them, their dog, Delsey, was whimpering and cowering while they watched it.

Barney could hear no sound coming from an engine and began to feel afraid of it, having the distinct feeling it was watching them. He got back in the car and resumed driving, but slowly, so he could keep his eyes on it. It paced them from about a hundred feet off the ground, some way off to the west. Betty saw a double row of windows on it, and coaxed Barney into stopping again so she could get a better look. Admitting it looked "like a big pancake," unlike any known craft, Barney was becoming visibly frightened and snapped at Betty, with whom he had been arguing about it since it first appeared, saying, "It must be a plane or something." It descended out of the sky in a spinning top kind of motion similar to that described by Boas.

Despite his fear, Barney was unaccountably drawn to the object as it approached, and walked across the field toward it, ignoring Betty as she called out to him. When he was about fifty feet away, it was hovering at treetop level, and he could clearly see the occupants and machinery inside. The leader looked "like a German Nazi" in a "black, black shiny jacket," and he saw another he called "an Irishman" for no reason he could really fathom except that he got the impression it had red hair and a round face. The crew wore "blue denims . . . dark clothing. And they all dressed alike." He noticed the crew had "slanted eyes . . . But not like a Chinese," and inexplicably felt that "the Irishman" felt friendly towards him. He also felt "like a rabbit" which Barney once "threw my hat on . . . and captured the poor little bunny who thought he was safe." He described the leader, especially, as having "wraparound eyes," which he was sure communicated to him in some way to "Stay there—and keep looking . . . just keep looking."

Betty also later noted that the leader spoke to her directly in her head, as if by telepathy. Neither saw the mouths of the crew ever move, which were "only a slit, completely without lips, and with a vertical line on each side," that "part[ed] slightly" as they communicated among themselves. When they spoke with each other, "they made this mumumumming sound," according to Barney, a distinctive trait that will be noticed in later cases. Betty's description tallied with Barney's, except that she at first remembered them as having "Jimmy Durante"-like noses, but decided later that they had virtually no noses at all and that she was just attempting to ascribe human faces to them before. Both said that the occupants of the craft were "bluish gray," Barney making the observation that they were "almost metallic looking." Betty added, "Their bodies seemed to be a little out of proportion, with a bigger chest cavity, broader chest." In height, they were between five and five and a third feet tall. In common with later abductees, they said that none of the occupants were recognizably identifiable as male or female or had any sort of facial expression, yet feelings that one or another was male or displayed amusement or annoyance were commented upon.

His fear giving him new strength, Barney screamed and ran back to the car after the leader had mentally commanded him to stay in place and "just keep looking." He tore off down the road and asked Betty to look behind them. She saw nothing, but soon after they both heard an irregularly rhythmic beeping sound and felt drowsy. Some time later they heard it again, and found themselves home at 5 AM—two hours late.

Dr. Simon's hypnotic regression sessions brought out what had happened in the two or more missing hours. After the first beeping sounds were heard, the Hills fell into a sort of trance, and Barney stopped the car at a roadblock on a dirt road. The crew members described earlier unhurriedly approached the car, opened the doors, and escorted them to their landed ship, nearby in the woods. Barney fainted and was dragged most of the way, causing scuffs on the tops of his shoes that puzzled him the next day. Betty sleepwalked, semiaware and apparently thinking more or less rationally. They walked up a ramp into what both agreed was unquestionably a metal ship, and were escorted to separate rooms, Betty being told that they could not be examined together because it would take too long and they were pressed for time. In common with every known abduction case on record, no relief or recreational facilities were noticed, nor any food storage or preparation area.

Betty was placed on a plain metal table in a sterile room, extremely similar to that described by Boas and many later abductees, down to the round stools that Boas had said were like barstools. She was assured that they only wanted to do some tests, and then would return the two unharmed. Stripped naked, Betty had a strand of hair and a nail clipping taken from her, and implements were used to check her skin and nervous system. Most interestingly, "they took something like a letter opener—only it wasn't—and they scraped my arm here . . . and there was like little—you know—how your skin gets dry and flaky sometimes, like little particles of skin? . . . they scraped, and they put this that came off on this plastic." This obscure detail has recurred in numerous abduction cases since, remarkable for the witnesses referring to the same area affected and the same curious effects resulting. (Other details, not mentioned here, also remain consistent in separate cases. As in police work, investigators keep some of these secret as a control.)

Then a pregnancy test was conducted by inserting a large needle in Betty's navel. This caused her to cry out in tremendous pain, though she had been assured she would be caused none. The leader was surprised, and placed his hand on her forehead, causing the pain to cease instantly, another common feature to many abductions. At the time the Hills' story became public, this revelation was considered sensationalistic and incomprehensible. Betty had told her abductors that no pregnancy test she knew of was conducted in such a fashion, which indeed, in 1961, it wasn't. Today we have a procedure known as "egg harvesting" that is virtually identical to that which Betty reported. It is used to select a precise egg for fertilization. Barney recalled a cup being placed over his groin to take a sperm sample, a detail left out of Fuller's account to spare Barney embarrassment but included in later recountings of the story. It left a ring of warts around his groin, which Fuller did mention. What is interesting to note is that, as in the Boas case, human reproduction is of interest to the UFO occupants, though here it is not as direct.

The next thing she knew, Betty was having a conversation with the leader in the main chamber. There was some brief confusion on the crew members' part as to what Barney's dentures were, which caused her some amusement. The leader asked her simple questions about her diet, what various colors were, and the like. She asked him where they were from, and he gestured to a star map. When she said she couldn't say where she was on the map, he replied that he couldn't very well tell her where he was from if she didn't even know where she was from, which he and Betty both laughed at, and she expressed some regret that, even though she had a postgraduate education, she didn't know more science to conduct a really interesting conversation with him.

Betty was also shown a book, the characters of which she couldn't read: "[I]t had sharp lines, and they were, some were very thin and some were medium and some were very heavy. It had some dots. It had straight lines and curved lines." She compared it to Japanese, and felt it was read up and down instead of from side to side. She was first given permission to take it with her as proof of her adventure, but was then denied it, making her quite upset. This parallels the Boas case with the clocklike device, and at least one other on record where an object first permitted to be taken by an abductee was retrieved by the same UFO occupants before it could be shown to humans as evidence of the abduction. Jacques Vallée calls attention to this and many other similarities between UFO abductions of today and fairy abductions of all cultures down through the ages—the fairies or little people frequently gave gifts with peculiar stipulations, or retrieved items they had given in a contrary fashion. That this pattern is so consistent raises important questions. Surely beings this advanced would agree to a policy beforehand, and not have to repeatedly debate whether to allow evidence to leave with the witnesses, or change their mind after giving it? Perhaps, in each instance, it is an object lesson intended for the witness, since there does seem to be some indication that the occupants are engaged to some degree in a program of educating their unwitting "guests." Or perhaps their type of being thinks in different patterns from those of human beings, and this behavior could be a critical clue as to just what they are.

By this time having come to somewhat enjoy her experience, realizing that neither she nor Barney were in fact going to come to any harm, she asked the leader if he would ever come back. He responded that it was a distinct possibility: "Don't worry, if we decide to come back, we will be able to find you all right. We always find those we want to." (This could well be one purpose for implants, given subsequent abductee testimony for their existence.) The leader advised her to forget her experience, which Betty swore she wouldn't do, and he laughed and said, "Maybe you will remember, I don't know. But I hope you don't. And it won't do you any good if you do, because Barney won't. Barney won't remember a single thing. And if you should remember anything at all, he is going to remember it differently from you. And all you are going to do is get each other so confused you will not know what to do. If you do remember, it would be better if you forgot it anyway."

Barney was returned, and they were marched back to the car where they stayed to watch the craft depart. Resuming their drive, Betty asked Barney if he believed in flying saucers now, to which he replied, "Oh, don't be ridiculous!" though he did comment that there had been nothing for them to be afraid of and asked Betty to look behind them for the object. Shortly, they heard the beeping sound again, and forgot all that had transpired as they found themselves near home later than expected.

After going through the sessions with Dr. Simon, Barney's headaches and sleeplessness lessened, and both their nightmares diminished. Simon never disclosed whether he thought their encounter had been real or simply imagined, but admitted the possibility that it could have been an actual occurrence. Unbeknownst to either John Fuller or Dr. Simon, New Hampshire's Pease Air Force Base considered the incident real, as is evidenced by the only official document on file of the case, in the records of SAC's 100th Bomb Wing, report number 100–1–61. The Hills' UFO had been recorded on radar. Betty reported the sighting soon after to the base, and her report is included with the official record of the radar confirmation. What is not included is any mention of the occupants or the abduction, showing how reluctant the Air Force was to consider such information as valid even when accompanied by solid physical evidence of the craft itself.

The mechanism for inducing amnesia in abductees is not completely understood, but seems to involve hypnosis, which is why regression therapy works in bringing it out—using the same key that locked the memory in the first place. The beeps before and after in the Hill case may have served to induce and end the trance, since it was precisely at that signal that they both forgot and then began to remember again. In some cases, gas is used to at least render victims unconscious, as will be seen, and may have some effect on later memory loss. There are drugs and procedures within our own technology that impair or erase memory, including electroshock (or electroconvulsive) therapy.

It has been charged that investigators utilizing hypnosis on suspected abductees may be leading unwitting subjects or planting false memories. In some instances this may occur, but approximately one-third of reported abductions are remembered with no hypnosis at all. Those memories tend to be recalled as especially vivid dreams or nightmares, as Betty Hill's first were. Their details match those retrieved hypnotically, in most cases.

The next most important case to emerge in the modern era was probably that of Betty Andreasson, documented in three ongoing books by investigator Raymond E. Fowler—*The Andreasson*

Affair; The Andreasson Affair, Phase Two; and *The Watchers*—spanning from 1979, when the case first was published after years of research, to 1990. Betty Andreasson was seven years old in 1944 when her first abduction experience occurred. She first investigated her experiences after a much later abduction, which occurred about 6:35 PM on the evening of January 25, 1967, a major flap year in UFO history. Her entire family—Betty's own parents and her seven children, aged three to eleven—except for her husband, who was in the hospital, witnessed the arrival of something strange outside her South Ashburnham, Massachusetts, home in the country. The house lights blinked on and off as a pulsing reddish orange light was seen at a small hill in the large field behind the house. Betty's father went to look and saw some strange, almost comical creatures: "These creatures that I saw through the windows of Betty's house were just like Halloween freaks. I thought they had put on a funny kind of headdress imitating a moon man. It was funny how they jumped one after the other—just like grasshoppers. When they saw me looking at them, they stopped . . . the one in front looked at me and I felt kind of queer. That's all I know." Like many abductees and abduction witnesses, his mind blanked from that point on.

Beings identical in appearance to the Hills' description—short, thin, gray, Mongoloid-looking, with oversized pear-shaped heads and giant black teardrop eyes—entered through the wooden front door . . . without opening it. This is another feature frequently reported in abduction cases: creatures capable of passing through solid walls or other obstacles as if they weren't even there. It is also another connection to fairy stories of old. An added feature Betty remembered is that their dark blue uniforms had an emblem of a Phoenix with outstretched wings on the left sleeve.

Their leader was taller, and different in appearance. He looked like a giant insect, rather like a bumblebee, with visible "feelers" on his head—i.e., "antennae"—and had one black eye and one white eye. The Hills had also said the leader was different from the others, agreeing that he was taller, adding that he was shiny and black, but were utterly unable to describe him any further. Both had been too frightened by him for some reason, even after knowing they were safe, to break through that particular mental block. Betty Andreasson's central abductor even had a name, "Quazgaa," making him the only known named being on the abduction phenomenon record. Some of Betty's recollections are wildly hallucinatory, with indications of a certain degree of confabulation—the name might be one of them, or it might not. Confabulation is not lying, but rather filling in by the rational mind after the fact, in an attempt to make sense out of something that doesn't seem to make sense at the time. It is one of the pitfalls of hypnotic testimony. A good example of confabulation later recognized by the witness is Betty Hill's realization that the beings she saw did not have large noses, as she first thought; she was just imagining that they did to try and make them human.

With the rest of the household more or less deactivated or switched off—another similarity to later cases—Betty's will was commandeered and she was led outside to a small oval craft, which rose so fast that she felt the G-force effects. It connected with a larger craft. She was exposed to strange machinery and put through a variety of medical procedures, including the retrieval from her nose of a BB-sized metal ball with tiny wires sticking out of it that had been placed there sometime before in a previous abduction.

Afterward, she was put into a tank of liquid (reported by many later abductees, with no professed knowledge of its purpose) "to protect her from harmful effects during transit," and taken by spacecraft into a cave hewn out of solid rock. Beyond was an alien landscape, over which she floated between two escorts, to see domed structures, trestlelike skyrails, water, vegetation, and flying craft, and "a pyramidlike structure with a sculptured head affixed to its apex," about which Betty said, "It looked sort of like an Egyptian head, and it had like a, you know, how they wear those hats?" Taken into a beautiful crystalline structure, she saw an enactment of the death and rebirth of the Phoenix, including the interesting feature of seeing not a new bird, but a worm emerging from the ashes. This point is interesting because it is obscure—and historically accurate. Another interesting feature, especially in light of the rest of her reported surroundings, is that the myth is not Greek; it is Egyptian, originally called not the Phoenix, but the Bennu bird. Betty was overwhelmed by the display and was bombarded by a chorus of voices in her head that blended together as one, asking her if she understood, and telling her, "I have chosen you to show the world."

Vallée, who has no difficulty drawing lengthy and well-researched attention to the similarities between UFO and religious apparition phenomena, and who is well known for studying any and all cases, does not mention the Betty Andreasson case anywhere in his voluminous writings. Keith Thompson also ignores it in his study of exactly such comparisons, *Angels and Aliens*. Just as there was a tremendous resistance on the part of early UFO investigators to consider first occupant and then abduction reports, there is similarly today an extreme reluctance to consider the overtly religious nature of many of them. It is especially interesting in Vallée's case, given not only his study of the similarities of Virgin Mary apparitions with UFO appearances and his attention to Aimé Michel's historical and anthropological study of the subject, but also his willingness to study two aspects of the UFO phenomenon that almost no other researcher is willing to touch: the initiatory and social control aspects. The Andreasson case is connected to all of these.

Betty Andreasson is a devout Catholic, and she interprets her experiences in that context. The control voice that speaks to her in her abductions relates itself to that, whether there is a connection or not, and she considers her abductors to be angels, whatever their methods or appearance. She feels certain that the Intelligence behind these encounters is friendly to man and working for the benefit of the species, having been our caretakers since ancient times. Her second husband, Bob Luca, also claims to be an abductee, and has had extremely similar experiences to Betty's. This too seems to be a not uncommon phenomenon: abductees coming to know each other, frequently to become extremely good friends or mates, neither initially knowing the other is an abductee.

When her 1967 encounter was concluded, the leader returned her safely home and told her, "Child, you must forget for a while." She suffered numerous mental blocks in her early hypnotic therapy, which over the years have lessened, until more and more of her encounters have been remembered. "They are going to come to the earth," she said. "Man is going to fear because of it ... He says that he had had others here (on the ship and other experiences) and many others have locked within their minds, secrets. And he is locking within my mind certain secrets. *And they will be revealed only when the time is right.*" Fowler agrees with her that the entities are "a certain class of angelic *beings* ... The Chaldean name for [which] is 'ir which translated means *Watcher,*" a subject that will be dealt with in greater detail in the second part of this book. Fowler asked her specifically at one point if the beings had any connection with what we refer to as the Second Coming, and she said, "They definitely do."

Any of this could be simply the religious passion of either Betty Andreasson or Raymond Fowler, but on the other hand it might actually be the case. In any event, it cannot simply be rejected without due consideration. Even the usually noncommittal J. Allen Hynek wrote, in the preface to *The Andreasson Affair,* "In the area of UFOs, deeper acquaintance reveals a subject that has not only potentially important scientific aspects but sociological, psychological, and even theological aspects as well. The Andreasson case involves all these aspects . . . It is not nonsense . . . Neither is there the slightest evidence of hoax or contrivance . . . More and more of these high-strangeness cases are surfacing. Like the Andreasson case, they outrage our common sense and . . . constitute a challenge to our present belief systems." Betty and her daughter Becky both underwent a battery of psychological and medical examinations, and were considered to be neither ill nor lying.

One of the "ongoing revelations" of Betty Andreasson's case came in 1987, matching a claim made by "Kathie Davis" (pseudonym—most abductees seem to prefer anonymity) in the same year in Budd Hopkins' *Intruders.* The timing could be coincidental; it could be a deliberate part of a concerted "time-release" plan, as Ms. Andreasson seems to believe; or it could be a straight copycat claim. The timing has to be mentioned, in the interest of fairness, since it is just a little bit suspicious. That reported revelation has since become common coin in the abduction phenomenon: the production of offspring.

Andreasson did not use the word "hybrid," which most abductologists have tacked on to the reports in spite of the mixed nature of the children described and the abductees' uncertainties. She said the baby the abductors produced from her could not be distinguished as either male or female, and looked neither exactly like them nor like a human fetus, but closer to the latter. Her impression was that it would grow up to be one of them, implying either a hybrid or surrogate.

While some abductees do upon occasion call these reported babies hybrids, most often they admit to being confused about them. Kathie Davis' report was the first published, in 1987, though others had been making the same claim. She reported it to Budd Hopkins without the aid of hypnosis in January of 1985. By her recollection, the child presented to her by the abductors was unquestionably hers, about four years old, "and she didn't look like them, but she didn't look like us, either." Her report, however, and her drawing of the child seem altogether human: "She was real pretty. She looked like an elf, or an . . . angel . . . a little teeny-weeny nose, just so perfect . . . And her hair was white and wispy and . . . real thin and fine . . . The forehead was just a little bit bigger . . . but she was just a doll . . . Her eyes were so blue and huge . . . Her skin was creamy . . . it wasn't gray [like the abductors]. She was pale and soft and creamy . . . Her face is shaped like a heart . . . tiny, tiny little mouth. Perfect lips. Blue eyes. White hair." The gray being told her, "A father . . . has to take care of his children," and told her he would bring it back for her to see again but had to take her away soon because "She has to stay with us." Kathie was told she would get sick if she stayed too long, and that she would be unable to feed the child.

It was Hopkins who asked her if the gray abductor being was the girl's father, but Kathie did not confirm it. She was certain she hadn't had sex with it, considering the idea "gross." "He just said she was a part of me," was her only explanation as to how or why the girl had come to be, or what its exact parentage was. Later she said, "That man just can't be the father. Maybe he donated some cells or something. Maybe that's what he told me." Other abductees have been as uncertain as Kathie, many reluctant to call them "hybrids" and not sure what precisely the babies should be called.

It should be noted that the girl was completely unlike the abductors in every regard. Kathie said she displayed emotion, was active, showed fear and joy, smiled, her eyes blinked; the gray beings never show any facial expression in any report, and are almost never reported to blink. The only emotion in the abductor-beings is expressed "If you look at their eyes," as Kathie Davis and Barney Hill and many other abductees put it. Similarly, their sex is determined solely in those eye-expressed emotions, since no physical difference is apparent. Considering the eyes are completely black, opaque, and do not blink, and the faces show no change of expression, this is a neat trick. There must be something in the "telepathic" transmission the abductees are receiving. It must also be noted that the physical description of the child given by Kathie Davis—and other abductees—matches very closely that of the woman who abducted and had sex with Antonio Boas.

Later reports of offspring as a by-product of the abduction experience have added details. The babies are placed in some kind of liquid vat, after being taken from the mother's womb early in her induced pregnancy; it happens so early that she will generally perceive the loss of the baby either as a false pregnancy, or as some kind of miscarriage leaving no remains. The offspring are brought back on a regular or semiregular schedule from then on, to meet with their parents as they develop. There are reports of abductees having sex with other purely human beings during their abduction experiences, very much like Boas'; in some cases abductees are certain these sexual partners are from Earth (often people they know, who are also abductees). There are also reports of abductees having sex with the gray beings. Any or all of these claims may or may not be true, are frequently obtained under hypnosis, and are certainly open to interpretation. Even when recalled consciously, the probability of drugs having been employed in combination with hypnotic techniques (narcohypnosis) must be weighed in when evaluating abductees' memories. But the reports must be considered, to find what common patterns or singular pieces of evidence emerge.

One other often-overlooked report should be considered, which does not appear to be disputed by anyone as genuine and is more or less standard—the case of Nebraska highway patrolman Herbert Schirmer. A little after midnight on December 3 of that major flap year, 1967, twenty-two-year-old Herbert Schirmer of the Ashland Police Department noticed a bull in a corral "kicking and charging at the gate. He was really upset." He made sure the corral was secure and drove on. About two and a half hours later, at the intersection of Highway 63 on the edge of town, his lights illuminated what he first thought was a stalled truck. When he turned his spotlight on it, "I just couldn't believe what I saw there . . . I had never really thought about flying saucers one way or the other . . . When I snapped on my high beams and spotlight, the vehicle took off into the sky and disappeared. That is all I remember until the Condon Committee came out to Ashland." When he returned to the station at 3 AM, he wrote in the logbook: "Saw a flying saucer at the junction of highways 6 and 63. Believe it or not!"

The Condon Committee had Schirmer brought to Boulder, where they were convened. Apparently it had been the fact that there were missing minutes in his report log that caught their attention. "They really hammered me on those missing minutes," Schirmer said. This is interesting, since it wasn't until the publication of Budd Hopkins' *Missing Time* in 1981 that the phenomenon was publicly recognized as a frequent feature of UFO abductions. In addition, "They spent a lot of time just measuring [my cruiser] . . . They also kept after me about the red welt on my neck nerve cord. They had found out that these welts were a part of a pattern among contactees. Another thing they kept asking about was the tingling sensation I felt all over my body. I had mentioned this and they kept asking about it." They put him under time-regression hypnosis and then let him go.

He returned to Ashland, and soon became head of the department and the Midwest's youngest police chief. But he quit shortly thereafter because he found himself suffering from continuing headaches that had begun the night of his saucer incident and inhibited his concentration. He was "gobbling down aspirin like it was popcorn." Convinced there was something vital about that night that he couldn't recall, he contacted Eric Norman, author of several published articles on flying saucers, who suggested he go through another hypnosis session. Schirmer underwent hypnosis by professional hypnotist Loring G. Williams, which was witnessed by Norman and author Brad Steiger. The session was tape-recorded and transcribed in two of Norman's books, *Gods, Demons and Space Chariots* and *Gods and Devils from Outer Space*.

After Schirmer saw the object, which was "metal and . . . shaped like a football" (not unlike the egg shape formerly described by other witnesses), it zoomed over to him at tremendous speed and landed near him. Occupants that he could not clearly see at the moment, but later described as being more or less identical to the "Grays" so far described, disembarked and approached his vehicle. Schirmer couldn't move and was quite terrified. The lead occupant produced a green gas from some object in its possession, which enveloped the car. Then it pointed a rodlike device from a holster at its hip at him, and he was actually paralyzed by a flash from it. This same device will be noticed in later reports, and in fact was brought up by the Hills. Additional features about the occupants not yet reported included an antenna sticking out of the left side of their helmets, which he took to be a radio antenna for their private communications though he could not remember them speaking among each other at any point. Also, their eye pupils widened and narrowed "like a camera lens adjusting," the latter being something hinted at by Betty Hill. They moved stiffly and mechanically like professional soldiers. A most interesting feature he noticed, especially in light of Betty Andreasson's experience, was the emblem of a winged serpent on their right breast area: the symbol of Quetzalcoatl, the culture god of the Americas.

He hesitated before drawing it while under hypnosis, mumbling, "Better not ... something ... " as if he were under a compulsion not to, but put it in place when coaxed by Williams to finish what he intended to draw.

The leader "pushed against the side of my neck [which] hurt for a minute," at the spot where Schirmer's welt later appeared. Unidentified body markings (UBMs) are also now recognized as a fairly standard indicator of UFO abductions. He wasn't sure what scratched him. Given later testimony by other abductees, it could have been an implant. "Maybe there was something about his glove that scratched my neck," Schirmer speculated, which is an interesting observation—an abductee interviewed by Jacques Vallée in South America was scratched by a UFO occupant after it had removed its glove, and developed essentially the same marks and symptoms as Schirmer. Schirmer never knew how the leader communicated with him—perhaps the scratch at his neck, if it was an implant, was a receiver of some sort.

Schirmer, like many abductees, was uncomfortable with the way the leader's eyes stared at him. The leader asked, "Are you the watchman over this place?" and whether or not a nearby power station he indicated was the only source of power they had, to which Schirmer replied yes. Schirmer asked him if he were real, and the occupant replied that he was very real and squeezed his shoulder to prove it. Then he asked if Schirmer would open fire on a flying saucer, and when Schirmer said no, the leader took him aboard.

He observed numerous video consoles, each showing different areas outside the ship from external cameras and automated probes, some of which sound like the smaller objects ejected from UFOs in flight. He was told that the ship was a small observation craft; some details about its construction and operation, including that the saucers are made from 100 percent pure magnesium (in some cases verified by later analysis, such as a case in Ubatuba, Brazil); that they generate protective force fields around their ships while landed, often taking the power from local electrical sources (such as the one Schirmer had been asked about); and that "they have bases on Venus and some of the other planets in our galaxy," including underground bases on Earth at one of the poles, and off the coasts of Florida (the Bermuda Triangle region), and Argentina.

Among the many things he was told was that "to a certain extent they want to puzzle people. They know they are being seen too frequently and they are trying to confuse the public's mind." And, "They put out reports slowly to prepare us . . . Everyone should believe in them some, but not too much." Considering that this was an overt admission to disinformation techniques on the part of the UFO crews, Schirmer added, "Maybe this is the part where they want to puzzle people. Why would they tell where their bases are located? That would be endangering themselves and I know they are very conscious of protecting themselves . . . I'm not even certain they are from the places they said [an unspecified nearby galaxy]. This might be something to throw us off guard."

The occupants were as vulnerable to bullets as human beings (some definitely are not, as will be seen in the next chapter). They guaranteed that any of their downed craft would not be recovered due to built-in booby-trap devices. "Your people are very hostile," the leader said. When asked if the saucers could be fought, Schirmer responded, "I would not even disclose that to the Air Force because they would try and destroy them." Schirmer was shown what were called warships in space, but was assured there was no hostility on the UFOnauts' part. He was also told that the smaller craft such as he was on were carried to and from bases by motherships that were much larger.

Schirmer felt aches and pains in his head while the leader pressed buttons and spoke to him: "[He's] saying that while we talk and he shows me things they will be putting things in my mind . . . He's saying they do this with everyone they contact." The leader's voice came out strangely, something like broken English, and seemed to come from his oversized chest area. This latter observation has occurred in many other reports, and Betty Hill also said her abductor spoke English "with a foreign accent, but very understandably," and somewhat brokenly. Schirmer observed, "They walked around as if they could breathe our atmosphere," and he was under the impression he could see the breath of the guards outside, though this might have been an illusion or a confabulation. Later, Schirmer admitted the discrepancy himself: "They wore no device that looked like it might be used for breathing. Fact is, I never really noticed whether they were breathing or not. Hmm. That puzzles me. Hmm. I can't forget those eyes. He is looking at me and he is not blinking or anything. . . ." And then later, again: "When they were outside the ship they did not wear a breathing device. One thing puzzles me. All the time I was looking at them I didn't notice whether they were breathing or not. Maybe I can't remember that well . . . or was interested in other things. I don't recall seeing them take a breath like we do." Like all other abductees, he saw no food, relief, or recreation facilities aboard the craft. "They could not have been earth people," he concluded. "They were just too different from us."

He was told that contactees were picked entirely randomly, which, to all appearances in subsequent investigations would indeed seem to be the case. Abductees are male or female, all races, all ages, all socioeconomic backgrounds. The only things they seem to have in common are having been in the right place at the right time—generally someplace very isolated—or else being the son or daughter of one or both abductee parents. "He said they left things to pure chance," said Schirmer. "I was told that I just happened to be in the wrong place at the right time or something like that. They have no plans for patterns for contacting people. It is by pure chance so the government cannot determine any patterns about them. There will be a lot more contacts." He added at another time, "If there isn't any rhyme or reason to something it is bound to puzzle the governments of the world and UFO investigators." The reason for the numerous contacts was that "They have been observing us for a long period of time and they think that if they slowly, slowly put out reports and have their contacts state the truth it will help them." Schirmer noted elsewhere, "The public should . . . have no fear of these beings because they are not hostile." This corroborates some of the statements made by Betty Andreasson and her husband. Schirmer also added, "Most of our people will not remember talking with them unless they want them to remember."

Schirmer was led to believe that the saucer occupants had devices enabling them to see anywhere they wanted to, in any facility or private domicile, which gave them the ability to pick moments for arrival and departure that would ensure they would not be detected. "I think some people have been picked up and their brains have been changed some way," said Schirmer. "They were able to control my report of the sighting. I did exactly as they told me, so I was like one of those robots you hear about."

Adding to the reproductive testimony that has been coming out on abductions, Schirmer stated: ". . . he said they had a program known as 'breeding analysis' and some humans had been used in these experiments. He didn't say if humans were kidnapped and taken away. We didn't discuss that any further, probably because I didn't want them to get any funny ideas."

One especially interesting thing was noticed by Schirmer before his excursion's end, in line with observations made of "hieroglyphics" at Roswell, "Japanese writing" in the book seen by Betty Hill, several occurrences that happened to Betty Andreasson, and numerous others. "There were some books which looked like log books, note books, on the tables," he said. "This stuff was more like symbols, like stuff you see in the movies about Egypt." He drew some of them, which resembled an abductee's sketches from Brooksville, Florida, with geometric shapes and "double-L's."

When the tour and briefing were concluded, totaling about twenty minutes, Schirmer was told they would be back to see him again twice more in his life. The leader said to him: "I wish that you would not tell that you have been aboard this ship. You are to tell that the ship landed below in the intersection of the highways, that you approached, and it shot up into the air and disappeared. You will tell this and nothing more. You will not speak wisely about this night."

The "missing time" aspect of UFO abductions was known at least ten years before Budd Hopkins first popularized the knowledge. Eric Norman wrote in 1970, having spoken to "several well-respected scientists involved with UFO research," that a great many sightings were more than mere sightings—they were actually forgotten abductions. "We're finding this trend in not only the United States," they told Norman. "Our colleagues are coming to the same conclusion in other countries. Memories of these contacts are being erased, or suppressed, in the contactee's mind."

Norman made an interesting observation, which might partly explain the hostility of scientists and other authorities to examination of the entire UFO phenomenon, although it should interest them more than anything that has ever happened in the history of the human race: "The occupants of flying saucers have a marked tendency to select ordinary people as their contacts. Contactees are hillbillies instead of important government officials. Community leaders are passed by while a television repairman or a grain salesman is given a ride in space. Believers are by-passed while unbelievers are selected for these experiments."

Jacques Vallée concurs: "They spoke to us 'in smooth English.' They did not speak to our scientists; they did not send sophisticated signals in uniquely decipherable codes as any well-behaved alien should before daring to penetrate our solar system. No, they picked [average people like] Gary Wilcox instead. And Joe Simonton. And Maurice Masse."

And as amazing as any of the contacts documented so far may seem, they pale beside those to be considered next. For the cases described in this chapter have been the more common contacts and abductions. A comparison of these with the less common—and sometimes much more frightening—occurrences discussed in the next chapter lead us to the likeliest explanation of the true nature of the beings seen aboard UFOs.

5

Humanoids

T HIS ISN'T THE first of it, you know," Sheriff Fred Diamond, a Mason in an all-Masonic office, told author and UFO researcher Ralph Blum forty-four hours after the Pascagoula, Mississippi, incident of October 11, 1973. T.V. units from Mobile, Alabama, and New Orleans were present outside the Pascagoula courthouse, and former Blue Book scientist J. Allen Hynek was in an inner room with Berkeley Professor of Engineering and APRO consultant Dr. James Harder and psychiatrist Dr. William D. Bridges, hypnotizing Charlie Hickson and Calvin Parker. Hickson, forty-two, was foreman of Walker Shipyards, where nineteen-year-old Parker worked. While fishing at the shipyard, both men claimed to have been abducted for twenty to thirty minutes aboard a glowing egg-shaped craft that alighted beside them out of the sky. Shaken and badly frightened, the two quickly reported the incident to the sheriff's office, even though they knew they would probably be "the laughing stock of the country."

"We been getting these reports for the past forty days," Diamond continued. "So has Harrison County. And Hancock County. And now this has happened. On a normal, routine day, we handle maybe four hundred calls. Yesterday, there must have been near two thousand come in from all over the nation."

Indeed, so many sightings of anthropomorphic but absurd occupants near flying and landed objects of an unidentified nature had been recently reported that 1973 was dubbed "The Year of the Humanoids" by UFO researchers and the press. On the same day Hickson and Parker claimed their abduction took place, close to sixty people in two different Indiana cities reported seeing what to all appearances sounded like the same object in the sky: two witnesses in Connersville saw "a disc-shaped object with a seg-mented compartment on the bottom"; an "oval-shaped object with . . . a segmented compartment on the bottom" was witnessed three hours later by fifty people; soon after, five witnesses in Laurel saw an object that "looked like two saucers put together . . . the bot-tom was segmented." In Boulder, Colorado, two witnesses saw a "slowly rotating craft [with] . . . a string of lights on the bottom that divided it into thirds."

Among others, Kevin D. Randle, in *The UFO Casebook,* com-piled the following occupant reports in the United States for Octo-ber 1973 alone: near an egg-shaped object (which left landing traces) three men saw "a huge creature that walked mechanically"; a "humanoid creature in a silvery wet suit" was seen inside a clear bubble-top dome atop a triangular hovering craft; someone else saw five yellow-clothed humanoids which may have been wearing helmets, but the witness couldn't be sure; a "creature with a glow-ing white head" was seen in Berea, Tennessee, which left tracks along with those of a vehicle that had blinking lights; a cabdriver's truck stalled and a "crablike claw" tapped his windshield; a tall creature with "clawlike hands and wide, blinking eyes" reached out of a UFO in an attempt to grab two children; a Georgia man reported vehicular abduction by "several robotlike creatures" who seemed to read his mind (an Oklahoma couple also reported, with-out sighting any humanoids, that a UFO over their truck some-how "knew everything they were thinking"); two "small creatures in silver suits and white gloves" were fired on from a revolver with no noticeable effect; a "humanoid with a wide mouth, flipper feet and webbing between the legs" stalled a car from a UFO; a Utah woman and her family claimed to have been taken from their home by "several tiny creatures" at night, in an early bedroom visitation report; two Virginia boys reported being chased by a "white thing about three or four feet tall [with] a large head [and] no eyes [that] ran sideways"; a "small man in metallic clothes with a bubble head and rectangular eyes" appeared outside a stalled car in Georgia; a "small humanoid in a gold metallic jumpsuit" was seen next to a landed UFO by a frightened North Carolina couple; "small gray men with big, dark eyes, no facial features, and pale skin" (stan-dard "Grays") abducted a couple from a stalled vehicle in part of what turned out to be repeat abductions; ground traces were found in Ohio where a mother and son saw a gray humanoid and landed UFO; a college student, missing for days, claimed she had been subjected to painful "stress tests" on board an "alien craft"; four different people in three different Indiana locations reported what appeared to be the same creatures, within two and a half hours— "four feet tall, with egg-shaped heads and gas masks with tubes running to their chests"; two other occupant sightings were reported in Kentucky; and a witness from a stalled car in North Carolina reported "a huge creature with blazing red eyes" from a UFO.

In addition, from September and November 1973, other interesting reports: a "limping creature with red glowing eyes, long hair, pointed ears, and a hook nose on a gray face, missing a hand but [capable of leaping] fifty or sixty feet at a time," seen by a North Carolina family and witnessed also by a group of boys and a radio disc jockey, who fired six shots at it with a pistol to no stated effect; a New Hampshire sighting of a "motionless creature wearing a black coat and wide-brim hat pulled down over a face that looked as if it had been covered with masking tape"; a "creature with gray wrinkled skin and large slanted eyes" reported behind a nearby porthole in a hovering sphere; and "two small creatures wearing silver suits gathering samples" frightened a couple and their dog outside their home at night.

And on the same day as Charlie Hickson and Calvin Parker wandered into the Pascagoula Sheriff's Office to make their frightening report, a three-year-old boy in neighboring Tanner Williams, Alabama, told his mother that he "had been playing with a nice monster that had gray wrinkled skin and pointed ears," which tallied identically with the shipyard workers' description of their abductors: they were "grayish, like a ghost," with "pointed ears and noses and a pale skin-type covering," and had "clawlike hands [pincher things]" with "feet *shape*" that "didn't have toes . . . more or less just a roundlike thing on a leg—if you'd call it a leg. . . ."

Artist James Flynt, a foreman at the shipyard, did a rendering which Ralph Blum said "looked like somebody's idea of a wrinkled robot," which is exactly the word both Hickson and Parker used to describe their assailants. "Calvin and me's talked about that too," Hickson said. "We've put our minds together and we've come to the conclusion it was robots. We think they might have been programmed. That they had a specific thing to do, and they done it. And they wasn't distracted one way or the other. They just done it and that was it. I'll believe until the day I die that they was robots and that they was communicating with somewhere else."

Both Hickson and Parker impressed all observers as earnest,

intelligent, and entirely truthful. They passed their polygraphs, and their stories matched both before and after hypnosis, though Parker—like Barney Hill—fainted before being taken aboard the craft and didn't remember much. They had gone to the shipyard to fish, and their attention was caught by a blue light in the sky. After a while, it settled two or three feet above the bayou, twenty-five or thirty yards away, and could be discerned as "oblong, sort of oblong . . . about eight feet tall." It made "a little buzzin' sound—*nnnnnnnn-nnnnnnnn*—just like that, that's all . . . And, you think you *dreamin'* about something like that, you know," Hickson related.

An opening suddenly appeared in the egg-shaped object, and three of what they described as robots emerged, floating down to the two men. Calvin "done went hysterical on me" and Hickson heard "one of 'em [make] a little buzzin' noise . . . Just *zzzZZZ zzzZZZ*," like a machine. "It might have been contactin' the others. See, I don't know. By then I was so damn scared I didn't know anything."

The two men were floated up into the craft without force, guided by two of the robots. Parker was unconscious, presumably with fright. Hickson was kept levitated and paralyzed in a prone position in midair while "some kind of instrument" scanned up and down his body. "It looked like an *eye*. Like a *big* eye. It had some kind of attachment to it. It moved. It looked like a *big* eye. And it went all over my body. Up and down."

The robots left for twenty to thirty minutes, "came back, [and] laid me back over again." Hickson tried to talk to them, but the only response he got was "a buzzin' sound out of one of 'em. That's all. They didn't pay me no attention, my talkin' or anything."

The next thing he knew, he was standing back on the riverbank, with "that kid, Calvin, just standing there. I've never seen that sort of fear on a man's face as I saw on Calvin's. It took me a while to get him back to his senses, and the first thing I told him was, Son, ain't nobody gonna believe this. Let's just keep this whole thing to ourselves. Well, the more I thought about it, the more I thought I had to let some officials know."

The pair was so shaken that they waited an hour before making a report, having a drink first to settle themselves. Hickson was so upset, he forgot to call his wife before reporting to the authorities. He called Keesler Air Force Base, who referred him to his local sheriff's office. He tried the *Mississippi Press* first, and was told by a man at the desk that no reporters would be around before morning. Finally, he and Parker went to the sheriff's office and had their statement witnessed and tape-recorded by Sheriff Diamond and Captain Glen Ryder at 11 PM, about three hours after the incident. "I guess there's no way I could have lived with it for the rest of my life. I couldn't keep it on my conscience. I felt I'd be doing my country an injustice if I didn't let someone know. I told Calvin, 'They're gonna call us crazy, but come hell or high water, I'm gonna contact some authority.'"

The next morning, the story was national news, and a flight of F-111s combed the area for some time, which was highly unusual. Keesler Air Force Base had announced as soon as Hickson and Parker's story hit the press that the case was closed, yet the two of them were spirited away to Keesler even as the announcement was issued. The shipyard's lawyer, Joe Colingo, called the base for a radiation check on their employees, since the incident had happened at Walker and the local hospital didn't have the right facilities. Police detective Tom Huntley, who received reports confirming Hickson and Parker's UFO from five different people in three locations, accompanied them to Keesler.

"When we got there, it was something amazing," said Huntley. "We were in an unmarked car, but the guards were expecting us and waved us through the moment I said who we was. I looked back through my rearview mirror, and damn if two cars full of air police hadn't fallen in behind us. They had more air police stationed at each crossing all along the road. We pulled up in this concrete area behind a building. The police had halted all traffic. Doctors were waiting, and man, *they* looked like space creatures—all wrapped in white and masked and gloved. They went over Charlie and Calvin from head to toe. They ran a radioactive check. They swabbed between the boys' fingers, along the tops of their shoes, even under the heels. Then they put each swab into a little bottle and labeled each bottle. Some officer came and took us into the building. I tell you, it was something. Armed air police at each door and all along the route! Four of 'em in the conference room! And the brass—colonels, majors—the whole base command must have been there. And a heap of doctors."

The head of base intelligence interrogated them, waiting until they had told their story without interruption to ask any questions. Huntley said he was "just cool. Like he'd heard it all before." The only thing that caught his attention was Charlie's mention of the claw hands. "Two colonels exchanged looks over that." Routine questions were asked about the craft's interior, and the doctors asked what the men had eaten and had to drink before their encounter.

Everyone was dismissed, and a promised report from Keesler to the sheriff's office never arrived. Ralph Blum was told later by a base PR officer that the case was closed and there was nothing to say about it.

J. Allen Hynek publicly declined to offer any confirmation of the reality of the UFO, "the physical nature of which I am not certain about." All he would publicly affirm was that "under no circumstances should these men be ridiculed. They are absolutely honest. They have had a fantastic experience and also I believe it should be taken in context with experiences that others have had elsewhere in this country and in the world."

Once again, in a painfully repetitive pattern, the Air Force publicly denied any interest or research, let alone conclusions in a UFO case, while privately proving the exact opposite. And yet again, Hynek failed to make a public stand of any consequence. Berkeley's Dr. Harder was far more courageous: "The many reports made over the past twenty, thirty years point to an objective reality that is not terrestrial. When you've eliminated all the probable explanations, and you still have something that you know is real, you're left with the less probable explanations, and I've been left with the conclusion—reduced, perhaps, to the conclusion—that we're dealing with an extraterrestrial phenomena [sic]. I can say so beyond any reasonable doubt."

Hickson appeared on the *Dick Cavett Show* in January of 1974, with Ralph Blum, shipyard attorney Joe Colingo, author John Wallace Spencer *(Limbo of the Lost), Apollo 9* astronaut Brigadier General James A. McDivitt, helicopter pilot and UFO-sighter Captain Larry Coyne, J. Allen Hynek, and Carl Sagan. Blum recounts the entire story in his book *Beyond Earth: Man's Contact with UFOs,* from which most of the information in this chapter is derived.

Cavett's approach was open and sincere, sympathetic to the witnesses. He began by mentioning the more than five hundred sighting reports in October 1973, showed some of the better photos authenticated by UFO organizations, and cracked a friendly joke, keeping the mood light. After a commercial, he became more serious and read polygrapher Scott Glasgow's legal affirmation of

Charlie Hickson's passing the lie detector test, about which Joe Colingo confided to Blum, off-camera, "Usually they do a polygraph test in about twenty minutes. But Glasgow kept old Charlie in that office for over *two hours.* Gave him the test over and over. Finally Glasgow came out of there white-faced and said to me, 'I'm afraid this son'bitch is tellin' the truth!'"

Hickson told his story to two million viewing Americans, with the same straightforward sincerity he always had. The audience listened attentively and only laughed where appropriate. They were with him.

The other guests were introduced and had their turns. Coyne recounted his near midair collision, Spencer talked of Bermuda Triangle disappearances, McDivitt described the "cylindrical object, white, with an antenna-like extension" he photographed during his *Gemini 4* mission command, and Hynek announced his formation of the CUFOS (Center for UFO Studies) organization.

Sagan went last, giving one of his standard, suave, debunking performances. He took dramatic pauses for serious effect to emphasize the scientific unlikelihood of interstellar visitation, chuckled dismissively in response to Hickson's story, shunted all of Spencer's findings aside with inappropriate jokes, and did everything but call Coyne a liar (responding to Hynek's observation that "altimeters don't hallucinate," he rejoined instantaneously with, "I don't mean to attack Captain Coyne, but people who *read* altimeters hallucinate"). Blum refers to Sagan in his book as "a Talmudic Jesuit in a white Palm Beach suit [who] certainly dominated the show ... disposing of the other guests by mocking their testimony, and he did it well," and to Dick Cavett as the man who "presided over the nation's first open meeting between scientists and UFO witnesses with skill, humor, and courtesy."

Hickson eventually stopped talking to callers about his experience, which he had done for a long time. He recorded his story for the oral history department of the University of Southern Mississippi at Hattlesburg, and recounts it on film in Blum's documentary, *Mysteries from Beyond Earth.* He received "... letters by the *thous*ands. And these people over here I rent my apartment from. They can't even use their telephone. They brought me *hun*dreds and *hun*dreds of calls. And not one of those calls from anyone who disbelieves us."

He had bad dreams for some time and went through a period when he couldn't sleep more than two hours a night, taking lots of aspirin for headaches. He kept wondering, *"what did they do to me?"* and if they would come back to get him. It has been discovered that UFO abductions are rarely, if ever, single-time occurrences, and Hickson's was no exception. He confided to *UFO Encyclopedia* editor and compiler John Spencer in 1990 that he believed repeat occurrences had continued throughout his life.

Calvin Parker spent time in the Laurel, Mississippi, mental hospital, and never did adjust to the experience as well as his older companion. "I tell you," Hickson said, "I've seen terror in my life. All the time I spent in Korea, in combat. I've lain out on a battlefield at night—pitch dark—fighting North Koreans and Chinese and I know what fear is. I lived twenty months and sixteen days in combat in Korea. I've got five battle stars. I know what terror is. I've seen 'em put in straitjackets. But I never seen that much terror and that much fear on a man's face as I saw on Calvin's."

In common with some abductees, Hickson found he couldn't keep a watch working. "Never could. People said I had electricity ... I tried every brand that I could find, but I never did find one that would keep correct time." He'd had the problem since long before his UFO encounter, but it should be mentioned in light of other reports. Given that most abductees' experiences seem to begin in childhood, it is also possible that Hickson had been an unaware abductee up to that point, and for whatever reason was not tranquilized or hypnotized in the Pascagoula incident.

Asked by Ralph Blum why he might have been picked up in the first place, Hickson replied, "I dunno. I think that they know more of what's goin' on on this Earth than we think, and I dunno, they might have been, you might say, lookin' for somebody that, uh—that could, uh—that could, you might say, hold up under the strain. And, uh—and convince people, that, that, uh—that, that there is another world, and there's some kind of life on that world." Brigadier General McDivitt had made essentially the same assessment privately to Blum backstage after Hickson finished his public testimony on the Cavett show. "That was just great!" he beamed, smiling. "They set down and picked up a man. Sure did pick up the right kind of man! That was fine!" McDivitt's statement and attitude indicate something more than a vague general awareness on the part of NASA as to just who "they" might be. McDivitt also implied agreement with Hickson and Parker's assessment of their abductors as robots, by telling Blum that the antennae the two men described sounded to him like advanced radar devices.

Though he was repeatedly offered money for movie deals on his story, Hickson always declined: "Making money is not what this experience is all about." He didn't get rich off his story. Neither did Parker, who not only avoided the limelight but suffered a nervous breakdown. They had no motivation for a hoax, and multiple witness confirmations of a UFO in their area corroborated their report. There is no recorded incident in history of two otherwise sane and healthy men developing sudden, simultaneous psychoses, let alone identical hallucinations. If the Air Force hadn't believed the two men, then why did they bother combing the area with jets and thoroughly interrogating and testing the witnesses the whole while they pretended publicly they had no interest at all?

Any single case this solid should be enough to convince a hardened skeptic that at least some UFOs are intelligently directed craft beyond our present ability to manufacture, that they sometimes abduct human beings for purposes not entirely known, and that at the very least the Air Force is intensely interested in them and engaged in concealing that fact from the public. The testimony and evidence for this one case are stronger than either the Boas or Hill incidents, and each one is strong confirmation of the other two, which in turn strengthen the thousands of similar reports worldwide. Why, then, are there still people who refuse to believe?

For most, it is probably a desire to disbelieve. That might well account for some of the government and press silence on the subject. The Hickson-Parker abduction, if acknowledged as true, forces the observer to admit that the universe is bigger than their present knowledge can comprehend, and that is a little bit frightening. The abductees themselves wish they hadn't been forced to think about it, as it causes them headaches and nightmares and sleepless nights. For the witnesses, the situation is not unlike having had a murder in the family: no one who hears of it really disbelieves that it happened, but the knowledge makes them uncomfortable and they avoid it at all costs.

Since the public at large has not had the reality of UFOs intrusively forced into their lives, they can construct rationalizations and assurances to ward off the unknown. The government, the military, and the press are all people, too, and are no more anxious to admit their fear of the unknown than anyone else. They are in fact far less inclined to do so, because their professions are based on the illusion of knowledge and authority, without which they have no base for their power. And if they are shackled by their fear of losing that power, scientists and academics are many times more so. Far easier to simply dismiss, ridicule, or suppress the evidence, from both sight and mind. As easy as whistling through a graveyard.

One of the earliest and most nightmarish of occupant encounters occurred on the night of August 21, 1955, at the isolated farmhouse of Gaither McGehe, in Kelly, near Hopkinsville, Kentucky. His renters, the Sutton family, were having a gathering with another family named Taylor. The witnesses of the events that night were eight adults and three children, between the ages of seven and fifty, and neighbors attested to the fact that the Suttons "weren't a drinking family." Subsequent to the events of their harrowing night, they reported everything in detail to the police, the Air Force, and the press, and were so ridiculed that they ultimately had to move away.

It began about seven that night, when Billy Ray Taylor went out to the well and saw a very large shining UFO, "all the colors of the rainbow," landing not far away. No one back at the house believed him, until about an hour later when the dog started barking. A creature with its arms stretched high was approaching: it was three or three and a half feet tall, with large round eyes on each side of its head that glowed yellow; the being itself shone silver, as if lighted from within; its head was bald and egg-shaped, narrowing to a pointed chin, with a horizontal slit for a mouth, a conical nose tapering to a point with a ball on the end of it, and enormous "elephant-like" ears. Its body was thin, with an oversized, muscular-looking upper torso and arms so long they practically dragged on the ground, with long, taloned hands; its legs were short spindles, with no feet—just round suction-cup-like endings. One critical feature almost never mentioned in written reports, but invariably in any rendering taken from the witnesses' testimony, are two antennae on top of the head.

Billy Ray and Elmer Sutton fired at it with a rifle and a shotgun. The thing—usually referred to as one of the "Hopkinsville Goblins"—"did a flip" and scurried away into the trees. When moving, the goblins did not walk, but "seemed to float" evenly, a feature that has been reported in a few cases. When hit by bullets or blasts, they dropped to all fours and locomoted away at tremendous speed, their arms doing most of the work.

Hearing something land on the roof, Taylor and Sutton went

outside and saw another of the things up there. They shot it off, and it did not fall, but floated gently to the ground. Once there, it scurried off like its identical twin before it. The two men ran back inside and bolted the doors.

For close to four hours, the farmhouse was besieged. It was about eleven o'clock that they made a break for it in their two cars and drove into Hopkinsville to get Chief Russell Greenwell, Deputy George Batts, more than a dozen officers, and a local reporter to come back with them. No one doubted the witnesses were telling the truth. The children were hysterical and the adults terrified. "Something frightened these people," Greenwell observed. "Something beyond their comprehension." No sign of the entities or any ship was present when the entourage returned to the scene, but the farmhouse was riddled with bullet holes and a "strange shower of meteors that came from the direction of the Sutton farmhouse" was noticed on their way out, which one officer testified made a "swishing sound," and two other sounds were reported "with a noise like artillery fire" passing overhead.

"I knocked one of them off a barrel with my .22," Taylor reported. "I heard the bullet hit the critter and ricochet off. The little man floated to the ground and rolled up like a ball. I used up four boxes of shells on the little men."

"Bullets just seemed to bounce off their nickle-plated armor," another witness concurred.

Several direct hits had been scored, none having any effect. At least one was point-blank, with a shotgun. Every time, the strange creatures would just "pop right up again and disappear into the darkness, away from the light." The things, it had been noticed, stayed in the dark, either light sensitive or simply anxious not to be seen clearly. Thirteen years later, in a Defense Intelligence Agency summary, bulletproof UFO occupants would also be reported: "La Razon (Buenos Aires) 27 July 68—Relates new sighting near La Pastora, Alvear, and Tapalque. The latter describes the crew and inability of machine-gun bullets to affect them...."

The nightmare seeming to be over, the law and the reporter returned to Hopkinsville, having decided to come back later in the day and examine the scene by daylight. But there was more to come. The new witnesses gone, Glennie Lankford, Elmer Sutton's mother, saw one of the goblins staring in her window at about 2:30 in the morning. She tried to persuade her son to attempt peaceful communication with it, but he resumed firing instead. As before, the shot had no effect, and the family merely sat around watching the creatures until dawn. They milled about to no noticeable purpose and made no move toward the farmhouse or any attempt at contact.

With nothing but their testimony and the evidence of their battle to go on, the community did not believe the witnesses, who nonetheless insisted on reporting everything that had happened no matter how ridiculous it sounded, just as Charles Hickson and Calvin Parker did nearly twenty years later. Sightseers harassed the Suttons regularly and they were charged with being religious hysterics. At least one of their neighbors corroborated part of their testimony, having seen strange lights that night and heard the shots. It had been so alarming that he considered going to their rescue, but in retrospect he said, "I am glad I didn't go out there— I might have been shot."

No abduction occurred in the Hopkinsville Goblins encounter, though one may have been intended. Like the Pascagoula incident, it is the sort of thing one might easily accept even an extremely poor debunking explanation to avoid thinking about. It was actually suggested that what the Suttons and Taylors confronted that night in Kentucky were escaped monkeys from a circus. Despite the fact that no circus was around, that monkeys do not glow in the dark or have lit-up eyes, that no animal carcass of any kind was to be found in the vicinity of the farmhouse even after four boxes and more of spent ammunition had been fired at and in many instances directly hit their targets, it appears that many were willing to accept the specious answer, or any other that may have suited them. And why not? What irrefutable evidence remained of the encounter, except for two terrorized families who risked their reputations to warn others, and their badly shot-up home? Just what constitutes "irrefutable evidence"?

Just by examining the three best abduction cases so far encountered—Boas, the Hills, and Hickson-Parker—even someone with a rigorous thirst for the truth, a hearty and brave disposition, and an openly inquiring scientific mind could easily manage to erect a mental shield. After all, how similar are they, really? In two cases an egg-shaped object, in one a pancake-shaped one; in one, sex with a human or very near-human female, in another, medical tests and telepathic communication, in the third no sex and no communication and no memory of medical tests. The humanoids are all different, and absurd on the face of it—

little men in pressure suits, identical beings with no pressure suits whose physiognomy suggests complete incompatibility with our atmosphere and specie, and weird silver robotlike things of only rudimentarily anthropomorphic form. What do they *really* have in common? But if one is truly a scientific observer, unafraid to follow evidence to whatever truth it may lead and patient enough to do a little detective work, the commonalities can be found. Just for starters, we know all three are connected to unidentified flying objects, for instance. And we might have noticed that, even if there are numerous different UFO configurations, the egg-shaped is definitely predominant.

Broadening the information base always helps. Perhaps the study of more cases than these three, unquestionably among the best, would help provide an answer. Analysis of added cases, however, only seems to make answers all the more elusive, not more concrete. There are a variety of craft—and by this point even the most hardened skeptic should be admitting that "craft" is the single best hypothesis for what these unidentified flying objects appear to be, given their attributes and physical traces left in the air and on the ground—and an even wider variety of increasingly more absurd humanoids. Surely, even if there were multitudinous varieties of craft, how many different races could there be flying around our planet? And how could they exist in our atmosphere, given the descriptions the witnesses report?

The Grays are only one variety, and arguably the most preposterous: three-and-a-half- to four-and-a-half-foot-tall ectomorphs, without pressure suits or breathing apparatus and utterly devoid of muscle tone or individuality, with immobile, fixed expressions and no emotions, telepathic (and just how is *that* supposed to work, anyway?) and reputed to be able to hybridize with man (which is unlikelier still, as has already been pointed out). Their eyes are so huge that if spherical like our own—and given the other obvious anthropomorphisms of their form, there is no theoretical reason they should not be—they would literally take up almost the entire skull, leaving no room for a brain. And what is one to make of the other "species" so far encountered? Forgetting the equally weird and improbable—and, like the Grays, identical— Hopkinsville Goblins, or the one-handed limping hooknose that can leap dozens of feet at a single bound and is as impervious to bullets as those same Goblins, what are we to make of such creatures as the "hairy dwarves" or the infamous "Mothman"?

Since the latter two have not yet been introduced, here is a good place for their inclusion in this study. In Point Pleasant, West Virginia, in 1966, a levitating, faceless gray creature, looking like a man with wings and glowing red bug eyes, was reported so often that the local press gave him a nomer: "Mothman." Sometimes described as a bird, Mothman was six to seven feet tall (or long— he was usually seen in flight), who swooped or hovered on wings spanning ten feet which never flapped, but only seemed to serve as gliding implements. He tracked cars at seventy-five miles per hour, giving some idea how anxious people were to flee him. His appearance was so startling that one mother actually dropped her newborn baby at the sight of him. A similar "birdman" (or "bat-man") was spotted at the same time in England's notorious UFO-haunt south of Warrington in Preston Brook/Daresbury, and later in southeast Texas in January-February of 1976, and the Russian taiga in 1991.

Hairy black dwarves have been reported by many witnesses. In Mexico, they are called *ikals,* a Tzeltal root word meaning "black," with connections to Quiché Mayan. American anthropologist Brian Stross heard about these beings on a night when his Tzeltal Indian companion and he saw "a strange light wandering about in the Mexican sky." Stross reported, "About twenty years ago, there were many sightings of this creature or creatures, and several people apparently tried to fight it with machetes. One man also saw a small sphere following him from about five feet." They live in caves the natives studiously avoid, their hovel since antiquity; they are three feet tall, fly through the air with a rocket on their backs, and kidnap the locals with the help of a paralyzing agent.

Similar black hairy dwarves set upon produce workers Gustave Gonzales and Jose Ponce on their way to a Caracas suburb at about 2 AM on November 28, 1954, from a hovering luminous sphere. A three-foot-tall hairy man-shaped thing with glowing eyes tried to grab Gonzales when he went to investigate the object. One blow from the dwarf was strong enough to reel Gonzales back fifteen feet. Gonzales stabbed it, but "the knife glanced off as though it had struck steel." The dwarf joined a like companion and escaped into the air in the sphere, leaving the men shaken but all right, the only injury being a deep red scratch on Gonzales' side from the creature's claws.

Many similar attacks occurred through December of that year. Two young rabbit hunters, Lorenzo Flores and Jesus Gomez, were attacked by four hairy three-foot-tall men from a hovering saucer near the Trans-Andean Highway in Venezuela. They seized Jesus, and Lorenzo bludgeoned one with his shotgun. "The gun seemed to have struck rock or something harder, as it broke in two," said Flores. Neither remembered how they escaped (they were probably abducted), and both were scratched and bruised in their encounter. They remembered only that the "little men" were of remarkably light weight for their incredible strength.

The sudden locomotion witnessed in the Hopkinsville Goblins was also reported by Officer Jeff Greenhaw of the Alabama State Police during the flap of 1973. A woman called with one of many reports of a "spaceship with flashing lights." Dispatched to the remote location, Greenhaw reported: "I saw it. It was just standing there in the middle of the road. I was scared stiff. It moved stiffly, like a robot, and didn't make any sounds." Greenhaw checked his fear, called "Howdy, stranger!," and as the silver-suited, antennaed figure advanced toward him, he snapped off four flash photos. He turned on his blue police light and the figure bolted down the road. "I jumped into my car and took after him, but I couldn't even catch up with him in a patrol car. He was running faster than any human I ever saw." It eluded him, and his wife didn't believe him later when he told her about the incident. "She wouldn't be laughing if she saw what I saw," was Greenhaw's comment to the *Birmingham News* on October 19, 1973.

When a newspaper offered to run Greenhaw's photos, other pictures which—based on his descriptions—were obvious fakes and of laughably poor quality appeared instead. One month later, as reported by the *Decatur Daily,* November 16, Greenhaw had literally been driven out of town. "I had planned to stay in Falkville in spite of all the problems I have been having, but now it doesn't look like I can." The problems to which he referred? Mayor Wade Tomlinson asked him to resign, which he did "under fire." His wife divorced him, and his car engine mysteriously blew up. Then his mobile home burned down and he suffered smoke injuries to his eyes. "So now I've lost my car, my wife, my home and my job. And I guess I'll just have to go where ever [*sic*] I can to find another job."

Greenhaw's case is an excellent example of media distortion and suppression of UFO evidence. He had no motive for a hoax, and not only didn't profit from his honest report, but lost everything he had. The papers ran pictures that weren't his own, designed to make him look like a fool. Who would want to do such a thing? Unless there was perhaps an official or unofficial policy against UFO stories? The running of false photos, the bombing of a car, and the burning of a house, though, go far beyond bad newspaper reporting. Any one of these things could be accidental. All together in the space of a single month could not.

Greenhaw's humanoid is but one more in a growing list of absurd UFOnauts. As Jacques Vallée asks, how many alien races can be hovering around our one little planet? Let alone in such numbers? And how could so many bizarre races all evolve in such absurd fashion? The answer, of course, is that they couldn't. The solution to this particular riddle becomes increasingly obvious the more one studies the reports at face value, and the very absurdity, itself, of the types of creatures.

How many different varieties are there? Vallée lists the following, in the index of *Dimensions:* "compared to animals; with oversize head; with flat faces, flat noses, and large mouths; with putty-colored face; with gray skin; greenish face, wide mouth like a fish; blonde hair; straight nose, prominent cheekbones, wide face; pointed ears; with tiny legs and long arms; body covered with fur; black, hairy dwarf; face covered with hair; dwarfs with human features; goat-like legs; luminous beings; aboard the airship of 1897; suffocating in England; in fairy stories; endowed with wings; similar to human beings; tall, thin and gentlemanly; extremely tall; Christ-like; clawmen; robot-like; equipped with rockets; carrying a torch or lamp; carrying a rod-like pistol; carrying a luminous wand; expelling a paralyzing gas; objecting to iron."

For the category of "eyes," alone, Vallée has sixteen separate listings: "with horizontal slits; large and sensitive; no pupils and no eyelids; huge, round, no eyelashes, no eyebrows; large, slanted; blue, slanted; large; large, round, glowing red; reddish-orange; huge, round, prominent, yellow-green; protruding, with small irises; like human eyes; frog-like; small, bright, like burning coals; like cat's eyes; in the forehead."

These lists can probably be considered redundant, and therefore reducible. For instance, the Grays fit several separate categories at once: "with oversize head; putty-colored face; gray skin; wide face [according to who does the reporting]; tiny legs and long arms; dwarfs with human features [more or less]; similar to human beings [again, more or less]; carrying a rod-like pistol [often]," etc. Their eyes also fit more than one of the listed descriptions. And there are a few that may or may not apply, like "flat faces."

If we weigh in that the witnesses who are abductees are probably drugged and certainly hypnotized, not to mention initially traumatized, we might account for a few more features on the list. Barney Hill remembered no noses, someone else remembers a small or nearly invisible nose, etc. One sees red hair, the other blonde or none. Some of these factors seem to become clearer under hypnosis, removing inconsistencies such as Betty Hill's initial confabulation of large noses on her abductors. Add in another factor, which is poor viewing conditions and no immediate reference point to describe what has been seen, not to mention that many sightings are of exceedingly brief duration. Looking at the same more or less formless humanoid mass with, oh, say, an Ace bandage on it, one witness may see eyes with no face, another eyes above a bandaged face, another still a face with stripes across it (regular or irregular), and so on. In some instances, "hair" may be strangely cast shadows on an uncertain surface in bad lighting, an optical illusion. And a certain number of hoaxes and frauds are possible. Adding to that confusion is *informed* fraud, better known as "disinformation," some of which has already been demonstrated.

In most instances, any report will have an historical precedent. Barney Hill's report of the leader being "an Irishman," or more specifically "a redhead," for instance, can be found published in the *Steep Rock Echo* (Ontario) of September-October 1950, which it is doubtful he would have seen. It ran the story of a man and wife who claimed to have seen, at dusk on July 2 of that year, a flying saucer resting on the surface of a lake, with strange beings working on it: "The operator was a midget figure on a small raised stand. He wore what seemed to be a red skull cap, or perhaps it was red paint, the caps worn by others were blue. I should say the figures were from 3 feet 6 inches to 4 feet tall, and all were the same size. We could not see their faces. In fact, the faces seemed just blank surfaces! It was odd that the figures moved like automata, rather than living beings. Over their chests was a gleaming metallic substance, but the legs and arms were covered by something darker. These figures did not turn around. They just altered the direction of their feet. They walked on the angle, or camber surface of the disk, and the leg on the higher side seemed shorter, so that the compensation—real or apparent—provided against any limp."

And the hairy figure with a frightening visage that could leap sixty feet at a time, seen in North Carolina in September of 1973, seems also to have been reported in 1837, under a most famous name: "Springheel Jack." Jack was first witnessed in November of that year in the dark lanes of London suburbs, making remarkable leaps seemingly impossible for any human being to accomplish—hence his name—and actually flying and swooping, in some incidents, summoning to mind the feats (and, in most regards, physical description) of the "Mothman." Journalist John J. Vyner reports that "The old Duke of Wellington himself set holsters at his saddle bow and rode out after dark in search of Springheel Jack," after authorities could no longer pretend that the frequently reported strange being did not exist. A reward fund, which was never claimed, was set up by Admiral Codgrington in response to a letter written by a Peckham resident to the Lord Mayor, which finally broke the official censorship on the subject.

On February 25, 1838, in Old Ford, London, Jane Alsop opened her violently ringing front door to be confronted by "a most hideous appearance." The figure before her had clawlike fingers with a vise grip, eyes that glowed like balls of fire and shining clothes with a flashing lamp on the chest. It rendered Jane unconscious with a burst of fiery gas to the face before her sister ran to the rescue and chased the figure off, quickly enough that he dropped his cloak, which was instantly retrieved by another figure that ran off after him.

The most detailed report of Jack's appearance, matching others such as Miss Alsop's, was the following: "The intruder was tall, thin and powerful. He had a prominent nose, and bony fingers of immense power which resembled claws. He was incredibly agile. He wore a long, flowing cloak, of the sort affected by opera-goers, soldiers and strolling actors. On his head was a tall, metallic-seeming helmet. Beneath the cloak were close-fitting garments of some glittering material like oilskin or metal mesh. There was a lamp strapped to his chest. Oddest of all: the creature's ears were cropped or pointed like those of an animal."

An article on the Alsop incident caused two witnesses to reveal that one of them had been attacked two nights previously in Green Dragon Alley. A loiterer who was "tall, thin, and (save the mark) gentlemanly" threw aside his cloak to reveal "a lantern flashing on the startled girl . . . Jack's weird blue flame spurted into his victim's face and she dropped to the ground in a deep swoon. Whereupon, Jack walked away calmly."

Two days after the assault on Miss Alsop, Jack terrified the butler of a Mr. Ashworth by doing nothing more than knocking on the door and inquiring for him. The servant screamed upon opening the door and seeing him, and Jack fled, having made his last London appearance.

He reappeared in 1877 in Aldershot, Hampshire, England, where he was fired upon by two sentries he swooped over. Jack stunned them with a "burst of blue fire" and disappeared. How could anyone be certain it was the same figure? Had Jack been a man, and begun his small reign of terror in 1837, he would have to be in his sixties at least when seen in Aldershot. But the description is the same: "wearing tight garments and shining helmet."

Jack becomes more intriguing and impossible, by any standard we know, at least, if Vyner is correct in his fingering of the shiny flier as the author of a wave of terror in Mattoon, Illinois, in late August of 1944. A Peeping Tom, "as in search of someone known to him by sight," was witnessed by many people, primarily women, who were rendered unconscious by some kind of device. Either the device, or the nocturnal prowler himself, was said to leave behind "a strange cloying smell."

Springheel Jack? In 1944? After first being reported in 1837? Supposing he began at age twenty, that would make him 127 years old at Mattoon, a bit spry for still peeking in women's windows at night. And the description also matches several of the sightings in the 1973 flap, as has already been pointed out. A 156-year-old man? Capable of leaping tall buildings in a single bound and impervious to bullets, who isn't fazed by the loss of a hand and can fly through the air? What sort of creature, if we rule out Clark Kent's alter ego, could we be dealing with? And what does such a being have in common with all these other most bizarre humanoids associated with the UFO phenomenon?

But we still haven't muddied the waters sufficiently. Let us add four more widely divergent reports, and see if their vast differences don't point more to a single underlying similarity than to a mystery too diffuse to understand.

The first comes from Cisco Grove, California, September 4, 1964. Authors Coral and Jim Lorenzen called it "the most spectacular report we have examined," leaked to them via Jacques Vallée after that most estimable scientist and J. Allen Hynek failed to get Blue Book to investigate it. The witness, twenty-eight-year-old Donald Schrum, was separated from his hunting party in the mountains when night fell. He lit signal fires and saw a light in the sky which he took to be a helicopter seeking him. Its hovering was not like that of a helicopter, though, and Schrum climbed a tree to get a better look. There was a flash from the object, accompanied by some kind of dark object falling to the ground. Two figures converged upon the tree from different directions to look up at him; they were a little over five feet tall, in silver uniforms that covered their heads.

What followed was a nightlong siege. The small beings, which by surface description could be typical Grays, were joined by a being "behaving more like a mechanical being than an animal or a man," according to Vallée. "It was darker and had two reddish-orange 'eyes.' It had no mouth, but rather a slit-like opening that would drop open like an oven door . . . the 'robot-like' entity would let its lower 'jaw' drop, then place its 'hand' inside the rectangular cavity thus revealed, and emit a puff of smoke in [Schrum's] direction. The smoke spread like a mist and, upon reaching him, made him lose consciousness. The effect of it was comparable to being suddenly deprived of oxygen." Consciousness-depriving gas appears in many UFO abductions.

Schrum tied himself to the tree with his belt to keep from falling out when he intermittently fell unconscious from the ongoing attack. He threw lighted pieces of his clothes at his attackers, and fired arrows from his quiver at the robot, which predictably clanged off with no effect except to make sparks and throw the thing back a few paces. Schrum awoke still in the tree at morning, the evidence of his ordeal all around.

The second case involves a woman in Loire, France, May 20, 1950. On her way home through the countryside one afternoon, she found herself grabbed from above by hands over her mouth which were "very cold and their touch made me think that they were not made of flesh." They were black with a yellowish tinge, "somewhat like copper. They pulled my head back against a very hard chest—one that seemed to be made of iron; I felt the cold through my hair and behind my neck, but no contact with clothes." Surrounded by "a strong, blinding light," she felt she "had been paralyzed, and when the hands touched me, I had the distinct impression of a strong electric discharge, as if I had been shaken by a lightning bolt. My whole body was annihilated, helpless, without reflexes."

At one point she was released, after having been dragged some distance. She heard laughter and was struck in the back "as if from a metallic object," but at no time saw any sign of her assailant. Her movement restored, she rambled home for fifteen or twenty minutes in shock, and didn't look back. What little was described of the attacker fits an overall UFO-related pattern: not only the paralysis and sudden blinding light, witnessed independently by others, but an abrupt departure consisting of "a great noise, like a violent wind during a storm, a sudden displacement of warm air or a violent whirlwind . . . I had the feeling something flew through the air very fast, but I saw nothing." Her attacker also was invisible, except for the hands, otherwise evident only by the displacement of grass and brush like a ghost, or something out of an *Invisible Man* movie. Vallée records numerous reports of roughly this type from the former Soviet Union. The astute reader will notice a similarity between this report and others of diabolical occult phenomena.

It must be noted that abductee Kathie Davis attested to cold, hard fingers, as well: "Whoever's touching me . . . I feel touching . . . I feel cold touches on both sides of my chest . . . and fingers or something cold touching me." She was asked specifically by Budd Hopkins if they felt like fingers, and answered, "Yeah, sort of, but they're cold . . . Not real soft . . . " And a twelve-year-old abductee in Argentina named Oscar saw a "giant" and a small "robot" in a landed craft, the hand of the giant being green with "nails like conical dark blue metallic claws" when a heavy glove was pulled off it; Oscar never saw the body of the giant properly— it was suited the entire time he was with it. He tried to make off with the glove, but a small sphere and another object flew over to him and sucked the glove out of his hand to retrieve it, recalling the failed attempts by both Antonio Boas and Betty Hill to take an object as proof of their experience. Marks were left on Oscar's body like those on Gustave Gonzales from where the metallic nails scratched him. Six days before Oscar's fully-conscious meeting of the beings, a cow had been found dead on his father's property, and Oscar saw the giant cutting up cow parts on board the craft. Oscar had nightmares and possible later abductions after his initial encounter.

The third incident took place at Voronezh, two hundred miles south of Moscow. In September and October of 1989, a major UFO flap occurred there, with as many as five hundred witnesses to any given sighting. Landing traces estimated to be from an object weighing eleven and a half tons were found, consistent in their quadruped dimensions with those in Quarouble, France, in 1954, and readings similar to Rendlesham Forest were taken. Ten- to twelve-foot-tall humanoids were seen walking about the landed, roughly egg-shaped objects, and both the landed objects and the humanoids sported a symbol associated with previous sightings (at least one series of which was dismissed as a hoax). The humanoids had round, flattish dome-shaped heads, with three eyes and no faces, no necks, and arms ending in pincer clamps extending all the way to their ankles. They were outfitted in foil-like silver suits, not unlike our own radiation suits. These humanoids never displayed hostility, but their appearance understandably frightened witnesses. They collected samples of dirt and plants, and were seen leading people to spots where they seemed to just disappear into thin air. The missing people invariably returned, none the worse for wear, but dazed and confused and lacking any memory at all of their encounter.

An interesting footnote to this flap is that J. Allen Hynek's Center for UFO Studies refused to examine evidence from it, having determined it must be false on the basis of the humanoids reported. They had decided that the well-known Grays were the only viable candidates for study, and were using certain anatomical knowledge in their possession as a criterion for testing validity of reports. This is a prime example of how UFO investigators fall into the same traps as more respectably viewed scientists and academicians, entrenching themselves in dogmas every bit as unreasonable.

The major media were no better. Tass put the story on wire as it was in progress. Britain's ITN News, the *Washington Post,* and the *New York Times* initially gave it a great blitz of coverage, impressed by the fact that it was Tass doing the reporting, but never did any follow-up. Proof of an eleven- or twelve-ton object flying around the sky and burning asphalt, matching previous evidence from other times and countries and with plainly no connection to any known terrestrial technology, would seem to constitute "news." Is there an official or unofficial order at the executive level not to run or investigate such stories? Or is there reluctance on the part of any investigative reporter to chase such leads, out of fear of ridicule or fear of the unknown, or on a more mundane level, simply the lack of personal resources? Maybe a combination of the above?

Our final example in this series is a little-known case from

John Spencer's *UFO Encyclopedia:* in Livingston, Scotland, on November 9, 1979, forester Robert Taylor was inspecting plantations between Edinburgh and Glasgow and found a large, strangely designed globe hovering just over the ground, which became partly transparent and then opaque again as if trying to camouflage itself. Two small spheres with grappling spikes rushed toward him on the ground from its vicinity, wrapped about his ankles, and dragged him toward the globe, and a choking smell caused him to fall unconscious. He awoke later to find his dog madly barking. Taylor had a headache and thirst that lasted for two days, and was unable to walk, talk, or drive his truck satisfactorily. The spiked spheres left rips in the grass and in Taylor's pants, but no other sign of the encounter or the globe remained.

What can be deduced or inferred about the nature of UFO occupants from all these wildly different reports? Perhaps everything. If one ignores appearances, the underlying similarities become crystal clear. Take the occupants' most obvious characteristic: *they are superhuman.*

Aside from their ability to walk through walls, enter and exit private domiciles undetected, drug, paralyze, and hypnotize witnesses into amnesia and the like, all of which appear to be accomplished by technological means, they *themselves* are superhuman. They can be stabbed with knives, shot with arrows, have gun butts broken off against them, be unfazed by pistol, rifle, machine-gun, or shotgun blasts, and can leap incredible bounds, run superhuman speeds, and in some cases even seem to fly more or less under their own power. They occupy craft which can accelerate or decelerate from thousands of miles an hour to a dead stop, without being pulverized by inertia. All of these things seem to hold true, despite varying outward appearances. Hairy dwarves, Hopkinsville Goblins, and hook-nosed, one-handed, hairy leapers all display the same characteristics. In addition, they seem unhampered by our gravity or atmosphere, and in some instances are even reported to not be breathing at all.

Zecharia Sitchin, in *Genesis Revisited,* makes the next most logical conclusion in analysis of the Grays: "[There is] an important clue to the identity of the small creatures with smooth skins, no sex organs, no hair, elliptical heads, and large odd eyes that are supposed to be operating the purported UFO's. *If the tales be true, then what the 'contactees' have seen are not the people, the intelligent beings, from another planet—but their anthropoid robots.*"

In other words, not only do these bizarre humanoid occupants exhibit the characteristics of artificial beings *despite* their appearances, they also exhibit all the same characteristics *by* their appearances. Consider all the descriptions so far: glowing eyes; glowing bodies; identical appearances; no sex organs; no digestive tracts, no functioning mouths, and no anuses; metallic look; metallic feel; masklike faces with no expression; no discernible emotions; physically cold bodies; hobbling, awkward walks, stiff and mechanical, even overtly compared to "automata" in some instances; hums, buzzes, and clicks for audible communication among themselves, like binary computers. What is the logical conclusion? Like the grappling spheres in Scotland, like the figures that seized Charles Hickson and Calvin Parker, like the hairy dwarves, like the Voronezh giants and the faceless midgets and the one-handed leapers and the Mothman and all the rest, the Hopkinsville Goblins and the famous Grays are *robots.* Different makes, yes, various exteriors, but all the same kind of creature: *mechanical.*

Amazingly enough, the researchers closest to the problem seem to have actually come to the same conclusion themselves, almost from the beginning. "It is odd that the creatures seen coming from these craft should resemble our own *homo sapiens* race so closely," J. Allen Hynek commented in an issue of *UFO Report,* perhaps not realizing his unconscious slip in admitting that he thought UFOs were "craft." He continued, "It is also peculiar that they would be able to adjust to our gravitational pull or breathe our air so easily. This could only mean that they are mechanical creatures—robots—or they originate from a habitat whose environment is very similar to ours here on Earth." In fact, Hynek's own definition of a "Close Encounter of the Third Kind" was specifically one in which "the presence of animated creatures is reported" around a UFO, an extremely interesting choice of words.

In his journal entry for December 5, 1965, Jacques Vallée wrote, "Over lunch Bill Powers and I have been talking about the operators of the craft. 'In some cases,' I said, 'it almost seems that they are not real beings, but artificial humanoids.' 'Yes,' he replied, warming up to the subject, 'they could be noticing machines with fast pattern recognition abilities! In a few minutes on the ground they could gather reams of data about us, couldn't they?'"

In one of his later books, Vallée hinted at the possibility, without any overt reference to automata, by writing about the

Everittstown, New Jersey, occurrence of November 6, 1957, as "another of the tantalizing coincidences with which UFO researchers are now becoming familiar." At 6:30 that morning, a twelve-year-old boy named Everett, in Dante, Tennessee, saw people talking between themselves "like German soldiers in movies" trying to catch his dog. They had several dogs from the neighborhood with them, and took off in an oblong object. In Everittstown that same night, John Trasco saw tam-o'-shantered green men outside an egg-shaped object by his barn. "We are peaceful people," one said in broken English. "We only want your dog." Trasco chased them away. Why on the same day would occupants from UFOs attempt to acquire dogs from a place and a boy that share an identical name? Perhaps because they are *computers,* thinking too literally, told to get "Everett's dogs." This might also explain some of the seemingly contradictory or childish behavior of the beings, who capriciously give an item one minute and retrieve it the next—their program sometimes can't recognize they have done something they were not supposed to, until the act has first been done. Put another way: if the robots were programmed for "courtesy," they might hand over an object on request; but if they were also programmed never to let an item leave the ship, then they would retrieve that object before the human "guest" to whom they had handed it was escorted back to his or her pick-up point. That the Everittstown humanoids were *disguised* to look like classic elves is apparent from both Trasco's and his wife's testimony that green powder came off the "man's" wrist when Trasco grabbed it. It would be interesting to ask Trasco if the wrist felt more like flesh or metal. Recall also Antonio Boas' remark about the beings that abducted him looking like elves.

Dr. Felix Zigel, Russia's equivalent to Jacques Vallée, came to the ultimate conclusion that UFO occupants were of four basic types: tall humanoids, small grays, spacemen indistinguishable from our own terrestrial *homo sapiens,* and "crews of robots or androids." If the tall humanoids include entities like the Voronezh giants, and the Grays are just another form of robot, as has been discussed, that leaves only two types: human and artificial (robot/android). In the publication *Gente* of July–August 1981, Zigel said he believed that these robots were "deliberately constructed in order to confound all our notions of space, matter, time and dimensions," with the ability to appear and disappear at will. The "deliberately constructed" comment sounds extremely like that given by Robert Sarbacher in Chapter 1, about the same occupants. "I have come to similar conclusions [as Felix Zigel], after more than thirty years of research," concurs Timothy Good in *Above Top Secret. UFO* magazine editor Richard Hall voices agreement in his book *Uninvited Guests.*

The explanation that UFO occupants are in fact robots answers two particularly knotty questions: one, what is the purpose of the implants; and two, how does their form of communication, their "telepathy," work? There may be more than one implant placed in individuals, or a single implant may serve several purposes, but at least one of them could answer the telepathy problem. Remember that Nebraska highway patrolman Herbert Schirmer didn't hear them say anything until after they had pressed against his neck, where a welt remained. It could have been an implant— which might have been nothing more than a *radio receiver.*

And that would also explain why so many of the occupants, whatever their appearance, sport *antennae.* Similarities can even be noticed between dissimilar humanoids: Antonio Boas' humanoid abductors had three "hoses" sticking out of their heads, which bent backwards into their shoulders and backs with no indication of being attached to any sort of apparatus; the robots that picked up Charles Hickson and Calvin Parker had three conical projections that would seem to serve no better purpose than antennae; the Hopkinsville Goblins had two antennae on top of their heads, and conical noses with small knobs on their tips, similar to the projections from the Pascagoula abductors—again, three antennae. And the Voronezh entities had three "eyes." The UFO humanoids also frequently are reported as having round, featureless feet, with which they levitate, as in Hopkinsville and Pascagoula.

Michael Lindemann, founder of California's future-studies organization, the 2020 Group, asked Budd Hopkins at a Santa Barbara UFO conference in November of 1990 whether or not "the suggestion of Linda Moulton Howe and others that the little gray beings usually associated with abduction are perhaps not fully conscious, but may actually be some kind of biological robot," and was answered with, ". . . whether the thing is a robot or whatever, it's alien. Calling it a non-living whatever doesn't really help, because it doesn't clarify anything. The point is that the alien nature of this means they simply are not like us." Linda Moulton Howe's suggestion of "biological" robots stems from comments made by abductees she has worked with. She has also heard them referred to simply as robots, serving as "bellhops" to escort the abductees to and from the craft, which appears to be exactly what they are. As to whether or not the fact that the occupants are robots would clarify anything, plainly it does.

Hopkins has even acknowledged the probability of robot UFO occupants himself, without realizing it. When his *Intruders* was filmed as a CBS miniseries in May of 1992, a real attempt was made to model the "aliens" as close as possible to abductee reports. They finally had to change them. "The first aliens built by the prop department very closely followed the descriptions given by abductees," Hopkins told *UFO* magazine a week after the telecast. "But when filmed, those 'aliens' looked lifeless, more like alien dolls or puppets than living entities." *Dolls or puppets.*

How certain is it that robots are the occupants being witnessed from these craft? Recall Robert Sarbacher's letter, quoted in Chapter One: he put the word "aliens" in quotes, denoting that it was inadequate or somehow inaccurate in its use, adding that the "instruments or people" operating the saucers were "constructed like certain insects on earth"—i.e., exoskeletal, which would also apply to *metallic*—specifically in order to withstand the tremendous G-forces of their craft. "Constructed like" could simply be defining an inherent biological framework, though it sounds more like an engineering reference—but how can one confuse "instruments" with "people"?

There are additional pieces of corroborative evidence. Randle and Schmitt, in *UFO Crash at Roswell*—who never indicate any belief that the recovered bodies from that crash were anything other than biological—mention that a technician at NORAD came across a peculiar item while computerizing the complex's files. The particular file in question was accompanied by black-and-white pictures, and dealt with recovered bodies which were only about five feet tall, with big heads, matching the description of those found in Roswell. The label on the file was "USAAF Early *Automation*." (Emphasis added.) This would seem to provide confirmation of the high-level CIA rumors about "little gray men" that author Victor Marchetti specifically heard were kept at Wright-Patterson's Foreign Technology Division. What would deceased alien life forms be doing in an Air Force base's division of foreign *technology?*

Additionally, Randle and Schmitt relate the testimony of CIC Master Sergeant Lewis S. Rickett, who escorted Lincoln La Paz—

the same Lincoln La Paz who would soon investigate the green fireballs of New Mexico—in September of 1947 to investigate the Roswell crash. La Paz's conclusions at that time were that a craft had indeed come down and been repaired by its crew, but not so well that it didn't crash anyway after taking off again. He also believed that the crew had ejected in an escape pod. One year later, Rickett met up with La Paz again. In that time, La Paz had decided that the craft was in fact remotely controlled. He "believed the object was unmanned but that it was some kind of extraterrestrial probe . . . La Paz was sure that it was remotely controlled and he was satisfied with that theory." In a seeming contradiction, he had said, "It had touched down briefly as those controlling it tried to make some long distance repairs." How could the controlling Intelligence make long distance repairs, without some form of remote-controlled arms or legs? Which, by definition, would be robots?

Bob Oechsler, a former Air Force intelligence man who goes around stirring up the disinformation waters of EBE/Area 51/MJ-12, claims to have inside knowledge on UFOs. Given his background, his testimony can only be considered questionable, but is interesting nevertheless for the elements it contains. By his own account, he introduced himself to Admiral Bobby Ray Inman on May 13, 1988, when Inman was giving the keynote address for the groundbreaking of a new top-secret NSA computer complex. For ten years, Inman was the number one or number two man of the most top-secret agencies in the United States: CIA, NSA, DIA, ONI. If anyone would know about a secret UFO group, Inman would definitely be the man. Retired from intelligence (at least officially) in 1982, Inman went on to become the chairman, president, and chief executive officer of a company in Texas specializing in microelectronics. After the ceremony, Oechsler handed Inman his card and said, "Excuse me, Admiral, I would be deeply appreciative if at some point you'd have someone contact me about how I can get closer to MJ-12." Checking over his credentials, Inman smiled a knowing smile and said, "O.K." And just what were Oechsler's credentials? In his own words, he was a NASA mission specialist and project engineer, "with . . . limited involvement with the mechanical-arm assembly created for the shuttle project by a Canadian firm, and . . . robotics expertise regarding sophisticated remote-control devices for character robots . . ." Author Timothy Good adds that Oechsler specialized as "a prototype designer of sophisticated control systems and mobile surveillance systems." In other words, one of the principle sources of intelligence disinformation on the subject of UFOs claims to be an expert in the very fields most closely associated to their apparent reality: microelectronics, mobile surveillance systems, remote-control devices, and character robots.

It is certainly interesting, in light of apparent UFO realities, that Admiral Bobby Ray Inman is head of a microelectronics company. And mathematician John von Neumann, who is *not* listed on the MJ-12 documents but was said by Robert Sarbacher to be "definitely involved" in the government's most secret UFO investigative group, was most famous until his death in 1957 as an early pioneer of digital computers. For that matter, if the MJ-12 documents were legitimate, it would be unusual that the only biologist on their listed team was Detlev Bronk: If alien life forms were recovered from the crash, they would probably have been the most important field of study, especially if they were as complex as later disinformation has led UFOlogists to believe, and more so given that at least one of the bodies was intact while the craft itself was nothing but wreckage. Jacques Vallée also was getting his advanced degree in computer science when he was picked up by Blue Book, and afterward went on to work for the Department of Defense (for which can be read the NSA).

A better question than asking how much evidence there is to confirm the identity of these creatures as robots might be whether or not there is any evidence for UFO occupants being "aliens" in the colloquially accepted meaning of that term as a nonhuman life form. The answer is no, not really. The only testimony for having seen retrieved bodies from Roswell or other possible crashes comes to us second- and third-hand, or at even a greater remove. The nurse at the Roswell "autopsy" (and that word was never used in the original testimony) was so rattled by what she saw that she couldn't even testify to whether the bodies were dressed or not. She never made any reference to internal structures, i.e., organs, except for their cartilaginous-seeming bone structure—and we don't even know that she referred to it as "bone structure," since the story comes to us secondhand from mortician Glenn Dennis, who may be interpolating the phrase himself, simply relaying it as best he understood what she was describing. Dennis specified that she never used the word "aliens," but only referred to them as "foreign bodies." For that matter, we don't even know that the men at the "autopsy" were doctors—the nurse had never seen them before.

The testimony of all concerned refers to at least one of the bodies being in very good shape, which is extremely unusual considering it had been lying exposed in the desert sun for almost a week. The others were not referred to as being decomposed, only mangled—and not very badly, if General Exon's testimony is accurate—which is easily explained by saying that they were simply less crash protected, or not thrown clear. Why would two or more bodies decompose, and one be intact? The nurse made reference (according to Dennis) to the doctors in the examining room saying the lack of genitalia on the bodies may have been due to predators, since they attack soft tissue first; but if that is the case, why did they leave one body alone, and attack the others? And why was there no mention at all of the eyes being absent, when these are the first tissues to decompose or be consumed by scavenging birds? The nurse did say that the bodies' heads were as pliably moveable as a newborn baby's—but that could more easily be explained as a durable plastic covering, especially given their formed-out-of-a-mold identical appearance and the fact that they should have been too far decomposed to have sufficient skin for testing pliability in the first place. The overpowering odor that drove the nurse from the examination room could as easily have been ammonia or some other chemical smell from an internal lubricant or medium as that of actual decay, and it is interesting that not one statement refers to the distinctive rotting stench of decomposition coming from the bodies.

Glenn Dennis was asked by the military about the preservation of tissue, and whether or not numerous bodies could be fit into a single hermetically sealed casket. But then, they would also have been anxious to instill the idea that a conventional crash had occurred if any word at all were to leak out—which they had to anticipate would happen—and, in fact, Dennis was summoned to convey one pilot to the base with only "minor injuries and a broken nose" on the same day as the Roswell remains were recovered, which most clearly would seem to indicate that the Army wanted to convince someone on the outside that this had been the case. What about the crates of ice into which the bodies were placed at the crash site? The Army wouldn't need those for nonbiological bodies. But then, they probably didn't know yet what they were dealing with, either.

What have we learned so far? The evidence leaves no doubt that unidentified flying objects are a physical reality; that a great many of them are intelligently controlled craft; that many, perhaps nearly all, of their occupants are mechanical—or at least artificial—in nature, and the intelligence exhibited in their actions is not inconsistent with artificial intelligence; that human beings—or beings so close to human that they are indistinguishable from us by appearance and function—are connected to their operation; that they have kept watch on our military-industrial power from the beginning, and periodically (or perhaps even regularly) sabotage our bases; that they collect biological samples from human beings and other animals; that in the case of human beings, at least one purpose for the collection of biological samples is the reproduction of human life; that those humans abducted by them are most often, if not always, lifelong repeat contacts for purposes not entirely known, but to all appearances benign; that they are not hostile to us, but neither are they reluctant about taking what they want; that they prefer to operate in secret, without detection, and take elaborate precautions to remain concealed, though there are some indications that they have a time schedule for the release of information from their end.

In short, we have essentially determined the mechanisms attached to the phenomenon and much of what UFOs are doing, and can make educated guesses at the technology involved even when we don't fully understand it for lack of concrete evidence. What we don't know yet (though we have already encountered some clues) are answers to three remaining questions: *Who* are "They"—the Intelligence behind the interplanetary craft and their automated occupants? *Where* do they come from? And, most important of all, *why* are they doing all this?

Perhaps the best place to start answering these questions would be to examine the history of UFOs before the modern era, with a specific emphasis on bizarre humanoids and their interactions with the human race. Just as patterns have so far developed by observation and examination in this study, perhaps they will continue to do so on these subjects. We have met the puppets—now we must find the curtain to peer behind that will reveal the puppet master: "The Wizard of Oz," as it were.

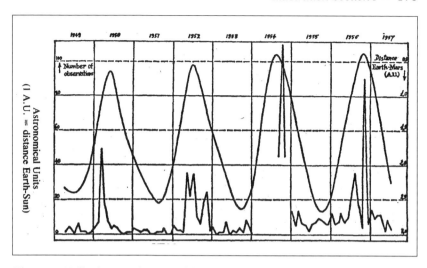

Figure 1. Vallée's correlation tables between UFO waves and oppositions of the planet Mars. The regularity is as consistent as a heartbeat. From Jacques and Janine Vallée, *Challenge to Science* (New York: Ballantine, 1966).

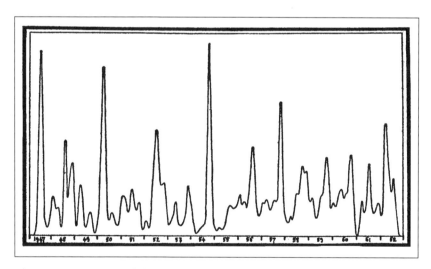

Figure 2. Structure of the wave phenomenon, 1947–62.

Figure 3. The Grays, reported by many abductees. Barney Hill's description was extremely similar to this skull-like or skeletonic variation. Like the rest of the beings reported, they appear to be robots. Barney included the fact that their surfaces were bluish and metallically shiny, and both he and Betty described a "shiny black-jacketed" leader like the insectoid (opposite). Other frequently reported features include antennae, arms that are longer from wrist to elbow than from elbow to shoulder, and long, suction cup-tipped fingers, matching eyewitness description of the recovered Roswell saucer occupants in 1947. Sketch by Tim Hogan, based on abductee testimonies.

Figure 4. A large black insectoid is reported with some frequency in UFO abductions, as a more advanced form of creature than the standard "Grays." This figure is generally of gleaming black metallic appearance, considered to be "the leader," and is most often thc "controller" of the abduction process. In American Indian mythology, such a being fits the description of Koko Pilau or the "Ant People," and in ancient Egypt an identical creature fulfilling the same functions was called simply "Mantis." A surprising number of abductees report witnessing Egyptian hieroglyphics or being shown scenes of ancient Egypt during their experience. Sketch by Tim Hogan, based on abductee testimonies.

Height: 2½ to 3½ feet
Sex: No indication

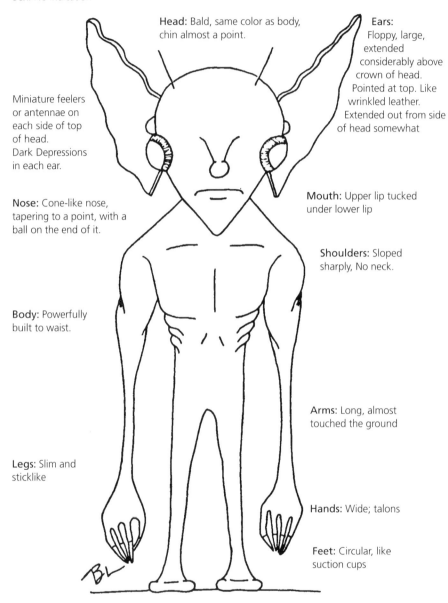

Head: Bald, same color as body, chin almost a point.

Ears: Floppy, large, extended considerably above crown of head. Pointed at top. Like wrinkled leather. Extended out from side of head somewhat

Miniature feelers or antennae on each side of top of head. Dark Depressions in each ear.

Nose: Cone-like nose, tapering to a point, with a ball on the end of it.

Mouth: Upper lip tucked under lower lip

Shoulders: Sloped sharply, No neck.

Body: Powerfully built to waist.

Arms: Long, almost touched the ground

Legs: Slim and sticklike

Hands: Wide; talons

Feet: Circular, like suction cups

Figure 5. One of the Hopkinsville Goblins. Note the two antennae and the third in front as a conical "nose." The feet are round and featureless, looking like suction cups, matching descriptions given researcher Len Stringfield of other UFO occupants. From John Spencer, *The UFO Encyclopedia* (New York: Avon Books, 1991).

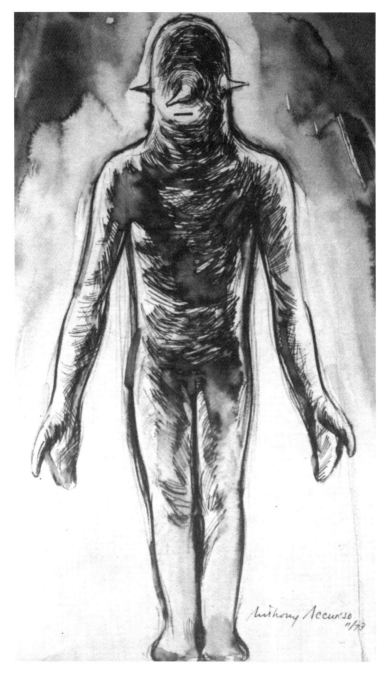

Figure 6. One of the Pascagoula entities. Like the Hopkinsville Goblin, it has three antennae and suction cup feet. In both cases, the beings floated. From Ralph and Judy Blum, *Beyond Earth* (New York: Bantam, 1974).

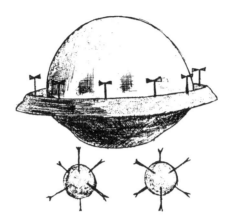

Figure 7. In 1979, in Livingston, Scotland, Forester Robert Taylor encountered what appeared to be a mechanized floating sphere with automated grappling hooks attached to metallic balls that gassed him into unconsciousness and left him with symptoms matching those of a standard UFO abduction. From John Spencer, *The UFO Encyclopedia* (New York: Avon Books, 1991).

Figure 8. The Voronezh entities. Again, three "eyes" that equate to the other beings' antennae, and sporting the frequently reported clamp "hands." Voronezh sketch from Jacques Vallée, *Revelations* (New York: Random House, 1991).

Pre-Knossos Vinca masks from Yugoslavia and the Cucuteni region.

Figure 9. Circa 5,000 BC, black with white-filled incisions and red painted bands at top corners and center.

Figure 10. Fifth Millennium BC, with meander symbol of the cosmic waters on its forehead.

Figure 11. Black, circa 4,500–4,000 BC. Note resemblance to UFO Grays. All images from Marija Gimbutas, *The Goddesses and Gods of Old Europe* (Berkeley, California: University of California Press, 1982).

| *Figure 12* | *Figure 13* |

Figure 12. Sketch of Sumerian clay figurine approximately 5,500 years old. Note the rod in the figure's hand, as described by the Paiute Indians and UFO abductees. Courtesy of Zecharia Sitchin, *The 12th Planet* (New York: Avon Books, 1978).

Figure 13. Japanese Kappa. From Peter Kolosimo, *Timeless Earth* (Secaucus, New Jersey: University Books, 1974).

Figure 14. Three views of the North American Indian figure Koko Pilau, the "humpbacked flute-player" who carries the seeds of reproduction. Sketches by Tim Hogan.

Figure 15. Left: Ancient Egyptian painting representing an invocation to the sun god. *Right:* A plasma generator. From Robert Charroux, *Forgotten Worlds* (New York: Popular Library, 1973).

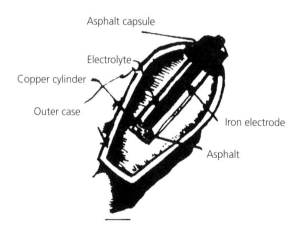

Figure 16. Electric battery found in a Baghdad museum. From Peter Kolosimo, *Timeless Earth* (Secaucus, New Jersey: University Press, 1974).

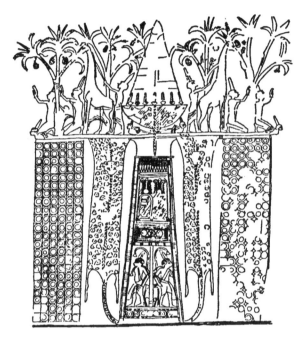

Figure 17. Tomb decoration of Ethiopian Viceroy Huy from the time of King Tut. NASA aerospace engineer Stuart W. Greenwood saw this reproduction in Sitchin's *The 12th Planet* and discovered four distinct similarities to a contemporary three-stage rocket, the nose-cone above ground and the rocket below in a shaft. Courtesy of Zecharia Sitchin, *The 12th Planet* (New York: Avon Books, 1976).

Figure 18. Wall sculpture of the goddess Ishtar, from her temple at Ashur, looking distinctly aeronautical. Courtesy of Zecharia Sitchin, *The 12th Planet* (New York: Avon Books, 1976).

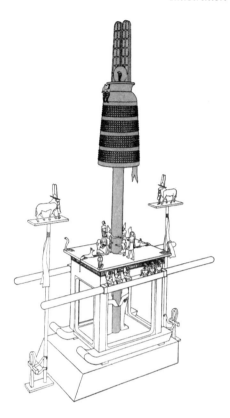

Figure 19. The fetish of Abydos known as the *ta-wer* ("Eldest Land"), by which Osiris rose to heaven. It, too, remarkably resembles a modern three-stage rocket, and can be seen on the Twenty-fifth Dynasty coffin of Nes-mutaatneru from Deir El-Bahari in the Boston Museum of Fine Arts, and on the Twenty-first Dynasty sarcophagus of Pameshem in the Cairo Museum. Reproduction after H.E. Winlock, from Richard H. Wilkinson, *Reading Egyptian Art* (London: Thames and Hudson, 1992).

Figure 20

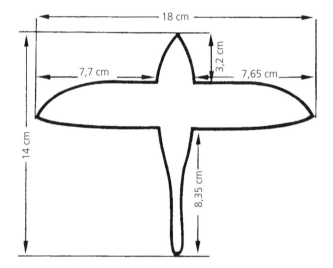

Figure 21

Figures 20 and 21. An Egyptian wooden "bird" model discovered in 1898 in a tomb near Saqqara. Catalogue #6347 in the Cairo Museum, it was reexamined by Dr. Khalil Messiha in 1969 and found to be aerodynamically sound by an interdisciplinary scientific team. The model was exhibited with thirteen others like it in 1972. Reproduction courtesy of David Hatcher Childress *Vimana Aircraft of Ancient India and Atlantis* (Stelle, IL: Adventures Unlimited Press, 1991).

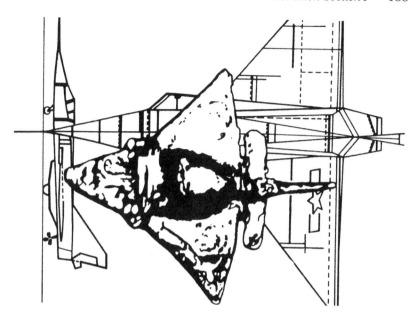

Figure 22. Gold peruvian artifact displayed in the State Museum of Bogota, Columbia. Usually considered to be a hummingbird, bee, or flying fish, it also is aerodynamically sound and remarkably similar in design to modern jet aircraft. Reproduction courtesy of David Hatcher Childress *Vimana Aircraft of Ancient India and Atlantis* (Stelle, IL: Adventures Unlimited Press, 1991).

Figure 23. Unknown object from central Europe, believed to depict a "cosmogonic myth" because it shows the "cosmic waters" above. Its shape, the cosmic water motif and the face of a probable god-figure within at bottom, are virtually identical to the sacred Egyptian Benben stone. From *Goddesses and Gods of Old Europe* by Marija Gimbutas (Berkeley, California: University of California Press, 1982).

Figure 24. Replica of the most sacred object in Egypt, the Benben stone, which brought Ra to Earth. It is usually depicted with a god or goddess in a square hatchway, and resembles a Saturn rocket nose-cone. Courtesy Zecharia Sitchin, *The Stairway to Heaven* (New York: Avon Books, 1983).

UR

In the Beginning:
Visitors from Heaven

6

Controls

T HE ESTIMABLE ITALIAN author of several well-researched
books on ancient civilization and celestial phenomena Peter
Kolosimo relates the following story in *Not of This World,*
which was told by an American traveler named William Thompson to a review publication of the time called *Adventure.* Thompson, referred to as "an honest businessman," had for several months
been a guest of the famous lamasery of Tuerin in Mongolia in 1920.
During his stay there, an adventurer of unsavory reputation named
John Spencer also became a guest, brought there by the lamas
when they found him dying of fever after a long trek from
Manchuria. Newspapers of the time had linked Spencer's name to
drug and arms dealing, and possibly counterfeiting as well. His
flight from Manchuria was probably connected to such activities.

Spencer soon recovered sufficiently to explore the grounds
on his own, presumably in search of treasure. Discovering a worn
stone staircase not far from the monastery, he followed it to a narrow door entering a polygonal room of twelve or more sides. Strange
designs on the walls he eventually determined were the constellation of Taurus, recognized from identical symbols on a Chinese
watch chain in his possession. Casually tracing the patterns, he
found that the wall silently opened when he hit the Pleiades, at
the end of the line.

Propping the wall open with a stone from outside, Spencer
followed a dim green glow, discernible in the distance of a dark
passageway. Of several available tunnels at the end of this central, narrow gallery, Spencer took the one on the far right, which
happened to have the sign of the Pleiades above it.

Finding himself in a chamber where the green glow was much

stronger, Spencer examined a line of twenty-five or thirty rectangular boxes along the wall, which turned out to be biers he believed could yield funeral treasures. There were no regularities to the bodies in the coffins, save two: none had any jewelry or treasure, and all were somehow perfectly preserved. They were not of the same epoch, becoming older the farther down the line he went. The most recent were deceased lamas, dressed like those presently in the lamasery. There was an Indian in a red silk cloak; a man dressed in garb of the 1700s; and two women, one dressed as a man and the other of some "origin he could not establish."

The final coffin in the line contained something not even human, except in form, "dressed in a sort of silver mail and who in place of a head had a ball of pure silver, with round holes where the eyes should be and an oval thing full of small holes in lieu of a nose—and there was no mouth!" Spencer no sooner got over this shock than "the big round eyes were wide open and emitting a horrifying green gleam."

Spencer screamed and fled, discovering to his further amazement that it was now night outside, when it had been bright morning just a short time before. "I must have walked for two or three hours all told," he later related. "It is impossible that I could have lost all sense of time to such an extent in there!"

Returning to the monastery, Spencer told his entire story to Thompson, who in turn told the monks. The next morning, the monks, not at all upset and actually smiling, said to him, "My poor friend, your fever has played a dirty trick on you! Why didn't you expect to be cured by visiting our holy places?" Spencer inquired about the "corpse without a mouth" and was told, "There are neither corpses nor vaults down there: come with me if you feel strong enough."

The head lama accompanied Spencer to the star chamber, touched a wall with his finger, and walked through a different gallery than Spencer had traversed. After fewer than ten minutes, they reached a small room in which there was a ledge of boxes perhaps a foot each in length. "This is what you really saw," said the monk, lifting the lids to reveal perfect miniature replicas of the bodies Spencer had seen. "They are images of people who have enriched the world with their wisdom and so we honour them. It was your fever, my poor friend, which made you think you were standing in front of real sarcophagi. And as you can see, there is no green light but only the yellow one from our humble lamps."

Sure the lama was wrong but not wishing to contradict him under the circumstances, Spencer asked who the silver, round-headed, mouthless figure was. The lama pointed to the Pleiades on the map, and said, "a high lord from the stars."

Later, rejoining Thompson, Spencer said, "It might easily be that I still had some fever, but I absolutely reject the idea that I dreamt it all or was the victim of delirium. I lost the heel of one of my shoes down in the labyrinth and scratched my hands at least a dozen times when I was feeling the stones for any possible snags. I touched the clothes on that corpse and noticed the veins and wrinkles . . . the piece of wall which opened was on the left of the entrance whereas the opening the lama stood in front of was almost right in front, slightly to the right . . . the monk has tried to convince me by showing me a miniature copy of what I actually saw."

The next week Spencer left, and Thompson never heard of him again. He asserted the truth of Spencer's story, however, in the retelling: "I have on some occasions myself seen corpses in Mongolian monasteries, preserved intact for centuries, perhaps for thousands of years, and have heard people talk several times about silver men who had come from the stars."

Kolosimo uses this story to illustrate the likelihood that Spencer saw a man in a spacesuit, but one vital part of the incident would seem to invalidate that: the figure's eye-lights came on while he was looking at it. Reflection of the light off of stationary glass or plastic eyepieces? Possibly. But Spencer was definite that they suddenly and abruptly were *blazing* green light, where before they had been dark. The implication is that something switched on, activated by Spencer's near proximity to it. Kolosimo's rendition says, specifically, "Spencer, recovering from his surprise, *was about to touch the object* [the "corpse"] when he changed his mind suddenly as the big round eyes of the dead man were wide open and emitting a horrifying green gleam." (Emphasis added.) That means that when Spencer said, "I touched the clothes on that corpse and noticed the veins and wrinkles," he must have been referring to one of the many others he rifled along the line for jewelry and treasure. The "corpse without a mouth," the "high lord," and "silver man who had come from the stars" may well have been a robot.

On the surface, the mouthless, silver-headed figure matches the description of many UFO occupants: the metallic silver suit;

the blazing eyes, apparently lit from within; the smooth, round, ball-bearing head; its "home in the stars." And which seems likelier? That a man would meditate in a helmeted spacesuit, in a coffin in an isolated mausoleum, lying in wait for unsuspecting tourists to scare by somehow turning on green eye-lights from a hidden switch at just the right moment? Or that a machine of some sort was sensor activated when its path was crossed?

American Indians and Australian Aborigines both refer to "creatures without mouths" who come down out of the heavens. For example, the kachinas—deified ancestral spirits—fall into the category of otherworldly beings that could perhaps be robots. Anthropologist Frank Waters writes about the kachina in *The Book of the Hopi,* "It is distinctly Hopi . . . when in a kiva we hear the strange falsetto yell announcing a presence above, feel the stamp on the roof demanding admittance, and see coming down the ladder a spirit whose manifested form has never been glimpsed among the figures of this mortal world . . . Even as they come down the ladder one by one, they utter their low eerie moans and move restlessly about, spirits of planets from the depths of space." Though believed to have "bases" in the San Francisco mountains of present-day New Mexico and other locations on Earth, the kachinas are considered to come "from much farther away, a long, long way—from neighboring stars, constellations too distant to be visible, from mysterious spirit worlds."

The chief earthly kachina, who led the Hopi to their present locations to live according to their lore, is the most interesting of all for his resemblance to reported insectoid UFO occupants. His name, *Koko Pilau,* means "wood hump," which he has on his back. He is also known as "the humpbacked flute player," images of which can be seen all across the American Southwest, and carved on rocks from South America to Canada. Koko Pilau is an entirely benign creature, one of the two *mahu* or "insect people resembling the katydid or locust" that proved their strength and indestructibility to "the eagle," causing the eagle to tell the mahu, "Now that you have stood both tests, you may use my feather any time you want to talk to our Father Sun, the Creator [on behalf of the Hopi], and I will deliver your message because I am the conqueror of air and master of height. I am the only one who has the power of space above, for I represent the loftiness of the spirit and can deliver your prayers to the Creator." In other words, the insect people serve more or less the purpose of "the Holy Spirit" to Christianity:

a power left behind to supervise, instruct, and guide the people in the great god's absence.

Koko Pilau is always depicted playing the flute, since his presence is announced by enchanting music—signifying, perhaps, hypnotic effect. The hump on his back contains the "seeds of plants and flowers," and he is often depicted with an enormous penis, because he carries "the seeds of human reproduction also." He is the one referred to as the "locust" of the insect pair. In drawings, he is almost never depicted without antennae on his head, often with knobs on the end of them. Of course, robotic UFO occupants match a similar description, involving themselves in human reproduction and in collecting plant and soil samples as well as biological material from other animals.

The kachina itself is an eerie creature with a masked face that doesn't speak as men do. Their language is no longer known to man, though it is believed that it once was: "His [Koko Pilau's] song is still remembered, but the words are so ancient that nobody knows what they mean," writes Waters. "The *kachinas* ... may be invoked to manifest their benign powers so that man may be enabled to continue his never-ending journey. They are the invisible forces of life—not gods, but rather intermediaries, messengers." In other words, what our Judaeo-Christian culture might refer to as an "angel." Their origin is unknown, lost in the prehistoric past along with the understanding of their language. "Kachina" is merely a word meaning "respected spirit"; and a kiva is the sacred underground chamber in which all religious mystery plays are enacted, "like a womb," representing "the previous underworld" through which the Hopi emerge into "the world above" following the rituals. (For more details, see Chapter 10.) These "spirits"—men and women of the tribe, in costume (though, in antiquity, someone or something else might have gotten them started)—initiate all their children aged six to eight into the society of the Kachinas or Powamus; every boy and girl must belong to one or the other society, by that age.

These initiations, like most in tribal societies, are not entirely pleasant. Being stripped naked and whipped is part of the process, frequently hard enough to let blood. Some of the kachinas are downright frightening, including a variety that are actually called "monster kachinas." These creatures, in a ritual not unlike our own Halloween, go from door to door in the village on prearranged nights, scraping implements of dismemberment along the walls as they go, their purpose being to frighten. They demand entrance to given hovels, insisting a named child be handed over to them for listed transgressions. In some cases the child is stripped naked in the street and whipped or doused in cold water, and admonished to behave better in the future. Sometimes they are merely frightened for a few minutes—given the distinct impression that they are to be carried away and cut to pieces—before the mother is allowed to placate the avenging spirits with food offerings that they will ultimately accept. There are moderate variations of this ritual, one of which is allowing the child to offer some food or a given penance for their misdeeds, which will be refused before he or she is given a memorable, but not severe, punishment.

In European culture, this was the original role of "Father Christmas" or "St. Nicholas," corrupted to our present "Santa Claus." Like our Christmas, the Hopi kachina rituals ("night dances") are held in the winter. Father Christmas was a much more ambivalent figure than today's jolly, sanitized version of Santa. He carried with him both presents and birch rods, and rewarded each child according to his deeds of the year. The monster kachinas do the same. As the kachinas are servants or intermediaries of the great sky god, so does Father Christmas have his elves—which, as we have noticed, is not an uncommon description of UFO entities. In both cases, a wise and benevolent sky god keeps tabs on his people, specifically to reward or punish them in accordance with their deeds. In essence, the Judaeo-Christian tradition is based on the same tenets. And in all cases, as the famous yuletide song goes, "He knows when you've been sleeping, He knows when you're awake, He knows when you've been bad or good, So be good for goodness' sake."

In the early or initiatory stages, the kachinas taunt or praise their young candidates, comparing them to bean sprouts that must be properly cared for and nurtured that they may grow straight and tall. The kachinas enter the kiva without being granted permission and without warning. The initiates are told a story by the Kachina Chief, virtually indistinguishable from the Christian tale of Adam and Eve's and the world's Fall from grace, and the exodus of the Hopi people from the old world into this new one. It is especially interesting to note the similarities between the Hopi religion and Christianity, considering there should be no connection at all between them. But not only do they begin their legends with the story of being driven from the paradisiacal garden, they also have an identical apocalypse. The final ritual of the Hopi mystery plays, signifying the world's coming end, begins with "a low hum and a strange blowing of breath sounding like the winds from outer space," into which "a lone white-robed figure wearing a large white star quietly enters the kiva and announces, 'I am the Beginning and the End.' He is Nutungtatoka (First and Last). . . ." Then the figure exits, the kiva is slammed shut by a rock above, which thrusts it into total darkness, and everyone inside screams and throws off their clothes, "leap[ing] for the ladder to get out unscathed before the world is destroyed." In the Christian religion, Jesus is a white-robed figure who calls himself "the Alpha and the Omega"—the Beginning and the End—and is present at the end of the world.

After the initiates are told the story of the Fall from grace, they are then led into the center of the kiva to be whipped. Their whippings vary in severity according to the dictates of their parents and godparents, and should any blow land too harshly, the godparent will frequently express sorrow and take the remaining lashes. In all ways, a sense of justice and fairness is imparted, and therefore a sense of community. Since the kachinas return at regular intervals, there is also a sense of continuity and permanence. "I am the Father of all of you," the Kachina Chief intones, when the ceremony is concluded, "yet as a father I have failed to protect you as my children, and it makes me sad to see this happen to you." The initiates are warned to keep private the proceedings they have undergone, on threat of more dire punishment in the future. This pattern is consistent with all secret societies, the world over.

The purpose for such initiations is *socialization;* or, put another way, *social control.* Our own socialization rituals, both religious and secular, have died out or been reduced to nothing more than a salutory nod with little if any meaning. The only societies who truly "initiate" anymore are criminal societies. To the tribal society, or that more advanced civilization that has not lost sight of higher goals, initiation rituals and societies serve the function of forming identity for the individual and common purpose and cohesion for the larger community.

Something of importance to note is the Hopi's belief in other planets containing life which bear significant relationship to life on Earth. They believe man literally began on another world and "is rooted in this world until he is planted on another world or planet at a future time." Other American Indian tribes have similar legends. The epic *Chon-oopa-sa,* attributed to an unknown poet called Pa-la-ne-a-pa-pe, states that, "In the remotest past / Millions and millions of moons ago / The first of mortal men was cast down / On this world by the great Wo-Kon. / The first Dakota was formed from a star; / He hurled him and watched him as he fell / Through the darkness until he rested / On soft soil. He was not wounded / Wa-kin-yan, the first Sioux. / From afar we see the days of summer / Setting in a golden splendour / Towards the mystic region of the legend / That remote land in the West, / The land of the house and the story of the Red Man, / Country of myths and strange customs, / Valley of dark unwritten history." The significance of "That remote land in the West" will be considered at greater length in Chapter 10.

The similarity of kachina initiation to UFO abduction should be apparent at a glance. The initiatory aspect of abductions has been noticed by a few researchers in the field, but little attention has been paid to it. Vallée draws attention to ten points involved in ritual initiation, which vary only slightly from tribal secret societies to any other form of occult initiation: the candidate is confronted by costumed members of the society into which he is considered for induction; blindfolded; led through a tortuous and uncertain route; brought into a special chamber, generally without windows, and allowed to see only portions of it; brought before the master; given a test and made to indicate that he has learned the correct answers; shown death symbolism; made to feel he may not survive the experience he is undergoing, to feel his own helplessness and vulnerability; given ritual food and drink; blindfolded again and returned from whence he came.

Abduction researcher David M. Jacobs has compiled a similar list of "mental" activities performed by UFO occupants on their selected subjects. Not all abductees undergo them. There is some indication that, like occult rituals, certain rites of passage must occur for abductees before moving on to higher levels of awareness. In these procedures, there is a mental communion between the abductee and his "controller," a leader-being such as has been described in the more thorough accounts. Members of the smaller, select subset then undergo what Jacobs calls "secondary" and "ancillary" experiences, such as imaging, envisioning, staging, and testing in the former category, and being shown media displays, given special knowledge, and/or undergoing an intimate and intensive "information transfer" in the latter category, before being returned. In these experiences, the subjects are shown various enacted scenes or put into interactive situations, seemingly for purposes of instruction or to determine responses; they are shown symbols or books which they find themselves able to read despite the fact that they have no idea how they are doing so; they find themselves (like Herbert Schirmer or Betty Andreasson) implanted with knowledge of things they should not know, and yet seem to; they are led into special chambers to communicate with higher beings in something akin to a chamber of judgment; and, most interestingly, they are sometimes tested on their knowledge of the ships' machinery and operation, including flight. This latter activity shows marked indications less of testing than of *training,* which may be of some significance.

The Iban of Borneo and the Aborigines of former Arnhem Land in northern Australia have beliefs in benign spirit beings who bear them aloft in the sky while they sleep in order to bestow powers and abilities on chosen members of the tribe, and be "initiated into the select groups of knowledgeables." Given that UFO abductees often have implants put in their ear, it is interesting that the Australian Aborigines report that their spirit abductor "inserts a very thin bamboo, often identified as a spirit snake, into the man's head; then he blows into the victim's ears giving him 'breath,' thus endowing him with magic powers."

Otto Billig, in *Flying Saucers—Magic in the Skies,* writes, "The encounters of primitive people with their ancestral predecessors take place under circumstances that are similar to the encounters reported with flying saucers. The ghosts are beings from another world, counterparts to the spaceships or the extraterrestrial humanoids that meet modern contactees. The contacts take place when the chosen individual walks alone in the bush country. Upon meeting the ghost, the person contacted falls asleep or 'acts as if dead,' a condition that corresponds to an alternate state of consciousness. After awakening, he is endowed with unusual powers. The contactee with a flying saucer, like primitive man, feels he is chosen to see what is invisible to others. When he climbs into the sky, he does it with the tools of his time; the chosen of the twentieth century is moved to other planets by propulsion faster than jets, while the aborigine depends on the strength of the ghost. The extraterrestrial beings that land on earth are made of the same superior and moral fiber as figures from folklore and mythology; they are good and evil, benevolent and malicious, but they are always endowed with supernatural qualities. Some of the modern visitors from outer space kill animals, scorch the earth, and torture people, but most are godlike, far superior to man, wise, and of high intelligence; the purpose of their appearance here is to better man and to warn him of his dangerous ways."

One way to look at these similarities—as Billig does (and often Jacques Vallée as well)—is that each age projects a psychological attribute in the trappings of its time, or that the phenomenon adapts itself to each separate day and age. Another angle is that it has been exactly the same occurrence in every age, but described in the only terms that the given society knows to express it. In other words, each of these societies is encountering the same controlled aircraft we have, piloted by the same beings, performing the same acts, and for the same purposes. Or, put another way, Koko Pilau is a robot, and the sleep paralysis and amnesia were performed in antiquity by means of more or less the same technology then as now.

All of which is to dance around and evade the obvious: what we are encountering in UFO phenomena is indistinguishable from what comprise the fundamental tenets and trappings of religion, whether it be Judaeo-Christian tradition, the mythologies of the ancients, or the folk beliefs of indigenous peoples the world over. The response of Western civilization to this similarity has been to dismiss it as psychological projection. Given that the reality of the unknown aerial craft is indisputable, perhaps it is cowardice on our part not to examine our mythologies and religions in a more realistic light, and admit that there may be a hard objective reality behind them differing from what is commonly accepted. Our discomfort in dealing with the subject comes from the fact that the modern orthodoxy of scientific enlightenment has deposed a former orthodoxy based on faith in a higher power, and any indication that there may be even the slightest relevancy to a preceding orthodoxy is never greeted well by the ruling one.

"Many descriptions of UFO phenomena," writes Vallée, "force us to deal simultaneously with two categories we always attempt to separate: the physical (or technical) and the spiritual (or divine). Numerous witnesses, in their statements after a close encounter, claim bluntly that the experience of the phenomenon has a religious meaning to them. Perhaps it does. Perhaps we need not only a scientific breakthrough here but a consciousness breakthrough as well, a global, historical grasp of the beliefs—materialistic as well as idealistic—among which we have been groping for ten thousand years."

Jacques Vallée sometimes refers to the UFO-religious connection as "the physics of the B.V.M. [Blessed Virgin Mary]," which is most apparent at Fátima, Portugal; Lourdes, France; and Guadalupe, Mexico. He was so certain that Fátima was a UFO encounter that he wrote in his journal on May 14, 1967, "The news media report that the Pope went to Fátima yesterday. Fifty years ago three little shepherds saw a UFO and its occupant there, with the theological implications we all know. The Pope visiting a saucer landing site . . . and American crowds watching the event through the wonders of the Early Bird artificial satellite. I find the mixture of mysticism and technology quite amazing."

Prior to the three shepherd children being surprised by a bright flash on May 13, 1917, beginning the series of apparitions that culminated in the "miracle" witnessed by seventy thousand people on October 13 of that year, at least one of them, Lucia dos Santos, had been the recipient of previous visitations. Three times in 1915, when she was eight years old (note the age in comparison with Hopi kachina initiations, and the apparent fact that virtually all UFO abductions begin in childhood and are repeat lifelong occurrences), and three times the following year, she was visited by "a youth of admirable beauty" that she called an angel. She and three girls of the village were halfheartedly reciting the rosary when a powerful wind and a white light brought the angel to them. It was described as "a statue made of snow . . . rendered almost transparent by the rays of the sun." It had been amused at their cheating on the rosary and taught them a new prayer, identifying itself as "the Angel of Peace." In this and the later recurrences, Lucia did not want to discuss what had happened with anybody, which is typical of UFO abduction. The others were similarly reluctant to discuss it even among themselves, but not so much so that they didn't tell their families about the occurrence. Also typical were Lucia's being "quite abstracted" in her ability to concentrate and inwardly self-absorbed following the encounter, the temporary paralysis that struck them all, and the extreme fatigue they suffered. One of them said, "I don't know what is happening to me. I cannot speak, nor play, nor sing, and I haven't the strength to do anything." Subsequent meetings with the angel, where the girls were given communion and taught to imitate his actions (a similarity to the "training" of UFO abductees), left them ecstatic but drained.

It was following these six visitations that Lucia with two other children, Jacinta and Francisco Marto, encountered the next visitant in 1917. Out tending the sheep on May 13, they saw a bright flash which they followed to the Cave of St. Irene, considered a sacred site since pagan times. (A well-publicized fact that is nevertheless not known by many is that modern Church holidays and sacred sites were all appropriated from their pagan predecessors; this will be brought out at greater length in Chapters 9 and 10.) At the cave, they were blinded by a glowing light, in the center of which was a small woman. She never, either at this time or in future encounters, identified herself as the Virgin Mary. In fact, rarely do apparitions attributed to being the Virgin Mary actually use the name; the Church simply accepts that the entity in given sightings is the Virgin Mary, and later ratifies various apparitions as having been her. If we take the Fátima apparition's own word for her identity, she referred to herself by no name at all, and said only that she came "from heaven," promising one day to take her young witnesses there with her. The children simply called her "the Lady," which other visitants of the Blessed Virgin (as she has been dubbed) also call her.

In Mexico, she did call herself "the blessed and ever-Virgin Mary of Guadalupe" (at least according to Catholic literature), apparently a misunderstanding by the Spaniards of the local Aztec language—*te coatlexopeuh,* meaning "who crushes the stone serpent," signifying that she was there to replace the idol of Quetzalcoatl—which they heard as "de Guadalupe." Quetzalcoatl had been the recipient of uncounted human sacrifices in the region (which had never been originally demanded in that god's mythology). The year of the Guadalupe visitations was 1531, and whatever one's religious viewpoint, the sociopolitical fact is that in the ensuing six years, eight million Indians were baptized into Christianity, effecting a relatively peaceful conversion from a primitive (and, in this case, barbaric) culture to a more technologically advanced one. This meeting of two cultures could have been far messier than it turned out being, as it initially was when Cortés brutally subjugated and slaughtered the Aztecs in 1519. Up to fifteen hundred persons daily still visit the shrine that the apparition calling herself the Virgin Mary ordered built there to commemorate her. If the UFO phenomenon is tied in any way to a social control mechanism, then the Guadalupe apparitions are one of the best examples on record.

The Lady made Lucia and her companions promise to return to the same spot every month, where she would meet them again. They agreed to tell no one of their experience, but Jacinta immediately broke her promise and the three children became the subject of ridicule. Lucia's sister noted at the time that she "seemed unusually sad and didn't want to talk of the experience." For the next six months, however, the children kept their promise and returned to the site, except for their August 13 appointment—a local official had arrested them to put an end to their "nonsense." On that occasion, phenomena were observed by other witnesses, who by that time numbered eighteen thousand people. One witness swore to a canonical inquiry that he saw "a luminous globe spinning through the clouds." Many people tried to catch falling flower petals that disintegrated in their hands or before touching the ground, and saw "angel hair" descend at the site (the unknown substance sometimes encountered in the atmosphere around UFOs). A clap of thunder and a bright flash preceded the appearance of a cloudlike apparition over the tree that was the usual perch of the Lady, and colorful irradiations of the clouds occurred. Such phenomena manifested at all arrivals and departures of the apparition.

When the children were released six days later, the phenomena repeated, as if having waited for them. Typical of all encounters was the appearance of the Lady to Lucia alone (Jacinta could see and hear her and Francisco could only see her, but neither attempted any conversation), though many witnessed the formation of a spherical cloud over the tree, and evidence of the topmost branches having supported some great weight was seen by everyone who looked. Lucia and the children would look in her direction and Lucia would kneel and listen to messages she later reported, which Francisco and Jacinta—and often many others in the crowd—heard only as a slight buzzing sound like the "buzzing of a bee" or "a mosquito in an empty bottle." At the apparition's departure, Lucia would kneel, "pale as death," suddenly cry out in terror, "Our Lady!" and then the children would look off to the east and point, Lucia saying, "Look, there she goes!" and finally, "There, now we can't see her anymore. She has gone back into heaven, the doors are shut!" The sound reported to accompany the Lady's departure was "rather like a rocket, a long way off, as it goes up." A priest at the next-to-last Fátima appearance was shaken by its departure straight toward the sun, saying that "it was a heavenly vehicle that carried the Mother of God from her throne above to this forbidden wasteland."

Two days of rain preceded the final appearance, the clouds parting and the rain stopping to reveal a brilliantly silver disk, "a weird disk that turns rapidly on its own axis and casts off beams of colored light in all directions." As opposed to previous reports of the apparition coming from a globe, this time it was recorded as a flat disk. It stopped spinning and "plunged downward in zig-zag fashion toward the earth and the horrified spectators," the motion frequently associated with landing UFOs. It was perceived by the crowd as being the sun itself, falling out of the sky. No one in the crowd of seventy thousand was unaffected, all falling to the ground in fear and most praying, believing they were about to die. Finally the disk reversed direction and sped back off into the sky, the real sun emerging, and everyone's clothes were discovered to have been dried by the heat that had come from the descending disk. Vallée makes special note of the testimony of two witnesses who looked directly at the disk with binoculars and saw "a ladder and two beings."

During the six-month course of the apparitions, a great many healings, conversions, and the like were reported, typical of a Marian apparition cycle—the term given to appearances of the "Virgin Mary." Messages were imparted and prophecies made, also typical.

Almost sixty years earlier, on February 11, 1858, illiterate, fourteen-year-old Bernadette Soubirous had her first encounter with "the Lady." She was gathering firewood in Lourdes and heard "a great noise, like the sound of a storm." Seeing no sign of disturbance whatsoever, she returned to her chores. Then, hearing it again, she looked up and "lost all power of speech and thought." A golden-colored cloud was approaching from a nearby grotto, to rest on top of a bush. A beautiful lady appeared there, and Bernadette found herself suddenly unafraid but also completely dazed and unsure who or where she was. She tried to cross herself and found that she couldn't—her arm was paralyzed—until the lady saw what she was trying to do and crossed herself first. Each morning from February 18 to March 4, Bernadette returned to the grotto at seven, as per the Lady's instructions, each time acquiring more of a crowd of onlookers. The only one able to see or hear the Lady, Bernadette said she was all in white and was the Mother of Angels; only late in the series of apparitions did the vision name herself as "the Immaculate Conception," which was an established dogma of the Church for four years at that time, though Bernadette may not have known that. (Church dogmas were priestly affairs, not commonly known among peasants.)

True to the loose pattern of UFO abductees, recipients of Martian visitations tend to be just any average layperson on the street. The various children at Fátima who encountered "the angel" or "the Lady" were simple peasant children; Bernadette was one more face in the anonymous peasant crowd, with nothing to distinguish her from any other young girl; the Indian known as Juan Diego, at Guadalupe (actually Tepeyac, Mexico), was a fifty-seven-year-old widower, also a peasant, to whom the lady identifying herself as the Virgin Mary said, "Listen, little son. There are many I could send. But you are the one I have chosen for this task." In every instance, the visitant serves more or less an ambassadorial function, and in virtually every instance they are persecuted, ridiculed, and harassed. This is as true for Marian visitants as it is for UFO contactees/abductees. Juan Diego, atypically, was quickly accepted and little ridiculed in his role.

Bernadette Soubirous, like Lucia dos Santos and the other Fátima children, was threatened by authorities, laughed at and despised by many; Lucia had even been beaten by her mother until she was black and blue, and treated with derisive scorn. To some extent, "the Lady" seems to intend this to happen. Like the Fairy Folk of old, or more modern occult initiators, she made requests of Bernadette that were seemingly designed to make her look foolish or mad. At one point, in front of the crowd, she was instructed to wash herself in a nonexistent spring, and Bernadette did so in the dirt at the spot indicated, finding just enough water to smear her face with mud. Shortly after, water ran at the spot, and slight digging revealed a natural spring beneath the surface. It was these waters that proved to have miraculous healing powers, attested to then and now.

Bernadette's encounters continued irregularly after the appointed fortnight of meetings, and the authorities persecuted her with increasing vigor. Apparent in the historical accounts is a tremendous amount of bourgeois contempt for her lower-class upbringing, especially by the police commissioner, Jean Dominique Jacomet, who actually referred to her and her family as "miserable," "disgusting," and "vile." Such attitudes and persecutions are exhibited toward today's UFO witnesses, for at least one of the same stated reasons: fear of such occurrences achieving cult status, threatening the status quo. The Church no less than the secular authorities were as threatened by such visionaries as Bernadette and Lucia as they had been by Joan of Arc centuries before: so long as any common peasant can find themselves in direct contact with supernatural powers, of what importance is the Church as an intermediary? The eventual inclusion of such occurrences in the official canon may be more a product of the Church gaining belated legitimacy off a cult experience, in anticipation of its potential rivalry, than of an actual belief in heavenly visitation or the sanctity of its recipients.

Perhaps this is an effect desired by the apparitions. The Lady asked Bernadette to "kiss the ground for sinners," about which Stephen Breen commented, "They were setting an example of prayer and humility which could save Europe if applied to the social problems of the time, which, after all, are only a collection of personal problems, in the final analysis." Vallée brings up this quote in his research, and adds, ". . . the point made here is the illustration of a mechanism through which phenomena such as UFO sightings and contacts with paranormal entities *can play a role far beyond their local impact.*" Among that "collection of personal problems" Breen refers to is class snobbery. The entity contacting Bernadette Soubirous would likely have known exactly what sort of effect thrusting her in the public spotlight would have. In other words, part of the purpose of a religious visitation or a UFO encounter—which might be the same thing—may well be to make the contactee an object lesson for those around them, partly as an ambassador and partly as the mirror or stage upon which all observers find themselves reflected.

In 1968, an analyst for the NSA put together a paper called "UFO Hypothesis and Survival Questions," dealing in part with the ambassadorial liaison aspect. It concluded that UFOs may well be related to "Intraterrestrial Intelligence," an undefined phrase with connotations such as those presently being discussed here. "Serious survival implications" were decided to be at stake should the public ever acknowledge UFOs as the technological product of a superior civilization. The stated belief was that, by historical example, technologically superior civilizations "absorb" lesser ones, causing the "less virile culture [to] most often suffer a tragic loss of identity." The paper's author cites Japan as one good example of a "technologically and/or culturally inferior" nation that survived such an encounter, "equal[izing] the differences between them and their adversaries," betraying an attitude that the Intelligence behind the UFO phenomenon was officially considered to be necessarily adversarial—a curious stance, given their lack of hostility, perhaps referring to the military sabotage and cattle mutilations. The analyst's conclusion as to why Japan survived the sudden culture shock after WWII involved national solidarity of opinion concerning the other power, acceptance of their differences and eagerness to learn from them via "highly controlled and limited intercourse with the other side," and rapidly adapting the other side's best cultural advantages to their own. "This often involves sending selected groups and individuals to the other's country to become one of his kind, or even to help him in his wars against other adversaries," the analyst added.

Remarking on the "serious survival implications," Victor Marchetti stated that he felt world intelligence agencies overreact to perceived potential threats to economy more than safety, worrying most about "retain[ing] institutional control over their respective populations . . . Such extreme conclusions are not necessarily valid, but probably accurately reflect the fears of the 'ruling classes' of the major nations, whose leaders (particularly those in the intelligence business) have always advocated excessive governmental secrecy as being necessary to preserve 'national security.'" This echoes the comment given Jacques Vallée by the French Air Force about "society working just fine the way it is," and not "encouraging all this saucer business." Philip Klass expressed it in deliberately more alarming terms, saying at the 1994 CSICOP conference in Seattle that "the consequences [of UFO beliefs] will be as serious as Jonestown, and Waco, Texas," which certainly the intelligence agencies would like everyone to believe.

The author of the NSA paper sums up by stating that mankind's attitude to the UFO question has been too leisurely for its potential seriousness, but seems to think that any threat involving them comes from ourselves. He offers the example of chimpanzees brought up in captivity, for whom sex becomes a daily preoccupation instead of the seasonal madness they experience in the wild; if released, these animals would soon die, because they have not been socialized into proper behavior for their specie, and their immune systems can no longer resist the diseases to which their bodies are naturally subject. "Do the captivity characteristics of modern civilization," the author asks, "cause a similar lessening of man's adaptive capability, of his health, of his ability to recognize reality, of his ability to survive? Perhaps the UFO question might even make man undertake studies which could enable him to construct a society which is most conducive to developing a completely *human* being, healthy in all respects of mind and body, and, most important, able to recognize and adapt to real environmental situations." In other words, he seems to be saying, perhaps we could learn something from them—not about aliens, but about *humans.* And that bespeaks a certain belief about the occupants of the craft: what "aliens" could teach man about man? Especially about man's *civilization,* which in the present day the author overtly compares to "unhealthy captivity"?

This paper was one of only two—out of a reluctantly admitted 279 on file—released by the NSA under the Freedom of Information Act. The other was a short and heavily censored paper citing Vallée's psychological evaluation of "high strangeness" in witnesses, discussing his opinion that amnesia is a natural result of UFO encounters owing to the traumatic nature of the contact. Vallée omits mention of the possibility of additional technological or hypnotic influences being involved, but these may have been edited out.

It has sometimes been suggested that, in a "first contact" scenario, we would observe essentially what we are observing in the UFO phenomenon. First would be probes from the other Intelligence to gain relative technological and sociological standing, then the testing of opposing weaponry and/or a feeling out of relative receptivity. A welcome reception failing to be present, a series of mass sightings, followed by lengthy disappearances, and interspersed periodically with isolated individually arranged sightings would tantalize the populace for inevitable contact in a gradual fashion. And during this process, the careful—or perhaps merely advantageous—selection of individual locals for clandestine and repeat contacts would create a network of ready ambassadors for the eventual open meeting between the two civilizations.

Vallée has often commented in his work on the social control aspect of UFOs, citing a pattern in their appearances indicative of a behavioral learning process. In *Forbidden Science,* he writes: "A new computer analysis of historical trends, compiled in the mid-seventies, led me to plot a striking graph of 'waves' of activity that was anything but periodic. Fred Beckman and Dr. Price-Williams (of UCLA) pointed out that it resembled a schedule of reinforcement typical of a learning or training process: the phenomenon was more akin to a control system than to an exploratory task force of alien travelers." Earlier, in *Dimensions,* he observed, ". . . certain ways of reinforcing behavior lead to better learning than others. If the training is too even and monotonous the subject may stop in its development or even return to an earlier state. *The best schedule of reinforcement is one that combines periodicity with unpredictability.* Learning is then slow but continuous. It leads to the highest level of adaptation. And it is irreversible." He states that it is entirely possible we may never meet our teachers. It could instead be suggested that perhaps we are just now starting to meet them, and that the lengthy learning process has been the history of our civilization, preparing us for precisely that meeting. Fátima and Lourdes may well have been ongoing acts in a drama that must eventually conclude. In the meantime, as religion has always served man when at its best, it has kept us essentially well regulated, and perhaps relatively protected as well.

There are other famous occurrences connecting religion with UFOs, generally indicative of cautious or failed attempts at establishing or continuing a liaison with mankind. Early in the ninth century, a bishop named Agobard saved the lives of four men and women who claimed to have been abducted by the Sylphs of the air to their wonderful sky city, Magonia, where they were shown many marvelous things; upon their return, the populace wanted to stone them as witches, until Agobard convinced them the witnesses were insane and so deserving of compassion. The biblical *cherubim,* meaning "full of knowledge," were called by the Hebrews *Sadaim,* with the same meaning, and the Greeks transposed the letters into *Daimonas,* from which we derive the word "demons." As intermediaries with heaven—believed to be spirits inhabiting the air—they transmitted heavenly wisdom to chosen individuals. The Muslim *jinn* (more familiar to us as "genies") are equivalent creatures, as are Norse and Celtic trolls, elves, kobolds and other "little people," many of which are described in terms suspiciously like those of UFO occupants. Aimé Michel discovered a great many prehistoric cave drawings with shapes similar to reported flying saucers, sometimes even depicted in flight. Some of them show occupants. One famous Paleolithic cave drawing in the Pech-Merle shows what looks very much to be a landed UFO with what is now recognized as a typical Gray standing beside it—the occupant is shot through with arrows or spears.

Some reports seem to signify a desire on the part of UFO occupants to stimulate not only our physical development in reproduction, but our intellectual development as well. In 1896 and 1897—the latter being the same year a mysterious craft made off with Alexander Hamilton's cow—several hundred reports were made all across the United States of a famous airship. It apparently had aerofoil wings and some kind of what we would call today a turbofoil propellor, as well as several side attachments of unspecified purpose. The ship was about sixty feet long, cigar-shaped and metallic, and had extremely powerful searchlights brighter than any electrical light, calling to mind the ghost rocket appearances in the 1930s. In common with modern UFOs, the airship would cruise over onlooking crowds' heads, and then suddenly shoot off and out of sight faster than a bullet. Its flight attributes were plainly superior even to our own aircraft a century later, yet by appearance it looked not too far beyond what might have been built in its own day and age . . . if airplanes had then existed. Could someone have been trying to plant ideas in mankind's collective head? If it weren't for the phenomenal sudden propulsion of the mysterious airship, it could have been a prototype experimental craft built by some Jules Verne with tremendous genius and technological resources.

The airship's occupants were sometimes encountered on the ground by individual witnesses, who found them speaking English and being polite, dressed as any other men would dress. Sometimes they asked for water or equipment, sometimes they offered onlookers rides, other times they refused requests for rides but promised to come back in the future to take the witnesses on a trip. In one instance an occupant was said to be wearing a sailor suit, and another was bearded and quite debonair. Other equally everyday men and women were stated to be among them. More than once the airship was seen to be dragging an anchor, attested to by a great many people. In one of those cases, the anchor snagged and was cut loose by the aforementioned man in the sailor suit, who climbed down a rope to accomplish his task. The anchor was kept and put in a blacksmith's shop.

The anchor occurrence is recorded happening twice before in the year 1211, once in Ireland and another time in England. The latter is found in Gervase of Tilbury's *Otis Imperialia.* Both cases occurred in a churchyard, the Irish one during mass. Both concerned strange "cloudships." In England, the occupant climbed down a rope and cut the anchor loose (as in 1897) where it had snagged in a mound of stones. The Irish incident was witnessed by the entire congregation, who saw several men and women floating in the air around the ship as if it were water, one of them swimming down to cut loose the anchor caught in the church door flukes. As in the religious events mentioned earlier in this chapter, all of these airship appearances—mediaeval or modern—seem to be, more than anything, theatrically contrived.

Without overtly stating the thesis himself, Vallée seems to make the same implication in *Anatomy of a Phenomenon*—that our intellects have been stimulated for an educational purpose—interestingly enough, using the primary example of *robots:* " . . . *the 'dead' period of UFO activity (1914–1946) has been one of the richest in science-fiction stories of all kinds,* and has seen the growing interest of the motion-picture industry in fantastic and 'horror' tales which might have resulted in an increasing number of hoaxes and hallucinations, and even in UFO waves, if the 'psychological' theory of UFOs were correct. As early as 1916, Otto Ripert's [*sic*] film *Homonculus* was about the creation of an artificial man by a mad scientist. In 1914 and 1920, the German industry produced two films on the subject of the 'Golem' (Paul Wegener and Henrik Galeen). In 1924 the film *Orlac's Hands* was made, after a novel by Maurice Renard. In 1926 Fritz Lang created *Metropolis,* and we should not forget that 1920 saw the introduction of the word 'robot,' with a play by Karel Capek, *Rossum's Universal Robots (R.U.R.).* In 1928, Fritz Lang did *The Woman in the Moon (Die Frau im Mond).* The first 'trip to the moon' had been made by the French pioneer Melies in 1902, and the celebrated series of Frankenstein and John Carter of Mars were created during this period." Vallée also notes that Arthur Koestler's 1933 play, *Twilight Bar,* has the first "blackout caused by a UFO" in drama or literature. Abductors identical to UFO occupants were first seen in 1949 in Jean Cocteau's *Orphee,* taking the title hero to the Underworld.

Probably the most famous pulp writer in this time period (specifically the 1930s) was H. P. Lovecraft, one of the earliest of a number of writers whose work bears an eerily prescient correspondence with UFO abduction phenomena. Almost all of Lovecraft's stories centered on ancient gods from outer space that made man in antiquity for their own purposes, leaving their megalithic cities behind, occasionally returning to hybridize with unfortunate females (or males) on Earth in preparation for their return. These stories have since been collectively called the "Cthulhu Mythos," after the chief god of Lovecraft's fictional pantheon.

Lovecraft wrote that he was repeatedly visited at night by strange humanoid demons, the physical reality of which he seemed to believe in, according to biographer L. Sprague de Camp (parenthetical inclusions and emphases Lovecraft's own): "When I was 6 or 7 I used to be tormented constantly with a peculiar type of recurrent nightmare in which a monstrous race of entities (called by me 'Night-Gaunts'—I don't know where I got hold of the name) used to snatch me up by the stomach (bad digestion?) & carry me off through infinite leagues of black air over the towers of dead and horrible cities. They would finally get me into a grey void where I could see the needle-like pinnacles of enormous mountains miles below. Then they would let me drop—& as I gained momentum in my Icarus-like plunge I would start awake in such a panic that I hated to think of sleeping again. The 'night-gaunts' were black, lean, rubbery things with horns, barbed tails, bat-wings, *and no faces at all.*" The falling and starting awake are found in numerous abduction accounts, not published until David Jacobs' *Secret Life* in 1992, and Lovecraft's humanoid descriptions—barring the barbed tails and possibly the bat wings—are similar to those of UFO abductors. Lovecraft thought he must have derived the memory of their appearance from the drawings of Gustave Dore, insisting that they "[came] in flocks" and never spoke with him (they "had no voices"), only "tickling" his stomach for a while before dropping him back in bed. It should be noted that Lovecraft died prematurely, of stomach cancer.

Robots are no strangers to human history. "We know from classical authors that the Egyptians possessed the most wonderful skill in the manufacture of automata," notes famous turn of the century mythologist Lewis Spence. Oracle statues were famous for moving and speaking. A papyrus in the British Museum describes a moving oracle-god discovering the identity of a thief who stole from Amenemwia's storehouse. The dispute over the tomb of a workman named Amenemope, in the time of Ramses III, is recorded both on a piece of pottery in the British Museum and a papyrus in the Berlin Museum as having been settled by an oracle statue's personal writing of the verdict. An illustrated papyrus in the Brooklyn Museum clearly denotes a statue of Amon-Ra moving toward its suppliant priest, Harsiese, under its own power. The animated broomsticks in "The Sorceror's Apprentice," made popular in *Fantasia,* actually come from the Egyptian story of Eucrates (related by Lucian), who animated pestles to do his work and could not make them stop.

Tibet's *Epic of Gesar of Ling,* Central Asia's *Iliad, Ramayana,* or *Aeneid,* refers to its title god-hero employing "enchanted dolls" in his adventures. Diodorus Siculus' *Biblioteca Historica* records Queen Semiramis' military usage of mechanical elephants against Strabrobates, so real that they fooled actual elephants into attempting copulation with them. John Lloyd Stephens and Frederick Catherwood wrote as recently as 1840 that Uxmal's Pyramid of the Dwarf, or House of the Magician (in Mexico's Yucatán peninsula), was believed by local Indians to be haunted by "animated" ornaments that walked at night, which they constantly disfigured with their machetes in an attempt to "quiet their potentially wandering spirits." Pope Sylvester II was reputed to have built a mechanical head "under certain stellar and planetary aspects," which answered simple questions. Albertus Magnus claimed to have built mechanical men, by alchemical (for which, read "scientific") precepts. Eighteenth-century Germany was world famous for its realistic character robots, capable of playing chess or musical instruments, some even executing fairly complicated dance maneuvers; Mary Shelley was likely exposed to them in her travels, inspiring *Frankenstein.* The golem of legend was an entirely animated figure performing its maker's will.

The lame Hephaestus was said to have made two realistic facsimiles of human females out of gold to assist him in walking. He also made the bronze bull-man, Talos, who patrolled Crete thrice daily protecting the treasures of King Minos, clutching interlopers to his breast and leaping with them into the fire. Talos is connected to the legend of the Minotaur, graphically memorialized in modern cinema by Ray Harryhausen in *Jason and the Argonauts* and *Sinbad and the Eye of the Tiger.*

Zecharia Sitchin compares the UFO occupants he labels as robots to a great many figurines found throughout the Middle East, especially from ancient Ur, the biblical birthplace of Abraham. They are "sky gods," though no one knows exactly what they are supposed to be, and are dated at approximately 3,500 BC. They are humanoid in shape, but not human. They are extremely slender and smooth, with tall, domed heads and huge, slanting eyes, vaguely human faces, and circular outcroppings of indiscernible function on their shoulders. And they hold a rod, just as so many UFO occupants are reported to possess. Another example of such a rod, connected both to UFOs and ancient history, comes from California's Paiute Indians. They claim an ancient, superior civilization preceded their own—the *Hav-musuvs*—who flew in silvery sky canoes, and carried "a small tube that could be held in one hand and would stun their enemies, producing lasting paralysis and a feeling similar to a shower of cactus needles," as Vallée writes.

And in the heart of Europe, where civil war now rages and a new, ongoing series of Marian apparitions has been occurring since 1981, is evidence of a culture and civilization which the late Marija Gimbutas believed predated that of Knossos. The Bosnia region of the former Yugoslavia sports hundreds of weird masks, called Vinca masks after the area in which they were first found, most often fashioned out of black clay. Earlier representations of the same style are found in Cucuteni art, throughout the western Ukraine and eastern Romania. "To us they appear unfamiliar, even ugly," Gimbutas comments in *The Goddesses and Gods of Old Europe—Myths and Cult Images,* "presenting an uncomfortably non-human visage suggestive of a mask." That they are clearly intended to portray sky gods is indicated by the frequent inscription on their foreheads of the double meander symbol for "the cosmic waters," associated with the virtually indistinguishable great bird and snake goddesses. This symbol is supposed to represent "two snakes with their heads meeting but not touching," and closely resembles a swastika, which—in a potential UFO connection—is found "also incised upon discs." These same symbols are found in other supposedly diverse ancient cultures, examples being swastikas in Tibet, India, and the Americas, and double snakes in the Greek staff of Hermes. Vinca masks are tall, smooth, and conical, like the figurines found in Ur, or else triangular, pentagonal, or diamond shaped. In any event, they are highly stylized and do not look human. "Was it the sculptor's intention to portray on the mask an animal or half-animal, half-human creature?" Gimbutas asks. "Though we cannot know for certain, we feel that the creature is endowed with an awe-inspiring power, the very essence of the significance of the mask. . . ." They have "Almond- or egg-shaped slanted eyes," also described as "large, elliptical-shaped eyes," or "enormous semicircular eyes." In most cases they have only small bumps for noses, and in all but the earliest representations they have *no mouths;* in those early cases where mouths are shown, they are mere slits. This description matches almost word for word the majority of UFO occupant reports, especially those of the Grays. The Vinca masks are also physically very similar to the Ur figurines, but date much further back, as far as approximately 6,000 BC.

Another creature closely matching such a description appears on an ancient cave wall near Ferghana in Uzbekistan, on the Sino-Russian border. Before ceding the territory back to the Chinese, Russian anthropologists meticulously reproduced the petroglyphic figures painted on the wall. There appears to be a very human man in a spacesuit, a clear visor in front of his face, and with much more clarity off to the side two other figures: one is a disk-shaped object, aloft, with flamelike rocket exhaust shooting out the direct center of its underside; the other is a diminutive humanoid, suited or metallic in appearance, with huge round eyes, a boxlike object on its chest, and two antennae on top of its head. *Pravda Vostoka* reported it as looking like "a man wearing an air-tight helmet with two antennae and on his back some sort of contraption for flight." A reproduction can be seen in the film version of *Chariots of the Gods.* Nor is this the only instance of UFO symbolism in religious paintings of that period, various occurrences being widely scattered. One excellent example, reproduced in the photo section of George C. Andrews' *Extra-Terrestrials Among Us,* is a fifteenth-century fresco from Greece's Mount Athos Monastery, depicting the dictation of the Apocalypse to a young disciple by St. John. Haloes surround both their heads, and classic UFO symbols are behind them: a sphere emitting rays converges directly on John's head, and he turns to see it; and what looks exactly like the famous disk-shaped flying saucer—also emitting a beam—is in the air behind the younger man.

From the Middle Ages we have entire treatises, such as Ludovico Maria Sinistrari's *Demoniality,* discussing creatures called incubi and succubi (or succubae). These were spirits that changed their sex from female (succubus) to male (incubus), in order to first obtain the seed of man, then transplant it to the womb of a woman, obviously for the purpose of reproduction. They visited their prey at night, while the targeted men and women were asleep. Given the superstitious religious climate of the time, all things were understood only within a rigid and narrow preconception of the universe, and any phenomena not immediately seen to be inside those operating parameters were either summarily rejected or else attributed automatically to the devil. As with the sylphs and their human guests in Magonia, edicts and laws were passed against any sort of congress with these unearthly beings, supposing such contacts to be voluntary. They may simply have been honestly reported and poorly understood phenomena, just as they are now, with the Church of that age showing no worse response than our present church of Science. Author Howard Blum reports that in contemporary Elmwood, Wisconsin, there have been so many UFO sightings that the city counsel voted on whether or not it was legal for them to land, and decided by one vote that it was, demonstrating the same assumption shown in the Middle Ages that we have any say in the matter.

Peter Kolosimo writes that eminent Japanese archaeologist and historian Professor Komatsu Kitamura defended a *Mainichi Graphic* (a serious weekly magazine) article in which he discussed whether or not Japan might have been the recipient of visitations from space until sometime around 3,000 BC. Kitamura wrote, "I was led to this hypothesis in the first instance by a print illustrating an old work on the history of the legendary Kappas or 'men of the cane-brake' who are said to have inhabited Japan in the Heian period (ninth to eleventh century AD). They are described in the old text as web-footed bipeds with three hooked fingers on each hand, the center digit being much longer than the others. Their skin is brown, smooth, silky and lucent; their heads are elongated, they have large ears and strange eyes of triangular shape. According to all reports, they wear a curious kind of hat 'with four needles in it'; their nose is like a proboscis and is connected to a casket-shaped hump on their backs. The old writers add that they could move with equal rapidity by land and sea." Kitamura was struck by their resemblance to modern naval frogmen. They could also be robots. The hump on the back is noteworthy in recalling Koko Pilau, as is the shape of the head and eyes. The long middle finger has been reported in several abductions, and we have noticed at least one UFO occupant with "flipper feet" and a description not unlike Kitamura's. "As for the four needles," concluded Kitamura, "I am tempted to believe that they were radio antennae."

In Mongolia, shamans claim to be able to communicate with "a nightmare world of spirits ... black, hunchbacked, with long claws [that] have the power to cast their skin and assume human form. Thus transformed, they go about unrecognized; but when clad in their 'dark skin,' they are said to be invisible and to sail or fly in great shells, over the waters or through the clouds, 'summoning the dead.' These shells are mentioned in the *Ghal Sudur* ('Book of Fire'). . . ."

Tibetans and American Indians both refer to "shining beings" they encounter in isolated spaces during secret religious rituals. Little description is ever given of them, except that they are humanoid and lit from within. They guard sacred sites on Earth, "holding them in trust for a future of wonders," and are bearers of great wisdom. W. Y. Evans-Wentz, a great scholar and student of world folklore, believes these beings have direct counterparts in the Celtic fairy faith. Some abductees, including Betty Andreasson, have reported such beings.

Science fiction writer Philip K. Dick wrote letters at great length beginning in February of 1978 referring to encounters with just such a shining being he was quite sure that he had experienced, which sound like what we now recognize as abductions. He wrote half a million words on these incidents over a four-year period before his death in 1982. Vallée records some of them in his book *Revelations.* Dick found himself kept awake at night by "violent phosphene activity . . . within my head it communicated with me in the form of a computer-like or AI [Artificial Intelligence]-system-like voice, quite different from any human voice, neither male nor female, and a very beautiful sound it was, the most beautiful sound I ever heard . . . the imposition—that is the right word—the imposition of another human personality unto mine produced startling modifications in my behavior . . . Some living, highly intelligent entity manifested itself inside me and around me, but what it was, what its purpose was, where it came from . . . each theory leaves some datum unexplained . . . and *I know this is not going to change.* I have the impression that a master gameplayer and magician and trickster is involved." Dick's insistence that it was both another *human* personality, and that it had a *computerlike* voice, supports the theories being presented here. If the shining being that "imposed" itself was both a robot and an emissary from a human source, this makes perfect sense.

Philip K. Dick, like Lovecraft, was a very influential writer, so much so that an annual award is given in his name. His stories were made into the movies *Blade Runner* and *Total Recall,* featuring accurate UFOlogical elements. That the boom of science fiction (especially robots and space travel) as a genre in this century could have resulted from ideas "planted" in our minds in just the manner Dick describes is a thesis subtly suggested by Jacques Vallée and more explicitly being addressed in this book.

But most interesting of all in this cavalcade of potential historical robot-beings is the creature called *abit,* or *Bebait,* from ancient Egypt. He is referred to in Chapters 76 and 104 of the Book of the Dead, the actual name of which is "The Book of Coming Forth by Day," which might have entirely different implications. His name means "Mantis"—i.e., the praying mantis, like Koko Pilau and the "ant people" of other tribes which fit the same description and functions. Foremost Egyptologist E. A. Wallis Budge said, "This insect was greatly honored in Egypt and Nubia, and the Greeks attributed to it supernatural powers. . . ." In Chapter 76, the mantis brings the deceased into heaven, where the deceased addresses the gods: "I have come into the House of the King by means of the mantis which led me hither. Homage to thee, O thou who fliest into heaven, and dost shine upon the son of the white crown, and dost protect the white crown, let me have my existence with thee! I have gathered together the great god(s), I am mighty, I have made my way and I have travelled along thereon." In Chapter 104, two different vignettes are shown in different recensions: one has the deceased seated between two "great gods" who are seated on their thrones; the other has the deceased "seated on a low pedestal before three gods." The deceased is in the judgment hall, declaring his purity and the right to take his place among the gods: "I sit among the great gods, and I have made a way for myself through the house of the *Seheptet* boat; and behold, the mantis hath brought me to see the great gods who dwell in the underworld, and I shall be triumphant before them, for I am pure."

There are a great many connections in the abduction phenomenon with ancient Egypt. We have already encountered Betty Andreasson's remarkable testimony, and that of several abductees such as Herbert Schirmer and Betty Hill who reported seeing what they thought were Egyptian hieroglyphics or some kind of Japanese or Sanskrit-like writing. In addition, everyone who saw the Roswell crash wreckage up close described something resembling either Egyptian or Japanese symbols on pieces of it, and Antonio Boas reported something of the sort as well.

A tremendous number of more recent abductees have been making exactly the same sort of claims, some with much more detail. Dr. John E. Mack, the Pulitzer Prize-winning Harvard psychiatrist, has discovered many of these Egyptian references in his case studies. Like Betty Andreasson's claims, they are often confusing, the abductee being unaware as to whether what they are being shown are memories from some past life, or another in a number of screened images designed somehow to instruct them. Shown "nature images," for instance, one abductee noted, "like okay, great. I've seen this on T.V. It's going to the desert. It's going to be pyramids. I'm seeing more Egyptian, ancient things, like hieroglyphics and pictures, pictures of pharaohs and things . . . this makes sense to me . . . This is not a trick. This is like useful information. This is not them pulling a bunch of shit like everything else." The stated answer commonly given to abductees as to why they are being shown these scenes from ancient Egypt is "to make you understand, to comprehend the implications. To put you in the right frame of mind." Considering the tremendous time and trouble being gone to, we must presume the abductors are trying to enlighten us to some connection.

The accuracy of these viewed images, on later analysis, is mixed. Some could be known from casual reading, such as the relative size of tomb paintings, but other details such as specific paint mixtures involved and exact dress for obscure rituals are remarkable for an average person to know. Betty Andreasson's use of the worm instead of the more commonly known self-renewing bird in the Bennu bird/Phoenix myth is an example of such astonishing awareness. In other instances, details described are inaccurate, though in almost all of these cases the abductee prefaces their recollections with a disclaimer stating that they are themselves unsure of their knowledge. One woman called a Pharaoh "Amon-Ra," which is a god's name and could never in any way be used by a man, and she also described someone who could only be King Akhnaton as a Middle Kingdom Pharaoh, when actually he was New Kingdom. She admitted uncertainty in both cases, however, and in the latter instance simply might have been describing what she witnessed from her own limited comprehension. This same abductee knew details, down to colors and styles of dress and implements used, of a ritual to Anubis for the acquisition of eternal life. Not only is such knowledge not common, it goes beyond even being considered "rare." Very few books carry such information.

One of the most interesting facts coming from these testimonies is something the abductees do not themselves connect to

Egypt, but which has a connection nonetheless: Dr. Mack has noted that many abductees identify themselves as being one of the abductor-beings. He mentions "an increasing group of abductees that I have been encountering who have discovered that they have a dual identity as an alien (they do not use that word) and a human being." The parenthetical inclusion is Mack's own: *abductees do not tend to call their abductors "aliens."* "I have to go with him," says one abductee of the being who comes to fetch him, "because I'm—we're—linked in some way." Another talks about being "intimately involved [with them] . . . in cahoots . . . [a] double agent . . . working with them. I'm split. I lead this secret life, and the secret life is that I've spent a lot of time with them." This abductee claimed to actually be "one of them" and to be more comfortable in their presence than on Earth, having "a foot in both worlds." In one specific case, Mack relates, "The figure told [the abductee] 'it's me,' and that he has 'the power to make this thing [the figure], and I can't see how I do.'" E. A. Wallis Budge notes that the determinative given for an *ushabti* figure in identifying with "the deceased" Pharaoh in the Book of the Dead is identical: "The variants are of interest, and not the least remarkable are the last two words, 'I am thou' in which the figure makes itself identical with the deceased."

And what is an ushabti? *Ushabtiu* (plural) are animated, artificial figures in "the Afterlife." They can be made to look like anything, including the Pharaoh himself. They may be the mysterious "porters of Horus" in the Coffin Texts, which bring magic to "the deceased," telling him "what I should know and what I should forget," which is comparable to the training and amnesia aspects in UFO abductions. One ushabti in the image of Tut was in the King's burial arrangement, now displayed on the second floor of the Cairo Museum. By his time (the Late Kingdom) the figures—as well as everything else in Egyptian religious ritual—had become simply one more in a long line of little-understood ceremonial items. That late in Egyptian history, elaborate models of seafaring ships were buried with Pharaohs, to represent "the solar barque of millions of years," originally a curved vessel occupied by gods which ferried him to the *Tuat* (the Underworld) on his way to heaven. The solar barque as depicted in the Book of the Dead does not match the characteristics of a sea ship, quite possibly having once represented something else. In its earliest known history, Egypt had no such figures as the ushabtiu in its burial accoutrements, though the belief in them and the solar barque extend back to antiquity. It is not unreasonable to assume that there once was clear knowledge of what these were, and that in later years, removed from the source, the Egyptians' diminished understanding caused these items to be regarded with superstition. Considering their decline in architecture, astronomy, and medicine from the Old Kingdom on, this hypothesis is even likelier. It may also be noteworthy that depictions of the gods performing special embalming ceremonies around the funeral slab of the Pharaoh are reminiscent of paralyzed abductees on a similar slab, while medical procedures of an unknown nature are performed on them by their abductors. "Sleep" and "death" have often been compared, in all times and cultures.

Budge relates the following tale of the ushabtiu, in *From Fetish to God in Ancient Egypt:* "An official of Sa-Amen called Hor, the son of Paneshe, was also greatly learned in magic. He went into the temple of Hermopolis and having made offerings to Thoth that God appeared to him and told him where to find the great Book of Magic. The Ethiopian sorcerers had sent their sorceries to Egypt intending to spirit away Pharaoh to Ethiopia. But as Hor had bound amulets on Pharaoh the sorceries of Ethiopia were powerless to carry him off. When Hor heard this from Pharaoh he determined to do to the governor of Ethiopia what the governor had tried to do to Pharaoh. He had a large quantity of pure wax brought to him and made a model of a litter and models of four men to carry it. Then he recited spells over all these, and so endowed them with life, and he ordered them to go to the Sudan (Nehes), and to bring the Viceroy to the presence chamber of Pharaoh. When there they were to give the Viceroy a beating with sticks, five hundred strokes, and then to carry him back to the Sudan. All this was to be done in six hours. The wax figures set out by night with the litter and accompanied by the sorceries of Hor they traveled through the clouds straight to Ethiopia. They seized the Viceroy, brought him to Egypt, administered the five hundred strokes with sticks, and then carried him back to Ethiopia within the six hours. The following morning the Viceroy assembled his nobles, and showed them his back, and they saw the weals and wounds which the sticks had made on it, and seeing them, they uttered loud cries of horror. The Viceroy sent for his chief sorceror, who was also called Hor, and cursed him by Amen, the Bull of Meroe, and commanded him to save him from further disgrace and suffering at the hands of the Egyptian sorcerors. Hor promptly prepared amulets and bound them on the Viceroy and so protected him."

The prologue to this same story is given in Lewis Spence's *Myths and Legends of Ancient Egypt,* providing the one element of the story missing in Budge's version that makes it identical to modern UFO abductions: it states definitely that the abductee was as horrified to discover his body in its wounded state upon awakening as his nobles were. The abductee in this case is the same Pharaoh later protected by his magician's sorceries from further assault, the abduction and beating of the Ethiopian Viceroy being his act of revenge against him. Specifically, Spence recounts that, "wakening the next morning . . . he lay in great pain, his body sorely bruised. Bewildered, he asked his courtiers how such could have happened in Egypt. They, thinking some madness had fallen upon their king, and yet ashamed of their thoughts, spoke soothingly to him, and said that the great gods would heal his afflictions. But still they asked him the meaning of his strange words, and suddenly he remembered all that had happened to him and recounted it to his courtiers." In every particular, the Pharaoh's and Viceroy's abductions are the same as the UFOlogists' established model of a "bedroom visitation" or "bedroom abduction." Abductees in such an experience frequently awaken to discover marks on their bodies they have no idea the origin of, appropriately called UBMs—unidentified body markings. Eventually, the experience comes back to their conscious recollection. And the reaction of the courtiers, initially believing their Pharaoh mad, also is the same as that given today's UFO abductees.

Many clues to the UFO phenomenon seem to lead to ancient Egypt. There are indications in the mythical record that this prehistoric culture was not primitive, but actually quite advanced. Allusions to space travel are so pervasive as to be inescapable, and the "magic" the Egyptians speak of sounds more like what we recognize as technology. "Model men" that fly "on the clouds" and abduct given targets for specified procedures are a phenomenon that, if the evidence so far considered is all correct, we continue to experience as much today as when they wrote of it. Unfortunately, the subject of ancient astronauts has become as unpopular and ballyhooed as that of flying saucers, guaranteeing it no audience among status-conscious scientists and academicians. If there were only some proof that the Egyptians of prehistory were actually capable of space flight, we could ignore their objections and study the theory with freedom from any fear of ridicule.

In fact, such evidence does exist. Like all the rest we have been examining, it has been ignored since its discovery, which is all the more inexplicable since the most curious—and costly—of incidents have continually occurred in connection with it. Just what is that evidence, and where might it be? Perhaps an innocent comment by Ralph Blum concerning the sky above him on the night Charles Hickson and Calvin Parker were giving their testimony to the press in a Pascagoula courthouse contains a vital clue: "An airplane was coming in from the south, heading toward Mobile, and I could see its red and green winking lights. In the western sky, Venus was bright. There was Jupiter, much higher, and in the east, glowing reddish and large, was Mars."

7

Correlations

J ANINE AND I are now doing a study of the correlation between the frequency of sightings and the distance of planet Mars," Jacques Vallée wrote in his diary on November 25, 1961, "which comes closest to the earth every twenty-six months. The resulting curve is striking. Guérin tells us he had not expected such a clear-cut relationship." The following year, Jacques and Janine Vallée published their findings in the September 1962 issue of *Flying Saucer Review.* One year later, he showed trepidation about the findings in his journal entry of November 17: "I often hit theoretical snags, as I did in the correlation between the frequency of sightings and the distance of Mars." He also stated concern that he not inadvertently lead future researchers astray with mistaken findings at his early stage of investigation.

In 1965, in his first published book on the subject of UFOs, *Anatomy of a Phenomenon,* he had rethought his position once again, stating, "We feel that our documents for the period between 1870 and 1914 are sufficient to justify an attempt to correlate UFO activity with the oppositions of Mars. Correlation of these limited data has so far given negative results . . . One should use extreme caution in interpreting in any direction, the existence or absence of correlations such as these." An accompanying table showed the seven peak UFO waves from 1881 to 1913. One of those waves was exactly one year distant from the best opposition; one was exactly at best opposition; one was five months past, two were four months from best opposition (one preceding and one following); one was only two months past the opposition; and the remaining one (1905) was apparently invalidated by the year's wave remaining consistently high throughout, though Vallée made no comment one way or the other about it. Despite his "negative results," Vallée, with his wife, Janine, was soon to reevaluate his position once more, coming to different conclusions.

Admitting for the moment that Vallée's findings at the time were not solidly "positive," two things about them must still be noticed. One is that five of the seven charts have Mars either at best opposition to Earth, or within one-third of that distance (four months in either direction is approximately a third or less the optimum Mars-Earth distance); the other is that Vallée thought there might be any correlation at all. On what "documents for the period" might he have been basing his assumption that there could be such a correlation?

Among the multitude of sightings made during the time period (and shortly before and after) in Vallée's table were the following: A "long train of clouds" was sighted by two different astronomers, Sir Norman Lockyer and a man named Sacchi, four days apart, on the Martian surface in 1862. On two different occasions—October 24, 1864, and January 3, 1865—red lights were seen on opposite sides of Mars. Then the *Journal of the British Association* published that on June 17, 1873, a much more impressive and frightening display was witnessed officially in England by a Dr. Sage, who saw a luminous object issuing from Mars which arrived in the skies of Austria-Hungary, in the startling space of five seconds, then exploded. Sage commented, "It seemed as if Mars were breaking up under the force of the impulsion of this object, and dividing into two parts. The concussion of the firing was sharp." On June 10, 1892, beams as if from a searchlight were projected from Mars to Earth, a phenomenon that was witnessed again in 1928 and the winter of 1936 by French astronomers and confirmed by Professor Robert Damion, an astronomer and editor of a then-popular scientific journal. And on August 3, 1892, witnesses in Manchester and Loughborough, England, saw rapid flashes of light on Mars that were not aurorae. At least from this period through 1936, occasional "flaming up" of a "queer bluish light" was noticed on the Martian surface, recurring at regular intervals for up to forty seconds. Brilliant, clearly defined bright spots of temporary duration, in locations of obviously nonrandom distribution, were reported by astronomers to be moving or changing color in 1890, 1892, 1894, 1900, 1911, 1924, 1937, 1952, 1954, 1967, and 1971. Transient, intensely dark spots were witnessed on the planet's surface in 1925, 1952, and 1954.

On March 9, 1901, the *Colorado Springs Gazette* reported that Nikola Tesla believed he was picking up intelligent radio signals from Mars, something he considered true for some time before he admitted to it, due to fear of ridicule. Ridicule was exactly what he got, until May 18, 1902, when Lord Kelvin publicly announced that he agreed with Tesla and made worldwide front-page news. The critics did not necessarily believe either man was right, but Kelvin's vocal support did silence them. The *New York Tribune* of September 2, 1921, stated that Dr. Frederick H. Miller had attempted communication with Mars for several weeks from his giant wireless station in Omaha, but had given up for lack of success; the report went on to say, however, that the owner of Marconi Wireless Telegraph Company, Ltd., "believed he had intercepted messages from Mars during the recent atmospheric experiments with wireless on board his yacht *Electra* in the Mediterranean." What had impressed Signor Marconi was that the signals received were 150,000 meters, when the maximum wavelength of that time was 14,000.

On June 30, 1908, an atomic explosion occurred over the Tunguska region of Siberia that science writer and science fiction author Alexander Kazantsev would say in the early 1960s might have been caused by a crashing spaceship which he speculated could have come from Mars. Not one to mince words, Kazantsev is on record as saying, "Highly advanced creatures from Mars have visited the Earth many times until today." The Irkutsk newspaper of the time, *Sibir,* recorded that peasants had seen, high above the northwest horizon, "a body shining very brightly (too bright for the naked eye) with a bluish-white light. It moved vertically downwards for about ten minutes. The body was in the form of a 'pipe' (i.e. cylindrical) . . . when the shining body approached the ground it seemed to be pulverized and in its place a huge cloud of black smoke was formed and a loud crash, not like thunder, but as if from the fall of large stones, or from gunfire, was heard. All the buildings shook and at the same time, a forked tongue of flames broke through the cloud. The old women wept. Everyone thought the end of the world was approaching." Half a dozen aftershock waves were recorded around the world; people were able to read the *London Times* at midnight by the explosion's glow; the light was enough to take photographs by throughout the night in Stockholm; and clouds sufficiently bright to interfere with astronomical observations persisted till the next morning in Holland. More than fifty years after the fact, two separate reports were conflicting as to whether or not abnormal radioactivity was at the site though there seemed general agreement that electromagnetic disturbances were severe, and growth of the local flora was unusually accelerated in much the same way as can be witnessed at many crop circle locations today. The cause of the explosion is still unknown, but there is no question that it caused burns and apparent radiation sickness in the local population at the time, devastated the region for approximately thirty-seven square miles from a blast epicenter about one mile high, and caused an aurora on the magnetic opposite side of Earth consistent with atomic explosions that was witnessed by the British explorer Ernest Shackelford at the Antarctic volcano Mount Erebus.

The most intriguing observations in this time period, though, were by Dr. William H. Pickering, who was the first man on record to witness "many geometrical figures, seen on Mars, that could not have been just produced by nature." Reported in 1907 and 1924 were "a vast octagon replaced by a five-pointed star" on Mars, and over the years other configurations were observed. By 1954, respected avant-garde English archaeologist-mythologist Harold T. Wilkins had recorded in *Flying Saucers on the Attack* that equilateral triangles, a cross in a circle, and other geometrical patterns had repeatedly been observed on the Martian surface. On November 24, 1894, Pickering saw from Lowell Observatory a self-luminous object approximately twenty miles above the unilluminated portion of Mars' surface. He also witnessed one of the many "absolutely inexplicable" light displays from the planet's surface, which played for seventy minutes on the night of December 7, 1900. He believed he detected an intelligent pattern behind them, in flash variations of two-thirds, one and one-third, and one and a half intervals, similar to the signals Tesla claimed to have received on his wireless as "a series of triplets." Japanese astronomer Tsuneo Saheki, professional observer of Mars since 1933, witnessed a similar display accompanied by intermittent radiation bursts that he took to be signals; on January 15, 1950, he reported seeing what he thought could be "an atomic explosion on Mars." It was a brilliant flare attaining the brightness of a sixth-magnitude star, lasting for five minutes. Thirteen years later, author V. A. Firsoff agreed with Saheki's assessment in his *Life Beyond Earth:* "No terrestrial volcano could produce a light of such brilliance; a megaton hydrogen bomb could."

Curiously, given both the Vallées' and Pierre Guérin's developing interest in the planet Mars and the fact that UFOs display inordinate interest in our atomic and weapons development, Vallée subtly suggested in 1965 the possibility of the entire modern era of UFO sightings having been triggered by our atomic bomb blasts—and that there was a connection with Mars. He brought up the fact that by 1947 a total of five atomic bomb explosions—Alamogordo (July 16, 1945), Hiroshima (August 6, 1945), Nagasaki (August 9, 1945), Crossroads A, and Crossroads B—had taken place. He then quoted from the declassified Appendix D to Project Sign's Report on Unidentified Flying Objects (proving that the military were not as lacking in interest on the subject as Vallée elsewhere commented): "Of these, the first two were in position to be seen from Mars, the third was very doubtful (at the edge of Earth's disk in daylight), and the last two were on the wrong side of the Earth." For the first, Mars was 165 million miles from Earth; for the second, it was 153 million. He avoided any conclusions, but referred to the author of the Appendix's "suggestion" that "other galactic communities" may have been keeping an eye on us . . . by tacit implication, from the planet Mars.

Vallée did not mention a fact that would have made this "suggestion" much more important: atomic explosions create aurorae disturbances in the ionosphere on the magnetic opposite side of Earth, causing extraordinarily bright lights, as were witnessed in the Siberian explosion of 1908. These would be at least as visible to a planet as close as Mars, if not more so, than the atomic explosions themselves. Weighing the aurorae into the equation, that means that out of the first five atomic explosions on our planet, all but one—80 percent—would have been in ideal position to be seen from Mars, with the remaining one a viable possibility.

In 1966, the Vallées were more decisive, though Jacques Vallée still exhibited his usual reserve. In their joint book, *Challenge to Science: The UFO Enigma,* they wrote: "According to our previous experiments, it would seem that the coincidence with the Martian cycle is very well verified for the period covering the four peaks of 1950, 1952, 1954, 1956, but loses its validity beyond this period. This would explain why more roughly made studies over a wider period have sometimes seemed to result in a reasonable correlation." After a tremendous amount of overly cautious and highly technical doubletalk designed to make it appear as if their results might somehow be an accident, they presented a graph of UFO waves from 1947 to

1962 with sharp spikes showing pronounced increase in sightings, precisely and unfailingly, during closest oppositions between Earth and Mars. The graph not only showed a marked increase during the peak opposition periods, but another peak during the "half period." Mars has an elliptical orbit bringing it closest to Earth every twenty-six months (the oppositions), at distances varying from approximately thirty-four to sixty-four million miles, and the thirteen-month, or "half periods," exactly between those oppositions—as Mars was just starting on its next close pass—also showed lesser but regularly noticeable upsurges in UFO appearances.

The Vallées explain, "The problem of [this] study of the cyclic variations is essentially a question of finding some period that 'best' represents the curve [of 1947–1962]. Our approach to this problem may be described in the following way. Choosing some arbitrary period, we compute the resulting error by the difference (or its square) between this theoretical curve and the curve [of 1947–1962]. Then we take a slightly different period and compute this error again, and so on. The minimum error corresponds to the theoretically 'optimum' representation. When these computations are performed two minimums are found, and the corresponding periods are *one year and three months* and *two years and two months* (fifteen and twenty-six months, respectively). The second value is precisely the period of the Martian oppositions. The first value is very close to the half period. When the error is evaluated by least squares, the first minimum vanishes. The fact that a period very close to that of the Martian cycle has been found is clearly important. It could be regarded as a confirmation of the correlations found earlier. . . ."

Applying two further scientific tests to the same curve, cross- and auto-correlation, "we found an interesting confirmation of the results discussed in the preceding section; we again obtained a period of one year and one month, the half period of the Martian cycle. The second experiment [cross-correlation] was conducted using a list of the distances of Mars, using four values per month. Again, a good correlation was obtained; in view of the preceding results, this cannot, of course, come as a surprise. As a test we ran the same calculation with the distance of Venus, and we found only a poor correlation." Applied to Vallée's 1965 chart of 1870–1914, the figuring-in of the Martian half period brings the seemingly furthest figure off—the one an entire twelve months away—almost perfectly into place.

Typically, Vallée wrote that ". . . [the] cycle is interesting, but it is far from being absolutely demonstrated." If by "absolutely" he meant 100 percent, then of course he is correct; but at the very least, the Vallées' findings demonstrate an *extremely probable* connection between the UFO phenomenon and the planet Mars. This is further emphasized by their assertion that no apparent relationship exists between the phenomenon and other planets: "Indeed, in a psychological theory, there is no reason for these two planets [Venus and Jupiter] to play a less important role than Mars." Of the Mars-Earth correlation, they added, "the current military investigations ignore [it] entirely," which certainly was true of Blue Book, but the subject couldn't possibly have been outside of someone's official research jurisdiction, as the aforementioned Appendix D proves.

Nor was this the only correlation Vallée found with Mars. On April 5, 1962, he wrote, "Today Guérin called me at work with an exciting observation. He had noticed that the three great circles I had computed divided the equator according to a defined scale, with a basic unit of 12.4 degrees which turns out to be related to the Martian mean time. Could we have found a genuine law? The elegant geometric pattern formed by these three great circles does seem to be more than the product of coincidence." What precisely those three great circles represent is not clearly expressed, but seems to have had to do either with sightings or landing patterns, probably the latter.

And Pierre Guérin and the Vallées had not been alone in discovering a connection between Mars oppositions and UFO waves, though apparently the others who noticed it did not continue to chase the lead. As Nigel Blundell and Roger Boar wrote, in *The World's Greatest UFO Mysteries,* "UFOlogists noted that the sighting peak years of 1967 and 1973 coincided with the time when the orbit of Mars brought it closest to Earth; they wondered whether Martians had to wait for suitable conditions to travel, just as Russia and America had to select exactly the right moments to launch their Venus probes." The 1967 wave alone answers Vallée's only stated objection to pronouncing his Mars correlation results "reliable" as opposed to "an interesting experiment": "[T]his time interval [1947–1962] is not long enough to test a period in excess of two years; a time span at least ten times longer than the period is generally recommended. This means that we should at least consider all sightings between 1946 and the end of 1966. But all the

1966 cases will not be known and coded before 1967 or 1968. The problem will then have reached maturity and it will be very interesting to resume this research on a larger scale." If the inclusion of four more years would have satisfied Vallée that "the problem had reached maturity," then the inclusion of the two biggest subsequent UFO waves in the modern era over the next five to eleven years—1967 and 1973, both occurring during peak Mars oppositions—surely make his findings "reliable."

Vallée wrote no further on Mars correlations in his research, instead focusing on occupant reports and their history for the remainder of his career. Mars research in the space age was just beginning, however. *Mariner 4* brought back the first observations of the planet in July of 1965, followed by *Mariners 6* and *7* in 1969. The unmanned robot probes beamed back a dismal landscape of a dead world, nothing like the romanticized images of Percival Lowell a century before, who had envisioned a Martian civilization with structured canals from the icecaps and geometrically designed surface features. Despite this dismal evidence, Carl Sagan addressed the 1966 American Astronautical Society Meeting with the words, "[T]he earth may have been visited by various galactic civilizations many times (possibly in the order of 10,000) during geological time. It is not out of the question that artifacts of these visits still exist, or even that some kind of base is maintained (possibly automatically) within the solar system to provide continuity for successive expeditions." What might have given this hard-boiled scientist, publicly disbelieving of the entire flying saucer phenomenon, such an idea?

In 1971, *Mariner 9* beamed back much different pictures of the Martian surface, cleaner, more detailed, and covering a greater and more interesting surface area. Among the images it returned were what appeared to be regularly spaced pyramidal objects, in rhombus formation, in the Elysium area. Additionally, frame 4212–15 showed a formation on the south of Mars dubbed "Inca City" after the acute resemblance to what NASA geologist John McCauley called "continuous [ridges], show[ing] no breaching . . . out among the surrounding plains and small hills like walls of an ancient ruin." And on frame 4209–75 at longitude 186.4 could be seen what NASA described as "unusual indentations with radial arms protruding from a central hub," which to all superficial appearances resembled what we would recognize as an airport terminal, though of course the explanation given by NASA was much more mundane: it was simply an unusual formation, admittedly rather regular looking, caused by the melting and collapse of permafrost layers. It wouldn't be for some time yet that the former speculation would sound less like science fiction than a very real possibility. Sagan lost no time publicizing the Elysium pyramids on his T.V. series, *Cosmos,* rallying public support for future unmanned missions to examine the objects and televise them for all the world to see. Author-lecturer, science writer, and present civilian Mars Mission group head Richard C. Hoagland mentioned in his book *The Monuments of Mars* that neither Sagan nor anyone else honestly believed the objects were real pyramids.

But others noticed mathematical connections with the Red Planet, and with unquestionably real pyramids—on Earth. The first notable publication of such findings came from British researchers M. W. Saunders and Duncan Lunan in 1975, in the book *Destiny Mars.* Extremely difficult to find in the United States, its central findings as relate to this study can be found published in George C. Andrews' *Extra-Terrestrials Among Us.* Duncan Lunan first observed that the Great Pyramid at Giza in Egypt and the Pyramid of the Sun in Teotihuacán aligned, and that their alignment "defined an orbital period which locked with the rotation of Mars." Further, "There seem to be relationships between the Great Pyramid, the Martian moons, and the largest volcanoes on Earth and Mars." By their measurements, the Great Pyramid's base-length times 1,000 million was found to be within 1 percent of the mean distance between Mars and the Sun; 1,000 million times its height equaled the mean Earth-Sun distance, with an error of 2 percent; and the maximum Mars-Earth distance was equivalent to 1,000 million times its height plus base-length, with an error of only 0.14 percent. The cubit itself, the measurement by which the Pyramid was built, was found to equal the Mars-Earth indicated base-length divided by 440, with tolerances for error beneath 0.1 percent (plus 0.04 in one instance). They also found that the eccentricity of Mars' orbit was equivalent to the displacement of the center of the Pyramid's innermost (King's) chamber from the east-west center line, divided by the mean semibase, to a tolerance of 0.0023 percent, and other more complex ratios. And Earth's Moon figured into at least one of their Pyramid calculations: the added equatorial radii of Earth and its Moon, divided by Earth's equatorial radius, equals the slope of the Great Pyramid to within 0.06 percent.

Other points of mathematical correlation were discovered by Saunders and Lunan between Earth and Mars. For one thing, the north slope of the Great Pyramid, which is a 2 *pi* pyramid, "points to a height above the equator equal to 2 *pi* times the equatorial radius of Mars" with a 0.5 percent margin for error. They observed that the Pyramid's longitude is almost exactly opposite that of Earth's largest volcano, Mauna Loa, approximately 19.6 degrees north of the equator, and that the largest volcano on Mars, Olympus Mons—which is also the largest known volcano in our solar system—is the same number of degrees south of the Martian equator. Hoagland later measured a more precise 19.47 degrees north and south, and found it to be an apparent universal constant for maximum volcanic activity of planetary bodies, being the location of the Great Red Spot on Jupiter, the Great Dark Spot of Neptune, and the Alpha and Beta Regios of Venus, among others.

Saunders and Lunan also found the following *pi* correlations (among others), all with a margin of error of 0.5 percent or less, for the two Martian satellites Phobos and Deimos: the mean height of Deimos' orbit equals *pi* times Earth's equatorial radius, and if a satellite in Earth's orbit were at the same height as that of Deimos, it would revolve twice for every rotation of Earth; for every rotation of Earth, Phobos orbits Mars *pi* times, and if Earth had a satellite at the same height as Phobos, it would revolve two *pi* times in the time it takes Earth to rotate once.

The significance of this is that Phobos and Deimos may not be natural satellites, but manufactured ones, which was seriously proposed—at least in Phobos' case—by Russian scientist I. S. Shklovskii in a book coauthored with Carl Sagan in 1966, *Intelligent Life in the Universe*. It was suggested that Phobos either had an ice center or was hollow, which was roundly attacked by the scientific community, and the idea that it might actually be some kind of manufactured satellite—or, by implication, a converted planetary body—was met with even more scorn. But it was admitted that Phobos did not act as any other moon in the solar system, and in fact was inexplicably gaining speed in its orbit. Its small size should either have caused it (as well as Deimos) to be cast away from Mars or to have crashed into its surface long ago; its orbit is too circularly perfect, not elliptical, directly in the equatorial region between the sixty-fifth parallels north and south, and unnaturally fast at approximately three and a half orbits in each Martian day. Counter to every known body in the Universe, Phobos rises in the west and sets in the east. There is evidence that activity has taken place on its surface that is in no way natural, and that it is ongoing: grooves and track marks mapped on Phobos by *Mariner 9* were discovered to have increased in number by the time that *Phobos 2* arrived at Mars eighteen years later, and these all lead to a mammoth "crater" on one end of the moonlet that is perfectly circular and takes up more than an entire third of Phobos' diameter. And, interesting to note, Phobos and Deimos were not discovered until 1877, though astronomers had been observing Mars for some time before that and arguably had sufficient lenses to see its satellites. Even the conservative Vallée admitted it was conceivable "that the 'saucers' are interplanetary craft that use either a satellite of Mars or that planet itself as a base in their exploration of our solar system. In our present state of the ignorance of the nature of the Martian satellites it is not impossible to think that they are large interstellar vehicles, placed into orbit more than a century ago . . . by an advanced scientific community coming from elsewhere in the universe." In short, nothing seems "natural" about Phobos.

For that matter, a great many questions have been raised about our own Moon that have yet to be answered. As NASA scientist Dr. Robin Brett puts it, "It seems much easier to explain the nonexistence of the moon than its existence." The Moon functions as a stabilizing brake on Earth's rotation, by its effect on our oceanic tides. To say the least, it is "convenient." So much so that, were such a thing possible, one might almost suggest its function had been deliberately calculated. A more curious feature about it is its perfectly synchronous rotation about Earth—meaning that it turns once on its own axis in exactly the time it takes to revolve once around the Earth—which causes it always to show the same face to our planet. Theoretically, there is no reason this cannot occur in nature, but its exceptional improbability has always left science seeking a plausible answer for it. This is especially true since our discovery that the Moon lacks the proper composition for it to have assumed such an orbit. Having been to the Moon, we have explored only a very small portion of it, leaving a great many fundamental questions unanswered; we are not even sure of its core, it being one-quarter the diameter but only one-eightieth of Earth's mass, indicating it is most probably hollow . . . as, it would also appear, is Phobos.

It would be some time yet before Phobos was more fully studied, but in the meantime, Mars had greater surprises to yield. In the summer of 1976, the orbiter *Viking 1* was placed over Mars, a second orbiter within a month of assuming position. *Viking 1* dropped a robot probe on July 20, and on its own thirty-fifth orbit photographed something from about a thousand feet up in the planet's Cydonia region, approximately forty-one degrees north of the equator. Imaging team member Toby Owen found it on frame 35A72 on that Sunday afternoon, and took it to show Viking project leader Gerry Soffen, whose exact reaction was, "Oh my God, look at this!" What the frame showed was a mesa more than a mile across, two miles long, and half a mile high that looked exactly like a human face. An international press conference was held the same afternoon, at which time Soffen—renowned for his integrity—displayed the photo, saying, "Isn't it peculiar what tricks of lighting and shadow can do. When we took a picture a few hours later, it all went away; it was just a trick, just the way the light fell on it."

In fact, they had not. It wasn't until thirty-five days later that Viking frame 70A13 was photographed of the same area, with a lighting change of twenty degrees—and the face not only wasn't gone, it was clearer, especially given the original image to make stereoscopic comparison with. As Richard C. Hoagland says in *The Monuments of Mars,* this was not so much a deliberate lie or concealment as it was an "overwhelmingly favored presumption" on the part of the Viking team. "This tendency to presume, rather than to check, would manifest itself again and again in the course of events surrounding investigation of this enigmatic landform." Hoagland had been one of the press conference reporters on the day Soffen issued his pronouncement, and accepted it at the time on the senior man's word.

It was three years after that conference that two scientists, Vincent DiPietro and Gregory Molenaar, unearthed the second NASA frame for independent study. To clarify the image, they pioneered a new computer graphic technique called Starburst Pixel Interleaving Technique (SPIT). In four months they had developed suitable evidence that the face was bisymmetrical and had created some striking three-dimensional computer facsimiles of it. After only four people—two of whom were reporters—turned out to see them display their findings, DiPietro and Molenaar were invited to speak at the American Astronautical Society's June 1980 meeting. Approximately 10 percent of the thousand nationwide members remained behind to get a better look at the pictures the two men had developed, and some ordered copies. The scientists continued to apply new techniques following the meeting, but failed to rally the support for further Mars exploration to closer examine the Cydonia anomalies. They revealed heightened detail on the face with the assistance of Dr. Mark J. Carlotto, of the Analytic Sciences Corporation, eventually including the pupil in the eye cavity, teeth in the mouth, cheekbone delineations, and clearly marked darkened bands on what increasingly appeared to be an Egyptian-style headdress or helmet (previously thought to be the face's "hair"). They also discovered something else that shouldn't be there: a pyramid.

The pyramid was immense, approximately 1 by 1.6 miles. Situated about ten miles southwest of the face, its four sides were aligned to the spin axis of Mars, as the Egyptian pyramids are precisely aligned to Earth's cardinal points. This pyramid was not one of the formerly seen Elysium pyramids, which were three-sided, Elysium being almost directly opposite the Cydonia region. They also had discovered what they took to be several smaller pyramids in the area. DiPietro and Molenaar published their findings in 1982, complete with numerous computer-enhanced photos, under the title *Unusual Martian Surface Features.*

In 1981, Hoagland met the two men at a "Case for Mars" conference in Boulder, Colorado, and thought he detected more in the photos they presented than had yet been seen. Unsure of himself, it was two more years before he detected, in updated editions of their work and additional original photos from the Viking mission, what looked to him very much like a city of intelligent construction. Detail on the newly processed photos showed two clear impacts on the pyramid, with ejecta, high toward the top and lower down on the flank of its eastern face; the violence of the higher impact had thrown debris clear over onto the western face. From high-contrast photos in the NASA files, ironically unretouched by DiPietro and Molenaar, Hoagland saw numerous geometrical features in an area of roughly five square miles of right angle-aligned structures in a rectangular area: objects on the perimeter were oblong, one in the center was exactly circular, additional aligned four-sided pyramids were at exact right angles to the face, a square-shaped complex precisely on an east-west right angle to the bridge of the face's "nose," and two pentagonal pyramids (one of enormous size), among others, all at precise angles to the face. Some of these, like the central pyramid, showed evidence of violent damage.

Detailed analysis showed the entire complex to be built on what is called a Fibonacci, or "golden mean," spiral. This is a precise mathematical configuration deriving from the *e/pi* ratio, which equals the number 0.865. In its relation to Mars, this recurring geometrical constant is referred to by Hoagland as the "tetrahedral Message of Cydonia." Defense Mapping Agency cartographer and systems analyst Erol Torun confirmed this formula in 1988, also demonstrating that the Giza complex in Egypt—the pyramids and the Sphinx—were built on exactly the same principle. Torun also did extensive geometrical analysis of the largest pentagonal pyramid (approximately ten times the size and one thousand times the volume of the Great Pyramid of Giza), called the "D&M Pyramid," and found overwhelmingly redundant mathematical constants both internally and in relation to the Cydonia complex. Chief among these constants was the 19.5-degree angle—which is the latitude north or south of any planetary body, at least by superficial observation, where maximum volcanic activity occurs, as previously mentioned. Translated into the simplest of what are called Plato's geometric solids, these mathematical figures become a spherically circumscribed tetrahedron—a three-sided pyramid of four equilateral sides (one the base), which intersect at sixty-degree angles—in Mars' case, specifically oriented to the magnetic poles. The most striking evidence of this in Cydonia is the 19.5 minutes of arc between the D&M Pyramid, the Face, and the complex itself, the distances between them equaling 1/360th the polar diameter of Mars.

In 1991, Carl Munck publicized for Hoagland's group (the Mars Mission) his finding of this same geometry in Britain: at Stonehenge. The northeast avenue of this famous megalithic complex—by which it is used as a solar solstitial marker—is off true north by 49.6 degrees, which is the *radians* of *e/pi*. He also claims to have found a geodetic pattern connecting megalithic sites in Britain and the Americas. As of 1992, Munck was at work, with the aid of David Myers, in extending what he calls "the Global Grid" of other *e/pi* megalithic sites to the Near East and Japan. Myers discovered that if the best (and longest held) estimate as to the original exterior angle of the Great Pyramid of Giza (~51.9 degrees) is divided by the tetrahedral sixty-degree angle of Cydonia, the result is *e/pi*. He also discovered that a "great circle" drawn to pass through the Great Pyramid and intersect the equator 19.5 degrees east of Giza will have a precise sixty degree tilt to the equator, and that a great circle drawn to connect Stonehenge and Giza intercepts the equator at precisely 22.5 degrees east (22.5 divided by 19.5 equals *e/pi*). Livio Catullo Stecchini, a specialist in ancient measurements, wrote in 1971 that ". . . the [Ancient] Egyptians used a system of right triangles, in which one side was one of the three axes of Egypt and the other a perpendicular to it; the hypotenuse usually indicated the course of a segment of the east coast of Africa. The most important of these triangles was one obtained counting from Behdet 19 degrees 30 minutes south along the central axis of Egypt and then 19 degrees 30 minutes to the east . . ." Nineteen degrees 30 minutes is 19.5 degrees.

In 1974, civil engineer Hugh Harleston, Jr., gave a paper on Teotihuacán to the Forty-first International Congress of Americanists, reporting his discovery that the values *e* and *pi* were redundant; the 19.5-degree angle was found on the fourth-level angle of stones at both the Pyramid of the Sun and the Pyramid of the Moon, the latter showing several redundancies in geodetic markers throughout its site. He also found the number 19.69 encoded in the fourth-level steps of the Pyramid of the Sun, which is important because that is the exact latitude on which that pyramid is built, proving that the builders knew precise spherical measurements of Earth.

Hoagland found the tetrahedral Cydonia Message popping up in crop circles as well, which have long been connected to UFO activity. The August 3, 1990, Cheesefoot Head crop circle in central England, for instance, contains a great many redundancies of the Cydonia figures. More impressive, on July 17, 1991, in an English field called Barbury Castle after a mediaeval ruin, a number of "bull's-eye"-arranged circles appeared, which Hoagland turned into a cosine polar projection of equivalent latitudes. The numbers which appeared were 19.5, 22.5, 45.0, 49.6, 52.0, and 69.4 degrees, which amounted to a three-dimensional representation of Cydonia's geometry. It may be a matter of some interest that six days before, on July 11, 1991, a total solar eclipse occurred in Mexico City, precisely on the date predicted in stone by the Mayans as the Prophecy of the Sixth (New) Sun, which was the day on which a new age of enlightenment would begin. At least 110 people videotaping the event picked up UFOs on their cameras that day, which appeared in "wave after wave" according to T.V.'s *Sightings*. They have not departed since. So many videotapes of these UFOs have been taken, week in and week out, that no one is even interested in seeing them anymore. They are discussed openly on Mexican T.V. and have gained international attention.

Another extremely important feature of Cydonia is an artificial cliff on the edge of a crater, precisely along a sightline so as to form a backdrop beyond the Face for the setting sun, when viewed from the center of the main pyramid complex. Mars Mission member Daniel Drasin discovered that its proportions were incremental in relation to the rest of the complex. Drasin and Carlotto noticed that a photo taken of the same cliff from the south at about twenty degrees off the surface, blown up for detail, showed that the cliff also appeared to be a stylized human face. Eyes, a long nose with round nostrils, prominent cheekbones, a short, smiling mouth, and the cleft in the chin are clearly visible. Given their situation, both faces appear to have been positioned for precise monitoring of the rising and setting sun, as do the pyramids of Earth, Stonehenge, the Anasazi sun-dagger near Holly House at Hovenweep National Monument between Utah and Colorado, and various other temples and mounds. The only evident difference in Cydonia is its incredible size and complexity, and its use of actual faces instead of the simpler markers on our planet.

It is my own contention that the two faces show sufficient detail to darken the lines and reveal extremely clear images of precisely what they are, which is in neither case a human face at all, but the faces of a hawk and a baboon—the Egyptian gods Ra and Thoth, respectively. Once delineated, the details become clear to the naked eye even on unretouched photos, except for the main Face, the Ra face, which has to be computer enhanced to see plainly. The lines are so clean that the additional details of a five-pointed star-shaped human-faced diadem is evident on the center of Ra's helmet, similar in design to the golden sun-face found in Cuzco's Temple of the Sun which was melted down by the Spaniards in the sixteenth century, after the conquistador Leguizano lost it in a gambling match. That famous sun-face bore a human expression with a radiant smile, as is witnessed by old Spanish woodcuts reproduced in the works of Potsdam astronomy professor Rolf Müller and in Zecharia Sitchin's *The Lost Realms,* and so it appears does the face of the Ra diadem. The overlapping of the projecting beak can be seen in the "figure-eight" formation of the mouth with a definite point hanging over its center line. The Thoth face shows marked and even horizontal striping across it—making it clearly a mandrill—and has two other simian faces above it, a chimpanzee over the right eye and a gorilla over the left. Baboons, and so possibly other simians, were sacred to Thoth.

Though their identities have not been officially verified (plainly not a possibility, when the faces themselves have yet to be officially acknowledged), the faces will be referred to in this study as being those of Ra and Thoth. Hoagland believes the central Face to be an image of *Homo erectus,* the theoretical evolutionary stage of man at the estimated time of the Cydonia complex construction, circa 450,000 years ago, but admits in his text that the central Cydonia Face may indeed be "Horus of the Horizon" from Egyptian mythology, and Horus is essentially another manifestation of the hawk god Ra. He makes mention of the fact that the actual Egyptian name for Horus is *heru,* the sun god, which Robert K. G. Temple comments in his book *The Sirius Mystery* is also synonymous with "face." Egyptian hieroglyphs communicate on more than one level at once and are extremely sophisticated, employing what many researchers have referred to as "sacred puns." As Temple puts it, "In Egyptian the letter 'l' and the letter 'r' are entirely interchangeable and have the same hieroglyph. Consequently, Heru could just as reliably be Helu. If one takes Helu and puts a Greek ending on it one gets Helios . . ."—who was the Greek god of the sun.

One geometrical feature publicized by NASA as early as August 18, 1976, was "parallel contours [that] look very much like an aerial view of ploughed ground . . . in a shallowed depression or basin," found on Viking frame 52A35. These are a series of what seem to be concentric semicircles, about a half mile from end to end, not unlike those in the mountains of Peru's Sacred Valley. There are a great many more mathematical and geometrical points of interest in this ongoing study, such as evenly spaced mounds indicative of aerial runway markers and a cleanly pentagonal (or imperfectly seen heptagonal) structure in the Utopia region. Interested readers should consult the aforementioned researchers for more details. For the purposes of this study, it is sufficiently demonstrated that the faces and complex in the Cydonia region of Mars are clearly the product of a designing intelligence. The findings of the Mars Mission have been independently verified by scientists in other countries, including geologist Dr. Vladimir Avinsky in Russia in 1983.

Predictably, while public interest on the subject has moved in cycles, official interest has been lacking. It cannot be doubted that behind the scenes, as in UFO investigations, there is a team of some sort that is the equivalent of Hoagland's Mars Mission, or that at least keeps tabs on their research. The ever-debunking Carl Sagan, who once observed that "Intelligent life on Earth first reveals itself through the geometric regularity of its constructions," referred to the central Mars Face as "merely seeing Jesus Christ on a tortilla chip" in a *Parade* article. Once he publicly scoffed at Hoagland's findings, only to privately corral Hoagland later to ask him just what findings he had, anxious to be the first to read his manuscript before it was submitted for publication, as he did at a 1985 conference. Articles periodically appear in various popular science magazines such as *Omni* and *Discover,* but no public scientific debate has occurred on the subject other than at amateur meetings and conferences such as Hoagland's Mars Mission group. One place the Face and pyramids did make frequent guest appearances was in the tabloids, which Hoagland has charged is a deliberate move to deflect public attention by ridiculing the subject. It should be mentioned that one of the biggest disinformation sources on the UFO subject, William Cooper, has stated outright that tabloids are sometimes used for precisely that purpose. Hoagland published his book on the subject in 1987, updating it in 1992 before the failure of the next Mars probe, the *Observer,* in August of the following year.

As Hoagland's book was being published, NASA put out an article and photograph in the September 1, 1987, *New York Times:* the picture was of a football-shaped fragment of rock—one of several discovered in Antarctica in 1979—that could plainly be seen to be the corner connection between four separate blocks, not unlike the appearance of pre-Inca ruins on Earth or the aptly named "Inca City" on Mars. The Antarctic rocks had formerly been believed to be SNC meteorites, the name given to eight fragments discovered in India, Egypt, and France from 1815 to 1865 that had been unique for their 1.3-billion-year-old age where most meteorites are 4.5 billion years old. The Antarctic and SNC rock samples (the *Times* article no longer made any pretense to their being called meteorites) both proved to have rare gas content virtually identical to the atmospheric composition of Mars, containing traces of isotopic Nitrogen-14, Argon-40 and -36, Neon-20, Krypton-84, and Xenon-13. The possibility of such combinations occurring randomly is astronomical, leaving the conclusion that these are, in fact, Mars rocks. Any remaining ambiguity is removed by U.S. Geological Surveyist Jeffrey S. Kargel's unequivocal comment, on the May 20, 1995, edition of *Sightings* on CBS, that "We have in our laboratories and museums chunks of Mars that have come to the Earth. Maybe terrestrial life has its roots on Mars. Maybe we're all evolved Martians." That fragments of Martian rock should be on Earth at all is a mystery, to say the least, let alone that they should be nearly 1.5 billion years old, and it is especially amazing that one sample (that we know of) should plainly show evidence of intelligent construction.

Between the publication of Hoagland's book and the launching of the *Observer* probe, the Soviets sent a mission to Mars on July 12, 1988: the probes *Phobos 1* and *Phobos 2*. Several other countries had an investment in the Phobos project, including the European Space Agency, France, and West Germany. After two months, *Phobos 1* was reported lost, presumably due to loss of the radio link—the same reason given in 1993 for the loss of *Observer* by the Americans. *Phobos 2* arrived at Mars in January of 1989 and established stable orbit. On March 28, it left the Martian orbit to establish a new orbit around its curious moonlet Phobos—the probe's primary mission, hence its name—and then "failed to communicate with Earth as scheduled," according to the news service Tass. Again, the stated reason was loss of the radio link, but no explanation as to why the link should have been lost was available. Despite reassurances that the probe link would probably be reestablished, Glavkosmos (the Soviet NASA) agent Nikolai A. Simyanov stated that he believed the spacecraft was lost for good.

The Soviets were no strangers to failed Mars probes: they lost six starting in October of 1960, ending with *Zond 2* in April 1965. These failures did not go unnoticed by American scientists, who uneasily began joking about the "Great Galactic Ghoul," but managed their own successful Mariner series following the loss of *Mariner 3* in November of 1964 when its protective shroud didn't open. *Mariner 4's* twenty-two successfully returned images of Mars in 1965 were followed by almost ten times as many from *Mariners 6* and *7* in 1969. As *Mariner 9* orbited Mars in 1971, the Russians succeeded in being the first to land on the Red Planet. Their missions, *Mars 2* and *Mars 3*, arrived about two weeks after *Mariner 9*. *Mars 2* crashed, reportedly due to a Martian dust storm, but *Mars 3* landed its rover, becoming the first transmitter of images from the Martian surface. It was not revealed until the Americans lost their *Observer* probe in 1993 that *Mars 3's* rover ceased transmission just twenty seconds into its debarkation, for reasons unknown.

On March 31, 1989, the European press ran a number of articles concerning an inexplicable object that *Phobos 2* had photographed between itself and Mars in its last few seconds of transmission. A thin ellipse with sharpened points (the points in a shape gem cutters call a "marquise"), about twelve and a half miles long, was the object in question. It was symmetrical, unlike the shadow Phobos itself casts, which is in a larger potato shape. Nor was this the only object of its sort that *Phobos 2* had photographed: a few days earlier, an identical shadow between sixteen and nineteen miles long was captured by the cameras. The Soviets were clearly convinced it was not the shadow of the moonlet Phobos, as they referred to this recurring, symmetrical shadow as a "phenomenon." A *Vremya* reporter inquired directly whether or not this was a rocket ship of some sort, and the space agency representative refused comment, other than to say it would be "to fantasize." *Aviation Week and Space Technology's* April 3, 1989, issue ran a story about the loss of the radio link, and the April 7 issue of *Science* ran the same story but added one new detail: that the probe's signal was weakly detected for a brief time a few hours after its loss, implying that it was in a spin. Further confirmation of this came from Paris in the April 10 *Aviation Week and Space Technology*, from sources quoting the Soviets as saying they were "tracking a spinner," which greatly puzzled the French because the satellite's stabilization system had performed so well for the Soviets on their Venus missions. It did admit to the presence of the unknown shadow, but implied that it was the satellite's jettisoned propulsion system (which was an impossibility). Aside from these, American news carried no stories at all on developments in researching the *Phobos 2* loss for some time.

Again ignored by the American media were further reports issued by the Soviets in response to international pressure about three months later, which ran in Europe and Canada as curiosities. Except for the final few frames, which still have not been released, *Phobos 2's* final transmissions were aired on television. In the equatorial region of Mars (where all the unusual surface features so far discovered on that planet occur, and over which Phobos regularly orbits), what appeared to be an intelligently designed area of more than 230 square miles was plainly visible, consisting of rows of parallel straight lines and rectangles of varying length. The most curious thing about them was that only infrared cameras, and not standard cameras, had photographed them— meaning that they were a heat source, and by implication beneath the Martian surface, though this suggestion tends to remain unvoiced by most. Radio Moscow's science correspondent Boris Bolitsky said that the "quite remarkable features" were either on the planet's surface or "in the lower atmosphere," a strange comment indeed. Dr. John Becklake of the London Science Museum made comments on Canadian television about them, describing them as puzzling and saying that he certainly didn't know what they were. "The city-like pattern is 60 kilometers wide," he said, "and could easily be mistaken for an aerial view of Los Angeles."

Of the actual probe loss, Becklake confirmed the "thin ellipse" seen between *Phobos 2* and the Martian surface and added that it was picked up both by visual and infrared cameras, verifying that it was not the shadow of the Martian moonlet to anyone who may have been in doubt. He also gave out some additional information, such as the fact that the ellipse had been seen just as *Phobos 2* was aligning itself with Phobos, and that "As the last picture was halfway through, [the Soviets] saw something which should not be there. [They] have not yet released this picture, and we won't speculate on what it shows." Where Becklake would not speculate, the Soviets themselves confirmed in the October 19, 1989, issue of *Nature* that one of two things took out their probe: it was a computer malfunction, or else some object "impacted" the probe. Computer malfunction seems unlikely, since the probe was spinning at one point and its signals were detected pointed at Earth— which would mean that radio contact should have been reestablished, or at least could have been. The Glavkosmos chairman reluctantly admitted, in explaining the probe loss to *Aviation Week and Space Technology,* that the last frame taken by *Phobos 2* "appears to include an odd-shaped object between the spacecraft and Mars." All possible known sources—including "space dust"—were ruled out as causes for the photographed object or the loss of the probe that imaged them. Which leaves, by strict definition, an unidentified flying object—or more than one, given the differences in size and dates of the objects photographed.

One item of importance was noticed before the loss of *Phobos 2:* there were more of the regular grooves or trenches in the moonlet's surface than had been there at the time of the Viking mission thirteen years before. "New grooves can be identified," were the Soviets' exact words. The mission had confirmed that they were in fact regular, of a uniform width of seven hundred to one thousand feet, and seventy-five to ninety feet deep. The material in their sides is brighter than the surface of Phobos, and they run parallel to each other, all converging on the gigantic crater "hole" at Phobos' tip. Something else the Viking mission discovered was that chains of small craters were in tandem with the grooves. How these could occur in nature, on an astral body with no volcanic activity, is a mystery. Similar craters have been discovered on our own Moon, believed to be the product of volcanism, but those seen on Phobos bring this interpretation into question. As to the fabled canals of Mars itself, there is no clear answer concerning them. Where the prevailing opinion is that astronomers had simply been perceiving an illusion since first spotting them, there is presently no proposed explanation as to just what landforms or conditions could have caused such an illusion, let alone one perceived by all observers in all ages, including our own.

NASA launched the last probe to Mars on September 25, 1992, at the cost of more than a billion dollars. Having first been delayed by Hurricane Andrew, NASA discovered on a safety check that the specially filtered nitrogen hoses meant to keep out any external debris had somehow failed in their job: bits of fiber, metal filings, dirt, paper, and even plaster of paris were discovered inside. The probe's special high-resolution camera was similarly contaminated. NASA investigated the highly suspicious debris, obviously more indicative of deliberate sabotage than hurricane damage, but never announced their findings publicly. Shortly after launch, the probe was believed "blown up" when it failed to respond to radio signals for over a half hour, according to Reuters news service. Somehow contact was reestablished, and *Observer* winged its way to Mars. Then, on August 21, 1993, three days from its destination, *Observer* was permanently lost. The radio link was first to be blamed, followed by later speculations that one or another system had leaked and caused an explosion. No final determination was possible.

Nor could the *Observer* loss even be considered an exceptional incident. Since the explosion of the shuttle *Challenger* in 1986, NASA was unable to accomplish a successful major launch until after the *Observer* disappearance. A number of satellites were lost, including a $1.5 billion CIA satellite that exploded less than a minute into launch, recalling such "deflections" as the *Juno 2* in 1959, the tracking by Cape Kennedy of a UFO which followed a Polaris missile over the south Atlantic in 1961, and the sabotage of Atlas and Minuteman missiles in 1966 and 1975 at Malmstrom Air Force Base. In fact, until the repair of the Hubble Space Telescope after the *Observer* loss—which also initially failed—NASA had nothing but a string of seemingly cursed ventures. NASA's official stance has always been (like all other government agencies) that it has no interest in (or investigative body into) UFOs, though its 1967 Management Instruction states plainly that "it is KSC (Kennedy Space Center) policy to respond to reported sightings of space vehicle fragments and unidentified flying objects as promptly as possible," adding that "under no circumstances will the origin of the object be discussed" with any observer reporting them.

Charges of sabotage and withholding of evidence were inevitable in the wake of *Observer's* loss, especially when it was discovered that, against protocol and the advice of the manufacturers (though NASA claims it was General Electric's and Martin Marietta's idea), the radio link had been ordered shut off at Mission Control, ostensibly because it would somehow assist the probe in the automatic pressurizing of its fuel system. This is utterly inexplicable, since telemetry (as it is called) is simply never shut off during any mission, for exactly the reason that became apparent with *Observer:* it may never come back on.

Richard Hoagland and Professor Emeritus Stanley McDaniel from Sonoma State University (Department of Philosophy), another major proponent for increased study of Cydonia, were quick to point out the tremendous convenience in timing concerning *Observer's* telemetry loss. It occurred on the eve of a press conference in which McDaniel's lengthy report challenging NASA candor with the public was to be discussed between Hoagland and Observer Mission scientist Dr. Bevan French (who did not read or discuss the report on the air) on *Good Morning America,* and was not announced until the day after the telecast, despite the fact that the radio link was lost the night before. It also did not go unnoticed that the link was intact until *Observer's* controllers had managed to upload the probe's commands and complete all necessary manipulations to get it into its prearranged orbit, meaning that *Observer* would automatically continue its mission, but Mission Control would not be able to receive the images it transmitted—

or, that someone at Mission Control might know exactly how to retrieve those images, but without the public (or possibly even most of NASA) ever knowing it. In short, that *Observer* could be privately monitored.

It didn't help matters any that the head of NASA, Admiral Richard Truly, was fired by President George Bush while he was investigating Congressman Howard Wolpe's (D-MI) allegations that the Space Agency had been officially ordered to circumvent the Freedom of Information Act. Wolpe had discovered a two-page set of instructions while Congress was looking into ways to develop the SP-100 nuclear space reactor. "This NASA document," he was quoted by Associated Press from his letter to Truly, "instructs government employees to: 1, rewrite and even destroy documents 'to minimize adverse impact'; 2, mix up documents and camouflage handwriting so that the document's significance would be 'less meaningful'; and 3, take steps to 'enhance the utility' of various FOIA exemptions." Truly, who was committed to openness and honesty, was replaced by Daniel Goldin, a quarter-century TRW defense industry contractor of top-secret satellite equipment with a history of "black-op" (secret operations) experience.

The subject of Professor McDaniel's concern was a 1958 NASA-commissioned Brookings Institute report (available to Congress three years later) on potential pursuits in space. Exceeding two hundred pages in length, the document discusses the possibility of encountering "artifacts left at some point in time" by intelligent extraterrestrials, which "might be discovered through our space activities on the Moon, Mars, or Venus." Like the 1968 NSA paper on "UFO Hypothesis and Survival Questions," it asked which circumstances would justify withholding information from the public, citing anthropological examples of "societies sure of their place in the universe, which have disintegrated when they had to associate with previously unfamiliar societies espousing different ideas and different life ways. . . ." Fundamentalist religious and other "antiscience" sects were considered the highest risk group to exposure of such information, followed by—interestingly enough—scientists and engineers, since "these professions most clearly associate with the mastery of nature," and so might be "the most devastated by the discovery of relatively superior creatures." Another study, done by Marshall Space Flight Center's design engineer, Joseph F. Blumrich, concluded after eighteen months that we would eventually find evidence of extraterrestrial visits on the Moon, and that both it and Earth had been regular visitation sites. Yet another study—Technical Report R-277—also undertaken by NASA, compiled by Barbara M. Middlehurst and called the "Chronological Catalogue of Reported Lunar Events" (currently available through the Sourcebook Project), listed 579 reliable sightings of unusual lunar phenomena from 1540 to 1967.

It should be noted that, like all other agencies involved in any of the myriad aspects of UFO investigation, NASA is demonstrably somewhat schizophrenic. There was never any attempt to conceal either the Elysium or Cydonia pyramids, or the now-famous Face in that region, only an attempt to downplay them, and to "ignore them and maybe they'll go away." The photos are published and discussed, at quite some detail and length, in many sources, and copies of the pictures can be obtained by interested researchers. The Space Agency has even volunteered such information as the rocks of Martian origin discovered in Antarctica, without any external prompting. Yet, on the *Observer* probe, evidence of possible sabotage before launch, inexplicable breach of protocol and suspicious activity during, and cover-up following can be seen, with papers brought to light by a congressman proving attempts to circumvent the Freedom of Information Act after the fact. The lattermost could easily be explained by there being a former CIA head as president of the country at the time, but the no less conservative Ronald Reagan was in office when NASA publicized the Antarctic Mars rocks—though, it should be noted, Reagan witnessed a UFO while governor of California and is on record as having a great interest in the subject, and so may have been less hostile to openness concerning it. It most appears that there is no standardized policy on how to treat such information, and its availability is entirely dependent on who is asked about it.

Written coincidentally with the formation of NASA, the Brookings Institute report stated that man will not come face to face with intelligent extraterrestrial life "within the next twenty years," as though this were somehow an eventual certainty, but emphasized the likelihood of encountering artifacts on our three nearest celestial neighbors. And, given the current evidence for there having once been a civilization, or at least a base, on Mars, the obvious question should arise: wouldn't such a race, if they had built structures on Earth as well (as the evidence indicates), also have used our Moon as a base? And where we have sent only robot probes to Mars and Venus, information on which is only now beginning to be processed and studied, we have actually set foot on the Moon. Our astronauts never reported finding any artifacts there. But we have reason to suspect NASA has not told us everything they discovered on the Moon.

Again, we have evidence not so much of cover-up, but of less than total candor. The Brookings Institute and Joseph Blumrich seem to have actually anticipated our finding artifacts beyond Earth. On what might they have based that assessment?

As with Mars, but stretching much further back, the Moon has been the subject of a variety of anomalous historical reports. The discoverer of Uranus, Friedrich Wilhelm Herschel, saw many small, bright, luminous points on the Moon, in 1783, 1787, and finally on October 2, 1790, during a total lunar eclipse. On March 7, 1794, Dr. William Wilkins of Norwich saw a light so bright he equated it with a star, on the dark of the Moon's disk, visible to the naked eye. "It lasted for 15 minutes," he said, "and was a fixed and steady light which brightened. It was brighter than any light part of the moon, and the moment before it disappeared, the brightness increased. Two persons passing also saw it." So did a servant of Sir George Booth, in England, who reported it in virtually the same words, as "a bright light like a star in the dark part of the moon."

Throughout the nineteenth century and into the twentieth, reports of such strange lights continued, growing in complexity due perhaps to the improved technology of telescopes. To mention a few: an intermittently appearing bright light, at times flashing, was seen on the dark part of the moon from Holland on October 20, 1824; on January 22 of the following year, two officers aboard the *HMS Coronation* in the Gulf of Siam witnessed two different lights, one in the crater Aristarchus; Thomas G. Elger reported in the *Astronomical Register* of April 9, 1867, that he saw a light like a star of the seventh magnitude flare out of the moon—"I have seen lights before on the moon, but never so clear as this," he wrote; in 1869, Great Britain's Royal Astronomical Society began a three-year investigation into a "sudden outbreak" of mysterious lights witnessed in the Mare Crisium (itself anomalous in that the Mare Crisium is in a cleanly hexagonal shape); on May 13, 1870, several English astronomers saw lights in the crater Plato, numbering from four to twenty-eight at any given time; in March of 1877 there were several reports of bright lights in the craters Proclus and Picard, specified not to be reflections of the sun; and shortly after, on June 17, 1877, New York's Professor Henry Harrison saw a light "like a reflection from a moving mirror" on the dark of the moon, as England's Frank Dennett saw the same thing in the crater Bessel.

UFO activity about the Moon was also plentiful: September 7, 1820, numerous French observers reported seeing objects flying precise maneuvers in a straight line and at regularly spaced intervals from each other during a lunar eclipse; *Le Monde* of Paris and the *Journal of the Franklin Institute* reported that a Professor Swift of Illinois and Professors Hines and Zentmayer in Europe witnessed the same phenomenon, in several formations, moving in straight and parallel lines during a solar eclipse on August 7, 1869; Monsieur Lamey reported vast numbers of dark bodies crossing the Moon, in an 1874 *L'Annee Scientifique;* on April 24, 1874, Professor Schafarik of Prague "saw an object of so peculiar a nature that I know not what to make of it. It was dazzlingly white, and slowly traversed the disk of the moon. I watched it after it left the moon's face"; the *Journal of the Liverpool Astronomical Society* reported South African Colonel Marwick's sighting near the Moon of something like a comet that moved rapidly; in 1892 and 1896, the same phenomenon was witnessed in the Netherlands and in America, of an object one-thirtieth of the Moon's diameter traversing the disk of that planetary body in three to four seconds; Arizona gave several reports during 1899 of luminous objects moving across the Moon; in November of that year, France reported an enormous object that moved like a kite and changed color from white to red to blue; on May 10, 1902, Colonel Marwick reported many brilliantly colored objects like little suns about the Moon; on November 26, 1910, the *Journal of the British Association for the Advancement of Science* and *La Nature* in France both reported a brightly luminous object seen during a lunar eclipse, one publication adding that it left the Moon's surface; F. B. Harris reported in England's January 27, 1912, *Popular Astronomy* that he saw an incredibly black object about 250 miles long and 150 miles wide on or over the Moon "like a vast crow poised . . . An extremely interesting and curious phenomenon must have happened"; and the *Bulletin de la Soc. Astron. de France* of August 29, 1917, reported bright objects seen traveling close with the Moon.

And, as with Mars, unusual geometrical features were also witnessed on the Moon. Baron Franz von Paula Gruithuisen thought he had discovered a lunar city between 1822 and 1824, based on a series of parallel mounds and configurations north of the crater Schröter. Over the years, scrutiny of the area in question gave conflicting results from different observers. Another astronomer named Gaudibert saw a similar enough configuration to produce a remarkably close sketch to that made by Gruithuisen, but given the lack of consistency, Gruithuisen's discovery was deemed fanciful. Mädler, one of the authors of the classic 1838–39 lunar mapping work *Der Mond,* drew a geometrically shaped enclosure with surrounding structures or marks remarkably similar to Gruithuisen's, only on the shore of the Mare Frigoris to the immediate west of the crater Fontenelle and northeast of the crater Plato.

Controversy occurred in 1866 over Athens Observatory director Julius Schmidt's reported disappearance of the crater Linné, an extremely deep depression, to be replaced by a small whitish patch for a brief time. Later observations confirmed that it had not changed, and any observers who discovered a difference were considered for whatever reason to simply have been incorrect in their assessment. Yet Linné, originally described in Beer and Mädler's *Der Mond* as "the second most conspicuous crater on the plain," at four and a half miles across and a depth so great its bottom could not be seen, is today a smallish white crater of merely one and a half miles across, with almost no height or depth at all. In 1877, two different observers at two different times noticed strange objects in craters: Meudon Observatory's Monsieur Trouvelot saw what appeared to be a luminous cable in Eudoxus on February 20, and a Doctor Klein reported in *L'Astronomie* seeing a luminous triangle on the floor of Plato on November 23; on the same night, observers across the United States reported seeing "flakes" of light converging from all lunar craters into the floor of Plato, where they formed into a triangle.

Between February of 1885 and December of 1919, a great many geometric and other unusual phenomena were noted in craters of the Moon, including what appeared to be a curved wall, a luminous cable in Aristarchus like that witnessed by Trouvelot in 1877, synchronous lights, color areas on the surface changing from light to dark or vice versa, a black wall in Aristillus, reddish smoke and shadows, intense black spots in and about various craters (some with cleanly defined, bright borders), and shafts of light projecting from given areas (witnessed at two different geographical locations). *Sky and Telescope* recorded a cross seen at the crater Fra Mauro, and volume 20 of the *Astronomical Register* mentioned "a geometric object shaped like a cross," or possibly a letter "X," seen in the crater Eratosthenes, along with "an acute-angled triangle" formed by the three lower embankments of a group of hills.

One feature was spotted by so many astronomers at so many times that in the last century it was simply referred to as "the Railway." Almost seventy miles in length, it is a straight wall approximately five hundred yards high, with steep edges rising steadily for about twelve hundred feet at about forty-five degrees from the Moon's surface. The consensus today seems to be that this is a fault line, caused by something pushing its way up through the surface. No logical proposal as to what or how that might be has been forthcoming. It is perhaps of note that around the wall are a great many of the seemingly symmetrical domes that still mystify lunar landscape watchers. Almost exactly opposite the wall, on the backside of the Moon, is a gigantic crack stretching approximately 150 miles, up to five miles wide in places. Soviet scientists Vasin and Shcerbakov seriously suggest that the crack and wall are evidence that the Moon is a hollowed-out asteroid being used as a spaceship, the wall being an armor plate that buckled under the force of some impact, the crack a resonant structural failure. Such a proposition may not be so far-fetched, given that the Moon does indeed show signs of being hollow, and NASA has reported that it "rings like a gong or a bell" when hit by spent rocket stages or landed upon by modules—reverberations of from one to four hours were picked up by *Apollo 12.*

The modern era brought far better observations of the lunar surface, and accordingly far more unusual reports. Arizona's American Meteorite Museum director, Dr. H. H. Nininger, discovered a twenty-mile tunnel in 1952 with walls smooth as glass connecting the two unusual craters Messier and Pickering in the Sea of Fecundity. The craters differ from other craters in having unnaturally extended lips in the same direction. The entrance and exit of this tunnel, he asserted, were clearly visible with any good telescope. Nininger suggested the formation of the tunnel was the passage of a meteorite moving twenty to thirty miles per second on almost a perfect horizontal plane, vaporizing and making into smooth glass the dust in its wake. The logistical problems behind this suggestion are immense, and it is questionable whether anyone really believes it or not, but the only other possibility is intelligent construction—then as now a forbidden topic to discuss in public, or even in most private confines. But the mountain range separating these two craters is fifteen to twenty miles wide and several thousand feet high, extremely unlikely to have been cleanly breached by a meteorite in the proposed fashion.

On July 29, 1953, former *New York Herald Tribune* science editor John O'Neill saw an approximately twelve-mile-long bridge-like structure over the Sea of Crisis, which was confirmed by more than one leading astronomer within even a month. The British Astronomical Association's Lunar Section head, H. P. Wilkins, referred to it as an artificial structure, not a natural one, and alluded that he thought it looked like an engineering job made fairly recently, owing to the fact that the oft-observed lunar surface had not formerly revealed it. He stated on BBC radio that sunlight could clearly be seen streaming in beneath it.

Soon more regular shapes began to be seen. Apparent structures seeming to form squares or rectangles were reported—not unlike those drawn by astronomers over a century earlier—as well as "domes" that were seen first in one spot, then another, as though they were moving. Science writer Joseph F. Goodavage noted in 1954 that "more than 200 circular dome-shaped structures have been observed on the moon and catalogued, but for some strange reason they often vanish from one place and reappear somewhere else."

On September 29, 1958, Dr. Kenzahuro Toyoda of Japan's Menjii University discovered actual letters on the Moon's surface, so huge and black that he could easily read them: PYAX JWA. The newspaper *Mainichi* carried the report, Toyoda not being the type to perpetrate a joke. The probe *Ranger 7* crashed into the Moon in 1964, but not before relaying pictures of the inside of a crater filled with a cluster of objects that have yet to be satisfactorily identified, appearing to be round, smooth, and symmetrical. Other craters seem to show similar features at different times.

On February 4, 1966, the Soviets' *Luna 9* probe photographed in the Sea of Storms regular, towering structures that *Argosy's* science editor Dr. Ivan Sanderson called "two straight lines of equidistant stones that look like markers along an airport runway," similar to what was later discovered in the Utopia region of Mars. In both cases, the structures are identical, and positioned so as to produce tremendous shadows. Russian Laureate State Prize winner Dr. S. Ivanov compared photos taken at two different times for stereoscopic effect and discovered that the spires were approximately fifteen stories high, evenly spaced and identical, concluding that "in three-D [they] seem to be arranged according to definite geometric laws." The news was not published in America, and the authors of *Psychic Discoveries Behind the Iron Curtain* claimed that NASA was "not at all happy about its publication," apparently there or anywhere else. In his authoritative *Our Moon,* the same Dr. Wilkins who publicly discussed O'Neill's artificial land bridge in 1953 described a gigantic hole in the center of crater Cassini A, on the edge of the Sea of Storms, more than six hundred feet across, the surrounding crater itself being "as smooth as glass" and a mile and a half across at the outer rim. There are many other holes of this sort visible in craters of the Moon. Wilkins was convinced that the Moon had substantial subterranean pits or hollows, with openings to the surface. The Sea of Storms is also a hotbed of UFO activity.

If NASA was unhappy about the publication of details about spires on the edge of the Sea of Storms, their own publication on November 2, 1966, of what have since been dubbed "the Blair Cuspids" seems schizophrenic. Boeing Institute of Biotechnology's William Blair discovered these objects in the Sea of Tranquility in a photograph taken by *Lunar Orbiter 2.* Seven obelisks (as they have since been called) were found in all, one of extreme height (about 213 meters) and six smaller ones, arranged in such a fashion that the three outer ones form an equilateral triangle, the other four triangulating to create a prismatic-pyramidal configuration. Blair countered arguments that the obelisks were natural landforms by saying that if they were, "the triangulation would be scalene or irregular, whereas those concerning the lunar objects lead to a basilary system, with coordinates x, y, z, to the right angle, six isosceles triangles and two axes consisting of three points each." In other words, their mathematical/geometrical correlations could not have occurred by accident. In close proximity to the obelisks is a gigantic rectangular depression with four 90-degree corners "persuad[ing] one to think it is like an excavation whose walls have been eroded or fallen inwards," as Blair put it. Soviet space engineer Alexander Abramov claims these markers are positioned identically to the Pyramids in Giza.

Discoveries made since man's landing on the Moon have added more to its mystery than brought desired answers. The odd resonation the Moon makes when struck has already been mentioned, arguing, as does other evidence, for its being completely hollow or—as Wilkins suggested—containing a great many sub-stantially hollowed pits or subterranean chambers accessed by "plugholes." There is considerably less dust on the surface of the Moon than should be present for its age. Now utterly devoid of dis-cernible water, sinuous rilles in the Moon's surface (and that of Mars) attest to the likelihood that water was once present, and inexplicably, after *Apollo 15,* NASA experts detected one hundred square miles of water vapor on the Moon's surface that still has not been accounted for. Almost 100 percent of the Moon's rocks are older than 90 percent of Earth's rocks—from 4.6 billion years old, compared to Earth's 3.7 billion-year-old rocks—making the Moon far older than our own planet, probably captured in our orbit from elsewhere in antiquity and not generated from Earth as was once believed. The soil of the Moon seems to be a billion years older than the rocks on its surface. Though the Moon is considered to have little or no magnetic field, its rocks seem to be highly mag-netized, and there are massive concentrations ("mascons") of mat-ter beneath the Moon's seas sufficient to gravitationally affect passing satellites. Among the rock samples brought back by both Soviet and American missions were found pure iron particles, which have not oxidized (rusted) at all. Though rustproof iron is completely unheard of in physics, the Moon's iron particles have an earthly counterpart in the thirty-foot-high solid iron Ashoka Pillar of indeterminate age (at least sixteen hundred years old) in the courtyard of Qutb Minar in New Delhi, India, that is also com-pletely free of rust.

But the most curious of our lunar neighbor's mysteries are a series of anomalies that seem to tie together. Many of the Moon's craters appear too round and too symmetrical to have been formed by meteor impacts, as was long supposed; Mars and Venus have similar craters, dispelling the idea that their perfection on the Moon was caused by its utter lack of atmosphere. The Moon's seas are fused plains of soil, requiring there at one time to have been a temperature of forty-five hundred degrees Fahrenheit or greater; this fused soil is loaded with rare metals and elements such as zirconium, titanium, yttrium, and beryllium, and is next to impos-sible to drill through. Substantial areas of the Moon's surface seem to be "paved with glass," as one scientific expert put it, positing that heat from a fantastically awesome solar flare may have scorched the Moon's surface about thirty thousand years ago. But there is also tremendous radioactivity in the upper eight miles of the Moon's forty miles of crust. Uranium, thorium, and potassium are present there in great quantities, creating an "embarrassingly high" radioactivity level read by *Apollo 15's* thermal equipment that caused one expert to exclaim, "My God, this place is about to melt!" The Moon's desolate and radioactive surface, according to NASA, was brought about in antiquity by "the violence of [multiple] cosmic bombardment[s]" which "exploded with the power of billions of H-bombs."

We have seen such fusion of sand into glass in our own age, at Trinity test site with the atomic bomb. Some of the Gobi Desert near Lob Nor Lake, where the Chinese have run their atomic tests, also has become glassine. But there are large areas of the Gobi, equally scarred, that were never visited by atomic weapons in the present day. The Gobi has long been a place of mystery. French Astronomer Royal and mayor of Paris, Jean-Sylvain Bailly, determined in 1778 that star maps brought back by missionaries in India were not only "many thousands of years old," but that "they showed stars which could not have been visible from their place of origin"; his conclusion was that the Indians had taken them from some more ancient civilization, and that the maps had to have been drawn from somewhere in the Gobi. The Gobi figures in ancient legends from central Asia concerning white men who came from the skies, about which Peter Kolosimo writes: "Many Soviet scientists are convinced of the existence of such visitors and have devoted much effort to finding their traces upon earth, and the Gobi Desert has been one of their favorite hunting grounds." There and in the caves of Turkestan, Russian investigators found what they believed could have been navigation instruments for cosmic vehicles, in the form of cone-shaped objects of glass or porcelain with a drop of mercury inside, corresponding to descriptions in the Sanskrit *Samaragansutradhara* and the *Ramayana* and *Dronaparva* texts of the *Mahabharata*.

In 1960, mathematician and physicist Professor Mikhail Agrest published in Moscow's *Literaturnaya Gazeta* his belief that Sodom and Gomorrah were nuclear blast sites, and that the mammoth Baalbek terrace of antiquity (in present-day Lebanon) was designed as a spaceship landing platform. Zecharia Sitchin concurs with this assessment of Baalbek, and cites a miles-wide area of scorched, blasted, and broken black rocks in the Sinai Peninsula that defy explanation. The Baalbek terrace is the most massive megalithic structure known in the world. Called the Heliopolis by the Greeks

("Sun City"), it consists of Roman temples built in succeeding ages to Jupiter and Venus (mostly destroyed in a 1759 earthquake), erected over an original prehistoric structure that was the temple dedicated to Astarte and Baal referred to in the Bible's Book of Kings. It is composed of limestone blocks too massive to accurately gauge in size or weight, but by the most conservative estimate they are approximately ten by thirty by sixty feet and 750 tons each, some estimates reaching as high as 1,500 tons. Baalbek's enclosure includes three of the largest stones ever used for such construction, called the Trilithon. About 13 feet high and 10 feet thick, they are 64, 63.5, and 62.5 feet long. These were somehow raised and put into place at a height of twenty-six feet. In their nearby quarry is another such stone that was never transported, thirteen by fourteen by seventy feet (approximate), conservatively estimated to weigh a thousand tons. The quarry is half a mile away. There are no cranes or instruments in the modern world capable of lifting, let alone transporting, more than perhaps one hundred tons.

The Russian investigators also considered North America's Death Valley between California and Nevada to be another possible nuclear site. "Around an imposing central building are the remains of a city that extended for about a mile," summarized adventurer William Walker in 1850 of damage to an unspecified area in this region. "There are . . . carbonized or vitrified blocks, the result of some terrible catastrophe. In the center of this city . . . is a rocky spur twenty or thirty feet high, on which the ruins of gigantic constructions can be seen. The buildings at their southern extremity look as though they had been in a furnace, and the rock on which they are built itself shows signs of having melted. Strange to say, the Indians have no tradition concerning the people who once lived here. The dismal ruins fill them with superstitious terror, but they know nothing of their history." Walker attributed the damage to volcanic eruption, not knowing that Death Valley has never experienced such activity, and couldn't have suffered the type of destruction evidenced even if it had.

There are a great many vitrified sites around the ancient world, for which there has never been a satisfactory explanation. Vitrification is the fusing of brick or stone into glassine glaze by extreme heat, which is common to nuclear destruction but has otherwise never been duplicated artificially despite many attempts. It is still considered a "phenomenon." In addition to the locations already mentioned, the ancient Hittite cities of Turkey are vitrified, as are forts found in Peru, Scotland, Ireland, France, and India. Historical sources in the Mediterranean attribute vitrification to the unknown chemical substance called "Greek Fire," which was reportedly able to burn underwater and was catapulted by ships against fortress walls. It was a weapon employed by the "Sea Peoples" (believed to be the ancestors of the Phoenicians and Carthaginians), who were as advanced, unknown, and migratory a race as the mysterious Aryan Indo-Europeans historically credited with the building of the Old World megaliths and the founding of Western civilization.

Among the most important of the world's vitrified sites is the advanced city of Mohenjo-Daro ("Mound of the Dead") in modern Pakistan, estimated to date from 2,500 BC or earlier. According to ancient texts and esoteric tradition, it was one of the seven cities of India's Rama Empire. When the city was excavated, skeletons scattered about the site were found lying together openly in the streets, unburied, no visible damage evident to signify what killed them. They were holding hands, as if having died suddenly and in full anticipation of their swift end. A. Gorbovsky's *Riddles of Ancient History* reported that skeletons found by Soviet scientists at nearby locations tested fifty times above the normal level of radioactivity. Thousands of clay vessel fragments were fused together into what have been labeled "black stones." There is no indication of volcanic activity having occurred in the region.

Accepting India's historical epic, the *Mahabharata,* at face value, descriptions of what happened to the site are reminiscent of the destruction wrought by modern weapons in 1945: ". . . [it was] a single projectile / Charged with all the power of the Universe. / An incandescent column of smoke and flame / As bright as the thousand suns / Rose in all its splendor . . . / . . . it was an unknown weapon, / An iron thunderbolt, / A gigantic messenger of death, / Which reduced to ashes / The entire race of the / Vrishnis and the Andakhas. / . . . The corpses were so burned / As to be unrecognizable. / The hair and nails fell out; / Pottery broke without apparent cause, / And the birds burned white. / After a few hours / All foodstuffs were infected . . . / . . . to escape from this fire / The soldiers threw themselves in streams / To wash themselves and their equipment." Not only is this description of destruction identical to that at Hiroshima and Nagasaki, but the survivors of those explosions also threw themselves into the water to try and ease the burning. The A-bomb's inventor, Dr.

Robert Oppenheimer, famous for his familiarity with ancient Sanskrit literature, was asked seven years after Alamogordo by a Rochester University interviewer whether that had been the first atomic detonation in the world, and he replied, "Well, yes, in modern history." After the first atomic test, Oppenheimer quoted the *Bhagavad Gita:* "Now I've become Death—the destroyer of worlds." He later added, "I suppose we all felt that way."

Other cities and sites of antiquity, and the substantial apparent impact damage on many of Mars' surface structures, would lend credence to the biblical "war in the heavens." These include an extremely dramatic hole, one thousand feet in diameter, in Cydonia's D&M Pyramid, with structural and surface damage and debris, looking very much like it was caused by explosive penetration. Numerous midair explosions, usually attributed to meteorites destroyed by the atmosphere, also have left their mark on the surface of Venus.

The list given of the anomalies on Mars, and on both its moons and Earth's, is only partial. NASA has investigated them, officially in some instances and most assuredly unofficially in others. A package of seventeen photos was given to the *Apollo 15* crew for study in 1971, with instructions to observe and report on them. These are mostly the areas mentioned so far where anomalies exist. It is noteworthy that the Sea of Tranquility, where the Blair Cuspids are located, was the first landing site of the Apollo missions. One drawing made by the astronauts of an eight-foot-high layered outcropping of rock near *Apollo 15's* landing site bears a remarkable resemblance to the polygonal walls of Sacsayhuaman in the Peruvian Andes. The mission's findings were not made public, and probably will not be without congressional pressure, but the areas in question and instructions for study are indicative of NASA's awareness of their significance.

Occasional glimpses of what might have been witnessed by the astronauts can be found in transcripts, such as *Apollo 17's* Ron Evans' report of a flashing light at the edge of the Orientale Basin, and the firsthand confirmation by *Apollo 11* astronauts of independently corroborated fluorescences on the lunar surface of up to fifty thousand square miles at a time, a phenomenon often observed from Earth and never adequately explained. In 1979, the former chief of NASA communications specialists, Maurice Chatelain, alleged that Neil Armstrong filmed UFOs on the Moon during his historic Moon walk, backing similar statements made earlier by another former NASA employee, Otto Binder. "The encounter was common knowledge in NASA," Chatelain said in his book, *Our Ancestors Came from Outer Space,* "but nobody has talked about it until now." The Space Agency and Armstrong himself dismissed the claim, but physicist and professor of mathematics at Moscow University Dr. Vladimir Azazha, ancient astronaut theorist Alexander Kazantsev, and Professor Sergei Boshich in Russia were certain it was true. Chatelain went on to say that, since astronaut Walter Schirra and *Gemini 8,* the term "Santa Claus" was employed to signal NASA that UFOs had been spotted, and that "all Apollo and Gemini flights were followed, both at a distance and sometimes also quite closely, by space vehicles of extraterrestrial origin—flying saucers, or UFOs ... if you want to call them by that name. Every time it occurred, the astronauts informed Mission Control, who then ordered absolute silence." *Apollo 14* lunar module pilot Edgar Mitchell, in a December 1972 BBC radio interview, answered in the affirmative to a caller's question as to whether or not NASA had any provisions for encountering extraterrestrials on the Moon or anyplace else in the solar system. Astronaut Gordon Cooper never claimed to have seen UFOs while in space, but testified to a United Nations committee that other astronauts had, and that he had seen them himself while still only a pilot in 1953 in Germany. "NASA and the government know very well that intelligent beings from other planets regularly visit our world to enter into discreet contact and observe us," Cooper is on record as saying. "They have an enormous amount of evidence, but have kept quiet in order not to alarm people."

The last live launch broadcast from NASA, done primarily to foster public and financial support for the Space Agency, was the Hubble repair mission on December 8, 1993. Since that time, all space transmissions have been scrambled and time delayed before release to the public. The repair shuttle photographed two rapidly moving white objects across Earth's horizon around 11:30 PM that startled the live commentator into silence. A few moments of confusion followed, the camera suddenly going fuzzy, shots of Mission Control and what was perhaps a cargo bay being shown with no word spoken before the crew of the shuttle were put on camera, all looking intently at their panels until one turned around to face the lens, smiling and saying, "You have to see this to believe it, J.T.!" Two years before, on September 15, 1991, the shuttle *Discovery* photographed strange glowing lights on Earth's horizon, which first slowed and stopped, then sharply changed both speed and direction in response to an unidentified flash from the lower left of the screen leaving a visible streak of light shooting through the space vacated by the central object. To all appearances, it looked like nothing less than a controlled object intelligently avoiding a hostile shot.

Mere weeks after WWII's end, the U.S. War Department secretly imported Nazi scientists in "Operation Paperclip," overseen by none other than Hitler's master spy, Reinhard Gehlen, who went on to become one of Allen Dulles' closest confederates when the CIA was formed two years later. S.S. elite Major Werner von Braun was brought to America with about 120 other German rocket scientists, lionized as one of the "100 Most Important Americans of the 20th Century" by *Life* magazine in 1990 for his building of the Saturn V rockets that took man to the Moon. Twenty to sixty thousand slave laborers at von Braun's Mittelbau-Dora factory died under the Nazi "extermination by work" program, with his full knowledge and unrepentant consent, building his V2 rockets that murdered about five thousand people in Belgium and Britain during the war. How could so execrable a record be sanitized as to make von Braun a great American hero, when so many others were executed and imprisoned at Nuremberg for exactly such acts? "Can there be any justification . . . for using men who worked with conviction for a criminal system?" asked Germany's Museum for Transport and Technology, at the fiftieth anniversary of the downfall of the Third Reich. "It was as if they had only ever thought of going to the moon," was the museum director's answer. Obviously, there had to be some practical reason for their wanting to do so.

Military involvement in space considerations has been intense from the beginning, and the suggestion made in 1994's sci-fi blockbuster film *Stargate* may not be as fictionally removed as it appears. In it, the military secretly send a nuclear device to the Egyptian planet of man's origins, in anticipation of a war with its occupants. Howard Koch, the playwright of Mercury Theatre's famous 1938 *The War of the Worlds* "Invasion from Mars" show, wrote in *The Panic Broadcast* (1970) that, "Not long ago there was a chilling prediction by an official in the American State Department. He projected a plan, which apparently his science advisors considered feasible, for launching a spaceship armed with nuclear missiles that could push the moon Phobus [*sic*] out of the Mars gravitational field across space and into our orbit." He suggested that the military would intend to use the satellite for a ready-made orbiting defense station. But given that the government must have strongly suspected at least by the time to which Koch was referring that Mars, and Phobos in particular, was the primary base of operations for the flying saucers visiting Earth on a regular basis, it could instead be interpreted that there may have been a more immediate and practical military reason for our probes to Phobos having been taken out by someone else's spaceships. This theory becomes all the easier to accept when it is realized that United States defense experts complained about a laser and ion emitter the Soviets had placed on *Phobos 2*, so powerful that they believed the Soviets were simply looking for an excuse to experiment with their own Star Wars weaponry. The ostensible reason for the probe's lethal equipment was given as the need to pulverize part of Phobos' surface for analysis of the gas that process would produce, and the dissenting experts were overruled by the White House "due to the improvement in Soviet-American relations."

What can we safely conclude from the evidence? The masses, including the vast majority of the scientific community, comfortably accept that there are no geometric anomalies on the surface of Mars at all, let alone on its moons or our own. But mathematics does not lie. It cannot. No natural formations could accidentally create precise angles and shapes, let alone relationships between objects. The faces of two Egyptian gods could not inadvertently erode into place, any more than could Mount Rushmore. A dying Pharaoh could not accidentally design his burial chamber according to mathematical correlations with the planet Mars, which in any event should have been beyond his ability to know. Rocks from the surface of a planet 34 million miles away, at its closest, some even joined together artificially in an intelligent structure, could not have gotten to Earth blown on a summer breeze. Tricks of light and shadow do not consistently remain at 19.5 degrees, or rocks line themselves up at uniform height. And that megalithic structures of precise astronomical orientation could be identical on two separate worlds is absolutely impossible . . . unless the builders on both worlds were the same, or at the very least in contact with each other.

That coincidence could play any part in all this becomes all the more unlikely when Ian Ridpath's *Journal of the British Interplanetary Society* article, "Signpost to Mars," is taken into account.

Ridpath writes that the name "Cairo" was originally "El-Kahira," from the Arabic "El-Kahir"—which means "Mars." The city was renamed in the tenth century AD, from a word loosely translated to mean "the camp," that has the same Arabic root-stem as "Mars"— *Masr*—which is confirmed by J. Aldridge's *Cairo: Biography of a City*. Its full name, according to the Encyclopedia Americana, is *Masr el Kahira,* the latter two words translated as "the victorious." With *Masr* being derivative of "Mars," the meaning becomes perfectly obvious.

In addition to the overwhelming geometrical and linguistic evidence, we have Vallée's Mars correlations to take into account, which are more astounding when combined with the fact that other UFOlogists noted the major flaps of 1967 and 1973 also occurred during the closest passings of Mars to Earth. There was unquestionably a link between Mars and Earth in antiquity, and the modern UFO evidence seems to indicate as strong a link in the present, as well. What remains to be seen is if the modern astronauts, piloting craft in our skies beyond twentieth-century terrestrial man's ability to construct, are the same as those from centuries past— and if so, to determine as much about them as possible from the ancient records in order to better understand their motives and relationship with us today.

8

Origins

I N THE EARLY 1970s, an independent Egyptologist named John
Anthony West made a discovery in the symbolist writings of
Alsatian mathematician and philosopher Schwaller de Lubicz
(1891–1962). Lubicz's arguments concerning the advanced mathematical knowledge of the ancient Egyptians in connection with
their architecture were not well received by traditional Egyptologists, because they flew in the face of established wisdom. Equally
unwelcome had been Lubicz's belief that the Giza Sphinx was
eroded not by wind, but by water. West, impressed with Lubicz's
mathematical findings, brought the water erosion theory to the
attention of an Oxford geologist via a mutual acquaintance. Receiving confirmation from the man that, yes, the difference between
wind and water erosion was not difficult to determine in virtually
all cases, West submitted a photograph to him, admitting up front
that he was pulling a bit of a trick on him. West had taken a picture of the Sphinx, using masking tape to conceal its head and
paws, revealing only the heavily eroded midsection of that structure. Could the geologist be certain what the cause of this particular erosion was? The geologist was quite definite that he could,
and determined immediately that it was done by water. After he
explained the differences between water and wind erosion and
demonstrated how this information applied to the photo, West
removed the tape to show him what he had been examining. The
geologist's eyes widened, and he said simply, "Oh."

The controversy over the ongoing exploration of this amazing anomaly is recorded in West's book, *Serpent in the Sky,* and
an Emmy Award-winning T.V. documentary called *Mystery of the
Sphinx.* The conclusions so far reached by him and his primary

colleagues in the investigation, Houston geophysicist Dr. Thomas L. Dobecki and Boston University geologist Dr. Robert M. Schoch, are as follows: the face of the Sphinx is not that of the Pharaoh Chephren, as long supposed, which was one of the primary (but flimsy) pieces of evidence for attributing its construction to him and therefore estimating its construction date sometime in the middle of the third millennium BC; at least three separate repair operations have been performed on the Sphinx in its long life (Chephren having done one); water is decidedly the cause of its erosion, almost certainly from a tremendous amount of precipitation; and the geological conditions of the Sphinx and its surrounding structures prove its construction to have been undertaken circa 10,000–5,000 BC. The dating is Schoch's, and was endorsed by nearly three hundred of his peers at the 1992 annual Geological Society of America meeting.

Admitting that these findings have not yet been established as absolute fact, what is most interesting about them in regards to this study is the official scientific and academic reaction to them. Intellectual opposition to West and his colleagues has been frankly violent, where they have not been completely ignored. Why? The commonly held theory that Chephren was the builder of the Sphinx has come from virtually nothing but gossip in ages long past Chephren's time, and in fact there is ancient documentary evidence in Cheops' famous "Inventory Stela" which plainly verifies that the Sphinx was in existence before Chephren was born. Put bluntly, the evidence—even on the traditional level—has always been more in opposition to the theory of Chephren's having built the Sphinx than in favor of it. Given this obvious discrepancy, one would think an historian would be ecstatic to discover actual evidence that Chephren did not build the Sphinx, because it would resolve that discrepancy and focus attention on better information from which a more accurate picture of ancient Egypt could be derived. Instead, the ranks of historians close against exactly such evidence, defending a picture that was never satisfactory in the first place.

This irrational rigidity is to be found everywhere in Egyptology. The more one studies the subject, the more apparent it seems that historical findings concerning ancient Egypt have come from about 10 percent fact, and 90 percent notion. Dating in any ancient history is notoriously precarious business, but even more so in Egypt, which may be far older than any civilization on Earth and was famous for intense secretiveness. Ancient Egypt is probably the most esoteric and occult of ancient civilizations, with initiates and priests concealing their knowledge in mathematical and hieroglyphic riddles and puns. Not a single record—down to monetary transactions or simple inventory or contracting, which we have in abundance on lesser structures—is left anywhere in all that sand, rock, or papyrus on the method of building their greatest monument, the Great Pyramid of Giza, which we cannot ourselves duplicate with all of our modern technology and equipment. Dating is so arbitrary that, between 1830 and 1880, four expert Egyptologists—Champollion, Lepsius, Mariette, and Brugsch—gave dates for the beginning of the First Dynasty that were two thousand years apart, the closest estimates being more than eight hundred years removed from each other. No standardized dates, or even names, have yet been agreed upon, making all the more inexplicable the certitude with which individual Egyptologists assign arbitrary dates, almost never with any kind of corroboration or even an explanation as to how they were arrived at.

The first thing one learns on a trip to Egypt is how little anyone knows about it. The ancient historians from whom we derive our knowledge of the country in antiquity, primarily Herodotus and Strabo, learned what they knew from nothing more than local gossip while passing through. Strabo seems to have had the more accurate knowledge, but we have fewer of his writings. Much of what was told Herodotus can be demonstrated to be false, but unfortunately has become a cornerstone of modern Egyptology. Herodotus was told that Cheops prostituted his own daughter to pay for the Pyramid, that the workers' food consumption while building it was recorded in hieroglyphs on the outer casing of the structure, that Cheops was buried beneath the Pyramid on an island in the middle of an underground lake, and other items of information that have since proven to be untrue, all relayed to him by his Egyptian guides.

Writing in 1946, L. Sprague and Catherine C. de Camp gave an excellent example of Egyptian guides that has not changed in the ensuing fifty years: "[O]ur guide . . . lectures us on pyramid lore while we are inside. His voice reverberates hollowly in the King's Chamber. His information is fifty years out of date and inaccurate to begin with, but there is no use questioning him on doubtful points. If we interrupt his well-rehearsed speech, which is all he really knows, he gets confused and has to go back to the beginning and start over like a phonograph record."

If a guide is asked how the pyramids were built, he will probably answer honestly that he does not know, but may venture an explanation concerning elaborate lever and pulley systems while admitting that the ancient Egyptians did not have such tools, or even the wheel. He will definitely say that the Great Pyramid of Giza is the oldest such structure, barring four previous attempts of laughably inferior quality (Saqqara, Meidum, and two at Dahshur), followed by the almost equally impressive pyramid of Chephren that is next to it, and that of Mycerinus—the third of the Giza complex—which is far less impressive. The Pharaoh Cheops (Khufu) will be named as the builder of the Great Pyramid, which was intended to be his burial place. The fact that neither his body nor anything else was ever found to have been in it will be ascribed to the work of grave robbers, despite a lack of evidence for anyone being inside the Great Pyramid before the Caliph al-Mamun broke into it in 820 AD. The fact that no record whatsoever of the Pyramid's construction exists to name Cheops as its builder will be answered by the belief that his cartouche (an oval-shaped enclosure of hieroglyphics spelling a name) was found in a remote chamber of the structure by Colonel Howard Vyse in 1837, even though that evidence is almost certainly fraudulent. As to why the Great Pyramid—inarguably the most impressive structure in the world, let alone the best of its type—was followed by a number of pyramids that did not improve but actually became worse in each succeeding generation, there will be no answer at all, even though the fact is undisputed.

Howard Carter, the discoverer of King Tutankhamen's tomb in 1922, was reputed to have said, "We do not know Egypt. We only think we do." The late E. A. Wallis Budge, formerly keeper of Egyptian and Assyrian antiquities at the British Museum, was honest enough in his volumes to admit that he did not have all the answers about ancient Egypt, offering as explanations for the strangeness of the country's beliefs only his best guesses and encouraging future investigators to follow after him and learn more. Unfortunately, Egyptology made the same mistakes as Herodotus, taking everything the ancient historian said to be undeniable truth instead of the several-times-removed conjecture that it was. John Anthony West has berated Egyptologists for wasting time debating how many asps bit Cleopatra instead of asking more serious and fundamental questions that have never had satisfactory answers. Those questions connect inextricably to all we know of ancient civilization in general.

For instance, if the pyramids were not designed to be tombs, what were they designed for? As early as 1813, astronomer Richard Proctor had discovered from ancient records that the Great Pyramid was used in antiquity as an astronomical observatory. Later researchers have confirmed that not only the pyramids but many ancient temples served the same function. Stonehenge, Woodhenge, and numerous other mounds and structures of the ancient world, from India to Mexico, have been shown to be accurate observatories, though the fact is not often discussed by traditionalists because it is an embarrassment. They have no ready answer for it, given that the people theorized to have existed at the time of their construction were supposed to be considerably less advanced. How could the Egyptians have perfect geodetic knowledge of Earth, without aerial surveys? Yet their monuments smile in elegant silence, bridging the centuries with ineradicable truth, obvious to the eye, the compass, and the logarithmic tables. The medical scrolls discussing pulverized scarabs and crocodile dung seem, at first glance, to be dreadfully primitive abominations, but on closer scrutiny, the compounds prove to be similar in chemical composition to our own antibiotics of today. Sumerian, Babylonian, and Egyptian astronomy (among others) were more accurate six thousand years ago than was ours until the eighteenth or nineteenth centuries, and in some regards we are still evidently behind them.

Any student of ancient history—whether of Egypt or any other long-supposed "primitive" civilization—is left with an increasing mountain of evidence that does not merely suggest, but clearly demonstrates, superior scientific wisdom in antiquity that we are only now beginning to appreciate sufficiently as our understanding and technology develops. It quickly becomes apparent that we have never had any reason to believe these civilizations to be primitive, other than their chronological age. The reasoning goes that, since civilization is a long, uphill evolution, then all which came before is automatically inferior to that which has followed. If the central premise were true, then the conclusion would be also. But any faulty premise can only lead to faulty conclusions, and it seems more and more that we have been working on faulty premises. This is perfectly understandable, since no one's first thought is that visitors from another planet, or perhaps even solar system, are connected to terrestrial occurrences, either past or present. Barring evidence for such a theory, it is nothing more than an entertaining hypothesis. But we now have evidence for exactly that theory, which gives us a mandate to explore if we are honestly to call ourselves seekers after the truth.

The greatest problem in introducing new theories is that, ironically enough, nothing is more irrational than science. It rivals religious faith in certitude on matters it cannot by its own admission fully know, tending to make sweeping intellectual decisions on evidence so scanty it is almost inconsequential. The entire theory of evolution is based not even on complete skeletons or skulls, but mere bone fragments in most instances, and not enough of those to cover a pool table. The beliefs, similarly, that Cheops and Chephren were the builders of two of the pyramids in the Giza complex in the third millennium BC are also based on virtually no evidence, but are so rigorously held to be true that any other suggestion is regarded as heresy.

The only evidence of the Great Pyramid having been built by Cheops was discovered by Colonel Howard Vyse, the ambitious black-sheep adventurer of an aristocratic English family, whose character was sharply impugned by former colleague Giovanni Battista Caviglia. Vyse admitted in his journal entry of January 27, 1837, that "I naturally wished to make some discoveries before I returned to England." On the evening of March 30, 1837, he did. They were in the latter four of the five so-called "relieving spaces" above the King's chamber discovered on the expedition, which Caviglia actually pointed out must exist before Vyse dismissed him from the site and blasted into them. The first such space had been discovered by Nathaniel Davison in 1765, and it was as conspicuously absent of any markings as Vyse's chambers were conspicuously rife with them.

From the first, Vyse's discovered quarry markings and cartouches in these chambers were suspicious. No other inscriptions have ever been found in any of the Giza pyramids, only those chambers opened by Howard Vyse. Vyse was aware that the particular red ochre paint in which the names on the cartouches were written was impossible to historically date, and he had seen similar genuine markings a few weeks before at a site discovered by Caviglia called Campbell's Tomb. Vyse mysteriously dismissed all of his foremen during the time his finds were made. Vyse's companion, copper mill superintendent and general go-between J. R. Hill (who ended up owning the Cairo Hotel after his association with the man), was documented in Vyse's own chronicles as going in and out of the chambers with red paint, ostensibly to write in them the names by which they were being christened. Even one of Vyse's conveniently arranged witnesses to the discovery of the cartouches, Egyptian Public Works Department engineer John Perring, voiced a veiled misgiving about the find in *The Pyramids of Gizeh,* remarking that such paint, called *mograh,* was still in use and that "such is the state of preservation of the marks in the quarries, that it is difficult to distinguish the mark of yesterday from one of three thousand years." Vyse repeatedly stalled experts from copying his discovered inscriptions, for no fathomable reason, and the discovered cartouches are unlike those found anywhere else in Egypt— being large, crude and sloppy, and uniquely upside down or vertical, as though made hastily at an awkward angle, which the cramped spaces of the relieving chambers would necessitate should the markings have been made after the chambers had been sealed. These stand in sharp contradistinction to actual quarry markings on the stones that are right-side up and cleanly legible. Only the eastern walls had no markings on them, as if the ancient builders had anticipated the chambers being blasted into in exactly that location and obligingly left them bare.

But most conspicuously, the Pharaoh Cheops' name is *misspelled* in these cartouches, misspellings identical to those in Leon de Laborde et Linat's *Voyage de l'Arabie Petrie* and John Gardner Wilkinson's *Materia Hieroglyphica* (the standard book on the subject at the time), both or either of which would have to have been in Vyse's possession, and neither of which was updated and corrected before Vyse's most fortuitous finds. Moreover, no other spelling of Cheops' name in Egypt matches those found by Vyse. The misspelling was soon to be confirmed by Lepsius' *Denkmaler,* Kurt Sethe's *Urkunden des Alten Reich,* and A. H. Gardiner and T. E. Peet's *The Inscriptions of Sinai.* Wilkinson's *Manners and Customs of the Ancient Egyptians* published the correct spellings at virtually the same time as Vyse's cartouches were being studied by the experts—and found wanting.

The British Museum's hieroglyphic expert, Samuel Birch, was lengthy and thorough in his analysis, the conclusions of which were somehow taken by most Egyptologists as confirming the authenticity of Vyse's discovered cartouches despite the fact that he voiced a great many misgivings. The chief problem he found was that the styles of the writings were semihieratic and hieratic, which did not come into use until many centuries after the Fourth Dynasty in which Cheops lived. Many of the symbols following the cartouches had no discernible parallels anywhere else in Egypt, and were all but illegible. A hieroglyphic meaning "good" or "gracious," simultaneously used as a numeral, had never been found before and has never been found since. And a royal title written in the same anachronistic hieratic hand employed a phrasing found only in one other place: the coffin of the ruler Amasis in the sixth century BC, 2,000 years following the reign of Cheops.

In other words, the scripts were from multiple time frames, often illegible and other times indecipherable, and without precedent or parallel. Birch also found not one name but *two* inscribed in the Pyramid's markings, which he noted were identical to those found in Wilkinson's *Hieroglyphica.* One of these would have been the name of Cheops' brother, who it was conceivable could have completed the work begun by Cheops, but the inscription could not have been his for the very simple reason that it was found in a lower chamber than the one in which Cheops' name was inscribed—i.e., in chronologically reverse order. Unable to reconcile this discrepancy, Birch concluded that "the presence of this [second] name in the quarry mark, in the Great Pyramid, is an additional embarrassment."

Germany's leading Egyptologist, Carl Richard Lepsius, independently came to many of the same conclusions as Birch. Close to a century after Vyse's finds, Gaston Maspero was still commenting on the unresolved "Problem of the Second Name," which, as he agreed, "has caused much embarrassment to Egyptologists." Similarly, Sir Alan Gardiner's *Egypt of the Pharaohs* made specific comparison between the correct spelling of Cheops' name and the former incorrect one that Vyse claimed was genuine. He mentioned the cartouche of Cheops being found "in various quarries, in the tombs of his kinsfolk and nobles, and in certain writing of later date," but made no mention of its being in the Great Pyramid. Gardiner also completely omitted any mention of Vyse's name in general, let alone of the next discovery he was to make—an omission which speaks eloquently in its silence.

Even though Vyse's cartouches were deemed "embarrassing" by so many experts, both at the time and after, his "discovery" was widely taken as confirmation of Herodotus. What made the virtually unquestioning acceptance of the anomalous cartouches all the more difficult to understand was the fact that, in July of that same year, Howard Vyse suspiciously made another incredible find: in the third pyramid of the Giza complex, he claimed to have

discovered the body of Mycerinus, that structure's supposed architect. Despite Giovanni Belzoni's having been in the very chamber
Vyse said he found the body, finding nothing himself but an empty
granite coffer and its lid in 1818, Vyse somehow miraculously discovered there, in a rubbish pile, nineteen years later, a wooden
coffin lid with the inscription "Men-ka-ra" (Mycerinus) and fragments of skeleton and mummy-cloth. Soon after, on the ceiling of
the second subsidiary pyramid of the Giza complex, which he
blasted into, Vyse also found Mycerinus' name—in red ochre paint.
Before that, the third pyramid's attribution to Mycerinus was no
more certain than was Cheops', written of only as hearsay by
Diodorus Siculus and—once more—Herodotus.

The sarcophagus lid was lost at sea on its way to the British
Museum for authentification, but the wooden lid (still at the
museum) and the remains were examined. Wilkinson accepted the
mummy case as genuine, but noticed that the grave cerements
looked too modern for such an ancient date, and Birch found "considerable difference of style" between the coffin and Fourth Dynasty
monuments—in fact, the lid's style was not used before the Saite
period, almost a full two thousand years later. It wasn't until 1883
that Gaston Maspero determined the lid to be a Twenty-fifth
Dynasty restoration job, and in 1892 Kurt Sethe pronounced the
consensus of Egyptologists that it could only have been fashioned
sometime after the Twentieth Dynasty. In our own century,
K. Michaelowsky, in *Art of Ancient Egypt,* confirmed that carbon
dating showed the lid "certainly dates from the Saitic period" of
660 BC or later, and I. E. S. Edwards stated in *The Pyramids of
Egypt* that the bones radiocarbon-tested to early Christian times.

In short, the Mycerinus find was determined to be false within
about fifty years and swept under the rug, a much more noticeable "embarrassment" than the previous Cheops cartouches—but
it was detected too late to prevent Vyse's promotion to general.
Today, no one accepts that the body found by Vyse was that of
Mycerinus. Despite that fact, no professional Egyptologist will officially pronounce Vyse's find by the only word that accurately
describes it. But, as Zecharia Sitchin so succinctly puts it, "If the
remains were not of an original burial, then they must have been
of an intrusive burial; but in such a case, mummy and coffin would
be of the same period. This was not the case: here, someone had
put together a mummy unearthed in one place, a coffin from
another place. The unavoidable conclusion is that the find

represented a *deliberate archaeological fraud.*" In 1983—three years after publishing his excellent study of Vyse's obviously questionable work in *The Stairway to Heaven*—Sitchin was approached by the great-grandson of a master mason named Humphries Brewer, who held contemporaneous family records confirming that Brewer had been engaged by Vyse as one of his gunpowder blasters, and been fired from the Pyramid site because he objected to J. R. Hill's entering the newly opened chambers with a bucket of red paint on the night the cartouches were forged.

Given the uncertainty of Herodotus' original information, the unquestionable lack of authenticity of the Mycerinus find, and the severe doubts from the very beginning concerning the veracity of the Cheops inscription discovered in the Great Pyramid by the same man in the same year, it should have been a matter of some relief for Egyptologists to find other evidence that Cheops definitely built the Pyramid, or that he did not. In fact, such proof was found in 1850 by Mariette in a limestone tablet in the nearby ruins of the Temple of Isis. Called the "Inventory Stela," it presently resides in the Cairo Museum. A self-laudatory document commemorating the temple's restoration, it bears the cartouche of Cheops in its opening statements, reading, "Live, Horus Mezdau. (To) King (of) Upper and Lower Egypt, Khufu, is given Life! He founded the House of Isis, Mistress of the Pyramid, beside the House of the Sphinx." In that phrase alone, it is established that both the Pyramid and the Sphinx were already standing when Khufu (Cheops) did his restoration, and before Chephren—the theoretical builder of the Sphinx—was even born.

However, rather than accept the Inventory Stela as proof of these facts, thereby upsetting the status quo, the stela was pronounced a forgery, and Vyse's finds were upheld as being legitimate. Despite the stela's exclusion from the accepted canon of authentic items, and having some personal doubts himself, James H. Breasted included it among his records of the Fourth Dynasty in his standard work, *Ancient Records of Egypt.* Maspero's comprehensive *Dawn of Civilization* in 1920 also took the stela's information on Khufu and his times as factual. But to this day, the supposed find of a man shown to have perpetrated at least one archaeological fraud is accepted as more legitimate evidence than the Inventory Stela, even though that stela shows all the earmarks of authenticity.

Why has there been such refusal to revise, or even reconsider, previous erroneous assumptions, especially those that had only the most questionable evidence to back them in the first place? Why accept the word of so unreliable an adventurer as Howard Vyse, over that of a seemingly much more authentic limestone stela, that is probably—or at the very least *possibly*—contemporaneous with the very Pharaoh in question? Especially when Egyptology's foremost experts have consistently expressed grave doubts? Sir Gardner Wilkinson suggested early on that the Great Pyramid was never intended to hold a corpse. Sir Flinders Petrie, in *The Pyramids and Temples of Gizeh* concurred, saying that "the coffer has certain remarkable cubic proportions which show a care and design beyond what could be expected in any burial coffer," noting also that the ventilation shafts appeared to imply frequent usage, possibly for some initiatory purpose. With two such preeminent names in the field willing to consider alternative explanations for the Great Pyramid from the start, why would their colleagues—then and now—be so reluctant to engage in reexamination of highly tenuous initial theories?

Perhaps the answer can be found in another question: how is it that countless trained geologists—who know, by sight, the difference between water and wind erosion—can have missed the water damage on the body of the Sphinx that is as plain to the naked eye today as it has been for thousands of years? Quite simply, the answer can only be because the *idea* of "Sphinx" preempts its actual appearance. When anyone looks at the Sphinx, scientist or not, they don't see the physical components of its being and construction—they see, instead, *Sphinx.* And the *idea* of "the Sphinx" as a structure eroded by centuries of wind is stronger than the *reality* that it is in fact a structure eroded centuries ago by water.

But, as Sir Mortimer Wheeler once said, "Archaeology is not a science, it's a vendetta." He might as well have been speaking of science, alone. Anyone naive enough to believe that Science is a temple devoted to truth and open enquiry has never encountered the tribunals held on the works of Immanuel Velikovsky or Wilhelm Reich. Reich was imprisoned for two years for contempt of court, where he died. His lab equipment was smashed with an axe and his books burned. His only crime had been to suggest that there was a natural force (which he called "orgone energy") that could be harnessed for the physical and emotional well-being of living organisms, curbing aggressive and destructive impulses— the apotheosis, it could be argued, of the "Make Love, Not War" philosophy. Timothy Leary was similarly persecuted, and in fact spent several years in jail, merely for advocating continued study of lysergic acid diethylamide (LSD) in a controlled setting. The Temple of Science's treatment of these pioneers is indistinguishable from that given Copernicus and Galileo by the Church of centuries past.

Arguably, this irrationality stems in large part from individual egos, but it is not unlikely that a certain amount of everyday fear enters into it as well. Not only fear of new ideas, which threaten carefully circumscribed belief systems, but also, on the more mundane level, the simple fear of peer pressure and ridicule. Status anxiety is connected to career advancement, and it never helps a career-minded individual to break ranks. Most academics' work is built on theories of established predecessors, and to acknowledge those predecessors' assumptions as false is to risk invalidating their own work, thus dooming it to the dustbin of history. Finally, in a world where money flows most easily to those who best hew to the party line, new ideas are going to be difficult to brook. On the personal level, it is frequently argued that there is no need to "drag extraterrestrials into the picture," which even Jacques Vallée has gone on record as saying. But the answer can only be that there is no *need* to *exclude* them, either. The only "need" of science is to explain the facts, having first defined them.

A century ago, the acknowledged authority on Egypt—Sir E. A. Wallis Budge—did not exclude the very possibility now under our scrutiny. In *The Gods of the Egyptians,* he wrote, "It may be urged that Tattu was merely the seat of the shrine of the god Osiris in the northern kingdom, just as Abydos was his sanctuary in the southern kingdom, but this explanation of the title is insufficient. It may further be urged that, inasmuch as the titles 'lord of Abydos,' 'lord of Tattu' occur in connection with others which have reference to Osiris in his capacity as governor of the Underworld, the Abydos and Tattu here mentioned are mythological cities and not cities upon Earth." If myth can be construed as another form of actual history, then this is a frank admission to the possibility of other planets entering into Egyptian writings.

One can save the price of a ticket to Egypt to discover how little agreement exists among Egyptologists on their own fundamental tenets by examining Budge's work alone. As stated above, he was at least honest enough to admit that he was offering only best guesses, not certainties. For starters, Budge offers a guess as to how the name Egypt even came about: "Naville suggests that the name Egypt is derived from Ageb, and that the country was the 'land of the flood,' *i.e.* the Inundation, which was poured out over the whole land by the Flood-god Ageb. Masr, the Arab name for Cairo, means to many Muslims all Egypt, and it is probable that Hekaptah did the same to the old inhabitants of the country." Peter Tompkins, in *Secrets of the Great Pyramid,* offers that the most ancient legends of the Arabs and the Jews were that the Pyramid "was erected to memorialize a tremendous cataclysm in the planetary system which affected the globe with fire and flooding," which could offer another meaning for Naville's "land of the flood." Records of these legends are preserved at Oxford's Bodleian Library, in a tenth-century manuscript by the Arabic writer Masudi, and in writings by Abou Balkhi. Tompkins reports these writers stating that a king (sometimes referred to as Surid or Saurid) had a vision in antiquity about the world being turned upside down when "the Heart of the Lion would reach the first minute of the head of Cancer," or when the precession of the stars went from Leo into Cancer (an idea also held by Plato and the later Hermetic Order of the Golden Dawn). This king built the pyramids to incorporate all the world's learning in astronomy, geometry, and physics. Also supposedly placed in the pyramids were treatises on various machines such as "celestial spheres and terrestrial globes," as well as on precious stones and such technology as "malleable glass." This idea seems less far-fetched when one takes into account the discovery of perfect mathematical relations between the Great Pyramid and the measurements not only of our own planet, but at least one other in our solar system and apparently even between Earth and the sun.

Egypt was most famous as "the Two Lands." Here, Budge cannot even agree with himself as to just what those Two Lands are supposed to be. There is no question that one is called "the Red Land" and the other "the Black Land," but just what those are has never been clearly defined. He first said, in *The Mummy,* that "the Egyptians gave many names to their land, but the commonest was Kam-t [Khem], *i.e.* the 'Black,' because of the dark colour of the soil; the deserts on each side of the Nile were spoken of as Tesher-t [Dvrt], *i.e.* the 'Red,' because of the lighter colour of the sand and stones." Thirty-seven years later, in *Amulets and Superstitions,* he seems to have changed his mind: "The word 'Alchemy,' *i.e.* the 'Black Art,' or rather the 'magical craft of the

Black Country,' is derived from one of the names of Northern Egypt, which was called the 'Black Country' because of the brownish-black colour of the soil in the Delta, as opposed to the 'Red Country,' which was given to Upper Egypt because of its reddish-yellow sand." This explanation cannot by traditional theory be accurate, because the Pharaonic Pa-Ra-Emheb Stela places the Sphinx, which is in Lower Egypt, in the "Sacred Desert" (another name for the Red Land), and also because it would assign the red crown to the Black Land, which makes no sense at all.

Upper Egypt refers to the southern end of the Nile, closer to that river's source, and Lower Egypt refers to the Delta at the northern end, where it empties into the Mediterranean. These are also sometimes referred to as the "northern kingdom" and the "southern kingdom," the northern (or Lower) being represented by a red crown and the southern (or Upper) being represented by a white crown. It is interesting that not only is Budge uncertain whether the Two Lands are the Nile itself and the desert on either side of it, or the Upper being one and the Lower the other, but—even reversing the associations he gives them—he has no explanation why the Red Land would be represented by a red crown while the Black Land is represented by a *white* one. For that matter, no other Egyptologist has an answer to that question, either—in fact, the question has never been raised at all. Clive Barrett does bring up the folkloric fact that the Egyptians so feared the Sacred Desert, the Red Land, that black and red were their respective colors for good and evil, and other sources make mention that the Arabs called Ra (the Sphinx), who resided in the Sacred Desert, the "Father of Terror" *(Abu Khawl);* but just how the white crown came about—and other religious associations utilizing the same color—remains a mystery.

The origin of the word "pyramid" is also in question. Budge believed it to have been a Greek word, derived from the Egyptian *peremus,* meaning either the slope or height of the structure. Theologian Joseph Seiss defined it by the Coptic *pyr-met,* "division of ten." Author Tom Valentine suggests that it may derive from the Hebrew-Chaldeaic *urrim midden,* or "light measures." Adventurer-archaeologist David Hatcher Childress says the word is Greek, meaning "fire in the center." One Egyptian word for the pyramids, *khuti* or *khufu* (the latter also the Egyptian name of the Pharaoh supposed to have been entombed in the Great Pyramid), meaning "glorious light," corresponds also with the Mayan name for their pyramids, *pirhua manco,* "revealer of light." Other authors have suggested the Greek word *pyramis,* meaning "wheaten cake," which makes little sense.

The actual Egyptian term for the structures was *mer,* meaning "Place of Ascension," which has always been taken to be a reference to the soul's ascension to the semicircular ocean of the heavens over Earth after death, one of the reasons the pyramids were believed to be tombs. Another reason for associating them with tombs was that the largest cemetery in the world, the Necropolis, is situated directly adjacent to the Giza pyramid complex, but as author and historian J. David Davis has commented, this logic is akin to stating that the Cathedral of Notre Dame is a burial complex because there is a graveyard beside it. Where bodies of royalty were plainly buried in the Valley of the Kings and Queens (hence the name), they have never been found in the pyramids. Nor are any funerary inscriptions inside them, or any decoration whatsoever, or any funerary offerings or implements. Traditional historians blame grave robbery for this, but until the Caliph al-Mamun forcibly broke his way into the Great Pyramid in 820 AD, there was no indication that anyone could have been, or ever was, inside it since the time of its construction. It was as barren then as it is today, the only access to the so-called burial chamber blocked by three red granite stones so immovable that al-Mamun had to go around them to gain access—with no evidence existing that anyone before him had done so.

Of particular interest in the word *mer* is that *To-mera,* or "land of the mer," was another name the Egyptians gave to their country. It is believed to refer to the pyramids, owing to its use as a term for the pyramidical meridian triangle, while also meaning "Place of Ascension." The word obviously is also part of the name Sumer (Su-Mer), called Shinar or Shumer in the Bible and known to us as Sumeria. The name specifically translates as "The Land" and "ones who watch," the significance of which will be discussed in more detail shortly.

It is not at all difficult to understand why erroneous assumptions were made in Egyptology's infancy. Extraterrestrial contact would have been the furthest idea from anyone's mind in Napoleon's time, when Egypt was first scientifically explored by the savants. But even then, mathematical knowledge of Earth was sufficient to determine that the Great Pyramid was oriented accurately to the planet's cardinal points, that the Egyptians had obviously used the baseline meridian for their measurements, and that it neatly cut the Delta region perfectly in half and enclosed the entire region in right-angled diagonals drawn through it. It was even suspected that the Great Pyramid might be sited more or less at the exact geodetic center of the world, which on some map projections it is, though geodesy is not a precise science. It would be some time yet before the omphalos stones of sacred temples ("oracle" stones, "navels" of the world connecting the sites to heaven, from which voices were said to emanate), which can be used for mathematical computations in the same way as an abacus, would be found to be situated at precise latitudinal increments for thirty degrees with two more equidistant from east to west. The frequently bizarre-seeming hieroglyphic drawings in the walls of temples, showing such things as kings at odd angles with erect phalli resting against right-angled serpents, had not yet been seen to represent precise *pi* and *phi* ratios as noticed by Schwaller de Lubicz, and Stecchini had yet to discover that the Book of the Dead contained elaborate and accurate mathematical formulas concealed in symbols (specifically, that the numbers ascribed to the spirits of the Netherworld in Chapter 64, multiplied together, provide correct ratios of Earth's measurements). And even having been discovered, each new find about this ancient civilization was—and is—disputed among experts, generally to be derided, ridiculed, or completely ignored, despite the fact that mathematics is incapable of lying.

But we are no longer in Napoleon's time, now having not only sufficient geodetic knowledge and mathematical precision to prove the Great Pyramid's astounding measurements on our own world, but equivalent measurements from the planet Mars, and even rocks of Martian origin on Earth to help us focus our Egyptology. In addition, there is ample record of the Egyptians possessing "magic" that we would call technology. Plutarch, Lucian Samosotan, Pausanias, and St. Augustine wrote of temples around Greece and Egypt which had perpetual lights, unaffected by wind or rain. Underground chamber number seventeen of the Temple of Hathor at Dendera shows priests carrying what look exactly like giant halogen lamps, their filaments depicted as snakes, which are attached by braided cords to pillars that could be batteries—this would easily explain how the Egyptians were able to paint the deeply recessed cavern-tombs in the Valley of the Kings when it has been demonstrated that refraction of light by mirrors was not possible, and no soot is in evidence to signify the use of torches.

In 1938–39, German archaeologist Wilhelm Koenig discovered several earthenware jars in Baghdad, containing iron rods encased in copper cylinders and covered with asphalt. The following year he published the opinion in *9 Jahre Irak* that they were electrical batteries. General Electric's Willard Gray duplicated them after the war, filling them with copper sulfate (the original electrolyte could not be determined), and found them capable of electroplating objects. Since many finds from the area turned out on examination to be gold plated, it was determined that the batteries had indeed been used for that purpose, and their having been found in magicians' huts testified to just what sort of secrets the high priests were guarding.

Moses himself received a Pharaoh's education, in mystery school, which is to say in science. Moses learned sufficient science to construct the Ark of the Covenant, when given instructions by God. There are many chests in Egypt, identical to the description of the Ark in the Bible, called *tabots,* and there is no way Moses would not have recognized these as what was being described by Yahweh. We have long supposed these merely to be ornamental chests, with no other function, and indeed in later history perhaps that is all they became; but they may well have been something else to an older and more technologically advanced Egypt, just as the "solar barque of millions of years" and ushabti figures may actually have been something far more in antiquity than they came to be regarded in later dynasties.

The Ark is perhaps the best connecting ground between the seemingly opposed schools of science and religion, demonstrably being a giant capacitor—i.e., "loudspeaker." The Hebrews even called the part of the Ark from which God's voice came the *Dvir,* meaning "speaker," in exactly the same way we would refer to that functional device on our own electronic instruments. Maurice Denis-Papin, descendant of the famous inventor, determined that the Ark was exactly such a device, capable of holding five hundred to seven hundred volts per vertical meter when contained in a dry space, dischargeable to the earth by means of its garlands. Peter Tompkins notes that such a device, insulated from the ground, acts like a Leyden jar, "giving off fiery rays" as the Bible says it did, acting more or less as an "energy accumulator" not unlike Wilhelm Reich's "orgone box" which Albert Einstein was quite intrigued with. The British inventor Sir W. Siemens discovered the Leyden jar effect independently of these theories, when he found his wine bottle became one simply by being held over his head while he stood on the Great Pyramid's summit. The pyramids may actually be such accumulators of energy, as 1968 Nobel Prize-winner in physics Dr. Luis Alvarez discovered when he attempted to find hidden chambers in Chephren's pyramid (as it is called) by means of a cosmic ray device, considered foolproof, which worked everywhere but in the pyramids. It "defied all known laws of physics," according to the international team involved in the project.

It was the Ark that caused the walls of Jericho to fall when God's people—at a time of his command—gave a great shout together. Why wouldn't they fall, if bombarded by amplified sound waves at the right frequency? And why wouldn't someone drop dead on the spot, as anyone did (having been commanded not to, on pain of their life), if they were to touch the two opposing plates of a high-voltage capacitor, completing the circuit and discharging the electricity through their bodies? For the religious to admit that their God uses science is to dismiss him as being God, at least by their narrowly circumscribed prejudices, and for scientists to admit the same thing is for them to acknowledge that someone with superior technology was meddling around in human affairs, at a time when all men were supposed to be superstitious primitives.

Neither science nor religion are demoted by the incorporation of extraterrestrial intervention theory, but are actually made more sensible by it. There is evidence of science and technology in the Ark of the Covenant. Its science could well answer a few questions, such as how great weights were lifted by the ancients in the construction of their megaliths. John Anthony West suggested that sound may have been used for that purpose, based on two pieces of evidence: one is that we are today capable of lifting miniscule objects of negligible weight by the employment of sound technology, holding them in "pockets" created by reflection of sound waves between two amplifying disks; the other is that Egyptian artifacts, especially the gigantic obelisks, are demonstrably harmonic, meaning that they resonate on an audible frequency (a musical note) when struck. Partially supporting West's idea is mythology itself. Merlin was said to have "danced" the stones of Stonehenge into place by his magic, and that magic—the magic of the Fairy Folk—was "music." (See Chapter 9.) Apollo, similarly, employed "music" in building, as recorded in H. A. Guerber's *The Myths of Greece and Rome*: "Apollo . . . went to assist Neptune, who had also been banished to earth, to build the walls of Troy. Scorning to perform any menial tasks, the God of Music seated himself near by [*sic*], and played such inspiring tunes that the stones moved into place of their own accord."

West did not mention, as other authors have, that the so-called King's coffer in the Great Pyramid also is harmonic. That "coffer" has the exact same dimensions as the Ark of the Covenant, as Worth Smith, Joseph Seiss, Peter Tompkins, and others have noticed. When given a sound slap with the open hand, the coffer can be heard to give off a low note which lasts for a considerable time, all the more remarkable for the fact that it has suffered considerable structural damage over the years. And this theory might also explain what the mysterious "dead spaces" are above the King's chamber in the Great Pyramid. Called by some "relieving spaces" for their supposed purpose of serving as an earthquake buffer—which may actually be one of their functions, there being no reason why they must be present only for one single reason— and called "spirit stones" by the Egyptians, these are five narrow air spaces, separated by eight to nine fifty-ton blocks of granite forming floors and ceilings between each. There is no reason they could not also be resonance chambers, as Zecharia Sitchin has suggested, each successive one resonating the sound for greater amplification. We would do well to recall the substantial evidence for the moons of both Earth and Mars being hollow, our own Moon known also to resonate. Sound resonation could have applications in physics for the movement of tremendous masses that we are only now beginning to suspect.

Indeed, the brilliant inventor Nikola Tesla considered exactly such a thing, when he experimented with his theory of "telegeo-dynamics," in 1898. He attached a tiny electromechanical oscillator to an iron pillar that went through the basement of his loft building, and in minutes, the oscillatory vibrations were carried through the substructure of Manhattan, shaking buildings and shattering windows in the immediate vicinity. Tesla turned the pocket-sized device off as soon as he realized the destruction it was causing, but boasted after similar later experiments. In one, he had broken a steel link two feet long and two inches thick with the resonance from a like device no bigger than an alarm clock and with no more than 2.5 horsepower; in another, with the same device, he had set up a vibration in a matter of minutes in the steel scaffolding of a ten-story building under construction that drove the workers off in panic that it was about to collapse. Tesla claimed that not only could he destroy the Brooklyn Bridge with his device in under an hour, but he could eventually even split the Earth itself in two. All with "but a fusillade of taps, no one of which would have harmed a baby." In fact, though he failed to interest Westinghouse in developing it, he described to the press an apparatus based on the same principle that was "a cylinder of finest steel—suspended in midair by a type of energy which was old in principle but which had been amplified by a secret principle—combined with a stationary part. Powerful impulses impressed upon the floating cylinder would react on the stationary part and through it, on the Earth."

The question of extraterrestrial contact in antiquity is essentially one of *context*. If one assumes, from the outset, that the study of ancient civilization is that of agrarian societies in stages of evolutionary progression, then that becomes the filter through which discovered facts are established, and anything contrary to that idea will be ignored, dismissed, or forgotten as an anomalous misperception. That same filter is the reason why the eyes of trained geologists missed the water damage to the Sphinx. This presumption of evolving civilization has ruled all scholarly and scientific enquiry from the beginning, for the quite understandable reason that, without any evidence to the contrary, it would seem likelier that man is an isolated creature on a planet fortunate enough to have evolved him. Though evidence has emerged for the alternate argument of extraterrestrial intervention and/or colonization in antiquity, counterresearch has been slowed by the tremendous opposition it faces from the scientific and academic communities.

In actuality, some serious research into the question of extraterrestrial intervention was done at least fifteen years before Viking's Martian discoveries. At that time, chief spokesman Erich Von Daniken's lack of scholarship was used as an excuse to dismiss the entire subject, ignoring the much better—but sometimes flawed—work of Maurice Chatelain, Jean Sendy, Robert Charroux, Jacques Bergier, Andrew Tomas, W. Raymond Drake, Peter Kolosimo, Barry H. Downing, and others, all of whom wrote at length on the subject since the late 1960s. Alexander Kazantsev, Aimé Michel, I. S. Shklovskii, and one or two other Russian scientists predated them, unashamed to go on the record with their belief that ancient astronauts were involved in man's early development. Carl Sagan, as Shklovskii's translator, even brought up the ancient divinity Oannes in regard to the theory.

Oannes is the most ancient legendary creature, or race, credited with the founding of human civilization on Earth, according to the Babylonian historian-priest Berossus, with roots going all the way back to the beginning of Sumer as the god Enki. Certain tribes of Africa refer to him as Nommo, and to his race as the race of Nommos. One of these tribes, the Dogon, alternately call this race "the Masters of the Water," "the Instructors," and "the Monitors." His race is sometimes referred to in Babylonian writings as "the Annedoti," for which no proper translation is available, but which Robert K. G. Temple believes is a form of *annedotus,* or "repulsive one." It may instead be a derivation of the Sumerian "Anunnaki," meaning "they who from heaven to earth came," in probable closest translation. The American Indian "Anasazi" (to which the Hopi tribes belong) sounds much like the latter, with a similar meaning to the Sumerian term: "the Ancient Ones." A form of Oannes, deteriorated into an agricultural deity with few of his former attributes, is better known to Western society as the Bible's Philistine god, Dagon, who is the "Odacon" of the historian Apollodorus' writings. Representations of him have been found on Assyrian cylinder seals, and at least part of one giant statue of him was found at Kouyunjik sometime around 1853.

Oannes fell from the sky into the water, from whence he came on land to teach man the arts of civilization, returning to the sea in which he preferred to live at the end of each day. Depictions of him show a muscular, bearded man, holding a basket in one hand with the other outstretched in greeting. Sometimes the outstretched hand holds an unidentifiable object which may or may not be associated with the Egyptian ankh. Described as amphibious, Oannes is specifically shown and described as wearing a fish skin over his own skin, which he could remove and put back on at will. On the cylinder seals, this frequently looks exactly like a Catholic bishop's miter and robe. Since he took it off after coming on land and put it back on when he returned to the sea, it seems only reasonable to assume this was a wet suit of some sort. His symbol, the fish, is still used by certain African tribes, drawn so that it looks simultaneously like a bearded human face and a sky rocket, on which he is specifically said by them to have arrived—their exact word for his ship is an ark. Members of his race are never referred to by the tribes as gods (though, for convenience, we continue to use the term), but as "semi-demons, personages or animals endowed with reason," with superhuman knowledge and life span, who eventually returned to the gods taking various samples of the earth's flora and fauna.

Statues discovered in the Yucatán at Tzekelna and Oxkintok, at least one of which is on exhibit at the Mérida Museum, depict what appears to be the same figure as a goggled man in a helmet and some sort of ribbed or scaled wet suit, holding a five-pointed star. Some of these statues also appear on Yucatan's offshore island of Jaina to the northwest, in temples dedicated to the Itzá god, Itzamna ("He Whose Home Is Water"), an ancient divinity who came ashore from the sea. The goggled Aztec rain god, Tlaloc, may be another representation. The symbolism can be shown to have survived in Egyptian hieroglyphs of the goddesses, who have visible fish tails sticking out the back of their headdresses. It is also almost certainly the origin of the Christian fish symbol, used as an underground code sign by the earliest believers. Oannes' symbolism is reminiscent of Poseidon or Neptune, and certainly of the mer-goat representing Capricorn.

The mer-goat's single fin is a recurring motif. The Australian aboriginal star god, Turunbulun, is a one eyed, one-footed god who is lord and protector of the Pleiades, that series of stars which figures so prominently in the world's oldest religions; the Greek Hephaestus was lame-footed, and the great god Pan had a single goat foot; the Hindu god Aja-Ekapada, meaning "One-footed Goat" or "Birthless One-footed One," was the apex of the cosmos and the eternal foe of the "Dragon of the Deep," another figure of universal significance; both the Egyptian Osiris and Ptah are always shown mummified, their feet wrapped together into a single foot; Odin and the Cyclopes were one eyed, and Odin's forerunners, Tiwaz and Tyr, were one-handed—some variants have one normal hand and one artificial hand of metal, such as Nuada of the Celts. The Celtic historical source, *Lebor Gabala Erenn,* also describes the demon-race of the Fomorians (discussed in the next chapter) as beings with single arms and single legs.

It is worthy of note that our present use of the word *mer*—which in antiquity defined the gods' ascension into the heavens—is connected to water. This may signify an ancient link between the two meanings. A mermaid (or "maiden of the mers"), for instance, appears as a woman's upper body attached to a fish tail, which is not unlike the Egyptian goddesses with fish tails in their headdresses. According to legend, the Frankish Merovingian kings were descended out of a line of sea gods. King Arthur's chief wizard, without whom he could not have risen to power, was called Merlin. The most important of these "mer" names is that of the first Egyptian Pharaoh, "Narmer," with whom written history in Egypt begins and about whom more will be said in Chapter 10.

Under the name "Nommo," Oannes would appear to be the same demigod reputed with teaching culture and astronomical wisdom to four Mali tribes in the French Sudan of Africa: the Dogon, the Bozo, the Minianka, and the Bambara. In 1954, the anthropologists Marcel Griaule and Germaine Dieterlen were shown the advanced astronomical knowledge of these tribes, and published their discovery of it under the title "A Sudanese Sirius System." Robert K. G. Temple read their obscure report in the original French and wrote his own study, published in 1976 as *The Sirius Mystery*. Griaule and Dieterlen discovered that not only did the star Sirius play a major role in these tribes' religious rituals, but their people had a knowledge of that star system equal to if not more advanced than Western science. They knew Sirius was a binary star system, with Sirius B (as we call it—they call it by the name of their smallest grain, *po*) being incredibly small and invisible, but also the heaviest thing in the sky, affecting the orbit of Sirius A (better known as the highly visible "Dog Star"). They knew the fifty-year cycle of the orbit of these two stars, and that they rotate on their own axes. They were even positive that there was a third star in the same system, which is still being debated by astronomers today. Sirius B, a white dwarf, was not photographed until 1970—and then only with extreme difficulty—by Irving W. Lindenblad of the U.S. Naval Observatory in Washington, D.C. How was it that these four Mali tribes were in possession of knowledge for countless generations that modern man was still having difficulty proving himself?

Temple's answer, accompanied by excellent but sometimes confusing research, is that Egypt was visited by a superior race from the Sirius star system sometime around 3,000 BC. He draws examples from Egyptian symbols in hieroglyphs, the use of sacred puns, and recurrences of numbers in the religious and astronomical system of Egypt to prove his point. While questions of interpretation remain open, Temple's research is certainly fascinating and worthy of serious study. It appears reasonably certain that the pyramid builders did not come from this planet, so they may well have come from another star system.

Some corroborative evidence comes from Robert Bauval and Adrian Gilbert's *The Orion Mystery,* if their theory holds true that the three pyramids of the Giza complex mirror the three stars of Orion's belt. According to computer analysis, the first such time the Orion belt matched the complex—and the only time it did so identically—was in 10,450 BC, which is the First Time of Osiris in Egyptian mythology. The three stars of the belt would have reached virtually the same position in approximately 2,450 BC (when Cheops supposedly built the Great Pyramid), and they are due again to reach it in about the year 2,000 AD. The date 10,450 BC corresponds to when Edgar Cayce, "the sleeping prophet," claimed the Great Pyramid was built, and dovetails very closely to the end of the last Ice Age. Bauval and Gilbert's theory is at least well thought out enough to have impressed Dr. I. E. S. Edwards, the British Museum's keeper of Egyptian antiquities from 1954 to 1974, who in a letter to the authors went on record saying that the theory may well be correct. There is no question that the Egyptians believed in the Hermetic "as above, so below" doctrine, reflecting it throughout their mythology. The Nile, for instance, was for them the earthly counterpart of the Milky Way, so the idea that the Giza complex mirrors a star system prominent in their religious writings is not an unlikely suggestion.

Certainly the most thorough and compelling research into the question of ancient astronauts is the work of Zecharia Sitchin, who has written six volumes on the subject, called collectively *The Earth Chronicles,* with a companion piece, *Genesis Revisited.* Richard Hoagland has correctly observed that no summary of Sitchin's research can do it justice, and anyone interested in pursuing the question of ancient extraterrestrial contact in man's history could not do better than to read it. Sitchin is a scholar of ancient languages who translates from the original cuneiform and hieroglyphs in many cases. He also demonstrates superior knowledge of the Old Testament. In addition to the depth of his own knowledge, he quotes extensively from acknowledged academic experts in various fields. Where he makes an occasional leap or stretch in interpretation, Sitchin straightforwardly admits it, and he is careful to document his steps in arriving at his conclusions. It would do us well to outline his basic findings, based on Sitchin's research from the original Creation tablets and other myth texts of the Middle East. We can also use the opportunity to examine corroborating evidence for his theories from other sources.

Central to Sitchin's thesis is the argument that there is another planet in our solar system, which he calls Nibiru (or Marduk) after the Sumerian/Babylonian mythologies. It is not necessary to believe, as he does, that a human race originated on that planet and traveled to Earth from it; it is sufficient within his own guidelines to believe simply that this race came from outside our solar system (as Temple contends), or at least beyond its farthest presently acknowledged limits. Whether this other race came from Sitchin's tenth planet (he calls it the twelfth, using the ancient annotation of the Sun and the Moon as planetary), the Sirius system, the Pleiades, or Orion is unimportant—they came from beyond the farthest reaches of our known solar system. Even this point could be argued, but both Sitchin and Temple present the case convincingly. This theoretical planet's existence is used to explain the origin of our present solar system in a cosmic cataclysm, for which there is a tremendous amount of evidence. It is possible that the central Sumerian god, Anu, is actually this planetary body, being one of those gods to whom personality is rarely ascribed but who seems to display truly cosmic power. (The derivations of the name "Anu" will be considered more thoroughly in the next chapter.) The scientific community has not determined that the present arrangement of planets was caused by cataclysm, and established academics are well known for arguing against it. Velikovsky proposed exactly the same thing in 1950, positing that the cause was the planet Venus originating as a comet. Alexander Kazantsev, in the January 1959 *Pravda,* wrote an article which put forth a similar theory.

The theory of a cataclysmic origin for our present solar system does answer many questions. For one thing, the Sumerians, generally considered to be the first advanced civilization on Earth, knew the number of planets in our solar system and depicted them around our sun. But the arrangement, by size, on such depictions as a third-millennium BC Akkadian cylinder seal (VA/243) in the State Museum of East Berlin shows the planets in a different order than they are presently found, with Pluto preceding Neptune. Pluto has a massive seventeen-degree orbital variation from the rest of the planets and is so erratic that in 1976 it moved closer to the sun than Neptune. Three of Uranus' four moons show unquestionable evidence of violent collision; one of them, Miranda, estimated to have been hit no fewer than five times, shows considerable signs of collision, including a titanic gouge in a chevron shape on its surface. Uranus itself has an extreme rotational inclination to its magnetic axis of fifty-eight degrees, as does its virtual twin, Neptune, at fifty, both planets lying virtually on their sides in comparison to the rest of the solar system. The asteroid belt situated between Mars and Jupiter has long been considered even by opponents of collision theory to be the remains of a shattered planet, which is exactly what the Babylonian myth of the war in the heavens between Marduk and Tiamat says it is, according to Sitchin: they call it the "hammered bracelet" in the heavens, as does the Bible. Pluto's discoverer, Clyde W. Tombaugh (himself a recorded witness of a UFO), summed up the evidence in *Out of the Darkness: The Planet Pluto:* "All in all, there are indications that strange events have taken place in the outer reaches of the Solar System."

According to Sitchin's reading of the myth, Tiamat was an astronomical body with too many moons and too much gravitational mass that threatened the stability of the other planetary bodies. It was eventually struck by a much larger body, called Marduk, that smashed it into two remains in the solar system—one, the nearly obliterated fragments that are the asteroid belt, and two, the planet Earth. Tiamat's moons were thrown far away, becoming captured by the other planets, and the orbit of the outer planets was changed and reestablished. One of Tiamat's moons, called in the myth Kingu, became Earth's Moon. As we have already seen, the evidence is in favor of our Moon having been captured in antiquity, and it is older than our own planet, which means the mythical tablets are not in conflict with modern scientific perceptions. Additionally, the Moon's glassine surface may have been caused by heat in that collision, or subsequent bombings in a planetary war, or both.

Myths the world over echo this same story. The Mali tribes tell it as the story of the pale fox, after which Griaule and Dieterlen published their 1965 book of the same name (*Le Renard Pale,* unavailable in English). In their version, the fox—Ogo—was mutilated in a fight, his falling blood creating the present planets of our solar system. The African stories are quite specific, delineating spatial bodies that rotate on their own axes and have orbits and moons, including details that could only be known by scientific means. They draw Saturn with rings and call it "the star of limiting the place," which is how the Sumerians described it (calling Saturn "Foremost Prince of the West"), attributing to it the quality of being the solar system's anchor. Exactly like the ancient

Egyptians, the Mali tribes consider the Milky Way to be the progenitor of life. They believe that Earth is "Ogo's placenta" connecting mankind to the Nommos, and that the star Sirius (known to them as the "land of the fish") is "Nommo's placenta," who is the "monitor of the universe." This is of extreme significance because of a longstanding debate as to whether or not the ancient Egyptians were solar- or stellar-oriented in their architecture, it showing evidence of both—the Mali tribes have *four* accurate astronomical calendars, each used for a different purpose: one solar, one lunar, one for the planet Venus, and the other Sirian.

The Mexican pyramids also can be used to intercalate these bodies, and possibly Mars as well. Venus is especially important to Mexican mythology, being the origin of Quetzalcoatl and his race and also their planet of war and catastrophe. Given the textual (and perhaps physical) evidence for cosmic warfare in antiquity, it is possible that one body of people lived on one sphere and another somewhere else. The Mali are quite certain that there is life on other planets, ascribing different attributes to each which are couched in metaphor.

Possible further evidence for the tenth planet exists in Mexico, based on mathematical measurements of the Teotihuacán pyramid complex. In 1972, American engineer Hugh Harleston, Jr., who had lived in Mexico twenty-five years seeking a constant measurement at Teotihuacán, discovered one in the proportions of large measurements in the Citadel, the largest complex in the area. He called his unit the *hunab* (Mayan for "unified measure"), equivalent to 1.059 meters, and in utilizing it found elegant and consistent mathematics throughout Teotihuacán. When used to measure other Mexican sites, such as Palenque, *hunab* measurements came out in uneven numbers—but when converted to ancient Egyptian geographic feet or cubits, the numbers came out even and round. Triangulating measurements inside the Citadel, Harleston found numerous universal constants, including the Einsteinian constant of the speed of light within −1.0028. *Pi, phi,* and *e* constantly recurred, and the entire Citadel appeared to be an advanced computer incorporating major universal constants on every level. Experimenting, he found what he was looking for as a base measurement for Earth along one side of the base of the Pyramid of Quetzalcoatl. Harleston then applied triangulated ratios within the Citadel to come up with correct integral proportions among various markers equating to the planetary orbits in the solar system.

Harleston extended the proportional measurements outside the Citadel and found them echoed along the popularly named Way of the Dead. There, he discovered markers whose placement gave mathematical values—when measured against the intersection of the Citadel's center line with the axis of the Procession as point zero—accurate for the orbits of all the planets. Since modern man did not discover more than five planets other than Earth until late in the eighteenth century (Uranus was found in 1787), this was quite impressive, especially given the accuracy of Neptune at thirty astronomical units and Pluto at thirty-nine, which were not discovered in our era until 1845 and 1930, respectively. But Harleston also found a ruined and plundered structure in the Procession, called by the local natives the Temple of Xochitl ("Flower"), at the site where another planet would be. His estimate was that this planet "X," which he called Xiknalkan ("Flying Serpent"), was seventy-five astronomical units from the sun, with a diameter approximately three times that of Earth at a 4.74 plane of the ecliptic. Though there are numerous different calculations for the possible tenth planet, its presence has been proposed by many leading astronomers, including J. J. See, W. Peck, T. Gugril, G. Forbes, and Dr. William H. Pickering (who even gave it the name of "Pan"), as well as mathematicians Joseph L. Brady and Dr. Charles Muses, all of whom have theorized its existence as an explanation for the perturbation of the outer planets and the major irregularities in the orbit of Halley's comet.

Some additional confirmation of Harleston's figures came from his friend Arthur Schlemmer, who had been seeking recurring patterns between earthquakes and planetary motions. Dividing the number of minutes in a day, 1,440, into the tropical Earth year of 365.242189, Schlemmer came up with the number 0.2536404097, with which he was able to accurately extrapolate orbital distances of the planets. This gave him a list of thirty-eight numbers which appeared to be constants, nineteen of which coincided with those of Harleston in Teotihuacán.

Harleston and Schlemmer had what they thought was a "far out" reading of Aztec mythology, which is related by Peter Tompkins in *Mysteries of the Mexican Pyramids:* they interpreted Xipe Xólotl, the "flayed red god of the east" (Mars), and his planetary twin, Quetzalcoatl (also called "Sumer")—the latter's outer surface "peeled off like an orange"—to be mutually mutilated bodies that gave birth to Earth as we know it and left the Moon a sterile core (which is designated as hollow and having arrived from the west, an orbit farther from the sun). This was the result both of cosmic catastrophe and deliberate activity by an extraterrestrial society. Osiris in Egypt is sometimes represented by a flayed ram skin on a pole, with a "twin" in Anubis—one or both of whom appear frequently to represent Saturn. Osiris is the dead god, mutilated by his brother Set, but who rises again to give new life. (This will be considered at greater length in a discussion on the Underworld in Chapter 10.) How "Quetzalcoatl" and "Sumer" come to be the same is not given in Tompkins' relation of the theory, but plainly it is a matter of some interest.

In other mythologies of the world, the planetary collision story—using castration or other mutilation, with life emerging from the drops of blood that fall from the act—can be found in Cronos' castration of Uranus in Greece, the war of the Rishis ("primeval flowing ones," or planets) in the Hindu Vedas, Kumarbi's castration of his father Anu in the Hittite, and a great many others. That these are not mere psychological projections is evident by the scientific accuracy the stories embody about the solar system. That they are not isolated mythologies with similarities, but rather variations of the same story emanating from one central source in antiquity, becomes increasingly apparent as we consider all the evidence for a single original civilization.

The biblical Creation myth picks up the thread of human origins from this point in Genesis. Voltaire observed that, in his century, every educated person knew that the passage did not read, "In the beginning, God created the heavens and the earth," but actually said, "In the beginning, *the gods* created the heavens and the earth," the actual word being *Elohim,* a plural. As Robert Charroux notes, referring to Hebrew scholar J. M. Vaschalde in *Masters of the Earth,* a second meaning is incorporated into the phrase, the Hebrews having learned from the Egyptians the art of sacred puns: "The word translated as 'in the beginning' . . . is a compound word which can have two meanings (as is true of the first word of many initiatic and hermetic texts). It can be divided into a particle and a noun, the latter meaning 'beginning.' But the particle can mean either 'in' or 'with,' so the compound word can mean either 'in the beginning' (the usual translation) or 'with what remained from the past' (a translation closer to a historical truth) . . . Here then, is an alternate, grammatically possible translation of the first verse of the Bible: 'Using what remained (after the

ARCHITECTS OF THE UNDERWORLD

cataclysm?), beings from the sky (re-)created the sky and the earth.' . . . The recreation probably took place after a cataclysm, since it was done with 'what remained,' that is, with the debris of an earlier world that had been destroyed." (All the parenthetical enclosures are Charroux's own.) This reading of the Hebrew predates by almost ten years the research of Sitchin and Temple, who both first published in 1976. Neither Sitchin or Temple quotes from Charroux or mentions Vaschalde, indicating they were unaware of the two men, and plainly Charroux did not know their work, meaning that a third party studying Creation myths from the original texts came to the same conclusions, entirely independently.

The Creation story of the Bible, the *Enuma Elish,* is derived from more ancient Mediterranean texts, with either the Egyptian or the Sumerian being the oldest. It is identical to the Egyptian myths, for instance, in the separation of the earth from the sky during one of the epochal "days," but the Egyptian story uses anthropomorphisms to express it in the forms of the sky god (Shu) lifting the arch of heaven (the goddess Nut) away from the earth (Geb). As "the earth was without form and void" (Genesis 1:2), all was nothingness in the empty chaos of Nu, the abysm of space in the Egyptian cosmogony. As God spoke commands and they instantly became reality, so did Thoth, the head of the primeval *Ogdoad* of gods ("original eight") in the oldest (Heliopolitan) Egyptian myth. The "Divine Command," or "the Word," were terms by which this eldest god was known, which should be familiar to a Christian readership by reference of John 1:1: "In the beginning was the Word, and the Word was with God, and the Word was God." The holy Trinity of the Father, the Son, and the Holy Spirit can be found in the original Sumerian Anu, Enlil, and Ea, or the Assyrian Anu, Bel, and Ea, in both cases (and all others where this same pattern recurs) a Trinity of equal but separate gods.

Sitchin and Temple diverge at this point, the former believing the Elohim came from the planetary body that caused the wreckage of our solar system and then restored it into a semblance of order, the latter believing they came from Sirius. This author finds the planet Nibiru/Marduk an unlikely body to support life, having an orbit Sitchin calculates at thirty-six hundred years, but agrees with Sitchin as opposed to Temple in reading the history of the Anunnaki—as the Sumerians called this race—in personal rather than mathematical terms. Temple sees the Anunnaki merely as numerical ciphers in a formula, without personality. But given the ancients' tendency to incorporate at least two meanings into every element in a story, they are probably useful both as a mathematical equation and as actual historical figures. Twelve central Anunnaki are always mentioned as a ruling body, which could as well apply to the zodiac as to a governing body of men. The goddess Ninti ("lady life," also called Ninharsag, the Great Mother goddess, whose symbol was the knife which cut the umbilical cord, identical with our zodiacal sign for Leo), for instance, is credited with having accomplished the medical creation of man, along with the god Enki ("lord" or "Prince of earth" and "lord of the Deep," also called Ea, "Lord of the Saltwaters," or "house of water," recalling Oannes/Nommo). These Anunnaki are ascribed definite roles in the story and definite personalities; it is possible that they may be not only actual personages at a given time in history, but that they represent all medical personnel. Or, put more simply, Adam and Eve may represent an entire specie of man and woman, not merely two people. "Adam," from the original "Adama" (or Adapa, "model man"), literally means "Earthman" (*Adamah*-"Earth"), and "Eve" means "she who has life" in the Hebrew, which is derived from the Sumerian word for both "life" and "rib," *ti,* from which we get the seemingly garbled biblical account of Eve having been made from Adam's rib.

Temple's definition of the mysterious Sumerian word, *Nebiru,* would seem to be likelier than Sitchin's. Where Sitchin ascribes it to the theoretical planetary body at the outer limits of our solar system, Temple finds it a contraction of the Egyptian *Neb-Heru* (Neb-"Lord," Heru-"Sun"), from which we also derive our word "hero." The symbol used for Nebiru [Nibiru] is the cross, usually made as we make a plus sign: + . The Mesopotamian "Epic of Creation" gives Nebiru fifty epithets—including "god who maintains life," "bestower of cultivation," and "creator of grain and herbs who causes vegetation to sprout"—along with the name *Asar,* "lofty bright watery king whose deep is plentiful," which is the Egyptian name for the great god of these same attributes: *Osiris,* the culture god of resurrection and eternal life. The cross is a worldwide symbol for eternity, life, creativity, and renewal, not limited to Christianity. Nebiru is described as being "most radiant of the gods," an accurate description of the Sun. Asar's Sumerian "water" meanings could as well apply to the Sun's plasma as to an actual ocean, or perhaps to the depths of space itself; it could also apply to Enki/Oannes/Nommo. As should be increasingly apparent by this point, the symbolism we take for granted in our own traditions goes much further back, and carries deeper connotations, than we may have hitherto suspected.

Wherever they came from, the Anunnaki—which can be equated with the biblical *Nefilim,* generally translated as "giants" but signifying also more literally "they who from heaven to earth fell," as well as "brilliant ones" and "workers of wonders"—came to Earth from outside our solar system, or at least traveled extensively throughout it. As already mentioned, the astronomical knowledge recorded in the Sumerian tablets describes Saturn accurately in gravitational effects and appearance, as well as other planets. Also, as Sitchin notes, they appear to have added one ray to every star symbol for each planet *in,* from the outside—meaning that Saturn is depicted as having four rays, Jupiter five, Mars six, and so on. Earth is the seventh planet—"the seventh heaven," literally.

Using the computations in Berossus' account of the arrival of Oannes, Sitchin came to a date 445,000 years ago, which fits almost perfectly with the estimated age of the Cydonia complex on Mars. At that time, man was in his first evolutionary stages, according to our understanding of that developmental theory. The Creation tablets state that the Anunnaki created man out of potentially useful primitive animals on Earth, for their own reasons. Either the demolished planet Tiamat contained enough DNA material from its own previous life to have begun evolution anew (it is not impossible it was the original home of the Anunnaki, with Mars a temporary base of operations where they rode out the catastrophe), or else it was helped along for some time by the Anunnaki.

The original purpose of the Anunnaki's visit to Earth, aside from the likeliest possibility of colonization, seems to have been for industrial development. One of the mysteries of the world's megaliths has only recently been noticed by academia, which is their frequent proximity to mining sites. Sitchin notices the peculiarity of statues of the gods made with one gold hand, signifying them to be lords of metal. Indeed, if megalithic construction is one critical key to understanding the Anunnaki, then metal is another. The serpent of Genesis is referred to as *Nahash,* meaning "he who knows secrets" and also "he who knows copper." The Lord in the Bible is referred to occasionally as the one who knows the hidden places of the metal in the mountains. Job 28:1–2, for instance, reads: "Surely there is a vein for the silver, and a place for gold where they [re]fine it. Iron is taken out of the earth and brass is molten out of the stone." And in verses 6–9: "The stones of it [earth] are the place of sapphires: and it hath dust of gold. There is a path which no fowl knoweth, and which the vulture's eye hath not seen: The lion's whelps have not trodden it, nor the fierce lion passed by it. He putteth forth his hand upon the rock; he overturneth the mountains by the roots."

Eventually the Anunnaki wearied of the mining and rebelled. Several medical attempts were made to create the perfect slave out of various animals, which only resulted in grotesque hybrids and mutations ("chimeras") that were of no ultimate use and had to be destroyed. (This element can frequently be seen in Hollywood movies about Atlantis.) "Let us make an Adamu in our image," they said, showing the exact inspiration for the Biblical "Let us make man in our own image," which shows God referring to himself in the plural. "He" was a race of people, the Anunnaki, who are referred to biblically as either angels or "the sons of god." An experiment performed by their chief medical personnel, Enki and Ninti, produced a "lulu" ("the mixed one"), the first man, out of a mix of Anunnaki genetic material and the more primitive human form native to Earth. The result were called the "black-headed people" in the Sumerian texts, who were used as mining slaves.

Enki became their leader, teaching them all the finer arts of civilization as well as their work and craft, again obviously reminiscent of Oannes/Nommo. He taught them brickmaking, construction, and metallurgy. The terms used in the Creation texts appear quite scientific, referring to moulding the essence of the Anunnaki with the egg of their wombs, purifying it in a bath, and creating an eventual bond, and the glyphs accompanying them show laboratories with vases like test tubes, cauldrons of fire, and the like. Their most complex phrase for the process was the special attention paid to "that which houses that which binds the memory," which Sitchin points out would most closely translate to "genes."

The demand for the "black-headed people" became too great for the Anunnaki to produce on a regular basis, since they had to be individually birthed using willing surrogate mothers, and the process was as painful as any childbirth. Eventually the slave people were given the gift of "knowing," i.e., self-reproduction. Enki appears to have been the one to upgrade the native human specie, making him the serpent in the Genesis garden. As a sentence for passing on this knowledge, Enki was to labor in the mines for the rest of his days—"Because thou hast done this, thou art cursed ... upon thy belly shalt thou go, and dust shalt thou eat all the days of thy life," as Genesis 3:14 puts it. That Enki is the serpent should not be surprising: his symbol, later the symbol for Thoth/Hermes and used today by the medical profession, is two intertwined snakes around a winged rod (the caduceus), which by appearance alone strongly suggests the DNA molecule.

Additionally in the sentence was that his seed should be at war ("enmity") with "the woman's" seed, which implies race or tribal warfare. It is possible that Enki was also known in another guise: the god we recognize as Hephaestus or Vulcan from Greek and Roman mythology. Hephaestus was thrown out of heaven by his mother, explaining the "enmity between thee and the woman." Hephaestus/Vulcan lived in the mines beneath the earth as the artificer of the gods, famous for the permanent limp caused by his fall from heaven. That limp, attributed to his "Fall from grace," was also a feature never lacking in Mediaeval dramatic portrayals of the devil.

If any of this seems contradictory to Bible students, it is because the text of Scripture is a condensation of far more extensive Sumerian and other Mesopotamian Creation texts that predated it by thousands of years. The reason God first creates mankind, then repents of having done it, decrees his destruction in the Flood, and yet preserves a remnant, is precisely because he is not perfect. "He" is a council, a society of coeval "gods," explaining how it is that actions occur without his awareness though he is attributed with omniscience. God has to *find out* that man has disobeyed him and eaten of the tree of knowledge; he has to *find out* what happened to Abel, not knowing upon his arrival that Cain has slain him; he sends "angels," indistinguishable from men, to *find out* if things are as bad in Sodom and Gomorrah as the angels have heard they are. It is by this token that the same God who made man can also be the serpent in the garden cursed by God. There is more than one of "Him," and they have not always been in agreement about what to do with us, mankind, since our creation.

The Egyptians and the Hindus, among the oldest civilizations on Earth if not actually the oldest, both believed that their pantheons of gods were what has been termed a "henotheism" by such notable scholars as Professor Max Mueller and E. A. Wallis Budge.

This term refers to a number of gods who are all equal as "God," though none of them are the one sole, original creator of the universe; they are the "limbs" of the one Great God, who is invariably invisible, unknowable, and unknown—the creative force of the universe itself. "The Primal Chaos," to the Egyptians. Which means that if the theory that the Anunnaki are a superior technological race that engendered us in antiquity and were termed "gods" or "angels" is true, then it would appear they are as much in the dark as to the actual origins of man as we are ourselves, expressing it in essentially the same terms. This theory does not eradicate the theory of evolution, or necessarily confirm it—it extends it much farther out into space and much further back in time than we are presently capable of studying. Budge asserted that the Egyptians were really monotheistic, never worshipping any of their gods as that central creative force, which was more of a philosophical concept. Their image of the "gods" with whom they had commerce was the same as that of men like themselves, except that the gods were longer lived and intellectually and technologically ("magically") superior, which we find to be true of all ancient beliefs in the gods.

Two vital pieces of evidence, from Scripture itself, demonstrate the henotheistic nature of the biblical God: God's many references to himself in the plural, and the phrase "the sons of god." The name *Elohim* itself is a plural, as already noted, and God plainly says, "Let *us* create man in *our* own image" in Genesis (1:26), and in the Tower of Babel incident (Genesis 11:7), "Let *us* go down and confuse their speech." The phrase "the sons of god" is used in Genesis and Job in reference to their rejoicing at their handiwork, measuring the firmament and the like. In Genesis 6, verses 2 and 4, we have the single most enigmatic phrase in the Bible: "And the sons of God saw the daughters of men, that they were fair, and took of them wives whichever they chose . . . There were giants in the earth in those days; and also after that, when the sons of God came in unto the daughters of men, and they bare children to them, the same became mighty men which were of old, men of renown."

Those two short verses caused church fathers no end of headaches, since the standard Judaeo-Christian theology is that angels (as well as God) are incorporeal beings, creatures of spirit entirely with no flesh or fleshly desires, which Genesis clearly contradicts. No bodiless spirit could "come in unto" earthly women, nor should it have the remotest desire to do so. But the phrases obscenely hang there, drawing attention to themselves, demanding an explanation. It was for precisely this "crime" that God ordained the destruction of all mankind by the Flood. Attempts to reconcile these two contradictory ideas—the Scripture as it stands and the theology which is its precise opposite—have produced only superstition and confusion.

Sitchin's reading of the biblical Flood is that it was caused by the return of the distant extra planet in our solar system. Passing too close on this particular orbit, its gravitation caused a slippage of the Antarctic icecap, creating the rise of the oceans and the abrupt end of the last Ice Age approximately thirteen thousand years ago. That date dovetails nicely with the preliminary water-damage estimates of West and Schoch, and is within about five hundred years of Bauval and Gilbert's dating of the First Time of Osiris pyramidal star configuration at 10,450 BC. This concurrence is the more impressive for the latter two's utter lack of recognition of Sitchin's work in either their text or their bibliography, and the former pair's independent paralleling of it. Nor are they alone in arriving at this period as the time of some major planetary catastrophe. Peter Kolosimo reports, "Some decades ago a map of the heavens was found in a cave at Bohistan in the Himalaya foothills. Its accuracy was confirmed by astronomers, who also noted that it diverged from our own maps in that it showed the position of the heavenly bodies 13,000 years ago. Another curious feature of the map, which was published in the *National Geographic Magazine,* was that lines were drawn on it connecting the earth and Venus." Brasseur de Bourbourg, decipherer of Mayan hieroglyphics, provides some circumstantial confirmation only about five hundred years off the same date, believing that the Troano Codex "contained descriptions of part of a catastrophe which had resulted from the end of the last glacial period," as Peter Tompkins explains in *Mysteries of the Mexican Pyramids.* "According to Brasseur, the Troano Codex placed the disappearance of [Atlantis] in the year 9937 BC."

With minor differences, A. T. Wilson of New Zealand's Victoria University proposed Sitchin's Antarctic icecap theory in 1964, including the Arctic icecap as well. The University of Maine's Dr. John T. Hollin has made similar propositions, as have others over the years. Some, like Hugh Auchincloss Brown, Charles Hapgood, and Peter Warlow, have included the possibility of shifts of the earth's polar axis.

The question of a universal, worldwide Flood—and its dating—remain open. Sir Leonard Wooley reported in his *Excavations at Ur,* in 1929, that he found a former civilization at the site beneath eleven feet of mud, circa 4,000 to 3,500 BC, initially believing it to be evidence of the biblical Flood. Kish, Erech, and Shurrupak had a similar mud stratum dating approximately 2,800 BC, and thirteen separate mud strata, alternating with riverine sand, were found at Nineveh at dates estimated between 4,000 and 3,000 BC. The discrepancy in dates led scholars to conclude that local inundations had occurred at varying times worldwide, since similar finds both in geology and mythical literature attest to a cataclysmic flood.

However one wishes to interpret it, evidence does then exist for the reality of the biblical Flood, including the precipitation damage to the Sphinx. The rain of forty days and forty nights may have been caused by the passage of the proposed extra astral body in our solar system, or some other cosmic catastrophe. Since the most conservative datings of regionalized inundations accepted by archaeologists predate by approximately half a millennium the standard dates for the construction of the Great Pyramid, this may be regarded as further evidence that these structures are in fact considerably older.

The point of the story as related in the Creation texts of the ancients is that the Flood was caused by cosmic means, not as a result of any action of the Anunnaki but as a force of nature. They could have saved mankind or they could have left him to die, and they chose the latter. Their entire council was not in agreement, and Enki being known for his wiliness—"the subtlest of God's creatures," as Genesis 3:1 describes the Serpent—was forced to agree not to intervene on man's behalf, as he never failed to do. He vowed not to tell anyone, but of course had a plan in mind to circumvent his promise even as he made it. Enki chose to save an especially righteous man and his family—Noah, called in the texts Sisythrus, Ziusudra, or Khasisatra, and with counterparts in all the rest of the world's mythologies, including that of the Hopi Indians. He arranged for Noah to be kept waiting behind a screen, while Enki, who on the Sumerian cylinder seals is literally depicted with a serpent's body, entered and discussed the coming catastrophe with a compatriot on the other side of the screen. Lamenting that he could not warn mankind (which of course he was doing), he outlined a hypothetical way man could save himself, being the instructions for the Ark. Enki even provided his compatriot as the pilot of the craft, which seems more or less to have been a primitive but effective submarine. The Hebrew word used for Noah's Ark is *tebah,* the same as the basket in which Moses was found among the bulrushes, generally read as "container"—which Jean Sendy notes would as accurately read "capsule"—and there are other connotations of the Ark that are discussed in Chapter 10. The Gilgamesh Epic does not say that Noah took two of every animal on board the ship with him, but rather "the seeds of life," which makes considerably more sense if a highly technical DNA preservation scenario is allowed. In the Hindu rendition of this myth, the righteous fisher-king Satyrivata ("the man who loves justice and truth") is warned and saved by the "fish god"—recognizable to us as Oannes/Nommo.

Thus prepared, Noah escaped the catastrophe undetected by the other Anunnaki until it was all over. By that time, Enki's compatriots forgave his deception, having themselves repented of their rash decision to let mankind be destroyed. The burnt offerings given by Noah as sacrifice were meat for the returning Anunnaki, who had taken to orbiting positions in the skies until the floodwaters below abated. What had been strained relations between mankind and his progenitors became newly cemented into a mutual bond of trust, beginning a pact between the two races that is the history of our Bible.

That history is one of shifting allegiances and conflicts between the technologically superior Annunaki and their human counterparts, to be examined in light of the world's mythologies in the next chapter, defining the problem of "the sons of god who came in unto the daughters of men" among other occurrences. This interbreeding component is the key to understanding the overall relationship between the two races, which appears to be ongoing. Before discussing this, however, Sitchin's explanation for the purpose of the Sphinx and the pyramids should be related, especially since it was our departure point.

In Sitchin's reading, Enki, as the maker of waterways—under the new name Ptah (who closely resembles Hephaestus)—built the pyramids after reclaiming the flooded Earth. The construction of the two greatest pyramids, those believed to belong to Cheops and Chephren, was accomplished in part to serve as a new landing beacon for the Anunnaki spaceport. The Bible implies in Job 38:25 that God did precisely such work: "Who hath divided a watercourse for the overflowing of waters, or a way for the lightning and thunder . . . ?" Many sacred cities of the ancients, Sitchin notes, lie along the thirtieth parallel—Giza/the Heliopolis, Eridu, Persepolis, Harappa, and Lhasa in Tibet, among others—which is exactly the latitude down which the Sphinx gazes eastward. Our own Cape Kennedy (Canaveral) is on the thirtieth parallel, for the same reason: it is an ideal launching spot. Part of the evidence for a spaceport could well be that the two Great Pyramids have exactly the same height, making them excellent landing guides from a great distance. Mark Antony recorded that the pyramids were visible from a hundred miles outside of Egypt. From space, covered in one hundred inches of white limestone that has since been stripped from them, the Pyramids could have been visible up to several million miles out. Sitchin shows a precise geometrical landing grid formed by Mount Ararat at one end, extending at an angle to connect with Giza directly through the Baalbek terrace at the second point, with the third point of the triangle being Mount St. Catherine and the city of Umm Shumar. Jerusalem lies in the center of this triangle, directly between Mount St. Catherine and Baalbek. A line then extended from Giza, east along the thirtieth parallel, has a geometric center in the smaller internal triangle formed between Giza, Mount St. Catherine, and Jerusalem, in the middle of the Sinai Peninsula, which is the exact site where miles of oddly blackened rock are visible from space to this day. It is this that he designates as the Anunnaki spaceport, blasted in antiquity by nuclear weapons. Further, connecting the equidistant sites of this proposed spaceport to Jerusalem and Baalbek, then connecting the outer two points to Delphi in Greece—the location of the oracle of the gods—another landing corridor of exactly the same dimensions as the first is formed.

Sitchin is not the only one to have thought of mathematically connecting ancient sites, and to discover surprising and elegant geometry emerging in the process. Demonstrated in *In Search of Ancient Astronauts,* Maurice Chatelain found that connecting twelve sacred temple sites of Greece formed a perfect Maltese cross when viewed from the air. He also found that three prehistoric megalithic sites in France connect to form a triangle hundreds of miles across, in exact proportion to the measurements of the Great Pyramid. Along the connecting lines are the known uranium mining sites in that region. An extension of one of its lines leads exactly to Peru's Nazca plain, where straight-line drawings on the barren earth form pictures of great size, visible only from the air. NASA calls such geometrical configurations as demonstrated by Sitchin and Chatelain "footprints," easily recognizable sites for landing.

There is expert testimony to support Sitchin's propositions, both from the Old Testament and ancient mythology scholars, as well as the scientific community. For instance, Job 38:4–7: "Where wast thou when I laid the foundations of the earth? Declare, if thou hast understanding. Who hath laid the measures thereof, if thou knowest? Or who hath stretched the line upon it? Whereupon are the foundations thereof fastened? Or who laid the corner stone thereof; when the morning stars sang together, and all the sons of God shouted for joy?" These passages demonstrate that the God of the Old Testament was a measurer, an architect— in short, that he employed geometry and stargazing in his design— and that he had others helping him. Moreover, he had his eyes on the particular stars and clusters that are of supreme significance not only to the religion of ancient Egypt, but the rest of the world as well, as he says in Job 38:31—"Canst thou bind the sweet influences of Pleiades, or loose the bands of Orion?" The gods as "measurers" who want man to "keep their days"—i.e., their calendar—can also be found in the Mayan Creation epic, the Popol Vuh ("Book of the People"), and will be discussed at more length in the next chapter.

Sitchin notes that the world's leading biologist, Nobel laureate Sir Francis Crick, in a paper coauthored with Leslie Orgel in 1973 titled "Directed Panspermia" (after Nobel laureate chemist Svante August Arrhenius' *Worlds in the Making*, written in 1908), determined that life on Earth could not have developed in the time the planet has existed. They argued it was likely "that technological societies existed elsewhere in the galaxy even before the formation of the Earth," and urged that the scientific community accept the logical conclusion: "... namely, that a primitive form of life was deliberately planted on Earth by a technologically advanced society on another planet." Specifically, that it was done by "the deliberate activity of an extraterrestrial society." In the October 26, 1981, *New York Times*, Crick stuck to his guns, saying, "Even though it sounds a bit cranky, all the steps in the argument are scientifically plausible."

It is quite conceivable—even likely, given what seems to be the highly advanced age for the Giza complex—that these Egyptian sites predate all others and were built, as the folklore suggests, before the Flood and in anticipation of it. As already mentioned, there is a tremendous body of lore attributing the building of the Great Pyramid to a wise king (or the gods) before the Flood, to incorporate and keep safe all the learning of man, which we can determine mathematically (at least to some extent) it does. It is possible, as the legends say, that there are other chambers in the Pyramid yet undiscovered, containing a rumored hidden library and samples of such items as "malleable glass," which is perhaps what we rediscovered as plastic. The precipitation damage to the Sphinx and the probability that it dates back perhaps twelve thousand years make the Flood story if not a certainty at least not improbable—the Sphinx is known to have been buried up to its neck, and often over its head as well, for most of its long life, which has preserved that water damage for us to witness today. We have no reliable documentation for who built the entire Giza complex, let alone why, so it is hardly out of bounds to propose the legendary theory for its construction as the possible correct one. All the world's mythologies contain a Flood myth, the Celtic one even using Noah's exact name as the survivor, and others have names almost identical—like the Hawaiian "Nu'u," the Chinese "Nu Wah," and the dead city of Ma Noa ("waters of Noah") in the Sierra Parima between Venezuela and Brazil. The pyramids could have been used as landing beacons before the Flood just as well as after. And there are other myths which strongly suggest Egypt as the earliest location of the Anunnaki.

It would be beneficial to investigate some of those other myths, and perhaps come to understand this legendary race through them. The closer they are scrutinized, the more a single picture emerges, rather than a number of divergent and separate ones. Of special interest is the question of "the sons of god" and "the daughters of men," and the "giants that once walked the earth." Coming to know them makes the Bible much clearer and more precise, not a generalized book of morals, but an often poorly recounted history more easily understood in light of other cultures' myth cycles. Answers seem to emerge by connecting the mythologies of the Egyptians, the Celts, the American and Mexican Indians, and the Norse/Teutonic peoples, as well as the Mesopotamian (biblical) myths already discussed. Not only are their stories and central gods recognizably the same, but so are the symbols associated with them—and some of these may give us a clear connection to our discoveries on Mars.

9

Rivalries

THERE ARE THREE basic ways to look at the similarity between the world's mythologies: one, each myth cycle is indigenous to a given people, beginning with features unique to them that then become influenced by invaders or assimilated tribes; two, myths are all psychological projections (called by Jung "archetypes") of man's innermost psyche, showing the universality of the human soul; or, three, they are all the same myth from great antiquity, becoming individually corrupted in various ways over the ensuing centuries. The first two theories are the prevailing ones today, being the anthropological and psychological schools of thought. The latter is generally dismissed without much consideration, since it brings to mind Atlantis (and other seemingly fabulous theories), which has become excluded from the accepted canon of theories though there is a tremendous amount of evidence to suggest it once existed.

If the academic orthodoxy shows shortsightedness in dismissing or ridiculing the universal first civilization theory, those who research it as the theory of Atlantis show equal shortsightedness in insisting on strictly factual interpretations. Myth is subtle and all encompassing, as are the sacred puns which express it. They are riddles and codes, understood by those who have the key or the perception to decipher them. The secret society of the Masons used the term "the Widow's Son" to identify themselves, understood as their connection with Christ and to a more distant heritage in Egypt, the myth of Osiris, Isis, and Horus. Osiris was murdered by his scheming and envious brother Set, leaving Isis a widow who nonetheless sired a son from her dead husband—Horus, "the Widow's Son." The connections to Christianity are obvious. This is an excellent example of the use of myth, and perhaps to the unriddling of its mysteries.

Taken in that light, Atlantis need not be a Greek island that sunk in the Atlantic Ocean. The story of Atlantis is that it was the first great and mighty civilization among men, which fell into irrevocable evil and perished beneath the sea in a cataclysm. According to Plato and occult tradition, its heritage was continued in Egypt. If we take into account that we may very well be dealing with a spacefaring race, then space itself may have been thought of by them as an "ocean," and planets as "islands." If Earth was engulfed in a Flood, such as we have just discussed, then that could be related as the sinking of the island civilization beneath the waves; if it began in Egypt—or was simply continued there by the same ones who founded it in the first place—then that would make sense according to the theories we have encountered.

Do the world's mythologies describe outer space as an ocean? We have already seen examples that they do. The central god of Sumerian mythology is *Anu,* progenitor of all the other gods. *Anunnaki* is a plural of the same word, as *Elohim* in the Bible is the plural of the word *El,* meaning the supreme "God." El is represented by a bull, which in Egypt is called "Amen, the Bull of Meroe," or "the Bull of Heaven, with his seven kine"—i.e., the constellation Taurus, in which the seven stars of the Pleiades are located. The Celtic gods, or "Fairy Folk" as they came to be known, were called the *Tuatha de Danaan* (pron: thoo-AH-huh duh-DAH-nun), meaning "Children of the Goddess Anu" (in some translations, "Ana," "Dana," or "Danu," called "Brigit" or "St. Brigit" in Christian times) with exactly the same spelling, just as *Tuatha* and the Egyptian *Tuat* have identical spellings. In the Hindu Vedas, which are scriptures believed to have been authored by the gods and not by men, *Danu* is the name of the goddess who gave birth to Indra's chief opponent, Vrtra. And *Don* is the equivalent race in the Welsh Mabinogi (myth cycle) to the Celtic Danaan, meaning "the wizard children."

Anu or Danu are also found to mean "the waters of heaven or space," which is exactly where the legendary Tuan Mac Carell said the Danaan descended from in the Book of the Dun Cow. Alwyn and Brinley Rees, in *Celtic Heritage,* state that in the Vedas "*danu* signifies 'stream,' and 'the waters of heaven,' and the same root is to be seen in the names of rivers, from the Russian Don, Dnieper, and Dniester to the Danube and to several rivers in England known as Don." Egyptian mythology relates the same meaning to their word *Nu,* the "primal waters of chaos." The goddess *Nut* was the personification of the sky, or the heavens. Both "Nu" and "Nut," it can easily be seen, are only one letter removed from "Anu." The race called the Fomorians—longstanding mortal foes of both the Partholanians and the Danaan—were "Children of the Goddess *Domnu,*" another name signifying water and space, meaning "abyss," or "deep sea." "Fomor" itself was a contraction of two Gaelic words meaning "under sea." The Fomorians (sometimes called "Fomors" or "Fomoir") were a race of hideous or misshapen giants, which is one translation of the biblical *Nefilim,* and they are equated by some scholars as being the equivalent of Vrtra, the offspring of the Vedic Danu already mentioned. They are found in all mythologies, two examples being the Titans of Greece and the Norse/Teutonic Frost Giants, and are associated with conflagration—Titan, Etin, and, Jotunn (the Scottish and Scandinavian forms) all derive from the Sanskrit *tith,* "to burn." The apparent Saxon name for them and their original abode is almost identical to the Bible's: *Nifelheim.*

The Goddess Anu of Celtic mythology, being the feminine principle of Creation, "the waters of heaven or space," had a male counterpart in her father, the Dagda Mor, meaning "the Good" or "the Wise," sometimes also rendered as "Fire of God." Like Anu in the Sumerian mythology, he is rarely accorded any real personality, though this depends largely on who is relating the tales. His principal function in all the myths—from which he soon vanishes— is to bestow legitimacy on claimants to the throne through his lineage. As T. W. Rolleston's *Myths and Legends of the Celtic Race* describes him, "A certain conception of vastness attaches to him and to his doings," making him more a primal force of nature, the "great overlord." He is referred to not by name, but by title: *the* Dagda Mor. His most famous possession (or feature) was a "cauldron" which could feed all men without ever being emptied, representing, perhaps, the endless bounty of the universe. Like Anu, he annually returns to see that all is in order. On those visits, though propitiated by his children, he is known to make huge gouges in the earth with his spear, like those "which mark the mearing of a province" as he is "trailing it on the march," and consumes the very earth—gravel, dirt, and all—without care or comment. A telling clue that he represents a planet or universal power is that all of his many children were mothered by *rivers,* the sea being the simile for outer space and rivers for regions therein.

Even in the rare instances where the Dagda is represented as a personal being, it is more as a force of nature. The Dagda Mor destroys "nine Fomorians" (misshapen giants) with the "music" from his "harp," which he calls to him in passing. The Fomorians were a rival race to the Danaan, but in this instance—numbering exactly nine—the metaphor may well refer to the planets of our solar system, the Dagda Mor (or Sumerian Anu) being that tenth planetary body proposed by Sitchin and other astronomers. The "music from his harp" could be the force of gravity, disordering or destroying the nine planets, making huge gouges without concern. "Music" means more than song in Celtic mythology; it is the very essence of the Danaan's magic, all of their spells said to be worked by it. Given the theory already discussed that this race may utilize sound waves in order to move large masses, "music"—which is, after all, only controlled manipulation of sound waves—could apply equally well to the forces of gravity, the "music of the spheres." This is especially interesting to contemplate since it was the Dagda Mor that ultimately destroyed the race of the Fomorians on Earth, "his blows sweeping down whole ranks of the enemy" on his passing over the battlefield, which was "Moytura," meaning "Plain of the Towers."

The Tuatha de Danaan, like the gods of other mythologies (especially the Egyptian), were not the first god-race in Ireland. They were preceded by a race called the Partholon (also referred to as Partholanians), who came from the Other World across the Western Ocean—which was an actual, physical location to the Celts, their "Land of the Dead" and "Land of Eternal Life," alike—on Beltaine, the day sacred to the God of Death or Ruler of the Underworld, from whom the Celts and Gauls believed themselves descended. The Partholon were the most ancient race, considered to be the builders of the megalithic temples in antiquity. "At this remote time," writes Charles Squire, in *Celtic Myth and Legend,* "Ireland consisted of only one treeless, grassless plain, watered by three lakes and nine rivers." Ancient Egypt is just such a country: a flat desert, fed only by the Nile River, which has its origin in Lake Tana in Ethiopia and Lakes Albert and Victoria in Uganda, emptying to the Mediterranean in nine rivers and three more lakes in the Delta, Lakes Mareotis, Bourlos, and Menzala. Nine rivers are frequently shown on maps, though seven (a holy number) were usually designated by the ancients: the Pelusiac, the Tanitic, the Mendesian, the Sebennytic, the Canopic, the Bolbitine (also called

Rashid or Rosetta), and the Pathmitic (also called Dumyat or Dami-etta), of which only the latter two rivers remain today. Building and expanding their kingdom, the Partholon eventually warred with another god-race, the Fomorians, and were driven off this world or simply left it to go back to the Other World (or, in later versions, died of plague), first building a special mound in their original land, the "Old Plain." Whether to death and the afterlife, or back to their Other World in their still-living physical bodies, it was from this Old Plain that they disembarked. If the Great Pyramid is indeed an astral marker, it would correspond with that special mound that saw them on their way home.

Certainly, that is the Pyramid's exact function in Egyptian mythology: to be the place of departure for the Pharaoh (and later, all deceased) to the Afterlife. Both the Celts and the Egyptians believed this Underworld, or Other World, was a physical location and the home of the gods, to which one traveled on "the solar barque of millions of years," the same curved glyph for which can be found not only in Egypt and Ireland, but in other countries as well. The British Museum has several Egyptian solar barques depicted on papyri from the nineteenth to the twenty-second Dynasties. New Grange, Dowth, and the tumulus of Loughcrew sport the glyph in Ireland, as does Locmaricquer in Brittany, and in Sweden it can be seen in Hallande, Ryxo, and Scania. R. T. Rundle Clark, in *Myth and Symbol in Ancient Egypt,* describes a funerary ritual in which a statue of the deceased "was crowned during the final ceremony inside the pyramid [and] was vested with the red crown of Lower Egypt," so as to be recognized by the gods as they came down to pick him up for the trip to heaven. The hieroglyphs used in this ritual are indicative of the Egyptian use of sacred puns: the deceased's destination is "*To*-land," meaning four things at once—"land," "God's land," "the World," and "the Two Lands." "The Land," we might recall, was also one of the meanings of the name "Sumer."

And in this "mound" or "mountain of the gods," we find a motif recurring in all the world's myths, without exception, tying in to another universal symbol: the cross. The cross always represents the four gardens, the four streams, or the four quadrants of life, at the center of which is the primal paradise and the mountain of the gods, connecting heaven and Earth. The mound is called by different names, most often a "mountain" or "the tree of life," and it is invariably in the center of these four quadrants—the center of Earth. The Greek Mount Olympus, the heavenly mountain abode of the gods, was believed to be at the center of the world. Asgard, the tree of life in the heavens populated by the Norse/ Teutonic gods, was at the center of the world, connecting all other worlds. So was the Chinese/Tartar "celestial mountain land," Tien-Chan; Tawrutsia of the Buddhist Sineru; Slavratta on Mount Meru of the Hindu Brahmas, connecting to the center of the earth; Osiris as the Tree of Byblos, the central pillar of the kingdom, in Egypt; Central America's "great mountain in the middle of the water," Culhuacán; Mexico's Miztec tribe's rock called "the Place of Heaven"; even the Celtic Maypole.

At least two American Indian tribes, the Oglala Sioux and the Nebraskan Great Plains Omahas, speak of the tree of life, "the living center of the nation," discovered once at "a time of tribal disruption, brought on by rivalries between the Omaha chiefs . . . One of their sons encountered a burning cedar tree. Although enveloped in flames, the tree did not burn up. The chief's son noticed that the forest animals had worn four trails to the tree, one leading to each cardinal direction, and in the tree's branches roosted thunderbirds, which are emblems of the sky and the talismans of warriors." The tree that burns but is not consumed is immediately recognizable as Moses' "burning bush," another in the growing list of anachronistic connections between the Old World and the New, to accompany such curiosities as the Paiute's "silver canoe to the Promised Land" and the Hopi's white-robed "First and Last" at the end of the world, among others.

Another universal connection to this central tree or mountain of the gods, is that its primary god died and rose upon or through it. As Osiris was dismembered by his evil brother Set and rose from the dead, continuing to feed his flock through the annual harvest, so did Zeus have his sinews hacked out by Typhon to be restored by Aegippas and Hermes, Odin rise from the tree of life after having been nailed to it by swords, and the pierced Cuchulainn, hung on a sacred pillar, return from hell after his death. It is recognizable to Christianity as both Petros, the rock on which Christ builds his Church, and Calvary Hill, the place of the cross: "calvary" means "mount" or "cone," and the cross is sometimes called the tree of life. The Third and Sixty-eighth Psalms (the "Lord's holy hill" and "the hill which the Lord dwells in forever") refer to the Garden of Eden being situated on a mountain. Even the previously mentioned Mali tribes (see Chapter 8) believe that Nommo died and rose for them, causing them to eat a eucharistic meal in his name, and the Aztecs practiced transubstantiation before Cortés.

Geodesy depends on artificially constructed spheroids designed to compensate for Earth's irregularities in shape, of which there is more than one model, so it cannot be said absolutely that the Great Pyramid is at the exact geodetic center of the planet—but the "Equal Surface Projection" model does put the Pyramid dead center of Earth's land mass, equidistantly dividing it at meridian 31 degrees, 9 minutes east of Greenwich, and 29 degrees, 58 minutes, 51 seconds north, as noted in the 1860s by Scotland's Astronomer Royal, Charles Piazzi Smyth, in *Our Inheritance in the Great Pyramid* and other of his works. Whatever its relation to world geodesy, the Pyramid is definitely at the exact center of the Nile Delta, and was the structure from which all the ancients took their measure. "The ancient geographer could establish his longitude with great precision on the basis of accurate tables of the nightly transit of celestial bodies as observed at the Pyramid," writes Peter Tompkins. "Because of the advanced geodetic and geographic science of the Egyptians, Egypt became the geodetic center of the known world. Other countries located their shrines and capital cities in terms of the Egyptian meridian 'zero,' including such capitals as Nimrod, Sardis, Susa, Persepolis, and, apparently, even the ancient Chinese capital of An-Yang . . . The same applies to the centers of worship of the Jews, the Greeks, and the Arabs." The thirtieth parallel referred to by Sitchin as being the orientation site of holy cities was that "meridian zero," off of which the Great Pyramid deviates only one-sixtieth of a degree south, and the supposed pyramid of Chephren next to it deviates only thirteen seconds more. In other words, it is within bounds to suppose that the Great Pyramid is the "mountain of the gods at the center of the world."

Further corroboration comes from the Piri Reis maps. The Turkish Reis and his uncle, Captain Kemal, captured rare and fascinating maps from a Spanish sailor during a naval battle in 1501. The sailor claimed he was one of Columbus' men, and that Columbus had used the maps to find America. He said Columbus had copied them from a translation of a book dating back to Alexander the Great. "If so," Andrew Tomas notes in *We Are Not the First*, "the words of Columbus' biographer Las Casas then become clear: 'He was as sure he would discover what he did discover as if he held it in a chamber under lock and key.'" Admiral Reis copied and included the surprisingly accurate maps in his cartographic compilation of 210 such well-drawn maps, the *Bahriye* or *Book of the Seas.* Two of these copies, dated 1513 and 1528, are presently in the National Museum of Turkey. These are both fragments, the former showing Brittany, Spain, West Africa, the Atlantic, parts of North America; the complete outline of South America's eastern half, including the unexplored Orinoco, Paraná, Uruguay, and Amazon rivers in that continent (among others); and the coastline of Antarctica *without its icecap,* extending eastward to a point beneath Africa and accurately depicting mountain ranges not detected until twentieth century technology could see beneath the ice. That Antarctica could appear at all on a map that old is amazing—the continent was not discovered in modern times until British and Russian expeditions between 1818 and 1820. The latter map shows part of Canada, the east coast of North America to Florida, Greenland, Labrador and Newfoundland. Tremendous precision is evident in these maps, with exact distances between Europe, Africa, and the Americas. The maps are complete and accurate enough to demonstrate that three more sections including the Indian Ocean and probably Australia, Europe, and Asia must once have existed. U.S. cartographic expert Arlington Mallery has stated, "We don't know how they could map it so accurately without an aeroplane." Projected by key reference points onto a grid, the Piri Reis maps proved to be all but identical to U.S. Air Force maps of the world equidistantly plotted from high above Cairo.

The destruction of the Fomorians ("giants") on the Plain of the Towers by the Dagda Mor may well have been the Flood caused by the proposed tenth astral body (or some other cosmic catastrophe), or the tale could represent an earlier Celtic myth concerning the destruction of the Nemedians and Fomorians by drowning: "The men of Erin were all at the battle, / After the Fomorians came; / All of them the sea engulphed, / Save only three times ten." The Nemedians, a god-race akin to the Partholon and the later Tuatha de Danaan, were the primary survivors, wandering in despair and eventually settling in various locations such as Britain. This story sounds a great deal like the Egyptian myth of Osiris' dismemberment after having been sunk in a chest in the sea, consigned there by his scheming brother, Set.

This myth can best be understood in its most thorough recounting: the pseudepigraphical (meaning that he himself did not actually write it) Book of Enoch. Until the discovery of many texts of the book in Qumran among the Dead Sea Scrolls, which were copies made about 200 BC from earlier versions, the Book of Enoch was believed by many to be a post-Christian text, owing to the remarkable number of New Testament quotes—more than a hundred—that emerge directly from it. A great many of Jesus' sayings are found in Enoch, in extremely close paraphrasings. This should be no surprise, since Jesus has long been supposed to have spent at least a few of his missing years among the Essenes, and theirs was the sect in Qumran. Aside from his use of Enoch, additional evidence for Jesus' having been an Essene are found in his specifically being said to wear white robes, which only the Essenes wore, and the fact that he was a healer, which was the special province of the Essenes. When exactly the Book of Enoch was written is unknown, but it is now generally accepted that it is very old. Much of Enoch's information, now that sufficient copies of it have been found for study, show it to incorporate a great deal of pre-Christian mysticism and even indirect but clear connections to prophets of the Old Testament. One of the pieces of evidence for this is its specific references to the Watchers, who were those enigmatic "sons of God who came in unto the daughters of men" and begat children from them in Genesis. In fact, we can quickly determine that the origins of the Book of Enoch go back to the earliest writings of man, as we shall soon see.

The Book of Enoch and its importance to the established canon of biblical writings was hotly debated by church fathers, obviously a matter of controversy since it contained so many quotes used throughout all the other "inspired" books of the Bible—including the direct quotes of Jesus, the Sermon on the Mount, and virtually the entire book of Revelation—yet it contained the single element that was anathema to them all: the embodiment of the angels. Why this should have been so intolerable to the early builders of the Church is a question that cannot readily be answered, except for the fact that they had by that time become quite accustomed to thinking of the angels solely as spiritual beings and simply did not want to consider that they may have been wrong all those years. Where Genesis, which could not be denied as a canonical book, contained references to bodily and sexual angels (both in lust and creation of offspring), it could at least be minimized and rationalized since only two sentences contained the offending material. Julius Africanus decided that the "sons of god" referred to the Cainites, which was satisfactory to all concerned, and Augustine—backed explicitly or tacitly by other church fathers—dismissed Enoch as hearsay, and therefore "apocryphal." So it was that the Book of Enoch was excluded from the official canon.

Enoch himself is an enigmatic figure to biblical scholars, referred to as being a descendant of both Sheth and Cain. It is possible that there were two Enochs, or that the scholars' understanding of him is imperfect. The pseudepigraphical Book of Jubilees confirmed him as the first man on Earth to learn writing, wisdom, and astronomy. (For the lattermost, in the Book of Enoch, he described being taught by the angels to utilize twelve "windows" that sound suspiciously like those found in megalithic monuments, in which he describes planetary bodies spending thirty days each.) His name means "foundation," as in the first, the beginning. He has a clear Sumerian equivalent in Enmeduranki, the first high priest taught by the gods all the wisdom and sciences known to man. He has an even clearer equivalent in Egypt.

Enoch's story, as rendered in the book bearing his name, is the story of the Watchers. "Before all these things Enoch was concealed," the book says (Chapter 12), "nor did any one of the sons of men know where he was concealed, where he had been and what had happened. He was wholly engaged with the holy ones, and with the Watchers in his days. I, Enoch, was blessing the great Lord and King of Peace. And behold, the Watchers called me Enoch the scribe." Enoch had been brought before the Most High, to have secrets revealed to him concerning the fate of fallen angels on Earth: the Watchers. "It happened after the sons of men had multiplied in those days," Enoch writes (we shall call him by name to avoid confusion, acknowledging that the actual Enoch did not pen the words), "that daughters were born to them, elegant and beautiful. And when the angels, the sons of heaven, beheld them, they became enamoured of them, saying to each other, Come, let us select for ourselves wives from the progeny of men, and let us beget children." Here, plainly, is a rendering of the scanty verses in Genesis that leaves no doubt whatsoever to their meaning, and is virtually word for word the same phrasing.

The leader of these angels, Samyaza, is named along with eighteen others as the head of a number of two hundred. Samyaza forced the other angels in agreement with him on this course of action to swear an oath of fealty and secrecy, lest he stand alone if they should be discovered. They took the oath and took the women of their choosing, "And the women conceiving brought forth giants . . . These devoured all which the labour of men produced; until it became impossible to feed them; When they turned themselves against men, in order to devour them; And began to injure birds, beasts, reptiles, and fishes, to eat their flesh one after another, and to drink their blood. Then the earth reproved the unrighteous. Moreover, Azazyel taught men to make swords, knives, shields [and] breastplates. . . ." Women were taught glamour in order to make themselves whores. "Impiety increased; fornication multiplied; and they transgressed and corrupted all their ways . . . And men, being destroyed, cried out; and their voice reached to heaven."

The Most High, the Great and Holy One (both names by which he is referred to in the text) sent an angel (Uriel) to Noah ("the son of Lamech"): "Say to him, in my name, Conceal thyself. Then explain to him the consummation which is about to take place; for all the earth shall perish; the waters of a deluge shall come over the whole earth, and all things which are in it shall be destroyed. And now teach him how he may escape, and how his seed may remain in all the earth . . . All the sons of men shall not perish in consequence of every secret, by which the Watchers have destroyed, and which they have taught, their offspring."

Azazyel was considered to be the central culprit behind the crimes of the angels, being the one who taught man war and abject prostitution. Raphael was dispatched to bind him and cast him into darkness on sharpened stones in "the desert which is in Dudael," there to remain forever until the "great day of judgment," at which time he would be "cast into the fire." Gabriel was sent to "destroy the children of fornication, the offspring of the Watchers, from among men" by "bring[ing] them forth and excit[ing] them one against another. Let them perish by mutual slaughter; for length of days shall not be theirs." The Most High tells Gabriel to be pitiless with them, for they will beg for their life of five hundred years, and eternal life to follow, but no mercy is ever again to be shown them. Michael was sent to pronounce doom on Samyaza and his cohorts.

"And when all their sons shall be slain," pronounces the Most High, "when they shall see the perdition of their beloved, bind them for seventy generations underneath the earth, even to the day of judgment, and of consummation, until the judgment, the effect of which will last for ever, be completed. Then shall they be taken away into the lowest depths of the fire in torments; and in confinement shall they be shut up for ever. Immediately after this shall [Samyaza], together with them, burn and perish; they shall be bound until the consummation of many generations. Destroy all the souls addicted to dalliance [lust], and the offspring of the Watchers, for they have tyrannized over mankind. Let every oppressor perish from the face of the earth; Let every evil work be destroyed. . . ."

Following this terrible judgment is pronounced a golden age for man: "The earth shall be cleansed from all corruption, from every crime, from all punishment, and from all suffering; neither again will I send a deluge on it from generation to generation for ever. In those days, I will open the treasures of blessing which are in heaven, that I may cause them to descend upon earth, and upon all the works and labour of man. Peace and equity shall associate with the sons of men all the days of the world, in every generation of it."

Bible students will already have recognized this as the substantive content of Revelation. Here, in the Book of Enoch, it is fully expounded upon. This fits not only Revelation, but the apocalyptic myths of the rest of the world. Ragnarok of the Norse and Teutons is an excellent example, being the time when Thor's great enemy, "the World Serpent" (who, as Apophis, was the eternal enemy of Ra in Egypt, and as Rahab was wounded by Yahweh in the Old Testament), will be unleashed, along with all manner of gods, demons and forces of nature, and a final showdown of sorts will be enacted. Loki, the evil one, is bound in a place where poison drips on his face, until that final judgment. Though this last battle is supposed to bring the death of all the gods, their righteous offspring are destined to survive and be immortal, along (seemingly) with some of the gods themselves. To the Hindus this apocalypse is the opening of the Eye of Shiva, which will burn Earth in fire as it did once in the past. The Eye of Ra did the same to Earth in Egyptian mythology, which could easily equate to Revelation's destruction of Earth by fire at the end of time. So did the Eye of Balor open and burn all it gazed upon in the Celtic cycle. In all myths, the world does not begin and end once, but over and over again in a number of repetitive cycles: Eliade's "Eternal Return."

One of the most interesting sights Enoch saw on one of his assumptions into heaven was "a lofty spot . . . a mountain, the top of which reached to heaven ... I surveyed the stone which supports the corners of the earth." He mentions this in conjunction with "the four winds, which bear up the earth, and the firmament of heaven." Again, the four directions of the "world cross," and the central mountain reaching to heaven. Isaiah (19:19–20) may well have been referring to the same "supporting stone" when he spoke of "an altar to the Lord in the midst of the land of Egypt, and a pillar at the border thereof to the Lord, and it shall be for a sign and a witness unto the Lord of hosts in the land of Egypt." As we have seen, the Great Pyramid stands in the middle of the ancient world (and, apparently, even the planet) and equilaterally marks the boundaries of the Delta, which would include the division between northern and southern Egypt—"Giza" even means "the border." It therefore meets Isaiah's qualifications. Could the "supporting stone" of Enoch also have been the Great Pyramid? There is one very good reason to think so, which is the same reason Enoch's story can be shown to have roots in man's earliest history: Enoch appears in the Egyptian Book of the Dead. Not under the same name, of course, but it is impossible not to recognize him.

Chapter 175 of the Theban Recension of the Book of the Dead contains Enoch's story. It can be found on the Papyrus of Ra in the Leyden Museum and the Papyrus of Ani in the British Museum, both from the Nineteenth Dynasty, the former written in Memphis, the latter in Thebes. In this chapter, "Ani, the Scribe"—as in, "the Watchers called me Enoch, the scribe"—stands before the god Thoth and says, "Hail, Thoth! What is it that hath happened unto the divine children of Nut? They have done battle, they have upheld strife, they have done evil, they have created the fiends, they have made slaughter, they have caused trouble; in truth, in all their doings the mighty have worked against the weak. Grant, O might of Thoth, that that which the god Tem (Atum) hath decreed (may be done)! And thou regardest not evil, nor art thou provoked to anger when they bring their years to confusion and throng in and push to disturb their months; for in all that they have done unto thee they have worked iniquity in secret. I am thy writing palette, O Thoth, and I have brought unto thee thine ink-jar. I am not of those who work iniquity in their secret places; let not evil happen unto me." Thoth answers, "I am going to blot out everything which I have made ... into the watery abyss of Nu by means of a raging flood. . . ."

That Thoth is the God we recognize as the central god of the Bible (Yahweh/Jehovah) has already been mentioned. He is the Logos, Hermes, the Divine Word of John 1:1—"And the Word was with God, and the Word was God." Further confirmation that the Bible's religion began in Egypt comes from analysis of the name under which Egypt's collective henotheism of gods was known: *Neteru,* from which we derive the word "nether," as in Netherworld. Neteru means, in literal translation, "Watchers." "Watchers" is also a meaning of the word *Essene,* the sect of the Dead Sea Scrolls that harbor the Book of Enoch, as denoted in Paul Carus' superior study, *The History of the Devil and the Idea of Evil:* "The word Essenes, or Essees . . . is derived by Ewald from [a Hebrew character meaning] preserver, guardian, a rabbinical term, because they called themselves 'watchers, guardians, servants of God.' " "Watchers" is one of the meanings of the name *Sumer,* as we have already noted: "land of the ones who watch." The Mali tribes refer to the Nommos as "the Monitors," another word for Watchers. The word *egregori,* from which we get "Gregorian"—as in calendar— also means Watchers. And, as was mentioned earlier, the Babylonian word for Watcher is *'ir*—as in "Ireland."

When Enoch/Ani made reference to Thoth's not being provoked to anger by the Watchers' "confusing and disturbing the months, working iniquity in secret" against him, he is almost certainly referring to the alteration of the accepted calendar, which governed the building of new temples oriented to different astral or stellar bodies. Thoth was the god associated with the Moon, who created a lunar calendar of fifty-two weeks of seven days; his brother Ra was a sun god with a solar calendar based on the number ten, and there is tremendous evidence in ancient texts (and historically in the periodic alteration of fundamental religious ideas) that Ra and Thoth vied for supremacy, with the choice of calendar—thus, style of temple—being evidence of it, along with the mythology. Sitchin writes on this particular subject at length in *When Time Began.*

Fifty-two was also the number of years in an Aztec religious cycle. The Hopi New-Fire festival, inherited from the Aztecs, begins exactly when Orion rises above direct center of their temple roof, a religious connection to ancient Egypt which adds weight to the theory that the Giza complex was intentionally built to mirror Orion's belt. As the Hopi inherited their culture and religion from the Aztecs, the Aztecs inherited (and corrupted) their entire culture from Toltec predecessors. Peter Tompkins points out in *Mysteries of the Mexican Pyramids* that the Aztecs never claimed to have built the pyramid complex in their area, but to have found those structures extant on their arrival. Laurette Sejourn's *Burning Water* discusses the fact that human sacrifice was abhorrent to their culture god, Quetzalcoatl, becoming implemented entirely on the bloodthirsty Aztecs' own initiative rather than a divine mandate. In line with stories of wars between rival gods, Mexican mythology records Quetzalcoatl's being driven out of Mexico and back to his original legendary home in the eastern sky (usually considered to be Venus) by the usurping war god, Huitzilopochtli ("Hummingbird-to-the-left," often equated with Mars), along with a second compatriot called Tezcatlipoca ("Smoking Mirror" or "Fiery Mirror") and a third called Tlacahuepan, who initiated the heart sacrifices. The original sacrifice Quetzalcoatl asked of his followers was only that of the first fruits, a simple festival of Thanksgiving for the harvest like those found the world over.

Quetzalcoatl's Sacred Calendar was based on fifty-two, and Thoth was famous in Egypt for "the Game of 52," which was his magical number. Quetzalcoatl was the "feathered serpent"—i.e., "flying wise man"—described as a tall white man with a red beard, who the natives said came from "the black and red land." In fact, so certain were the Indians of his appearance that they automatically assumed Cortés was Quetzalcoatl when he arrived on Aztec shores in their Year of 1 Reed (1519 AD)—which was exactly when Quetzalcoatl had prophesied his return. Pizarro was also confused to find his arrival in Peru in 1532 greeted with the salutation of "Viracocha" ("Foam of the Sea"), the Inca bearded white man from the sky who had been their "Ancient lord, instructor of the world, creator." (Viracocha has also been translated as "Windy Sea" and "White Master.") And the Spaniards found the exact same personage referred to as "Kukulcán" among the Mayans—of interest both linguistically and mythologically for his resemblance to the Celtic "Cuchulainn." They were equally baffled by the discovery that natives already worshipped the cross in other parts of the world, entirely independent of Christianity, which the Spaniards blamed on some subterfuge of the devil.

Maurice Chatelain found another link between ancient Mesopotamia and Mexico, being the number 2,268. In the Library of Assurbanipal is an enormous number, the significance of which was unknown until recently. Taken as seconds and then translated into days, the number becomes 2,268 million days. Teotihuacán's Grand Avenue measures 2,268 ancient Mexican yards, and all measurements in the complex are exact fractions of 2,268. The Nineveh Constant of the Sumerians contains the same number: 2,268.

Zecharia Sitchin believes that the biblical Cain ended up in the Americas, being the connection to the Middle East. He bases this idea on two strong pieces of evidence. One is a Babylonian tablet copied from an earlier Sumerian tablet around the third millennium BC and translated by W. G. Lambert from a copy by A. R. Millard, now in the British Museum (No. 74329) and catalogued as "containing an otherwise unknown myth." It relates the tale of a man named "Ka'in" doomed to roam in sorrow after murdering his shepherd brother, coming finally to rest in the land of Dunnu, where he builds a city with twin towers—a hallmark of architecture attributed to the Aztecs. The other evidence Sitchin offers is linguistic: the Egyptians used syllables interchangeably, meaning that "Ka'in" could as easily be "In'ka," or "Inca"; and the adding of a "T" prefix to words is a trait typical of the Aztecs, making the removal of it from "Tenochtitlán," meaning "City of Tenoch," instead the "City of Enoch." The Book of Jubilees also states that Cain built a city for his son Enoch, which would seem to support the theory of Cain's displacement to another hemisphere.

In Egypt, different times brought different Creation myths, prefiguring wars among the gods and ultimate apocalypses. Atum remained the greatest of these in all ages, the primal creator god, probably the equivalent of Anu or the Dagda Mor. Atum is that god who returns to create "a cosmic collapse and a 'Gotterdämmerung' from which only Atum and Osiris survive . . . destroy[ing] the world, submerging gods, men and Egypt in the Primal Waters *(Nun),* which were all that existed at the beginning of time," as George Hart's *A Dictionary of Egyptian Gods and Goddesses* puts it. This destruction is the equivalent of Revelation or Ragnarok. Atum is "the god Tem" referred to by Ani in the Book of the Dead, whose "decree" he asks Thoth to honor, destroying all that has been created in the Flood. More a principle and a force of nature, Atum's place as the head of the gods is as secure as that of all his counterparts around the world (the Dagda Mor, etc).

The other gods of Creation, however, vary in primacy from age to age. One era has Ra as the central god, another has Thoth. Eventually Osiris supplanted them all. The essential difference among these theologies lies in the Afterlife. Under Ra, only the Pharaoh and his immediate family and descendants could expect or hope for eternal life. His was an elitist view. Under Osiris, the Afterlife became democratized—any peasant could hope to please the gods sufficiently to join Osiris in heaven. Thoth was extremely instrumental in bringing Osiris' house to power, by enabling his dead body to sire an avenging son with his widow, Isis, eventually raising Osiris himself from the dead. Analogies to Christianity are obvious, especially in Osiris' death and rebirth. Osiris was the prototype of the dead or dying god, and the resurrection. The rivalry between Ra and Thoth equates to that between the Sumerian Enlil and Enki, or Balor and "Nuada of the Silver Hand" in the Celtic. All relate the same story, which is a battle for supremacy over the earth.

The Bible makes reference to this ongoing conflict, in its few actual namings of the devil. Isaiah (14:10–17) identifies Lucifer as an actual man on Earth: "All they shall speak and say unto thee, Art thou also become weak as we? art thou become like unto us? Thy pomp is brought down to the grave and the noise of thy viols [harps] . . . How art thou fallen from heaven, O Lucifer, son of the morning! how art thou cut down to the ground, which didst weaken the nations! For thou hast said in thine heart, I will ascend into heaven, I will exalt my throne above the stars of God: I will sit also upon the mount of the congregation, in the sides of the north: I will ascend above the heights of the clouds; I will be like the most High. Yet thou shalt be brought down to hell, to the sides of the pit. They that see thee shall narrowly look upon thee, and consider thee, saying, Is this the man that made the earth to tremble, that did shake kingdoms; That made the world as a wilderness, and destroyed the cities thereof; that opened not the house of his prisoners?" These same words are used in Enoch, pronouncing doom upon the fallen Watchers.

The oldest renditions of the wars of the gods in the Middle East are the Egyptian murder of Osiris by Set (from which "Satan" is derived) and the Sumerian defeat of Zu by Ninurta. In the Egyptian myth, Osiris was a good and just king. He taught civilization to all men, ranging far and wide over the whole world to do so. In his absence, his wife Isis was left in charge of the kingdom, and after his murder she continued his work. Osiris' brother, Set, lusted after both his power and his wife, and conspired with cohorts (he never acted alone) to trick Osiris into a precisely measured coffin chest. First he cast Osiris into the sea, where he washed up on the shores of Byblos and grew into the tree that supported the kingdom's vault—the "tree of life" referred to earlier. Isis, mourning and in fear, eventually found Osiris and tried to return him home so that Thoth could use his magic to raise him from the dead, but Set intercepted the body en route and dismembered it into fourteen pieces, burying them far and wide. Isis found the pieces anyway, all but her dead husband's phallus, which was claimed to be the reason the earth remained fertile. Thoth fashioned an artificial phallus and impregnated Isis with her dead husband's seed. This produced Horus, who later avenged his father's murder in a series of battles with Set.

In the fragments that survive of the Sumerian version, Zu, "his heart having thus plotted aggression," steals the Tablets of Destiny from Enlil. These tablets elsewhere appear to refer to a cosmic force, perhaps meaning the ordained orbital paths of the planets—Zu's name is Sumerian for "He Who Knows," and he is sometimes more specifically referred to as *Anzu,* meaning "He Who Knows the Heavens"—but in this myth they are presented as items of power, authority, and kingship. Having stolen the tablets, Zu flees in a "Bird" to the "Mountain of the Sky Chambers." Enlil's son and rightful heir, Ninurta, pursues Zu in a series of battles, most of which are aerially conducted from flying machines. Ninurta holds weapons which fire brilliant beams of light and ultimately succeeds in downing Zu's vehicle by hurling some kind of missile into its "pinions." The apprehended Zu is tried and convicted, his throat cut. Zu is recognizable to twentieth-century audiences from the famous Assyrian statue of Pazuzu, Demon of the Southwest Wind, exhibited in the Louvre and seen in the movie *The Exorcist.* Pazuzu was the most feared of demons, the storm devil. Another famous depiction of Zu is an archaic relief of his execution in central Mesopotamia, showing him as a demon-cock with a third eye in his forehead. This third eye is recognizable to occult students as belonging to the devil, and to devotees of Eastern religions as the third eye of Shiva or the open eye of enlightenment. Such connections (or confusions) between a benevolent god and the devil will be discussed in greater detail in the next chapter.

Babylonian and Assyrian sources identify the annual sacrificial bull of the ancient world as Zu. Having been chosen, the bull was whispered to in ritual fashion by the priests, who said, "Bull, the guilty Zu are you," prior to executing it in a reenactment of the trial before Enlil. In Egypt, the sacrificial bull was called Apis, or Serapis, whose dismemberment represented that of Osiris. Enlil (like Osiris) is recognizable as "the Great Shepherd," and can be equated to Ra ("Re") by the litany in his name found in Theban tombs declaring them as one divinity: "Re in Osiris, Osiris in Re." George Hart's dictionary also says that "The Egyptians gradually evolved a concept of synthesis between the chthonic god Osiris and the solar divinity Re." In later times, the "guilty bull" became the "scapegoat," a necessary sacrifice to appease not only the wronged central god, but also his entire company—the company of heaven, or what we would now call "the angels." The ritual slaughter completed, the priest washed his hands and became "now as Enlil ... [upon] the Earth," who promised a coming redeemer for the evil perpetrated by Zu. This ritual will be instantly recognizable to a Christian readership, Jesus being the promised redeemer who substitutes himself for the usual sacrifice. The Old Testament asserts that Abraham was asked by the Most High to slay his own son in place of the sin-offered scapegoat, but was checked from performing the deed at the last minute. In the same manner, Jesus sacrificed himself in an act of gallantry to appease his own father's wrath, serving as the final atonement.

This same messianic myth is found the world over, often down to particulars, especially in symbols. Enlil is the "Divine Shepherd." So is Osiris the shepherd of his flock. Jesus is "the Good Shepherd." The virgin-born son of the Shepherd King, who is a sun god and a god of light, avenging his father and restoring the rightful order, ultimately leading to resurrection and the eternal kingdom, is universal. In the Celtic, it is Lugh (pron: Loo) who is born of a virgin to defeat the tyrannical alliance of the evil half-Fomorian King Bres (Zu/Set) with his Fomorian kin, Balor (Enlil/Ra). His enemies try to kill Lugh in infancy, but by a ruse, his helpers smuggle him away to be raised in secret—as did the helpers of Moses, Krishna, Horus, and Jesus. As Jesus learned carpentry and Moses learned science while living with foster fathers and mothers, Lugh learned metallurgy and smithing under his foster father, Cuillan. He used his knowledge to forge metal weapons with which to arm his followers for revolt against the oppressive Fomorians, exactly as Horus forged metal weapons at Edfu and armed his followers, and Moses forged the Ark. Krishna (a shepherd in his youth) also armed his human forces, leading some of them in aerial combat in Vimanas. Jesus breaks the mold, being the first specifically *nonviolent* messiah, perhaps the chief reason the Jews, who were accustomed to militaristic judges serving as their deliverer in ages past, refused to accept him—though this is not entirely accurate, either, since Jesus said he would return to finish his militaristic business at the end of time. In his case, it is simply "postponed." He also said that his kingdom was not of this world, but that if it were, then his followers would take up arms and fight for him.

The universal messiah eventually goes to the Underworld for a brief rest in the sleep of death, or leaves Earth temporarily with a promise to return. Thus was it that Jesus' followers called him a reincarnation of Moses, and John the Baptist, Elijah. Lugh returned as his own son, Cuchulainn, who more or less repeated Lugh's heroic acts as these other messianic heroes did. Each is an avatar, a return of the same god from the past, but in a new form.

Given the sacred puns of the ancients, it cannot be an accident that "sons" are always these avatars. Ra's son is the "son of the sun." Cuchulainn is the "son of the son," or, Lugh being the solar god, the "son of the sun." The most sacred object in ancient Egypt was the *Benben* stone, only replicas of which any longer exist, such as the one on the main floor of the Cairo Museum. It was a conical pyramidion, in which frequently could be seen the figure of a god or goddess in a small rectangular doorway etched in the bottom. It was said to have fallen from heaven, bringing the gods. To all appearances and descriptions, it matches the nose cone of a Saturn V rocket, as does a tomb drawing in the resting place of Tutankhamen's viceroy, Huy, which NASA aerospace engineer Stuart W. Greenwood found to have four key points of resemblance to exactly such a rocket. It is shown being paid reverence by followers, buried in a shaft in the ground in three stages with only the nose cone visible above. "Benben," a word for which no linguist can exactly ascertain the Egyptian meaning, has an unquestionable meaning in Hebrew: "Ben" means "son." Benben, then, in addition to meaning the vehicle that brought the sun god to Earth, could also easily mean "son of the son"—or "son of the *sun.*" The name Kon-Tiki, the central god of the Polynesians, also means "son of the sun." "Tiki" was the prenomen to Viracocha's name, as well (*Kon Tiki Illac Viracocha*, "lightning son of the sun from out of the sea foam"). And "Sons of the Sun" is not only the title accorded the rulers of Egypt, Assyria, and Crete, Japan's Mikado, and some Chinese emperors (such as the Chou dynasty), but was also the very name by which the Incas called themselves.

The recurrent resemblance of biblical heroes to supposedly pagan ones raises obvious questions, as does the fact that the central elements of their stories keep repeating. Are we dealing with a single story from great antiquity? Or a number of renditions of the same story, each with local variation? King David—another shepherd king and a son of the son by being in the divine line—was called out of anonymity to slay Goliath and rise to kingship. Goliath was a "giant." David slew him with a slingshot, flinging a rock into his head. Lugh slayed Balor—a Fomorian, therefore a "giant"—by putting out his death-dealing fire-eye, also by flinging a rock through it, and in two later Celtic cycles the heroes Cuchulainn and Finn are both victorious over a one-eyed giant named Goll. Odysseus speared the Cyclops, another "giant," through its single eye. The race of Cyclopes, like the Watchers, were cast into Tartarus beneath Earth for their rebellion. When do coincidences cease to be coincidences? When do they become evidence?

The story of the Flood is the conclusion of one of those mythical, epic conflicts. There were others. Sitchin pieces together the story of two civil wars in his work, the "Pyramid Wars," taken largely from the Sumerian "Myths of Kur" tablets, the *Lugal-e* epic, F. Hrozny's *Mythen von dem Gotte Ninib*, J. Bollenrücher's *Gebete und Hymnen an Nergal*, and George A. Barton's *Miscellaneous Babylonian Texts*, as well as other fragmentary tablets from the region. These texts constitute strong evidence for the two Great Pyramids at Giza having been in existence long before Egyptology claims they were. A cylinder seal shows the symbol of Ninurta (Horus) with a victory wreath, between two objects which could only be pyramids—not only are they triangles, but they are composed of tiers of rectangular blocks. Reference to one of these is given as "the mountain the gods assembled." Inside it were lethal "stones," with which "the Great Serpent" nearly killed Ninurta in his battle against him, with their "strong power . . . to grab to kill me, with a tracking which kills to seize me," taken out and destroyed after Ninurta's victory. The stones glowed in the dark in different colors, set in various recesses which may be those found in the Great Pyramid. One of this "mountain's" weapons was a "net," referred to in other texts, emitting sound and measuring distances, that was kept in the innermost sacred chamber—

which would equate with an Ark in the "King's coffer," as discussed earlier.

Atomic weapons, or at the very least radioactive ones, are heavily implied in the central conflict: a "Killing Brightness" from "Ninurta's Brilliant Weapon" blinded onlookers, but "the House's platform withstood the lord," meaning the Pyramid was unaffected. Either this blast or another injured the eyes of Ninurta, "blowing fire" at him, conceivably the backblast of an atomic bomb. Ninharsag, his mother, feared the weapon would kill Ninurta, and he gave her "clothes which should make her unafraid" in order to enter the battleground and serve as peace envoy, which as Sitchin notes could easily be a radiation suit. Chemical weapons and missiles are distinctly alluded to, and light beams are described which caused people struck by them to clutch at their chests as they died.

The Great Pyramid—the *Ekur,* as it is called, or *Azag,* "mountain monster," possibly meant as an epithet for the Great Serpent—is referred to in these early Mesopotamian myths presented by Sitchin as "the Radiant House Where the Cord-Measuring Begins." It is one of the "two Great Houses" (the other being the pyramid supposedly built by Chephren), or the "House Which Is Like a Mountain." Enki (Thoth) identifies it as "the House that is like a heap, that which I have as a pile raised up." It is also referred to by Ninharsag as "Where Asar [Osiris] his eyes to Anu raised," which is another strong piece of evidence for the Giza complex being oriented to the constellation Orion. Osiris is represented as the eye atop the Pyramid (a symbol so common to us that we tend to forget it exists in our daily life, on the back of the dollar bill), and if "Anu" refers to the heavens, meaning "space," then this makes perfect sense. Its enemies even paid the Ekur the ultimate compliment, saying, "Like Anu art thou made."

This defeat of Enki in his "mountain" fortress concluded the second of the Pyramid Wars (the first apparently being the aforementioned conflict with Zu). These wars were ongoing disputes between Enlil and Enki, who are read here as Ra and Thoth, or Balor and "Nuada of the Silver Hand." *Nuada,* with his one metal hand (replacing the one he lost in combat during a brief early battle against the Fir Bolgs, prior to their subsequent easy submission), is obviously reminiscent of the Middle East figurines representing "lords of metal," and of *Nahash,* the Genesis serpent who "knew the secrets of copper." Also brought to mind in this symbolism are the Norse-Teutonic Odin's one-handed forerunners, Tiwaz and Tyr. H. A. Guerber, in *Myths of the Norsemen from the Eddas and Sagas,* solidifies this latter comparison by drawing attention to Tyr's connections with mined metal for weapons as well as the sun: "Tyr was identical with the Saxon god Saxnot (from *sax,* a sword), and with Er, Heru, or Cheru, the chief divinity of the Cheruski, who also considered him god of the sun, and deemed his shining sword blade an emblem of its rays." H. R. Ellis Davidson, in *Gods and Myths of Northern Europe,* equates the name Saxnot with *Sahsginot,* "sword-companion." This sun god "companion of the sword" is repeatedly encountered in the world's myths, the establisher of kings by the power of his unbeatable blade. Also in the myths is worldwide conflict between two central gods, eventually concluding with a kingdom of man established by the sword-bearer.

In this instance, Enki yielded in order to preserve his land from destruction. As the ravaged surfaces of Mars and the Moon suggest, his lands may have been much more than just Egypt. He was given Sumer as a peace settlement but was banished from Egypt. Enki also insisted that his submission was temporary, and subject to change on Anu's return (establishment/reestablishment of astral order, one of the laws of the gods concerning transferral of power on Earth—"as above, so below"), at which time proper authority would be established. In this, by Sitchin's reading, lay the seeds for the alteration of temples to try to gain ascendancy, with Enki traveling the world in exile and establishing lunar calendars to mark his space.

There is textual evidence in Middle Eastern tablets to support the position that calendars were changed to establish the ascendancy of new gods, and many uses of animals in the Bible make more sense by the interpretation. The "golden calf" that Moses' people resumed worshipping in his absence could be seen as worshipping the "son of the bull"—Enlil's avatar—as opposed to Yahweh. And the later "Lamb of God" referring to Jesus would be the "son of the ram," one of Osiris' many avatars. If Sitchin's reading is correct, then kingship or governorship among the Anunnaki changed hands with the equinoctial precession, and which son (or prince) was going to rise to power could have been intimately involved with the signs in the heavens. These animals are signs of the zodiac, each succeeding the last. Religious traditionalists who haven't given much thought to the question might wish to reflect not only on why there were Twelve Tribes of Israel and twelve apostles—the same as the number of signs in the zodiac—but also why they were represented by the animals of the zodiac (e.g., the Lion of Judah). The authors of the four Gospels are also assigned the symbols of the zodiac's cornerstones: the bull, the lion, the eagle, and the man, being Taurus, Leo, Scorpio, and Aquarius.

One of Enki/Thoth's appearances elsewhere in the world would seem to be as Quetzalcoatl, who according to legend was "exiled by the war god" at the time he was in the Americas. The Chiapas Indians of Guatemala—whose language has always confused scholars because of its strong resemblances to Hebrew—have a famous legend about an exiled king who came to stay with them, a white man-god who lived among them, traveling frequently, teaching them civilization and all their knowledge. His name was "Votan," and his people were called the *Chivim*, "Serpents." Not only is the name quite obviously the same as that of "Wotan" (which, in the German tongue, would be exactly pronounced "Votan") and "Odin," but it also cannot help but call to mind the great god of the American Indian Creation epic, the *Chon-oopa-sa,* named "Wo-kon." Votan told them the story of the Tower of Babel, as "a great city where a magnificent temple was under construction which was intended to reach to heaven, but was doomed by a confusion of languages." He was associated with jade and snakes, and with healing. Before his departure, he wrote a book in the Quiché language describing his travels and hidden treasures, which was burned by Bishop Nuñez de la Vega in 1691.

Ethnologist L. Taylor Hansen, in *He Walked the Americas,* documents North American Indian legends of an identical figure who taught wisdom, healing, and universal brotherhood to tribes throughout Georgia, Oklahoma, Mississippi, Dakota, and Wyoming, described most specifically by the Chippewa as a bearded white man with gray-green eyes and copper-colored hair, wearing a long white robe and golden sandals. In the Philippine Islands, he is known as "Wakea, the Fair God of the Ocean," also described with gray-green eyes, even said to have walked ashore on the water without getting his white robe wet. That robe is described as looking like "the foam of the sea," an obvious connection to Viracocha, and for that matter to Aphrodite, who was said to have been born of the sea's foam. An excellent stained-glass reproduction of Wakea can be seen today in New Zealand's St. Faith Church in Rotorua.

Another place this defeated exile would seem to have traveled was Britain, possibly as "Amergin the Poet" (Thoth was famous as the inventor of words and hieroglyphs, Odin the runic writing, Hermes words and communications, etc.), making him the probable Merlin of the Arthurian legends, themselves vastly corrupted and romanticized Celtic mythology. Geoffrey of Monmouth ascribes the building of Stonehenge to Merlin, the prefix of whose name *(Mer)* has connotations already discussed (see Chapter 8). The choosing of Arthur and his rise to power under Merlin's careful tutelage and guidance echoes those universal myths already encountered, such as King David or Lugh. As an example of the power and expression of myth, literalists might consider that Arthur's Knights of the Round Table may well have a much more commonsense meaning: the Round Table was Merlin's (Thoth's) idea, and Stonehenge is indeed a round *measuring* table, of *nights*— i.e., "moons." Also, there are two tales of how Arthur came by his sword of power, Excalibur. In one version, Arthur pulls it from the stone, which could easily be read as pulling metal from the rock for industrial might, exactly as the Anunnaki appear to have done in their mining; in the other, he is handed Excalibur by the Lady of the Lake, who lives under the water, signifying that his sovereignty was approved and granted by the fairy queens. In both instances, the literal is not intended to be taken as true, but rather the symbolic.

As a condition of surrender, before leaving Egypt, Enki appointed Ninurta the keeper of the Pyramid and of the "Place of Life." He gave him the ankh, the symbol of life itself and also an item of power—exactly like Merlin's bequeathal of Excalibur to Arthur, by enchanting the sword in the stone so that only Arthur could remove it—along with the new and exalted name and title, "Ningishzida," meaning "Lord of the Artifact of Life." Identified by one tablet (UET 6/1) as "the falcon among the gods," Ninurta/ Ningishzida becomes recognizable to us as Horus, "the avenger of his father," who is Osiris (an avatar of Enlil/Ra). Horus is depicted holding the ankh when on the throne, usually with his mother Isis standing behind him. The Book of the Dead attests that no one can come into the presence of Osiris (the Father) except through Horus (the Son), which should automatically be recognizable to students of Christianity.

The ankh, or *crux ansata* ("cross of life"), is one of the oldest of cross symbols. The universality of the symbol and its meaning have already been discussed (see Chapter 8). One extremely inter-esting connection the ankh has to a supposedly unrelated pagan culture is Thor's hammer. The symbol for the gods (*Neteru,* Watch-ers) in Egypt was what has been called an axe, though no one knows for certain exactly what it is supposed to be. The axe, which resembles a hammer, is also the European gods' symbol of author-ity, especially in the hands of Thor. More than one historian has noticed the resemblance of this hammer to a cross. H. R. Ellis Davidson, for instance, relates the story of a heathen who made the sign of the cross over his drink at mealtime, confusing a Chris-tian. A companion at the table explained, "The King acts like all those who trust in their strength and might. He made the sign of the hammer over it before he drank." She also relates how Ham-mers of Thor were popular amulets to be worn around the neck, "and there is an obvious resemblance between the little hammers and the square, equal-armed crosses with figures of Christ on them that were worn at about the same time." Elsewhere, David-son notes, "Like that of the Christian cross, the sign of the ham-mer was at once a protection and a blessing to those who used it." She attests to its being the direct equivalent of the thunderbolt weapon held by the ancient gods of the Middle East, which is also sometimes represented as a trident, and discusses smaller, but-terfly-shaped axe blades with short handles and small rings atop them seeming to have no purpose. These latter items look exactly like the crosses found engraved in stone by Coptic Christians, the small loop on top being clearly the loop of the ankh. That top loop is also identical with the symbol for omega, the Egyptian *shin,* which Horus of Behutet carries, and we might recall that Jesus called himself the Alpha and the Omega.

The ongoing rivalry between Enki/Thoth and Enlil/Ra was not the only conflict among the gods. Mesopotamian texts such as those referred to as *The Curse of Agade* tell of a war involving the goddess Inanna (who is Ishtar/Astarte/Venus). This goddess attempted divine usurpation of a kingdom for herself. Through seductions of kings, and her ruses and wiles, she secured mili-tary might from both men and gods to accomplish her ends. The verses of the texts relating this tale sound almost identical to those in the Bible about the whore of Babylon. "Babylon" itself means "Gateway of the Gods," and Inanna wanted to raise her own Baby-lon—i.e., "spaceport." The precise dating, or even the general, are difficult at best, so this may have occurred as part of the prior

Pyramid Wars or as a later, separate event. Sitchin equates it to the biblical wars of the kings, a coalition of four eastern against five Canaanite monarchs in the time of Abraham, which also is not known for certain but which is generally estimated to have been around the turn of the second millennium BC. What is known is the war's outcome, which was the destruction of Sodom and Gomorrah. Genesis 19:24–25 reads, "And the Lord rained upon Sodom and Gomorrah, from the skies, brimstone and fire that had come from Yahweh. And he upheavaled those cities and the whole plain, and all the inhabitants of the cities and all the vegetation that grows from the ground." The original Sumerian texts say that Lot's wife was turned into vapor, not salt, which makes much more sense if it was a nuclear holocaust.

Sitchin relates the Sumerian "lamentation texts" (called "The Destruction of Ur" or "The Destruction of Sumer") referring to Sumer's demise by an "Evil Wind": "An evil blast heralded the baleful storm, an evil blast the forerunner of the baleful storm was; Mighty offspring, valiant sons were the heralds of the pestilence," meaning it had been caused by "the gods." The blast, automatically reminiscent of atomic weaponry, is specifically said to have come in a "lightning flash," from "the Midst of the Mountains . . . from the Plain of No Pity." A great cloud of darkness and howling wind accompanied it, bringing death from no visible source. The victims not killed in the blast took more than a day to die. They coughed blood, barely able to breathe, their skin going deathly pale and their flesh numb. They suffered dizziness, nausea, and headaches—exactly what we would expect from radiation sickness.

Enlil—Ra, by this reading—sent the destruction via two of his sons, one of whom was Ninurta (Horus). "Seven awesome weapons created by Anu" were the cause, all unleashed at once. "Seven" is a number signifying a great and/or holy magnitude, and Anu could refer either to a personal inventor or to the harnessing of natural forces (as with an atomic bomb). Inanna fled the doomed city in a "submersible ship," according to her lamentation text, bewailing the catastrophic destruction of her capital city, "which in an instant, in a blink of an eye was created in the midst of the mountains." The *Uruk Lament* states that the gods themselves paled in horror at the devastation they had wrought, its "gigantic rays reach[ing] up to heaven . . . the earth trembl[ing] to its core." *The Khedorlaomer Texts* are quite specific that the target was a launching platform: "That which was raised towards

Anu to launch, they caused to wither; its place they made fade away, its face they made desolate." This recalls Nimrod's building of a tower to reach heaven, causing the gods to scatter mankind and confuse his speech, which it is difficult to interpret in any way except to say that the gods were afraid of man's rivaling them for power. (Sitchin baldly asserts that the loss of *Phobos 2* is another Tower of Babel incident.) The tower reaching to heaven that is destroyed by the gods is another mythological motif that can be found the world over. The Hindu variant has it specifically being built on Mount Meru (another "mer" derivation)—where the gods' own sacred stronghold was located—with its height intended to reach eighty-four thousand *yodshana,* a distance about equal to that between Earth and its Moon, according to nineteenth-century mythologist Karl Koppen.

In this capacity, Inanna/Ishtar embodies another universal archetype as the destroyer goddess. Still recognizable today as Kali or the Tibetan mKha'sGroma (pron: em-ma khas GROAM-muh), she was called by the early Akkadians Lilith or Lilitu, and by the Celts the Morrigan (corrupted in Arthurian romance to "Morgan le Fay"). The ancient Egyptians referred to her as Sekhmet, the destructive incarnation of the creation goddess Hathor. One myth of Ra tells of the world's destruction by fire out of his lethal eye, taken down to Earth by Sekhmet. Plainly the "eye" is a weapon, also belonging to the other great creator/destroyer gods, Balor and Shiva. In Egyptian myth, an "eye" can also be a planet, or a vehicle which travels through air or water. Ra destroyed the world for fear that man conspired against him, but having nearly eradicated the entire race in his rage, he repented and called Sekhmet back— albeit with some difficulty, owing to her innate blood lust. (For more on Sekhmet, see Chapter 10 on the Underworld.)

The flying Valkyries of northern mythology fought aerial battles and determined the fate of who would live and who would die; their very name meant "choosers of the slain," and they immediately took their chosen heroes to Valhalla after their noble despatch, there to be fed specifically on the meat of the boar (a point of some interest, given the object of the Wild Hunt, which is discussed below). They literally wove the fates of their chosen mortal men, prophesying for them and aiding them at crucial times in their lives, visiting them in their dreams, initiating, testing and trying them, and on their destined day of death, they were present to bear their hero's body aloft to Valhalla. Like their Hindu equivalent, the Apsalas (or Apsaras), and the Celtic fairy women, the Valkyries were notorious for taking mortal men to their beds, even bearing children to them.

Typically, the destroyer or warrior goddess is also the goddess of beauty, becoming hideous in her wrath, who progresses from being the persecutor of the messiah sun god to becoming his ally and/or protectress, with some variations: the goddess Athena carries the aegis of Medusa's hideous, paralyzing face when going to war, which turns its victims to "stone" in perhaps the same way as Lot's wife was turned to a "pillar of salt"; Inanna curses Gilgamesh for spurning her lust but eventually is impressed by his prowess; the Morrigán has an identical relationship with Cuchulainn, an incarnation of Lugh; Hera is the lifelong persecutor of Dionysus but eventually yields to his inclusion in Olympus.

Though the wars of the gods always centered on battles for supremacy, one of the important issues at stake was the disposition of man. The Watchers were perversely content to treat man not only as a slave, but as a plaything for their amusement. The most powerful of the gods, Enlil/Ra/Zeus or whatever other name applies, was afraid of man from the very beginning. The serpent's statement that the gods feared man's becoming like them was true. There seemed always to be one faction believing that man was entitled to the same immortality the gods possessed, and another believing that he was a dangerous and cunning animal that must not only be watched, but killed as well. In this aspect of the ongoing conflict, it was always Enlil/Ra who took the harder line against man, and Enki/Thoth who was his central advocate. Or, put into biblical terms, El tended to oppose man and Yahweh tended to favor him. Understanding this makes the seemingly schizophrenic dichotomy of God in Scripture perfectly understandable. Leviticus 16 shows this clear distinction between the two gods in the presentation of two scapegoats for sin offerings: "one for the Lord, and one for Azazel." The Lord was Yahweh, and Azazel was "the mighty one of the desert," El, the bull—the same "Azazyel" who led the fallen Watchers. As Zu was associated with the sacrificial bull, Azazel was associated with the scapegoat, and the goat became one of the best-known symbols of the devil. Azazel was also associated with the planet Mars in occult tradition, as will be noted in the next chapter. In the Christian faith, Jesus gallantly volunteered himself in place of the scapegoat as an offering to Yahweh, as mankind's final atonement to stay God's (Elohim/Azazel's) hand in the ultimate devastation of the race. (The Jews continued the annual sacrifice of two scapegoats to the two separate gods until the destruction of their temple by Rome in 70 AD.)

Whenever these rivalries occurred, there came finally a cessation of conflicts and a resolution between the warring parties, concluding when one or another of them withdrew. Periods of exile occurred for both of the primary gods involved. Enlil, Ra, and Zeus all were exiled to the Underworld for acts of rape, and Enki's probable sojourns during his exile as Votan, Quetzalcoatl, and Amergin or Merlin, we have just discussed above. The eventual outcome may have been creation of the worship of Osiris, who is in some cases another avatar of Enlil/Ra, though he may also be a synthesis of both central gods. "Osiris" may never have existed, but simply have been another name for Enlil/Ra and Enki/Thoth that recognized them both—a *convention*—just as Christians use the word "God" for a Trinity of three separate but equal divinities regarded as one. The gods in any mythology sometimes become slightly confused with one another, attributes becoming subsumed or redistributed periodically. That the primary gods had other avatars should be obvious by now, and that one or another of them may have changed identity more than once, or come to be recognized differently, is abundantly evident.

The god Amun is probably such a synthesis of Enlil/Ra and Enki/Thoth. Like Thoth, Amun is hidden and invisible, but also personal enough to impregnate chosen mortal women on Earth; like Yahweh (another avatar of Thoth), he is the god of the poor, instructing those who worship at his temple to give alms and take care of the needy; as Hermes (another avatar of the same god), he is famous as the "god of the crossroads," patron of travelers, and is also the god of magic and medicine. Most telling, Amun is the head of the Ogdoad, the company of eight original creator gods, which is the exact position held by Thoth. However, Amun's symbols are the ram and the bull, traditionally associated with Enlil/Ra and Osiris.

There are other examples of such fusions around the world. The ancient Inca god, Rimac, bears both the thunder-weapon trident and the magic wand, the separate symbols of the two principal gods. There is also the enigmatic Norse god, Heimdall. Like Osiris, he is represented by a flayed ram skin on a pole—quite possibly the same as Jason's Golden Fleece, which has solar connotations to be discussed in the next chapter—but, like Odin (who

more closely resembles Thoth, though he may be another synthesis), Heimdall occupies the central throne in all the realms,
seeing and hearing all that goes on in every world by virtue of his
extra-keen senses, traveling easily through all the worlds by virtue
of a magic horse, and siring divine lines of kings. "Heimdall has
several other names," says Guerber, adding elsewhere, "at times
he takes Odin's place and is identified with that god, as well as
with the other sword gods, Er, Heru, Cheru and Tyr, who are all
noted for their shining weapons."

Paul Carus cites perhaps the best example of this fusion:
"Prometheus and Hercules are combined into one person in the
Christian Savior, Jesus Christ. The similarity of the story of Gol-
gotha with the myth of Prometheus is not purely accidental. For
observe that in some of the older pictures, as for instance in the
vase of Chiusi . . . Prometheus is not chained to a rock, but tied
to a pole, i.e., to a cross, and Greek authors frequently use expressions . . . which mean 'to be crucified.'" Prometheus is the Great
Serpent (Enki/Thoth) who "stole fire from Olympus" to give to
mankind, and was punished by Zeus (the great sun god) only to
be freed later by Zeus' selfless and heroic son, Hercules. Hercules
is pictorially rendered, along with Gilgamesh and numerous other
savior-heroes in Assyria, Asia, Babylon, and Khorsabad, as defeat-
ing a lion. The lion is the symbol of the biblical House of Judah,
from which kings and saviors are born. In other words, a son of
the House of the Lion reverses his father's tyrannical edict by freeing a captive tortured for opposing the tyrant-father in the past,
and thereby effects redemption.

Osiris' being a fusion of more than one god, or representative of an entire race, would best explain the two dispositions of
his body after the murder: the first story (Osiris' sinking in the
chest and then growing into the pillar upholding the kingdom)
would constitute the disruption of the gods by the fallen Watchers and the Flood; the second story (that of his dismemberment)
represents the division of the gods into factions by Set, until Set's
overthrow by Osiris' avenging son, Horus, thus reuniting and resurrecting Osiris' body by the assistance of Thoth's magic. The argument for Osiris' representing a race of gods is strengthened by the
fact that Osiris was generally considered by the ancients to be
interchangeable with Poseidon, and Poseidon could only be
Oannes/Nommo, almost certainly an entire race—the "race of
Nommos," as the Mali refer to him—as opposed to a single

personage. Also, Poseid, Poseidonis, or Poseidon were the ancient names for Atlantis. An effective reading of the Trinity, then, would be two central opposing gods or parties, with the third god being the son of the ruler who restores the rightful order fragmented by the two primary gods' civil wars, helped to power by his father's former enemy, thereby ensuring the peace. Humanity's redemption is part of the kingdom of heaven's restoration, mankind having been involved in those wars, hence the "Fall from grace." "God," in the sense of the original unknown, unknowable, unseen creator of the entire universe—the demiurge, or prime mover—would be Anu, the Dagda Mor, Atum, perhaps sometimes "personified" in the form of the returning astral body that periodically reorders the solar system in apocalyptic fashion.

That demiurge is invariably the father of the one Great God, who is recognizable in all times and places by universal symbols and numerical associations, always head of the pantheon of gods, ruler of all the worlds, and master of life and death. The Great God usually seems to be yet another avatar of Thoth, though it is possible he is sometimes either a synthesis of the two primary gods or else is representative of his entire race, especially when depicted at war. The Great God is the inheritor of his demiurge father's attributes, which he personifies. Ean Begg, in *The Cult of the Black Virgin,* makes mention that the Dagda Mor's cauldron is found also in the possession of Wotan, and adds about the Dagda that, "His son, Ogma Sun-Face or Ogmias, god of literature and eloquence, was the inventor of Ogham, the Celtic alphabet. The Dagda's club, so big that it would have taken eight men to carry it, dealt death at one end and life at the other." Once more, there is the connection with the number eight (Thoth's Ogdoad), the "son of the sun," and "the Word," the "first to give utterance," the inventor of writing and eloquence: in this reading, the emergence and personification of the Great God from the chaos of the prime mover—the universe itself.

The widespread association of the number eight with this particular Great God is also found in his universal accoutrement of an eight-legged horse or eight-wheeled chariot (usually aerial), such as that of Shiva, or Odin's steed, "Sleipnir." Santa Claus' "eight tiny reindeer" are our folkloric remnant. Begg underscores Santa's connection to this original Great God, saying that "Wotan's great feast is Saturnalia or Yuletide, twelve nights at least which, disguised as St. Nicholas, he has wrested back from the encroachments of Christianity, replacing the cross with his world-tree." Odin (Wotan) can be seen in art spearing his enemy, the wild boar—representing Loki—from either Sleipnir or his eight-wheeled chariot. Thoth and Horus are seen spearing the pig of Set from the barque of the gods in Egypt, just as the archangel Michael in Christian statuary holds the pig of Satan beneath his foot while brandishing his sword. That spear or sword is the Spear of Destiny always wielded by the Great God, the aforementioned bestower of kingly power on Earth, and St. Michael is a Christianized version of that God. "The Franks were wont to celebrate yearly martial games in honor of the sword," writes Guerber, "but it is said that when the heathen gods were renounced in favour of Christianity, the priests transferred many of their attributes to the saints, and that this sword became the property of the Archangel St. Michael, who has wielded it ever since."

The spearing of the boar is the central act of "The Wild Hunt," a Celtic/European legend referring to a time when the Great God ("Herne" in England and Wales, perhaps a variation on "Hermes," or the Teutonic Erl-King) manifested himself, followed by his ghost train, and was not to be seen by mortals. Anyone foolish enough to be caught out of doors at the time of the hunt was driven mad and killed, their faces found frozen in great terror and their necks broken, when their bodies could be found at all. Associated with the hunt were all kinds of UFO phenomena, most notably terrifying winds, great thunder, and lights in the sky.

The hunt could be seen as an ethnic purge, with at least one precedent in Africa: the Zulus. Zulu oral tradition holds that the first act of their nation was to go to war with, and destroy, a race of ape-men. If not a purge, the Wild Hunt may have been a friendly warning to "stay off the streets" during the gods' business, perhaps at times of battle between warring parties—which is strongly implied by the fact that it specifically concerns Odin/Wotan's chase and spearing of the satanic boar. Precedent for this interpretation might be found in the Passover, that time in which the Israelites were ordered to remain off the streets and ritually mark their doors to avoid being caught by the "angel of death." Author William Bramley, in *The Gods of Eden,* suggests that the Black Death of the Middle Ages was exactly such a "thinning-out of the herd," citing historical sources reporting the frequent presence of strange lights in the sky (referred to, as were all unknown lights in the sky, as "comets") that killed trees, vegetation, and people in the wake of their noxious trails. Also reported in the historical annals were strolling black-robed "demons" in the mists, carrying scythes—he indicates that these could have been spray guns, creating the look of scythe blades in their arc. In this context, it is interesting how often UFO occupants are reported as having skull-like faces and skeletal physiques. In any event, it cannot be ruled out that all these were emissaries of the Great God.

Rolleston connects this same Great God to the Cymric "Gwyn" and Gaelic "Finn" (both meaning "white"), who has "impressed himself more deeply and lastingly on the Welsh popular imagination than any of the other divinities. A mighty warrior and huntsman, he glories in the crash of breaking spears, and, like Odin, assembles the souls of dead heroes in his shadowy kingdom, for although he belongs to the kindred of the Light-Gods, Hades is his special domain. The combat between him and Gwythur ap Greidawl (Victor, son of Scorcher) for Creudylad, daughter of Llud . . . is to be renewed every Mayday till time shall end. . . ." Llud is identical to Nuada of the Silver Hand, according to both Rolleston and Squire, called by Rome "Nodens," a forerunner to Odin.

Squire concurs that Gwyn and Finn MacCumhail (pron: Mick-COOL) are the same Great God, with the same functions: "The name of both alike means 'white'; both are sons of the heaven-god; both are famed as hunters. Gwyn, however, is more than that, for his game is man. In the early Welsh poems, he is a god of battle and of the dead, and, as such, fills the part of a *psychopompos,* conducting the slain into Hades, and there ruling over them. In later, semi-Christianized story he is described as 'Gwyn, son of Nudd, whom God has placed over the brood of devils in Annwn [pron: an-noon, meaning Chaos or the Abyss] lest they should destroy the present race.' . . . [H]e came to be considered the king of the *Twyleth Teg* [pron: TILL-ig TAY], the Welsh fairies, and his name as such has hardly yet died out of his last haunt, the romantic vale of Neath. He is the wild huntsman of Wales and the West of England, and it is his pack which is sometimes heard at chase in waste places by night. In his earliest guise, as a god of war and death, he is . . . perhaps the clearest figure of the British Pantheon, the 'mighty hunter' not of deer, but of men's souls, riding his demon horse, and cheering on his demon hound to the fearful chase. He knows when and where all the great warriors fell, for he gathered their souls upon the field of battle, and now rules over them in Hades, or upon some 'misty mountain top.'" One of this god's titles was "bull of conflict," the same animal we have seen attributed to God; as the psychopompos, we shall find him discussed in greater detail in the next chapter; and as the "mighty hunter of men's souls," we might recognize a familiar biblical phrase, in Jesus' telling Peter he will be made a "fisher of men's souls."

Alwyn and Brinley Rees also make the connection between Finn MacCumhail and King Arthur, the two being described with the same acts and attributes both in Nennius' *Historia Brittonum* and *mirabilia* ("Wonders of Britain") around the beginning of the ninth century: "Like Finn, Arthur is here a warrior who defends his country against foreign invaders . . . and also in 'Kulhwch and Olwen' which was probably written earlier than any other extensive Arthurian story, he figures as the hunter of a boar, Twrch Trwyd (or Trwyth) [pron: toorch troo-with]. According to the latter text this hunt, the greatest of several mentioned in the story, began in Ireland, where the boar had already lain waste a third of the country, and the chase was continued through South Wales and into Cornwall. It required the co-operation of Arthur, his huntsmen, his house-troop . . . and several other notables. Twrch Trwyd, a king transformed into a boar (according to this story), figures also in early Irish literature. In *Lebor Gabála Érenn,* [he] is described as the King of Boars . . . In any case, boar hunts have a prominent place in the Fenian literature. An account of a great boar-hunt in which all of the *fiana* of Ireland [pron: fee-anna, a military order of two clans devoted to the High King in the repelling of foreign invaders] took part is the prelude to the story of Finn's death, and Diarmaid's destiny is bound up with the life of a magic boar whose human origin and venomous bristles recall the Twrch Trwyth." The name of Finn's father, it must be noted, derives from the Gaulic *Camulus,* the heaven god the Romans equated specifically with Mars, and Rome also believed its own civilization's founders, Romulus and Remus, were fathered by Mars. It has even been suggested that "Camelot" derives from *Camulodunum*— literally, "City of Mars."

Given the king of the boar's symbolism as the eternally hunted enemy of the high king, it is interesting that his having "already lain waste a third of the country" so closely parallels Revelation's description of Satan as "a huge dragon, flaming red . . . [whose] tail swept a third of the stars from the sky and hurled them down to the earth" (Rev. 12:3–4), and its repetitions of a third of the sky being darkened, a third of the water being poisoned, a third of the earth being scorched, etc. There is probably more than a passing resemblance to the wild huntsman/sun god driving the boar king on in an endless chase, and Jesus' driving the demon-possessed Gadarene swine, "Legion," off a cliff.

It may also be of interest that the fairy king/wild huntsman of "the vale of Neath" resides in a place metonymic with the Egyptian Saitic creator goddess: *Neith*. Neith's title is the "mistress of the bow . . . ruler of arrows," considered by the ancients the equivalent of Athena (though she closely resembles Artemis/Diana, as well)—the universal destroyer goddess already discussed. Her name means both "that which is" (quite similar to "I Am") and simultaneously "the terrifying," like the wild huntsman himself. As will be noticed in the next chapter, it may be of additional import that this particular "terrifying" warrior goddess wears the red crown of Lower Egypt and was closely associated with Ra. *Neit* is also, in Cormac's glossary (a primary source material), the Celtic "god of battle."

In this context, it is significant to note that the sign of God's covenant with man in Genesis is that of a "bow" set in the heavens, the original Hebrew word being *keshet*—specifically, an archer's bow. This shows that the ancient "archer" motif refers at least partly to astronomy, almost certainly in a constellation known as "the bow," found in Mesopotamia and China pointing its arrow directly at *Canis Major*—Sirius, the "Dog Star"—the Babylonian prefix of which, *Kaksidi,* means "arrow." This would explain the religious significance of Sirius to the ancient world, God's covenantal "bow" in the heavens being an astronomically stable anchor of measurement after the cataclysmic Flood, there being some evidence (to be considered in the next chapter) that the catastrophe included a pole shift or some other disorientation of Earth's axes. This association is strengthened by the goddess Satit, a personification of Sothis/Sirius, being seen firing an arrow at exactly that star on the famous Egyptian "Round Zodiac" of Denderah, now at the Louvre. Other world myths use the arrow to refer also to the "slaying of the sun" before his "descent into the Underworld," such as the shaft that pierces and kills the sun god, Balder, in Norse mythology, specifically on the day of the summer solstice (Midsummer Eve).

In time, after their various wars both among themselves and men, this technologically superior race left Earth—more or less.

Written Egyptian history begins with the Palette of Narmer, circa 3,100 BC. This is the oldest pictorial document known to Egyptologists, commemorating the unification of "the two lands" under Menes, the first human Pharaoh. Egypt had been ruled for thousands of years entirely by the gods, then demigods, according to the priestly scribe Manetho (meaning "Gift of Thoth"), one of our historical sources. Other world mythologies contain the same lengthy periods of divine rule preceding that of man. The palette shows Narmer/Menes standing victorious over an enemy, under the auspices of the military savior god, Horus. It also has a depiction of a pyramid on its reverse side, another of several strong indicators that the Great Pyramid was built much earlier than Cheops. The name "Menes" ("Man") means "the Establisher," or "the Everlasting," just like the name "Enoch." In the Hindu he was called Manu, in the Greek, Minos (the Flood survivors).

In the Celtic mythology, the Tuatha de Danaan were finally persuaded to leave Ireland after conflict with an entirely human race, the Milesians, who were somehow connected to the gods and originated, like them, on another planet. Having won the land in ages past, and where once they had reigned supreme, the Danaan were forced first to acknowledge cohabitation with their Milesian cousins, and finally to leave the world in their hands. The negotiator of a failed treaty to forestall the war was the poet Amergin, almost certainly Enki/Thoth, who as ever was man's advocate. Amergin was famous for a poem identifying himself repeatedly with the phrase "I Am," giving him another solid link to the biblical Yahweh, whose name meant "I Am Who Am"—that same poem refers to Amergin as "the Word of Science," and "He who announceth the ages of the moon," Thoth's symbol and the basis of his calendar.

The exact dispensation of Earth was never clearly stated in the myths, some versions seeming to show more and others less hostility continuing between the two parties. "After their defeat in battle," write Alwyn and Brinley Rees, "Amairgen [Amergin], poet and judge of the newcomers [the Milesians], is said to have 'divided Ireland in two, and the half of Ireland that was underground he gave to the Tuatha De Danann, and the other half to the [Milesians].' The Tuatha then 'went into hills and fairy regions, so that fairies under ground were subject to them. . . .'" It was both to their original world and to the "underground" that the Danaan returned, the full significance of which will be pondered in the next chapter. It may be noticed that, like Egypt, the Ireland of myth was divided in two, and the half given to man was "upper" since that given the Danaan was clearly denoted as being "lower."

When the Danaan withdrew to the Other World from which they originally came, they pronounced the eventual doom of man through his own sins and lusts, and reserved the right for themselves to come and go in man's world as they chose but agreeing to keep their visits unobtrusive and infrequent. From that point on, the Danaan and the Fomorians essentially became synonomous as far as Ireland itself (Earth) was concerned. The Danaan occupied the places once held by the Fomorians, and did as the Fomoire had before them, sometimes promoting strife between factions of men, sometimes intermarrying with them, sometimes curing, and sometimes cursing. They also required recognition in annual offerings or tithes. The well-being of the crops remained theirs to bless or blight. In other words, the Danaan maintained some control even in their absence.

If we refrain from imposing our own psychological viewpoints or other assumptions on ancient texts and mythic traditions, what we have is a very clear story with admitted variations on particulars. Its origins concur with our own long-held beliefs about the cosmos and evolution: that in the beginning was primordial chaos, out of which stars and planets formed, eventually evolving human life. Discovering itself supreme among life forms, humanity fought with the forces of nature and created technology, extending its mastery. Human tribes fought other tribes for supremacy, made compromises, suffered losses, and enjoyed victories.

At this point, the mind of modern man rebels against the story told, because it adds a variation insulting to his narcissism: that the original human race preceded another, or perhaps several others, with our own being not only one more in a line, but the last in that line, and initially made to be mining slaves to boot. In addition, the original humans were a spacefaring race not originally from this planet, and they seem to have organized the solar system to order out of wreckage created in the annual (but tremendously rare) return of a devastating astral body in a phenomenally elliptical orbit.

A lengthy reign of that technologically advanced race of humans, who came to be called gods, is recorded with tremendous similarity in every culture. They accomplished great feats (by most accounts, even conquering death) and fought terrible wars in a variety of air, sea, land, and spacecraft, often described in detail. NASA engineer Joseph F. Blumrich, attempting to debunk ancient astronaut theory once and for all, discovered to his surprise that he could make a perfectly viable aircraft by the descriptions given in Ezekiel, and even patented it. After nearly obliterating their genetically engineered offspring more than once, and coming close to destroying themselves in cosmic conflicts (with the strong possibility that some of their races were completely killed off), this progenitor race eventually conceded to leave man to his own affairs after also warring with him, finally returning to the world they came from but maintaining a certain liaison in their absence.

They interacted with man at various times in his history, with what seems to be a strong consistency: priesthoods were established, being ambassadorial relations with scientifically educated members initiated into a bond with this race and preserving its secrets, and a chosen king was enthroned. This line continued by succession, until it was destroyed either by outside forces or internecine warfare and corruption, at which time new kings and new priesthoods were established. The textual evidence shows Sargon of Akkad to have been such a king, as was King David. How many times this was separately established in any given region, let alone around the world, is difficult to precisely tell, though all records seem to show a maintenance consistent within given bloodlines. The determination is made more difficult by the fact that all divine kings/saviors appear to have identical (or nearly identical) histories, raising the question of whether this is meant to establish the recurring pattern, or else to indicate that it is a single story from great antiquity being continually revived and retold in new settings and times; also, some of these may have been histories pertaining to their race instead of ours, evidenced in the discovery of texts placing Abraham's biblical argument with the "angels" instead between the gods in their heavenly stronghold. The unbeatable sword of Nuada and that of Odin are the same, and Arthur's pulling of Excalibur from the stone to establish his kingship under Merlin is no different from Sigmund's pulling of the sword from the trunk of Branstock (the tree of life) to establish his kingship under Odin; the magic sword given Sigurd for his unbeatable power is the same as the indefensible barbed spear, *gae bulga,* which the Valkyrie Skatha gives Cuchulainn.

Certain facts can be ascertained from the historical record about this other race's style of living and governing themselves.

Sitchin observes, for instance, that all royal courts of antiquity, from Sumer and Egypt to the Incas and the biblical patriarchs, had the same strict rules of succession, a legal heir being predestined only as the product of a particular genetic pairing: the son of a ruler from his *half* sister. There is a misconception that the Egyptians were all inbred, marrying their brothers and sisters, which accounts for the seemingly demented theologies they constructed. In reality, their matings for legal successors were produced with half sisters and half brothers, and their theologies appear not to have been demented at all, but merely reflections of a simple truth we are only now rediscovering—namely, that they were in congress with another race of men, much more technologically advanced ("magical"). Sitchin cites two strong pieces of scientific evidence that such a genetic pairing is far from undesirable, as we might believe, but actually preferable: one is Hannah Wu's 1980 discovery at Washington University that female monkeys, left to their own desires, will select their half brothers for mates—same father, different mother; the other is an article from the December 1988 *Discover* magazine, reporting that it is standard for male wasps to mate with their sisters—which, by definition, are actually half sisters, since every male wasp fertilizes many females, making the pairing one of same father, different mother. Lord Byron's overwhelming attraction to his own half sister—which was reciprocal—is well-known, and perhaps was more natural than we have yet come to understand.

Intermarriage between opposing factions, in the interests of lasting peace, is also shown in the myths of this race. One example is Bres' having a Fomorian father and a Danaan mother, and Lugh the opposite combination in his parentage. The textual evidence of this is the same around the world, which may be of some significance in light of the reproductive activity apparently going on in modern UFO abductions.

Their mating and establishment of lineage lead to another simple observation about this race: for a technological people, they operate almost entirely within natural law. Their Hermetic "as above, so below" doctrine appears to be not only a philosophy, but an actual way of life. If they are indeed utilizing sound to affect weight of massive objects, then this technology is nothing more than the controlled manipulation of a natural force. So is the laser beam, which many of the light weapons in cosmic warfare texts sound remarkably like. The evidence we can glean about the craft they are presently using—if they are the visitors in our modern skies, as seems probable—appears to show they have found a way to use the gravitational fields in nature for propelling themselves through space. Peter Kolosimo adds weight to the sound technology argument by quoting the La Paz Museum in 1974: "The Indians say that thousands of years ago their ancestors travelled on great golden discs which were kept airborne by means of sound vibrations at a certain pitch, produced by continual hammer blows." This sounds very much like Tesla's telegeodynamics, and his proposed apparatus suspended in midair by the same "interfere[nce] with cosmic processes" in "a fusillade of taps." The museum even suggested that perhaps sound frequency somehow altered the metal's "atomic energy," though of course this could only be considered speculation. Obviously, more cannot be known about this until such time as the race in question, or any government agency in possession of items of their technology, make available their craft for study.

The architectural layouts of this early race are determined by perfect observation of nature, geodetically centered and aligned, incorporating the total mathematics and geometry of the astral body on which they are built. If the Sumerian record is accurate, then the Giza Pyramid complex withstood atomic blasts, which is not incompatible with our own reasoning—its very structure makes its cohesion and strength optimum, its weight distribution, shape, and even the structural components of its individual building blocks anchoring it so solidly to the planet on which it is built that it is highly unlikely anything could ever destroy it, short of the literal breakup of the planet itself. The damage to the Martian pyramids appears to have required penetrating missiles, and these failed to do more than make surface holes, the depth of which, without closer inspection, cannot be known with certainty. In addition to the astounding architecture and mating/succession rules of this race, their dwelling places and records—built and etched in earthen bricks—have withstood the test of time far greater than our own could ever hope to. They also show an amazing efficiency. The Great Pyramid alone seems to have been a geodetic landmark, a space beacon, a solar/lunar/stellar observatory, a military stronghold, perhaps an initiatory structure or repository of some kind, a mathematical encoding device, an energy accumulator, and maybe a great many more things that we haven't even begun to guess.

In actuality, there is no less reason to believe the mythical accounts as true than there is to believe in blind evolution limited to the planet Earth. The archaeological evidence is not against it, and in fact is a great deal more for it. So, frankly, is the biological, according to the world's leading expert, Sir Francis Crick. The evidence so far discovered on and about the other planetary bodies in our solar system confirms a great deal of the theory of extraterrestrial contact with Earth in antiquity, though exactly how much is a matter for debate. The linguistic evidence is overwhelmingly in favor of a single original civilization, as is the mythological, unless credible explanations can be provided for the appearance of Votan in Mexico and Wo-Kon in North America, equating to Wotan/Odin in Norse mythology, or the proliferation of variations on the word "Watchers" and "Anu." Even then, the symbolic evidence cannot be explained away: the cross, the mound/mountain/tree/pillar of the gods in the center of Earth reaching to heaven, the axe/hammer/thunder weapon of authority of the gods, and others. And how can one explain the Hopi Indians having a white-robed figure who announces himself as the "Beginning and the End," exactly like Jesus' "Alpha and the Omega," at the end of the world?

The circumstantial evidence, above and beyond that so far encountered, is phenomenal. The famous Allagash UFO abduction in Canada occurred next to a mountain sacred to the Abenaki Indians, sounding very much like "Anunnaki." The Algonquins have as one of their gods Loki, the evil trickster from the Norse (and other exact elements from that mythology). Following a hunch, ethnologist L. Taylor Hansen showed pictures of Egyptian hieroglyphs to the Apache Indians and discovered that they recognized Ammon-Ra, by name, as their "god of light and fire." Another in the "Anu" names is "Ainu," the oldest race of Japanese. Intensely race conscious, the Japanese are reluctant to admit the Ainu's preeminence (but concede that it is true), because the Ainu are Caucasoid. Though their features are Mongoloid, their skin is as white as any European's, and they grow beards, giving them the nickname "the Hairy Ainu." They live on the northern Japanese island of Hokkaido in a simple and primitive manner. Their legends say that an ancient white god named Okiku-rumi-kamui descended at Haiopira in Hokkaido, aboard a shining "Shinta," an Ainu cradle. He created them, defeated an evil god, and taught them all the right and just way to live, and will one day return from the sky into which he was last seen leaving. Ethnologists would not much disagree with the legend. A. T. Sadler's *A Short History of Japan* says that the first ancestors of the Japanese race were the white-skinned Yamato, who overcame the aboriginal Ainu in much the same way as the Tuatha de Danaan overcame the Fir Bolgs, or the Hyksos the primitive Egyptians. Like the mysterious Indo-European/Aryans, no one knows exactly where the Yamato went, or who their descendants are today.

"White men from the skies" are another universal constant. Many tribes around the world, from Philippine to Native American, literally paint their skins white with a coat of mud, then either row out to sea and row back or else lower a circular gourd from the skies to symbolize "the arrival of the gods." White women with red hair are found painted in Aboriginal Australian rock glyphs and other places around the world holding symbols of the gods, and in Peru can be found Inca mummies with auburn or reddish blonde hair. The Peruvian mummies are often clothed in garments of red and white, with red and black turbans, the significance of which will be discussed in the next chapter. "The sun-god, their ancestor," wrote Pedro Pizarro, the conquistador's cousin, "sent them long ago a son and a daughter of his to teach them knowledge; they were perceived to be divine by their speech and fair complexion. The highest class among the Incas are light-skinned; their noblewomen are handsome and are well aware of it. Both men and women are blond as the standing corn, and some are lighter in complexion than Spaniards. I have seen in this country a white woman with a child of unusual fairness. The natives maintain that such people are descendants of the gods."

The complete range of ethnic types can be found carved, painted, or sculpted in the Americas and Asia, where theoretically no white men should have been, yet not only are they depicted, but in variations sufficient to distinguish Anglo from Semite. The Olmecs of the Americas more closely resemble Negroes than any other race, who by traditional theory should not have been living on that continent. Around the famous "Sleeping Buddha" of Grotto 58 at Tun-huang can be seen an entire spectrum of ethnic variety, including red men and one or two races completely unidentifiable to us today. Where white men are not specifically mentioned in Creation myths, "blue men" are, who may or may not have been Caucasians, though the evidence of archaeology and anthropology seems to indicate they were (the Aryans).

The very name "Fairy Folk," applied to the Tuatha de Danaan, is itself the most telling of clues. After their departure, they were demonized and diminished by Catholicism and superstition, shrinking in size from their formerly attributed tall human height to "little people," the "y" suffix attached almost certainly being a diminutive form of "fair": white skinned. For those unimpressed by such "coincidences," a simple scientific question suffices—if man evolved on this planet, then why did white men evolve so *badly?* Their skin is too fair for the sun, even in northern climes, burning easily. Their eyes are insufficiently pigmented to screen out the bright light radiation from that same sun. If evolution is a product of life adapting itself to existing conditions, then why is there such a diversity of racial types on this planet? Especially white people, who by any definition are poorly adapted to Earth's sun and climate?

There is a natural tendency to avoid exactly such questions as these, even when political correctness is not an issue, owing to the effects of racial divisions we have all been unfortunate enough to witness. But it would be as foolish to ignore the evidence as it would be to yield to racism's ugly personal and political potentials. If we accept that Jesus was a representative of this race, then we must also accept the teaching that, in Christ—or "the cross," if one prefers—there is no black or white, no man or woman, but only one body in the Lord. And if one accepts the thesis of an initiator race but cannot accept that it has had representatives among us, the philosophy should still hold true on its own merits—it no longer matters what race began the process of life on this planet, or the histories of the individual races that resulted. The white race presently on this planet has no more connection to the white-skinned race that created us all than does any other, and their having preceded us makes them neither morally superior (or inferior, for that matter) or even the foremost of all races—for all we know, a race as yellow as the Asians could have made them, or as dark as the blackest African. However any of us began, the message offered to us for at least the last two thousand years has been that our destiny is to attain the same birthright as our progenitors. Perhaps Zecharia Sitchin sums up the situation best when he says, "We are all, ultimately, Sumerians."

If we could determine exactly how Mars fits into this entire picture, we would have a final reason to suppose that this thesis is correct. There is a clear connection, which can be demonstrated by the myths, etymology, and the archaeological evidence we have already encountered. It also gives us some solid clues to answering questions that have never been raised—but should be—and closing the evidentiary circle between the European/Celtic myths and those of the ancient Egyptians. That evidence is the critical link they all share: the Underworld.

10

Underworlds

ERHAPS THE FIRST recorded incident of a crop circle appeared nine years before Newton's *Principia* was published, in an August 22, 1678, woodcut called *Mowing Devil,* showing a black, smiling, horned man cutting the crops with a scythe in a number of regular, oval patterns. Its similarity to the mysterious geometric patterns appearing in fields around the world with some frequency since about 1980 is immediately apparent. In his article "Clutching at Straws," J. M. Rickard notes with some amusement that social injustice between landowners and serfs was such that occurrences of this sort had to be expected. Labor unions weren't yet in existence, and the serfs had no legal recourse if their master took advantage of them, except for organized acts of vandalism. Particulars were not given in the story of the Mowing Devil, other than to say that the field owner would not cut in that field again. The landowner three hundred years ago no doubt believed the culprits, as the woodcut suggests, were the Good Neighbors. The Celtic and Gaelic, as well as Teutonic, Scandinavian, and Finnish folklore, are full of references to them under one name or another. No wise man would go against the Good Neighbors, since any sign of their displeasure was considered to be a friendly word of warning. "Good Neighbors" was just one of many euphemisms for a race we have been discussing: the Tuatha de Danaan, or the "Fairy Folk."

The fairies are intimately connected to the agricultural realm, and to social justice, according to all the lore about them. They are faithful to their word, rewarding good deeds among mortals and sometimes punishing evil ones. They have their sacred spaces and expect to be left alone there—any wayfarer into their territory

351

may be harassed or toyed with for their amusement, but they almost always leave their visitors with some benefit or present for their trouble, provided they accept their "initiation" with a modicum of good grace. Also known as the Gentry, they are considered to be a tall, aristocratic, and exceedingly handsome race, with extremely white skin. They reserve the rarely exercised right to take mortals of their choosing away with them—permanently. Warriors, poets, and musicians by former occupation (utilizing aerial ships, in many accounts), they are believed by some to be in exile, the fallen angels of Scripture, until such time as they may be redeemed, and their music is renowned for its ability to enchant all listeners. Odin, it must also be observed, was a warrior-poet, as essentially were the Druids. The idea that they were fallen angels appears to have been fostered by the Church, since it proved absolutely impossible to rid the populace of their belief in them. The fairy queen, it is commonly held, is what the Church calls the Virgin Mary, the Virgin's appearance sites invariably being former Danaan haunts. The story of St. Patrick driving the "snakes" out of Ireland seems to have been the destruction of altar stones at megalithic sites, mounds, and barrows (always associated with the Danaan) which were inscribed with snake glyphs when the Church invaded; no one among the common peasantry was ever in doubt that the Fairy Folk built them, which is why the sacred sites were the subject of so many horror stories involving witches and demons, such as Arthur Machen and M. R. James made famous.

Hunters since their exile, the Gentry live off the land and know how to keep themselves invisible from prying eyes. They watch mortal affairs for their amusement, or perhaps because they have an active interest of some sort in them. When they spirit away a mortal to join their ranks, it is because they find him exceptional in some regard, usually in learning, wit, and morality. "By tradition they favoured upright men," Rickard wryly observes, "even if they were Christians." Temporary abductions are also performed by them, sometimes for the specifically stated purpose of helping with a birth. There are implications of interbreeding, but—like many modern UFO abductees—no one who returns from Fairyland can remember what happened there; the Gentry have the power to erase guests' memories concerning events transpiring in their realm. Abductees disappear while in an isolated spot, especially if it is an old sacred pagan site, or even out of their beds in the middle of the night, sometimes to be returned by morning, sometimes not for several days. Sometimes the Gentry's abductees are terrified, other times merely dazed or foggy, and paralysis is frequently reported. There are tales of substitutions at birth between their infants and ours ("changelings"), or of mortals being secretly raised by them for their own purposes. These latter are found throughout Celtic and Arthurian mythology—for example, Arthur was raised by Merlin, and Lancelot by the Lady of the Lake.

Abduction is a constant element in all tales of the Fairy Folk. When it was prophesied to the Fomorian King Balor that his own grandson would overthrow him, he locked his daughter in a tower away from all men, attended entirely by women. Lugh's father, of the Danaan (Fairy) race, gained access to the virgin daughter by sorcery (technology), casting a spell that enabled him to impregnate her in the traditional fashion while leaving her consciously unaware. When she awoke, she told her nurse that she had experienced a most remarkable dream of exactly those events, so real she would have sworn it could not have been a dream. Contemporary UFO abductees frequently make exactly the same claim, confused not only by the reality of the seeming dream, but by the same result Balor's daughter discovered—actual pregnancy. In her case, she carried the child (Lugh) to term, when it was taken by its father to be raised in hiding, matching the particulars of the universal hero/savior myth already discussed. In the case of contemporary female abductees, the embryo seems to be taken from the womb before it becomes obviously visible.

Fairy women are notorious in the lore for abducting mortal men to be their mates or lovers, just like the Valkyries. One of the most famous stories is that of "The Sick-Bed of Cuchulainn," a Red Branch of Ulster hero bewitched by Fand, the wife of the great god, Manannan Mac Lir. Manannan is another Oannes figure, probably yet another avatar of Thoth. His name is given as "Manannan, Son of the Sea," and he identifies himself as "son of Ler, king of the Land of Promise." A great Danaan divinity and founder of one of the divine lines, he is clearly in a position to be one of the two great gods warring for supremacy. His son, Mongan, is a definite Christ figure, making the link stronger. The Great Sea God, "Lir" in this case, would seem to be that prime mover, the sea of space, fitting Thoth's position as first of the gods to give utterance—"the Word"—and gain supremacy. In this light, his name might translate to "Man of the Danaan race, son of the Great

Cosmic Waters." Manannan appears to be the closest Celtic equivalent of the enigmatic Heimdall in Norse mythology. W. Y. Evans-Wentz quotes Hippolytus' overt comparison of him to Hermes in his classic *The Fairy Faith in Celtic Countries:* "The Greeks saw in Hermes the symbol of the Logos. Like Manannan, he conducted the souls of men to the Otherworld of the gods, and then brought them back to the human world. Hermes 'holds a rod in his hands, beautiful, golden, wherewith he spellbinds the eyes of men whomsoever he would and wakes them again from sleep' in initiations; while Manannan and the fairy beings lure mortals to the fairy world through sleep produced by the music of the Silver Branch." This Silver Branch is the ancients' Golden Bough, sometimes referred to as "golden apples," or the caduceus or thyrsus of the Greek mysteries, the "magic wand" of all magicians or authority figures (crozier, staff, etc.). The bough or "twig" was a sacred talismanic passport to and from the Fairy World.

Cuchulainn, believed by many to be a reincarnation of the sun god Lugh (the recurrence of the divine bloodline), was sleeping against a pillar stone after hunting (a sacred spot, such as Jacob slept in, awakening to see the ladder to heaven), when he awoke to find two fairy women in green and red standing over him. They mischievously whipped him with rods while he lay helpless and paralyzed. Interestingly enough, modern UFO abductees frequently are not only preoccupied with sex, but have a marked proclivity for bondage or mild sadomasochistic activities. This is another connection between Egypt and the Celts: The English are still known for erotic corporal punishment, and Herodotus (Chapter 61) reported that the Egyptians were sadomasochistic as well. Otto Neubert commented on the "flogging [which] provoked desire and self-satisfaction in the few [of the ruling class]," in *Tutankhamun and the Valley of the Kings:* "When the guests at a party had been made really cheerful with drink, they usually called for a naked slave to be lashed for their entertainment. Yet it must not be forgotten that many of those who enjoyed seeing others whipped got considerable satisfaction out of being whipped themselves." Also, there is an initiatic aspect to this behavior, such as in the Hopi kachina rites. Cuchulainn lay sick until Samhain (Halloween), at which time a messenger appeared and told him he would be cured if he accepted the fairy women's invitation to join them for a time. Fand—one of the women who had whipped him—had taken a liking to him, and he would have her love as a prize if he assisted them in a battle against their father's enemies. He accepted, and when that battle was over, he enjoyed Fand's company for a month, at which time he had to return, but Fand continued to tryst with him. Cuchulainn's wife was jealous, and Manannan nearly went to war with him over the incident (probably an inspiration for Arthur and Lancelot's conflict over Guinevere), but instead he placed a mantle of forgetfulness between the two lovers, erasing their memories of the encounter. The Fairy Folk returned to their Other World and Cuchulainn to his, the war over before it began. There was no rancor after the fact, Cuchulainn being given his eternal life in the Other World after dying a noble death many years later.

By all accounts, fairy women have a tendency to pick destined heroes for lovers, or to make their chosen ones great in the world of men. Their visits are characterized by many of the same traits as UFO abductions: paralysis, initiation, sex and sometimes reproduction, and hints that training is given for certain "otherworld" activities. Amnesia is the typical ending, though return visits appear to be the norm. An interesting item common to many abductions not only concerns having sex, but specifically having sex *under water,* yet somehow being able to breathe throughout the encounter. Evans-Wentz reports Cormac, an initiate, "behold[ing] 'the loveliest of the world's women.' After she has been magically bathed, he bathes. . . ." Presumably this is their prelude to sex, since all other particulars so closely resemble the modern abduction phenomenon, especially (in this instance) the Boas case. Evans-Wentz makes clear that initiation is the goal, since "The warrior-messenger who *took* them all is none other than the great god Manannan Mac Lir of the Tuatha de Danaan . . . They enter the Otherworld in a trance state, and on waking are in Erin again, spiritually enriched." Manannan states, in Cormac's tale, ". . . to see the Land of Promise was the reason I brought (thee) hither . . ." Signs of such initiation have been encountered in Betty Andreasson and Herbert Schirmer. This aspect has been ignored or passed over by most abductologists in favor of the more sensationalistic sexual aspects.

The same phenomenon is at work in the Bible between prophets and angels, which is not surprising if Manannan is Yahweh. Visitants are greeted with "Fear not," or "Be not afraid," implying something frightening about divine appearances. Paralysis is reported, along with amnesia and other symptoms of UFO abduction. Numbers 12:6–8 has Yahweh distinguishing between his method of talking to Moses and to other prophets: "If I find a prophet among you I make myself known to him in a vision, I speak to him in a dream. Not so with my servant Moses: he is at home in my house; I speak with him face to face, plainly and not in riddles, and he sees the form of Yahweh." In other translations, the phrase is, "I speak with him face to face, and not in the dark speech," a good description in either rendering for exactly what is said to happen in both fairy and UFO abductions. It is interesting that Yahweh indicates he is *looking* for "prophets among you" and admits to speaking in riddles, which Thoth and Hermes were famous for. Zeus was believed to have spies so good they didn't know themselves that they were spies. Many UFO abductees feel that information is taken from and imparted to them regularly in the process, indicative of their being potential spies and prophets, fitting the pattern perfectly.

The Fairy Folk are famous for always looking out for the poor, regarding charity and hospitality as the greatest virtues, with greed and vulgarity held in equal contempt. If a farmer falls ill, then the fairies do his work for him while he recovers. Invisible spirits, going by many names—*kornbocks* or *hausbocks* in Norse and Teutonic Europe, or the Irish and Welsh *pookas*—are sent to help the short-handed while they are asleep. The appearance of these creatures, when haplessly encountered, differs from report to report, but there are a great many descriptions that tally with those of modern UFO occupants.

The trolls are of special interest, along with other "elemental spirits" being indicative of robots, as Elsa-Brita Titchenell's *The Masks of Odin—Wisdom of the Ancient Norse* makes clear: "Among the elemental dwarfs (those belonging to kingdoms of life less evolved even than the minerals) are *trolls* which are said to be inimical to humans and *tomtar* which serve and help man in many ways. In popular stories, the troll is depicted as a hideous monster, the tomte as an appealing little sprite in a gray suit with a red Phrygian cap. Every farm of old had its tomte which protected the livestock and the crops, kept the horses from slipping on ice in the winter, and performed numerous other services throughout the year . . . It is noteworthy that in all such folklore there was no real exchange between humans and dwarfs on an emotional or mental level. Whether useful or harmful, dwarfs are not intentionally either benevolent or malevolent but simply unthinking nature forces, acting automatically and without amity or malice, so that man's regard for them was a curiously impersonal one. You would not become fond of a tomte, though you might well be grateful for his actions."

The Fairy Folk have been known to bequeath endless supplies of money to various poor people, so long as they never spend more than they need for simple living and are generous with their goods. Towards determining any given soul's worthiness, they are reputed to test them without warning and in disguise, reminiscent of the Bible's admonition to treat strangers hospitably in case they be angels. The tomte's fee for services rendered was never more than "a plate of hot rice porridge by the barn door on Christmas Eve," an offering of a hot meal to the poor who may pass by. Our "trick or treat" is a surviving ritual associated with the fairies—anyone found not to be charitable with their food had a trick played on them by their ill-treated visitors.

This famous "impishness" associated with the Fairy Folk, as well as many of their other attributes, is automatically reminiscent of Hermes (Thoth), "the trickster," and Odin, who by this reading are the same personage. One of the interesting details reported by a surprising number of UFO abductees that was not published prior to David Jacobs' *Secret Life* in 1992 is that they at least once in their history of abductions have awakened to find themselves turned wrong-way-around in bed. Such an occurrence can only be regarded as both a practical joke and a signature trademark, having no other obvious purpose, and cannot have been picked up by hysterical contagion since it only very recently was made known.

Like the Hopi "monster kachinas" and the European "Father Christmas," the Fairy Folk exercise a social control function, as well as being a poor-man's labor board. Harvard anthropologist Wade Davis, in *The Serpent and the Rainbow,* documented a secret Haitian society's use of a homemade—and very advanced—drug to create zombies. It was used exactly as a social justice tool, and only in the direst of circumstances. The drug puts the victim in a state of paralysis and suspension bordering on death, making him extremely susceptible to suggestion. Used in a particular manner, it can all but permanently destroy the victim's will, after which he is put to work as a slave in the cane fields for the rest of his life. The recipients of this severe judgment are only those who have destroyed their communities for their own enrichment, and even then, they must be exceptionally evil before such a sentence is passed on them, with numerous opportunities and warnings to reform beforehand. It is the priests of the *humfos,* the sorcerors *(bocors),* who pass judgment, they being the only ones with knowledge of how to produce the drug. That knowledge is secretly passed on from generation to generation, along with initiation into the society and proper teachings of all the obligations and responsibilities attached to it. They may have acquired their advanced medical knowledge by trial and error; they may also have acquired it from Legba, the lame god of the crossroads, who as the exact *vodun* ("voodoo") equivalent of Hermes/Thoth/Yahweh would also have been the god of social justice and medicine.

In tribal civilizations, medicine is one of the great gifts of the gods. Another is agriculture. Corn—yellow corn, maize, as opposed to the Old World use of the word for wheat—is a miracle of science, not nature. There is no such thing as "wild corn," as there is wild wheat. There is a primitive form of corn, being a small, hard ear which is inedible by human beings, but it did not evolve into corn and could not on its own ever become what we recognize as corn. Uncultivated, corn would not revert back to this primitive state, but would die out altogether. It relies on careful maintenance, from generation to generation, for its continued existence. Yellow corn stretches back as far as the records of man in the Americas. Since it could only have begun as a successful hybrid, the obvious question arises: who did the hybridizing? The answer of American Indians everywhere yellow corn exists is the same— it was a gift from the gods.

In all cultures, there is a god of the Underworld. He is the agricultural god and the god of plenty. He represents increase and wealth. Pluto, the Roman derivation of the Greek Hades, is one, often symbolized by the horn of plenty, the cornucopia overflowing with food that we associate with Thanksgiving. Dionysus, who some believe is merely a variation of Hades, is another. Nommo of the Mali tribes is one of the best examples, believed by the people to continually die, crucified on a tree, and resurrect to become their eucharistic meal. He annually repeats this death and resurrection, dying and falling into the earth, like the seeds of all vegetation, rising again each new season as the tribe's food. He is also the god of fermentation, becoming universal drink from the grain. As previously mentioned, the Philistine degeneration of Nommo was as Odacon or Dagon, who had lost all but the agricultural aspects of the same god in other cultures. He can be recognized in the Persian Mithras, the bull annually sacrificed to rise again; the Sumerian Tammuz, who the grieving goddess Inanna traveled to the Underworld in order to raise from the dead, herself dying and resurrecting in the process; Adonis, of Babylon and Syria, whose name so closely resembles one of the many names of God in the Bible, "Adonai"; Odin; Attis; Baal. In all cases, this dying/reborn god is associated with a tree—the tree of life. Adonis/Tammuz was born from the trunk of a tree, on the eve of December 24, underscoring the obvious connection to Christ.

The prototype of all these would seem to be Osiris, god of the corn (generally regarded as wheat and barley), the fermentation, the annual harvest, and the Underworld. As in all the other forms, he is the culture god who abolished human sacrifice (substituting his own body) and taught mankind civilization. He is also the hope for bodily resurrection and eternal life for his followers. The Greeks recognized their own Dionysus as a derivation of Osiris, representing him as a bearded face cut into a tree. In this form he can be found in Celtic lands as "the Green Man," John Barleycorn, or Jack-in-the-Green, the god of vegetation (Osiris' skin was painted green). His face is found in orthodox Christian churches in Britain, cut into the very masonry. He is Robin Wood, from whom Robin Hood (*Oodin,* "Odin") is derived—which should be no surprise if he is connected to the Fairy Folk, since they are intensely interested in helping the poor. Robin Hood's style of cap is Phrygian, the same cap worn by Mithras and sometimes Adonis, with an accompanying short tunic and cloak. Hermes is depicted wearing exactly such a cap, with wings on it (where Robin Hood's has a feather), as is Odin. Two much later groups adopted this distinctive headgear as their trademark, as Michael Howard notes in *The Occult Conspiracy:* the revolutionary guard of the French Revolution, and the mediaeval Masons.

It is no secret that the Church adopted pagan holidays as Christian ones, as is plainly evident by the date chosen for Christmas. What is less well known is that 90 percent of mediaeval churches, at least in England, were deliberately built on former pagan sites. This was discovered for a fact by Cambridge University's Professor Gregory Webb, who as the secretary of the Royal Commission on Historical Monuments in 1946 was sent by the government to assess damage to mediaeval architecture caused by Nazi bombing. Beneath a dislodged fourteenth-century altar stone, he found a stone phallus. All but 10 percent of pre-Reformation churches turned out to have them, too. Obviously, the Masons were the builders of those churches.

Christians are painfully unaware of their own origins, generally having no more awareness of the Old Testament—which is the history directly preceding and connected to their religion—than some vague (and primarily superstitious) idea of Adam and Eve, Moses, and as much knowledge of the Ark of the Covenant as fits into a Cecil B. DeMille or T.V. movie. The mere notion that their God has connections—let alone identical ones—to a universal "pagan" god of death and resurrection is automatically dismissed by them as a heresy, when it is clearly demonstrated by even a superficial examination. A reading of 2 Kings 23:4–7 reveals that Solomon built shrines to the goddess Ashtoreth, who is Ishtar/Aphrodite/Venus. 1 Kings 3:3 states that "Solomon loved the Lord, walking in the statutes of David his father: only he sacrificed and burnt incense in high places," which were dedicated to the goddess. The destruction of altars to these gods and reestablishment of another king by Yahweh in this instance are one example of the recurring pattern so far discussed in the conflict between the two central gods. 2 Samuel 24:1 reads, "The anger of the Lord was kindled against Israel, and he moved David against them to say, Go, number Israel and Judah." The recounting of that same incident in 1 Chronicles 21:1 reads, "Satan stood up against Israel and provoked David to number Israel." There is also the previously mentioned dual sacrifice made to both Yahweh and Azazel.

If the Bible can itself confuse "the Lord" and "Satan," it should not be any great surprise to either a Christian or a Jew that their god may also be the Lord of the Underworld. There are other folkloric reasons to accept that the underworld/fertility god may be the Judaeo-Christian God, or at the very least intimately connected to him. The very word "God" actually comes from *Deus,* which is a corruption of the Indo-European *Dyaus.* Combined with the word *Pitar,* "Father," they become "God the Father." The corruption of Dyaus-Pitar creates "Jupiter"—*Zeus,* or *Deus.* "Deuce" has since become a word connoted with the devil. Our terms "boogeyman" or "bogeyman" and "spooky" are a corruption of the Irish or Welsh *pooka,* which is itself derived from the Slavic word for God, *Bog.* That the name "Peter" *(Pitar)* is given to the first vicar of Christ should be of quite some interest to a Western audience.

Also of interest is the fact that, the world over, the gods are always represented as *horned*. Where did that idea come from? Everyone thinks of the devil as horned, but not many stop to realize that the ancient gods of the Middle East, Europe, Ireland, the Americas, and Australia were also horned. Ram horns, bull horns, stag horns, whatever animal was prevalent in the region of the god depicted, were seen on the head of the god. This was partly (according to legend and Sir James Frazer) the result of Isis instructing people to substitute animals for Osiris in sacrifice, which is the origin of the hind being substituted for Iphigenia in Greek mythology. Some of these may have been directly chosen to correspond with an animal of the zodiac, the gods' reigns showing some evidence of being linked to the precession of the equinox, as has been discussed. Sometimes these horns are so thin and angular that they have actually caused anthropologists to compare them with antennae, which they may be. One famous Tassili rock painting in the Sahara is even nicknamed "the Martian." There are statues of Hera or Athena from Minoan Greece that show three thin lines leading out from her headdress, topped with small balls. These are considered to be poppies. Why? There is no textual evidence to support their being flowers, or any logical reason to assume it. Whatever they are, they are certainly another variation of the horns.

Cernunnos, his name and function obviously reminiscent of Chronos (who would be the Anu/Dagda Mor figure), is probably the oldest representation of the Lord of the Underworld in Gaulic/Brittanic Europe, famous as the god of the witches and one of the prototypes for our modern image of the devil. The horns became synonymous with the devil when "the gods" were demoted to pagan mythology by the Church, the same way the Fairy Folk shrunk in size and came to be regarded as fallen angels. Satan's pitchfork was what had formerly been the symbol of authority of the chief god, the thunder weapon or trident seen carried by Zeus or Poscidon. His cloven hoofs were borrowed from the feet of Set, who was depicted as a speared boar after his betrayal of the gods in Egypt.

The equation of the Underworld and heaven is found throughout the ancient world, the two in the Afterlife not being removed from each other, but one and the same place. The souls of all the deceased went to Hades, not just those of the evil. It was generally believed that there was a place of torment for the workers of evil, but its depiction as a place completely removed from the souls of the virtuous developed later.

Complicating matters is the fact that ancient texts use earthly locations interchangeably with those of the Underworld. We have already encountered Budge's assessment that Osiris' kingdom in the Underworld may have been called by earthly locations, but was more likely to have been another, separate world. In de Jubainville's *Irish Mythological Cycle,* he quotes Nennius as saying that "'Spain' . . . is a rationalistic rendering of the Celtic words designating the Land of the Dead." Rolleston quotes de Jubainville and concurs, as does Charles Squire, in *Celtic Myth and Legend:* "It is sufficient for us to find the first men in Spain, remembering that 'Spain' stood for the Celtic Hades, or Elysium." The human-god race that succeeded the Danaan, the Milesians (and the earlier, lesser race, the Fir Bolgs), were said to have come "from Spain," and all sources seem agreed that "Spain" is the Underworld. The only consistent clue is that it is "in the West."

Every location of the Underworld is given as being in the west. It is the "happy land across the Western ocean" that is the location of the lotus flower from which Ra and the Buddha sprung; the Tir na Nog (Land of Eternal Youth), the Plain Agreeable (Happy), Land of the Living, Land of Promise, Other Land, Other World, and Great Plain of the Celts; the Happy Otherworld of Scandinavian, Iranian, and Indian mythologies; the First World of the Hopi; Amenti (the Tuat) of Egypt, across the Dark Sea—all are in the west. The Hades of the Greeks, said by both Plutarch and Caesar as well as Procopius' *De Bella Gothico* to be in the west, was separated from the east by the impassable barrier of the River Styx, crossed only in magic boats. The Chinese western paradise was Hsi Wang Mu, headquarters of the "Ancient Ones" and "Abode of the Immortals" (traditionally believed to be in the Kunlun Shan mountains in northwestern Tibet) where lived Kuan Yin, the Merciful Guardian and Queen Mother of the West. Mayan Lord Shield-Pacal, of Palenque—a nonindigenous man with an atypical height of five-foot eight, whose teeth were discovered to be painted bright red—is depicted on his famous twelve-and-a-half-foot-long, five-ton sarcophagus lid in what looks suspiciously like a rocket ship, traveling to the Underworld in the west.

Lord Shield-Pacal's height and red-painted teeth denote him as one of the "Red Paint People." The Red Paint People were written of around the turn of the century by such notable scholars as Lewis Spence in *The History of Atlantis,* and then appear to have been ignored or forgotten until such anthropologists as Richard

Cavendish (*The Black Arts,* 1967) and Franklin and Mary Folsom (*America's Ancient Treasures,* 1971) brought them up again. Harvard's controversial epigrapher, Barry Fell, discusses them in his works, and they have been publicized on PBS. Also known as the "Maritime Archaic" culture circa 5,500–2,000 BC, they were a comparatively tall white race (five-foot eight or taller) who employed megalithic burial chambers, used metal weapons and tools, and got their nickname from their practice of sprinkling red ochre paint (common to ancient Egypt, as noted in Chapter 8) over their dead. Referring to "the prehistoric custom of coloring corpses red," Cavendish writes in *The Black Arts:* "In a prehistoric graveyard near Nördlingen in Bavaria thirty-three human skulls were found embedded in red ochre (and all facing west, where the sun dies in the evening). Finds at Grimaldi in Italy included a boy's skeleton stained red with peroxide of iron, three bodies in a grave lined with red ochre and the scarlet skeleton of a man whose bones had been covered with powdered haematite." University of Alabama's craniotemy expert, Dr. Albert E. Casey, determined that the Red Paint Peoples' skull measurements and medical defects most closely approximate those of the Irish, though some of their artifacts appear to be Scandinavian. Their remains have been found in Canada, Labrador, Finland, Newfoundland, Norway, New England, central Siberia, northeastern Honduras, and Europe. They are found buried with their faces to the west, as Cavendish notes, and the significance of the color in which they are painted is discussed below.

A mysterious "Land of the West" is also frequently encountered without being referred to as the Underworld. Egyptian inscriptions circa 5,000 BC refer to "Urani Land," a "Land Beyond the Western Sea." Pazuzu was the "Demon of the Southwest Wind." Lugh approached the Fomorians for combat from the west. King Bran, renowned traveler to mysterious regions and brother of Manannan Mac Lir, took a winged chariot to a land in the west. In the Danaan-Milesian war, their leader saw Ireland by looking west from the tower his grandfather built, and Herakles "is also associated with a cauldron-shaped vessel which he borrowed from the sun in order to make his voyage to the west." The Cherokee *Tsunil-kalu* ("Slant-eyed people"), their race of giants equating to the Fomorians, "lived very far away in the direction in which the sun goes down"—the west. Timagenes and Diodorus quoted Gaulic traditions that the Hyperborean "Lands of the West" were invaded by "warlike giants" from the "Western Ocean." Easter Island's culture god, Hoto Matua, "looked to the west when he called to the spirits who hovered over his submerged home," and the only outward-looking *moai* heads there face west from a large platform.

Hercules' tenth labor was the freeing of the oxen of Geryon from Erytheia, the "Red Island," known as the "Land of the Sunset Beyond the Western Sea." This same myth is found in the Adityas' liberating of the *kine* from the Asuras' Celestial Abode, a word traditionally meaning "cow-cattle," but equivalents such as Odysseus' liberation of his men turned to swine by the witch Circe, and Momotaro's freeing of captives from the demon king's island (also associated with the color red), strongly imply more the meaning "kin." Hermes' theft of Apollo's cattle is another version of the same legend, and Jason's stealing of the Golden Fleece. "To us alone assuredly belongs this world!" the *Satapatha Brahmana* of the Hindus records the Asuras saying, after the younger Adityas had stolen back their kine from them. "Well then, let us divide this world between ourselves." They are then specifically written of "dividing it from west to east"—perhaps meaning a separation of the west *from* the east.

We have already mentioned that the Celts and Gauls regarded themselves as the descendants of the Dis Pater (another "God the Father" derivative of Dyaus-Pitar), the Bile of the Britons, Baal or Bel of the Middle East, Cernunnos/Chronos/Anu/the Dagda Mor. Where this Dis Pater is known to be the invisible prime mover force of the universe, he is also regarded as a person when discussing the Lord of the Underworld, who is also the culture or fertility god: Osiris, Odin, Oannes/Nommo, etc. Zeus and Ra both ruled from the Underworld for a time, as have their other equivalents around the world. This world was a very real place to the Egyptians and Celts, an actual, physical location. No matter its name, its location was in "the west," under the sea or ocean, or beneath the earth. All these locations were one, used interchangeably. Since "sea" or "ocean" can also mean "space," and there is no up or down in space, it is certainly possible that this Underworld is actually beneath the earth—another planet.

This Other World was no less a real location to the Hopi Indians or the Buddhists. The Hopi even have distinguishing characteristics attached to it. For one thing, they are in agreement that it is beneath the earth—their kivas are designed in such a way that the central chamber is underground, which is vital for the annual reenactment of their ascent into this present Fourth World: they came up from below. More importantly, when they came to this world, the kachinas gave them four ears of corn, each a different color. One was black, one white, and one yellow, each representing the color of a race they would encounter in the course of their migrations, each with a separate destiny tied into that of the Hopi toward the completion of all things. As for the Hopi, "They themselves were represented by the red corn," according to Frank Waters' *Book of the Hopi,* "whose color symbolized the west from which they had come to this Fourth World," i.e., from the Underworld to this one. They also have "hundreds of tales" about a mysterious Red City of the South from which the kachinas came, where the highest learning and moral instruction were taught in structures specifically designated as pyramids. This may or may not have been the once-red Mayan city of Tikal.

Nor are the Hopi the only tribe with legends telling of a lost Red Land: the "Weeping God" on the Gateway to the Sun at Tiahuanaco is said to cry for "the sunken Red Land." L. Taylor Hansen, in *The Ancient Atlantic,* quotes a Sioux chief as saying,". . . this is the land of our beginning, where we went from the old Red Land before it sank, because this land is as old as the dragon land of the fire god." The Apache myth is the same: "Long before the Deluge, we used to live in the land of red fire, in a city whose entrance was hard to find . . . the mountains were the highest in the world in those days, and deep down in them was the abode of the fire-god [Amon-Ra]. It was through his rage that our old land was destroyed: the god left his underground cave, rose up through the mountain and poured fire and death on the terrified people." This last could mean a volcano, if the other legends agreed with its particulars—or it could mean something else. The Arawak Indians' myth is the same, with "Aimon" burning and submerging the world.

Red was the color worn in battle by both the Valkyries and Sekhmet, who the "Father of Terror," Ra, sent with his eye to burn the human race. Sekhmet wore red specifically because it was the color of her homeland, according to the texts. Red was the color of Tiwaz's (Odin's) horse—an animal associated with Mars, in occult tradition—such as the one carved on Banbury's Tysoe Hill that was scoured every Palm Sunday until it all but eroded away at the end of the eighteenth century. (Banbury's red horse is counterparted by an ancient white horse in Uffington whose jagged style remarkably resembles mysterious "Anubis" figures discovered in Oklahoma caves.) Red was the color of one of the Two Lands of Egypt, *Teserh-t* or *Dvrt,* from which we derive our own word "desert." The Red Land was the Sacred Desert in which the Pharaonic Pa-Ra-Emheb Stela named Ra as the engineer who measured the land and built the "protected place" from which he could "ascend beautifully and traverse the skies," and the Sphinx in his own image and name (Ra-Harakhte). Red was also the original color of the Sphinx itself, evidenced by traces of the bright scarlet paint still found on its uraeus crest and beard in the British Museum. Presumably because the Red Land was the home of Ra and Sekhmet, who destroyed the earth with fire, the Egyptians associated the color with evil and feared it so.

Ayers Rock, a giant mass of granite in the center of Australia, is red. Geologically anomalous, the sandstone sediment inside the rock is unnaturally vertical as opposed to horizontal. Now a tourist attraction, Ayers Rock is still a sacred site to the local Aborigines, who say it is where supernatural races waged cosmic war with poison clouds of death and hot winds in the prehistoric "Dreamtime." In the weirdly eroded and vitrified streets and caves of a geologically curious area called Moon City, north of Roper River in Aboriginal Land (formerly called Arnhem Land), similar legends are told of the sun god coming down out of heaven and vanquishing the earth god with intense heat after a mighty and terrifying conflict. Such legends closely resemble those of the destruction of India's mythical Rama Empire. Like Ayers Rock, red sandstone is also what the capital Jaipur is constructed of in India, giving it the name "Pink City," and all Rajasthani cities have what is called a "Red Fort."

Red is the color of the clay from which Adam was made, and the color associated with the sea Moses crossed in the Exodus. Red is also the color the Egyptians painted the males of their race in hieroglyphs (with the females painted white). In addition to its aforementioned meanings, *Adom* means "he of the ruddy complexion," or "he who is red." *Adama,* and its parallel Akkadian word, *Adamatu,* both had the distinct meaning of "dark red soil" or "dark red earth." That red soil was taken by Enki from the *Apzu,* or Lower World, where he lived, and it was there that he made mankind. This may be of interest, considering that in Celtic mythology a human race (as in "non-god"), the Nemedians, came from the Other World of the gods and became the race that finally drove the gods from Earth. *Apsu,* apparently a word for the sun—a planetary word for "one who exists from the beginning"—is also the word used for a boat which reaches Enki's world; and the completely sealed Ark in which Noah was preserved was to be made "like an Apsu boat," which, given the connotations, could quite possibly be a "solar barque" or "boat of the sun" such as ferries the deceased to the Afterlife both in Egyptian and Celtic tradition.

Together with white, red is one of the colors on the striped barber's pole, traditionally a place of surgery and healing, its spiral design a hangover from the caduceus of Hermes. These same colors today belong to the most famous charitable healing organization in the world, the Red Cross. Red and white are the colors of the "Land of the Rising Sun," Japan. Red and white are also the colors of Santa's costume, like the Underworld god a lord of plenty, even with an old name of the devil: "Nick." The Valkyries wore only red in combat and white in Valhalla and were famous for their phenomenally white arms. Red, white, and black—the colors of Egypt—are still the predominant rock colors in the Canary Islands and were said by Plato in the *Critias* to be the primary colors of stone construction in Atlantis, a land which itself "flashed with the red light of orichalcum." The black Easter Island *moai* heads have red topknots and red pupils in their white eyes. Red and black are also the colors of the two "meals" in the Tibetan *chod* mystery ritual, the black too secret to reveal to the uninitiated and the red—accompanied with "white food"—specifically meant to feed demons. Red, white, and black are the colors the Fon tribe of West African Benin (formerly Dahomey) say the Great Serpent who holds up the four corner-posts of the sky wears, and which he told them were the three colors of the sky. Red, white, and black are also the colors of three of the cardinal heavenly points in China and of the Nebraska Great Plains Skidi Pawnee tribe, the remaining color green in the former and yellow in the latter. Together, all five are the central colors of Taoist and pre-Taoist China, found also on Mayan stelae and in Hopi planting rituals. All five colors bedeck the Shaanxi Province of China's enigmatic Great Pyramid of Xian as well, the largest earthen structure of its type in the world (approximately 1,000–1,200 feet high, 1,500 feet per base side), fully accurate dimensions of which are not known because it remains in restricted territory.

Red has a surprising number of connections to the color white around the world, none of which have any explanation. "What exactly is signified by this Ganesha, or Ganapati—Lord of the Multitudes, or was it primarily Lord of the Territory?" asked Ananda K. Coomaraswamy and Sister Nivedita, in *Myths of the Hindus and Buddhists*. "Ganesha" means "Lord of Hosts," one of the epithets of God in the Bible and of Zeus and the world's other chief ruling gods, represented as an elephant in the east where he is a bull in the west. "What is the meaning of that white elephant-head borne on that red body? Vast and cosmic he certainly is. Is he at bottom the white cloud glistening in the evening against the crimson sun?" The authors might better have asked the question Egyptology never has: why are the Two Lands, called Red and Black, represented by a red and *white* crown? As with the elephant-headed Ganesha, white is above, red below—white head (upper), red body (lower), and White "Upper" Egypt, Red "Lower" Egypt. So was Japan's decapitated tyrant goblin king, Shutendoji, "of gigantic stature, with bright red skin and a mass of white hair," white above, red below.

China also has two dragons: the red and the white. The mythology of the Celts and Britons has a red dragon and a white dragon, and a red clan (Arthur's heroic "Red Branch of Ulster") and a white clan. The story of their conflict will be familiar to anyone who remembers the Mesopotamian texts referring to the battle around the *Ekur,* the Pyramid which binds heaven and earth: "As for the shriek, Llevelys [the king of France] explained it to be raised by a dragon," as Charles Squire relates it. "This monster was the Red Dragon of Britain, and it raised the shriek because it was being attacked by the White Dragon of the Saxons, which was trying to overcome and destroy it. The French King told his brother to measure the length and breadth of Britain, and, when he had found the exact centre of the island, to cause a pit to be dug there." Llud (Nuada of the Silver Hand) and "a mighty man of magic" made "careful measurements [which] proved that the centre of the island of Britain was at Oxford, and there he caused the pit to be dug. . . ." The dueling dragons were both lulled to sleep and buried "in a stone coffin in the strongest place in Britain," in "a strong fortress." Merlin dug them up five hundred years later, when they continued their fight until the red dragon drove the white dragon out of Britain. The measuring and placing of a magic structure in the exact center of an "island" is, by now, a familiar motif, as is a civil war with interims.

Given the evidence presented in this study, it should be increasingly obvious that we are begging the question of the planet

Mars. Like the Egyptians' "evil" Red Land, from which a wrathful god (Ra) destroyed them with fire, the Greeks and Romans named Aries' (Mars') attendants *Phobos* and *Deimos:* "Fear" and "Terror." The Norse/Teutonic Tiwaz or Tyr was the equivalent, a one-handed god like Nuada of the Silver Hand, whose Roman day of the week ("Tiw's-day") was that to which Mars was sacred; among his Roman titles was *Mars Thingsus,* "Thing" being the name for the supreme Assembly of Justice, and he was represented with a red horse such as the aforementioned one at Edge Hill. Ra was specifically mentioned in Egyptian stelae as erecting a Sphinx in his own image in a "protected place," i.e., a place of pyramids. Until the discoveries of the Viking probe, we had nothing but Giza to equate that to. But the Cairo sphinx does not look like Ra, who was depicted as a hawk—the Cydonia Sphinx on Mars *does*. The very name of this Sphinx is given as Ra-Harakhte: "Falcon of the Horizon." More to the point, Ra was said to wear a diadem on his forehead, from which he could fire a bolt to kill his enemies—the Cydonia sphinx appears to have exactly such an item sculpted on its forehead.

On the painted papyrus of Queen Nejmet in the Egyptian Department of the British Museum is a red planet to the right, surmounted by Harpokrates, the young Horus—it is called the "Red Eye of Horus." Horus is sometimes referred to as having "two red eyes" or "two blue eyes," or as having one red eye with the other blue. Ra's "right eye" and "left eye" being used to refer to the Sun and the Moon respectively, and "Thoth's eye" used to refer to the Moon, we know that "eyes" are sometimes used by the ancient Egyptians to refer to planets. Horus lost one of his eyes in battle with Set during the civil wars, having it restored to him by the magic of Thoth. In Nejmet's papyrus, the Red Eye of Horus has a cord extended to it from the upper left, which goes back around to the lower left, both points manned by a holder of the cord. Between the cords, led by twelve gods (presumably the zodiac), the solar barque travels to the Red Eye of Horus. This papyrus specifically illustrates the Pharaoh's (or deceased's) final stage on the journey to the Tuat, the "Place of Ascending" to "the Imperishable Star." Given that we have already encountered evidence for the Great Pyramid of Giza and the Pyramid of the Sun at Teotihuacán describing an orbital cycle between Earth and Mars, it is not unreasonable to assume that the papyrus of Queen Nejmet is depicting exactly that. Horus' blue eye would of course be the blue planet, Earth. As reasonably, his red eye would be Mars.

An "eye" also can represent a weapon and/or a ship, as has been demonstrated. The Mali tribes sometimes refer to Nommo's ark as his "eye," and to Nommo as "the Word," another connection to both Yahweh and Thoth. Similarly, "an eye of Horus is an object existing independently of him," as Sitchin notes in *The Stairway to Heaven,* "an object into whose insides the king can enter, and which can change hues from blue to red as it is 'powered.'" In other words, one enters the vehicle which is "the eye of Horus," it powers up, and one goes from the blue to the red—more specifically, in the typical dual meaning of ancient sacred puns, from his "blue eye" to his "red eye," or from Earth to Mars. It is when spoken of in this context that the eye of Horus is also known as the "celestial ladder" for the deceased, a vehicle for attaining heaven, as a spaceship would accurately be described.

The trip to the Afterlife—the Underworld—is connected to a number of rituals in ancient Egypt. One of these is the erection of the *ded* pillars, which are equated with Osiris as the tree of life. "Ded" is obviously metonymic with "dead," as in Osiris' being the Lord of the Underworld, or "Lord of the Dead." As with everything else historians and anthropologists cannot discern any immediate practical use for—which comprises virtually everything in Egypt—these pillars have been called "religious objects," meaning no one has any idea what they were meant for and therefore they must have been superstitious representations of something. The best explanation for the ded pillars has been that they represented the "backbone of Osiris," or the "strength of the king." There has never been any reason to believe this, except that no other answer was evident.

There is nothing connected to the many supposed superstitious funerary rituals of Egypt that cannot also be interpreted as pertaining to space travel or some more advanced scientific accomplishment. The ded pillars could as realistically be stabilization pillars for a rocket as any meaningless symbolization of an unknown religious impulse. We have simply become accustomed to the latter interpretation, which was never a satisfactory one. Of course, it cannot be automatically assumed that the more advanced, technological interpretation is correct either, but in light of everything else discovered in the course of this study, it seems perfectly possible, perhaps even likely. In *The Stairway to Heaven,* Sitchin calls attention to an especially interesting item discovered among "other unusual copper objects" in a First Dynasty tomb in 1936. Walter

B. Emery's *Great Tombs of the First Dynasty* and Cyril Aldred's *Egypt to the End of the Old Kingdom* found the item impossible to describe, and speculate that it is an imitation of a form originally made of metal (the object was of brittle schist stone). It most closely resembles a rotary flywheel, with a rim and a hub and folds in the spokes indicating it was meant to be used while immersed in some fluid. That anyone, even invaders in Egypt, could have been making items of this type in metal is beyond the capacities we have ascribed any race in the world at that time. Objects such as these and the original Benben object—which, like most religious items of veneration of the ancients, presently exists nowhere in the world—were usually found or described as being in priestly temples, i.e., as objects of the gods.

What the ded pillars most resemble, intrinsic to ancient Egyptian symbology, is Old and Middle Kingdom representations of the "Ladder to Heaven," without which Osiris could not reach the sky. Specifically, Osiris "would never have reached heaven at all had not Ra provided him with a ladder." The Papyrus of Ani has the deceased say, "I have set up a Ladder among the gods, and I am a divine being among them." Like the ded pillar, this ladder has a narrow base widening to a ridged top, and the two are so similar in appearance it is very difficult not to equate them. The ladder is one of the oldest symbols in Egypt, its iconography surviving in triple-barred Orthodox crosses. Some illustrations in the Book of the Dead actually show the lower portion of the ded pillar as having the straight rungs of a ladder, strengthening the connection between the two, and other illustrations show it with fins exactly like those seen on rockets. The Ani papyrus, among others, shows the ded pillar surmounted by an ankh, arms uplifted to hold the sun. Pyramidal-shaped radiation waves surround it; baboons (sacred to Thoth) and human worshippers kneel in adoration of it with their hands raised. Robert Charroux has shown its appearance to be identical to the diagram of a contemporary plasma generator, which is not an unlikely guess, given the text, "The sky god has strengthened the radiance for the king that the king may lift himself to Heaven like the Eye of Ra."

Another unknown object associated with the journey to the Afterlife is a strange, loopy red object called the *tet,* referred to as "the blood of Isis" because of its color and no other reason. More or less, the implication is that it is supposed to be the goddess' genitals or perhaps some kind of tampon, which seems frankly sillier than the idea that it may be some object associated with space travel. It is called a "buckle" or "tie," closely resembling the shape of a harness (which the words could easily mean) seen on the famous three-dimensional, life-size statue of Ishtar, *The Goddess with a Vase,* unearthed at her temple in Ashur in 1934. A similar sort of harness called a *menat* is seen on representations of the creator god, Ptah, who holds three items of no discernible terrestrial purpose that could easily be technical devices, their exact use as yet unguessed by us. Hathor is also associated with the menat, bearing a red disk between her horns—a connection to her other identity as Sekhmet (the two are considered to be one goddess), who is probably also Ishtar. Ishtar wears a helmet called a *shugarra,* meaning literally "that which makes go far into universe." It stylistically curves up at the front edges in the shape of horns; if not actually antennae, perhaps still the inspiration for horns on the gods. A wall sculpture in the same temple shows Ishtar in a tight-fitting helmet with large goggles over her eyes like those of modern aviators, something very much like earphones at its sides with what appear to be antennae. A box of some sort is on the back of the helmet, with a long vertical hose leading down the back. The "headdress" on the Cydonia Face also more closely resembles a helmet in Egyptian style, Ra's "beak" looking not unlike the oxygen mask our own jet pilots wear. That the red tet of Isis is of that color and is probably a harness is reminiscent of Sekhmet's wearing red because it was the color of her homeland— which would be the Tuat destination in the Afterlife journey, Mars, if this reading is correct—and also recalls that the ritual performed in the Pyramid for the journey into heaven involved placing the red crown on the image of the deceased.

It is also the red crown that is shown on the head of Narmer (Menes) as he takes command of his newly conquered lands, on the reverse side of the famous palette bearing his name that begins written Egyptian history: to the right of his head is his new epithet, "Nar-mer," and to the left, a hieroglyph of a pyramid, specially isolated. As will be remembered, *mer* ("Place of Ascension") is the name the ancient Egyptians gave to the pyramids, further ensuring that the hieroglyph could mean nothing else, and providing even stronger evidence that the Great Pyramid was in existence well before Cheops. *Nar* is an Egyptian word meaning "Fiery Pillar." Put together, then, Menes' title, "Narmer," meant something like "Lord of the Fiery Pillar at the Place of Ascension," giving the red crown in the journey to heaven ritual conducted in the Pyramid even more significance.

Sitchin refers to Sumerian *me,* "divine power objects" for "swimming in celestial waters," called by Inanna a "celestial garment" for travels in her "golden chamber in the sky." *Me* has also been read more or less as "Divine measures of the depths of the spacial seas," in connection with ancient temples. The Sumerian Enoch's name, "Enmeduranki," meant "Ruler whose Me connect Heaven and Earth." Gudea's sacred temple for the gods was a secret enclosure ("strong stone resting place for the Mu") for their comings and goings in their "divine black wind bird," the Bible's whirlwind that took Ezekiel bodily into heaven. As the Lord asks Isaiah (60:8): "Who are these that fly as a cloud, and as a dove to their windows?" "Clouds" are used repeatedly throughout the Bible as a metaphor for something which flies. It was the glory cloud that led the Israelites out of Egypt by day, becoming a "pillar of fire" by night (as the silver canoe of the *Hav-musuv* led the Paiute to their Promised Land), and Jesus departed from Earth on the clouds, prophesied to return the same way. The *mu* ("that which rises straight") were these flying machines in the original texts, depicted in a hymn to Inanna/Ishtar: "Lady of Heaven: She puts on the Garment of Heaven; She valiantly ascends towards Heaven. Over all the peopled lands she flies in her Mu. Lady, who in her Mu to the heights of Heaven joyfully wings. Over all the resting places she flies in her Mu."

The Semitic derivative *shu-mu* ("that which is a Mu") was vulgarly translated in the Bible as *shem,* "that by which one is remembered," or "name." G. M. Redslob's *Zeitschrift der Morgenlandischen Gesellschaft* pointed out over a century ago that "that which is highward" is more correct, and many places where "name" is found in Scripture make imminently more sense when interpreted instead as aerial vehicles. It was a *shem* that Nimrod wanted to place on "a tower whose top shall reach the heavens" (Gen. 11:4), and an aerial vehicle is more sensible a threat or concern to the Elohim than a "name." Also, one couldn't very well fly around heaven in a "name." An ancient coin from Byblos ("Gebal" in the Bible, the Shriners' "El Jebel") shows a conical object enclosed in the Temple of Ishtar's innermost walls, immediately reminiscent of the pyramidal Benben that was the vehicle of Ra—sculptures and stelae show gods standing inside these objects, as they are seen inside the Egyptian Benben. Cuneiform mus look remarkably like three-stage rocket ships, and an identical tower is often depicted behind the dead Pharaoh as he is being prepared for his journey to the Tuat. The Osirian fetish of Abydos, the *ta-wer* (sounding like our own "tower," meaning "Eldest Land" or "Great Land," equivalent to the Celtic "Old Plain"), another ladder of life by which Osiris attains heaven, is a gigantic pole held straight in a shaft, topped by a conical object and the heaven plumes of Amun; it also bears a remarkable resemblance to modern manned rockets. The heaven plumes were sometimes called the "testicles of Set"—Set lost his testicles to Horus in combat, explaining how it was he fell from heaven and lost his place with the gods.

At present we do not fully understand the codes and riddles used to describe the Tuat/Afterlife journey, but we do have sufficient clues to see that it involves another planet, and it is defined as the last stop of a space journey on the way to heaven. There are self-propelled magic boats that are voice activated, doors that open and close by themselves with no visible seam, and gods whose faces are concealed behind faceplates. Various descriptions refer to Earth, and others to "the lake that is the heavens" and "the shores of the sky" upon arrival, which is further evidence of space being described as waters and planets as islands with atmospheric "shores." Part of the Tuat is space itself, attested to by the Papyri of Ani and Ra, with the scribe Ani (Enoch) brought before Thoth and describing the fearful journey: "What kind of place is Augert (the Underworld) whereto I have come? There is neither water nor air in it. It is an unfathomable abyss, it is dark with the blackest darkness, and a man wandereth about helplessly therein. There is (no) life whatsoever therein. . . ."

The term "Tuat" seems to contain not only the Underworld itself, but also the journey to reach it and locations along the way. It may be of some significance that there were fourteen "states" in the Tuat, each governed by a different god, and this is the same number of pieces into which Osiris' body was dismembered by Set—possibly signifying the civil war, fourteen divided states, reunited and resurrected by Horus. The Tuat is shown pictorially as an enclosed oval formed by the body of Nut, ending with an opening to "the imperishable star" surmounted by Osiris holding aloft the solar disk. One of the first taking-off points is "the two that bind closer the heavens," which may refer to a launch from Earth to the Moon to get to Mars, or from Earth to Mars to the actual final "Heaven," or both, or neither—it is impossible for us to know without better information. But we do have evidence of space travel on Mars and the Moon, so attempting to fit them into the journey is certainly credible. The last "division" of twelve such divisions (or "hours") on the journey is called *Tesert-baiu*, meaning "Red Souls," obviously a term of some interest.

Of special note is that the trip to (or through) the Tuat not only involves one sphinx—it involves *two*. A double sphinx *(Aker)* can be seen depicted in the Pyramid Texts and the Book of the Dead, being either two sphinxes back to back with a solar disk between them, or else a single body with one head gazing eternally east (as ours does at Cairo), and the other gazing eternally west (which may be the Face on Mars). It is referred to as the "Great God who opens the Gates of Earth." The stela of Thothmes IV, dedicated to the Winged Disk (or Celestial Globe), shows the double sphinx as the guide of the Celestial Barge from "yesterday to tomorrow," the association by which it is connected with a sealed chamber of Sokar in the Sacred Desert—Sokar is a hawk-headed version of Osiris. The Pa-Ra-Emheb Stela—which refers to Ra's building of the Sphinx in his image amid a "protected place in the Sacred Desert" with a "hidden name," the place of the "King of the Gods" in the "secret Underworld"—mentions the extension of cords and a crossing of the sky to the subterranean world where secret things are made. This is extremely similar, if not identical, to the Red Eye of Horus in Queen Nejmet's papyrus, which also depicts fourteen gods that could be those of the Tuat.

Interestingly enough, possible confirmation of a hawk-headed sphinx on Mars comes from the foremost authority on Egyptology, E. A. Wallis Budge, who wrote in 1934 that "Mars . . . was called Hor-Tesher, the 'Red Horus.' He was said 'to journey backwards in travelling,' and he was also known as 'Harakhti,' 'Horus of the Two Horizons.' The god of this planet was Ra; he had the head of a hawk with a star above it." The Cydonia Sphinx of Mars is to all appearances exactly that: the head of a hawk with a star above it, the star (diadem) containing a stylized human face. The "Two Horizons" applies equally well to sunrise and sunset on the one planet, as it does to the horizons of two planets connected by travel. Mars is referred to as the "Star of the East" (Saturn is the "Star of the West") in Egyptian mythology, and east is also the direction given for the deceased's travel to the Tuat in the Book of the Dead. The Nejmet Papyrus illustration is identical but reversed in the tomb of Ramses VI, with the inscription, "The god is like this. He bends over the mysterious mound, in the interior of which is the great secret." Another inscription reads, "Horus of the Horizon is his name, / A Star in the East of Heaven / He sails backwards. / He who crosses the sky is his name / A star in the West of Heaven / Horus the Bull of Heaven is his name." Since "Heaven" is in the west, and the Tuat is the last stop on the way there, this may well indicate that Heaven "in the West" is Saturn or beyond, possibly outside our solar system, since Saturn is elsewhere referred to as the "star of limiting the place."

E. C. Krupp, in *Echoes of the Ancient Skies,* observes that "Both Mars and Saturn were called the Eastern Star and the Western Star in various inscriptions, however." This is important to note, because there is textual evidence for Earth more than once having had opposite polar orientations than it has at present. The southern panel of Queen Hatshepsut's architect's tomb shows the position of the zodiac and other constellations in reverse, as A. Pogo recorded in "The Astronomical Ceiling Decoration in the Tomb of Senmut." He wrote that the panel's orientation is such that one has to face north to see south, and that Orion is incorrectly moving eastward, instead of west. There cannot have been an error in his interpretation, since J. H. Breasted's *Ancient Records of Egypt* (III, 18) records the tomb's inscription as saying, "Harakhte, he riseth in the west," where Harakhte is traditionally considered to set. Herodotus provides additional confirmation in his *Histories* (II, 142), quoting the priests concerning both dynastic and predynastic Egypt of prior to the fifth century BC, "four times in this period (so they told me) the sun rose contrary to his wont; twice he rose where he now sets, and twice he set where he now rises." Several Egyptian papyri also speak of exactly such an event occurring, one example being the Papyrus Anastasi IV in the British Museum, recorded in Adolf Erman's *Egyptian Literature:* "The winter is come as summer, the months are reversed and the hours are disordered." The Harris Papyrus, the Ipuwer Papyrus in Leyden, and the Ermitage Papyrus in Leningrad make statements regarding the south becoming north, the earth turning over, and the land being upside down, and the Pyramid Texts as recorded by L. Speelers in 1923 say specifically at one point that the sun "ceased to live in the occident, and shines, a new one, in the orient." Even the Bible records such an event in Isaiah 24:1: "Behold, the Lord maketh the earth empty and maketh it waste, and turneth it upside down, and scattereth abroad the inhabitants thereof."

The Hopi tradition of the destruction of Tokpa, the Second World, has it that "Sotuknang called upon the Ant People to open up the underground world for the chosen people. When they were safely underground, Sotuknang commanded the twins . . . to leave their posts at the north and south ends of the world's axis, where they were stationed to keep the earth properly rotating. The twins had hardly abandoned their stations when the world, with no one to control it, teetered off balance, spun around crazily, then rolled over twice. Mountains plunged into the seas with a great splash, seas and lakes sloshed over the land; and as the world spun through cold and lifeless space, it froze into solid ice." Velikovsky reports worldwide myths from Finland's *Kalevala,* Iceland's *Voluspa,* oral traditions of Greenland Eskimos, Andaman Island natives, Mayans, Aztecs, Chinese, and many other peoples that Earth has turned upside down.

It is not the purpose of this study to further examine catastrophe theory in this light, merely to demonstrate that textual evidence does exist to explain reversals of the stars in ancient maps of the constellations. The Third World that the Hopi went to as their Second World was destroyed was colored red and was in the *east;* now, in the Fourth World—our Earth—they refer to that former red world as being in the *west.* This, along with the description of a world destroyed by spinning off its axis and perishing in a Flood, make for a good argument that Earth was abandoned for Mars, then was returned to when Mars itself was later destroyed—or perhaps that the Hopi Second World was that shattered planet (mythically referred to in Babylon as Tiamat) which is now the asteroid belt between Mars and Jupiter. The argument could be furthered with the Sumerian relation of the same myth placing Noah in a boat "like an Apsu boat," which in one translation would be a "boat of the sun" such as Enki used to travel to his home in the Lower World, the place of the red clay from which mankind was made. In fact, the Hopi tradition has it that the death of the Third World— in accordance with the observations made of Mars' surface in this study—came about "when the people began to use their creative power in another evil and destructive way," specifically in aerial warfare, "so fast no one knew where they came from," and when all the cities and countries became corrupt and murderous in war, then that world, too, was lost in a Flood ordered by Sotuknang.

Where Kukulkan and Quetzalcoatl were said to have come from and returned to Venus or the east, their exact equivalent,

Viracocha, returned to the west. Perhaps the "east" refers to an earthly location (likely Egypt, given that this god was also said to come from "the red and black land"), and the "west" to another world, or vice versa. It may be that directions became reversed due to a change in the poles, or that both Venus and Mars were once occupied and are being separately referred to. The Great Lakes Indians believe their ancestors came from a land "toward the rising sun," the Iowa say that "At first all men lived on an island where the day star is born," and the Sioux claim that "The tribes of Indians were formerly one, and all dwelt together on an island ... toward the east or sunrise." Harleston and Schlemmer's Aztec theory had both Quetzalcoatl/Sumer (probably Venus, by traditional association) and Mars, "the flayed Red God of the East," giving life to Earth. It is important to note that Venus, "the Great Star" and the "Lord of the Dawn" (i.e., east), is colored red, black, and white in Mexican art. Venus, or the "Star of the East," was also the Egyptian Bennu bird, the Phoenix, "the soul of Ra and the living symbol of Osiris," perishing in flame and rising anew from its own ashes—a destroyed and resurrected civilization. As Spell 17 of the Book of the Dead describes the cosmic war of antiquity, "The Children of Heaven entered into the eastern part of the sky, there straightway taketh place a battle in heaven and in the earth to its whole extent."

Like the reversed zodiac found in Egypt, Chinese red-white references are opposite those we have been studying—the white moon in the west and the red sun in the east, as seen on the domed ceiling of the tomb of the Princess Yung Tai, near Xian on the Wei River. And in yet another of a growing number of ignored connections between China and the Americas, Bruce Hunter's *A Guide to Ancient Maya Ruins,* published in 1986, cited the identical custom in both cultures of burying the dead with pieces of jade in the mouth and each hand, adding that, "Before the tomb was closed, the whole chamber was sprinkled with powdered red cinnabar, widely used in burials throughout Mesoamerica. The red color symbolizes the east, the rising sun and resurrection." The direction, obviously, remains in question, the red-painted Lord Shield-Pacal departed for the Underworld to the *west.*

One more such reversal is found in Maui, Maori, and Samoan myths regarding the location of the *Fare-kura,* the "red" or "purple house" (where the Hopi's highest moral instruction also was said to take place). It was in Hawaiki, the supernatural "abode of the venerated learning of the gods—there in the spirit world," a temple "in the spot where the teaching of [man] originated, where man was first taught the doctrines brought down from Heaven by Tane," a world referred to alternately as being either in the east or the west. "Tane-of-ancient-waters," of the "sacred tree"—obviously the same as Manannan Mac Lir—sings of a resurrected "way-opener," who is "the first . . . who came at last," plainly a point of interest. S. Percy Smith's *The Lore of the Whare-wananga* in 1913 specified that this Fare-kura—under several different names with the same meaning—was the "gathering place of the spirits" and "primordial home," but indicated that there was at some point a separation between it and another world, their Hades then becoming "fixed at the east" where "those spirits which by their evil conduct on this earth . . . left the [red house] temple . . . by the [long, rapid descent]," the others ascending slowly to the "realm of Io the Supreme God," the "All-Source of Tuamotu." This last sounds not unlike "Tuat," and the whole shows the occasional confusion of the fabled Red Land's location between east and west in space, and its function in heaven and the Afterlife.

In any event, if Mars is not the actual Underworld itself, it is at least a stop along the way. It seems certain that it is the "Red Land" of "the Two Lands" of Egypt, the "Sacred Desert." That Mars could be the Tuat and/or Lower Egypt fits the multiple-entendre sacred pun pattern of this race: half the size of Earth, Mars is "lesser," which could be rendered as "lower"; "lower" is also "under," and our Mars probes indicate that if there is life on Mars, it is beneath the planet's surface, making the Underworld an underworld.

There are other indications that the journey to the Afterlife extends at least into space, if not beyond the solar system. Egyptologists G. A. Wainwright, Rundle Clark, and Samuel A. Mercer (translator of the Pyramid Texts in 1952) all noticed that the *adze,* another one of those odd implements associated with the Afterlife that no one can satisfactorily explain, was shaped like Ursa Major (the "Great Bear," the Big Dipper), and the German Egyptologist L. Borchardt modified their view by saying it more closely resembled Ursa Minor. The adze was used for the "Opening of the Mouth" Ceremony before the deceased began his journey and was made of meteoritic iron *(bja)*—i.e., metal from space. A god, either Anubis or Horus, is the "opener of the way" who touches the adze to the deceased's mouth, and mortal priests perform the same task with the foreleg of a cow, which has much the same shape but is not "divine." This ceremony takes place before a towering obelisk topped by the pyramidion (Benben). Taken altogether, they could easily signify preparing for an astral journey directed by the constellations, "opening the way" to heaven as a map which Horus would be able to read. Horus is the way to the Father, Osiris, as Jesus is to the Father in Christianity, and it is he who takes the deceased to the Tuat in the Divine Eye, which has already been denoted as a vehicle.

Some mythology might be clearer with astral connotations taken into account. Herodotus was certain that the Greeks had borrowed their mythology from the Egyptians. In Greek mythology, Zeus preserved his savior-figure demigod son, Dionysus, by hiding him from his enemies in his youth. He "sewed Dionysus in his thigh" to keep him safe until he could be born. The Egyptian name for the constellation of Ursa Major is *meshtw,* "the Thigh," and sacred births were said to be "born upon the thigh" of Osiris. Jesus also was concealed in infancy, and discovered only by three kings, who were Zoroastrian priests—i.e., astronomers—who found him by following a star, or the stars.

Almost all of Judaeo-Christianity can be traced to Egyptian origins, which has been noticed by many scholars reluctant to accept it. That versions of the Book of the Dead have Thoth ordering the Flood as occurred in Scripture is a fact so obscure not many Egyptologists know it. It is clearly written out in the Papyrus of Ra at the Leyden Museum, but popular translations omit it completely. Budge quotes the much shorter text in his translation, saying only that longer versions exist, but then he fails to mention anything at all about the Flood being in it. Only in his last book, *From Fetish to God in Ancient Egypt,* does Budge finally provide the omitted text. Then he does his best to stress that it must not be the biblical Flood, even as he admits that other Egyptian texts seem to confirm that a flood did occur and that there are numerous comparisons between the Bible and ancient Egyptian myths. Egyptologists generally ignore the idea of an Egyptian Flood myth, or state that it was only alluded to in the Byblos chest or Sekhmet and the Eye of Ra myths.

The fact that Moses was trained in Egyptian mystery school came from both the Bible and the historical sources Manetho and Josephus, but took time to be written about by modern historians. Sir Gardner Wilkinson was one of the first to make the overt observation that "Many of the religious rites of the Jews bear a striking resemblance to those of Egypt," and then it was in a footnote to an edited professional journal. Circumcision, as Herodotus informs us, was originally an Egyptian practice which the Hebrews picked up during their bondage. Budge sometimes noted the evidence, but generally tried to explain it away as coincidence, which has been the prevailing practice in academia. Sitchin has begun opening the doors to such evidence, bringing up many ancient Egyptian texts that are found virtually word for word in Psalms and Scripture, and many from Sumer as well. As has been discussed, the Book of the Dead can plainly be shown to have been the origin of the Book of Enoch, and so at least some of Genesis and related books of the Bible. Many of Jesus' quotes can be found not only there, but in Egyptian myth. One example is Jesus' warning that "out of your own mouths will I save you, with your own words will I condemn you" (Matthew 12:37), which is a direct paraphrase of Ra's words upon discovering Set's treachery when Isis became a bird and brought Set's exact words to Ra's ears, proving him a liar and hypocrite when he contradicted himself in the court of the gods.

Jesus' frequent references to the tree and the vine, the harvest of time, reaping as one sows, the separation of the wheat and the chaff at final judgment, and the like come from other Egyptian and ancient texts and occult mysteries. Jesus fits the same position in mythology as Horus, being the son of the fertility god (Osiris) who dies and rises again. When the god of the Underworld (or the demiurge/prime mover) is personified into the fertility god, these allusions become obvious. Cronos was the symbol of vast ages of time, like Anu or the Dagda Mor, shown pictorially as the old man with a scythe: the reaper. The historical source Varro, in *De Lingua Latina,* stated that the Roman equivalent of Cronos, Saturn, was derived from the word *satus,* meaning "sowing." Similarly, *kraino* means "completer" or "ripener," perhaps as valid a root word for the fertility god as *kronos* ("time"). The Protestant and Catholic apostolic creed both contain the statement of belief that "Jesus descended to the dead. On the third day he rose again and ascended into heaven." A descent to the dead is exactly the same as a descent into the Underworld. In Egypt, the annual spring festival commemorating the death and resurrection of Osiris corresponded with our own Easter, three days of mourning being observed between his death and rising, exactly as between Good Friday and Easter Sunday.

Ecclesiastes, in its famous verses about everything being in its own season, makes reference to there being "a time to gather stones together" (Eccles. 3:5). For what purpose? The megaliths of the world provide an answer, embodying the work the sons of god performed in measuring the sacred places, and explaining what rocks Jesus said would "suddenly cry out" (in their mathematics and geometry) were no one to bear witness to the Lord (Luke 19:40). As astronomical calendars, the megaliths would also provide an explanation for Jesus' reference to the end times occurring "before this present generation is passed" (Matthew 24:34). Where his followers took that to mean their own lifetimes, the generation to which he was referring could have been the age of the ruling sign in heaven, the precessional equinox (in his time, just becoming Pisces, the sign of the fish), which is now passing into Aquarius.

When Daniel explains to King Belshazzar what the prophetic writing on the wall means (Dan. 5:27), Belshazzar is told that he has been "weighed in the balances, and found wanting." Weighing in the balances is the Judgment in the Hall of Osiris. The deceased is led before Osiris (the Father), by Horus (the Son), and has his heart weighed in the balance against the feather of Ma'at (Truth). If he fails, if he "does not speak true" or is "an utterer of falsehood," then Ammit (the Devourer) consumes him and his soul is consigned to torment or oblivion. Exactly this same arrangement is found in the Bardo Thödol, the Tibetan Book of the Dead, even including the supervisor of the procedure being the monkey god, Shinje, where it is the baboon (Thoth) in the Egyptian.

The Hebrew mysticism that rabbis study is very similar to that of the Egyptian priests. Like hieroglyphics, Hebrew is a language with several meanings at once. It has a phonetic and numerical value (the Gematria or Caballah), as well as a pictorial one. Also like the Egyptian, Hebrew written language has no vowels. Both priesthoods were characterized by intense secrecy, as were the Druids, who were forbidden to commit any of their learning to writing.

Thoth, Ra, Osiris, and Amun were so prominent as predynastic rulers that all Pharaohs affixed one or another of their names to their own to signify the original link between heaven and earth. So it is that we have Pharaohs named Thothmes ("beloved of Thoth"), Menkaura ("Men, soul of Ra"), Hatshepsut sa Amen ("Hatshepsut, united with Amen"), etc. Tutankhamen meant "Tut, life of Amen." It wasn't until Akhnaton, Tut's predecessor in the New Kingdom, that the practice of god-names affixed to the Pharaoh's own was abolished in favor of solar monotheism. Akhnaton was dubbed "the heretic" and universally hated by virtually everyone in Egypt, proving that it was not the sun they worshipped when they worshipped Ra, since the sun was the one god Akhnaton insisted on swearing allegiance to. After his premature death all of Akhnaton's reforms were abolished. The same basic practice of affixing god-names (changed to saints' names) is still in evidence with Catholic popes, as are at least two particular symbols from ancient Egypt: the shepherd's crook (crozier), and the papal crown, which is almost identical to the white crown of Upper Egypt that Osiris always wears. "Thy rod and thy staff" of the twenty-third Psalm are the emblems of authority for Osiris and the Pharaohs: the flail and the crook. The very word that ends Christian prayers is the name of the great hidden Egyptian god: "Amen."

But the most striking of all similarities between the Egyptian and the Judaeo-Christian religions is their belief in a bodily Afterlife. Many sects of both Judaism and Christianity debate or disagree with the idea, yet it is at the core of their very belief system. C. S. Lewis, the most popular modern apologist of Christianity, has noted in his work that the sole area of agreement between Christians is the central tenet of the Resurrection. Without it, Jesus is only a philosopher, no matter how holy or admirable. The various sects in Jesus' time were in no more agreement on the issue than those of today, but he praised the ones who believed in bodily resurrection and condemned the others. There are admittedly grounds for believing that reincarnation and rebirth are the bodily resurrection referred to, in all of these sects and the Druidic Celts as well, but when taken back to the Egyptian roots, the evidence is for resurrection in the same body—even though that same body is a *different* "same body."

Exactly what the Egyptians believed concerning their Afterlife has always been a point of contention. Popular misconceptions hold that the Egyptians were preoccupied with preserving their bodies because they believed those same bodies would resurrect for their Afterlife. In fact, they were intensely preoccupied with the preservation of their earthly bodies—but not because they thought those same bodies would rise again. They believed their new bodies would be *created* from their old bodies. Their personality and soul would be rejoined to the duplicate body by means of some magic of the gods, and the magic of the gods would also create the new body from their old one in the first place. It has only been in the last twenty-five or thirty years that such a "magic" has become conceivable to modern minds: cloning.

Biologists of the University of Oklahoma confirmed as early as March of 1963 that the Egyptian Princess Mene's skin cells were still intact—in essence, alive enough to be potentially cloned. The cloning of mummy tissue is no longer a question of science fiction but in 1985 became science fact, recorded in the British science journal *Nature.* Swedish scientist Svante Paabo, inspired by a Berkeley team's successful cloning of two hundred subunits of quagga (primitive zebra) tissue in 1984, applied the technique to skin taken from the left leg of an infant mummy in the Egyptian Museum in Berlin. More than three thousand subunits of mitochondrial DNA were successfully grown and activated in the process.

Anubis, the black jackal- or dog-headed deity, officiated over the rites of death and embalming. Osiris is sometimes also represented as black, where he is at all other times green. Anubis and Osiris both bear the title "Foremost of the Westerners" at different times. Osiris and Anubis are sometimes portrayed as brothers (like the "flayed" brothers who gave life to Earth in Harleston and Schlemmer's reading of Aztec mythology), and other times as one god in different forms—"An" or "Asar" prefixes refer to Osiris, the "Temple of On" in the Bible being one such occurrence. Anubis also frequently holds the same position held by Osiris' son, Horus, being called "the Avenger of His Father," and like Horus is often shown applying the adze to the mouth of the mummy. In this capacity, he is also called *upuaut,* "the opener of the ways," and occupies Horus' position in the boat to the Afterlife. His color, black, is the color of death, the Black Rite of Isis being the magic by which Osiris was raised from the dead. Robert Temple interprets the rite as having astronomical significance concerning the possibly trinary Sirius system, and his research is certainly thorough and intriguing. Given the ancients' tradition of ascribing more than one meaning to nearly everything, it is possible the Black Rite has both that significance and a more immediate earthly one. In astronomical terms, it would have something to do with the heliacal rising of Sirius in relation to Orion, if Temple's interpretations are correct. It may also have other astronomical interpretations closer to home.

Anubis in earliest times was believed to ritually kill the Pharaoh with an asp after twenty-eight years' reign. He came by night and painlessly dispatched the king in his sleep, then removed the body to a secret chamber for mummification. The number of years between Osiris' becoming king and his later murder, in some versions of the tale, is twenty-eight. Twenty-eight is also twice the number of pieces into which Osiris' body was dismembered, twice the number of gods and states in the Tuat, and the number of cubits' height that the Nile annually reached at Aswan (where it was measured) on the seventeenth of the month of Athyr. And it is only one and a half years less than the twenty nine and a half years it takes Saturn to "return," or complete one circle around the zodiac. "According to Plutarch," E. C. Krupp elucidates, "Osiris was slain—suffocated in the box—on the seventeenth day of the month of Athyr, when the sun was in Scorpius, in the twenty-eighth year of his reign. The numbers are significant. Although the moon completes its phases in 29½ days, the number 28 was used symbolically for this interval." The same numbers used to signify the days of the waxing and waning of the moon equate exactly to the number of years Saturn takes to complete its circuit—which means that Saturn's twenty-nine-and-a-half-year orbit could as readily be rendered by the Egyptians as twenty eight.

The little-understood Egyptian jubilee festival, the *heb-sed,* when the king annually renewed his reign (and which was somehow connected to the Afterlife, but no one is certain exactly how) by running a complete circuit around the open courtyard of the Saqqara step pyramid, was also enacted "for the first time thirty years after his accession," and was then repeated at slightly shorter intervals thereafter—which may mean that the "renewed king" was not the earthly Pharaoh, but the heavenly Saturn. The Pharaoh carried with him implements associated with the dismembered Apis bull, Osiris, in the *heb-sed,* and Saqqara's probable connection to astronomical observation is evident from a statue of Zoser positioned sitting in a side structure to the pyramid, looking out through two siting holes over the horizon. Saturn was connected with the color black and death, and was the "Star of the West," where Osiris or Anubis were "Foremost" in the Afterlife, the Sumerians also calling Saturn "Foremost in the Heavens" and ascribing its rulership to Ninurta (Horus, who is sometimes Anubis). Saturn was the Roman name given to Cronos, the "sower," "the ripener," and "the reaper," who harvests at a specific time. Clearly,

Saturn bears some significant role in the Afterlife journey, as does Mars. If the adze does represent Ursa Minor and astral navigation, then "the opener of the ways" in connection with "the star of limiting the place" being employed at a predestined time, and involving the "Star of the West" where the gods live, implies a great deal.

One definite astromathematical explanation of the role of Saturn, already partly discussed in this study, is made clear by Jane B. Sellers in *The Death of Gods in Ancient Egypt:* "Returning to the account of Osiris, son of Cronos, god of Measurable Time, Plutarch takes pains to remind the reader of the original Egyptian year consisting of 360 days ... described as being '12 months of 30 days each.' Then we are told that Osiris leaves on a long journey, during which Seth, his evil brother, plots with 72 companions to slay Osiris. He also secretly obtained 'the measure' of Osiris and made ready a chest in which to entrap him ... (It is) an observable fact that Saturn has the longest sidereal period of the known planets at that time, an orbit of 30 years. Saturn is absent from a specific constellation for that length of time. A simple mathematical fact has been revealed to any that are even remotely sensitive to numbers: if you multiply 72 by 30 ... the resulting product is 2,160, the number of years required for one 30-degree shift, or a shift through one complete sign of the zodiac. This number multiplied by the twelve signs also gives 25,920 ... If you multiply the unusual number 72 by 360, a number that Plutarch mentions several times, the product will be 25,920, again the number of years symbolizing the ultimate rebirth. This 'Eternal Return' is the return of, say, Taurus to the position of marking the vernal equinox by 'riding in the solar bark with Re' after having relinquished this honored position to Aries, and subsequently to the 10 other zodiacal constellations. Such a return after 25,920 years is indeed a return to a Golden Age. . . ." In other words, observation of Saturn marks the precessional equinox.

Sellers brings up the point that all the numbers in this formula redact, in occult fashion, to the number nine, which recurs mythologically as a number of lunar wisdom according to mythologist Robert Graves, the Moon in many traditions being the parent of Earth whose "substances and vital essences are still being transferred to its successor" as Titchenell puts it. Nine is the number of days Odin hung crucified on the world tree before rebirth, the number of nights upon which his magic ring eternally regenerates eight more like itself, and the number of Mimer's ("matter" or "memory's") worlds with which Odin daily "conferred" (or worked with intimately), all of which may signify the reordering and rebuilding of our solar system after each Ragnarok brought about by the proposed tenth body—it was "time," Saturn/Cronos, that dismembered Mimer and cast his lifeless body into space, and Odin's conferring with Mimer's head would equate with the reshaping of a world to new life.

Graves' *The White Goddess* recalls numerous other repetitions of Sellers' ancient Saturnian numbers, particularly in five, nine, and seventy-two. One in particular is that the aggregate number of letter strokes in the twenty-two-letter Celtic Ogham alphabet is seventy-two, and the Celts have five basic dialects. Another is the Dionysian Celtic hero Feniusa Farsa, who has seventy-two assistants to help him decipher the seventy-two languages left in the aftermath of the Tower of Babel, which was made of nine elements—nine, the lunar number, being a multiple of seventy-two. The Pentateuch's (the first five books of the Bible) translation into Greek for Ptolemy by Hellenistic Jews, circa 250 BC, was said to have taken seventy-two scholars seventy-two days.

Renaissance occult historian Frances A. Yates wrote that, "It is no accident that there are 72 of Pico's [Della Mirandola, a magus of the time] conclusions, for the fifty-sixth conclusion shows that he knew something of the mystery of the Name of God with 72 letters," remarking also that seventy-two is the number of angels ascribed to the Sephiroth, the "powers of God." Sellers notes that the multiple 432 is of equal astronomical significance, stating that a prominent Jewish Assyriologist of the last century claimed mathematical encoding in the number of patriarchs from Adam to the Flood: 1,656 years, which are 86,400 seven-day weeks, dividing to 43,200. This number is exactly twice that ascribed by the Indian yogic schools (21,600) to every human being's number of breaths per day. Joseph Campbell's *Occidental Mythology* volume of his Masks of God series notes the importance of the date St. Patrick came to Ireland—which was 432 AD.

Additional confirmation of the number's significance comes from Titchenell, who remarks, "Valhalla presents yet another aspect which links it with Eastern scriptures of remote antiquity: Odin in Grimnismal tells his pupil that 'there are five hundred doors and forty more' to Valhalla; and that eight hundred warriors issue from each when Odin goes to war with the wolf. Further we are told that there are five hundred and forty halls in bulging Bilskirner (the shining abode), the largest being 'my son's'—the solar deity's. Multiplying 540 x 800 we get 432,000 warriors and the same number of halls. In both Babylonian and Indian chronologies this figure occurs in numerous ways. Multiples of it define specific astronomical cycles while, divided by various numbers, it applies to terrestrial events of greater frequency, even down to the pulsebeat of the human heart, generally reckoned as 72 beats per minute. It is itself the length assigned in human years to the length of the Iron Age, in Sanskrit the *kali yuga,* when the forces of darkness are most challenging ... It certainly hints vigorously at some common source from which these widely separated traditions have descended and at some hidden meaning which makes this figure recur in them."

The Rig-Veda consists of 10,800 stanzas of forty syllables each—432,000 syllables. Four hundred thirty-two thousand years was the number given by Berossus as making up one Babylonian Great Year. Variations of 108 recur with equal frequency. Heraclitus' duration of the Aion, according to Censorinus, was 10,800, and the same number of bricks are specified as belonging to the Indian *Agnicayana,* or "fire-altar." The Cambodian temple complex of Angkor has five gates reached by an equal number of roads, each road bordered by fifty-four giant stone figures of Devas and Asuras on either side, or 108 per avenue, for a combined number of 540. And each road has a nine-headed Naga serpent at its end. "To quibble away such a coincidence," F. R. Schröder comments in *Altgermanische Kulturprobleme,* "or to ascribe it to chance, is in my opinion to drive skepticism beyond its limits."

Some of these same numbers—along with other correspondences we have been studying, such as the connections between red and black and the planets Mars and Saturn—become much clearer with just a little more reading into both ancient astronomy and occult mysticism. Giorgio de Santillana and Hertha von Dechend's landmark study of ancient astronomy and the question of original wisdom, *Hamlet's Mill,* notes that "the character of Heimdall raises a number of sharp questions. He has appeared upon the scene as 'the son of nine mothers' ... a rare distinction even in mythology, and one which Heimdall shares only with Agni in the *Rigveda,* and with Agni's son Skanda in the *Mahabharata. Skanda* (literally 'the jumping one' or 'the hopping one') is the planet Mars, also called *Kartikeya,* inasmuch as he was born of the Krittika, the Pleiades. The *Mahabharata* insists on *six* as the number of the

Pleiades, as well as of the numbers of Skanda and gives a very broad and wild description of the birth and the installation of Kartikeya 'by the assembled gods . . . as their generalissimo. . . .'"

Santillana and Dechend elucidate the *Mahabharata's* saying that "Mars was 'installed' during a more or less close conjunction of all planets . . . it is stressed that the powerful gods assembled 'all poured water upon Skanda, even as the gods had poured water on the head of Varuna, the lord of waters, for investing him with dominion.' And this 'investiture' took place at the beginning of the Krita Yuga, the Golden Age." The Golden Age, of course, would equate with Atlantis before its cataclysmic fall. It is interesting that Heimdall was also known as "Rig," in which guise he was a beam of light or fire that impregnated Earth, connecting both to the Hindu Rig-Veda and to the god *Agni,* whose name means "fire." And in Egypt, the "nine mothers" would equate with the theological *Ennead,* "the nine," mystically connecting with "the eight" of the *Ogdoad* in the same way as Odin's eight rings regenerate every ninth night in the Norse mythology. The connection with the Pleiades is more interesting still. The authors state, "It should be emphasized, aloud and strongly, that in Babylonian astronomy Mars is the *only* planetary representative of the Pleiades," which is affirmed also by P. F. Gössmann's 1950 study, *Planetarium Babylonicum.* The ancient writer Lucian Samosota also "remarked once that the ludicrous story of Hephaistos the Lame surprising his wife Aphrodite in bed with Mars, and pinning down the couple with a net to exhibit their shame to the other gods, was not an idle fancy, but must have referred to a conjunction of Mars and Venus, and, it is fair to add, a conjunction in the Pleiades."

The "Mill" of Santillana and Dechend's study is the "grinding" of Amlethus/Cronos, or Saturn, marking measures of time and crushing the body of the god John Barleycorn/Osiris. "What kind of grinding could it have been?" they ask. "Surely the lament referred to in popular consciousness to the death of a corn god, called also Adonis (the Lord), slain by a wild boar, but the celestial aspect is predominant to the agrarian one, and more ancient, too; the more so as that 'wild boar' was Mars." We have already encountered the wild boar as the enemy of the Great God in the Wild Hunt. Emphasizing this is the authors' bringing up, without recognizing the connection themselves, "that we do not know more about Inanna's (Venus/Ishtar) unwelcome subtenants in her huluppu-tree [another "tree of life"], about Lilith, and about the dragon at the root; that he corresponds to Nidhoggr of the *Edda* does not enlighten us concerning his identity. The Zu-bird [corresponding to these others] at least is known to us; the planet Mars it is," which is confirmed by Gössmann.

J. A. Eisenmegger's magnum opus of 1711, *Entdecktes Judenthum,* discloses "the identity (as claimed by rabbinical literature) of the planet Mars with the serpent in Paradise, with Kain, Esau, Ebemelech, Goliath, Samael, the Scape-Goat, and many others." The Zohar, or Sepher-ha Zohar ("Book of Splendor"), an Aramaic book of rabbinical occult doctrine believed to have been written sometime after 1275 AD by cabalist scholar Moses de Leon, makes the statement (confirming earlier remarks from Rabbi Eleazar b. Pedath circa 270 AD) that "Pharaoh raised his eyes to heaven and saw the Egyptian Angels take flight in the skies," in regard to the Exodus. *("Als der Pharaoh aus Agypten auszog, die Israeliten zu verfolgen, erhoben sie ihre Augen gen Himmel und sahen den Engelsfürsten Ägyptens in der Luft fliegen.")* In this light, the crossing of the "Red Sea" takes on a whole new meaning. G. Rabuse, in *Der komische Aufbau der Jenseitsreiche Dantes* in 1958, drew the same corollary in explaining Dante's placing of Lucifer in the frozen ice of Tartarus in his *Divine Comedy:* as explained in *Hamlet's Mill,* "Rabuse has solved this puzzle in a careful analytical study of Dante's three worlds. First, he has found by way of a little-known manuscript of late antiquity, the so-called 'Third Vatican Mythographer,' that the circular territory occupied by the Red River in Hell was meant by 'certain writers' to be the exact counterpart of the circle of Mars in the skies 'because they make the heavens to begin in the Nether World.'"

Psalms 24:21 refers to the same final judgment decreed earlier in the Book of Enoch when it says, "On that day, the Lord will punish the host of heaven, in heaven, and the kings of the earth, on the earth." Among these, in the occult tradition, are various "guardian angels," about whom Santillana and Dechend remark, "These 'guardian angels' will be identified sooner or later, insofar as this has not yet been accomplished in older literature which our contemporaries disdain as 'obsolete'; one among them, the angel-lord of Esau/Edom, with whom, according to the Zohar, Jacob wrestled (Gen. XXXII.24–33), is the planet Mars. How the whole system really works—e.g. these punishments first in 'heaven,' subsequently 'on earth'—will not be understood before Plato's *Timaeus* is taken as earnestly as it was taken by the Pythagorean

Timaios himself, whom Plato introduced as 'astronomikotaton hemon,' i.e. the most astronomically-minded among us, and before it is accepted as the foundation from which to proceed further."

It is the combination of legend and astronomy that may make sense of the connection between the religious importance of the precessional equinox measured by the planet Saturn, and its significance in combination with Mars: "There are no Powers more diverse than Saturn and Mars," remark the authors of *Hamlet's Mill,* "yet this is not the only time they will appear as a confusing and unexplained doublet of the two. One of the motifs, destruction, is often associated with the Amlethus [Kronos/Saturn] figure. The other belongs more specifically to Mars. There is a peculiar blind aspect to Mars, insisted on in both Harranian and Mexican myths. It is even echoed in Virgil: *'caeco Marte.'* But it does not stand only for blind fury. It must be sought in the Nether World, which will come soon. Meanwhile, here is [a] presentation of the double figure of Mars and Kronos. In Mexico, it stands out dreadfully in the grotesque forms of the Black and the Red Tezcatlipoca. There is a certain phase in the Great Tale, obviously, in which the wrecking powers of Mars unleashed make up a fatal compound with the avenging implacable design of Saturn." In other words, a predestined astral correlation prefigures Ragnarok/the Apocalypse.

In terms of actual bodily resurrection, Anubis (in some versions Thoth), who we have been regarding as Saturn, is the originator of embalming. How much of the myth and symbolism refers to space travel and how much to physical revivification is a matter for conjecture, but the possibility of a body rising from the dead is not out-of-bounds. Jesus was reported to have raised men from the dead, and to have arisen himself, the latter feat possibly assisted by the one or two "angels" in white robes in Jesus' tomb (the number varying from gospel to gospel), as Anubis and his assisting train were portrayed doing for the deceased in Egypt. The white robes could signify that these "angels" were Essenes, the famous sect of healers. There are Sumerian texts and cylinder seals showing Inanna raised from the dead in the Underworld by a device which emits rays. The controversial Shroud of Turin, Jesus' supposed burial wrapping, is believed by many to have had its image formed by some kind of radioactive photoeffect such as is caused by nuclear blasts. And, of course, the question of cloning remains.

One thing is definite: the Black Rite was the most closely guarded secret in Egypt. Only an elite few priests were ever allowed to know it, and they were forbidden to reveal anything about it. The ancient Egyptians believed their Afterlife was directly connected to it. Embalming itself was as closely guarded. Most of the preservation secrets are known by us today, but these are later techniques and not necessarily the original ones. Given the remarkable similarity between the Egyptians and the Hebrews, there may have been more than a mere sanitary consideration in the practice of circumcision. The priest performed the act and disposed of the tissues. The priesthood—being the preserver of the secrets—may have had a purpose for those tissues. If they had a liaison with a superior race of humans from another planet that knew the secret of cloning tissues, then the flesh and blood sample taken from every male member of the tribe by circumcision would ensure their Afterlife. Since the female members also were assured a rebirth, then if this theory is correct there would have to be an equivalent tissue sample taken from them. Whether the Hebrews have such a ceremony for their females is unknown to the author, but the Egyptians, Mayans, Aztecs, Incas, Polynesians, Dogon, and other tribes around the world did and do have ritual mutilation of both men and women.

As with all other things Egyptian, both interpretations could be correct: the Afterlife as a bodily resurrection, and also as a journey through space. "Supernatural" beings have always been connected with graveyards and places of the dead, perhaps because they have some business there. They could be periodically gathering tissue samples, as there is no question the UFO occupants we have encountered are doing. World religions seem to agree that, once raised from the dead to live with the gods, returning to this world rarely if ever occurs, and when it does, it is at specific times of year (perhaps with planetary correlations). It would be far more feasible, if strenuous and lengthy trips are involved, to transfer tremendous numbers of people in the form of their compact cellular bodily essence, rather than in their living bodies. In that fashion, the process could be accomplished entirely by automata, requiring no food or relief facilities and precious little space aboard their craft. Where men and women from Earth are on record as having bodily left this world (if one accepts religious texts), these instances are remarkably few—Enoch, Elijah, Jesus, the Virgin Mary (according to tradition), a few others. Jesus repeatedly referred to man's having to die first in order to rise again to eternal life. The economic needs of space travel may well be the reason.

It is difficult to say exactly what may safely be known from all this, a certain amount of speculation being unavoidable. The archaeological evidence leaves extremely little doubt that Mars is the Red Land of "the Two Lands" of Ancient Egypt, and the final area of the Tuat—the "Place of Ascending"—traversed in the journey to the Afterlife. The Underworld or Other World "across the Western Ocean" or beneath Earth that figures so prominently in the world's mythologies may also be Mars. Saturn obviously plays an important role in the journey, possibly being "the Imperishable Star" to which the deceased ascends from the Tuat.

It may be of interest that the Elysian Fields of the Tuat, the *Sekhet-hetep* ("Field of Offerings"), was famous as a place intersected by canals—like Mars. It is worth noting as well that the land of Colchis—historically, an Egyptian colony—in the myth of Jason (whose name Robert Graves translates as "healer," like Jesus) was said to have a falcon (Circe, *kirke,* "falcon," or "hawk") presiding over its cemetery. As a sphinx presides over the Giza cemetery complex, which appears also to be a spaceport, so does a hawk-headed sphinx preside over the Cydonia complex on Mars. Robert Temple notes that the Greek *erion,* "woolen fleece," is a *heru* (the sun) derived word, and the sun daily stabled in Colchis where the fleece was located—specifically "in the grove of Ares (Mars)."

As to the nature of the Afterlife, textual evidence is plentiful but interpretations are questionable. The connection to space travel seems powerfully apparent. Bodily resurrection or reincarnation are not within our present understanding, but are within our speculation. Immortality, or phenomenal longevity, are not beyond current scientific consideration as real possibilities. It is consistent with the reading so far given the available evidence that death itself was an implanted safety device or control, intended to keep superior power in the hands of our makers. If that is so, then the idea that the device may be removed at a future time is perfectly feasible, as is the idea that duplicates of the body can be formed, which is what the Egyptians (and apparently the Celts) believed.

The connections between the Celts and the Egyptians are strong archaeologically, mythologically, and theologically. To those connections may be added the metric. Nineteenth-century mathematician and astronomer John Taylor, Scottish Astronomer Royal Charles Piazzi Smyth, and astronomer John Herschel discovered, independently of each other, that the British inch was within one-thousandth of the twenty-fifth part of the Egyptian sacred cubit, by which the Great Pyramid was built. Also, Taylor found that the King's coffer in the Pyramid was almost exactly four times the standard measure of grain in Britain: eight bushels, or a quarter.

The UFO abduction phenomenon especially has strong connections to Celtic tales of the Tuatha de Danaan—the Fairy Folk. Strong connections are also found between the Hebrew religion and its resultant Christian offshoot/progression, and ancient Egyptian theology, symbolism, religious texts, and occult mysticism. The means by which the Judaeo-Christian God communicated with his prophets bears all the earmarks of UFO abduction, and so does that of the great god of the Danaan, Manannan Mac Lir.

The idea that the Egyptians and the Celts were connected in antiquity—and that they spread much farther across the world than is commonly believed—is not a new one; it has been noticed by many scholars over the years. Rolleston, in 1911, said, "The facts at present known do not, I think, justify us in framing any theory as to the actual historical relation of the dolmen-builders of Western Europe with the people who created the wonderful religion and civilization of ancient Egypt. But when we consider all the lines of evidence that converge in this direction, it seems clear that there was such a relation." In *The Mediterranean Race,* Sergi noted that the "Two Feet" symbol of Osiris, by which the god denotes taking possession of a land under the guise of the god "Temu" in Chapter 17 of the Book of the Dead, appears in India as the footprints of the Buddha, and is found on dolmens in Brittany and in the Scandinavian rock carvings of Lokeberget and Bohuslän. Rolleston equated them with the footprints of St. Patrick or St. Columba in Ireland, and Lord Kingsborough's *Antiquities of Mexico* and Tyler's *Primitive Culture* refer to them as the prints of the sun god Tezcatlipoca in Aztec ceremony. Letorneau noted in the April 1893 *Bulletin de la Soc. d'Anthropologie* that "the builders of our megalithic monuments came from the south, and were related to the races of North Africa," and Sergi recorded finding the sign of the ankh and other hieroglyphic signs on French dolmens. Sir Flinders Petrie wrote in *Egypt and Israel* that he believed the Madonna derived from Isis, which is now little disputed. Professor J. Morris Jones confirmed, in *The Welsh People,* the suggestion of Sir John Rhys that Celtic languages preserved Egyptian Hamitic syntax: "The pre-Aryan idioms which still live in Welsh and Irish were derived from a language allied to Egyptian and the Berber tongues." Fernand Niel's *The Mysteries of Stonehenge* recorded the finding of small blue beads in a Wessex burial ground, discovered on close examination to have been made in Egypt.

W. Y. Evans-Wentz noted in 1911 at the very beginning of his *The Fairy Faith in Celtic Countries* that plainly there had to be some significant connection between Brittany and Egypt. In Upper Egypt, *Karnak* is the site of one of the world's most impressive sun temples from the New Kingdom, oriented to both solar northwest and solar southwest for the solstices; in Brittany, *Carnac* is composed of thousands of east-west aligned menhirs and dolmens in straight lines, extending fifteen miles even out beneath the sea, extremely similar or identical to such sites as the Blair Cuspids and Sea of Storms structures on the Moon and those of the Utopia region of Mars. Professor and Dr. A. S. Thom believe that Carnac was a lunar observatory site focused on a variety of stones in the complex, the largest one of which was the now-fallen seventy-foot-long stone in four pieces called *Er Grah* ("the Stone of the Fairies") or *Le Grand Menhir Brise* ("the Great Broken Menhir"). When whole, this stone would have weighed approximately three hundred tons. Evans-Wentz also believed there was a planned solar construction similarity between New Grange (a solstitially aligned megalithic burial mound located twenty-six miles north of Dublin) and the Great Pyramid, basing that belief on the oft-suspected but unproven theory that the Pyramid is connected by a hidden causeway to the Sphinx—if true, then its orientation according to Evans-Wentz is identical to the neolithic (c. 3,300 BC) New Grange.

Nor are these building or calendrical similarities restricted to the British Isles, Brittany, and Egypt. Celtic scholars and anthropologists have long worked at proving that the Celts were in North America in antiquity. Retired ranger Erlen Trekell wandered the miles around southeastern Colorado's Crack Cave in the 420,000-acre Comanche National Grassland near Springfield for fifteen years, finding drawings of longships with dragon's-heads and what he believes are messages in several ancient languages about stellar conjunctions. Retired engineer William McGlone and Phillip Leonard, authors of *Ancient American Inscriptions: Plow Marks or History?,* believe the scratch marks at many separate sites in the same region are *ogam,* an early Celtic alphabet apparently sometimes using no vowels—the same "Ogham" referred to earlier as the invention of the Dagda's eldest son, the Great God. While the traditional view is that they are plow marks, or an early American Indian form of counting, McGlone and Leonard stated in the

March 21, 1994, *Rocky Mountain News* that more than one Celtic scholar has confirmed their translations of the rock scratches as accurate predictions of equinoctial solar activity.

"It's an old form of Celtic, and says things about the sun will happen," says McGlone. "And they do happen . . . At three sites at equinox, the sun interacts with the writing as the writing predicts. It doesn't prove there were Celts here, but it makes the objective person want to look at it." One of these sites is at the sun temple near La Junta, where the sun fills a slot between the horizon and a rock outcropping only on the days halfway between solstice and equinox, as its Ogham inscription says it will. The most impressive among dozens of these sites is Crack Cave, where for nine minutes every fall and spring equinox the scratches are visible, by virtue of the shadows cast across them by the sun. The Ogham inscription accurately describes the course daylight will follow across its hidden pattern at equinox sunrise, the only time at which the pattern is visible. Equally impressive is Rochester Creek, where a number of petroglyphs are found with remarkable similarity both in subject and composition to Egyptian hieroglyphs. Oklahoma also has such sites. One of these, "Anubis Cave"—so named for its rock carvings closely resembling that god, even with attendant flail—depicts what seems to be an Egyptian *serakh,* or sun temple, which are also seen on Semitic coins. It is accompanied by what appears to be a Libyan inscription, *ata laila dayan Bel yafidu antana,* which Harvard's Barry Fell translates as "Enact at sunset the rites of Bel, assembling at that hour in worship." Cecil Pascal's *The Cults of Cisalpine Gaul* documents Anubis altars found in Celtic territories of France, Spanish Granada, and Hungary. Meter-high inscriptions of Egyptian nature on barely accessible rock faces of the Amazonia-Brazilian federal state of Mato Grosso, apparently four to five thousand years old, are meticulously collected and studied in Alfredo Brandao's two-volume *A Escripta Prehistorica do Brasil.*

Not only Ogham and Egyptian, but also Arabic, Phoenician, Libyan, Tifinag, Chinese, Burmese, and Paliburmese inscriptions (and a few that are unknown) were discovered by Mexican archaeologist Neil Steede and San Diego's Epigraphic Society on 3,671 bricks of the Mayan port city of Comalcalco (about 3 percent of the total then excavated and analyzed), listed in Steede's 1984 *Preliminary Catalogue of the Comalcalco Bricks* for the Mexican National Institute of Anthropology and History. Like numerous other sites in the Americas, Comalcalco also depicts a great many elephants among its hieroglyphs, which by all traditional theories have never lived in the Western Hemisphere. The fact that the writing is on comparatively few bricks, placed in buildings so as not to be visible, leads Fell to conclude that they were first used for practice in a language school, then employed for building. Fell and Steede believe that the languages employed necessitate the dating of the city to at least 0–400 AD, rather than the presently held 700–900 AD.

Though the archaeological and anthropological communities are generally opposed to the theory of Celts in the Americas and contend that there is no hard evidence for it, they admit that "the slashes deserve more study." As the *News* article so neatly summarized about Crack Cave, "Lost among the debates about artifacts, linguistics, astronomy, [and] old world contamination of new world cultures is any discussion about the theoretical Celts: What were they doing in southeastern Colorado, and how did they get there?" Ogham inscriptions have been discovered not only in Scandinavia, Malta, and even New England, but also North and South Africa, standing as strong evidence that a single original culture must once have existed that traveled all over the world.

South African Bantu tribal historian and anthropologist Credo Mutwa, author of *Indaba, My Children,* shows his people's "magic slate" in Witwatersrand is a record of Ogham, and says that Zimbabwe's people are descendants of red-haired, red-skinned men who knew all about space travel, radioactivity, and robots. They also have "thunderbird" totems like those of North American Indians, which may well be the legacy of Horus in Egypt. An Ogham rock inscription on the Riet River at Driekops Eiland in the Republic of South Africa was discovered by Barry Fell to be in three-thousand-year-old Canaanite language, saying, "Under constant attack, we have quit this place to occupy a safe stronghold," and Orville L. Hope's *6000 Years of Seafaring* cites an interesting Celtic custom practiced as recently as 1983 by Swaziland natives, learned from a race of "Pink Men" (who he says are Mutwa's "red-skinned" men), of stiffening and bleaching their hair with lime. The Pink Men had red, yellow, or black hair, and blue, green, or brown eyes, and Hope believes they formed the Sabean civilization in southern Arabia sometime around 2,000 BC.

Other formerly supposed "Celtic" inscriptions can be found the world over: "cup marks." Sometimes referred to as "mazes" or "cup-and-ring" markings, these are semicircular (in more or less a "hoof" shape), square, or rectangular and are self-replicating patterns diminishing inside the enclosure of the glyph, looking rather like a target zeroing in toward its "bull's-eye." They almost all have an opening in one side, some of them with curved lines attached to a central dot that look either like a snake or a spermatozoa. Some are instead spirals, but otherwise similar. In addition to Brittany, Great Britain, and Ireland, these patterns can be seen in Dupaix's *Monuments of New Spain* and Lord Kingsborough's fourth volume of *Antiquities of Mexico,* and J. Simpson's *Archaic Sculpturings* shows them in India, where they are called *mahadeos.* Charles Berlitz's *Mysteries from Forgotten Worlds* has comparative reproductions from pre-Columbian Ecuador and the Hopi dwellings of North America. They are also found plentifully throughout the Mediterranean, especially in the ruins of Minoan Crete, and in ancient terra cotta "intestine-faced" masks of the Sumerian Humbaba (or Huwawa), the "Creator/Guardian of the cedar of paradise," strengthening the connection with the maze. Humbaba's "intestine"/maze-face also bears a remarkable resemblance to that of the goggled Aztec rain god, Tlaloc, which is formed by two sinuous serpents.

The ancient Egyptians—who, as should have been demonstrated, are almost certainly the same people as the Celts—are equally proven to have traveled the world over, despite the insistence of traditional theory that they had no transoceanic contact. The Cairo Museum's mummy room exhibits dehydrated grains found in tombs and pyramids, among which is maize: yellow corn. It is plainly marked as such by the exhibit's card. Perhaps Osiris' being referred to as "the god of the corn" is more literal than has hitherto been supposed. This standing contradiction begs the question of why history books still hold that yellow corn was uniquely a product of the Americas, and that there was no connection between the Old World and the New until the last five hundred years.

The same museum's famous King Tut exhibit on the second floor also displays, in two wall cases, up to perhaps thirty "magic wands" discovered among the pharaoh's burial accoutrements—not only are they identical to boomerangs, but David Hatcher Childress reported in *Lost Cities and Ancient Mysteries of Africa and Arabia* that at least as recently as 1989, there was even an Australian boomerang between the two cases to graphically illustrate their resemblance. The second volume of Gaston Maspero's *History of Egypt* clearly showed as early as 1906 an illustration of an Egyptian with a boomerang, accompanied by the specific caption, "Hunting with a boomerang and fishing with a double-edged harpoon." The Anthropology Museum in Mexico City depicts the Hopi using boomerangs, and Mayan hieroglyphs indicate their use in Mexico as well. Childress' *Lost Cities of North and Central America* documents Dr. Carl Clausen's discovery both in western Texas and Little Salt Springs, Florida, of curved throwing sticks, bull-roarers, and nonreturning oak L-shaped killing boomerangs, carbon-dated between 9,080 and 9,572 years old. He also discusses the Egyptian/Australian boomerang connection in *Lost Cities of Ancient Lemuria and the Pacific,* commenting that they have been found in Denmark as well. Pawel Valde-Nowak of Krakow's Polish Academy of Sciences reported, in issue 132 of Science News in 1987, the discovery of a curved mammoth tusk approximately twenty-three thousand years old in southern Poland, 27 inches long, 0.6 inches thick, and 2.3 inches wide, which he and his colleagues called "the world's oldest boomerang." After Thor Heyerdahl proved that the simplest reed raft can cross the oceans, it is absurd for even the most conservative of historians not to at least consider the plentiful evidence for Egyptian transoceanic voyages in antiquity.

A connection between ancient Egypt and Australia would also answer with ease a question that has always plagued Egyptologists: what is the Set animal? All the gods of Egypt are represented by animals that are easily identifiable—except Set. His animal, seen either fully reclining or sitting on its haunches, has long ears, a long, bent snout, a very long, powerful-looking tail, and enormous feet. It has been compared by various Egyptologists to a camel, a giraffe, a jerboa, a pig, or even a warthog, and even in desperation to some form of extinct dog, none of which it really looks like. There is no animal it clearly resembles in Egypt, but there is one it is virtually identical to in Australia: the kangaroo. What makes this most interesting is the frequency with which the Set animal appears on the "magic wands" that so closely resemble boomerangs. Budge even refers to the magic wands as "throw sticks" involved in hunting, specifically calling attention to one in the British Museum upon which is plainly depicted the Set animal (which he uses as evidence that it must be an extinct hunting dog, suggested to be related to the Arab saluki even as he admits that the ears and tail are not quite correct), yet no Egyptologist has advanced the simple proposition that these are Australian boomerangs, and Set, a kangaroo. From the Fifth to the Nineteenth Dynasties, Set was extremely popular, kings especially delighting in attaching his name to their own for his outstanding character-istics of valor and military prowess. In that light, the kangaroo and the "magic wand throw sticks" being associated with him make perfect sense: kangaroos are among the fiercest fighting creatures on the face of the earth.

But there is one other extremely important piece of evidence connecting the Celts with Egypt, and it is the strongest: it is the Egyptian history of the Hyksos, an invading people called "the Shepherd Kings," represented pictorially with a shepherd's crook among the cartouche items of their name, but whose nomer derives from the words *hekau,* or "magician" (specifically technological magic, as we would understand it), and *khaswt,* meaning "foreign hill countries." In other words, they were the "wizards of the hills," the same title given the "Don" branch of the Welsh Mabinogi. They first ruled Egypt, peacefully, in its remote prehistory, then returned after a long absence to establish a much more oppressive rule for perhaps two hundred years before the New Kingdom was estab-lished. Some historians believe the Hyksos to have been the advanced Hittites of Turkey. Josephus thought the Hyksos rule was when Moses and the Exodus occurred, an opinion shared by some other ancient historians. Many Egyptologists consider the entire story of the Hyksos to be mythical, meaning in their view that it never happened, where more likely it did actually transpire in our understanding of mythology as forgotten history that has simply been misunderstood.

No one questions that the Hyksos were superior in weaponry to the Egyptians, which was how they effortlessly took over. They taught the Egyptians metalworking and technological advances, as did Cuillan and Lugh in the Celtic mythology. One of their kings was named "Khian," meaning "Prince of the deserts" (the last word having connotations beyond the mundane which have just been considered), whose symbol was the lion—as in "the Lion of Judah," the house from which the biblical savior is born. "Kian" is also the name of one of the Danaan, who sired Lugh, the avenger (Horus), and the Hyksos' conquering of the Egyptians matches the myth of the Danaan's conquest of the equally primitive and weaponless Fir Bolgs. The Thebans eventually rose up and overthrew the Hyksos exactly as Lugh overthrew the tyrannical Bres and the Fomorians, and for the same reason of gross economic oppression.

Another of the Hyksos kings was Apophis or Apepa, the exact name of the sea serpent with which Ra daily did battle. Another still was Nubti, "but some think that Nubti was the god Set," as E. A. Wallis Budge says. And Sutekh—who is simply another avatar of Set—was the god most worshipped during the Hyksos occupation. It was after the Hyksos were expelled that idols of Set were savagely defaced and he came to be regarded as the god of evil. Formerly, as just mentioned, he had been held in equal esteem with his brother Horus, with whom he was often depicted establishing the foundations of Egypt and escorting the deceased up the ladder to heaven. He is seen with Horus pouring life over Pharaoh Seti I, and an illustration exists of him personally teaching Pharaoh Thutmose III archery. He was even shown spearing Ra's enemy, the aforementioned sea serpent Apep, from the prow of the solar barque—the same position where later Horus and Thoth would be shown spearing Set, as a wild boar. Not only do these parallels connect the Celts and the Egyptians more strongly, but they suggest greater connection with the fall of Lucifer in the Bible, strengthening the Egyptian origin of that book's history and teachings, and once more raising the question as to whether or not some of its characters are actually of the Danaan race.

That the ancient fertility cults are the original practices and beliefs upon which all of the Judaeo-Christian tradition rests there can be no doubt whatsoever, and that Egypt was the origin of those fertility cult beliefs is highly probable. One could question their inspiration being the Danaan/Watchers, but the evidence is greatly in favor of it. Though fragmentary, the Celtic texts and lore give us one of the best examples for studying the race apparently behind both the ancient religions and the modern UFO phenomenon, largely because the supposedly pagan roots in Celtic countries are still extremely strong and the belief in the Fairy Folk is very much alive.

That evidence—which is not in conflict with any provided by the Egyptians or Hebrews—shows the Danaan to be a nature-loving race, well bred, naturally aristocratic, cultured, and mannered, to whom good morals and good fellowship are extremely important, as are social equality and learning. As the name "Watchers" implies, the Danaan keep an eye on human affairs and take it upon themselves to serve as behind-the-scenes instructors, guides, testers, and even sometimes judges. They form liaisons with chosen individuals in the human community, up to and including ongoing sexual relations resulting in offspring, and recruit people to help them in their battles and other concerns, even (in extremely rare instances) taking human beings away to live with them permanently. They prefer to remain an unseen influence, but are fond of practical jokes as a signature of their presence. An interesting side note is that the circular phosphorescent fungal growths referred to as "fairy rings" not infrequently appear at the sites of reported UFO landings.

Having considered the ancient evidence and brought it back full circle to the living Fairy Faith of Celtic countries, it is time to consider what has been learned, summarize findings, and contemplate what it all means.

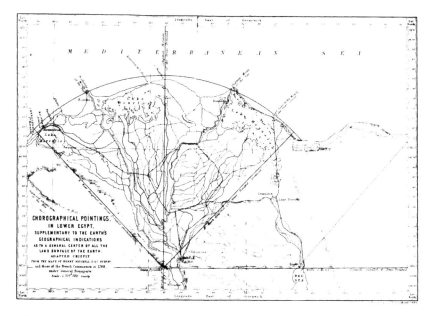

Figure 25. Rendering by Napoleon's savants showing the Pyramid's accurate orientation to the four cardinal points, its neat division of the Delta region in half, and its geometrical centering in the region. None of this could have been accomplished without advanced geodetic and astronomical knowledge. From Peter Tompkins, *Secrets of the Great Pyramid* (New York: Harper & Row, 1971).

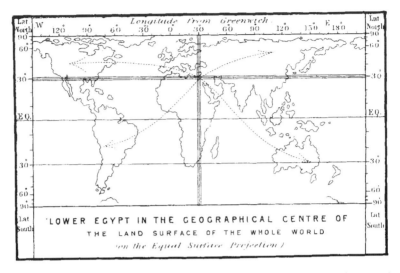

Figure 26. Charles Piazzi Smyth, Astronomer Royal of Scotland, recorded in *Our Inheritance in the Great Pyramid* (1864) that the ancient wonder of the world was situated dead center of the Earth's land mass, as depicted on the Equal Surface Projection map. All world mythologies place a sacred tree or Mountain of the Gods at the center of the world, which connects the Earth with the worlds of Heaven.

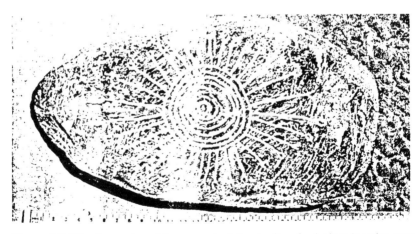

Figure 27. "Tjuringa stone" from central Australia, depicting Atonist sun art from Egypt circa 1,000 BC. From the *Australian Post,* Dec. 12, 1981, p. 9.

Figure 28. "Hunting with a boomerang and fishing with a double-edged harpoon," an illustration from Volume 2 of Gaston Maspero's *History of Egypt* (London: Grolier Society, 1906).

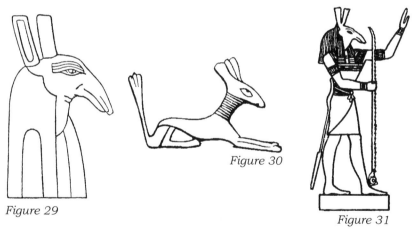

Figure 30

Figure 29

Figure 31

Figures 29–31. Three images of Set and a "throw stick" (usually referred to as "magic wands," see Figure 30, page 406) from the British Museum. The Set animal has never been identified, but most closely resembles a kangaroo, which exhibits Set's most notable characteristic, ferocity in battle. Despite boomerangs having been documented in ancient Egypt, maize being found in Egyptian tombs, and Thor Heyerdahl's successful traversing of the oceans on simple rafts, traditional theory does not accept contact between Egypt and other continents in antiquity. (E. A. Wallis Budge, *The Mummy* (1893) (New York: Dover Books, 1989) and *From Fetish to God in Ancient Egypt* (1934) (New York: Dover Books, 1988).

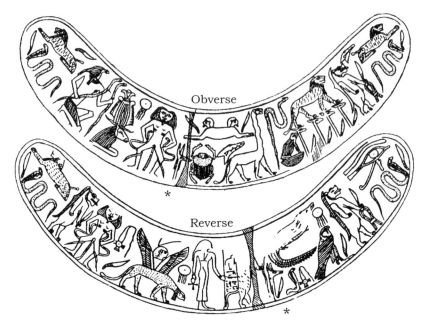

Figure 32. See caption for figures 27–29. The head of Set is shown by the asterisk.

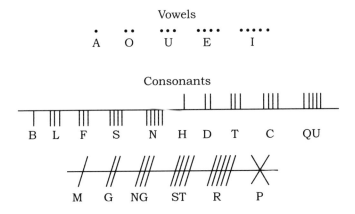

Figure 33: Ogham Alphabet. Scholars disagree as to the antiquity of this Celtic script, but it has been found in South Africa and in Colorado caves.

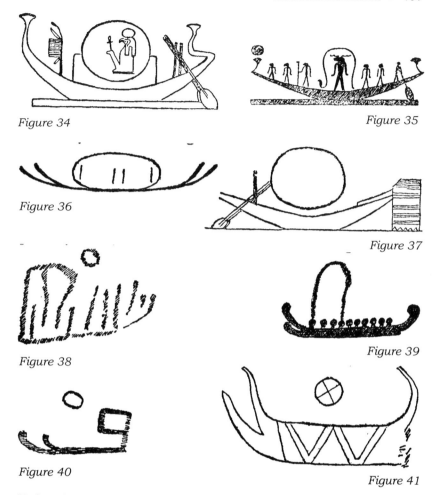

Figure 34

Figure 35

Figure 36

Figure 37

Figure 38

Figure 39

Figure 40

Figure 41

"Solar Ships" around the world, illustrating that the ancient Egyptians were far more traveled than traditional theory can account for. The similarities are startling.

Figure 34: Egyptian Bark, with figure of Ra holding an *Ankh,* enclosed in Solar Disk. XIX Dynasty. From the British Museum.

Figure 35: Egyptian Solar Bark, with god Khnemu and attendant deities From the British Museum.

Figure 36: Ship Carving (with Solar Emblem?) from Scania, Sweden. (after Du Chaillu).

Figure 37: Egyptian Solar Bark, XXII Dynasty. From the British Museum.

Figure 38: Solar Ship (with Sail?) from New Grange, Ireland.

Figure 39: Ship (with Sail?) from Ryxö (after Du Chaillu).

Figure 40: Solar Ship from Loc mariaker, Brittany (after Ferguson).

Figure 41: Solar Ship from Hallande, Sweden (after Montelius).

Figure 42: "Cup-and-ring" markings, theoretically Celtic, also are found around the world. The ancient Celts and the ancient Egyptians were the same people.

Figure 43: Labyrinth designs used in pre-Columbian Ecuador (left) compared with two labyrinth patterns traditionally employed by the Hopi Indians. Other designs showing labyrinth appear throughout the Mediterranean, especially centered in the Minoan civilization of ancient Crete, with its fearsome legend of the Minotaur.

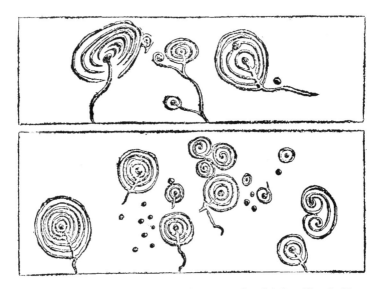

Figure 44: Cup-and-ring markings from Scotland (after Sir. J. Simpson).

Figure 45

Figure 46

The "Blair Cuspids" discovered on the moon.

Figure 45: The photos taken by artificial satellites.

Figure 46: Their triangulation. From Peter Kolosimo, *Not of this World* (Secaucus, New Jersey: University Books, 1971).

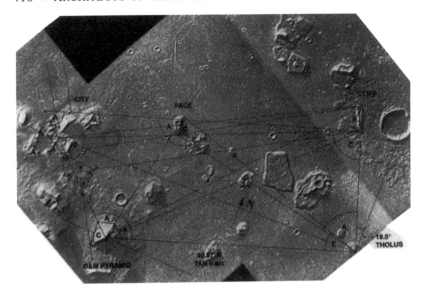

Angles		Angle Ratios	Trig. Functions
degrees	radians		
A = 60.0	= π.3	C/A = √2	TAN A = √3
B = 120.0	= 2π/3	B/D = √3	TAN B = –√3
C = 85.3		C/F = √3	SIN A = e/π
D = 69.4	= e/√5	A/D = e/π	SIN B = e/π
E = 34.7		C/D = e/√5	TAN F = π/e
F = 49.6	= e/π	A/F = e/√5	COS E = √5/e
G = 45.1		H/G = e/√5	SIN G = √5/π
H = 55.3		C/B = √5/π	SIN C = 1
I = 100.4		D/F = π/√5	TAN G = 1
			TAN I = –2e
			TAN 40.87°w = e/π

Figure 47

Figures 47 and 48: Mathematical correlations of the Martian Cydonia region discovered by Erol Torun, confirmed by him and Richard Hoagland, and later modified and updated by the Mars Mission group. Original Viking photo enhancement by Dr. Mark J. Carlotto. David Myers proposed the polar diameter correlaries, confirmed by Hoagland and Torun. From Richard C. Hoagland, *The Monuments of Mars* (Berkeley, California: North Atlantic Books, 1987, 1992). Used by permission of the publisher and the photographer.

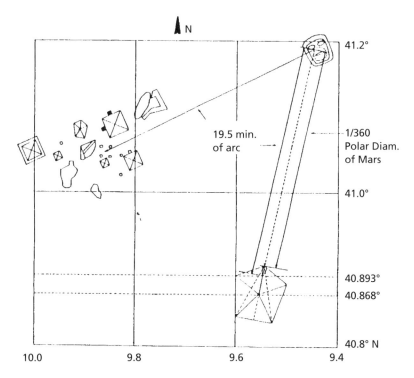

Figure 48

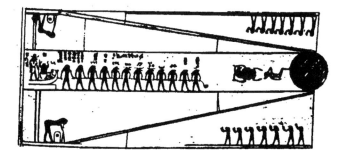

Figure 49. Illustration from the Papyrus of Queen Nejmet, showing "the Red Eye of Horus." The same illustration can be found reversed in the tomb of Ramesses VI, with the caption "The great secret." The accompanying inscription reads, "The god is like this. He bends over the mysterious mound, in the interior of which is the great secret." Courtesy of Zecharia Sitchin, from *The Stairway to Heaven*.

Figure 50. Ancient Egyptian rendering of Ra-Harakhte, considered to be the Sphinx, built by Ra in his own image (a hawk) in the Sacred Desert, also called "the Red Land." The enormous serpent-encircled disk is red. Also known as Hor-Tesher, Ra-Harakhte was the god of Mars in Egyptian mythology, specifically described as a hawk-head with a star above it. From *Myths and Legends of Ancient Egypt* (1915) by Lewis Spence, courtesy Dover Books (New York: 1990).

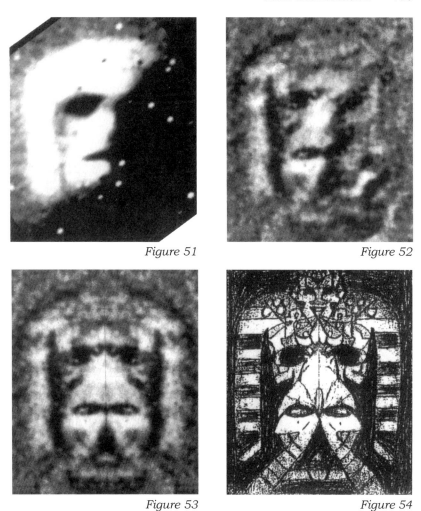

Figure 51

Figure 52

Figure 53

Figure 54

Figure 51: Original NASA photo of the Face in Cydonia.

Figure 52: Photographic enhancement by Dr. Mark J. Carlotto of The Analytic Science Corporation.

Figure 53: Richard Hoagland's mirror-imaging of Carlotto's enhancement, showing the lit side in complete symmetry.

Figure 54: The author's own sketch enrichment, detailing and cleaning-up the information already in the picture. It is Ra-Harakhte, the hawk-headed Sphinx, complete with the diadem of legend as the star-shaped human face on the forehead. The overlapping of the beak is evident even in the cruder enhancements. From Richard C. Hoagland, *The Monuments of Mars* (Berkeley, California: North Atlantic Books, 1987, 1992). Used by permission of the publisher and the photographer.

Figure 55. A reproduction from Rolf Müller of a sixteenth-century Spanish woodcut illustrating the gold sun face that used to hang in the Holy of Holies at the Temple of the Sun in Cuzco. Note its resemblance to the solar diadem on Ra's forehead in Cydonia.

Figure 56

Figure 57

Figure 58

Figures 56, 57, and 58. Different contrasts of the Cliff face in Cydonia discovered by Daniel Drasin and enhanced by Mark J. Carlotto, further enhanced by the author to reveal its configuration as the striped face of a mandrill baboon, an avatar of Thoth. The enhancement shows what appear to be two additional simian faces above it, a chimpanzee and a gorilla. (From Richard C. Hoagland, *The Monuments of Mars* Berkeley, California: North Atlantic Books, 1987, 1992). Used by permission of the publisher and the photographer.

ARQ UR

Tomorrow Is Yesterday

11

Conclusions

I N JULY OF 1947, a piloted, maneuverable aerial vehicle, originating from somewhere off this planet, crashed near Roswell, New Mexico, concluding the prologue to a longstanding government question as to the nature of unidentified flying objects officially witnessed worldwide for over a decade previous. Wreckage and robot pilots were recovered from that craft, and swiftly sequestered by the Army Air Corps at various locations, most material going to Wright (now Wright-Patterson) Field, where it probably remains to this day. Technical laboratories experimented with the recovered material primarily for weapons exploitation, with knowledge of the results and ongoing investigation going to an elite group of top brass, research scientists, and government representatives, membership rotating as necessary. Witnesses to the Roswell crash were heavily intimidated and/or bought, though their later testimony and that of government representatives at varying levels on the inside have made the evidence clear enough to determine the truth today.

Added bureaucracy immediately following the Roswell crash, in the form of the Air Force (newly separated from the Army) and the Central Intelligence Agency, helped compartmentalize, prioritize, and make more secure the protection of this elite knowledge, which was and is classified higher in secrecy than the H-bomb. Simultaneously, sham investigative units such as Project Blue Book were arranged by the Air Force to speciously examine the UFO question and offer palliatives to both the public and the government itself. The FBI was duped for a brief time into making their hoaxed frauds look authentic toward this end, and a handful of scientists were bought to make appearances even better. Two highly visible and publicized appearances of UFOs over the White House (and other world government centers), combined with the discovery of ongoing monitoring and sabotage activities at military and industrial atomic sites, contributed to the creation of an even more powerful research unit, the National Security Agency—then as now the world's largest and most secret intelligence branch with no available charter or public accountability, answerable solely to the president. While this was done almost completely behind closed doors, the public was given a palliative in the 1953 CIA-sponsored Robertson Panel, which debunked the subject altogether for the press while giving recommendations to the government on how to continue its investigations in private. The sheer hypocrisy of the government alienated some of its best men into quitting the military in order to independently speak out on what facts they knew.

The Robertson Panel recommended that the media be used disinformationally to deflect attention from the subject. This manifested in documentaries as specious as the panel itself and in the filming of deliberately comical or just plain bad movies centering around UFOs. Prior to this, the medium had been tested as a method to safely introduce some of the facts that were being discovered in an effort to prepare the public for eventual disclosure of the reality at hand. Extending to cartoons and television shows, this policy remains in effect today but undergoes periodic changes in focus of intent depending on the political undercurrent. Civilian UFO groups were infiltrated by the CIA according to the panel's suggestion, and private citizens involved in UFO research were illegally spied upon. To what extent this activity continues is unclear, but can be presumed as still highly active if the large number of ex-intelligence people in UFO organizations today is any indicator.

The government began investigating the possibility that the race behind the unknown spacecraft was one parallel to our own, and connected to human life from antiquity, no later than 1958. In that period NASA was formed for space exploration and the Brookings Document speculated that our discovery of alien artifacts on Mars, the Moon, and Venus was inevitable. By 1966 the presence of a past celestial race became a certainty, when Soviet lunar probes photographed regular structures in the Sea of Storms and the Blair Cuspids were discovered in the Moon's Sea of Tranquility, the latter being the first landing spot of the Apollo missions. Astronomers' records make it conceivable that limited government study of some of these extraterrestrial artifacts began many decades prior. Additional circumstantial evidence exists, in both the production and handling of the earliest flying saucer movies (e.g., *Invaders from Mars* of 1953), that reveals the government was aware that UFOs were robot-piloted spacecraft, which were guided by another race of humans coming from Mars, abducting human beings and implanting them. It is impossible that officials had not discovered the Martian connection any later than 1961, because they could not have been unaware of the findings of Jacques and Janine Vallée and Pierre Guérin. It is more likely they made those same discoveries independently much earlier. Given the intense interest and secrecy concerning the subject of UFOs, and its being of worldwide concern for every conceivable reason, it seems a safe bet to assume that any discovery announced publicly was always made far earlier by the intelligence teams. Government awareness of the Martian connection continues to be evidenced in the dissembling over the discoveries of the Viking probes in 1976, as well as subsequent Mars probes.

By the late fifties and early sixties, it appears that the media experimented with a more genuinely informative program, a forerunner to a later-proposed educational program. Intelligent science fiction was produced in Britain and the United States that explored the secretly known UFOlogical themes and elements in government files in such a way as to begin subtly acquainting the public mind with them. The disinformational/deflectional entertainments never ceased, though their proportion to the informational pieces varies. The worldwide-disseminated *Star Trek* was produced in a period spanning the discovery of the Blair Cuspids and man's first landings at that location on the Moon. Under President Jimmy Carter—who had promised to open files on UFOs since he was himself a witness to one—probably the best-budgeted informational media program was implemented, no doubt given an assist by the discoveries of the Viking probes the very year of his election. The reversion of science fiction to Us vs. Them shoot-'em-ups occurred under Ronald Reagan and George Bush, coincidentally with greater blockages of the Freedom of Information Act, increased (and virtually unchecked) intelligence and disinformational activity, and the largest military buildup in history with the High Frontier/SDI/Star Wars program.

Reagan's own political attitude against the Russians changed by the end of his administration, and to just what extent the discoveries of the Russian probes *Phobos 1* and *2* altered subsequent international diplomacy cannot be judged but can be assumed to have been of some importance. There is every indicator that all world governments are aware of the reality of UFOs and have always taken them very seriously, but it is debatable exactly how much they know or what influence the knowledge has had politically. The likelihood of military exploitation for personal profit, given their control of information and history of exactly such manipulation, must seriously be considered. Elected officials seem to have little knowledge of the subject, and are blocked in every instance that they try to gain more. The military, the intelligence agencies, and the president (by virtue of executive privilege with the NSA) are therefore in a unique position of power in their isolated knowledge of the subject, and potentials for exploitation are immense.

In 1958 Aerial Phenomena Research Organization investigator Olavo Fontes put it this way: "Only the persons who work on the problem know the real situation: intelligence officers in the Army, Navy and Air Force; some high-ranking officers in the High Command; the National Security Council and a few scientists whose activities are connected with it; and a few members of certain civilian organizations doing research for military projects. All information about the UFO subject from the military is not only classified or reserved for official uses, it is *top secret*. Civilian authorities and military officers in general are not entitled to know. Even our President is not informed of the whole truth." Concurring with Fontes' assessment is author Timothy Good, who was told by "a high-ranking defense official" that "he was once privy to above top secret [*sic*] information (*not* UFO-related) that only about fifty people had access to. The 'compartment' list did not include either the Minister of Defense or the Prime Minister."

As to the nature of the interplanetary craft in question, both they and the traces they leave behind are consistent. Reputable scientists have gone on record from the earliest sightings as being certain that these UFOs are intelligently controlled vehicles, even speculating on the nature of their propulsion and equipment based on the observable data. Though there are variations, sufficient reports exist in the public realm to determine their reality. The craft are most often described as egg-shaped; they move silently and with phenomenal accelerations and decelerations, wobble periodically in flight, and are usually seen as glowing brightly red at some point in the encounter; they frequently employ remote-controlled objects both in the air and on the ground—the latter being robots, also of recognizable and generally consistent designs; and the UFOs are most often perceived as being helicopters until their behavior proves otherwise. They have technology enabling them seemingly to pass through solid matter and levitate objects, and to paralyze the will and all but completely repress the memories of human beings.

Their full agenda cannot presently be known, but a great deal is apparent and certain deductions can be made both from their actions and witness testimony. Foremost, they plainly have no hostile intent. They evade when pursued, fire only when fired upon, and despite unquestionable superiority do not exploit their advantage in any discernible attempt for invasion or conquest. They are plainly unfriendly to American military buildup, and all indications are that their inimical nature to military forces is unilateral around the world. They have continually and persistently monitored the development of Earth's industrial and military capacity from their first appearance in the modern age. Sabotage of nuclear weaponry appears to be a regular occurrence. So is the mutilation of cattle and other animals, seemingly for the purpose of appropriating genetic material. What specific use that material has for the intelligence operating the craft cannot be ascertained.

Human liaison is one of their primary concerns, a number of people being repetitively visited and temporarily abducted. One of the purposes of this contact seems to be the establishment of ambassadors between them and us, the indications being that the extraterrestrials are in the process of gradually preparing our world for a more open relationship. Human reproduction is involved in this program, for reasons not fully clear. So is a certain amount of training in the operation of the visitors' craft and equipment. These are both indicative of a long-term relationship, not a transitory phenomenon. Robots are used as escorts to and from the ships, and for virtually all activity requiring any form of manual manipulation on Earth. Surgery is often employed on abductees, apparently to assist the reproduction program and to secure implants, the probable purpose of the latter being for location in subsequent visits and communication. While the contacts due to their very nature sometimes frighten or confuse the participants, the portrayal in the media of the experience as an inescapable nightmare is more indicative of a disinformation program than the long-term experience reported by the abductees.

The likeliest candidates for the intelligence behind the craft are that race historically called "the gods," under a variety of names: Anunnaki, Elohim, Nefilim, Watchers, Tuatha de Danaan, and the like. The rationale for this is the continuity of historical precedent, the demonstrably human intelligence exhibited in the aliens' knowledge and behavior, the ongoing nature of the activity (which argues against an alien survey mission that would long ago have obtained all the information it needs), descriptions from witnesses, and the apparent fact that reproduction is occurring between our two species. Acknowledging limitations and hidden codes within mythology, a great deal can still be learned about this race from combining myth texts about them with observational science and some intuition. First, more than one race may be involved in UFO activity. Though there is a tremendous consistency in behavior on their part, there are rare exceptions. This could denote either a lack of complete solidarity concerning us, on the part of a single race, or more than one race. Little or no evidence exists for races other than human in origin behind the UFOs, either in the present day or in antiquity, though of course the possibility cannot be ruled out entirely. An early generation of this race, along with Earth's human race that appears to have been created initially to be mining slaves, was all but completely destroyed in a cosmic catastrophe which we remember as the Flood, between (at best present guesses) approximately six thousand to thirteen thousand years ago. Many among this early extraterrestrial community became hopelessly corrupt and subverted our race into criminal behavior like their own.

Survivors from both their race and ours eventually met again, beginning with their reeducation of our race in the arts of civilization and the elimination of human sacrifice. At least three or four generations or different races of technologically advanced people are listed in the Celtic mythology, with counterparts in other world myths, as well as our own primitive Earthbound race, which they (Danaan and Fomorians) conquered with extreme ease and ruled over in peace for some time before being torn apart themselves by civil war. At one point, their fear of our potential to rival them caused them to disperse us over the Earth and "confuse our speech." Man became embroiled in their conflicts, which appear to have been between two central gods, political parties or races, or combinations thereof. A second world conflagration, apparently nuclear, occurred at some later time (perhaps four thousand years ago), which may even have extended to our Moon and Mars, the latter a base of theirs for at least the last 450,000 to half a million years if the historian Berossus' dating and that of the Cydonia complex are correct. The conflict went into abatement under terms, but never fully concluded.

Though communications between the space races and our own continued, they were severely curtailed and went underground. Man's civilization degenerated, his science becoming all but nonexistent for hundreds of years. The Danaan (a collective convention-name, to avoid confusion), always jealous of their technology and secrets, were demonized by the various religions that guarded the traditions established by them long ago, since corrupted by man through ignorance. From active persecution by the Church of contactees between their race and ours in the Dark Ages, man progressed to the point that he dealt with the problem through ridicule or derision by Science instead, in time ascribing the space races to personifications of psychological projections (archetypes), bedtime fables, and sanitized surrogates such as fairies, the boogeyman, and Santa Claus.

One of these advanced races has from the earliest times taken mankind under their protection, for whatever reason. They have involved themselves in battles for liberty wherever oppression occurs, overtly in antiquity and covertly since, from the revolt of the mining slaves to the Exodus to (possibly) the French and American Revolutions, evidence for which is circumstantial but abundant. They keep an ever-watchful eye on us, probably because we are an ongoing concern of theirs. Being architects and engineers on a planetary scale, they seem to have literally made Earth a life-giving planet from the time of its origin in a cataclysmic cosmic collision. We are their descendants, a proxy colony of caretakers for their property.

The Danaan themselves are reported to be an aristocratic race of hunters, scientists, and poets, preferring their privacy and able to make themselves invisible but keeping touch with the human race. Having fought wars of their own in the past, they are opposed to them now. Their architecture is a marvel in mathematics and engineering beyond our own capacity to do anything more than appreciate. "Music" is their principal "magic," meaning the controlled use of sound waves to lift and move massive objects possibly up to and including planet-sized bodies, though the technology probably has its limitations. Their megaliths serve a variety of functions, being used for geodetic markers, recorders of mathematical measurements, observatories, and in some cases (at least at one time) as military strongholds. Everything about them is simultaneously simple and complex. Their graphics communicate on at least three levels at the same time, being pictorial, mathematical, and verbal. The verbal also communicates on at least two levels at once, almost invariably incorporating puns and double entendres.

When they interact with man, it is through his dreams and in riddles, a pattern consistent with Yahweh in the Bible and a variety of identical gods in all cultures, seeming to prefer inspiring from behind the scenes to any kind of direct communication. When overt contact is necessary, they assume the guise of the Virgin Mary, the Corn Mother, angels, kachinas, or whatever appropriate cultural equivalent exists. There is strong circumstantial evidence for this race's continual intervention on a number of levels in man's development, from the crudely physical to the artistic, scientific, and esoteric. They cover their tracks with hypnosis, and probably drugs or some other high technology, to cloud the memories of their visitants. Their rituals and ways of life derive from a worship of the harmony of nature, and the mastery of the mind of man (to which their race also belongs) over it. It was this particular quality about them that the Greeks embodied, albeit less than perfectly, causing modern-day man to mistakenly attribute Greece with the foundation of Western culture instead of Egypt—but it is typical of the Danaan to prefer it that way since they invariably hid their wisdom from all but the smallest circle of priestly initiates.

There has never been a time in (terrestrial) man's history when these people were absent, and nothing occurring in today's UFO and abduction phenomena has not been recorded throughout. The only difference today is that there is much more evidence of the encounters, and contact is becoming increasingly visible. The mythical record the world over speaks of a Golden Age in which man and the gods (or angels) freely and openly interacted, and all such records have prophesied that a time would come when a new Golden Age would occur, all former secrets being revealed. Given the tremendous increase of activity on the part of this ancient race, and especially its ongoing and intimately personal nature on a large scale, it is not unreasonable to assume that we are presently undergoing the transition into that new Golden Age.

Three notable prophecies that have never been clearly understood make perfect sense in light of these present-day phenomena. Two are quatrains of Nostradamus for the end times. Nostradamus cannot be considered solely a "metaphysical" source, since his exact prophecy of Louis Pasteur's fame, by name, month, year, and field came to pass centuries after his death. One quatrain—*Century X, 72*—specifically says that "Mars will reign for a good cause," usually given the inaccurate translation of "Fear and terror will reign," which is not at all what the words say *(Avant que Mars régner par bonheur)*. The other quatrain—*X, 42*—with "angel" usually considered to mean the Angel Isle and the Pax Brittanica, is "Humane realm and angelic offspring causes lasting peace and unity; war subdues under its control. Peace is maintained." Offspring between human and "angelic" realms is precisely what is occurring in UFO abductions, if reports are accurate. The myths show that the Danaan frequently intermarried with other races, such as the Fomorians, for diplomatic relations. And there is unquestionably a move on the part of the Danaan to unilaterally disarm the world's military forces, which is perfectly understandable if we are one of their territories and ongoing concerns. It also matches one of their nomers, "the People of Peace." The third prophecy, which ties in with the one just quoted, is from the Book of Enoch, 39:1—"In those days shall the elect and holy race descend from the upper heavens, and their seed shall then be with the sons of men."

This disarmament policy of the UFO occupants makes even more sense in light of the material now emerging concerning atomic testing during the cold war, and the incredible lack of safety and maintenance at chemical and nuclear production facilities. The repeated taking of cattle tissues over periods of time in localized regions could easily be for comparative tests to see how many chemicals or how much radiation were being absorbed. Continuing tests on the same abductees for the same contamination would of course be of even more interest to the Danaan, since mankind is their close cousin. Never in the history of our race or our planet have so many extremely dangerous products been manufactured, let alone in the phenomenal quantities that are now becoming part of the public record.

Where the common man's reaction to nuclear or environmental threats has been dulled into coma, that of the Danaan plainly has not. The frequently reported imagery of nuclear war seen by abductees makes sense, in that light. Abductee Judy Doraty and her daughter, taken during the major flap year of 1973, had medical tests performed on them by the Grays and witnessed their mutilation of a cow. Like the "Oscar" case reported by Jacques Vallée, the occupants Judy reported had long dark nails; like those reported in the 1950 Ontario *Steep Rock Echo* article, they pivoted "kind of like on their heel . . . swing rather than like we might turn slowly or take two or three steps to turn . . . it seems like they pivot"; and as in many other abductee reports, the beings' eyes seemed to open and close like a camera lens. "They go in and out real fast, like this," she explained, folding her fingers and then spreading them out several times in a repetitive gesture. "I believe from the way they talked," Judy said, "they're concerned about man for themselves. That men are going to kill themselves through polluting the earth area. Something, I don't know. I can't . . . it's going to get in the water. It's going to be in vegetation. Going to be, it is in vegetation . . . Their concern is loss of life. There is going to be a big loss of life due to this . . . it's already passed a certain state . . . it can be reversed, but there will be a loss of life because it already's filtered down to a certain point to where there is going to be so much pollution and so much of this poison in the water that people are going to die from it. And it has to do with somehow nuclear waste or testing or . . . causing a change in the chemical composition of something."

It would appear that the Danaan are working privately, on an individual grass-roots basis, to inform people in opposition to the disinformation the government is spreading, and that they are in the process of disarming the greatest oppressive power block in the history of man, which is consistent with what they have always done. The military's response has been to more tightly restrict all information of the Danaan's existence and agenda, probably while alarming successive presidents for an increase in their own funding. John Keel's "Mothman" was involved in the same kind of activity. UFOs followed Red Cross bloodmobiles during Mothman's brief reign, and domestic animals disappeared or were mutilated. In addition, Mothman's primary haunt was a manufacturing site for atomic bomb charges, storehouses of which he entered. "Insiders know," says Keel, "that the AEC [Atomic Energy Commission] and our nuclear industry have always been related to UFO activity . . . Maybe Mothman was just some atomic spy from some other dimension. History does repeat itself and in the 1980s the Soviet Union was suddenly engulfed in UFOs and monsters in a classic repetition of what had happened in the U.S.A. in the 1950s and 60s ... Bright lights were haunting Soviet atomic plants and hundreds of remote little Russian towns were plunged into the same kind of Twilight Zone horror that once gripped Point Pleasant."

Initial fears on the military's part are easy to sympathize with, though their later abuse of the secret knowledge in their possession for power and profit is not. By the time of the Roswell crash, most of the top brass in the military must already have known, or at least very strongly suspected, that aircraft not from this planet were traveling the skies. To recover wreckage from one would have been remarkable enough, when the atom bomb was only two years old and plastic was still in its earliest stages as Bakelite, jets were experimental, television was just being invented, and radios still operated on tubes. But to have recovered robot pilots from the wreck must have been alarming, to say the least. Their existence would have been mute proof of a civilization with technology so superior that they didn't even have to fly long-distance spacecraft in person. There would have been no clue as to what race invented them, since mannequins betray little in the way of features, made for function as opposed to realistic facsimile. The military wouldn't have known whether the intelligence behind them was truly "alien" (i.e., "nonhuman"), but must initially have thought so since no human beings we could immediately have theorized were capable of inventing such instrumentation. And in the absence of even that much knowledge, guessing their motivations could only have been a nightmarish experience. They would have to wonder whether they were here to survey, explore, invade, or conquer, especially in light of the craft being witnessed in such frequent proximity to military and industrial strongholds, and more especially in light of the sabotage activity that must have been taking place. From the start their own people did not handle the knowledge well. First Defense Secretary James V. Forrestal ran through the corridors of the Pentagon in 1949 screaming, "We're being invaded and we can't stop them!" He was institutionalized at Bethesda, and soon after either threw himself out of a window or was thrown. Shortly following Forrestal's death, the Rand Corporation think tank computer was assigned the task of fighting an imaginary war on the basis of the available UFO data. Its conclusion was that since we didn't know their location or technology, or how to attack them, we should surrender.

It can hardly be a coincidence that our own three-stage rockets so closely resemble the tomb paintings found in ancient Egypt. One drawing in particular, named after the region in which it was found, is even called "the Missile of Merowe." Following the recovery of the Roswell wreckage, the government investigators would have known to focus their studies on that country, if only because of the hieroglyphic writing discovered. That such recognition took place on the government's part is strongly implied by Hermann Oberth's comment in 1974 that the leaps in mankind's post-World War Two technology owed something to "the people from other worlds." Indication that government scientists knew even earlier than the war's end of a former advanced civilization on Earth is confirmed by A-bomb inventor Robert Oppenheimer stating that Alamogordo was not the first atomic detonation in the world, but only the first "in modern history."

It is questionable whether ongoing governmental investigation has determined the Danaan place of origin, any more than this study or others like it have been able to. Evidence appears equally strong for their planet of origination being inside or outside our solar system, though simple logic would favor the former. The Danaan could have begun on Mars and moved to Earth in antiquity, the evidence being that the ruins on that planet are a half million years old, or Mars may merely be one of their bases. Possible pole shifts on Earth further confuse the question of whether this race may have started on Mars or Venus. The demolished remains that comprise the asteroid belt between Mars and Jupiter, mythically referred to as Tiamat, are another credible possibility. Given our limited understanding of the planets, it is also possible that they came from an outer body in our system. An Upper, Lower, and Middle World being common to most mythologies, available myths can be read as indicating that a white race originally came to the Middle World of Earth from the Upper World of Venus, and established another colony of their own on (or in) the Lower World of Mars, all of which have served as homes at various times. It is possible that they originally came from Sirius, Orion, or the Pleiades, but the evidence of their use of three-stage rockets in ancient Egypt would seem to indicate their technology at that time insufficient to navigate farther than the closest planets. This ancient race could have originated within our system and later developed sufficient technology to conquer the stars, or come from beyond and suffered a dire setback due to unforeseen catastrophe, having to rediscover their technology afterward. Indeed, given the various American Indian legends and images of the gods weeping for their "sunken Red Land," the multiple mythical references to space as a vast ocean, and numerous occult connections, it is likely that Mars was the original "island" of Atlantis that "sank beneath the waves," with the name later applying to any similar global catastrophe which followed on our own world.

We know just as little about where this race is presently based. Mars, at least one of its moons, and the Earth's Moon definitely appear to be active bases, but whether the Danaan are living in these locations cannot be known. The surfaces of these astral bodies are uninhabitable, but certain evidence allows us to speculate on their living inside Mars or the Moon, or perhaps in protective surface structures. They could be elsewhere in the system, or could have moved to another solar system altogether (such as those just mentioned), leaving active bases here under robot control, as even Carl Sagan speculated in 1966. It is conceivable that they have artificial stations undetectable to us, with a technology capable of acquiring necessary resources from living planets to sustain such an environment. Since members of this race have been seen by abductees and in some instances had intimate personal relations with them, it must be concluded that they are either presently living within our solar system or else have technology capable of traveling at speeds beyond our comprehension—probably the former. Of all the possibilities, the evidence most strongly indicates they are living beneath the surface of Mars, and probably have been for a long time. The Martian surface could easily have been capable of sustaining life as we know it in the distant past, its atmosphere since destroyed either by cosmic catastrophe or technological devastation, or both.

Where the monitoring and dismantling of the world's nuclear war machine is unquestionably a major part of their present agenda, we can only speculate on the Danaan's present breeding program, or their training of abductees in the operation of their technology. World myth prophecies, not just the biblical, predict coming cataclysmic events that are at least partly cosmic in nature, as they have been in the past. The training of abductees in craft and instrument operation may have to do with preparation for such a coming catastrophe, in which case it appears we would have help from their race in the event.

Part of the Danaan's agenda may be simply to monitor our progress and/or development as a breeding project. Evidence being that they seeded Earth in antiquity with human life from else-where, this could mean that the offspring being produced between their race and ours at present is to begin human life on another planet. Echoing American Indian myths of Creation, Russian scholar Viaceslav Saitsev's *On Earth and Sea* quotes a Slavonic tale as stating that "man was created far from the Earth and very long ago. When God had finished creating He commanded the angels to take some human couples to Earth so that they should multiply there. The angels spread the couples over the world and wherever they set up home they multiplied. Perhaps when Earth is nearing its end, God will again take men somewhere else so that they may reproduce." Robert Charroux refers to experiments con-ducted by Professor Henry Harris and Dr. J. F. Watkins of Oxford in 1964 on hybridized crossbreeding as a possibility for space col-onization on other planets. "American and Soviet specialists," he writes, "have worked out a plan of hybridization in which a human fetus or fertilized ovum, brought directly from Earth, would be made to develop in an extraterrestrial plant or animal. It is quite possible that such a procedure could lead to the formation of a viable creature, assuming that the necessary chemical elements were supplied to the incubation medium. Development might also be favored by eliminating harmful secretions in the medium." If we have been experimenting with such projects on Earth, it is cer-tainly possible that someone more technologically advanced already has such a program in operation. Charroux also quotes Professor Andre Bouguenec's remarks about the more rapid fecundation and evolution of plant species being caused by "foreign" agents, and asks whether "that 'foreign' agent [is] analogous to the 'extrater-restrial lovers' who came and will no doubt come again to fecun-date the Earth . . . and our intelligences? Are hybridizations, transplants and mixtures necessary to the evolution of species?"

In support of the breeding and colonization theory, a 1986 issue of *Omni* quoted NASA's Jet Propulsion Laboratory head, Lew Allen, referring to the more fascinating research the civilian aspect of JPL had been involved with (as opposed to its Department of Defense-funded work): "One of the most exciting of these future programs, called Cassini, is an investigation of Saturn's moon Titan. Its atmosphere was too dense for the Voyagers to give us any clues about what lies beneath. The Cassini mission . . . would probe this atmosphere . . . we've concluded that it is very similar to what the earth's must have been at the earliest stages of its evolution." In other words, it has crossed NASA's mind to investigate planetary bodies capable of beginning to sustain life, in exactly the same manner as Arthur C. Clarke wrote about in his novel *2010* several years before. The plot of Clarke's story was that a former advanced civilization in our solar system was beginning life on one of Jupiter's moons, and gave terrestrial man the message to leave their new world alone so it could develop. Either Clarke was aware of the Cassini mission before it was publicized, or he had a very lucky guess. If he was in on the Cassini mission as it was in progress, perhaps he had an inkling as to what was actually going on there, as well. Even if he did not, it is easily within the realm of speculation, given the evidence, that our extraterrestrial visitors are in process of exactly such a project.

Vallée, after a lifetime of research into the question of UFOs, wrote his conclusions in *Forbidden Science,* before announcing retirement from the field. Those conclusions were in boldface and italics, the strongest emphasis ever given in his writings: "The UFO Phenomenon exists. It has been with us throughout history. It is physical in nature and it remains unexplained in terms of contemporary science. It represents a level of consciousness that we have not yet recognized and which is able to manipulate dimensions beyond time and space as we understand them. It affects our own consciousness in ways that we do not grasp fully, and it generally behaves as a control system." Charles Fort, perhaps the first man to seriously study such phenomena before, came to the similar conclusion that the human race was someone else's property. So did Vallée's contemporary, journalist John Keel, who is filled with forebodings about the fact. Author William Bramley concludes that Sitchin's Anunnaki have used religion to oppress man throughout human history, concurring with Vallée's control system thesis.

All have reached the same conclusion, but with different feelings about the fact. This study agrees with them, differing in that it does not see the control system being malefic in any way, and perhaps as actually being beneficial. Who could expect the Danaan to behave any differently as regards our nuclear capability than we do that of North Korea or Iraq? Our own missionaries, religious or medical, have found children living in such unsanitary squalor in Africa or India that they are going blind early in infancy; to save the infants' sight, the missionaries perform painful procedures for a brief time, during which the infants cry—but when they grow up, the pain is forgotten and their sight is saved. Most people wouldn't think twice about undergoing chemotherapy to put cancer in remission, yet it seems to alarm us that someone else's missionaries are performing medical procedures on our bodies for probably far more beneficial purpose, and are going out of their way to eliminate the cause of such grotesque diseases in the first place.

If we live in fear over the UFO question, it is fear born of ignorance, and knowledge dispels fear. The question has been sufficiently studied to make its conclusions known. First CIA Director Rear Admiral Hillenkoetter, who was in on the entire study from the very beginning, stated his opinion in 1960 that "The public has a right to know. It is time for the truth to be brought out in open Congressional hearings ... through official secrecy and ridicule, many citizens are led to believe the unknown flying objects are nonsense." If there was once reason to withhold information regarding UFOs from the public, it has since operated to our own detriment to continue doing so. The vacuum of ignorance has led people to speculate on the ugliest possible conspiracy scenarios, or to find dangerous if not actively hostile alien beings behind the phenomenon where none exist, working toward nefarious purposes rivaling those of the Nazis. None of the evidence supports such hypotheses, but then most of the evidence is still tightly held in secret.

Making matters worse, the very people holding that evidence have played in the worst ways on the misperceptions and fears created by their secrecy, under the guise of protecting the public, exploiting it to their own maximum advantage. Knowledge is power, and until the facts are made open, that power is maintained only by those who have all too amply demonstrated their irresponsibility to hold it. "It is self-evident that the public ought to be told the truth," Carl Jung wrote to Donald Keyhoe, "because ultimately it will nevertheless come to light. There can hardly be any greater shock than the H-bomb and yet everybody knows of it without fainting." Paris Flammonde writes, "The experience of what has happened to succeeding administrations [after Nixon's] in Washington and to the entire psycho-philosophic manner of modern America makes such things [as UFOs] appear insignificant by comparison ... Is it inconceivable that somewhere people who know something you should know about what has been happening in the skies across our land [since the beginning] are—only obeying orders? There are Unidentified Flying Objects . . . Something is happening up there. It is about time you knew what."

We can hardly expect the president of the United States, or any other world leader, to publicly admit, at this late date, any of the findings arrived at behind the scenes by the intelligence agencies on this subject. "[O]ur leaders [are presented] with an awesome dilemma," concedes Timothy Good. "Such an admission would lead to a deluge of questions, some of which simply cannot be answered without disclosing vital defense interests: alarming cases of missing aircraft; abductions; genetic experiments; and bizarre cases that will remain beyond our comprehension for centuries to come. In this respect I am fully in sympathy with the current official policy." But we can realize that what UFO facts have been discovered and studied behind the scenes all these years probably come close to the same conclusions we have reached. APRO's Dr. James Harder, in 1984, commented that, "From an intelligence point of view, the UFO phenomenon must be truly awesome—the worst of science fiction come to life . . . However, over the years, the intelligence agencies must have come to the realization that the strangers from space are nothing exactly new—that evidence from the past indicates that we are experiencing only an intensification of what may have been going on for centuries."

The best that can be expected of the government is that it open all of its files and assume a cooperative attitude with researchers and the press—in other words, that secret government be abolished and genuine democracy restored. Without doing that, the military-industrial complex remains empowered at the public's—and the government's—expense. That complex has been inadvertently assisted by members of every scientific and academic discipline, in their very cowardice to confront the subject and deal with it. Better to begin discussing it intelligently in the open than to continue the tragic errors started almost a full half century ago. In doing so, perhaps we can come to understand more fully the true history of the human race, its collective origins and destiny, as Children of the Cosmic Waters.

Notes

Chapter One: Recoveries

PRIMARY UFO BACKGROUND information in this and following chapters comes from Timothy Good's excellent *Above Top Secret,* and Captain Edward J. Ruppelt's indispensable *The Report on Unidentified Flying Objects.* Kevin D. Randle's *The UFO Casebook* is a worthwhile supplement. Documentary evidence acquired via the Freedom of Information Act comes mostly from Lawrence Fawcett and Barry J. Greenwood's groundbreaking book, *Clear Intent.* Information on the National Security Agency—which, even from the best sources, is sketchy—comes partly from cited articles in various periodicals, but almost exclusively from its only in-depth biography, James Bamford's *The Puzzle Palace: Inside America's Most Secret Agency.* The Roswell information is summarized from Kevin D. Randle and Donald R. Schmitt's *UFO Crash at Roswell* and *The Truth about the UFO Crash at Roswell,* the former being the overall better of the two for reasons cited in the text.

Page 3
"saucer skipped across water"—Edward J. Ruppelt, *The Report On Unidentified Flying Objects* (New York: ACE Books Inc., 1956), p. 27.
"It is the personal opinion of the interviewer..."—Timothy Good, *Above Top Secret* (Great Britain: Sidgwick and Jackson, Limited, 1987; New York: William Morrow, 1988), p. 253.

Page 5
"as many as fifteen airplanes..."—Ibid., p. 446.
"Taking into account our distance..."—Ibid., p. 16.
Stephen J. Brickner quotes—Ibid., p. 18.

Page 6
"proof that flying saucers were real"—Kevin D. Randle and Donald R. Schmitt, *UFO Crash at Roswell* (New York: Avon Books, 1991), p. 39.
Haut press story, "RAAF Captures Flying Saucer," *Roswell Daily Record,* 7/8/47.

"CEASE TRANSMISSION"—Good, *Above Top Secret,* p. 255.

"the story had been killed"—Ibid., p. 572.

Page 7

July 8, 1947 FBI document—Randle & Schmitt, *UFO Crash at Roswell,* p. 75.

"Happy in my retirement... I cannot talk to you"—Michael Lindemann, editor, *UFOs and the Alien Presence* (Santa Barbara, California: The 2020 Group, Visitors Investigation Project, 1991), p. 38.

"an interesting response indeed"—Ibid.

Page 8

Hoover/Tolson memorandum and quotes—Lawrence Fawcett and Barry J. Greenwood, *Clear Intent* (New York: Fireside/Simon and Schuster, 1984), pp. 147–149.

"the investigation of Unidentified Flying Objects"—Good, *Above Top Secret,* p. 475

"faked solutions..."—Kevin D. Randle, *The UFO Casebook* (New York: Warner Books, 1989), pp. 124–125.

"I never went to El Paso..."—Ibid., pp. 125–126.

Page 9

"The first document of any consequence... " Fawcett & Greenwood, *Clear Intent,* p. 147.

"Many documents have been withheld..."—Ibid.

1950 Hoover note—Ibid., p. 167.

Hottel memo—Good, *Above Top Secret,* p. 527.

Page 10

"anything written in intelligence channels ... may be highly distorted" —Ibid., p. 363.

Page 11

"A little sliver"—Randle & Schmitt, *UFO Crash at Roswell,* p. 200.

"Contrary to published reports"—Ibid., p. 201.

Page 12

"had touched down and skipped along"—Ibid., pp. 202–203.

"nothing from the earth"—Ibid., p. 54.

"It was something he had never seen..."—Ibid., p. 69.

Debris witness list—Ibid., p. 203.

Page 13

"It is still classified above Top Secret"—Good, *Above Top Secret,* p. 405.

"I have long ago given up..."—Ibid.

Wilbert Smith letter—Good, *Above Top Secret,* p. 464

"a very sincere interest..."—Randle & Schmitt, *UFO Crash at Roswell,* p. 69.

Page 14

"Jess Marcel has brought something in..."—Ibid.

orders came from "The Puzzle Palace" on UFOs—Dale Goudie and Jim Klotz, "Documents Trace NSA-UFO Connection," *UFO,* Vol. 9, No. 1, 1994, p. 26.

"watch-lists"—James Bamford, *The Puzzle Palace: America's Most Secret Agency* (New York: Houghton Mifflin,1982), p. 323.

Page 15
"...or otherwise undermine the national security of the U.S."—Ibid., pp. 323–324.

MacArthur *New York Times* quote—Good, *Above Top Secret,* p. 267.

Timothy Good IPU letter—Ibid., p. 484.

"enemies from outer space"— Presidential speech, May 5, 1988. The actual specific quote was "a [threat] by a . . . power from outer space, from another planet."

Page 16
"a bright, disc-shaped object"—Randle, *The UFO Casebook,* p. 19.

"metallic and tremendous in size"—Ibid., p. 20.

Page 17
9/23/47 Twining memo—Good, *Above Top Secret,* p. 477.

Page 18
"We have all of the other explained. . ."—Randle & Schmitt, *UFO Crash at Roswell,* p. 162.

"leave it alone"—Ibid.

Page 19
"As you will be aware, intelligence agencies are . . . compartmented. . ." —Good, *Above Top Secret,* p. 362.

"concentration of inquiries"—Ibid.

"under the umbrella of Air Force . . . rather than the CIA itself"—Ibid.

Page 20
"...that no indication of CIA interest or concern reach the public" —Ibid., p. 331.

Page 21
"To the extent that the presence of. . ."—"Are The Reasons for the Coverup Solely Scientific?," *Flying Saucer Review,* Vol. 28, No. 6, 1982, pp. 2–8.

"...if there wasn't an MJ–12, we'd have to invent one"—Lindemann, *UFOs and the Alien Presence,* p. 46.

"It requires, therefore, little imagination. . ."—Paris Flammonde, *UFO Exist!* (Canada: G. P. Putnam's Sons, 1976; reprint, New York: Ballantine, 1991), p. 422.

Page 22
"special project"—Randle & Schmitt, *UFO Crash at Roswell,* p. 110

"there was a top intelligence echelon. . ."—Ibid., p. 232.

"never heard what the results were . . . pieces were from space"—Ibid., p. 110.

"Blanchard could have cared less. . ."—Ibid., pp. 110–111.

Page 23
"oversight committee . . . to exploit it [the technology]"—Ibid., p. 111.

"We cannot take the credit. . ."—Good, *Above Top Secret,* p. 370.

"We find ourselves faced by powers. . ."—*Neues Europa,* 1/1/59.

"suggesting" that the station not air. . . —Randle & Schmitt, *UFO Crash at Roswell,* p. 71.

Page 24
"calls from London and Paris. . ."—Ibid., p. 70.

"Nobody, and I must stress this. . ."—Ibid., pp. 74–75.

configure the wreckage into a "kite"—Ibid., pp. 186–187.

Page 25

"was under a great deal of stress"—Ibid., p. 78.

". . .They weren't green"—Ibid., p. 79.

"We don't know if there are bodies. . ."—Ibid., p. 224.

Page 26

"the balloon"—Ibid., p. 78.

"They were three or four of them. . ."—Ibid., p. 89.

"pretty good sized . . . burst open"—Ibid., p. 90.

"patriotic duty . . . classified project"—Ibid.

". . .been there when the spaceship had come down"—Ibid., p. 115.

"like tar, thick and black"—Ibid.

Page 27

"crashed airplane without wings"—Ibid., p. 116.

"He was sure that if he told stories of crashed saucers. . ."—Ibid.,
    pp. 115–116.

". . .threats have silenced people for more than forty years"—Ibid.,
    p. 117.

Page 28

". . .bodies from the one that crashed"—Ibid., p. 91.

"in fairly good shape"—Ibid., pp. 91–92.

"there was some wreckage"—Kevin D. Randle & Donald R. Schmitt,
    The Truth About the UFO Crash At Roswell (New York: Avon Books,
    1994), p. 18.

"Looked like some particles or pieces from a crashed airplane. . ."
    —Ibid.

". . .it reminded me of Egyptian inscriptions"—Ibid., p. 19.

"very excited"—Ibid.

"How did you get in here?. . ."—Ibid.

Page 29

"Who are you? What are you doing here?"—Ibid.

"Looks like you've had a crash. . ."—Ibid.

". . .diggin' your bones outta the sand"—video, *UFOs—A Need To Know*,
    1990.

". . .I would like to know more about the incident"—Randle & Schmitt,
    The Truth About the UFO Crash At Roswell, p. 26.

"I understand you've been trying to call me . . . at the officers' club"
    —Ibid.

"I want to tell you what this is all about . . . ever seen in my life"—Ibid.,
    pp. 26–27.

"I don't think she said alien bodies . . . when she got involved in it"
    —Ibid., p. 27.

"You stay here. We've got to have you"—Ibid.

"didn't know what they were or . . . came from"—Randle & Schmitt,
    UFO Crash at Roswell, p. 92.

"She said it was so gruesome . . . never touched her food"—Randle &
    Schmitt, *The Truth About the UFO Crash At Roswell*, p. 28.

Page 30

"I didn't pay any attention and was so sick"—Ibid.

like the thumb was "missing"—Ibid., p. 27.

"very pliable . . . it would be movable"—Ibid., p. 28.

"very thin . . . even harder than the bone structure"—Ibid.

"They told me she wasn't working . . . big red print that said, 'Deceased'"—Ibid., p. 87.

Page 31

"Glenn is in some kind of trouble at the base. . ."—Ibid.

"would make good dog food"—Ibid.

". . .not only would we be killed, but they would get the rest of the family"—Ibid.

"clearly nervous"—Randle & Schmitt, *UFO Crash at Roswell,* p. 94.

"kinda little guys"—Ibid.

Page 32

". . .with slanted eyes and tiny mouths"—Ibid., p. 95.

"They did say there were bodies. . ."—Ibid., p. 110.

"very sensitive activities"—Good, *Above Top Secret,* p. 364.

"little gray men"—Ibid.

"high level" rumors—Ibid.

"autopsy" composite—Randle & Schmitt, *UFO Crash at Roswell,* pp. 105–106.

Page 33

The Robert Sarbacher letter—Good, *Above Top Secret,* pp. 183, 397, 525.

Page 34

Denver Post article that prompted Rep. Steven Schiff's inquiry—date unknown, but personally read by the author.

Chapter Two: Investigations

Ed Ruppelt's *The Report on Unidentified Flying Objects,* Timothy Good's *Above Top Secret,* and Jacques Vallée's *Forbidden Science* are the primary sources of information on this subject, with Kevin Randle's *The UFO Casebook* a satisfactory backup. Jenny Randles' (no relation) *The UFO Conspiracy* is a broad and general overview, providing a readable summary of UFO history in the modern era. Any of Donald Keyhoe's books are worth reading for acquiring a solid appraisal of the atmosphere of the time concerning the subject of UFO investigation, but like Ruppelt's book, are difficult to come by. *Project Blue Book,* edited by Brad Steiger, is fragmentary but informative, and a good source for original documents.

Page 35

"By the end of July. . ."—Ruppelt, *The Report on Unidentified Flying Objects,* p. 34.

"the reported phenomena were real," "The question 'Do UFO's. . ." —Ibid., p. 26.

Page 36

"The general said it would cause a stampede..."—Donald E. Keyhoe, *Aliens From Space* (London: Panther Books, 1973), p. 27.

"Project Saucer"—Jenny Randles, *The UFO Conspiracy* (New York: Barnes & Noble, 1987), p. 23.

Page 37

"proved non-existent," "No definite and conclusive evidence..." —Brad Steiger, editor, *Project Blue Book* (New York: Ballantine Books, 1976), p. 174.

"Evaluation of reports of unidentified flying objects..."—Ibid., p. 175.

"This attitude can be readily seen..."—Randle, *The UFO Casebook,* pp. 164–165.

Page 38

dropped the word "probable"—Ibid., p. 51.

The Condon Committee ... concluding "aircraft"—Ibid., p. 52.

Still, the answer was "aircraft"—Ibid., pp. 49–54.

Page 39

"the word 'Grudge' was no longer applicable..."—Ruppelt, *The Report on Unidentified Flying Objects,* p. 174.

"UFO's ... flying saucers"—Ibid., p. 7.

"...still would like us to call it the 'Arnold Phenomenon'..."—Jacques Vallée, journal entry dated 11/17/63, *Forbidden Science* (Berkeley, California: North Atlantic Books, 1992), p. 76.

Page 40

"Washington Nationals"—Ruppelt, *The Report on Unidentified Flying Objects,* p. 207.

"not enough information," "in hand," "being taken care of"—Randles, *The UFO Conspiracy,* p. 36.

"huge fiery-orange sphere"—Ruppelt, *The Report on Unidentified Flying Objects,* p. 212.

Page 41

"intercept and destroy"—Randles, *The UFO Conspiracy,* pp. 35–36 (a project called "Operation Intercept").

"no comment"—Ruppelt, *The Report on Unidentified Flying Objects,* p. 214.

Page 42

"I have no idea what the Air Force is doing..."—Randles, *The UFO Conspiracy,* pp. 35–36.

"stunned silence"—Jerome Clark, contributing writer, in *UFO Encounters & Beyond* (Lincolnwood, Illinois: Publications International, 1993), p. 44.

"very probably solid metallic objects"—Randles, *The UFO Conspiracy,* p. 38 (Dewey Fournet report).

Page 44

"When a ground radar picks up a UFO target..."—Ruppelt, *The Report on Unidentified Flying Objects,* p. 317.

"It did take pressure off Project Blue Book..."—Ibid., p. 228.

"We found out that the UFO's frequently visited..."—Ibid., pp. 224–225.

Page 45

"Had the press been aware. . ."—Ibid., p. 225.

"Most of the press, with some relief. . ."—Randles, *The UFO Conspiracy,* p. 38.

"front man"—Ibid., p. 39.

"there appear to be no confirmed saucer fans. . ."—Ruppelt, *The Report on Unidentified Flying Objects,* p. 316.

Page 46

"ah, Melbourne. . ."—Good, *Above Top Secret,* p. 177.

"At first I calculated that there were about fifty of them. . ."—Ibid., p. 142.

"angel hair"—Ibid.

"At the British War Office, they are concerned"—Ibid., p. 143.

"The Masters of Silence"—Ibid., p. 136.

Page 47

"In 1977 it was necessary. . ."—Ibid., p. 140.

Fatima miracles—Jacques Vallée, *Dimensions* (Canada: Random House/Ballantine Books, 1988), pp. 173–185.

"green fireball"—Ruppelt, *The Report on Unidentified Flying Objects,* pp. 66–67.

Page 48

"nuts and bolts spacecraft"—John Spencer, *The UFO Encyclopedia* (New York: Avon Books, 1991), p. 333.

"Why is Blue Book rejecting . . . landing reports?. . ."—Vallée, *Forbidden Science,* p. 86.

Page 49

"orthoteny"—Spencer, *The UFO Encyclopedia,* p. 233.

". . .rivalry with another species"—Steiger, *Project Blue Book,* p. 105.

George Adamski, "contactees," liaisons with "space brothers" et. al.—passim—Desmond Leslie and George Adamski, *Flying Saucers Have Landed* (Werner Laurie, 1953).

"space brothers," "the Venusians"—Peter Hough and Jenny Randles, *Looking for the Aliens* (London: Blandford Books, 1991), pp. 63–70.

"Aura Rhanes . . . tops in shapeliness and beauty"—Spencer, *The UFO Encyclopedia,* p. 27.

Glassboro, New Jersey case—Randle, *The UFO Casebook,* pp. 118–129.

Page 50

"the contactees . . . could have been set up in their roles. . ."—Jacques Vallée, *Messengers of Deception* (Berkeley, California: And/Or Press, 1979), pp. 202–203.

"muttering about a CIA experiment"—Clark, *UFO Encounters & Beyond,* p. 124.

Page 51

"After months of weary-eyed reading. . ."—Howard Blum, *Out There* (New York: Simon and Schuster/Pocket Books, 1990), pp. 60–61.

"weasel-worded"—Flammonde, *UFO Exist!,* p. 229.

Page 52

"swamp gas"—Vallée, *Dimensions,* pp. 191, 205.

"Hynek has been charmed and neutralized. . ."—Vallée, journal entry dated 9/14/69, *Forbidden Science,* pp. 408–409.

"Hynek remains very prudent. . ."—Ibid., journal entry dated 1/17/64, p. 86.

"when he witnessed the destruction of tracking tapes. . ."—Jacques Vallée, *Revelations* (New York: Random House/Ballantine Books, 1991), inside back cover.

"My interest in 'flying saucers'. . ."—Vallée, journal entry dated 9/1/58, *Forbidden Science,* p. 15.

Page 53

"Luciano has sent me. . ."—Ibid., journal entry dated 4/13/65, p. 133.

"Aimé does not trust any of these people. . ."—Ibid., journal entry dated 2/23/65, p. 129.

Page 54

"Dissatisfied as he may have been. . ."—Good, *Above Top Secret,* p. 339.

". . .seemed reluctant to give out much in return"—Ibid., p. 353.

". . .to the skeptical scientific fraternity," ". . .Obviously funds were adequate"—Ibid.

"Hynek's motives may well have been innocent. . ."—Ibid.

Page 55

"Comets seemed utterly fantastic. . ."—Vallée, journal entry dated 1/17/64, *Forbidden Science,* p. 86.

"Hynek is impressed by this argument, but. . ." "Carl Sagan himself. . ." —Ibid.

"[Moody's] universe. . ."—Ibid., journal entry dated 2/23/65, p. 129.

"Moody deserves a Nobel Prize. . ."—Ibid., journal entry dated 2/6/65, p. 126.

"The Mission of the Air Force. . ."—Ibid., journal entry dated 1/16/64, p. 84.

Page 56

"In December 1964 a huge craft. . ."—Ibid., journal entry dated 2/23/65, p. 129.

"The question we asked was. . ."—Ruppelt, *The Report on Unidentified Flying Objects,* p. 240.

Page 57

"To study UFOs is like studying meteorites. . ."—Vallée, journal entry dated 5/5/67, *Forbidden Science,* p. 260.

"We in the French Air Force. . ."—Ibid., journal entry dated 6/21/67, p. 282.

Page 58

"We're ordered to hide sightings when possible. . ."—Good, *Above Top Secret,* p. 339.

"Another question the panel had. . . ," ". . .obviously hadn't panicked" —Ruppelt, *The Report on Unidentified Flying Objects,* p. 285.

". . .to possible enemy psychological warfare"—Good, *Above Top Secret,* p. 337.

Page 59

"...aura of mystery they have unfortunately acquired"—Dale Goudie & Jim Klotz, "Documents Trace NSA-UFO Connection," *UFO*, Vol. 9, No. 1, 1994, p. 29.

"spread the gospel,"—Good, *Above Top Secret*, p. 338.

Walt Disney cartoons—Ibid., pp. 337–338.

"The debunking aim. . ."—Ibid., p. 337.

Page 60

"Because of Mr. Disney's position. . ."—photo section in Marc Eliot, *Walt Disney: Hollywood's Dark Prince* (New York: HarperCollins, 1994 [1993]).

"could reasonably be expected to disclose. . ."—Ibid.

"pledged to fight . . . domination by Communists," etc.—Ibid., p. 185.

"a valued contact of this office"—Ibid., p. 326.

Page 61

"Mr. Disney was on the Special Correspondents' List. . ."—Ibid., photo section.

Page 62

"The worst section of [Hynek's] files. . ."—Vallée, *Forbidden Science*, pp. 280–281.

"Let us go back to 1953. . ."—Ibid.

Page 63

"When he started reading from his notes. . ."—Ibid., journal entry dated 3/18/68, p. 338.

"Any work performed with NPIC. . ."—Good, *Above Top Secret*, p. 345.

"...How do you expect to counter all that?"—Vallée, journal entry dated 3/23/68, *Forbidden Science*, p. 340.

Page 64

"The cold, hard fact is. . ."—Ibid., journal entry dated 7/12/67, p. 295.

"...and have the decision made in Washington"—Good, *Above Top Secret*, p. 346.

"[Fuller] reveals the evidence. . ."—Vallée, journal entry dated 5/9/68, *Forbidden Science*, p. 347.

"The Condon Report assembled. . ."—Flammonde, *UFO Exist!*, p. 42.

Page 65

"grave doubts as to the scientific profundity. . ."—Nigel Blundell & Roger Boar, *The World's Greatest UFO Mysteries* (London: Octopus Books Limited, 1983; reprint, New York: Berkley, 1990), p. 200.

"...will die laughing at the Condon Report"—Ibid.

. . . and are not part of the Blue Book system" (Bolender memo)—Good, *Above Top Secret*, p. 443.

Chapter Three: *Installations, Mutilations, And Disinformations*

Ruppelt's book and Timothy Good's *Above Top Secret* are both solid sources on the subject of military sabotage by UFOs, with Lawrence Fawcett and

Barry J. Greenwood's groundbreaking publication of Freedom of Information Act-acquired documents on the subject being invaluable. The cattle mutilation phenomenon is covered in a number of sources, the best probably being Linda Moulton Howe's book *An Alien Harvest* (1989), which contains numerous photos (as does her first volume of *Glimpses of Other Realities,* 1993) and her videos *A Strange Harvest* (1980, 1988) and *Strange Harvests* (1993) (all Linda Moulton Howe Productions, Huntingdon Valley, Pennsylvania). The best books on UFO disinformation and counterintelligence are *Revelations* and *Messengers of Deception* by Jacques Vallée, the former being the better of the two. Jim Keith's *A Casebook on Alternative 3* is well worth reading, being the only objective criticism of that particular disinformational story in print. Howard Blum's *Out There* appears itself to have been sown as a disinformation source by Intelligence insiders, much in the same way that *Project Blue Book* and other specious investigations preceding it were, which Blum himself admits to suspecting; it is nevertheless a well-researched and worthwhile book. Blum's recounting of the Bennewitz Affair is the most thorough in print.

Page 67

"No matter what these green fireballs were. . ."—Ruppelt, *The Report on Unidentified Flying Objects,* p. 69.

Page 68

"seriously doubted"—Ibid., p. 70.

"The object was similar in appearance. . ."—Ibid., p. 71.

Page 69

". . .theory had to be abandoned by any objective person"—Tad A. Sherburn and Harvey M. Haeberle, "Los Alamos Overflights," *UFO,* Vol. 11, No.1, p. 33.

"This matter is considered Top Secret. . ."—Fawcett & Greenwood, *Clear Intent,* p. 159.

FBI list—Ibid., p. 169.

Page 70

"It seems incredible, but the blip . . . swallowed our F–89"—Clark, *UFO Encounters & Beyond,* p. 42.

"Well, we just cannot talk about those cases"—Ibid.

"Faded Giants"—Fawcett & Greenwood, *Clear Intent,* p. 29.

Page 71

SAC memo, "Suspicious Unknown Air Activity"—Blum, *Out There,* pp. 65–66.

Page 72

"lights . . . near the weapons storage area"—Fawcett & Greenwood, *Clear Intent,* p. 43.

". . .over the ammo storage area at 100–200 yards altitude"—Ibid., p. 53.

Page 73

"reddish orange" and incredibly bright—Ibid., pp. 18–19.

"We would launch. . ."—Ibid., pp. 20–21.

"We had reports . . . were some very exciting stories"—*UFOs: A Need to Know.*

Page 74

"I could hardly believe it . . . no turbulence, either"—Nigel Blundell and Roger Boar, *The World's Greatest UFO Mysteries* (London: Octopus Books, 1983), p. 201.

"A couple of days later . . . of a security breach"—Good, *Above Top Secret,* pp. 292–293.

Page 75

"a nervous battery commander . . . to be in working order"—Ibid., p. 227.

Page 76

"The wing leader reported. . ."—Ibid., p. 421.

DIA distribution list—Ibid., p. 319.

Page 77

"An outstanding report . . . in the DIA files at the Pentagon"—Ibid., p. 321.

". . .The article proceeds to quote from Air Force. . ."—Fawcett & Greenwood, *Clear Intent,* p. 54.

Page 78

". . .regarding the incidents described," "may not have happened at all"—Ibid.

"of transitory interest," "permanent files are not maintained"—Ibid., p. 55.

July of 1947, Roswell AFB possessed the atom bomb—Sherburn and Haeberle, "Los Alamos Overflights," op. cit., p. 36.

Page 79

"Last Monday night, about 10:30 . . . any more to do with them" —Jacques Vallée, *Anatomy of a Phenomenon* (Henry Regnery Co./Ace Books, 1965), pp. 33–34.

Page 80

"About 2:00–3:00 a.m., I saw three very bright. . ."—Linda Moulton Howe, *An Alien Harvest* (Huntingdon, Pennsylvania: LMH Productions, 1989), p. 3.

"cut from the neck down. . . ," "most amazing,"—Ibid., p. 4.

Page 81

"I have done hundreds of autopsies. . . ," "at the edge of the cut. . ." —Ibid.

"unbelievably frightened. . ."—Ibid., p. 5.

Page 82

". . .back to town and got a geiger counter. . . ," ". . .around here uptight"—Ibid., p. 22.

"the Red Sun that rises. . ."—Anton Fitzgerald quote in Vallée, *Messengers of Deception,* p. 165.

Atsil-dihye gi, or "Fire-carrier"—Linda Moulton Howe, *Glimpses of Other Realities, Vol. 1* (Huntingdon, Pennsylvania: LMH Productions, 1993), p. 115.

"...was of a dark reddish color"—Vallée, *Anatomy of a Phenomenon,*
p. 34.

Page 83

"Around the base. . ."—*UFOs: A Need To Know.*

"...this would be a neat place to have a cattle mutilation"—Vallée,
Messengers of Deception, p. 161.

Page 85

"biogeochemistry"—George C. Andrews, *Extraterrestrials Among Us* (St.
Paul, Minnesota: Llewellyn Publications, 1992, 1986), p. 187.

Page 86

"very dark greenish-black . . . no markings," etc.—personal letter to
author, 5/17/95.

Page 87

"out came articles describing a virus identical to the AIDS virus. . ."
—Jim Keith, *Casebook On Alternative 3—UFOs, Secret Societies and
World Control* (Lilburn, Georgia: IllumiNet Press, 1994), p. 93.

Page 88

"is made here, and it isn't from outer space. . ."—Andrews, *Extraterrestrials Among Us,* p. 192.

Mario Feola, cow hemoglobin—Howe, *An Alien Harvest,* p. 110.

Page 89

Jacques Vallée notes . . . to terrorize. . . —*Revelations,* p. 60; *Messengers
of Deception,* pp. 160–188 passim.

"paws and other body parts . . . strikingly similar arrangements"—
Howe, *Glimpses of Other Realities, Vol. 1,* p. 168.

Page 90

"The mutilations are one of the greatest outrages. . ."—*Meeker Herald,*
Colorado, 9/6/75.

"The amateur researchers. . ."—Andrews, *Extraterrestrials Among Us,*
p. 198.

Page 91

"The conference was designed to embarass the sincere. . ."—Ibid.

"...and still are protecting the mutilators"—Ibid., pp. 198–199.

Page 92

"Disinformation, as the Soviet term desinformatsiya. . ."—Blum, *Out
There,* p. 258.

asked to "cooperate," "Falcon," "...the only person we've ever heard. . ."
—Ibid., p. 252.

"...from a variety of agencies"—Ibid., p. 258.

AFOSI-Bennewitz plot—Blum, *Out There,* pp. 249–260; Vallée,
Revelations, pp. 41–50, 78–80.

"systematically to confuse, discourage and discredit. . ."—Blum, *Out
There,* p. 258.

Page 93

"Their work had been remarkably successful. . ."—Ibid., pp. 258–259.

Page 94

"Little Aunt"—Vallée, *Messengers of Deception,* p. 190.

Moore knowingly passed on . . . documents to him from Doty. . . —Blum, *Out There,* p. 259.

"What about the Constitution . . . to drive someone crazy?"—Vallée, *Revelations,* p. 79.

"If the Air Force . . . has not been documented at all"—Ibid., p. 80.

Page 95

concerted letter-writing campaign. . . , "his own worst enemy"—Blum, *Out There,* pp. 257–258.

Kirtland file, "For Official Use Only" et. al.—Fawcett & Greenwood, *Clear Intent,* pp. 224–225.

Page 96

"he had knowledge and evidence of threats. . ."—Ibid., p. 226.

"allegedly had a number of conversations with Senator Schmidt. . ." —Ibid., p. 227.

"Request a DCII check be made on Dr. Bennewitz . . . HQ CR 44"—Ibid., p. 226.

Page 97

". . .research into Aerial Phenomena for the last 15 months"—Ibid.

Donna Basset, Philip Klass, John Mack quotes and story—Geoff Olson, "'Psi-Cops' Bite Into Abduction Claims," and Richard Cutting, "Q&A: John Mack, M.D.," *UFO,* Vol. 9, No. 5.

Page 98

highly questionable abduction case under study by Budd Hopkins— Greg Bishop, "'History' Served Up At MUFON Event," Ibid.

Pages 99–101

MJ–12/EBE/Area 51—Blum, *Out There,* pp. 261–267; Vallée, *Revelations,* pp. 38–75 passim.

Page 100

"had been the victim of a neat bait-and-switch. . ."—Ibid., p. 43.

Page 102

"The report is true! Devastatingly true!"—William Cooper, *Behold A Pale Horse* (Sedona Arizona: Light Technology Publishing, 1991), p. 404.

"Who takes out the garbage"—Vallée, *Revelations,* p. 55.

"Trojan," "The German," and "The Instigator"—Leslie Watkins and David Ambrose, *Alternative 3* (Great Britain: Sphere Books, 1978), pp. 238–239.

Page 103

Lear . . . flew missions for the CIA by his own admission—Vallée, *Revelations,* p. 62.

. . . was an information analyst for the Air Force—Ibid., p. 181.

"an example of strange prescience"—Keith, *Casebook On Alternative 3—UFOs, Secret Societies and World Control,* p. 54.

Page 104

"fiendish double bluff inspired by the very agencies. . ."—Watkins and Ambrose, *Alternative 3,* p. 162.

"had hundreds of calls. The film was brilliantly done to deceive"—Ibid.

". . .Networks there want to assess its effect on British viewers"—Ibid., p. 164.

Page 105

Doty and ... Collins ... exposed as ... "Falcon" and "Condor"
—Vallée, *Revelations,* pp. 47–48.

"...actually saw Kennedy's driver shoot him..."—Cooper, *Behold A Pale Horse,* p. 14.

"Most UFO organizations..."—Vallée, *Messengers of Deception,* pp. 190–191.

Page 106

(the Franck Fontaine case)—Vallée, *Revelations,* pp. 133–166 passim.

"The Strawberry Ice Cream Show"—Ibid., p. 44.

Page 108

"The expectation of extraterrestrials..."—Ibid., p. 284.

"The American public is being taught to expect..."—Ibid., p. 288.

Chapter Four: *Abductions*

Except for the original March 1965 *Flying Saucer Review* published for exclusive readership in Britain, Coral and Jim Lorenzen's *Flying Saucer Occupants* is the only worthwhile journalistic report on the Antonio Villas Boas abduction. Ralph and Judy Blum's *Beyond Earth: Man's Contact With UFOs* is the only thorough recounting of the Hickson-Parker/Pascagoula, Mississippi case. Similarly, the only in-depth reports on the Betty and Barney Hill and Herbert Schirmer abductions are John G. Fuller's *The Interrupted Journey* and Eric Norman's *Gods, Demons and Space Chariots* and *Gods and Devils from Outer Space,* respectively. The books of researcher Raymond Fowler cover the Betty Andreasson Luca abduction history in detail, the best overall summary (owing to the case having matured and been studied at length) being that given in *The Watchers.* These books and researchers, in every instance, are those that first broke the stories they each have to tell, and as such are invaluable as primary investigative records. The mistake made by UFOlogists in studying both the occupant and abduction problems has been in reading watered-down and sometimes grossly inaccurate subsequent reports derived from these original sources.

Page 109

"pains throughout the whole body ... violet-tinged area"—Ralph Blum with Judy Blum, *Beyond Earth: Man's Contact With UFOs* (New York: Bantam Books, 1974), p. 184 (n).

Page 110

"no less than twenty times"—Coral and Jim Lorenzen, *Flying Saucer Occupants* (New York: Signet Books/New American Library, 1967), p. 44.

"The light kept still..."—Ibid.

"...before I could make up my mind what to do about it"—Ibid.

"a large, elongated egg"—Ibid., p. 45.

"a small figure in strange clothes"—Ibid., p. 46.

Page 111
occupant description, pp. 75–76—Ibid., pp. 51–53.

Page 112
"the same as broad daylight"—Ibid., p. 47.
"The only furniture visible. . ."—Ibid., p. 48.

Page 113
"no resemblance whatever to human speech. . ." ". . .ending in a tremor"—Ibid.
"They obviously couldn't understand me. . ." "scribbles . . . unknown to us"—Ibid., p. 49.
"like painted cloth burning"—Ibid., p. 50.
". . .a woman was coming in. . ."—Ibid., p. 53.

Page 114
"She came in slowly . . . nearly the color of blood"—Ibid., pp. 53–54.
pubic hair was also bright red—Ralph Blum with Judy Blum, *Beyond Earth: Man's Contact With UFOs,* p. 183.
"The woman came toward me in silence. . ."—Lorenzen, *Flying Saucer Occupants,* pp. 53–54.
"clearly giving me to understand. . ."—Ibid., p. 54.

Page 115
". . .a good stallion to improve their own stock," "animal growls"—Ibid.
"But before leaving, she pointed to her belly. . ."—Ibid., pp. 54–55.
". . .knew no harm would come to me"—Ibid., p. 55.
"Obviously . . . only when I behaved. . ."—Ibid., p. 56.
"machine"—Ibid., p. 57.
". . .a southerly direction in the sky"—Ibid., p. 58.

Page 116
". . .disappeared from sight in a few seconds"—Ibid., p. 59.
". . .unless they were of common genetic background"—Ibid., pp. 205–206.
"The overall genetic distance between us and chimps. . ."—Jared Diamond, *The Third Chimpanzee* (New York: HarperCollins Publishers, 1992), p. 4.

Page 117
". . .was in actuality a breeding experiment"—Lorenzen, *Flying Saucer Occupants,* p. 206.

Page 118
"the body of a helicopter," "My God. . . !" "like the door of a Convair. . ." —Ibid., p. 194.
"Did the female part of the experiment pick her companion"—Ibid., p. 206.

Page 119
"dressed in tight fitting clothes. . ." "camera-like device"—Vallée, *Dimensions,* p. 143.
". . .containers and many dials," "soldering operation," ". . .resistant to heat"—Ibid.

Page 120
"shaped like an egg laid horizontally"—Ibid., p. 141.
"gas masks"—Ibid., p. 142.
Joe Simonton case and quotes—Ibid., pp. 44–45.

Page 121
"an aluminum airliner . . . with no seams along the fuselage"—Ibid., p. 234.
"a man . . . or whatever he might happen to be on that crew"—Ibid.

Page 123
"like a big pancake"—John G. Fuller, *The Interrupted Journey* (New York: Berkley Publishing Corporation, 1966), p. 112.
"It must be a plane or something"—Lorenzen, *Flying Saucer Occupants,* p. 75.
"like a German Nazi"—Fuller, *The Interrupted Journey,* p. 115.
"black, black shiny jacket"—Ibid., p. 120.
"an Irishman"—Ibid., p. 114.
"blue denims . . . dressed alike"—Ibid., p. 145.
"slanted eyes. . ."—Ibid., p. 116.
"the Irishman" felt friendly—Ibid., p. 114.
"like a rabbit," ". . .the poor little bunny who thought he was safe"—Ibid., p. 116.
"wraparound eyes"—Keith Thompson, *Angels and Aliens* (New York: Ballantine, 1991), p. 66.
". . .just keep looking"—Fuller, p. 118
"only a slit, completely without lips. . ." "part[ed] slightly"—Lorenzen, *Flying Saucer Occupants,* p. 78.
". . .mumumumming sound"—Fuller, *The Interrupted Journey,* p. 305.
"Jimmy Durante"-like noses—Ibid., p. 344.

Page 124
"bluish gray"—Ibid., p. 309.
"almost metallic looking"—Ibid., p. 305.
". . .with a bigger chest cavity, broader chest"—Ibid., p. 310.
down to the round stools—Ibid., p. 192.
"they took something like a letter-opener—only it wasn't. . ."—Ibid., p. 193.

Page 126
". . .it had straight lines and curved lines" Ibid., p. 208.
"Don't worry, if we decide to come back. . ."—Ibid., p. 211.
"Maybe you will remember, I don't know. . ."—Ibid., p. 212.

Page 127
"Oh, don't be ridiculous"—Ibid.
SAC's 100th Bomb Wing, report No. 100–1–61—Vallée, *Dimensions,* p. 103.

Page 128
"These creatures that I saw through the windows. . ."—Raymond E. Fowler, *The Watchers* (New York: Bantam Books, 1990), p. 4.
"feelers"—Philip J. Klass, *UFO Abductions: A Dangerous Game* (Buffalo New York: Prometheus Books, 1989), p. 44.

"Quazgaa"—Fowler, *The Watchers*, p. 19. (She did name one other as "Andantio.")

Page 129

"to protect her from harmful effects. . ."—Ibid., p. 338.

"a pyramidlike structure with a sculptured head. . ."—Ibid.

"It looked sort of like an Egyptian head. . ."—Ibid.

"I have chosen you to show the world"—Ibid., p. 339.

Page 130

"Child, you must forget for a while"—Ibid.

"They are going to come to the earth"—Ibid., p. 340.

". . .And they will be revealed only when the time is right."—Ibid.

"a certain class of angelic beings. . ."—Ibid., p. 214.

"They definitely do."—Klass, *UFO Abductions: A Dangerous Game*, p. 48.

Page 131

". . .constitute a challenge to our present belief systems"—Fowler, *The Watchers*, p. 354.

"and she didn't look like them. . . ," Kathie Davis "hybrid" description —Budd Hopkins, *Intruders* New York: Ballantine Books, 1988), pp. 223–226.

Page 132

"A father . . . has to take care of his children," ". . .stay with us"—Ibid., pp. 225–226.

"gross"—Ibid., p. 230.

"He just said she was a part of me"—Ibid., p. 227.

"That man just can't be the father. . ."—Ibid., p. 230.

"If you look at their eyes"—Ibid., p. 227.

Page 133

"kicking and charging at the gate. . ."—Eric Norman, *Gods, Demons and Space Chariots* (New York: Lancer Books, 1970), p. 170.

"I just couldn't believe what I saw there. . ."—Ibid., pp. 170–171.

"Saw a flying saucer. . ."—Ralph Blum with Judy Blum, *Beyond Earth: Man's Contact With UFOs*, p. 110.

"They really hammered me on those missing minutes"—Eric Norman, *Gods and Devils from Outer Space* (New York: Lancer Books, 1973), p. 141.

"They spent a lot of time just measuring the car. . ."—Ibid., pp. 141–142.

Page 134

"gobbling down aspirin like it was popcorn"—Ralph Blum with Judy Blum, *Beyond Earth: Man's Contact With UFOs*, p. 110.

"metal and . . . shaped like a football"—Norman, *Gods and Devils from Outer Space*, p. 143.

"like a camera lens adjusting"—Ralph Blum with Judy Blum, *Beyond Earth: Man's Contact With UFOs*, p. 113.

Page 135

"Better not . . . something. . ."—Norman, *Gods, Demons and Space Chariots*, p. 190.

"pushed against the side of my neck. . ."—Norman, *Gods and Devils from Outer Space*, p. 144.

"Maybe there was something about his glove. . ."—Ibid.

an abductee interviewed by Jacques Vallée in South America ["Oscar"] —Jacques Vallée, *Confrontations* (New York/Canada: Random House/Ballantine, 1990), p. 139.

"Are you the watchman over this place"—Norman, *Gods, Demons and Space Chariots*, p. 179.

"they have bases on Venus and some of the other planets. . ."—Ralph Blum with Judy Blum, *Beyond Earth: Man's Contact With UFOs*, p. 115.

"to a certain extent they want to puzzle people. . ."—Norman, *Gods and Devils from Outer Space*, p. 147.

Page 136

"They put out reports slowly to prepare us . . . not too much"—Norman, *Gods, Demons and Space Chariots*, p. 179.

"Why would they tell . . . conscious of protecting themselves"—Ibid., p. 185.

"I'm not even certain . . . something to throw us off guard"—Ibid., pp. 184–185.

"Your people are very hostile"—Ibid., p. 186.

"I would not even disclose that to the Air Force. . ."—Norman, *Gods and Devils from Outer Space*, p. 148.

"He's pressing buttons again. . ."—Norman, *Gods, Demons and Space Chariots*, p. 180.

". . .saying that while we talk . . . with everyone they contact"—Norman, *Gods and Devils from Outer Space*, p. 148.

"with a foreign accent, but very understandably"—Fuller, *The Interrupted Journey*, p. 343.

". . .as if they could breathe our atmosphere"—Norman, *Gods, Demons and Space Chariots*, p. 184.

". . .that looked like it might be used for breathing. . ."—Norman, *Gods and Devils from Outer Space*, p. 152.

". . .I don't recall seeing them take a breath like we do"—Ibid., p. 158.

Page 137

"They could not have been earth people . . . too different from us" —Ibid., p. 157.

"He said they left things to pure chance"—Norman, *Gods, Demons and Space Chariots*, p. 185.

"I was told that I just happened to be . . . lot more contacts"—Norman, *Gods and Devils from Outer Space*, p. 148.

"If there isn't any rhyme or reason. . ."—Norman, *Gods, Demons and Space Chariots*, p. 185.

". . .contacts state the truth it will help them"—Ralph Blum with Judy Blum, *Beyond Earth: Man's Contact With UFOs*, p. 117.

"The public should have no fear . . . they are not hostile"—Norman, *Gods and Devils from Outer Space*, p. 147.

"Most of our people will not remember. . ."—Norman, *Gods, Demons and Space Chariots*, p. 192.

"I think some people . . . like one of those robots you hear about" —Ibid., p. 186.

"...had a program known as 'breeding analysis'..."—Ibid., pp. 185–186.
Page 138
"like stuff you see in the movies about Egypt," "double-L's"—Ibid.,
p. 192.
"...You will not speak wisely about this night"—Ralph Blum with Judy
Blum, *Beyond Earth: Man's Contact With UFOs,* p. 118.
"several well-respected scientists..."—Norman, *Gods, Demons and
Space Chariots,* p. 193.
"We're finding this trend ... erased, or suppressed, in the contactee's
mind"—Ibid.
"The occupants of flying saucers have a marked tendency..."—Ibid.
"They spoke to us 'in smooth English'..."—Vallée, *Dimensions,* p. 63.

Chapter Five: *Humanoids*

The best books dealing with UFO occupants are still the Lorenzens' *Flying Saucer Occupants* and the Blums' *Beyond Earth: Man's Contact With UFOs,* though Jacques Vallée's *Passport to Magonia* (see Bibliography) and *Dimensions* (virtually the same book) and *UFO* magazine editor Richard Hall's *Uninvited Guests* (see Bibliography) are also rather good. John Spencer's *The UFO Encyclopedia,* extremely useful in numerous areas concerning the UFO question, does a good job reporting occupants.
Page 141
"This isn't the first of it, you know..."—Ralph Blum with Judy Blum,
Beyond Earth: Man's Contact With UFOs, p. 14.
"the laughingstock of the country"—Ibid., p. 30.
"We been getting these reports for the past forty days..."—Ibid., p. 14.
Page 142
"disc-shaped," "segmented," "oval-shaped" (etc.) object—Randle, *The
UFO Casebook,* pp. 142–143.
October 1973 "Year of the Humanoids" descriptions—Ibid., pp. 140–147.
September & November 1973 "Humanoids" descriptions—Ibid., pp. 140,
147–148.
Page 143
"...that had gray wrinkled skin and pointed ears"—Ibid., p. 142.
"grayish, like a ghost"—Ralph Blum with Judy Blum, *Beyond Earth:
Man's Contact With UFOs,* p. 17.
"pointed ears and noses and a pale skin-type covering"—Ibid., p. 10.
"clawlike hands"—Ibid., p. 13.
"pincher things"—Ibid., p. 32.
"feet shape" that "didn't have toes ... just a roundlike thing..."—Ibid.,
p. 31.
"looked like somebody's idea of a wrinkled robot"—Ibid., p. 16
"Calvin and me's talked about that too..."—Ibid., pp. 136–137.
Page 144
"oblong, sort of oblong ... about eight feet tall"—Ibid., p. 34.
"...dreamin' about something like that, you know"—Ibid., p. 31.
"done went hysterical on me," "zzzZZZ zzzZZZ"—Ibid.

"It might have been contactin' the others..."—Ibid., p. 32.

"It looked like an eye..., ," "...back over again," "a buzzin' sound..."
—Ibid., p. 33.

"...I had to let some officials know"—Ibid., p. 34.

Page 145

"I guess there's no way I could have lived with it..."—Ibid., pp. 139–140.

"When we got there, it was something amazing..."—Ibid., pp. 16–17.

"...Like he'd heard it all before," "Two colonels exchanged looks..."
—Ibid., p. 17.

Page 146

"...nature of which I am not certain..." "this country and in the
world"—Ibid., p. 24.

"...I can say so beyond any reasonable doubt"—Ibid., pp. 24–25.

Page 147

"...'I'm afraid this son'bitch is tellin' the truth!'"—Ibid., p. 199.

"cylindrical object, white, with an antenna-like extension"—Ibid., p. 200.

"altimeters don't hallucinate ... people who read altimeters hallucinate"—Ibid., p. 204.

"a Talmudic Jesuit in a white Palm Beach suit..."—Ibid., p. 205.

"...UFO witnesses with skill, humor, and courtesy"—Ibid.

"...And not one of those calls from anyone who disbelieves us"—Ibid.,
p. 135.

Page 148

"what did they do to me?"—Ibid., p. 136.

repeat occurrences had continued throughout his life—Spencer, The
UFO Encyclopedia, p. 240.

Calvin Parker spent time in the ... mental hospital—Ralph Blum with
Judy Blum, Beyond Earth: Man's Contact With UFOs, p. 196.

"I tell you, I've seen terror in my life..."—Ibid., p. 136.

"...never did find one that would keep correct time"—Ibid., p. 138.

"I dunno ... there's some kind of life on that world"—Mysteries From
Beyond Earth.

"...Sure did pick up the right kind of man! That was fine"—Ralph
Blum with Judy Blum, Beyond Earth: Man's Contact With UFOs,
p. 200.

Page 149

"Making money is not what this experience is all about"—Spencer, The
UFO Encyclopedia, p. 240.

Page 150

"weren't a drinking family"—Steiger, Project Blue Book, p. 104.

"all the colors of the rainbow," "elephant-like ears"—Spencer, The UFO
Encyclopedia, p. 172.

"did a flip"—Vallée, Dimensions, p. 22.

"seemed to float"—Steiger, Project Blue Book, p. 104.

Page 151

"Something frightened these people"—Spencer, The UFO Encyclopedia,
p. 172.

"strange shower of meteors" "swishing sound" "like artillery fire,"

—Steiger, *Project Blue Book,* p. 104.

"I knocked one of them off a barrel. . ."—Ibid., pp. 103–104.

"Bullets just seemed to bounce off. . . ," "pop right up again. . ."—Ibid., p. 103.

". . .inability of machine-gun bullets to affect them. . ."—Good, *Above Top Secret,* p. 316.

Page 152

". . .I might have been shot"—Spencer, *The UFO Encyclopedia,* p. 173.

Page 154

"Mothman"—John A. Keel, *The Mothman Prophecies* (Avondale Estates, Georgia: IllumiNet Press, 1975; 1991), passim.

ikals . . . "black"—Vallée, *Dimensions,* p. 73.

"a strange light wandering about. . . ," "About twenty years ago. . ." —Ibid., pp. 73–74.

". . .as though it had struck steel"—Lorenzen, *Flying Saucer Occupants,* p. 103.

Page 155

"The gun seemed to have struck rock. . . ," "little men"—Ibid., p. 104.

"Howdy, stranger," "She wouldn't be laughing," etc.—"Falkville Chief Says 'Howdy' to Spaceman," *Birmingham News,* 10/19/73.

". . .stay in Falkville. . . ," "under fire," "get another job"—"Falkville Police Chief Resigns Under Pressure," *Decatur Daily,* 11/16/73.

Page 158

Springheel Jack and John J. Vyner humanoid descriptions—Vallée, *Dimensions,* pp. 89–90.

Page 159

Cisco Grove/Donald Schrum case and quotes—Ibid., pp. 92–93.

Page 160

Loire, France case and quotes—Ibid., pp. 108–109.

Page 161

"Whoever's touching me . . . I feel touching" ". . .cold . . . not real soft. . ." —Hopkins, *Intruders,* p. 97.

"giant," "robot," "nails like conical dark blue metallic claws"—Vallée, *Confrontations,* p. 139.

Page 162

Voronezh—Vallée, *Revelations,* pp. 235–245.

Page 163

Livingston, Scotland—Spencer, *The UFO Encyclopedia,* pp. 189–190.

". . .but their anthropoid robots"—Zecharia Sitchin, *Genesis Revisited* (New York: Avon Books, 1990), p. 292.

Page 164

"It is odd that the creatures seen coming. . ."—Steiger, *Project Blue Book,* p. 105.

"Close Encounter of the 3rd Kind . . . presence of animated creatures. . ." —Clark, *UFO Encounters & Beyond,* p. 72.

". . .reams of data about us, couldn't they"—Vallée, journal entry dated 12/3/65, *Forbidden Science,* pp. 161–162.

Page 165
  Everett/Everittstown "tantalizing coincidence" case and quotes—Vallée, *Dimensions,* p. 62.
  "crews of robots or androids"—Good, *Above Top Secret,* p. 241.

Page 166
  "I have come to similar conclusions [as Felix Zigel]..."—Ibid.
  "suggestion of Linda Howe...," "whether the thing is a robot..." —Lindemann, *UFOs and the Alien Presence,* p. 164.

Page 167
  "bellhops"—Howe, *Glimpses of Other Realities, Vol. 1.*
  "...like alien dolls or puppets than living entities"—George Earley, "Hopkins Rates Mini-Series: 'B+'", *UFO,* Vol. 7, No. 4, 1992, p. 11.
  "USAAF Early Automation"—Randle & Schmitt, *UFO Crash at Roswell,* pp. 106–107.

Page 168
  "believed the object was unmanned...," "...long distance repairs" —Ibid., p. 121.
  "Excuse me, Admiral..."—Timothy Good, *Alien Liaison* (London: Arrow Books Ltd., 1991), p. 187.
  "...remote-control devices for character robots..."—Ibid., p. 198.

Page 169
  "...and mobile surveillance systems"—Ibid., pp. 188–189.
  "minor injuries and a broken nose"—Randle & Schmitt, *The Truth About the UFO Crash at Roswell,* p. 18.

Chapter Six: *Controls*

Pages 189–191
  Adventure magazine John Spencer Mongolian monastery story—Peter Kolosimo, *Not of This World* (Secaucus, New Jersey: University Books, Inc., 1971), pp. 37–43.

Page 192
  "creatures without mouths"—Ibid., photo section.
  "It is distinctly Hopi. One cannot doubt [it]..."—Frank Waters, *The Book of the Hopi* (New York: Viking Penguin Books, 1963), p. 168.
  "...from mysterious spirit worlds"—Ibid., p. 165.
  koko pilau, "wood hump," "the humpbacked flute player"—Ibid., p. 38.
  mahu, "insect people resembling the katydid or locust," "the eagle" —Ibid., p. 37.
  "Now that you have stood both tests..."—Ibid., pp. 37–38.

Page 193
  "seeds of plants and flowers"—Ibid., p. 38.
  "the seeds of human reproduction also"—Ibid. (n).
  "His [koko pilau's] song is still remembered..."—Ibid., p. 38.
  "The kachinas ... may be invoked..."—Ibid., p. 166.
  "respected spirit"—Ibid., p. 167.
  kiva, "like a womb," "the previous underworld," "the world above" —Ibid., p. 127.
  "monster kachinas"—Ibid., pp. 185–187.

Page 194
("night dances")—Ibid., p. 165.

Page 195
"a low hum and a strange blowing . . . like the winds from outer space"
—Ibid., p. 145.
Nutungtatoka, "First and Last," ". . .before the world is destroyed,"
etc.—Ibid.
"The Alpha and the Omega"—Revelations 1:8.
"I am the Father of all of you . . . see this happen to you"—Waters, *The
Book of the Hopi,* pp. 178–179.
"is rooted in this world. . ." Ibid., p. 133.

Page 196
Chon-oopa-sa—Kolosimo, *Not of This World,* p. 213.
Vallée draws attention to ten points. . .—Vallée, *Dimensions,* p. 170.
David M. Jacobs' list—David M. Jacobs, Ph.D., *Secret Life* (New York:
Fireside Simon & Schuster, 1992), Appendix C, p. 330.

Page 197
"initiated into the select . . . knowledgeables," "inserts a . . . thin bamboo"—Otto Billig, *Flying Saucers: Magic in the Skies* (Cambridge,
Massachusetts: Schenkman Publishing Company, Inc., 1982),
p. 102.
"The encounters of primitive people. . ."—Ibid., pp. 102–103.

Page 198
"Many descriptions of UFO phenomena. . ."—Vallée, *Dimensions,* p. 173.

Page 199
"the physics of the B.V.M."—Ibid., p. 182.
". . .mixture of mysticism and technology quite amazing"—Vallée, *Forbidden Science,* p. 263.
"a youth of admirable beauty"—Vallée, *Dimensions,* p. 179.
"a statue made of snow. . ."—Sandra L. Zimdars-Swartz, *Encountering
Mary* (New York: Avon Books, 1991; 1992), p. 73.
"the Angel of Peace"—Vallée, *Dimensions,* p. 179.
"quite abstracted"— Zimdars-Swartz, *Encountering Mary,* p. 73.
"I don't know what is happening to me. . ."—Vallée, *Dimensions,* p. 179.

Page 200
"from heaven"—Ibid., p. 174.
"the Lady"—Ibid., p. 175. (Joseph Pelletier, *The Sun Danced At Fatima.*)
"the blessed and ever-Virgin Mary of Guadalupe"—Helen Behrens and
Dr. Charles Wahlig, *A Handbook On Guadalupe* (Kenosha, Wisconsin: Franciscan Marytown Press, 1974), p. 18.
te coatlexopeuh . . . "de Guadalupe" . . . "who crushes the stone serpent"—Ibid.

Page 201
"seemed unusually sad. . ."—Zimdars-Swartz, *Encountering Mary,* p. 78.
"nonsense," "a luminous globe spinning through the clouds"—Vallée,
Dimensions, p. 176.
"buzzing of a bee," "mosquito in an empty bottle," "pale as death"
—Zimdars-Swartz, *Encountering Mary,* p. 80.

"Our Lady," "...there she goes," "...doors are shut," "...rather like a rocket"—Ibid.

Page 202

"...heavenly vehicle...," "weird disk...," "ladder ... two beings," etc. —Vallée, *Dimensions,* p. 177.

"a great noise ... sound of a storm," "lost ... speech and thought" —Vallée, *Dimensions,* p. 182.

Page 203

"The Immaculate Conception"—Zimdars-Swartz, *Encountering Mary,* p. 55.

"Listen, little son..."—Vallée, *Dimensions,* p. 136.

"miserable," "disgusting" and "vile"—Zimdars-Swartz, *Encountering Mary,* p. 46.

Page 204

"kiss the ground for sinners"—Vallée, *Dimensions,* p. 184.

"They were setting an example of prayer and humility..." (Stephen Breen)—Ibid.

"...can play a role far beyond their local impact"—Ibid.

"UFO Hypothesis and Survival Questions"—Fawcett & Greenwood, *Clear Intent,* pp. 183–185.

Page 205

"retain[ing] institutional control ... to preserve 'national security'" —Good, *Above Top Secret,* p. 365.

"the consequences [of UFO beliefs] will be as serious..."—Geoff Olson, "'Psi-Cops' Bite Into Abduction Claims," *UFO,* Vol. 9, No. 5, p. 15.

Page 206

"Do the captivity characteristics of modern..."—Fawcett & Greenwood, *Clear Intent,* p. 186.

"high strangeness"—Ibid., p. 182

"A new computer analysis of historical trends..."—Vallée, *Forbidden Science,* p. 420.

Page 207

"...certain ways of reinforcing behavior..."—Vallée, *Dimensions,* p. 245.

cherubim..., "full of knowledge," Sadaim ... daimonas—Ibid., p. 16.

Page 208

airship of 1897—Ibid , pp. 38–43.

Page 209

"cloudships"—Ibid., p. 42.

"...the dead period of UFO activity..."—Vallée, *Anatomy of a Phenomenon,* p. 54.

"blackout caused by a UFO" (Vallée)—Per Schelde, *Androids, Humanoids and Other Science Fiction Monsters* (New York: New York University Press, 1993), p. 85.

Page 210

"I used to be tormented constantly ... 'Night-Gaunts'" etc.—L. Sprague de Camp, *Lovecraft: A Biography* (New York: Random House, 1975; 1976), pp. 32–33.

"...Egyptians possessed ... skill in the manufacture of automata"
—Lewis Spence, *Myths & Legends of Ancient Egypt* (Mineola, New York: Dover Publications, Inc., 1915; 1990), p. 142.

Page 211

"animated" ornaments, "...to quiet their potentially wandering spirits"—Peter Tompkins, *Mysteries of the Mexican Pyramids* (New York: Harper & Row, 1976), p. 99.

"under certain stellar and planetary aspects"—Andrew Tomas, *We Are Not The First* (New York: Bantam Books/G. P. Putnam's Sons, 1971), p. 123.

Page 212

"a small tube that could be held in one hand..."—Vallée, *Dimensions,* p. 74

"To us, they appear unfamiliar, even ugly..."—Marija Gimbutas, *The Goddesses and Gods of Old Europe 6500–3500 B.C.* (Berkeley, Los Angeles, New York: University of California Press, 1974; 1982), p. 57.

"cosmic waters," "two snakes ... heads meeting," "incised upon discs" —Ibid., p. 124.

"Was it the sculptor's intention ... significance of the mask..."—Ibid., p. 64.

"Almond- or egg-shaped," "elliptical-shaped" "semicircular eyes"—Ibid., pp. 63–64.

Page 213

"a man wearing an air-tight helmet ... for flight"—Gordon Creighton, "A Russian Wall Painting and Other Spacemen," *Flying Saucer Review,* 1965.

Page 214

Kappas, Professor Komatsu Kitamura, *Mainichi Graphic* article—Peter Kolosimo, *Timeless Earth* (Secaucus, New Jersey: University Books, Inc., 1974), pp. 63–64.

"a nightmare world of spirits..." Ibid., pp. 62–63.

Page 215

"holding them in trust for a future of wonders"—Vallée, *Dimensions,* p. 186.

"violent phosphene activity ... trickster is involved"—Vallée, *Revelations,* pp. 293–294.

Page 216

abit ... Bebait ... "Mantis"—E. A. Wallis Budge, *The Book of the Dead* (1899) (England: Penguin Arkana Publishing, 1989), p. 310 (n).

Page 217

"nature images," "like, okay, great. I've seen this on T.V...."—John E. Mack, M.D., *Abduction* (New York: Charles Scribner's Sons, 1994), p. 171.

"to make you understand, to comprehend the implications..."—Ibid., p. 173.

"Amun Ra"—Ibid., p. 172.

Page 218

"an increasing group of abductees that I have been encountering. . ." —Ibid., p. 217.

"I have to go with him. . ."—Ibid., p. 222.

". . .the secret life is that I've spent a lot of time with them"—Ibid., pp. 183–184.

"a foot in both worlds"—Ibid., pp. 217–241 passim.

"The figure told [the abductee] 'it's me'. . ."—Ibid., p. 232.

". . .in which the figure makes itself identical with the deceased"—E. A. Wallis Budge, *The Mummy* (1893) (Mineola, New York: Dover Publications, Inc., 1989), p. 255.

"porters of Horus"—Bob Brier, *Ancient Egyptian Magic* (New York: William Morrow & Company, Inc., 1980), p. 126.

"what I should know and what I should forget"— R. O. Faulkner, *The Ancient Egyptian Coffin Texts* (3 vols.) (Warminster, England, Aris & Phillips, Ltd., 1977), Spell 572.

"the solar barque of millions of years"—Veronica Ions, *Egyptian Mythology* (New York, Peter Bedrick Books, 1968), pp. 40–41.

Page 219

"An official of Sa-Amen called Hor . . . and so protected him"—E. A. Wallis Budge, *From Fetish to God In Ancient Egypt* (1934) (Mineola, New York: Dover Publications, Inc., 1988), pp. 123–124.

Page 220

". . .suddenly he remembered all that had happened to him. . ."—Spence, *Myths & Legends of Ancient Egypt,* p. 215.

Page 221

". . .glowing reddish and large, was Mars"—Ralph Blum with Judy Blum, *Beyond Earth: Man's Contact With UFOs,* p. 21.

Chapter Seven: *Correlations*

Information in this chapter comes from several principal sources, most of which are specified in the text. Jacques Vallée's *Anatomy of a Phenomenon* and Jacques and Janine Vallée's *Challenge to Science: The UFO Enigma* are the sources on the Martian UFO correlation, with peripheral confirmation from Nigel Blundell's and Roger Boar's *The World's Greatest UFO Mysteries.* The primary source for official NASA data on the Moon is Andrew Chaikin's *A Man on the Moon: The Voyages of the Apollo Astronauts.* For anomalies of the Moon, David Hatcher Childress' *Extraterrestrial Archaeology; UFO* magazine's March/April 1995 issue article "Long Saga of Lunar Anomalies" by Don Ecker; and Harold T. Wilkins' *Flying Saucers on the Attack*; the latter is indispensable not only on the subject of lunar anomalies, but those of Mars as well. The essential information on Mars and its anomalies is taken from Richard C. Hoagland's *The Monuments of Mars,* with most information on the *Phobos 2* loss coming from Zecharia Sitchin's highly informative *Genesis Revisited.* For the loss of the *Observer* probe and additional information on Martian anomalies, the following articles from *UFO* magazine's November/December 1993 issue:

Don Ecker's "The 'Galactic Ghoul': Superpower Problems in Getting to Mars," Don Ecker and Vicki Cooper's "Mission Improbable: NASA on the Mars Observer," Vicki Cooper's "NASA Accused of Hiding Facts—Mars Observer: What Went Wrong?" and "Did NASA Disobey the 'Prime Directive'?" by Richard C. Hoagland. The *Mahabharata* quotes in this chapter are taken from David Hatcher Childress' *Lost Cities of China, Central Asia & India.*

Page 223

"Janine and I are now doing a study. . ."—Vallée, *Forbidden Science,* p. 48.

"I often hit theoretical snags. . ."—Ibid., p. 76.

". . .for the period between 1870 and 1914. . ."—Vallée, *Anatomy of a Phenomenon,* pp. 63–64.

Page 224

"long train of clouds," "It seemed as if Mars was breaking up. . ." —Harold T. Wilkins, *Flying Saucers on the Attack* (New York: Ace Books, Inc., 1954), p. 231.

"flaming up . . . queer bluish light"—Ibid., p. 232.

Page 225

"believed he had intercepted messages from Mars . . . in the Mediterranean"—"Marconi Believes He Received Wireless Messages From Mars," *New York Tribune,* 9/2/21.

"Highly advanced creatures from Mars have visited. . ."—W. Raymond Drake, *Gods and Spacemen in the Ancient East* (London: Sphere Books, 1968), p. 90.

"a body shining . . . in the form of a 'pipe' . . . end of the world was approaching"—Simon Welfare & John Fairley, *Arthur C. Clarke's Mysterious World* (New York: A & W Publishers Inc., 1980), p. 154.

Page 226

"many geometrical figures. . .," "octagon/five-pointed star"—Wilkins, *Flying Saucers on the Attack,* pp. 232–233.

"absolutely inexplicable," "series of triplets," "atomic explosion on Mars"—Ibid.

"No terrestrial volcano could produce a light of such brilliance. . ." —Andrews, citing V. A. Firsoff, *Life Beyond Earth* (New York: Basic Books, 1963), *Extraterrestrials Among Us,* p. 103.

Page 227

"in position to be seen from Mars," "other galactic communities" —Vallée, *Anatomy of a Phenomenon,* p. 89.

atomic explosions create aurorae on opposite sides of the Earth—Welfare & Fairley, *Arthur C. Clarke's Mysterious World,* pp. 162–163.

". . .seemed to result in a reasonable correlation"—Jacques and Janine Vallée, *Challenge To Science: The UFO Enigma* (New York: Ballantine Books, 1966), pp. 161–162.

Page 228

"The problem of [this] study of the cyclic variations. . ."—Ibid., p. 166.

"we found an interesting confirmation of the results. . ."—Ibid., pp. 168–169.

Page 229

"...but it is far from being absolutely demonstrated"—Ibid., p. 171.

"...to play a less important role than Mars"—Ibid., p. 172.

"the current military investigations ignore [it] entirely"—Ibid.

"...seem to be more than the product of coincidence"—Vallée, *Forbidden Science,* p. 57.

"UFOlogists noted . . . years of 1967 and 1973. . ."—Blundell and Boar, pp. 222–223.

"reliable" as opposed to "an interesting experiment"—Vallée, *Challenge To Science: The UFO Enigma,* p. 168.

"...and it will be very interesting to resume this research on a larger scale"—Ibid.

Page 230

"...to provide continuity for successive expeditions"—Ralph Blum with Judy Blum, *Beyond Earth: Man's Contact With UFOs,* p. 203.

"...and small hills like walls of an ancient ruin"—Sitchin, *Genesis Revisited,* p. 242.

"...radial arms protruding from a central hub"—Ibid., p. 280.

Page 231

"...which locked with the rotation of Mars"—Andrews, *Extraterrestrials Among Us,* p. 113.

Page 232

"...to 2 pi times the equatorial radius of Mars."—Ibid.

Page 233

"...community coming from elsewhere in the universe"—Vallée, *Anatomy of a Phenomenon,* p. 172.

"It seems much easier to explain the nonexistence of the moon. . ." —David Hatcher Childress, *Extraterrestrial Archaeology* (Stelle, Illinois: Adventures Unlimited Press, 1994), p. 11.

Page 234

"Oh my God, look at this," ". . .just the way the light fell on it"—Richard C. Hoagland, *The Monuments of Mars* (Berkeley, California: North Atlantic Books, 1987), pp. 4–5.

"overwhelmingly favored presumption"—Ibid., p. 7 (n).

"This tendency to presume, rather than to check. . ."—Ibid.

Page 236

"the Global Grid"—Ibid., p. 358.

"great circle"—Ibid., p. 360.

Page 237

"...and then 19 degrees 30 minutes to the east. . ."—Ibid., p. 357.

Page 239

"...and puts a Greek ending on it one gets Helios. . ."—Robert K. G. Temple, *The Sirius Mystery* (Rochester, Vermont: Destiny Books, 1976), p. 116.

"parallel contours [that] look very much like. . ."—Sitchin, *Genesis Revisited,* p. 264.

Page 240
   "merely seeing Jesus Christ on a tortilla chip"—Hoagland, *The Monuments of Mars,* p. 329.

Page 241
   "failed to communicate with Earth as scheduled"—Sitchin, *Genesis Revisited,* p. 272.

Page 242
   "phenomenon"—Ibid., p. 275.
   a shape gem-cutters call a "marquise"—Ibid., p. 281.
   "to fantasize," "tracking a spinner"—Ibid., pp. 276–277.

Page 243
   "quite remarkable features . . . in the lower atmosphere"—Childress, *Extraterrestrial Archaeology,* p. 217.
   "The city-like pattern is 60 kilometers wide. . ."—Ibid., p. 220.
   "thin ellipse," probe "impacted," etc.—Sitchin, *Genesis Revisited,* pp. 282–283.
   ". . .object between the spacecraft and Mars"—Ibid., p. 277.
   "New grooves can be identified"—Ibid., p. 298.

Page 244
   "blown up"— Don Eckert, "The Galactic Ghoul: Superpower Problems in Getting to Mars," *UFO* Vol. 8, No. 6, p. 33.

Page 245
   "It is KSC [Kennedy Space Center] policy. . ."—Good, *Above Top Secret,* p. 367.

Page 246
   "This NASA document. . ."—*UFO* Vol. 8., No. 6, p. 35.
   "artifacts left. . ." "societies sure of their place. . ."—Brookings Document, p. 215.
   "anti-science," "professions . . . mastery of nature," ". . .superior creatures,"—Ibid., p. 225.
   "within the next twenty years"—Ibid., p. 215.

Page 248
   "It lasted for 15 minutes. . ." and "a bright light like a star"—Wilkins, *Flying Saucers on the Attack,* p. 218.
   "I have seen lights before on the moon. . ."—Ibid., p. 222.
   "sudden outbreak" of mystery lights in the Mare Crisium—Don Ecker, "Long Saga of Lunar Anomalies," *UFO* Vol.10, No. 2, p. 23.
   "a ball of fire the apparent size of the moon"—Wilkins, *Flying Saucers on the Attack,* p. 219.

Page 249
   "like a reflection from a moving mirror"—Ibid., p. 223.
   "saw an object of so peculiar a nature. . ."—Ibid., p. 225.
   "like a vast crow poised. . ."—Ibid., p. 226.

Page 250
   "the second most conspicuous crater on the plain"—Childress, *Extraterrestrial Archaeology,* p. 35.

Page 251

"a geometric object shaped like a cross," "an acute-angled triangle" —Ibid., p. 45.

"The Railway"—Ibid., p. 39.

"rings like a gong or a bell"—Ibid., p. 12.

Page 252

"more than 200 circular dome-shaped structures. . ."—Ibid., p. 40.

Page 253

". . .according to definite geometric laws"—Ibid., p. 98.

"not at all happy about its publication"—Ibid.

"as smooth as glass"—Ibid., p. 42.

"the triangulation would be scalene or irregular. . ."—Kolosimo, *Not of This World*, p. 147.

"persuad[ing] one to think it is like an excavation. . ."—Ibid.

Page 254

"plugholes"—Childress, *Extraterrestrial Archaeology*, p. 42.

"mascons" of matter beneath the Moon's seas—Andrew Chaikin, *A Man on the Moon: The Voyages of the Apollo Astronauts* (New York: Penguin Books, 1994), p. 70.

"paved with glass"—Childress, *Extraterrestrial Archaeology*, p. 14.

Page 255

"embarrasingly high," "My God, this place is about to melt"—Ibid., p. 13.

"the violence of cosmic bombardment"—Chaikin, *A Man on the Moon: The Voyages of the Apollo Astronauts,* p. 493.

"exploded with the power of billions of H-bombs"—Ibid., p. 539.

"many thousands of years old"—Kolosimo, *Timeless Earth* (Secaucus, NJ: University Books, 1974), p. 58.

". . .could not have been visible from their place of origin"—Ibid.

"Many Soviet scientists are convinced of the existence. . ."—Ibid.

Page 256

"Around an imposing central building . . . know nothing of their history"—Ibid., p. 60.

Page 257

Mohenjo-Daro ("Mound of the Dead")—David Hatcher Childress, *Lost Cities of China, Central Asia & India* (1985) (Stelle, Illinois: Adventures Unlimited Press, 1991), p. 239.

A. Gorbovsky, radioactive skeleton—Tomas, citing A. Gorbovsky, *Riddles of Ancient History* (Moscow, 1966), *We Are Not The First*, p. 54.

". . .a single projectile . . . wash themselves . . . equipment"—Childress, *Lost Cities of China, Central Asia & India,* pp. 243–244.

Page 258

"Well, yes, in modern history," Oppenheimer Sanskrit quotes, etc. —Ibid., p. 244.

the Biblical "war in the heavens"—Revelations 12:7.

Page 259

"The encounter was common knowledge in NASA. . ."—Good, *Above Top Secret,* p. 384.

"Santa Claus," "all Apollo and Gemini flights were followed. . ."—Ibid., p. 385.

"NASA and the government know. . ."—Blundell and Boar, p. 215.

"You have to see this to believe it, J. T.!"—*Encounters,* Fox TV, 7–24–95.

Page 260

"Operation Paper Clip"—Jonathan Vankin, Conspiracies, Cover-ups and Crimes (New York: Paragon House, 1992), p. 290.

Life's "100 Most Important . . . 20th Century"—Larry Thorson, "Space pioneer no hero, German exhibit suggests," AP, *Rocky Mountain News,* 4/12/95.

"Can there be any justification . . . for a criminal system?"—Ibid.

"It was as if they had only ever thought of going to the moon"—Ibid.

"Not long ago there was a chilling prediction. . ."—Howard Koch, *The Panic Broadcast* (New York: Avon Books, 1970), p. 144.

Page 261

"due to the improvement in Soviet-American relations"—Sitchin *Genesis Revisited,* p. 305.

"Signpost to Mars"/Cairo: Biography of a City—Hoagland, *The Monuments of Mars,* p. 289.

Chapter Eight: *Origins*

John Anthony West's *Serpent in the Sky* (Wheaton, Illinois: Quest Books, Theosophical Publishing House, 1993) is the most concise collection of criticisms against traditional Egyptology in print, enlivened by the inclusion of multiple cross-references from common accepted sources that appear comical in light of increased learning on the subject. His and his teams' theories on the Sphinx are more thoroughly presented in the NBC special/video *Mystery of the Sphinx*. Similarly, the CBS special *Mysteries of the Ancient World* (in book form by Charles E. Sellier, New York: Dell Books, 1995) is a very thorough overview of the problems with Egyptology as it is presently taught. Zecharia Sitchin's *The Stairway to Heaven* is the source from which the expose of Colonel Howard Vyse's Cheops forgeries is primarily taken; it is a scholarly and sometimes pedantic book, but worth the time to peruse. Sitchin's *The 12th Planet* (the first of his *The Earth Chronicles* series) is more accessible to the common reader and presents all of his fundamental theories.

The best overall book on the Great Pyramid is Peter Tompkins' *Secrets of the Great Pyramid,* with plentiful sketches and maps. Tompkins' subsequent *Mysteries of the Mexican Pyramids* is even better. Of the traditional Egyptology sources listed, probably the most accessible to the common reader are R. T. Rundle Clark's *Myth and Symbol in Ancient Egypt,* Bob Brier's *Ancient Egyptian Magic* (New York: Quill/William Morrow and Co., 1980) and Lewis Spence's *Myths and Legends of Ancient Egypt* (published as *Ancient Egyptian Myths and Legends,* Mineola, New York: Dover Books, 1990), though the works of E. A. Wallis Budge—which are admittedly very dry and long-winded—are overall the most informative, especially his last in-depth summary, *From Fetish to God in Ancient Egypt* (Mineola, New York: Dover Books, 1988).

E. C. Krupp's *Echoes of the Ancient Skies,* which eschews any connection to Ancient Astronaut theory, is an excellent book covering the topic of archaeoastronomy. Of the Ancient Astronaut theorists mentioned, Sitchin is certainly the best. Also worthy of note are the works of Jean Sendy and W. Raymond Drake (see Bibliography), though they are difficult to come by. Robert Charroux is more fragmentary and makes greater leaps, but is highly informative. Erich Von Daniken's works suffer from lack of hard scholarship, but are still worthwhile to look over. Ignatius Donnelly's *Atlantis: The Antediluvian World,* despite much adverse criticism over the years, is still an excellent preliminary study of diffusionistic anthropology, especially since E. F. Bleiler's 1976 introduction and footnoting in the Dover edition have cleaned up Donnelly's (mostly negligible and understandable) errors.

Bible quotes have not been standardized.

Page 265
"Oh."—*Mystery of the Sphinx,* NBC
"...our guide ... lectures us on pyramid lore..."—L. Sprague and Catherine C. de Camp, *Ancient Ruins and Archaeology* (New York: Doubleday & Co., 1946), pp. 36–37.

Page 266
"We do not know Egypt. We only think we do" (Howard Carter)—traditional.

Pages 268–272
Howard Vyse forgeries—Zecharia Sitchin, "Forging the Pharaoh's Name" in *The Stairway to Heaven* (1980) (New York: Avon Books, 1983), pp. 253–282.

Page 268
"I naturally wished to make some discoveries before I returned..." —Ibid., p. 261.

Page 269
"Such is the state of preservation of the marks in the quarries..." —Ibid., pp. 276–277.

Page 270
"good" or "gracious"—Ibid., p. 266.
"the presence of this (second) name ... is an additional embarassment"—Ibid., p. 267.
"has caused much embarassment to Egyptologists"—Ibid., p. 270.
"in various quarries ... and in certain writing of later date"—Ibid., p. 282.

Page 271
"considerable difference of style"—Ibid., p. 279.
"certainly dates from the Saitic period"—Ibid., p. 249.

"...were not of an original burial ... deliberate archaeological fraud" —Ibid., p. 280.

Page 272

contemporaneous family records ... [Brewer] fired from the Pyramid site—Zecharia Sitchin, *The Wars of Gods and Men* (New York: Avon Books, 1985), p. 136.

"Live Horus Mezdau ... beside the House of the Sphinx"—Sitchin, *The Stairway to Heaven,* p. 256.

Page 273

"the coffer has certain remarkable cubic proportions..."—W. M. Flinders Petrie, *The Pyramids and Temples of Gizeh* (London, 1883), p. 201.

Page 274

"...are mythological cities and not cities upon Earth."—E. A. Wallis Budge, *The Gods of the Egyptians, Vol. 1* (1904) (Mineola, New York: Dover Publications, Inc., 1969), pp. 103–104.

Page 275

"Ageb ... 'land of the flood' ... Masr..."—Budge, *The Mummy*, p. 2.

"...which affected the globe with fire and flooding"—Peter Tompkins, *Secrets of the Great Pyramid* (New York, Harper & Row Publishers, Inc., 1971), pp. 217–218.

"...the Heart of the Lion ... the head of Cancer..."—Ibid.

"the Egyptians gave many names to their land..."—Budge, *The Mummy,* p. 1.

"The word 'Alchemy,' i.e. the 'Black Art'..."—E. A. Wallis Budge, *Amulets and Superstitions* (1930) (Mineola, New York: Dover Publications, Inc., 1978), p. 443.

Page 276

"Father of Terror" (Abu Khawl)—Bob Brier, *Ancient Egyptian Magic* (New York: Quill/William Morrow and Co., 1980), p. 110.

peremus—Budge, *The Mummy*, p. 31 (n).

pyr-met, "division of ten"—Joseph A. Seiss, D.D., *The Great Pyramid: A Miracle in Stone* (1877) (Blauvelt, New York: Steinerbooks, 1989), p. 46.

urrim midden, "light measures"—Tom Valentine, *The Great Pyramid: Man's Monument to Man* (New York: Pinnacle Books, 1975), p. 57.

Greek for "fire in the center"—David Hatcher Childress, *Lost Cities & Ancient Mysteries of Africa and Arabia* (Stelle, Illinois, Adventures Unlimited Press, 1989), p. 99.

khuti or khufu, "glorious light"—Valentine, *The Great Pyramid: Man's Monument to Man,* p. 57.

Page 277

pirhua manco, "revealer of light"—Ibid., p. 58.

pyramis ... "wheaten cake"—Rosalie David, *Discovering Ancient Egypt* (New York: Facts On File Inc., 1993), p. 126.

mer... "Place of Ascension"—Ibid.

To-mera ... "land of the mer"—Tompkins, *Secrets of the Great Pyramid,* pp. 291–292 (Livio Stecchini).

Sumer . . . "The Land"—Zecharia Sitchin, *The 12th Planet* (1976) (New York: Avon Books, 1978), p. 97.

"ones who watch"—Hoagland, *The Monuments of Mars,* p. 290.

Page 278

omphalos . . . "oracle"—Temple, *The Sirius Mystery,* p. 130.

"navels"—Tompkins, *Secrets of the Great Pyramid,* p. 182.

Page 279

Wilhelm Koenig, Egyptian electricity, etc.—Tomas, *We Are Not The First,* pp. 93–98.

tabots—Graham Hancock, *The Sign and the Seal* (New York, Touchstone/Simon & Schuster, 1992), pp. 290–292.

"giving off fiery rays," "energy accumulator," "orgone box"—Tompkins, *Secrets of the Great Pyramid,* p. 278.

Page 280

"defied all known laws of physics"—Ibid., p. 273.

"King's coffer" . . . Ark of the Covenant—Tompkins, *Secrets of the Great Pyramid,* p. 278.

"pockets" . . . reflection of sound waves—*Mystery of the Sphinx* (NBC-TV).

Merlin "dancing" Stonehenge into place, magic of the Danaan—Nikolai Tolstoy, *The Quest for Merlin* (New York: Back Bay Books/Little, Brown and Company, 1985), pp. 127–129, 112. The "Giant's Dance" is a nickname sometimes given to the stones of Stonehenge themselves, though historical sources such as Geoffrey of Monmouth hint at the implication that supernatural movement is also involved. Tolstoy calls attention to the fact that *machinationes* (p. 128) and "superior engineering skills" (p. 129) were involved in Merlin's magic, involving some secret apparatus never specified in any of the sources, though he discounts the *Historia Brittonum's* rendering that it had anything to do with "timber and stones" (p. 112) as not credible. (Traditional Egyptologists have insisted from the beginning that the "rope and pulley" theories told Herodotus are credible for erecting the megalithic blocks of the Giza Pyramids.) The "sound levitation" theory has another potential backing in the Easter Island natives' explanation for how the giant moai (statues) were put into place: "They walked." See pp. 241–270 of Charles E. Sellier's *Mysteries of the Ancient World,* New York: Dell, 1995, and pp. 309–324 (Chapter 14) of David Hatcher Childress' *Lost Cities of Ancient Lemuria & the Pacific,* Stelle, Illinois: Adventures Unlimited Press, 1988.

". . .such . . . tunes that the stones moved into place of their own accord"—H. A. Guerber, *The Myths of Greece and Rome* (1907) (Mineola, New York: Dover Books, 1993), p. 48.

Page 281

"telegeodynamics"—Margaret Cheney, *Tesla: Man Out Of Time* (1981) (New York: Dell Publishing, 1983), pp. 117–118.

Page 282

"a fusillade of taps. . ."—Ibid., p. 116.

"a cylinder of finest steel. . ."—Ibid., p. 118.
Page 283
"the Masters of the Water," "the Instructors," and "The Monitors"
—Temple, p. 209.
annedotus . . . "repulsive one"—Ibid., pp. 205–206.
"Anunnaki . . . they who from heaven to earth fell"—Sitchin, passim.
Anasazi . . . "the Ancient Ones"—E. C. Krupp, Echoes of the Ancient
Skies (New York: Harper & Row, Inc., 1983), p. 150.
"Odacon"—Temple, *The Sirius Mystery,* p. 207.
their exact word for his ship is an ark—Ibid., p. 209.
Page 284
"semi-demons . . . endowed with reason"—Ibid., p. 17.
Itzamna ("He Whose Home Is Water")—Zecharia Sitchin, *The Lost Realms*
(New York: Avon Books, 1990), p. 92.
Aja-Ekapada, "One-footed Goat" or "Birthless One-footed One"—Ananda
Coomaraswamy and Sr. Nivedita, *Myths of the Hindus and Buddhists*
(1913) (Mineola, New York: Dover Publications, Inc., 1967), p. 388.
Page 285
po—Temple, *The Sirius Mystery,* p. 3 (Griaule and Dieterlin).
Page 286
Dr. Edwards potentially confirms Giza-stellar correlation—Robert Bau-
val and Adrian Gilbert, *The Orion Mystery* (New York: Crown Pub-
lishers, Inc., 1994), pp. 51–52; 127–128.
Page 288
". . .strange events have taken place in the . . . Solar System"—Clyde
W. Tombaugh and Patrick Moore, *Out of the Darkness: The Planet
Pluto* (1980) (New York: New American Library, 1981), p. 33.
Ogo—Temple, *The Sirius Mystery,* p. 31.
"the star of limiting the place"—Ibid., p. 29.
"Foremost Prince of the West"—Sitchin, *The 12th Planet,* p. 214.
Page 289
"Ogo/Nommo's placenta" "land of the fish"—Temple, *The Sirius Mys-
tery,* pp. 31–33.
monitor of the universe—Ibid., p. 31.
hunab (Mayan for "unified measure")—Tompkins, *Mysteries of the Mex-
ican Pyramids,* p. 247.
Page 290
Xochitl ("flower")—Ibid., p. 268.
Xiknalkan (Mayan for "Flying Serpent")—Ibid.
Dr. Charles Muses, "Pan"—Ibid., p. 269.
"far out"—Ibid., p. 271 (n).
Xipe Xolotl, the "flayed red god of the east" (Mars)—Ibid.
Quetzalcoatl (also called "Sumer," Venus)—Ibid.
"peeled off like an orange"—Ibid.
Page 291
Rishis . . . "primeval flowing ones"—traditional.
". . .the gods created the heavens and the earth" (Voltaire)—traditional.

"The word translated as 'In the beginning'. . ."—Robert Charroux, *Masters of the Earth* (1967) (New York: Berkley Publishing Corporation, 1974), p. 26.

Page 292

"Divine Command"—R. T. Rundle Clark, *Myth and Symbol in Ancient Egypt* (London/New York: Thames and Hudson Ltd., 1959), p. 36.

"In the beginning was the Word. . ."—John 1.1.

Page 293

Ninti . . . "lady life"—Sitchin, *The 12th Planet*, p. 105.

"Prince of earth" "lord of the Deep" "Lord of the Saltwaters," etc.—Ibid., p. 102.

"house of water"—Ibid.

"Adama" . . . Adapa, "model man"—Ibid., p. 349

Adamah—"Earth"—Sitchin, *Genesis Revisited*, p. 161.

"life," "rib," ti—Sitchin, *The 12th Planet*, p. 354.

Neb-Heru . . . "Lord Sun"—Temple, *The Sirius Mystery*, p. 117.

50 epithets of Nebiru, "god who maintains life," Asar, etc.—Sitchin, *The 12th Planet*, p. 255.

"most radiant of the gods"—Ibid., p. 244.

Page 294

Nefilim, "they who from heaven to earth fell"—Sitchin, passim.

Nefilim, "brilliant ones," "workers of wonders"—Charroux, p. 16

gods with one gold hand . . . lords of metal—*Talk Live*, NBC-TV, 1993.

Nahash . . . "he who knows secrets," "he who knows copper"—Sitchin, *Genesis Revisited*, p. 202.

Page 295

"chimeras"—Ibid., p. 179.

"lulu" . . . "mixed one"—Sitchin, *The 12th Planet*, p. 348.

"genes" . . . "that which houses that which binds the memory"—Sitchin, *Genesis Revisited*, p. 167

Page 296

"enmity" . . . "the woman's" seed, etc.—Genesis 3:15.

"henotheism"—Budge, *The Gods of the Egyptians*, Vol. 1, p. 136.

Page 298

Osiris star configuration—Bauval and Gilbert, *The Orion Mystery*, pp. 189–196.

"Some decades ago . . . connecting the earth and Venus"—Kolosimo, *Not Of This World*, p. 57.

"contained descriptions of part of a catastrophe. . ."—Tompkins, *Mysteries of the Mexican Pyramids*, p. 114 (n).

"According to Brasseur . . . (Atlantis) in the year 9937 BC"—Ibid., p. 115.

Page 300

tebah, "container," "capsule"—Jean Sendy, *Those Gods Who Made Heaven and Earth* (1969) (New York: Berkley Books, 1972), pp. 155–156.

"the man who loves justice and truth," "fish god"—Ignatius Donnelly (quoting Francois Lenormant), *Atlantis* (1882) (Mineola, New York: Dover Publications, Inc., 1976), p. 88.

Page 301
  Sitchin's "landing grids"—Sitchin, *The Stairway to Heaven,* pp. 232–233, 283–308.
Page 302
  "Directed Panspermia" (published in *Icarus,* Vol. 19)—Sitchin, *Genesis Revisited,* p. 152.
  "that technological societies existed . . . though it sounds cranky," etc. —Ibid., p. 156.
Page 303
  "malleable glass"—Tompkins, *Mysteries of the Mexican Pyramids,* p. 217.
  "Nu'u," "Nu Wah," Ma Noa ("waters of Noah")—Kolosimo, *Not Of This World,* p. 143.

Chapter Nine: *Rivalries*

Any mythical text serves as an excellent source for study on this subject— the *Mabinogion* (Welsh), *Mahabharata* (Hindu-Aryan), the Bible, etc.—all telling the same story with different emphases. As compiler and commentator, Zecharia Sitchin covers the topic most thoroughly in *The Wars of Gods and Men,* bringing Hindu and Greek mythology into the question, though the subject runs throughout his corpus. Sitchin's *The Lost Realms* is one of his best books, extending the study from the ancient Middle East to the Americas. From the Celtic standpoint, Rees and Squier are excellent sources, but W. Y. Evans-Wentz's *The Fairy Faith in Celtic Countries* is the best. The Egyptian aspect is covered thoroughly in the corpus of E. A. Wallis Budge. The Hindu mythology of the gods' conflicts can be found discussed in connection with UFO phenomena in Richard L. Thompson's *Alien Identities: Ancient Insights into Modern UFO Phenomena* (San Diego, California: Govardhan Hill Publishing, 1993). All sources noted below are good.

Page 305
  "The Widow's Son"—Michael Howard, *The Occult Conspiracy* (Rochester, Vermont: Destiny Books, 1989), p. 15, passim.
Page 306
  "fairy folk" . . . Tuatha de Danaan—W. Y. Evans-Wentz, *The Fairy Faith in Celtic Countries* (1911) (New York: Citadel Press, 1990), pp. 27–28, passim.
  "Children of the Goddess Anu"—Charles Squire, *Celtic Myth and Legend* (1905) (Van Nuys, California: Newcastle Publishing, 1975), pp. 48, 50–51.
  "Brigit" . . . "St. Brigit"—T. W. Rolleston, *Myths and Legends of the Celtic Race* (1911) (Mineola, New York: Dover Publications, Inc., 1990), pp. 103, 126.
  Danu . . . Vrtra—Alwyn and Brinley Rees, *Celtic Heritage* (New York: Thames and Hudson, 1961), p. 53.
  Don . . . "wizard children"—Ibid., p. 176.
  "the waters of heaven or space"—Ibid., p. 53.
  "danu signifies 'stream'. . ."—Ibid.

Page 307

Nu, Nut . . . "primal waters of chaos"—Budge, *The Gods of the Egyptians.*

"Children of Goddess Domnu," abyss, deep sea, Fomor, under sea —Squire, *Celtic Myth and Legend,* p. 48.

Sanskrit tith, "to burn"—Lewis Spence, *History of Atlantis* (original publication date unknown) (London, Senate/Studio Editions Ltd., 1995), p. 193.

The Saxon name for them is almost identical to the Bible's: Nifelheim —Paul Carus, *The History of the Devil and the Idea of Evil* (1900) (La Salle, Illinois: Open Court Publishing, 1974), p. 246. Carus is unclear as to whether Nifelheim is used as a name for the original generation of giants in Norse-Teutonic mythology, but implies strongly that it is. Other sources give them no name, and very few even go so far as to mention that the later generation of giants were called Jotun and inhabited Jotunheim. But given the fact that the giants always inhabited the frozen wastes—hence their being called "Frost Giants" or "Ice Giants"—it only makes sense that they would have been in Nifelheim, which was the original frozen wasteland; and in Norse-Teutonic mythology, regions and the names of those inhabiting them are often synonomous: "Hel," for instance, is both the name of a region of the frozen wastes and the name of the goddess presiding over that region. It is also the name from which we derive "Hell."

"The Good" and "The Wise"—Rolleston, *Myths and Legends of the Celtic Race,* p. 103.

"Fire of God"—Rees, p. 30; Squire, *Celtic Myth and Legend,* p. 54 (n).

Page 308

"music from his harp," etc.—Rolleston, *Myths and Legends of the Celtic Race,* pp. 118–119.

"his blows sweeping down whole ranks of the enemy"—Ibid., p. 120.

"Moytura" . . . "Plain of the Towers"—Ibid., p. 106 (n).

"Land of the Dead" . . . "Land of Eternal Life"—Evans-Wentz, *The Fairy Faith in Celtic Countries,* pp. 332–357, passim.

". . .one treeless, grassless plain. . ."—Squire, *Celtic Myth and Legend,* p. 65.

Page 309

"Old Plain"—Ibid., p. 66.

". . .was vested with the red crown of Lower Egypt"—Clark, *Myth and Symbol in Ancient Egypt,* pp. 40–41.

"To-land," "land," "God's land," "the World" and "the Two Lands—Ibid., p. 41.

"mound/mountain of the gods," etc.—Donnelly, *Atlantis,* pp. 322–325 (quoting Plato).

Page 310

Tree of Life, "living center of nation . . . talismans of warriors"—Krupp, *Echoes of the Ancient Skies,* pp. 88–89.

Page 311

"The ancient geographer could establish his longitude. . ."—Tompkins, *Secrets of the Great Pyramids,* p. 183.

"If so, the words of Christopher Columbus' biographer. . ."—Tomas, *We Are Not The First,* p. 88.

Page 312

"We don't know how they could map it so accurately. . ."—Ibid., p. 89.

"The men of Erin. . ."—Eochy O'Flann, c. 960 AD (Rolleston, *Myths and Legends of the Celtic Race,* p. 102.)

Page 314

"foundation"—Sitchin, *The Lost Realms,* p. 40.

"It happened after the sons of men. . ."—Enoch 7:1–2.

Page 315

"And the women conceiving brought forth giants. . ."—Enoch 7:11–8:1.

"Impiety increased . . . and their voice reached to heaven"—Enoch 8:2–9.

"the son of Lamech," "Say to him, in my name, Conceal thyself"—Enoch 10:2–11.

"the desert which is in Dudael"—Enoch 10:6.

"great day of judgment," "cast into the fire"—Enoch 10:9.

"destroy the children of fornication . . . days shall not be theirs"—Enoch 10:13.

"And when all their sons . . . every evil work be destroyed"—Enoch 10:15–20.

Page 316

"The earth shall be cleansed . . . in every generation of it"—Enoch 10:27–29.

"the World Serpent"—H. R. Ellis Davidson, *Gods and Myths of Northern Europe.* 1964. (New York: Penguin Books, 1990), pp. 202–210.

"a lofty spot . . . the top of which reached to heaven"—Enoch 17:2.

". . .stone which supports the corners of the earth"—Enoch 18:2.

Page 317

". . .and the firmament of heaven"—Enoch 18:3.

"Giza" . . . means "the border"—E. Raymond Capt, *Study In Pyramidology* (Thousand Oaks, California: Artisan Sales, 1986), p. 11.

"Hail, Thoth! What is it that hath happened. . ."—Budge, *From Fetish to God in Ancient Egypt,* pp. 197–198.

Page 318

"Neteru" . . . "Watchers"—Budge, *The Gods of the Egyptians,* Vol. 1, p. 141, passim.

"Watchers" . . . Essene—Carus (quoting translation of Ewald), *The History of the Devil and the Idea of Evil,* p. 140 (n).

"The Monitors" . . . Watchers—Temple, *The Sirius Mystery,* p. 209.

egregori . . . "Gregorian" . . . Watchers—W. Raymond Drake (quoting Pandorus, Egyptian monk), *Gods and Spacemen in Greece and Rome* (London: Sphere Books, Ltd., 1976), p. 30.

Page 319

Huitzilopochtli, "Hummingbird-to-the-left," Mars—Lewis Spence, *The Myths of Mexico and Peru* (1913) (Mineola, New York: Dover Books, 1994), pp. 70, 72.

Tezcatlipoca ("Smoking Mirror" or "Fiery Mirror")—Ibid., p. 59.

"The Game of 52"—Zecharia Sitchin, *When Time Began* (New York: Avon Books, 1993), p. 294.

Quetzalcoatl . . . the natives said came from "the black and red land"— Berlitz, *Mysteries from the Forgotten Worlds,* p. 105.

"Viracocha," ("foam of the sea,") "Ancient lord, instructor of the world. . ."—Alan and Sally Landsburg, *In Search of Ancient Mysteries* (New York: Bantam Books, 1974), p. 47.

"Windy Sea"—Charles Berlitz, *Mysteries from Forgotten Worlds* (New York: Dell Books, 1972), p. 136.

"White Master"—William Bramley, *The Gods of Eden* (San Jose, California: Dahlin Family Press, 1989), p. 95.

2,268—Maurice Chatelain, "Our Mexican Ancestors," *Pursuit,* Vol. 18, No. 2, whole no. 70, pp. 78–84.

Page 320

"containing an otherwise unknown myth"—Sitchin, *The Wars of Gods and Men,* p. 112.

"Ka'in," "In'ka," "Tenochtitlan," "Tenoch," etc.—Sitchin, *The Lost Realms,* pp. 41–42.

"a cosmic collapse and a 'Gotterdamerung'. . ."—George Hart, *A Dictionary of Egyptian Gods and Goddesses* (New York, Routledge, Chapman and Hall, Inc., 1986), p. 47.

Page 321

"Nuada of the Silver Hand"—Squire, *Celtic Myth and Legend,* p. 51, passim.

Page 322

"his heart having thus plotted aggression"—Sitchin, *The Wars of Gods and Men,* p. 97.

Zu, Anzu, "Bird," "Mountain of Sky Chambers," "pinions," etc.—Ibid., pp. 96–98.

Page 323

"Bull, the guilty Zu are you. . ." Enlil is "the Great Shepherd"—Ibid., p. 100.

"Re [Ra] in Osiris, Osiris in Re"—Hart, *A Dictionary of Egyptian Gods and Goddesses,* p. 182.

"The Egyptians gradually evolved a concept of synthesis. . ."—Ibid., p. 181.

"now as Enlil [upon] the Earth"—Sitchin, *The Wars of Gods and Men,* p. 100.

Enlil is the "Divine Shepherd"—Sitchin, *The 12th Planet,* p. 98.

"the Good Shepherd"—John 10:11, passim.

Page 324

Kon Tiki Illac Viracocha, "lightning son of the sun from out of the sea foam"—Kolosimo, *Not Of This World,* p. 164.

"Sons of the Sun" . . . the very name the Incas called themselves—Marcel Homet, *Sons of the Sun* (London, 1963), passim.

Page 325

Enki/Ninurta conflict, Ekur—Sitchin, *The Wars of Gods and Men,* pp. 153–172 passim.

Page 326

> Azag, "mountain monster"—Tikva Frymer-Kensky, *In the Wake of the Goddesses* (New York: Macmillan, Inc., 1992), p. 15.
>
> "The Radiant House...," descriptions of "mountain"—Sitchin, *The Wars of Gods and Men,* pp. 158, 165–167.

Page 327

> "Tyr was identical with the Saxon god, Saxnot..."—H. A. Guerber, *Myths of the Norsemen from the Eddas and Sagas* (1909) (Mineola, New York: Dover Publications, Inc., New York, 1992), p. 87.
>
> Sahsginot, "sword companion"—Davidson, *Gods and Myths of Northern Europe,* p. 60.

Page 328

> Bull, Lion, Eagle, and Man being Taurus, Leo, Scorpio, and Aquarius. Where Scorpio is traditionally represented as the scorpion, the sign (unlike the rest) has two other representations: the serpent (or gray lizard) and the eagle. Any astrology book can be consulted for verification. See for example Linda Goodman's *Sun Signs* (New York: Taplinger Publishing, 1968), pp. 277–315.
>
> "exiled by the war god"—Sitchin, *The Lost Realms,* p. 7.
>
> "Votan," Chivim, "Serpents"—Tompkins, *Mysteries of the Mexican Pyramids,* pp. 78–80.
>
> "a great city where a magnificent temple..."—Ibid., p. 79.

Page 329

> "Place of Life," Ningishzida "Lord of the Artifact of Life"—Sitchin *The Wars of Gods and Men,* p. 176.
>
> "falcon among the gods"—Ibid., p. 177.

Page 330

> "sign of the hammer," "Like the Christian cross," etc.—Davidson, *Gods and Myths of Northern Europe,* pp. 80–81.
>
> "Babylon" ... "Gateway of the Gods" ... "spaceport"—Sitchin, *The Wars of Gods and Men,* p. 250 (Bab-Ili).

Page 331

> "lamentation texts" of Ur (from Sitchin)—Ibid., pp. 331–339.

Page 332

> "...its face they made desolate"—Ibid., p. 331 (final Sitchin quote).
>
> eighty-four thousand *yodshana* ... distance to moon, Karl Koppen —Sendy, *Those Gods Who Made Heaven and Earth,* p. 168.

Page 335

> "Heimdall has several other names..."—Guerber, *Myths of the Norsemen from the Eddas and Sagas,* pp. 150–151.
>
> "Prometheus and Hercules are combined into one person..."—Carus, *The History of the Devil and the Idea of Evil,* pp. 210–211.

Page 336

> "His son, Ogma Sun-Face, or Ogmias, god of literature and eloquence..."—Ean Begg, *The Cult of the Black Virgin* (London: Penguin Arkana, 1985), p. 76.
>
> "Sleipnir"—H. R. Ellis Davidson, *Myths and Symbols in Pagan Europe* (Syracuse, New York: Syracuse University Press, 1988), p. 90.

"Wotan's great feast is Saturnalia or Yuletide. . ."—Begg, *The Cult of the Black Virgin,* p. 90.

Page 337

"The Franks were wont to celebrate yearly martial games. . ."—Guerber, *Myths of the Norsemen from the Eddas and Sagas,* p. 89.

Page 338

". . .to be renewed every Mayday till time shall end. . ."—Rolleston, *Myths and Legends of the Celtic Race,* pp. 349–353.

Llud is identical to Nuada (and) "Nodens," forerunner to Odin—Rolleston, *Myths and Legends of the Celtic Race,* pp. 346–347; Squire, *Celtic Myth and Legend,* p. 253.

"The name of both alike [is] 'white' . . . 'misty mountain top'"—Squire, *Celtic Myth and Legend,* pp. 254–255.

Page 339

"bull of conflict"—Ibid., p. 256.

"fisher of men's souls"—Matthew 4:19, Luke 5:10, passim.

mirabilia ("Wonders of Britain")—Rees, *Celtic Heritage,* p. 70.

"Like Finn, Arthur is here a warrior . . . recall Twrch Twryth"—Ibid., pp. 70–71.

Camulus, the heaven-god Rome equated with Mars—Squire, *Celtic Myth and Legend,* p. 204.

Camulodunum, "City of Mars"—source unknown; but the rationale is legitimate: Dunum is "city," Camul is "Mars," and o denotes "son of" or "of."

Page 340

Neith, "mistress of bow, ruler of arrows," "that which is," "terrifying"—Hart, *A Dictionary of Egyptian Gods and Goddesses,* p. 131.

Neit, the Celtic "god of battle"—Rees, *Celtic Heritage,* pp. 30–31.

keshet, "bow"—Sendy, *Those Gods Who Made Heaven and Earth,* p. 158.

Sirius, Babylonian prefix of which, Kaksidi, means "arrow"—Giorgio de Santillana and Hertha von Dechend, *Hamlet's Mill* (1977, 1969) (Boston: David R. Godine, Publisher, Inc., 1992), p. 216.

"slaying of the sun," Balder, Midsummer's Eve, etc.—Guerber, *Myths of the Norsemen from the Eddas and Sagas,* p. 215.

Page 341

"Menes" . . . "The Establisher," or "The Everlasting"—George Rawlinson, *History of Ancient Egypt,* Vol. 2 (New York: J. W. Lovell, 1880), p. 26.

Amergin . . . "I Am"—Rees, *Celtic Heritage,* p. 98.

"After their defeat in battle . . . fairies underground were subject to them"—Ibid., p. 38.

Page 343

Joseph F. Blumrich . . . patented—Alan and Sally Landsburg, *In Search of Ancient Mysteries* (New York: Bantam Books, 1974), pp. 134–143. (Also see Blumrich's *The Spaceships of Ezekiel.*)

gae bulga, Skatha and Cuchulainn—Rolleston, *Myths and Legends of the Celtic Race,* p. 188.

Page 345

"The Indians say that thousands of years ago. . ."—Kolosimo, *Not Of This World,* p. 206.

"interfere[nce] with cosmic processes" in a "fusillade of taps"—Cheney, *Tesla: Man Out of Time,* pp. 116–117.

Page 346

UFO abduction . . . Abanaki Indians—*Unsolved Mysteries,* 9/18/94.

Algonquins have . . . the evil Trickster from the Norse, Loki. . . —J. F. Bierlein, *Parallel Myths* (New York: Ballantine Books, 1994), pp. 45–46.

Ammon-Ra . . . their "god of light and fire"—Kolosimo, *Not Of This World,* p. 213.

"the Hairy Ainu"—Rupert Furneaux, *Ancient Mysteries* (New York: McGraw Hill, 1977), pp. 112–116.

Page 347

paint their skins with a white coat of mud, etc.—*In Search of Ancient Astronauts* (NBC-TV).

"the sun-god, their ancestor . . . are descendants of their gods" —Kolosimo, *Not Of This World,* p. 166.

Page 348

"We are all, ultimately, Sumerians"—Hoagland, *The Monuments of Mars,* p. 291.

Chapter Ten: *Underworlds*

All listed Celtic sources are good for studying Otherworld or Underworld journies, especially W. Y. Evans-Wentz's *The Fairy Faith in Celtic Countries.* To these may be added Nikolai Tolstoy's *The Quest for Merlin* (see Bibliography). Zecharia Sitchin's *The Stairway to Heaven* is the best single study delineating the Egyptian Afterlife journey in a technological context, and George C. Andrews' *Extraterrestrials Among Us* (see Bibliography) also devotes its first three chapters largely to the same topic. The best book studying the connection of God as we recognize him to the "God of the Underworld," or the Devil, is Paul Carus' *The History of the Devil and the Idea of Evil,* though many of the books listed on the subject of the occult in the Bibliography also cover the territory rather extensively. The sources listed in the text connecting the ancient Egyptians to the ancient Celts are all worth reading. The works of David Hatcher Childress published by Adventures Unlimited Press in Stelle, Illinois, cover diffusionistic theory very well, but in scattershot manner. Probably the best of these are *Lost Cities of North & Central America* and *Lost Cities of Ancient Lemuria & the Pacific,* both of which discuss the widespread use of boomerangs around the world.

Page 351

"Good Neighbors"—Vallée, *Dimensions,* p. 64.

Page 352

"By tradition they favored upright men. . ."—Robert Rickard, "Clutching at Straws," p. 64, in *The Crop Circle Enigma,* edited by Ralph Noyes (The Hollies, Wellow, Bath, United Kingdom: Gateway Books, 1990), pp. 62–71.

Page 353

"Changelings"—Evans-Wentz, *The Fairy Faith in Celtic Countries,* passim.
"The Sick-Bed of Cuchulainn"—Ibid., pp. 345–346.
"son of Ler, king of the Land of Promise"—Ibid., p. 342.

Page 354

"The Greeks saw in Hermes the symbol of the Logos. . ."—Ibid., p. 343 (n).
"flogging," ". . .satisfaction out of being whipped themselves"—Otto Neubert, *Tutankhamun and the Valley of the Kings* (1954, English translation 1957) (New York: Granada Publishing, 1977), pp. 94–95.

Page 355

abductees specifically having sex underwater, yet being able to breathe—This is the only abduction fact taken by the author not from a published source material but from personal conversations with abductees, though the "breathing pool" itself comes from numerous published sources.
"behold[ing] 'the loveliest of the world's women'. . ."—Evans-Wentz, *The Fairy Faith in Celtic Countries,* p. 342.
"The warrior-messenger who took them all . . . the Land of Promise," etc.—Ibid.

Page 356

kornbocks . . . hausbocks . . . pookas—Robert Rickard, "Clutching at Straws," in *The Crop Circle Enigma,* p. 64.
"Among the elemental dwarfs . . . might well be grateful for his actions"—Elsa-Brita Titchenell, *The Masks of Odin: Wisdom of the Ancient Norse* (Pasadena, California: Theosophical University Press, 1985), pp. 59–60.

Page 357

"a plate of hot rice porridge by the barn door on Christmas Eve"—Ibid., p. 60.

Page 358

humfos . . . bocors . . . vodun—Wade Davis, *The Serpent and the Rainbow* (New York: Simon & Schuster, Inc., 1985), passim.

Page 359

Osiris, "god of the corn"—Hart, *A Dictionary of Egyptian Gods and Goddesses,* p. 158; E. A. Wallis Budge, *Osiris and the Egyptian Resurrection* (2 Volumes; 1911) (Mineola, New York: Dover Books, 1973), Vol. 1, p. 80. Hart's *Dictionary* specifically states, "The earliest unambiguous reference to Osiris and corn occurs in the Dramatic Ramesseum Papyrus, a commentary on, or directory of, ritual." Budge refers to Osiris as Lord of the Underworld, presiding over the "Field of Reeds": "Among these 'fields of reeds' there must have been many fair fields wherein grain of various kinds was grown, for in the text of Pepi II, 1. 1316, it is said that Osiris makes Pepi 'to plough corn and to reap barley.'"

"The Green Man," etc.—Sir James George Frazer, *The Golden Bough* (New York: Macmillan Publishing Company, 1922), passim.

Oodin, "Odin"—Donnelly, *Atlantis,* p. 210 (quoting nineteenth-century scholar Dr. Dasent).

Professor Gregory Webb . . . discovered a stone phallus. . . —Howard, *The Occult Conspiracy,* p. 19.

Page 360

Deus, Dyaus, Pitar, etc.—Drake, *Gods and Spacemen in Greece and Rome,* p. 24.

God, Bog—Margaret A. Murray, *The God of the Witches* (1931) (New York: Oxford University Press, 1952), p. 44.

Page 361

"the Martian"—Kolosimo, *Not Of This World,* picture section.

Page 362

". . .the Celtic words designating the Land of the Dead"—Rolleston, *Myths and Legends of the Celtic Race,* p. 102.

". . .remembering that 'Spain' stood for . . . Celtic Hades, or Elysium" —Squire, *Celtic Myth and Legend,* p. 121.

Page 363

"the prehistoric custom of coloring corpses red"—Richard Cavendish, *The Black Arts* (London: Routledge & Kegan Paul Ltd., 1967), p. 38.

"In a prehistoric graveyard near Nordlingen . . . with powdered haematite"—Ibid.

"Urani Land," as a "Land Beyond the Western Sea"—W. Raymond Drake, *Gods and Spacemen in the Ancient West* (London: Sphere Books, 1974), p. 103.

"is also associated with a cauldron-shaped vessel. . ."—Begg, *The Cult of the Black Virgin,* p. 76.

Tsunil-kalu ("Slant-eyed people")—Howe, *Glimpses of Other Realities,* p. 115.

Page 364

"Lands of the West," "warlike giants," "Western Ocean"—Drake, *Gods and Spacemen in the Ancient West,* p. 85

"looked to the west . . . hovered over his submerged home"—Spence, *History of Atlantis,* p. 188.

"Red Island," "Land of the Sunset Beyond the Western Sea"—Drake, *Gods and Spacemen in the Ancient West,* p. 85.

kine ("cow-cattle")—Sitchin, *The Wars of Gods and Men,* p. 64.

"To us alone assuredly belongs this world," "dividing it . . . west to east"—Ibid., p. 65.

Page 365

"They themselves were represented by the red corn. . ."—Waters, *The Book of the Hopi,* p. 69.

"hundreds of tales"—Ibid., p. 67.

"the sunken Red Land"—David Hatcher Childress, *Lost Cities & Ancient Mysteries of South America* (Stelle, Illinois: Adventures Unlimited Press, 1986), p. 145.

"...where we went from the old Red Land before it sank..."—Ibid., p. 104.

"god of light and fire"—Kolosimo, *Timeless Earth,* p. 213.

"Long before the deluge . . . fire and death on the terrified people"—Ibid., pp. 213–214.

The Arawak Indians' "Aimon"—Spence, *History of Atlantis,* p. 173.

Page 366

"protected place," "ascend beautifully and traverse the skies"—Sitchin, *The Wars of Gods and Men,* p. 149.

Original red color of the Sphinx . . . on beard and crest in British Museum—W. B. Crow, *A Fascinating History of Witchcraft, Magic and Occultism* (1968) (North Hollywood, California: Wilshire Book Company, 1972), p. 47.

India's "Pink City" of Jaipur, and Rajastani "Red Forts"—Childress, *Lost Cities of China, Central Asia & India,* p. 201.

Adom, "of the ruddy complexion," "he who is red"—Sitchin, *The 12th Planet,* p. 349.

Adama, Adamatu, "dark red soil," "dark red earth"—Ibid.

Apzu, Lower World—Ibid., pp. 358–359.

Page 367

Apsu, "one who exists from the beginning"—Ibid., p. 212.

"like an Apsu boat"—Ibid., p. 396.

Red, white and black . . . Plato called the colors of Atlantis—Berlitz, *Mysteries from Forgotten Worlds,* pp. 105–106.

Red and black "meals" with "white food," Tibetan chod ritual—Alexandra David-Neel, *Magic and Mystery in Tibet* (1932, 1929) (Mineola, New York: Dover Publications, Inc., 1971), pp. 151, 160.

Page 368

"What exactly is signified by this Ganesha..."—Coomaraswamy and Nivedita, *Myths of the Hindus and Buddhists,* p. 18.

"of gigantic stature, with bright red skin and a mass of white hair"—F. Hadland Davis, *Myths and Legends of Japan* (1913) (Mineola, New York: Dover Publications, Inc., 1992), p. 46.

"...the exact centre of the island, to cause a pit to be dug there"—Squire, *Celtic Myth and Legend,* p. 378.

"in a stone coffin in strongest place in Britain . . . mighty man of magic"—Ibid., p. 379.

Page 369

Mars Thingsus, "Thing" . . . the Assembly of Justice—Davidson, *Gods and Myths of Northern Europe,* pp. 57–58.

"Place of Ascending" to "the Imperishable Star"—Sitchin, *The Stairway to Heaven,* pp. 228–230.

Page 370

"an object into whose insides the king can enter..."—Ibid., p. 45.

"celestial ladder," Ded—Budge, *The Mummy,* pp. 307–325.

"backbone of Osiris," "strength of the king"—Budge, *Osiris and the Egyptian Resurrection,* Vol. 1, pp. 48, 24–61.

"other unusual copper objects"—Sitchin, *The Stairway to Heaven,* pp. 73–74.

Page 371

"would never have reached heaven at all. . ."—Budge, *The Mummy,* p. 324.

"I have set up a ladder among the gods. . ."—Ibid., p. 325.

Charroux . . . diagram of a contemporary plasma generator—Robert Charroux, *Forgotten Worlds* (1971) (New York: Popular Library, 1973), p. 93.

"The sky god . . . strengthened the radiance. . ."—the Pyramid Texts, Sitchin, *The Stairway to Heaven,* p. 63.

Page 372

Tet, "blood of Isis," "buckle," "tie"—Budge, *The Mummy,* p. 308.

menat—Budge, *The Mummy,* pp. 323–324.

"Shugarra . . . that which makes go far into universe"—Sitchin, *The 12th Planet,* p. 133.

Nar . . . "Fiery Pillar"—Sitchin, *The Wars of Gods and Men,* p. 45.

Page 373

me, "divine power objects," "swimming in celestial waters," etc.—Sitchin, *The 12th Planet,* p. 136.

Me . . . "Divine measures of the depths of the spacial seas"—de Santillana and von Dechend, *Hamlet's Mill,* p. 302.

"Enmeduranki," "Ruler whose Me connect Heaven and Earth"—Sitchin, *The 12th Planet,* p. 136.

"strong stone resting place for the Mu," "divine black wind bird"—Ibid., p. 139.

mu ("that which rises straight"), "Lady of Heaven. . ."—Ibid., pp. 141–142.

shu-mu ("that which is a mu"), shem, "name," "highward," etc.—Ibid., p. 143.

Page 374

the Osirian fetish of Abydos, the ta-wer, "Eldest Land"—Richard H. Wilkinson, *Reading Egyptian Art* (London: Thames and Hudson Ltd., 1992), p. 169.

"Great Land"—Budge, *From Fetish to God in Ancient Egypt,* p. 273.

heaven-plumes (of Amun) sometimes called the "testicles of Set" —Sellers, *The Death of Gods in Ancient Egypt,* p. 229. An obscure but definite reference, from the heb-sed: "From a Middle Kingdom 'dramatic' papyrus which describes the rituals for the coronation of Senusert I, we learn that the two scepters that accompany the two plumes at the coronation of the king are called the testicles of Seth." The scepters and plumes correspond.

"What kind of place is Augert. . ."—Budge, *From Fetish to God in Ancient Egypt,* p. 197.

"the imperishable star," "the two that bind closer the heavens"—Sitchin, *The Stairway to Heaven,* p. 49.

Page 375

Tesert-baiu, "Red Souls"—Budge, *The Gods of the Egyptians,* p. 203 (vol. 1).

double-sphinx (Aker)—Ibid., pp. 360–361 (vol. 2).

"Great God who opens the Gates of Earth"—Sitchin, *The Stairway to Heaven,* p. 304.

Pa-Ra-Emheb stela—Ibid., pp. 303–305.

"Mars, Hor-Tesher, 'Red Horus' . . . hawk with a star above it"—Budge, *From Fetish to God in Ancient Egypt,* p. 244.

Page 376

"The god is like this . . . in the interior of which is the great secret"— Jane B. Sellers, *The Death of Gods in Ancient Egypt* (London: Penguin Books, 1992), p. xiv.

"Horus of the Horizon is his name . . . the Bull of Heaven is his name" —Ibid., p. 322.

"Both Mars and Saturn . . . called Eastern Star and Western Star. . ." —Krupp, *Echoes of Ancient Skies,* p. 70.

". . .the months are reversed and the hours are disordered"— Adolf Erman, *Egyptian Literature* (Berlin, 1927), p. 309.

". . .and shines, a new one, in the orient"—Immanuel Velikovsky, *Worlds In Collision* (New York: Doubleday & Co. Inc., 1950), p. 120 (L. Speelers, *Les Textes des Pyramides,* Vol. I, 1923).

Page 377

"Sotuknang called on the Ant People . . . it froze into solid ice"—Waters, *The Book of the Hopi,* p. 16.

"began to use . . . power in [an] evil way . . . where they came from" —Ibid., pp. 17–18.

Kukulkan/Quetzalcoatl from the East, Viracocha from the West —Berlitz, *Mysteries from Forgotten Worlds,* p. 136.

Page 378

"toward rising sun," ". . .where the day star is born," "east or sunrise" —Ibid., p. 132.

Venus, "The Great Star" and the "Lord of the Dawn"—Spence, *The Myths of Mexico and Peru,* p. 96.

Venus . . . colored red, black and white in Mexican art—Ibid., pp. 96–97.

"the soul of Ra and the living symbol of Osiris"—Budge, *The Gods of the Egyptians,* p. 96 (Vol. 2).

"The Children of Heaven entered into the eastern part of the sky. . ." —Sellers, *The Death of Gods in Ancient Egypt,* p. 113.

"Before the tomb was closed, whole chamber was sprinkled"—Childress, *Lost Cities of North & Central America,* p. 197.

Fare-kura—the "red" or "purple house"—de Santillana and von Dechend, *Hamlet's Mill,* p. 445 (n).

Page 379

"abode of the venerated learning . . . brought down from Heaven by Tane"—Ibid.

"sacred tree," "Tane-of-sacred-waters," etc.—Ibid.

"way-opener," who is "the first . . . who came at last"—Ibid. (n).

"gathering place of the spirits," "primordial home"—Ibid. (n).

another world ... "fixed at the east"—S. Percy Smith, editor and translator, *The Lore of the Whare-wananga* (New Plymouth, Memoirs Polynesian Society 3, 1913), p. 101.

"those spirits which by their evil conduct...," "Io," "All-Source," etc. —Ibid., p. 113.

Wainwright, Clark, Mercer, adze, etc.—Bauval and Gilbert, *The Orion Mystery,* p. 206; Clark *Myth and Symbol in Ancient Egypt,* p. 122.

Page 380

meshtw, "the thigh"—Bauval and Gilbert, *The Orion Mystery,* p. 206.

sacred births were said to be "born upon the thigh" of Osiris—Clark, *Myth and Symbol in Ancient Egypt,* p. 130.

Page 381

"Many of the religious rites of the Jews..."—Budge, *From Fetish to God in Ancient Egypt,* pp. 40–41 (n).

Circumcision ... an Egyptian practice—Herodotus, Book 2, 103 (de Selincourt).

satus, "sowing"; kraino, "completer," etc...." kronos ("time")—Drake, *Gods and Spacemen in the Ancient West,* pp. 20–21.

Page 384

Nature, quagga, cloning of Egyptian infant mummy tissue—Bob Brier, *Egyptian Mummies* (New York: William Morrow, 1994), pp. 188–193.

upuaut, "the opener of the ways"—Ions, *Egyptian Mythology,* p. 84.

Page 385

Anubis ... was believed to ritually kill the pharaoh, 28 years, etc. —Ibid., p. 82.

"According to Plutarch ... 28 was used symbolically for this interval" —Krupp, *Echoes of the Ancient Skies,* p. 18.

the heb-sed, when the king annually renewed his reign—I.E.S. Edwards, *The Pyramids of Egypt* (1947) (London: Penguin Books, 1993), pp. 45–46.

"for the first time thirty years after his accession"—Wilkinson, *Reading Egyptian Art,* p. 146.

Page 386

"Returning to the account of Osiris ... return to a golden age"—Sellers, *The Death of Gods in Ancient Egypt,* pp. 204–205.

"substances and vital essences ... being transferred to its successor" —Titchenell, *The Masks of Odin,* p. 53

Mimer, "matter"—Ibid., p. 29.

Page 387

Mimer, "memory"—Guerber, *Myths of the Norsemen from the Eddas and Sagas,* p. 30.

"It is no accident that there are 72..."—Sellers, *The Death of Gods in Ancient Egypt,* p. 207.

"Valhalla presents yet another aspect ... recur in them"—Titchenell, *The Masks of Odin,* pp. 79–80.

Page 388

Agnicayana, or "fire-altar"—de Santillana and von Dechend, *Hamlet's Mill,* p. 162.

"To quibble away such a coincidence, or to ascribe it to chance. . ."
—Ibid.
"the character of Heimdall raises a number of sharp questions. . ."
—Ibid., p. 157.

Page 389
"Mars was 'installed'. . ."—Ibid. (n)
"It should be emphasized, aloud and strongly. . ."—Ibid. (n).
"remarked once that the ludicrous story of Hephaistos. . ."—Ibid., p. 177.
"What kind of grinding could it have been? Surely the lament. . ."
—Ibid., pp. 284–285.

Page 390
". . .The Zu-bird, at least, is known to us; the planet Mars it is"—Ibid.,
p. 443.
"the identity of the planet Mars . . . with the serpent in Paradise. . ."
—Ibid., p. 390.
Zohar, Sepher-ha Zohar ("Book of Splendor")—Cavendish, *The Black
Arts,* p. 98.
"Als der Pharaoh aus Agypten auszog. . ."—de Santillana and von
Dechend, *Hamlet's Mill,* p. 396.
"Rabuse has solved this puzzle in a careful analytical study. . ."—Ibid.,
p. 196.
"These 'guardian angels' will be identified sooner or later. . ."—Ibid., p.
396.

Page 391
"There are no powers more diverse than Saturn and Mars. . ."—Ibid.,
p. 176.
Shroud of Turin . . . formed by . . . radioactive photo-effect—Robert K.
Wilcox, *Shroud* (New York: Macmillan, 1977), pp. 122–127.

Page 393
Sekhet-hetep, "Field of Offerings"—Budge, *From Fetish to God in Ancient
Egypt,* p. 347.
"Jason" meaning "healer"; Circe, kirke, "falcon" or "hawk—Temple, *The
Sirius Mystery,* pp. 118–119.
erion, "woolen fleece," heru (the sun)—Ibid., p. 117.
specifically "in the grove of Ares (Mars)"—Ibid., p. 135.

Page 394
"The facts at present known, do not, I think, justify us. . ."—Rolleston,
Myths and Legends of the Celtic Race, p. 78.
"the builders of our megalithic monuments came from the south. . ."
—Ibid.
"The pre-Aryan idioms which still live in Welsh and Irish. . ."—Ibid. (n).

Page 395
". . .relation or identity between Carnac and Karnak"—Evans-Wentz,
The Fairy Faith in Celtic Countries, p. xxiii (n).
Er Grah ("Stone of the Fairies"), Le Grand Menhir, etc.—Krupp, *Echoes
of the Ancient Skies,* p. 43.

Page 396

"It's an old form of Celtic. . ."—Deborah Frazier, "Ancient scratches are Celtic, researchers say," *Rocky Mountain News,* 3/21/94.

"Anubis Cave"—Leonard McGlone, et.al., *Ancient American Inscriptions: Plow Marks or History?* (Salt Lake City, Utah: Publishers Press, 1993), pp. 139–182.

an Egyptian serakh, or sun temple—Ibid., pp. 147–148.

"Enact at sunset the rites of Bel, assembling at that hour in worship" —Ibid.

Brandao's A Escripta Prehistorica do Brasil studies—Childress, *Lost Cities & Ancient Mysteries of South America,* pp. 236–237.

Steede's Preliminary Catalogue of the Comalcalco Bricks —Childress, *Lost Cities & Ancient Mysteries of North & Central America,* p. 207.

Page 397

"the slashes deserve more study," "Lost among debates. . ."—Frazier, *Rocky Mountain News,* op. cit.

"Under constant attack. . ."—Childress *Lost Cities & Ancient Mysteries of Africa & Arabia,* p. 358.

"red-skinned" men, "Pink Men"—Ibid., p. 345.

Page 398

"intestine-faced" Sumerian Humbaba—de Santillana and von Dechend, *Hamlet's Mill,* p. 290.

"Creator/Guardian of the cedar of paradise"—Ibid., p. 289 (n).

corn (maize) in Egyptian tombs, boomerang in Tut exhibit—Childress, *Lost Cities & Ancient Mysteries of Africa & Arabia,* p. 96.

Page 399

"throw sticks"—Budge, *From Fetish to God in Ancinet Egypt,* p. 87.

Page 400

Hyksos, "Shepherd Kings"—Budge, *The Mummy,* p. 47.

hekau, "magician"—Budge, *From Fetish to God in Ancient Egypt,* p. 113.

Hyksos, hekau-khaswt, "foreign hill countries"—David, *Discovering Ancient Egypt,* p. 145.

"Khian," meaning "Prince of the deserts"—Budge, *The Mummy,* p. 47.

Page 401

"but some think that Nubti was the god Set"—Ibid., p. 48.

Chapter Eleven: *Conclusions*

Page 420

"In Brazil, only the persons who work on the problem. . ."—Good, *Above Top Secret,* pp. 426–427.

". . .include either the Minister of Defense or the Prime Minister"—Ibid., p. 437.

Page 425

"Humane realm . . . and angelic. . ."—*Mysteries of the Ancient World,* CBS-TV, 1994.

Page 426

"kind of like on their heel . . . rather than like we might turn. . ."—Howe, *An Alien Harvest,* p. 317.

"They go in and out real fast, like this . . . composition of something" —Ibid., 318–319.

"Insiders know . . . that once gripped Point Pleasant"—Keel, *The Mothman Prophecies,* pp. 274–275.

Page 427

"We're being invaded. . ." Rand Corp. think tank computer—Ibid., pp. 216–217.

Page 428

"the Missile of Merowe"—Kolosimo, *Not of This World,* picture section.

Page 430

"man was created far from the Earth . . . that they may reproduce" —Ibid., p. 196.

"American and Soviet specialists . . . secretions in the medium"—Charroux, *Masters of the Earth,* p. 66.

"that 'foreign' agent (is) analogous to the 'extraterrestrial lovers'. . ." —Ibid., p. 68.

"One of the most exciting of these future programs. . ."—Good, *Above Top Secret,* p. 382.

Page 432

"The public has a right to know. . ."—Good, *Above Top Secret,* p. 444.

"It is self-evident that the public ought to be told the truth. . ."—Major Donald E. Keyhoe, *Flying Saucers: Top Secret* (New York: G.p. Putnam's Sons, 1960), p. 236.

". . .It is about time you knew what"—Flammonde, *UFO Exist!,* pp. 422–423.

Page 433

". . .Our leaders [are presented] with an awesome dilemma. . ."—Good, *Above Top Secret,* p. 438.

"From an intelligence point. . ."—*APRO Bulletin,* Vol. 32, No. 4, 1984, pp. 6–7.

Bibliography

Adamski, George. *Inside the Space Ships.* New York: Abelard-Schuman, 1955.

Andrews, George C. *Extraterrestrials Among Us.* 1986. St. Paul, Minnesota: Llewellyn, 1992.

Bamford, James. *The Puzzle Palace: A Report on America's Most Secret Agency.* New York: Houghton Mifflin, 1982.

Barclay, David, and Marie Therese, editors. *UFOs: The Final Answer?* London: Blandford Books, 1993.

Barrett, Clive. *The Egyptian Gods and Goddesses.* London: HarperCollins, 1991.

Bartholomew, Alick, editor. *Crop Circles: Harbingers of World Change.* The Hollies, Wellow, Bath, United Kingdom: Gateway Books, 1991.

Bartimus, Tad, and Scott McCartney. *Trinity's Children.* Albuquerque, New Mexico: University of New Mexico Press, 1991.

Baudez, Claude, and Sydney Picasso. *Lost Cities of the Maya.* 1987. Translated by Caroline Palmer. New York: Harry N. Abrams, Inc., 1992.

Bauval, Robert, and Adrian Gilbert. *The Orion Mystery.* New York: Crown, 1994.

Begg, Ean. *The Cult of the Black Virgin.* New York: Penguin Arkana, 1985.

Behrens, Helen, and Dr. Charles Wahlig. *A Handbook on Guadalupe.* Kenosha, Wisconsin: Franciscan Marytown Press, 1974.

Bergier, Jacques. *Extraterrestrial Visitations from Prehistoric Times to the Present.* 1970. Chicago: Henry Regnery Company, 1973.

Berlitz, Charles. *Mysteries from Forgotten Worlds.* New York: Dell, 1972.

Bierlein, J. F. *Parallel Myths.* New York: Ballantine, 1994.

Billig, Otto. *Flying Saucers: Magic in the Skies.* Cambridge, Massachusetts: Schenkman, 1982.

Blum, Howard. *Out There.* New York: Simon & Schuster, 1990.

Blum, Ralph, and Judy Blum. *Beyond Earth: Man's Contact With UFOs.* New York: Bantam, 1974.

Blundell, Nigel, and Roger Boar. *The World's Greatest UFO Mysteries.* London: Octopus Books, 1983.

Bramley, William. *The Gods of Eden.* 1989. New York: Avon, 1993.

Brier, Bob. *Ancient Egyptian Magic.* New York: William Morrow, 1980.

—. *Egyptian Mummies.* New York: William Morrow, 1994.

Budge, Sir E. A. Wallis. *Amulets and Superstitions.* 1930. Mineola, New York: Dover, 1978.

—. *The Book of the Dead.* 1899. London: Penguin Arkana, 1989.

—. *Egyptian Hieroglyphic Dictionary.* Two Volumes. 1920. Mineola, New York: Dover, 1978.

—. *From Fetish to God in Ancient Egypt.* 1934. Mineola, New York: Dover, 1988.

—. *The Gods of the Egyptians.* Two Volumes. 1904. Mineola, New York: Dover, 1969.

—. *The Mummy.* 1893. Mineola, New York: Dover, 1989.

—. *Osiris and the Egyptian Resurrection.* Two Volumes. 1911. New York: Dover, 1973.

Campbell, Joseph. *The Flight of the Wild Gander.* Chicago: Regnery Gateway, 1951.

—. *The Hero With A Thousand Faces.* Princeton, New Jersey: Princeton University Press, 1949.

Capt, Raymond E. *Study In Pyramidology.* Thousand Oaks, California: Artisan Sales, 1986.

Carus, Paul. *The History of the Devil and the Idea of Evil.* 1900. La Salle, Illinois: Open Court, 1974.

Cavendish, Richard. *The Black Arts.* London: Routledge & Kegan Paul, 1967.

Ceram, C. W. *Gods, Graves and Scholars.* 1949. New York: Alfred A. Knopf, 1951.

Chaikin, Andrew. *A Man on the Moon: The Voyages of the Apollo Astronauts.* New York: Penguin Books, 1994.

Charbonneau-Lassay, Louis. *The Bestiary of Christ.* 1940. New York: Penguin Arkana, 1992.

Charroux, Robert. *Forgotten Worlds.* 1971. New York: Popular Library, 1973.

—. *Masters of the Earth.* 1967. New York: Berkley, 1974.

Cheney, Margaret. *Tesla: Man Out Of Time.* 1981. New York: Dell Publishing, 1983.

Childress, David Hatcher. *Extraterrestrial Archaeology.* Stelle, Illinois: Adventures Unlimited Press, 1994.

—. *Lost Cities & Ancient Mysteries of Africa & Arabia.* Stelle, Illinois: Adventures Unlimited Press, 1989.

—. *Lost Cities & Ancient Mysteries of South America.* Stelle, Illinois: Adventures Unlimited Press, 1986.

—. *Lost Cities of Ancient Lemuria & the Pacific.* Stelle, Illinois: Adventures Unlimited Press, 1988.

—. *Lost Cities of China, Central Asia & India.* Stelle, Illinois: Adventures Unlimited Press, 1985.

—. *Lost Cities of North & Central America.* Stelle, Illinois: Adventures Unlimited Press, 1992.

Clark, Jerome. *UFO Encounters and Beyond.* Lincolnwood, Illinois: Publications International, 1993.

Clark, R. T. Rundle. *Myth and Symbol in Ancient Egypt.* London: Thames and Hudson, 1959.

Coomaraswamy, Ananda K., and Sister Nivedita. 1913. *Myths of the Hindus and Buddhists.* New York: Dover, 1967.

Cooper, William. *Behold A Pale Horse.* Sedona, Arizona: Light Technology Publishing, 1991.

Crow, W. B. *A Fascinating History of Witchcraft, Magic and Occultism.* 1968. North Hollywood, California: Wilshire Book Company, 1972.

David, Rosalie. *Discovering Ancient Egypt.* New York: Facts On File, 1993.

David-Neel, Alexandra. *Magic and Mystery In Tibet.* 1932. Mineola, New York: Dover, 1971.

Davidson, H. R. Ellis. *Gods and Myths of Northern Europe.* 1964. New York: Penguin Books, 1990.

—. *Myths and Symbols in Pagan Europe.* New York: Syracuse University Press, 1988.

Davis, F. Hadland. *Myths and Legends of Japan.* 1913. Mineola, New York: Dover, 1992.

Davis, Wade. *The Serpent and the Rainbow.* New York: Simon & Schuster, 1985.

de Camp, L. Sprague. *Lovecraft: A Biography.* 1975. New York: Random House, 1976.

de Camp, L. Sprague, and Catherine C. de Camp. *Ancient Ruins and Archaeology.* New York: Doubleday & Co., 1946.

de Santillana, Georgio, and Hertha von Dechend. *Hamlet's Mill.* Boston: David R. Godine, Publisher, Inc., 1992.

Diamond, Jared. *The Third Chimpanzee.* New York: HarperCollins, 1992.

DiPietro, Vincent, and Gregory Molenaar. *Unusual Martian Surface Features.* Berkeley, California: North Atlantic Books, 1982.

Donnelly, Ignatius. *Atlantis.* 1882. Mineola, New York: Dover, 1976.

Drake, W. Raymond. *Gods and Spacemen in Greece and Rome.* London: Sphere Books, 1976.

—. *Gods and Spacemen in the Ancient East.* London: Sphere Books, 1968.

—. *Gods and Spacemen in the Ancient West.* London: Sphere Books, 1974.

Edwards, I. E. S. *The Pyramids of Egypt.* 1947. London: Penguin Books, 1993.

Eliot, Marc. *Walt Disney: Hollywood's Dark Prince.* 1993. New York: HarperCollins, 1994.

El Mahdy, Christine. *Mummies, Myth and Magic.* London: Thames and Hudson, 1991.

Erman, Adolf. *Egyptian Literature.* Berlin, 1927.

—. *Life In Ancient Egypt.* 1894. Mineola, New York: Dover, 1971.

Evans-Wentz, W. Y. *Cuchama and Sacred Mountains.* Athens, Ohio: Ohio University Press, 1981.

—. *The Fairy Faith in Celtic Countries.* 1911. New York: Citadel, 1990.

—. *The Tibetan Book of the Dead.* London: Oxford University Press, 1927.

Fagan, Brian M. *The Rape of the Nile.* London: Moyer Bell, 1975.

Faulkner, R. O. *The Ancient Egyptian Coffin Texts.* Three Volumes. Warminster, England: Aris & Phillips, Ltd., 1977.

Fawcett, Lawrence, and Barry J. Greenwood. *Clear Intent.* New York: Simon & Schuster, 1984.

Fell, Barry. *America B.C.* New York: New York Times Book Company, 1976.

Flammonde, Paris. *UFO Exist!* Canada: G. P. Putnam's Sons, 1976.

Flinders Petrie, W. M. *The Pyramids and Temples of Gizeh.* London: Field & Tuer, 1883.

Folsom, Franklin, and Mary Folsom. *America's Ancient Treasures.* Albuquerque, New Mexico: University of New Mexico Press, 1971.

Fowler, Raymond E. *The Allagash Abductions.* Tigard, Oregon: Wild Flower Press, 1993.

—. *The Watchers.* New York: Bantam, 1990.

Franklyn, Julian. *Death By Enchantment.* Great Britain: Hamish Hamilton Ltd., 1971.

Frazer, Sir James George. *The Golden Bough.* New York: Macmillan, 1922.

Frymer-Kensky, Tikva. *In the Wake of the Goddesses.* New York: Macmillan, 1992.

Fuller, John G. *The Interrupted Journey.* New York: Berkley, 1966.

Furneaux, Rupert. *Ancient Mysteries.* New York: McGraw Hill, 1977.

Gimbutas, Marija. *The Goddesses and Gods of Old Europe.* 1974. Berkeley, California: University of California Press, 1982.

Ginzburg, Carlo. *Ecstasies: Deciphering the Witches' Sabbath.* 1989. New York: Random House, 1991.

Good, Timothy. *Above Top Secret.* Great Britain; Sidgwick and Jackson, 1987.

—. *Alien Liaison.* London: Arrow, 1991.

Graves, Robert. *The White Goddess.* New York: Farrar, Straus and Giroux, 1966.

Guerbcr, II. A. *The Myths of Greece and Rome.* 1907. Mineola, New York: Dover, 1993.

—. *Myths of the Norsemen from the Eddas and Sagas.* 1909. Mineola, New York: Dover, 1992.

Gurney, O. R. *The Hittites.* 1952. London: Penguin Books, 1990.

Hall, Richard. *Uninvited Guests.* Santa Fe, New Mexico: Aurora Press, 1988.

Hancock, Graham. *The Sign and the Seal.* New York: Simon & Schuster, 1992.

Hansen, L. Taylor. *The Ancient Atlantic.* Amherst, Wisconsin: Amherst Press, 1969.

—. *He Walked the Americas.* Amherst, Wisconsin: Amherst Press, 1963.

Hart, George. *A Dictionary of Egyptian Gods and Goddesses.* London: Routledge, 1986.

Hill, Douglas, and Pat Williams. *The Supernatural.* London: Aldus Books Limited, 1965.

Hoagland, Richard. *The Monuments of Mars.* Berkeley, California: North Atlantic Books, 1987.

Homet, Marcel. *Sons of the Sun.* London, 1963.

Hope, Orville L. *6000 Years of Seafaring.* Gastonia, North Carolina: Hope Press, 1983.

Hopkins, Budd. *Intruders.* New York: Ballantine, 1988.

—. *Missing Time.* New York: Ballantine, 1981.

Hough, Peter, and Jenny Randles. *Looking for the Aliens.* London: Blandford Books, 1991.

Howard, Michael. *The Occult Conspiracy.* Rochester, Vermont: Destiny Books, 1989.

Howe, Linda Moulton. *An Alien Harvest.* Huntingdon Valley, Pennsylvania: LMH Productions, 1989.

—. *Glimpses of Other Realities. Volume I: Facts and Eyewitnesses.* Huntingdon Valley, Pennsylvania: LMH Productions, 1993.

Hunter, Bruce. *A Guide to Ancient Maya Ruins.* Norman, Oklahoma: University of Oklahoma Press, 1986.

Ions, Veronica. *Egyptian Mythology.* New York: Peter Bedrick Books, 1968.

Jacobs, David M., Ph.D. *Secret Life.* New York: Simon & Schuster, 1992.

Jung, Carl G., editor. *Man and His Symbols.* London: Aldus Books, 1964.

Keel, John A. *The Mothman Prophecies.* 1975. Avondale Estates, Georgia: IllumiNet Press, 1991.

Keith, Jim. *Casebook On Alternative 3.* Lilburn, Georgia: IllumiNet Press, 1994.

Keller, Werner. *The Bible as History.* New York: William Morrow, 1956.

Keyhoe, Donald E. *Aliens From Space.* London: Panther Books, 1973.

—. *Flying Saucers: Top Secret.* New York: G. P. Putnam's Sons, 1960.

Klass, Philip J. *UFO Abductions: A Dangerous Game.* Buffalo, New York: Prometheus, 1989.

Kolosimo, Peter. *Not Of This World.* Secaucus, New Jersey: University Books, 1971.

—. *Timeless Earth.* Secaucus, New Jersey: University Books, 1974.

Krupp, E. C. *Echoes of the Ancient Skies.* New York: Harper & Row, Inc., 1983.

Landsburg, Alan, and Sally Landsburg. *In Search of Ancient Mysteries.* New York: Bantam, 1974.

Lindemann, Michael, editor. *UFOs and the Alien Presence.* Santa Barbara, California: 2020 Group, 1991.

Lorenzen, Jim, and Coral Lorenzen. *Flying Saucer Occupants.* New York: Signet, 1967.

Mack, John E., M.D. *Abduction.* New York: Charles Scribner's Sons, 1994.

Maspero, G. *History of Egypt.* Three volumes. London: The Grolier Society, 1906.

Masters, R. E. L. *Eros and Evil.* New York: Julian Press, 1962.

McGlone, William R., P. M. Leonard, J. L.Guthrie, R. W. Gillespie, and J. P. Whittall, Jr. *Ancient American Inscriptions.* Salt Lake City, Utah: Publishers Press, 1994.

Murray, Margaret A. *The God of the Witches.* 1931. London: Oxford University Press, 1952.

Neubert, Otto. *Tutankhamun and the Valley of the Kings.* 1954. New York: Granada, 1977.

Niel, Fernand. *The Mysteries of Stonehenge.* New York: Avon, 1974.

Norman, Eric. *Gods and Devils from Outer Space.* New York: Lancer, 1973.

—. *Gods, Demons and Space Chariots.* New York: Lancer, 1970.

Noyes, Ralph, editor. *The Crop Circle Enigma.* The Hollies, Wellow, Bath, United Kingdom: Gateway Books, 1990.

Ostrander, Sheila, and Lynn Schroeder. *Psychic Discoveries Behind the Iron Curtain.* New Jersey: Prentice-Hall, 1970.

Pagels, Elaine. *The Gnostic Gospels.* New York: Random House, 1979.

Pym, Christopher. *The Ancient Civilization of Angkor.* New York: Mentor/New American Library, 1968.

Randle, Kevin D. *A History of UFO Crashes.* New York: Avon, 1995.

—. *The UFO Casebook.* New York: Warner, 1989.

Randle, Kevin D., and Donald R. Schmitt. *The Truth About the UFO Crash at Roswell.* New York: Avon, 1994.

—. *UFO Crash At Roswell.* New York: Avon, 1991.

Randles, Jenny. *Alien Contacts and Abductions.* New York: Sterling Publishing, 1993.

—. *The UFO Conspiracy.* New York: Barnes & Noble, 1987.

Rawlinson, Georges. *History of Ancient Egypt.* New York: J. W. Lovell, 1880.

Reich, Wilhelm. *Selected Writings.* 1942. New York: Farrar, Straus and Cudahy, 1960.

Rees, Alwyn and Brinley. *Celtic Heritage.* New York: Thames and Hudson, 1961.

Richelson, Jeffrey T., and Desmond Ball. *The Ties That Bind: Intelligence Cooperation Between the UKUSA Countries.* 1985. London: Unwin Hyman Ltd., 1990, Second Edition.

Ring, Kenneth, Ph.D. *The Omega Project.* New York: William Morrow, 1992.

Rogo, D. Scott, editor. *Alien Abductions.* New York: Signet, 1980.

Rolleston, T. W. *Myths and Legends of the Celtic Race.* 1911. Mineola, New York: Dover, 1990.

Romer, John. *Ancient Lives.* New York: Holt, Rinehart and Winston, 1984.

—. *Valley of the Kings.* New York: Henry Holt and Company, Inc., 1981.

Ruppelt, Edward J. *The Report On Unidentified Flying Objects.* New York: Ace, 1956.

Sadler, A. L. *A Short History of Japan.* London: Angus & Robertson, 1963.

Saunders, M. W., and Duncan Lunan. *Destiny Mars*. Surrey, England: Caterham, 1975.

Schellhorn, G. Cope. *Extraterrestrials in Biblical Prophecy*. Madison, Wisconsin: Horus House Press Inc., 1990.

Scott, Sir Walter, editor and translator. *Hermetica*. Boulder, Colorado, Hermes House, 1982.

Sellers, Jane B. *The Death of Gods In Ancient Egypt*. London: Penguin Books, 1992.

Seiss, Joseph A., D.D. *The Great Pyramid: A Miracle In Stone*. 1877. Blauvelt, New York: Steiner, 1973.

Sendy, Jean. *The Coming of the Gods*. 1970. New York: Berkley, 1973.

—. *The Moon: Outpost of the Gods*. 1968. New York: Berkley, 1975.

—. *Those Gods Who Made Heaven and Earth*. 1969. New York: Berkley, 1972.

Sitchin, Zecharia. *Genesis Revisited*. New York: Avon, 1990.

—. *The Lost Realms*. New York: Avon, 1990.

—. *The Stairway to Heaven*. 1980. New York: Avon, 1983.

—. *The 12th Planet*. 1976. New York: Avon, 1978.

—. *The Wars of Gods and Men*. New York: Avon, 1985.

—. *When Time Began*. New York: Avon, 1993.

Smith, S. Percy, editor and translator. *The Lore of the Whare-wananga*. N. Plymouth: Mem. Polynesian Society 3, 1913.

Smyth, Charles Piazzi. *Life and Work at the Great Pyramid*. Edinburgh: Edmund and Douglas, 1867.

—. *Our Inheritance in the Great Pyramid*. London: A. Stranam & Co., 1864.

Spence, Lewis. *History of Atlantis*. 1930. London: Senate/Studio Editions Ltd., 1995.

—. *Myths & Legends of Ancient Egypt*. 1915. Mineola, New York: Dover, 1990.

—. *The Myths of Mexico and Peru*. 1913. Mineola, New York: Dover, 1994.

—. *The Myths of the North American Indians*. 1914. Mineola, New York: Dover, 1989.

Spencer, John. *The UFO Encyclopedia*. New York: Avon, 1991.

Steiger, Brad, editor. *Project Blue Book*. New York: Ballantine, 1976.

Squire, Charles. *Celtic Myth and Legend*. 1905. Van Nuys, California: Newcastle Publishing, 1975.

Summers, Montague. *The History of Witchcraft*. 1925. Secaucus, New Jersey: Lyle Stuart Inc., 1956.

Temple, Robert K. G. *The Sirius Mystery*. Rochester, Vermont: Destiny Books, 1976.

Thompson, Keith. *Angels and Aliens*. New York: Ballantine, 1991.

Thompson, Richard L. *Alien Identities*. San Diego, California: Govardhan Hill Publishing, 1993.

Titchenell, Elsa-Brita. *The Masks of Odin*. Pasadena, California: Theosophical University Press, 1985.

Tolstoy, Nikolai. *The Quest for Merlin.* New York: Back Bay/Little, Brown and Company, 1985.

Tomas, Andrew. *We Are Not the First.* New York: G. P. Putnam's Sons, 1971.

Tombaugh, Clyde W., and Patrick Moore. *Out of the Darkness: The Planet Pluto.* New York: New American Library, 1981.

Tompkins, Peter. *Mysteries of the Mexican Pyramids.* New York: Harper & Row, 1976.

—. *Secrets of the Great Pyramid.* New York: Harper & Row, 1971.

Vallée, Jacques. *Anatomy of a Phenomenon.* New York: Ace, 1965.

—. *Confrontations.* Toronto, Canada: Random House, 1990.

—. *Dimensions.* Toronto, Canada: Random House, 1988.

—. *Forbidden Science.* Berkeley, California: North Atlantic Books, 1992.

—. *Messengers of Deception.* Berkeley, California: And/Or Press, 1979.

—. *Passport to Magonia.* 1969. Chicago: Contemporary Books, 1993.

—. *Revelations.* New York: Random House, 1991.

Vallée, Jacques, and Janine Vallée. *Challenge To Science: The UFO Enigma.* New York: Ballantine, 1966.

Valentine, Tom. *The Great Pyramid: Man's Monument to Man.* New York: Pinnacle, 1975.

Vankin, Jonathan. *Conspiracies, Cover-ups and Crimes.* New York: Paragon House, 1992.

Vankin, Jonathan, and John Whalen. *The 50 Greatest Conspiracies of All Time.* New York: Citadel Press, 1995.

Velikovsky, Immanuel. *Worlds In Collision.* New York: Doubleday & Company, Inc., 1950.

Von Daniken, Erich. *Chariots of the Gods.* New York: G. P. Putnam's Sons, 1970.

Waters, Frank. *The Book of the Hopi.* New York: Viking Penguin Books, 1963.

Watkins, Leslie, and David Ambrose. *Alternative 3.* London, Great Britain: Sphere Books, 1978.

Watson, Don. *Indians of the Mesa Verde.* Ann Arbor, Michigan: Cushing-Malloy, Inc., 1961.

Welfare, Simon, and John Fairley. *Arthur C. Clarke's Mysterious World.* New York: A & W Publishers Inc., 1980.

West, John Anthony. *Serpent in the Sky.* Wheaton, Illinois: Quest Books, 1993.

White, John. *Pole Shift.* Virginia Beach, Virginia: A.R.E. Press/Edgar Cayce Foundation, 1980.

Wilcox, Robert K. *Shroud.* New York: Macmillan, 1977.

Wilkins, Harold. *Flying Saucers on the Attack.* New York: Ace, 1954.

—. *Flying Saucers Uncensored.* New Jersey: Citadel Press, 1955.

Wilkinson, Richard H. *Reading Egyptian Art.* London: Thames and Hudson, Ltd., 1992.

—. *Symbol and Magic in Egyptian Art.* London: Thames and Hudson, Ltd., 1994.

Wilson, Colin. *Starseekers*. Great Britain: Hodder & Stoughton Ltd., 1980.

Wilson, Robert Anton. *The New Inquisition*. 1987. Scottsdale, Arizona: New Falcon Publications, 1991

—. *Wilhelm Reich In Hell*. Scottsdale, Arizona: New Falcon Publications, 1987.

Woods, William. *A History of the Devil*. 1974. New York: G.P. Putnam's Sons, 1975.

Zimdars-Swartz, Sandra L. *Encountering Mary*. 1991. New York, Avon, 1992.

Zimmer, Heinrich. *Myths and Symbols In Indian Art and Civilization*. Princeton, New Jersey: Princeton University Press, 1972.

Ancient And Historical Texts

Bhagavad Gita. Edited by Bhaktivedanta Prabhupada. 1965.

The Bible (King James Version)

Book of Enoch. Translated by Richard Laurence, LL.D. London: Kegan Paul, Trench & Co., 1883.

Corpus Hermeticum.Translated by Sir Walter Scott (c. 19th Century).

Demoniality. Ludovico Maria Sinistrari. 1622. Translated by Montague Summers. 1927.

The Egyptian Book of the Dead. Translated by Sir E. A. Wallis Budge. 1899.

Histories. Herodotus. Translated by W. G. Waddell. London, 1939.

Mabinogion. Edited by John Rhys and J. Gwenogvryn Evans. London: Oxford, 1887.

Popol Vuh. Translated by Dennis Tedlock. New York: Touchstone/Simon & Schuster, 1986.

Prophecies. Nostradamus. Translated by Erika Cheetham. New York: Bantam, 1973.

The Tibetan Book of the Dead. Edited by W. Y. Evans-Wentz. London: Oxford, 1927.

Periodicals

"America's Ancient Skywatchers," *National Geographic,* Vol. 177, No. 3, 3/90.

"Anomalous Table Procedures," *UFO,* Vol. 8, No. 1, 1993.

"Are the Reasons for the Coverup Solely Scientific?" *Flying Saucer Review,* Vol. 28, No. 6.

"Behind the Scenes at 'Intruders'," *UFO,* Vol. 7, No. 4, 1992.

"Bovine beasts, humans share 'perfect match' chromosomes," *Texarkana Gazette,* 2/27/84.

"Breaking Through Secrecy," *UFO,* Vol. 9, No. 1, 1994.

"Civilization Rethought," *Conde Nast Traveler,* 2/93.

Colorado Springs Gazette Telegraph, 9/24/75.

"The Common Ground of Abduction Support," *UFO,* Vol. 8, No. 1, 1993.

"Copters and Roberts," *Longmont Daily Times-Call,* 8/2/94, No. 214.

"Dead Horse Riddle Sparks UFO Buffs," *Pueblo Chieftain,* 10/7/67.

"Disinformation Games," "Former CIA Officer Talks," *UFO,* Vol. 6, No. 6, 1991.

"Documents Trace NSA-UFO Connection," *UFO,* Vol. 9, No. 1, 1994.

"DSP Satellite 'Spots' UFOs," *UFO,* Vol. 9, No. 1, 1994.

"Falkville Chief Says 'Howdy' to Spaceman," *Birmingham News,* 10/19/73.

"Falkville Police Chief Resigns Under Pressure," *Decatur Daily,* 11/16/73.

"'Fire In The Sky' Inquiry," *UFO,* Vol. 8, No. 3, 1993.

"The Galactic Ghoul: Superpower Problems in Getting to Mars," *UFO,* Vol. 8, No. 6, 1993.

"Gulf Breeze Photo Case Marred By 'Bad Science'," *UFO,* Vol. 9, No. 1, 1994.

"Harvest of Bones—Ritual Cave Burial in Honduras," *Archaeology,* Vol. 48, No. 3, 5/6/95.

"Hopkins Rates Mini-Series 'B+'," *UFO,* Vol. 7, No. 4, 1992.

"Iraq: Crucible of Civilization," *National Geographic,* Vol. 179, No. 5, 5/91.

"It's No Act—He's Into UFOs," *UFO,* Vol. 9, No. 4, 1994.

"Los Alamos Overflights," *UFO,* Vol. 11, No. 1, 1996.

"Our Mexican Ancestors," *Pursuit,* Vol. 18, No. 2, whole no. 70.

"Past, Secret UFO Study Confirmed," *UFO,* Vol. 8, No. 2, 1993.

"Possible 'Covert Ops' Target Researchers," *UFO,* Vol. 8. No. 1, 1993.

"'Psi-Cops' Bite Into Abduction Claims," *UFO,* Vol. 9, No. 5, 1994.

"Q & A: John Mack, M.D.," *UFO,* Vol. 9, No. 5, 1994.

"RAAF Captures Flying Saucer," *Roswell Daily Record,* 7/8/47.

"That Awful Alien 'Slime,'" *UFO,* Vol. 8, No. 3. 1993.

"The Sphinx Revealed," *National Geographic,* Vol. 179, No. 4, 4/91.

"UFO's vs. USAF, Amazing (But True) Encounters," *Parade,* 12/10/78.

"Uranus: Visit to a Dark Planet," *National Geographic,* Vol. 170, No. 2, 8/86.

"Venus Revealed," *National Geographic,* Vol. 183, No. 2, 2/93.

"Wreckage in the Desert Was Odd, but Not Alien," *New York Times,* 9/18/94.

Television Specials, News Shows, and Independent Documentaries

A Strange Harvest. Linda Moulton Howe Productions, 1980, 1988.

Ancient Mysteries. CBS-TV, 1994.

48 Hours: Are We Alone? CBS-TV, 1994.

Mysteries From Beyond Earth. 1977.

Mystery of the Sphinx. NBC-TV, 1993.

Overlords of the UFO. 1977.

Strange Harvests 1993. Linda Moulton Howe Productions, 1993.

UFO Coverup?: Live. Seligman Productions, 1988.

UFO Coverup: Live from Area 51. TNT, 1994.

UFOs—A Need To Know. Ted Oliphant Productions, 1989.

Index